Early Intervention
for Infants and
Children with Handicaps

Early Intervention for Infants and Children with Handicaps

An Empirical Base

Edited by

Samuel L. Odom, Ph.D.
Department of Special Education
George Peabody College for Teachers
Vanderbilt University

and

Merle B. Karnes, Ed.D.
Department of Special Education
University of Illinois
at Urbana-Champaign

PAUL H. BROOKES PUBLISHING CO.

Baltimore · London · Toronto · Sydney

Paul H. Brookes Publishing Co.
Post Office Box 10624
Baltimore, Maryland 21285-0624

Copyright © 1988 by Paul H. Brookes Publishing Co., Inc.
All rights reserved.

Typeset by The Composing Room, Grand Rapids, Michigan.
Manufactured in the United States of America by
The Maple Press Company, York, Pennsylvania.

Library of Congress Cataloging-in-Publication Data
Early intervention for infants and children with handicaps.

  Bibliography: p.
  Includes index.
    1. Handicapped children—Education (Preschool)—United States.   2.
Handicapped children—Education—Research—United States.   3. Handicapped
children—United States—Family relationships.   I. Odom, Samuel L.   II. Karnes,
Merle B., 1916–
LC4019.2.E26   1988   371.9   87-30947
ISBN 0-933716-87-7

Contents

Contributors

Stephen J. Bagnato, Ed.D.
Professor of Pediatrics and School Psychology
Coordinator, Toddler/Preschool Program
  Children's Hospital of Pittsburgh
University of Pittsburgh School of Medicine
Pittsburgh, PA 15261

Donald B. Bailey, Jr., Ph.D.
Director of Early Childhood Research
Frank Porter Graham Child Development Center
CB#8180
University of North Carolina at Chapel Hill
Chapel Hill, NC 27599

Patricia A. Barber, Ph.D.
Research Associate
Bureau of Child Research
University of Kansas
Lawrence, KS 66045

Shirley K. Behr, M.A.P.A., O.T.R.
Research Assistant
Bureau of Child Research
University of Kansas
Lawrence, KS 66045

Jeffri Brookfield-Norman, M.A.
Project Director
Human Development Institute
University of Kentucky
Lexington, KY 40506

Judith J. Carta, Ph.D.
Research Associate and Project Director
Bureau of Child Research
University of Kansas
Juniper Gardens Children's Project
1614 Washington Blvd.
Kansas City, KS 66102

Glendon Casto, Ph.D.
Co-Director
Early Intervention Research Institute
Developmental Center for Handicapped Persons
and
Professor
Department of Psychology
Utah State University
Logan, UT 84322-6580

Eugene Edgar, Ph.D.
Professor
Area of Special Education
Experimental Education Unit, WJ-10
University of Washington
Seattle, WA 98195

Rebecca R. Fewell, Ph.D.
Professor
Area of Special Education
Experimental Education Unit, WJ-10
University of Washington
Seattle, WA 98195

Charles R. Greenwood, Ph.D.
Associate Scientist and Research Director
Bureau of Child Research
University of Kansas
Juniper Gardens Children's Project
1614 Washington Blvd.
Kansas City, KS 66102

Michael J. Guralnick, Ph.D.
Director
Child Development and Mental Retardation
  Center, WJ-10
University of Washington
Seattle, WA 98195

Lawrence J. Johnson, Ph.D.
Associate Professor of Special Education
Chairperson of Early Childhood Education for the
  Handicapped
Department of Special Education
The University of Alabama
P.O. Box 2592
Tuscaloosa, AL 35486

Ann P. Kaiser, Ph.D.
Associate Professor
Department of Special Education
Box 328, Peabody College
Vanderbilt University
Nashville, TN 37203

Ruth Kaminski, M.S.
Research Assistant
Center on Human Development
University of Oregon
Eugene, OR 97403

Merle B. Karnes, Ed.D.
Professor of Special Education
Department of Special Education
University of Illinois at Urbana-Champaign
Colonel Wolfe School
403 E. Healey St.
Champaign, IL 61820

Georgia M. Kerns, Ph.D.
Faculty in Residence
Department of Education
University of New Hampshire
Durham, NH 03824

Frank W. Kohler, Ph.D.
Research Associate Principal
Western Psychiatric Institute and Clinic
University of Pittsburgh
Pittsburgh, PA 15213

Kathleen McCartan, Ph.D.
Assistant Professor
Department of Child Development
Iowa State University
Ames, IA 50011

Jeanette McCollum, Ph.D.
Associate Professor
Department of Special Education
University of Illinois at Urbana-Champaign
Champaign, IL 61820

Mary A. McEvoy, Ph.D.
Research Assistant Professor
Department of Special Education
Box 328, Peabody College
Vanderbilt University
Nashville, TN 37203

John T. Neisworth, Ph.D.
Professor
Department of Special Education
Room 226-A, Moore Building
Pennsylvania State University
University Park, PA 16802

Samuel L. Odom, Ph.D.
Assistant Professor
Department of Special Education
Box 328, Peabody College
Vanderbilt University
Nashville, TN 37203

Cordelia C. Robinson, Ph.D.
Director of Special Education
Meyer Children's Rehabilitation Institute
and
Associate Professor
College of Nursing
University of Nebraska Medical Center
Omaha, NB 68105

Steven A. Rosenberg, Ph.D.
Assistant Professor
Department of Psychology
University of Nebraska at Omaha
Omaha, NB 68182

Diane M. Sainato, Ph.D.
Research Associate Principal
Western Psychiatric Institute and Clinic
University of Pittsburgh
Pittsburgh, PA 15213

Rune J. Simeonsson, Ph.D.
Professor
Department of Special Education
University of North Carolina at Chapel Hill
Chapel Hill, NC 27514

Phillip S. Strain, Ph.D.
Associate Professor
Department of Psychiatry
Western Psychiatric Institute and Clinic
University of Pittsburgh
Pittsburgh, PA 15213

Ann P. Turnbull, Ed.D.
Acting Associate Director
Bureau of Child Research
and
Professor
Department of Special Education
University of Kansas
Lawrence, KS 66045

Steven F. Warren, Ph.D.
Associate Professor
Department of Special Education
Box 328, Peabody College
Vanderbilt University
Nashville, TN 37203

Mark R. Wolery, Ph.D.
Associate Professor
Department of Special Education
University of Kentucky
Lexington, KY 40506

Preface

PICTURE THE FOLLOWING SCENARIO: AT A NATIONAL CONFERENCE ON ISSUES RE-
lated to child development, three individuals are engaged in a spirited discussion. Questions being
bandied about include: Does early childhood special education work? Is it effective? What intervention or educational procedures within developmental skill domains produce the best results? What are
the effects on families? Where and how should interventions take place?

The participants present different perspectives in this discussion. One is a "believer." This
person has seen directly the positive effects of intervention programs for infants and young children
with handicaps and their families and believes strongly that early intervention works. The second
discussant is a "questioner." This person reflects the Missouri adage that you have to "show me"
that these procedures work and are worth the investment of valuable government funds. The third
participant is a "doubter"; this person believes strongly that early childhood special education is not
effective and is in fact a waste of money. These individuals reflect the positions that parents,
professionals, and policymakers take when the topic of early childhood special education arises, and
their conversation reflects issues debated at a national and international level. As the discussion
reaches a crescendo, a familiar question is offered: "Well, what does the research say? Let's look at
the empirical base for early intervention." A silence falls over the three individuals.

At this point, the discussants could have turned to this book for some of the answers to their
questions, for this book is about research in early childhood special education. The chapters have been
written by researchers, most of whom admittedly fit the believer or questioner roles. In organizing this
book, we intended that it be directed to several audiences. It should be appropriate for, and of interest
to, individuals in the advanced stages of master's training programs or doctoral training programs that
prepare professionals to work or do research in early intervention settings. It would also be of interest
to professionals from special education and related disciplines who are currently working or who have
interests in early intervention. In addition, this book would be of particular interest to researchers in
the field. In general, we are hoping that professionals and professionals-to-be in early childhood
special education and related disciplines will attend to the content and issues raised in this book.

Chapters in this book were solicited to address four topical areas: issues related to conducting
research with infants and young children with handicaps, research on instruction or intervention
practices within developmental skill domains, issues related to families, and a last miscellaneous set
of issues that are important for early intervention with infants and young children, but which defy
categorization.

The initial portion of the book, concerning issues related to research, begins with Odom's
chapter on the different methodologies used in early intervention research. In this chapter, he reviews
four research approaches that researchers use in their investigations, and cites examples of their use
from the early childhood special education literature. Odom notes that each design has its own unique
advantages and disadvantages for answering questions about early intervention. In the second chapter
in this topical area, Neisworth and Bagnato examine the range of assessment instruments and procedures that researchers and practioners use in early childhood special education. They make an
important and useful contribution to our understanding of the assessment enterprise by proposing a
typology of assessment approaches. In the third chapter, Casto examines the relationship between
traditional research methodology and program evaluation. He sees the two as very closely related, a
view that diverges somewhat from the models of program evaluation that are present in the educational research literature. Of particular note in Casto's chapter is an excellent discussion of how
stratification can be used to control for the heterogeneity found in most groups of children with
handicaps.

Edgar's chapter, which concerns factors influencing research in early childhood special education, continues the research issues portion of the book. Edgar brings a thoughtful and candid perspective to the often unclear relationship between social policy and research. His analysis of the research

questions that are taboo and of the motivations of educational researchers will surely provoke discussion, and possibly reflection, among researchers and consumers of research. Guralnick's chapter, which concludes this research issues section, notes that past efficacy research has attempted to provide a unitary and simplistic answer to what is actually a complex set of questions. He proposes that efficacy research in early intervention is probably best viewed as a matrix of questions related to program, subject, and goal variables. This chapter contributes both organizational and conceptual clarity to current discussions of efficacy research.

Authors of the next four chapters reviewed research on intervention procedures designed to promote skill acquisition within discrete developmental domains. In their scholarly chapter on early language intervention, Warren and Kaiser examine both didactic and naturalistic approaches to language training, reviewing the relative merits of each. Their discussion of research problems related to early language research and directions for future research should prove instructional for individuals interested in beginning a program of language research. Wolery and Brookfield-Norman review the literature on preacademic instruction for preschoolers with handicaps. An important contribution of this chapter is the delineation of the skills areas that should be identified as preacademic, and of effective strategies for promoting these skills. This chapter should introduce some conceptual clarity into an often nebulous area of instruction.

Strain and Kohler contribute a strong chapter on social interaction interventions for young children with handicaps. They identify a number of questions related to interventions and offer suggestions for ways the effects of these interventions should be measured. They also offer an interesting design for gauging intervention effects. To conclude this group of chapters, Fewell and Kaminski review the research on the development of play skills in young children with handicaps. Their chapter will be of great interest to professionals who wish to assess symbolic play of infants and preschoolers and to design programs to teach play skills.

Two chapters make up a brief grouping of reviews on issues related to families. Rosenberg and Robinson present the research on social interactions between parents and their infants and young children with handicaps. This review organizes a disparate literature that is growing rapidly. It should be of considerable interest to individuals who wish to work with infants and parents. In taking a broader view of the family as a whole, Barber, Turnbull, Behr, and Kerns offer a family systems perspective on early childhood special education. These authors delineate a conceptual framework for understanding family systems, and substantiate the model in a powerful way with case studies of individual families.

A last set of chapters addresses a number of important but only loosely related issues. Bailey and Simeonsson examine research related to the effects of home-based interventions for infants and children with handicaps and their families. Their conclusion—that the choice of the type of service delivery must correspond with the family's needs and abilities—provides nice support for the development of the individualized family service plan required by Part H of PL 99-457. In their chapter on ecobehavioral assessment of classroom instruction, Carta, Sainato, and Greenwood identify a number of ecological variables that have direct effects on children's behavior. Most notably, the authors present data from their research projects to illustrate their points.

Odom and McEvoy review the literature related to three rationales used frequently for the suggestion of mainstreaming or integrated programs as an option for some children. These authors found support for at least two of the three rationales and suggest that professionals use these data to work toward more integrated options for young children with handicaps.

In the last chapter in this group, McCollum and McCartan review the literature on an under-researched but vitally important area for early childhood special education: teacher education. In the absence of a clear empirical base, these authors extrapolate from the research in the regular education literature and propose directions for future research. A major contribution of this chapter is the organizational framework for conceptualizing research in the education of teachers in early childhood special education.

As a concluding chapter for the book, Karnes and Johnson consider a number of research related issues that point to future directions for research in early childhood special education. Their discussion of research concepts such as triangulation, social validity, and meta-analysis could serve as a guide for individuals entering the research field. In addition, their recommendations for the better utilization of research findings relate very directly to Odom's discussion of translative research discussed in the first chapter, and serve to bring the book around full circle.

We wish to acknowledge two omissions. Any coverage of instruction related to developmental skill training should include a chapter on motor skill development. Similarly, any grouping of chapters about families should have a chapter on siblings. We must admit that these were two gaps that we just could not fill.

We should also make a few points about the terminology used in this book. Because this field is interdisciplinary, we allowed the authors to choose their own style for talking about children who have handicaps. The issue of whether "handicap" or "disability" is the correct terminology has yet to be settled, so the two terms were allowed to vary freely across chapters. Similarly, in this book, the terms "early intervention" and "early childhood special education" are used synonymously, although there is no clear agreement about these terms. But clearly, early intervention with infants and young children is accomplished often by professionals other than educators.

We hope that the chapters in this book will prove useful for a wide range of professionals and professionals-in-training. It is also our hope that the book will ultimately benefit the individuals with whom these professionals work: the infants and young children with handicaps and their families. If this occurs, then the purpose of this book will have been met.

Acknowledgments

THIS BOOK IS A PRODUCT OF TWO COMMITTEES WITHIN THE DIVISION FOR EARLY Childhood. As such, we would like to acknowledge the support of members of the Executive Board of DEC, and members of the Research and Publication committees. Particularly supportive were the individuals who served as president of DEC during the time that this book developed: Warren Umanksy, Amy Toole, Lisbeth Vincent, and Corinne Garland. In addition, we acknowledge the support of individuals at our respective institutions. Support was provided initially by Susan Shuster and Henry Schroeder at the Developmental Training Center at Indiana University. Tracey Wagner provided expert secretarial assistance. At Peabody College of Vanderbilt University, Brenda Sims provided a great deal of secretarial assistance, and the Department of Special Education, under the leadership of Herb Rieth, has been very supportive. In addition, Paul Yoder contributed expert editorial assistance on one chapter manuscript. At the University of Illinois, the staff of the Colonel Wolfe School supplied much needed support for this project. In addition, members of the editorial staff of the *Journal of the Division for Early Childhood* assisted greatly with this project. Last, and most importantly, we acknowledge the hard work of the authors of the chapters, whose efforts have produced what we feel will be an important contribution to the research literature on early childhood special education.

*We dedicate this book to Samuel A. Kirk,
an early pioneer in research on education
of young children with handicaps.*

Early Intervention
for Infants and
Children with Handicaps

Chapter 1

Research in Early Childhood Special Education
Methodologies and Paradigms
Samuel L. Odom

IN THE LATE 1960S, WHEN SPECIAL ED-
ucators began to develop programs for infants
and young children with handicaps and their
families, they found that they could not rely on
the then current practices in the general field of
education. Their students differed so much
from nonhandicapped students that new, innovative procedures had to be developed. In the
absence of a data base, they borrowed information and theory from clinical and developmental psychology, sociology, speech pathology,
applied behavior analysis, nursing, pediatrics,
and other disciplines. The interdisciplinary
nature of both research and practice in early
intervention for infants and children with handicaps continues to exist today. Yet within the
discipline of special education, a group of professionals has begun to identify themselves as
specialists in the early childhood area.

As a subdiscipline, early childhood special
education has matured over the past 2 decades.
An early reflection of this maturational process
was the establishment, in 1974, of the Division
for Early Childhood (DEC) within the Council
for Exceptional Children. DEC has steadily
grown to become, at this writing, the fourth
largest division within the organization, containing over 4,500 members in 1987 (Division
for Early Childhood, 1987).

In 1976, the federal government, recognizing the need for research in early childhood
special education, created four Early Childhood Research Institutes as part of the Handicapped Children's Early Education Program.
This institute process, which entered its third
funding cycle in 1987, continues to operate and
to reflect the federal government's commitment to research and development in early
childhood special education.

A further step in the maturational process
has been the development of specialized journals for disseminating research and development information. In the early 1980s, the *Journal of the Division for Early Childhood* and
Topics in Early Childhood Special Education
were established to disseminate research in early childhood special education and to translate
research findings for teachers. The development of methods textbooks is another example
of the translation of research into practice. In
1977, there was only one early childhood special education text (Jordan, Hayden, Karnes, &
Wood, 1977); since that time, more than a
dozen texts have been published.

An important additional reflection of the maturation of this subdiscipline has been the development of an empirical base for early intervention. Ten years ago, the research base for
this field would not have supported the collection of reviews that appear in the current text,
although Tjossem's (1976) classic collection of
papers was early evidence of mounting interest
and activity.

The purposes of this chapter are to set the

The author thanks Cathy Alpert and Ann Kaiser for their comments on an earlier draft of this manuscript.

context for research in early childhood special education and to examine the most frequently used methods for conducting research. For each methodology, the author will identify basic design characteristics, the research questions that it is best suited to address, the questions that are not easily addressed by the design, and practical constraints in using the design. Examples of the use of the designs in research with young children with handicaps will be provided for each methodology.

THE CONTEXT AND CONSUMERS OF RESEARCH IN EARLY CHILDHOOD SPECIAL EDUCATION

Research in early childhood special education exists in a complex world in which a range of factors influence both the feasibility and the direction of the research activity. Two groups of factors that have an impact on research are the contexts in which the research occurs and the ultimate consumers for whom the research is intended.

CONTEXTS OF RESEARCH

Context refers to the "whole situation, background, or environment relevant to some happening . . ." (Guralnik & Friend, 1966, p. 319). Research, as a systematic process for generating knowledge, cannot be understood out of the contexts in which it exists. These contexts are multidimensional. They include the physical and social setting in which researchers work, the theoretical orientation or position with which researchers align themselves, the broader historical *zeitgeist* that dictates the acceptable paradigm of inquiry, and the sociopolitical climate existing at the time.

Physical and Social Context

Early childhood special education is an applied discipline, and as such its research is most often designed to answer pragmatic questions. Usually this research occurs in "real world" settings, such as in the homes of families with infants with handicaps, in preschool special education classrooms, in neonatal intensive care

units in hospitals, or in day care centers. The physical context of early childhood special education research is both beneficial and problematic. It is beneficial in that research conducted in the natural setting to answer applied questions may be presumed to have greater "ecological validity" (Bronfenbrener, 1976; Brooks & Baumeister, 1977) than if it were conducted in laboratory settings. Ecological validity refers to the degree to which results accurately reflect events or relationships in naturalistic settings. This "real world" context is sometimes problematic in that the researcher may have less control over the variables of interest in the natural setting than in a laboratory setting.

For example, if a researcher wanted to examine the social interactions that occur between mothers and their handicapped infants, they could take two or more approaches. Through naturalistic observations, researchers might watch mothers at home in a variety of activities during the day. Because social interaction occurs in varying amounts on different days, the researcher would probably have to spend a great deal of time in the home over a period of several days. In contrast, another researcher might ask mothers to come to the child development laboratory to participate in a study. In the laboratory, the researcher might ask the mother to interact with her handicapped infant for 15 minutes, and the research staff would videotape the interactions. In the first scenario described above, the process of collecting the information is labor-intensive, but it is more ecologically valid than the data collected in the second scenario (i.e., because the setting is less contrived, there may be fewer demand characteristics). In the second scenario, the research may be less ecologically valid, but it may enable the researcher to collect more information about the interaction and to later use the videotapes to analyze the data in different ways. In conducting research in early childhood special education, the researcher must decide when to sacrifice the ecological validity inherent in most classroom or home settings for the control offered by a laboratory setting.

Theoretical Context

Research also takes place in a theoretical context. The purpose of *basic* research is to build explanatory theories of certain phenomena (Kerlinger, 1986). The results of basic research support and/or extend theory or invalidate competing theories. In contrast, *applied* research is less directly related to theory development; its purpose is to answer more pragmatic questions (for example: Are half-day programs as effective as full-day programs? Does cognitively-oriented instruction promote language development more effectively than direct instruction?). Yet even with a pragmatic emphasis, applied researchers usually have hypotheses (i.e., theories that are less well developed than those formulated in basic research), about the research questions they are asking. The theoretical orientation of the researcher will exert a substantial influence upon the way the research is conducted.

Such influences are seen in the questions that the researchers ask, or do not ask, in their investigations. For example, when teaching social interaction skills to young children with handicaps, a researcher with a cognitive theoretical orientation might be interested in whether a child understands how to solve a social problem that may arise during interactions with peers in a play group. In contrast, an applied behavior analyst might be interested in the specific positive social interactions occurring in a play group. Though interested in basically the same phenomena, these two researchers would ask quite different questions.

Measurement instruments chosen for an investigation also reflect the investigator's theoretical orientation. In the example above, the cognitive researcher might use a role-playing assessment of social problem solving, whereas the behavioral researcher would probably directly observe children's social interactions with peers. In most studies, investigators choose a narrow range of dependent variables that are selected because they are consistent with the researchers' theoretical orientation. In part to counter the influence of the investigator's theory or values, a number of researchers

have called for the use of multiple dependent variables when investigating phenomena related to educational programs and young children with handicaps (Cronbach, 1982; Neisworth & Bagnato, Chapter 2, this volume; Odom & McConnell, 1985). However, even when multiple variables are used, consumers of research must understand through which theoretical ''lens'' the researcher is viewing the phenomena.

Paradigmatic Context

Research also exists in a paradigmatic context. Simply stated, a paradigm of research refers to the acceptable way in which one collects and understands information about a phenomenon. Kuhn (1970), a historian of science and a physicist, has proposed that as a science matures, it moves from a preparadigmatic state, in which there is no agreed-upon methodology, to a paradigmatic state, in which a method or methods for obtaining knowledge are developed and largely accepted. Also, he proposed that these paradigms change across time. Such a change is reflected in the current educational research literature, in which there is much discussion of the movement from a positivist paradigm to a postpositivist paradigm (Garrison, 1986; Phillips, 1983). In the positivist paradigm, theories are proposed and quantitative data (e.g., child performance on assessments or observations of child behavior) are collected and analyzed through statistical manipulations or direct observation of the graphed results. Conclusions are drawn directly from the results, answering the questions posed in the research or suggested by theory.

In the postpositivist paradigm, the way of knowing about relationships in the world differs. The conclusions drawn about relationships of phenomena in the real world cannot be obtained by the empirical method described above because: 1) results from any empirical investigation are heavily influenced by the theories themselves, and 2) the findings of any single empirical investigation are generally too narrow to explain the whole phenomenon under investigation. Broader, more elaborate understandings of the subjects of study—in this case, children or families—

must be employed. The clearest reflection in special education of the conflict occurring between the two paradigmatic positions appears in the debates over the use of quantitative or qualitative approaches to research (Simpson & Eaves, 1985; Stainback & Stainback, 1984, 1985), the use of holistic or behavioral approaches to educating children with learning disabilities (Heshusius, 1982,1986; Ulman & Rosenberg, 1986), and in the proposal to move toward a multiparadigmatic approach to special education knowledge (Skrtic, 1986). Researchers from both paradigmatic positions are represented in early childhood special education, although they may not openly align themselves with either position. The positivist paradigm is represented in the group, product-process, and single-subject design methodologies. The postpositivist paradigm is most clearly represented in the ethnographic/naturalistic methodology. Early childhood special education is clearly rooted in the positivist paradigm, although within the field this paradigm is beginning to be questioned (Edgar, Chapter 4, this volume) and other approaches are beginning to emerge (Odom & Shuster, 1986).

Sociopolitical Context

Sociopolitical context refers to the prevailing societal attitudes toward a particular issue or subject, or to the political climate in which the subject exists. In early intervention studies, sociopolitical context determines the support that the research will receive, the acceptability of the research activity, and the relative impact of the research findings.

Support for Research　Government funding agencies and, at times, private foundations provide support for research. As questions become important for policymakers or for society in general, funding agencies issue directives about the types of research they will support. Open competitions for research reflect a general societal interest in an area. For example, the Office of Special Education Programs of the Department of Education sponsors a field-initiated research competition, in which researchers propose topics of research across the general field of special education. Competitions with established priorities reflect interest in a specific research area. These specific interests may be generated by a need within society or by a theory that has become particularly visible and that needs to be tested. For example, in the 1982 competition for the Early Childhood Research Institutes sponsored by the Office of Special Education, one of the three funding priorities identified by the agency was efficacy of early childhood special education. This priority reflected the policymakers' need for more knowledge about whether early intervention actually had an effect upon children and families, and about the relative costs of such interventions. Similarly, there was a priority for research on mainstreaming and social skills training that reflected a need from the field for more information about strategies for providing early intervention in the least restrictive environment.

Acceptability of Research　The sociopolitical context also determines the acceptability of specific research practices. Current guidelines for conducting research reflect societal tolerance for research activities. Until the 1960s, relatively loose restrictions were placed on social science research with humans. Partly as a result of experiments conducted during that time (e.g., Milgram, 1963), discussion arose within psychology about ethical practices in research with human beings (Kelman, 1967), and in the early 1970s, the American Psychological Association (1973) published ethical guidelines for conducting research with humans. Currently, to conduct research with humans, researchers must demonstrate to institutional review boards (IRBs) that their practices are humane, that they will not harm the individuals under study, and that the individuals participating in the research have been fully informed about the purpose of the research and its potential risks. In conducting early intervention research, putting a child or family at risk for a poor outcome or denying services that are thought to be beneficial in order to test the effects of a treatment strategy would not be an ethical way of conducting research; in fact, this would be judged to be unethical by most IRBs. Another example of the sociopolitical influence on research, outside of education, is the growing practice of closely monitoring the use of animals in biomedical research.

Impact on Social Policy The sociopolitical climate will also determine the effect research may have on social policy. In her analysis of the impact of research on social policy, Bricker (1987) noted that the influence of research may occur either before or after policy is developed. Most often, societal opinion is expressed through social policy, and research follows to examine the effects of the implementation of policy decisions (Edgar, Chapter 4, this volume). For example, the least restrictive environment (LRE) provision of PL 94-142 was derived from a philosophical mandate rather than from a data base indicating it was the most effective program (Odom & McEvoy, Chapter 14, this volume). However, research may provide information that influences how such LRE placements may best be carried out.

At times, research may provide information for developing social policy. For example, in compensatory education programs of the 1960s, parents were involved in some programs and not in others; Bronfenbrener (1974) reviewed the research on early intervention for children from low income families and found that parent involvement was associated with the more effective intervention programs. His analysis of the research exerted a profound effect on subsequent policies for educating young handicapped children, and probably created a rationale and impetus for much of the family research literature in early childhood special education (see Rosenberg & Robinson, Chapter 10, this volume; Barber, Turnbull, Behr, & Kerns, Chapter 11, this volume). In fact, the family systems research with children with handicaps exerted a substantial influence on the creation of the requirement of an Individualized Family Service Plan in the Birth–2 portion of PL 99-457.

However, to influence social policy, research findings must be compatible with the prevailing values of policymakers and society at large (Dokecki, 1986). As Edgar (Chapter 4, this volume) pointed out, one reflection of this

value orientation is that some questions become "taboo" or unaskable. However, when research is conducted and the findings are at variance with strongly valued beliefs or positions, the probability of their producing an impact on social policy is very low. Cronbach (1982) suggested that the probability of evaluation research producing an impact on programs or policies was a function of the strength of the previously held societal belief, the strength of the research findings (i.e., in terms of methodology), and the compatibility of the two.

A clear example of the relationship between societal beliefs and research findings exists in the early childhood special education literature. In their meta-analysis of the effects of parent involvement, Casto and Mastropieri (1985) reported that programs not including parent involvement had greater effect sizes than programs that did include parents. This finding is so contrary to prevailing thought about effective practice in early intervention with young children with handicaps that the likelihood that it will have an impact upon social policy is not great. In fact, the standard reaction to a research finding that is incompatible with current societal opinion is that researchers give great scrutiny to the original researchers' methods of investigation (Dunst & Snyder, 1986) and reanalyze the original questions in a different way (Shonkoff, Hauser-Cram, 1987).

CONSUMERS OF RESEARCH

Research in early childhood special education has many consumers, and for each, the research findings have a different purpose.

Researchers

Researchers both inside and outside the field of early childhood special education may be considered consumers of research. Basic researchers use research to substantiate their theories, to create new theories, or to debunk competing theories. For example, Spieker (1986) investigated the attachment relationship of a group of high risk infants and found a behavior pattern reflecting insecure attachment that differed from the previous classifications of attachment. She used this research to propose an additional classification, which extended the theory of attachment initially proposed by Bowlby (1969) and refined by Ainsworth and colleagues (Ainsworth, Blehar, Waters, & Wall, 1978). Applied researchers use the information to derive answers about practical problems or to guide them in developing a further line of research that will answer applied questions. For example, to develop their model for family focused intervention, Bailey et al., (1986) used previous research and theory on family systems to determine the roles that parents and professionals should play in the intervention process.

Teacher Educators

Research in early childhood special education should have great relevance for teacher educators (i.e., professors in colleges of education). Given that this research, by definition, would provide information relevant for designing intervention programs for children with handicaps and their families, the current research literature, combined with their own practical experience, should be the pool from which teacher educators draw their knowledge about effective practices.

In analyzing the relationship between researchers and practitioners (i.e., teachers), several researchers have noted that researchers and teachers are parts of different cultures that interact only infrequently. This separation is manifested when teachers fail to use research-based technical knowledge (Lortie, 1975; Nemser & Floden, 1986). Applied researchers, unquestionably, have the responsibility of communicating the findings and implications of their research to service providers. However, teacher educators should be the active liaison between these two cultures. Through them, individuals in training, or those receiving inservice training, should become familiar with current research. Teacher educators must act as translators (see below) of current research, which makes their job more difficult than that of the researcher. They must be both well-versed in interpreting the quality of the research and able to derive

practical applications that are feasible in the real world.

Teachers

Contrary to Lortie (1975), it appears that teachers do make use of research findings at different points in their teaching careers. Early in their teaching careers, they appear to use "theoretical knowledge" (i.e., knowledge acquired through preservice training and the research literature) a great deal (Zahorik, 1986). As their classroom experience accumulates, they make less use of theoretical knowledge and greater use of practical knowledge (i.e., knowledge gained from directly working with children). Thus, information about current research may be used often by teachers early in their careers but rarely used by experienced teachers to guide their actions in the classroom, especially when a school district does not have an active inservice training program (Odom, 1987).

Policymakers

As noted above, policymakers may use research in two ways. First, they may develop policy directly from research findings, as long as the findings are not contrary to strongly held beliefs or values. When this occurs, as Bricker (1987) noted, research has a direct influence on policy. Second, policymakers may also use research to evaluate the policies that have been developed. This second use of research illustrates the reciprocal relationship that sometimes exists between research and policy (Bricker, 1987). Research activities come after policy has been established (i.e., they are influenced by the policy), yet the results may influence or redirect future social policy.

Parents

Parents may also be consumers of research. Some parents make active attempts to discern the best practice for their children by examining the applied research literature or by reading about research in summaries written in parent-oriented or popular magazines. Parents may use the research to advocate for the best services for their child.

Translating Research for Consumers

Consumer groups sometimes influence the way in which the research is conducted and the form in which it is reported. Because each consumer group has specific informational needs, it is difficult to conduct research that addresses the needs for more than one or two groups. In its purest form, research is reported in journal articles or research presentation at professional conferences. In these reports, the researchers fully describe research methods and discuss the relevance of the findings for theory or practice.

For some consumer groups research must go through a "translation" process before it can be used. This translation may take several forms. The process itself may be an organized research activity in which research findings are systematically tested in classroom settings and procedural manuals are developed to guide teachers or parents in the use of a specific intervention strategy. Such a systematic approach, which could be termed "translative", differs from other applied research in that it specifically takes theoretical findings and translates them into practical intervention techniques. The research and development process followed by the Center at Oregon for Research in the Be-

havioral Education of the Handicapped (COR-BEH) at the University of Oregon exemplifies this type of translative research (Walker, Hops, & Greenwood, 1984).

Translations of research also occur in other ways. The practical implications of research are usually described in articles that appear in applied professional journals. Volumes of research data are often reduced into executive summaries for policymakers in order to convey the essential findings without including information about technical methods. Editors sometimes summarize a line of research in brief articles for newsletters or technical journals. Researchers sometimes write descriptions of their research for popular magazines such as *Psychology Today, Scientific American,* or *Redbook.* For parents, research is sometimes summarized in magazines such as the *Exceptional Parent.* In addition, research implications are often presented at conferences of professional or advocacy organizations that have active practitioner and/or parent emphases (e.g., National Society for Autistic Children; The Association for Persons with Severe Handicaps; the Association for Retarded Citizens of the United States).

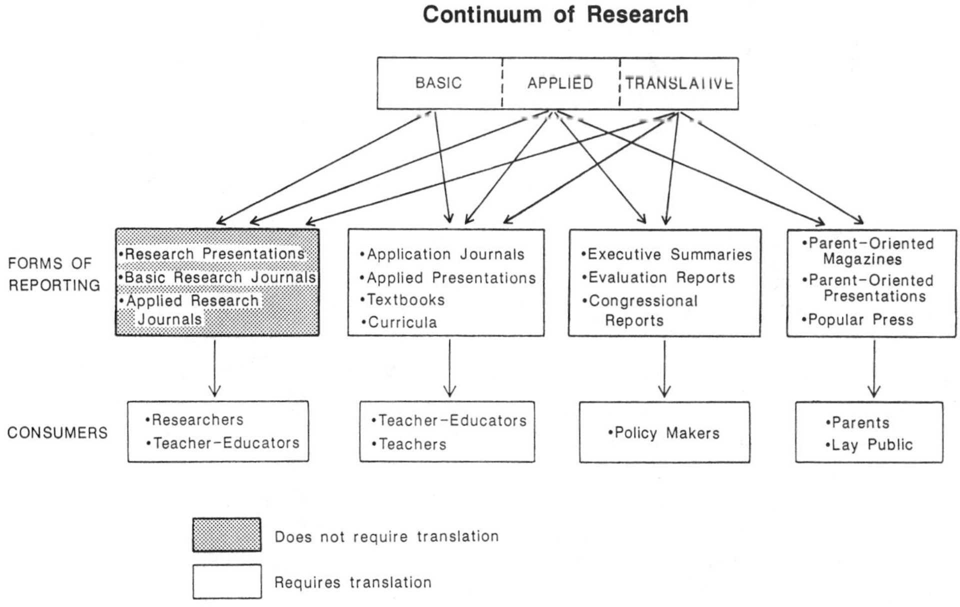

Continuum of Research

Figure 1. Relationship of research and consumers in early childhood special education: Continuum of research.

The process whereby research is communicated or translated to consumers is portrayed in Figure 1. For researchers and teacher educators, the need for translations would be less than for other consumers since the former should have received training in conducting or interpreting research. For parents, policymakers, and teachers, some form of research translation is often needed. This process is essential because without it, research will have little impact on consumer groups.

EXPERIMENTAL DESIGN IN EARLY CHILDHOOD SPECIAL EDUCATION

Research is designed to answer questions. The topics in early childhood special education range from issues that are theoretical in nature, such as the development of an interactionalist perspective on language acquisition (Warren & Kaiser, Chapter 6, this volume), to those issues that are very practical, such as a comparison of the relative costs and benefits of half- versus full-day programs for young children with handicaps (Barnett & Pezzino, 1987).

Researchers from a range of disciplines have created experimental designs and methodologies. These designs have two purposes. First, they give the researcher a framework for collecting information that will lead to an answer to the research question (i.e., that will support their hypothesis), and at the same time will rule out any other alternative answers. Second, they provide standards against which the reader of the research can judge how well the researcher matched the experimental design to the questions that he or she was originally asking. No single experimental design can answer every question within a discipline. In fact, active researchers will find themselves using different experimental designs to address different questions of interest. Some designs (e.g., single subject designs) are closely associated with specific theoretical orientations, while other designs are atheoretical. In the following sections, the designs used most frequently in early childhood special education research will be described and examples of their use in the literature will be provided.

Randomized Group Designs

In randomized group designs, participants (e.g., children or families) in the research are randomly assigned to different groups, exposed to different treatments, and assessed at different points in time with dependent variables designed to provide answers to the research questions (Neisworth & Bagnato, Chapter 2, this volume). Researchers then attribute differences that occur between groups as being "caused" by the independent variable or treatment.

If researchers use a randomized group design to test the effects of a treatment condition as compared with a nontreatment or contrast condition, and their hypothesis is that treatment effects were going to occur, then he or she can only "prove" that the treatment had an effect and cannot infer that the treatment did not have an effect (i.e., cannot prove the null hypothesis). When treatment effects are not found, the most that usually can be said is that no differences were found (Edwards, 1984), rather than that the two conditions produced that same effect. It is always possible that differences might have occurred if other dependent variables had been used. The acceptance of a no difference finding is important for early childhood special education. For example, in a study designed to compare the effects of an early intervention program for infants with visual impairments, infants are randomly assigned to treatment and no treatment groups, and assessments of child development are given at the beginning and end of the year. At the beginning of the study, the researchers hypothesize that there will be a difference between groups, with the intervention group scoring higher on the child development measures at the end of the year. At the end of the year, if the researchers find no statistically significant differences, they cannot say that their study proved that the early intervention program was not effective, because it could well be that there are other explanations for the results (e.g., the instruments were not sensitive, the program could have been effective with another group of children). The only finding that this type of study can confidently produce is when statistical significance is found between the groups on the child development measures at the end of the year. The exception to this rule would be if the study met the very specific criteria that Cook and Campbell (1979) have suggested for accepting "no difference" findings.

In their classic chapter on experimental methodology, Campbell and Stanley (1963) labeled randomized group designs as "true" experimental designs because they came the closest to controlling for unforeseen, extraneous variables through random assignment. Although there may be complex variations to this basic design (Sax, 1979), the premise is that comparable groups are compared after being exposed to different treatment conditions (e.g., intervention programs).

Randomized group designs do not guarantee that groups will be comparable after they are randomly assigned (White & Pezzino, 1986). This is a problem when conducting research with children with handicaps because the population is often very hetereogeneous. One way of controlling for this hetereogeneity is to stratify groups or subjects on relevant characteristics before randomly assigning them. Casto (Chapter 3, this volume) describes procedures for creating a stratified random assignment.

The issue of random assignment is a thorny one in early intervention research. While it appears to be an important practice, sometimes there may be ethical and practical constraints that prevent or limit the opportunity to assign participants randomly to conditions (Gray, 1986). As White and Pezzino (1986) noted, numerous researchers have expressed concern in randomly assigning children to treatment and nontreatment groups because of the ethics of denying treatment to one group of children. This concern is reduced in studies where the effects of two treatments are compared because, unless there is a clear inequity in treatment, both groups of children or families will receive an intervention.

An added concern may also be that when research is conducted in field-based settings,

school districts might be very hesitant to randomly assign children to treatments, preferring instead to assign children based upon the district's criteria. Parents may resist enrolling their child in a program that randomly assigns the child to a treatment, rather than placing the child based on individual needs. However, citing their work at the Early Intervention Research Institute, White and Pezzino (1986) reported that parents in their studies accepted random assignment of their children to experimental groups in efficacy studies of early intervention.

A final key issue related to randomized group designs, as well as to all of the experimental designs described below, is that of implementation of treatment conditions. Group designs are based on the presumption that a specific treatment will be fully implemented in the treatment condition, and a different treatment or no treatment will occur in the other conditions. This creates two concerns. The degree to which the treatment is fully implemented may well determine the magnitude of the treatment effect (Leinhardt, 1980). Also, the degree to which the control or contrast conditions occur as described will determine the conclusions drawn about the comparisons between the treatment effects and the contrast conditions.

For example, suppose a researcher is interested in examining the effects of an early intervention program with hearing impaired children. He or she randomly assigns young children with hearing impairments who are living in a large metropolitan area to treatment and control conditions. In the treatment condition the children receive speech and hearing evaluations, hearing aids or other necessary equipment, and a home-based language stimulation program. In the control condition, the children receive a speech and hearing evaluation. If the nature of the intervention in both conditions is not closely monitored by formally measuring implementation, two scenarios could develop, both leading to erroneous conclusions.

First, a significant number of children may not use their aids as prescribed by the program, or might only receive part of the language stimulation program because their mothers are too busy with their other children to carry out the program. A comparison of treatment effects without implementation measures might conclude that early intervention is a weak treatment, even though it has not been implemented as described. In a second scenario, suppose that the treatment group received the intervention as prescribed. However, after the control group children receive their hearing screening, their parents are not satisfied with the no treatment option. They actively seek and obtain audiological and language stimulation services for their child through other agencies that are available in the community. Again, a comparison of the two randomly assigned groups, without a measure of implementation for *both* conditions, could yield an erroneous conclusion that the intervention program had little or no effect.

Importantly, treatment implementation issues are not unique to randomized groups design. The same concerns exist for quasi-experimental designs, single-subject designs (Billingsley, White, & Munson, 1980), and certain types of correlational designs.

Examples within Early Childhood Special Education Randomized group designs have been used to examine a number of questions relevant for early childhood special education. In their examination of the effects of early intervention for children with handicaps, the Early Intervention Efficacy Institute has proposed conducting sixteen randomized group design studies across a 5-year period (White, Mott, Pezzino, & Behl, 1987). At this writing, the investigations are currently underway. In their analysis of a training package to increase parents' participation in individualized education programs (IEP) meetings, Brinckerhoff and Vincent (1986) randomly assigned parents to a treatment group that received the training package and a control group that only received a letter stating the purpose of the IEP meeting and the parents' role. Parents in the treatment group were significantly more active in the IEP meeting than were parents in the control group. To examine the effects of social integration

with normally developing peers on preschool children with mild and moderate handicaps, Jenkins, Odom, and Speltz (1987) randomly assigned 56 children to integrated and nonintegrated classes that received a social integration curriculum and to integrated and nonintegrated classes that received a contrast curriculum. Implementation measures for both curricular conditions were collected. The researchers found significant differences in the levels of social interaction between the two curricular conditions, as well as significant differences in social competence scores and language development measures in favor of the social integration curricular condition.

Quasi-experimental Group Designs

Quasi-experimental designs contain treatments, outcomes, and experimental units, but do not contain random assignment to groups (Cook & Campbell, 1979). Although Campbell and Stanley (1963) included time-series and correlational designs under the quasi-experimental descriptor, those designs will be discussed in a separate section. In this section, group designs that are parallels to the randomized group design, but that do not conclude randomization, will be discussed. The most common of these designs, and the one used most frequently in early childhood special education, is the nonequivalent control group design.

The nonequivalent control group design is identical to the randomized group design except that participants are not randomly assigned to groups. The groups in this design are often intact before the study begins. For example, an investigator may implement a specialized gross motor curriculum with children in one early intervention classroom and then compare the results to the motor performance of children in another early intervention classroom that did not implement the curriculum.

When using this type of design, the researcher must provide evidence that the participants in the intact groups are initially comparable (i.e., before the treatment) on relevant dependent measures, and that no extraneous variables affect the dependent variable. With randomized group designs having stratified samples, random assignment provides some control for comparability of groups and extraneous variables; with nonequivalent control group designs, the investigator must make greater effort to ensure that the appropriate controls are in place. In the example above, the two groups of children should be comparable on pretest measures of motor skills, and there should not be a disproportionately larger number of motor handicaps (e.g., cerebral palsy) in either group. If such controls are not in place, the final differences between groups could be due to the initial group differences, rather than to the treatment.

Examples within Early Childhood Special Education Investigators have used nonequivalent control group designs to answer a variety of questions in early childhood special education. Sometimes it is not possible to randomly assign children to treatment groups, and the investigator must conduct his or her research in the settings that are available. For example, in their review of early intervention programs that had been approved by the Joint Dissemination and Review Panel within the Department of Education, Odom and Fewell (1983) found that four programs had used intact control groups from the community against which to gauge the effects of their program. These programs provided evidence that the groups were comparable, at least on the dependent variables, before the intervention programs were begun. In a study of the longitudinal effects of early intervention with children who were autistic, Lovaas (1987) used a nonequivalent control group design in which the control group participants were located a greater distance from the treatment center and had received a less intense version of the treatment. In his study, he provided extensive evidence that the groups were comparable on most relevant variables except for the treatment differences. In their investigation of the effects of integration into special education programs on normally developing children, Odom, De-Klyen, and Jenkins (1984) identified a matched group of normally developing children enrolled in a high quality preschool to serve as

their standard for comparison (i.e., control group), and again presented evidence that the groups were comparable on most variables before the study began.

Single Group Designs

Single group designs do not include a separate comparison or control group. Campbell and Stanley (1963) referred to these as "preexperimental" designs because they could not be used to experimentally determine an effect. Single group designs may consist of a dependent measure being given to a group of children after a treatment has been implemented, or more commonly, of dependent measures given both before and after the treatment.

Developmental Change Designs The problem with most single group designs is that they do not have a standard (i.e., control group) against which the effects of the treatment may be compared. This problem is very serious for investigators in early childhood special education, because often control or comparison groups are not available. To address this problem, two approaches have been followed. In the first general approach, a number of statistical manipulations have been created to allow children in the program to serve as their own controls. With these designs, the rate of development prior to the child's entry into the program is compared to the child's rate of development after he or she has been in the program for a period of time. These statistical techniques, along with the formulas, are listed in Table 1.

Two studies have examined the relative use of these single group designs. In evaluating outcomes of their computer-based, infant intervention program, Fewell and Sandall (1986) compared the use of increases in developmental ages, changes in developmental quotients, and a prediction formula employed by Oelwein, Fewell, and Pruess (1985). They found that each of the formulas led to different conclusions about the effects of their project. Also, they questioned the use of developmental quotients and change formulas with infants for whom there is typically a deceleration in rate of development (e.g., Down syndrome infants),

Table 1.   Computational formulas for rate of developmental change analyses

Bagnato and Neisworth (1980)	Intervention Efficiency Index	$\dfrac{\text{Post DA} - \text{Pre DA}}{\text{Time in program}}$
Brassell (1977) Rosenberg, Robinson, Finkler, and Rose (1987)	Changes in Developmental Velocities	$\dfrac{\text{Post DA} - \text{Pre DA}}{\text{Time in program}} - \dfrac{\text{Pre DA}}{\text{Pre CA}}$
Irwin and Wong (1974)	Age—compensated scores	$\text{Post DA} - [\text{Post CA} - \text{Pre CA}) \times (\text{Pre DA/Pre CA})]$
Oelwein, Fewell, and Pruess (1985)	Difference between Actual Performance Age and Predicted Performance Age at PostTest	$\text{Post DA} - \left[\text{Pre DA} + \left(\dfrac{\text{Pre DA}}{\text{Pre CA}} \times \text{time in program}\right)\right]$
Simeonsson and Weigerink (1975)	Efficiency Index	$\dfrac{\text{Post DA} - \text{Pre DA}}{\text{Ideal progress}} \div \dfrac{\text{Pre DA}}{\text{Pre CA}}$
Wolery (1983)	Proportional Change Index	$\dfrac{\text{Post DA} - \text{Pre DA}}{\text{Time in program}} \div \dfrac{\text{Pre DA}}{\text{Pre CA}}$

Pre CA = Chronological age at the beginning of the program.
Pre DA = Developmental age at the beginning of the program.
Post CA = Chronological age at the end of the program.
Post DA = Developmentat age at the end of the program.

although the formulas have effectively measured change in older children with handicaps.

To examine the relationship among a number of formulas listed in Table 1, Rosenberg, Robinson, Finkler, and Rose (1987) identified those strategies that measured rate of development (Bagnato & Neisworth, 1980) and that measured changes in rate of development (Irwin & Wong, 1974; Rosenberg et al., 1987; Simeonsson & Weigerink, 1975; Wolery, 1983). They then used all the formulas to analyze the Bayley Scale test scores of three groups of infants and young children with handicapping conditions enrolled in early intervention programs. They found the rate of change scores correlated most highly with other rate of change formula scores, and that developmental rate scores correlated most highly with other developmental rate scores. These data supported the authors a priori classification of the formulae into the two groups.

A problem which Odom and Fewell (1983), Rosenberg et al. (1987), and Snyder-McLean (1987) have noted, is that these measures assume that child development is linear and has a positive trend. If, in fact, a child's development begins to spontaneously accelerate (e.g., as in the natural acceleration of children's language development around the second birthday) at about the time the intervention program begins, the acceleration in development may

be wrongly attributed to the intervention program. Similarly, if a child's development begins to decelerate at about the time the intervention program begins, an erroneous conclusion drawn from these formulas would be that the program is actually having a negative effect upon the child. The Fewell and Sandall (1986) study is an example of just such a case. In both situations, only the inclusion of a control/contrast group could control for these nonlinear trends in development.

Inclusion of Supportive Evidence   A second approach to making single group designs more convincing has been to draw from multiple sources for demonstrating the program's effects. A number of researchers have recommended that multiple data sources should be used in demonstrating a program's effects (Cronbach, 1982; Karnes & Johnson, Chapter 16, this volume), with the presumption that these multiple sources can serve to "triangulate" the effects. Although specific standards or procedures for accomplishing this triangulation have yet to be determined, many programs that have used single group designs in their evaluation plan also include follow-up data on the children and families who move through their program. The information often suggests that children are performing in a positive way that is different from children with similar disabilities who were not in the program, although the standard of comparison is suggested rather than substantiated. Such information is very important to collect, and may be the basis for a strong argument for the effects of the treatment, but it generally does not allow the critical reader of research to draw a firm conclusion.

Examples from within Early Childhood Special Education Although they are the weakest experimental designs, single group designs, by necessity, are sometimes used in research that is designed to demonstrate the effects of programs. Using these designs, a number of researchers have examined the effects of specific early intervention models for infants with handicaps (Fewell & Sandall, 1986; Hanson, 1985; Widerstrom & Goodwin, 1987) and for preschool children with a range of handicapping conditions (Bailey & Bricker, 1985; Hoyson, Jamieson, & Strain, 1984; Oelwein et al., 1985; Rogers, Herbison, Lewis, Pantone, & Reis, 1986). To substantiate the case for the power of their treatment, many of these authors have also provided evidence of the children's successful performance after they have left the program (e.g., Widerstrom & Goodwin, 1987).

Correlational Designs

In contrast to group designs, which have the purpose of demonstrating that one variable caused a change in a second variable, the primary purpose of correlational designs is to describe the relationships that exist between variables without making a causal inference (Sax, 1979). In this type of research, groups of participants are usually compared on a range of variables, but none of the variables are actively manipulated by the researcher. Correlational designs often include the use of correlation coefficients to describe this relationship, but other statistical procedures may also be used (e.g., analyses of variance).

Examples from within Early Childhood Special Education Researchers have used correlational designs for several purposes in early childhood special education. Psychometric analyses of assessment instruments typically employ a correlational design. To demonstrate test-retest reliability of an assessment,

a researcher may administer the assessment to the same group of children on two occasions and compute correlations between the two scores. For example, to determine the test-retest reliability of the "Evaluation and Programming System for Infants and Young Children," Bailey and Bricker (1986) had observers code the developmental skills that twenty-eight children with handicaps exhibited on two occasions, and then computed a correlation between the two scores. Across subtests, coefficients ranged from .42 to .94 for the group of children with handicaps, indicating moderate to high reliability for the test.

Researchers also use a correlational design to demonstrate the validity of assessment instruments. In these studies, children's scores on the assessment may be correlated with their scores on another test that claims to measure the same developmental skill (i.e., to determine concurrent validity) or with a criterion condition or behavior (i.e., to measure criterion-related validity). For example, in his examination of the construct validity of the Receptive-Expressive Emergent Language Scale (REEL) for young children with mental retardation, Mahoney (1984) correlated the REEL scores of 60 children with a language sample collected from videotape and their performance on measures of cognitive development. Similarly, in their restandardization of the DIAL-R, Mardell-Czudnowski and Goldenberg (1984) reported a high correlation of the DIAL R scores and Stanford-Binet IQ scores for 2,447 children, and used this data to establish criterion-related validity for the screening test.

Correlational designs, in the broadest sense of the term, have been used frequently in early childhood special education to measure relationships between certain organismic variables and dependent variables. An organismic variable (e.g., mental retardation, low socioeconomic status, parent of a handicapped child) is a particular characteristic of an individual, and thus cannot be randomly assigned by the experimenter. Although these studies at times appear to be similar to nonequivalent control group designs (i.e., performances of different groups of individuals are compared with others), the researcher cannot assign the condition to any single individual. Thus, the investigator cannot draw causal inferences and may only obtain descriptive information.

Many studies using this type of design have appeared in the literature. For example, Beckman, Porkorni, Maza, and Balzer-Martin (1986) examined the stress experienced by the families of 17 preterm infants and the families of 17 full-term infants, finding significant correlations between informal and formal measures of social support and the stress experienced by the family at different points during the first year. In a study of the relationship between developmental levels of young children with handicaps and their level of play skills, Odom (1981) observed the play of children with mental retardation who ranged across developmental levels. He found significant correlations between the level of play (i.e., both social participation and cognitive play) and the children's level of development.

A further type of correlational design has been used to determine the relationship between certain process or procedural measures of early intervention and outcomes for children. This general type of approach has its roots in the effective teaching literature with elementary-age normally developing children (Brophy & Good, 1986). In that literature, academic learning time is observed in the classroom and is correlated with scores on tests of academic achievement. Significant positive correlations reveal strong association between the two variables.

Within early childhood special education, Moore, Fredericks, and Baldwin (1981) have examined observationally 14 aspects of the instructional environment that could relate to the maintenance of treatment gains occurring from early intervention programs. Using a stepwise regression formula, they found the most variance explained by the number of individual programs for each instructional area, and the number of minutes taken to administer individual programs.

A more current example of the correlational approach to research appears in the chapter by Carta, Sainato, and Greenwood (Chapter 13, this volume). In proposing an ecobehavioral analysis of early intervention, Carta and her colleagues (Carta & Greenwood, 1985; Carta, Greenwood, & Robinson, in press) have developed a detailed observation system that describes the instructional classroom across a number of dimensions. By examining the relationship between the ecobehavioral characteristics of the classroom and children's performances in those classrooms, these researchers are attempting to identify potent instructional variables in early intervention settings. Because these relationships are only correlational, the next step in the research will be to demonstrate the causal nature of the relationships through the use of the experimental group designs noted above, or through the single-subject designs noted below.

Single-Subject Research Designs

Single-subject experimentation emerged from the applied behavior analysis literature in the 1960s (Tawney & Gast, 1984). These designs share several characteristics:

1. They are idiographic in that they usually examine the performance of a single individual at multiple points across an extended time period rather than groups of individuals at one or two points in time.
2. They depend on the direct replication of program effects either within a single individual or across a small number of individuals.
3. Statistical analysis is usually not used to interpret outcomes but rather a visual interpretation of graphed data is the most common form of analysis.
4. The designs are flexible enough to address questions that arise during the study.
5. The dependent variables are often, but not necessarily, observational in nature (see Neisworth & Bagnato, Chapter 2, this volume).

A considerable number of single-subject designs exist, and the reader is referred to several excellent texts for a detailed analysis of the methodology (Barlow & Hersen, 1984; Kazdin, 1982, Tawney & Gast, 1984). However, two frequently used designs will be presented below.

The *withdrawal of treatment* design, also called a reversal design, involves several phases. Usually in the first phase, called the A or baseline phase, the child is observed in a situation that approximates the normal preintervention setting. The child is observed in this phase until a stable baseline (i.e., consistent level of responding) is obtained. In the second phase (i.e., the B phase), an intervention is introduced, and its effects on the child's behavior are observed. When the child reaches a level of stable response in this phase, the researcher begins a second baseline in order to establish experimental control. Experimental control demonstrates that the changes in the child's behavior are due to the treatment rather than to other events in the environment. To this point, the design may be called an ABA design. When attempting to produce positive results for children, most researchers will reinstitute the intervention, again looking for the effects of the treatment on the child's behavior, thus creating an ABAB design. An example of an ABAB design is found in Figure 2.

Withdrawal of treatment designs are most effective for answering questions about interventions in which child behavior or performance will vary with the implementation of the treatment. A concern with these designs is that once a treatment has had positive effects for the

child, it may not be ethical to then remove the treatment and return to a baseline condition, even if the treatment is to be reimplemented later.

Multiple baseline designs (see Figure 3) are also frequently used in programs for young children with handicaps. These designs replicate the effects of an intervention across several children, or they replicate the effects of an intervention for a single child across different settings or different behaviors. Experimental control is established by staggering the onset of treatment. For example, in Figure 3, each of the children are initially in a baseline condition. The treatment will begin with one child, while the other two remain in the baseline condition. When the intervention effects are seen with the first child, the intervention is then begun with the second child, and the third child remains in baseline. Likewise, when intervention effects are seen with the second child, the intervention is begun for the third child, allowing a replication of effects across the three children.

The multiple baseline design may be useful for addressing questions about interventions that produce changes in children's behavior that will not decrease when the intervention is withdrawn. Also, an advantage of the multiple baseline design is that treatment does not have to be withdrawn to demonstrate experimental control. However, one concern with this de-

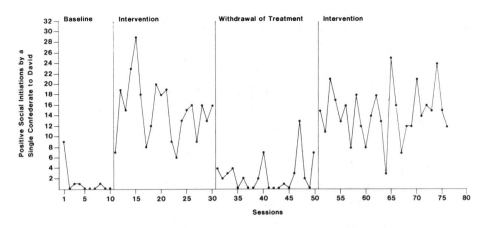

Figure 2. An example of a withdrawal of treatment single subject design.

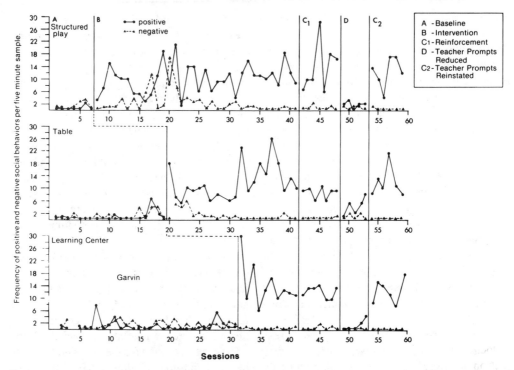

Figure 3.   An example of a multiple baseline single subject design. (This graph originally appeared in Odom, S. L., Hoyson, M., Jamieson, B., & Strain, P. S. [1985]. Increasing handicapped preschooler's peer social interaction: Cross-setting and component analysis. *Journal of Applied Behavior Analysis, 18,* 3–16.)

sign is that some children will have to stay in baseline an extended period of time (i.e., the second or third child). The advantage is that everyone will eventually receive intervention.

A concern often voiced about single-subject designs is that because they contain so few subjects, their results may not be generalizable beyond the subjects in the study. Single-subject researchers may attempt to build external validity for their results in several ways. First, studies may produce replications across several subjects. For most studies, the term "single subject" is somewhat of a misnomer because usually more than one subject is involved, although the number of subjects is almost always small. Second, single-subject researchers can provide detailed descriptions for individual subjects. Such descriptions may allow the reader of the research to understand for whom the interventions may or may not be effective. Third, single-subject researchers may describe their treatment in great detail in order to allow replication. Such detail should

give the reader of the research enough information to conduct the study, and thus would increase the likelihood that similar results could be achieved in another setting with similar children. As mentioned in the discussion of group designs, investigators have proposed that carefully documenting and measuring the implementation of the independent variable (i.e., the intervention) is a critical aspect of any single-subject design (Billingsley et al., 1980). Single-subject studies that include these features build a case for external validity, but even with these features, the small number of subjects in these designs is still a concern for many investigators.

Social validity is a concept that has emerged out of the single-subject design literature. It refers to judgments of the social importance of interventions. These judgments may occur at different levels: they may be judgments about the goals of programs or interventions, the methods employed in interventions, or the outcomes of interventions (Wolf, 1978). Such judgments may be made by comparing the different aspects of an intervention to a pre-established criterion, or by having individuals who are ultimately the consumers of the intervention directly evaluate the program's social importance (Kazdin, 1977). Thus, social validity represents a somewhat more conservative criterion for determining the success of a treatment than criteria used in other experimental methodologies. Not only must the primary data reflect a change in the child's behavior, but the behavior must produce a socially important change in the child's life. (See Karnes & Johnson, Chapter 16, this volume, for an extended discussion of social validity)

Examples in Early Childhood Special Education Single-subject designs are intervention oriented, and as such usually demonstrate the effects of a program or procedure. For example, Odom, Strain, Karger, and Smith (1986) used a withdrawal of treatment design to document the effects of using multiple peers to promote the social interaction of two children with handicaps. In a study of incidental teaching language facilitation strategies, Mudd and Wolery (1987) used a multiple baseline design to determine the effectiveness of an inservice training plus feedback procedure for training Head Start teachers to use such intervention approaches. Similarly, Strain and Kohler (Chapter 8, this volume) describe the use of a multiple baseline approach for answering a number of important questions about social interaction research with young children with handicaps.

A number of researchers have measured the social validity of interventions for young children with handicaps. Odom and Watts (1987) examined the effects of a strategy for reducing teacher prompts to peers in a social interaction training study for three children with autism. To determine the social validity of their intervention, these researchers compared the levels of social interactions of the children with autism in the study to normative data on young children's levels of social interaction (Greenwood, Walker, Todd, & Hops, 1981). In an examination of the social validity of outcomes of a unison responding and pacing strategy for

young children with substantial handicaps, Sainato, Strain, and Lyon (in press) had teachers from other classrooms rate videotapes of children in the treatment program who were at different stages of the treatment. These researchers found that during intervention teachers were significantly more likely to rate the subjects as children that they would like to have in their classes.

Qualitative Research

A huge range of procedures may be grouped under the general rubric of qualitative research. Research methodologies called naturalistic, ethnographic, interpretive, and descriptive all have been linked to this qualitative research paradigm at different times, although many researchers disavow the label (Erickson, 1986; Lincoln & Guba, 1985).

Ironically, qualitative research methodologies share several characteristics with single-subject design, even though applied behavior analysis is thought to be the antithesis of the qualitative approach. Qualitative research 1) is idiographic, 2) employs a methodology that is flexible to questions that arise during the study, 3) involves data collection at multiple points over extended time periods, and 4) depends primarily upon observation as a data collection device. However, it differs from single-subject methodology as well as all the other methodologies by its inductive approach to scientific inquiry.

Qualitative research often begins with *focusing* on the research question. The questions of interest are narrowed until they represent a realistic guide to inquiry (Lincoln & Guba, 1985). When the research question is determined, the investigator begins by collecting information from sources that should best be able to provide answers. The primary methods for collecting information are through participant observation and interviews (Dor-Bremme, 1985; Edgerton, 1985). From these data, the researcher forms his or her theory about the answer to the research question. This theory is "grounded" in the data (Glaser & Strauss, 1967), in that researchers base their theories upon the data they collect rather than initially collecting their data to substantiate a previously formulated theory. When a theory is established, the researcher systematically samples cases that will support or challenge the theory. As new data emerge, the theory may be confirmed, reshaped, or abandoned.

Qualitative research is often criticized because it lacks clearly established standards for its methodology. By design, qualitative research is characterized by methodologies that are very flexible. Such flexibility allows the investigation to move as the data indicate, but it discourages standardization of procedures. However, a number of researchers have begun establishing standards for acceptable methodology (Kirk & Miller, 1986; Levine, 1985; Lincoln & Guba, 1985).

Examples in Early Childhood Special Education   Qualitative research appears to be slowly gaining favor as a methodology in early childhood special education. As researchers begin to address questions for which there are not adequate dependent variables, or for which standard experimental designs are not possible, qualitative designs may provide a rich source of data (Odom & Shuster, 1986). For example, in their investigation of the reactions of parents to the diagnosis of their infants who were health impaired or who had other handicaps, Shuster, Guskin, Hawkins, and Okolo (1986) interviewed a number of mothers and physicians across multiple time periods. These researchers identified themes that occurred consistently across mothers. In a study of parental perceptions about mainstreamed programs for their children, Winton and Turnbull (1981) initially interviewed a number of parents and then developed a systematic questionnaire to collect further information that would substantiate their conclusions. In a further example of the qualitative approach to research, Barber and

her colleagues (Chapter 11, this volume) present an insightful review of family research that employs qualitative methodology to examine family systems and the reciprocal influences of the family member with a handicap.

CONCLUSION

Research in early childhood special education generates many questions, and no single experimental design or methodology will be able to answer them all. An effective researcher should have a working knowledge of all the designs identified above and should be skilled in matching the appropriate design to the questions under study. However, such a task is not easy. The feasibility of any single methodology will depend on the physical, sociopolitical, theoretical, and paradigmatic contexts in which the research occurs. In addition, the design must be chosen to yield results that are understandable to potential consumers of the research; again, this task is complicated, since most researchers in early childhood special education respond to the information needs of multiple consumer groups.

Conducting research in early childhood special education is often a balancing act wherein the investigator is weighing the need for methodological rigor against the contextual constraints of working in naturalistic settings. In the chapters that follow, the authors discuss the work of researchers who have achieved this balance in at least some of their investigations. As the demand increases for a respectable empirical base for early childhood special education, researchers must continue to be creative in their search for methodologies that will answer pressing research questions in a convincing manner.

REFERENCES

Ainsworth, M. D., Blehar, M. C., Waters, E., & Wall, S. (1978). *Patterns of attachment: A study of the strange situation*. Hillsdale, NJ: Erlbaum Press.

American Psychological Association. (1973). *Ethical principles in the conduct of research with human participants* Washington, DC: American Psychological Association.

Bagnato, S. J., & Neisworth, J. T. (1980). The intervention efficiency index: An approach to preschool program accountibility. *Exceptional Children, 46,* 264–269.

Bailey, D. B., Simeonsson, R. J., Winton, P. J., Huntington, G. S., Comfort, M., Isbell, P., O'Donnell, K. J., & Helm, J. M. (1986). Family focused intervention: A functional model for planning, implementing, and evaluating individualized family services in early intervention. *Journal of the Division for Early Childhood, 10,* 156–172.

Bailey, E. J., & Bricker, D. D. (1985). Evaluation of a three-year early intervention demonstration project. *Topics in Early Childhood Special Education, 5*(2), 52–66.

Bailey, E. J., & Bricker, D. D. (1986). A psychometric study of a criterion-referenced assessment instrument designed for infants and young children. *Journal of the Division for Early Childhood, 10,* 124–134.

Barlow, D. H., & Hersen, M. (1984). *Single case experimental designs: Strategies for studying behavior change.* New York: Pergamon Press.

Barnett, W. S., & Pezzino, J. (1987). Cost-effectiveness analysis for state and local decision making: An application to half-day and full-day preschool special education programs. *Journal of the Division for Early Childhood, 11,* 181–189.

Beckman, P. J., Pokorni, J. L., Maza, E. A., & Balzer-Martin, L. (1986). A longitudinal study of stress and support in families of preterm and full-term infants. *Journal of the Division for Early Childhood, 11,* 2–9.

Billingsley, F., White, O. R., & Munson, R. (1980). Procedural reliability: A rationale and example. *Behavioral Assessment, 2,* 229–241.

Bowlby, J. (1969). *Attachment and loss, Vol. 1: Attachment.* New York: Basic Books.

Brassell, W. R. (1977). Intervention with handicapped infants: Correlates of progress. *Mental Retardation, 15,* 18–22.

Bricker, D. D. (1987). Impact of research on social policy for handicapped infants and children. *Journal of the Division for Early Childhood, 11,* 98–106.

Brinckerhoff, J. L., & Vincent, L. J. (1986). Increasing parental decision-making at the individualized educational program meeting. *Journal of the Division for Early Childhood, 11,* 46–58.

Bronfenbrener, U. (1974). *A report on longitudinal evaluation of preschool programs: Is early education effective?* Washington, DC: Office of Child Development. (ERIC Document Reproduction Service No. ED 093 501)

Bronfenbrener, U. (1976). The experimental ecology of education. *Educational Researcher, 5,* 5–15.

Brooks, P. H., & Baumeister, A. A. (1977). A plea for consideration of ecological validity in the experimental psychology of mental retardation: A guest editorial. *American Journal of Mental Deficiency, 81,* 407–416.

Brophy, J., & Good, T. (1986). Teacher behavior and student achievement. In M. Wittrock (Ed.), *Handbook of research on teaching* (3rd ed.) (pp. 328–375). New York: Macmillan.

Campbell, D. T., & Stanley, J. C. (1963). Experimental and quasi-experimental designs for research on teaching. In N. Gage (Ed.), *Handbook of research on teaching* (pp.171–246). Chicago: Rand McNally.

Carta, J. J., & Greenwood, C. R. (1985). Eco-behavioral assessment: A methodology for expanding the evaluation of early intervention programs. *Topics in Early Childhood Special Education, 5*(2), 88–104.

Carta, J. J., Greenwood, C. R., & Robinson, S. (in press). Application of an ecobehavioral approach to the evaluation of early intervention programs. In R. Prinz (Ed.), *Advances in behavioral assessment of children and families.* Greenwich, CT: JAI Press.

Casto, G., & Mastropieri, M. A. (1985). The efficacy of early intervention programs: A meta-analysis. *Exceptional Children, 52,* 425–435.

Cook, T. D., & Campbell, D. T. (1979). *Quasi-experimentation: Design and analysis issues for field settings.* Chicago: Rand McNally.

Cronbach, L. J. (1982). *Designing evaluations of educational and social programs.* San Francisco: Jossey-Bass.

DEC membership chairperson report. (1987). Division for Early Childhood. *DEC Communicator, 13*(4), 2.

Dokecki, P. R. (1986). The impact of evaluation research on policymaking. In L. Bickman & D. Weatherford (Eds.), *Evaluating early intervention programs for severely handicapped children and their families* (pp.311–334). Austin: PRO-ED.

Dor-Bremme, D. W. (1985). Ethnographic evaluation: A theory and method. *Educational Evaluation and Policy Analysis, 7,* 65–83.

Dunst, C. J., & Snyder, S. W. (1986). A critique of the Utah State University early intervention meta-analysis research. *Exceptional Children, 53,* 269–276.

Edgerton, R. B. (1985). The participant-observer approach to research in mental retardation. *American Journal of Mental Deficiency, 88,* 498–505.

Edwards, A. L. (1984). *Experimental design in psychological research* (5th ed.). New York: Holt, Rinehart, & Winston.

Erickson, F. (1986). Qualitative methods in research on teaching. In M. Wittrock (Ed.), *Handbook of research on teaching* (3rd ed.) (pp.119–161). New York: Macmillan.

Feiman-Nemser, S., & Floden, R. E. (1986). The cultures of teaching. In M. Wittrock (Ed.), *Handbook of research on teaching* (3rd ed.) (pp. 505–526). New York: Macmillan.

Fewell, R. R., & Sandall, S. R. (1986). Developmental testing of handicapped infants: A measurement dilemma. *Topics in Early Childhood Special Education, 6*(3), 86–99.

Garrison, J. W. (1986). Some principles of postpositivistic philosophy of science. *Educational Researcher, 15*(9), 12–15.

Glaser, B., & Strauss, A. (1967). *The discovery of grounded theory.* Chicago: Adline Press.

Gray, S. W. (1986). Early intervention for children at educational risk: Some sidelights for learners with severe mental retardation. In P. Dokecki & R. Zaner (Eds.), *Ethics of dealing with persons with severe handicaps* (pp. 97–112). Baltimore: Paul H. Brookes Publishing Co.

Greenwood, C. R., Walker, H. M., Todd, N. M., & Hops, H. (1981). Normative and descriptive analysis of preschool freeplay social interaction rates. *Journal of Pediatric Psychology, 4,* 343–367.

Guralnik, D. B., & Friend, J. H. (1966). *Webster's New World Dictionary of the American Language: College Edition.* New York: The World Publishing Company.

Hanson, M. J. (1985). An analysis of the effects of early intervention services for infants and toddlers with moderate and severe handicaps. *Topics in Early Childhood Special Education, 5*(2), 36–51.

Heshusius, L. (1982). At the heart of the advocacy dilemma: A mechanistic world view. *Exceptional Children, 49,* 6–13.

Heshusius, L. (1986). Paradigm shifts and special education: A response to Ulman and Rosenberg. *Exceptional Children, 52,* 461–465.

Hoyson, M., Jamieson, B., & Strain, P. S. (1984). Individualized group instruction of normally developing and autistic-like children: The LEAP curriculum model. *Journal of the Division for Early Childhood, 8,* 157–172.

Irwin, J., & Wong, S. (1974). Compensation for maturity in long-range intervention studies. *Acta Symbolica, 5,* 33–46.

Jenkins, J. R., Odom, S. L., & Speltz, M. L. (1987). *Effects of integration and structured play on the development of handicapped children.* Manuscript submitted for publication.

Jordan, J., Hayden, A., Karnes, M., & Wood, M. (Eds.). (1977). *Early education for exceptional children: A handbook of ideas and exemplary practices.* Reston, VA: Council for Exceptional Children.

Kazdin, A. E. (1977). Assessing the clinical or applied importance of behavior change through social validation. *Behavior Modification, 1,* 427–451.

Kazdin, A. E. (1982). *Single-case research designs.* New York: Oxford University Press.

Kelman, H. C. (1967). Human use of human subjects: The problem of deception in social psychological experiments. *Psychological Bulletin, 67,* 1–11.

Kerlinger, F. N. (1986). *Foundations of behavioral research* (3rd ed.). New York: Holt, Rinehart, & Winston.

Kirk, J., & Miller, M. C. (1986). *Reliability and validity in qualitative research.* Newbury Park, CA: Sage Publications.

Kuhn, T. S. (1970). *The structure of scientific revolutions* (2nd ed.). Chicago: University of Chicago Press.

Leinhardt, G. (1980). Modeling and measuring educational treatment in evaluation. *Review of Educational Research, 50,* 393–420.

Levine, H. G. (1985). Principles of data storage and retrieval for use in qualitative evaluations. *Educational Evaluation and Policy Analysis, 7,* 169–186.

Lincoln, Y. S., & Guba, E. G. (1985). *Naturalistic inquiry.* Beverly Hills, CA: Sage Publications.

Lortie, D. (1975). *Schoolteacher.* Chicago: University of Chicago Press.

Lovaas, O. I. (1987). Behavioral treatment and normal educational and intellectual functioning in young autistic children. *Journal of Consulting and Clinical Psychology, 55,* 3–9.

Mahoney, G. (1984). The validity of the Receptive-Expressive Emergent Language Scale with mentally retarded children. *Journal of the Division for Early Childhood, 9,* 86–94.

Mardell-Czudnowski, C., & Goldenberg, D. (1984). Revision and restandardization of a preschool screening test: DIAL becomes the DIAL-R. *Journal of the Division for Early Childhood, 8,* 149–156.

Milgram, S. (1963). Behavioral study of obedience. *Journal of Abnormal and Social Psychology, 67,* 371–378.

Moore, M. G., Fredericks, H. D., & Baldwin, V. L. (1981). The long-range effects of early childhood education on a trainable mentally retarded population. *Journal of the Division for Early Childhood, 4,* 93–109.

Mudd, J. M., & Wolery, M. (1987). Training Head Start teachers to use incidental teaching. *Journal of the Division for Early Childhood, 11,* 124–134.

Odom, S. L. (1981). The relationship of play to developmental level in mentally retarded preschool children.

Education and Training of the Mentally Retarded, 16, 136–141.

Odom, S. L. (1987). The role of theory in the preparation of professionals in early childhood special education. *Topics in Early Childhood Special Education 7*(3), 1–11.

Odom, S. L., DeKlyen, M., & Jenkins, J. R. (1984). Integrating handicapped and nonhandicapped preschoolers: Developmental impact on the nonhandicapped children. *Exceptional Children, 51,* 41–49.

Odom, S. L., & Fewell, R. R. (1983). Program evaluation and early childhood special education: A meta-evaluation. *Educational Evaluation and Policy Analysis, 5,* 445–460.

Odom, S. L., & McConnell, S. R. (1985). Performance-based conceptualization of social competence of handicapped preschool children: Implications for assessment. *Topics in Early Childhood Special Education, 4*(4), 1–19.

Odom, S. L., & Shuster, S. K. (1986). Naturalistic inquiry and the assessment of young handicapped children and their families. *Topics in Early Childhood Special Education, 6*(2), 68–82.

Odom, S. L., Strain, P. S., Karger, M., & Smith, J. (1986). Using single and multiple peers to promote social interactions of young children with behavioral handicaps. *Journal of the Division for Early Childhood, 10,* 53–64.

Odom, S. L., & Watts, E. (1987). *Cross-setting generalization of autistic preschool children's social interactions in peer-initiation interventions: Using correspondence training with peer-intervenors.* Manuscript submitted for publication.

Oelwein, P. L., Fewell, R. R., & Pruess, J. B. (1985). The efficacy of intervention at outreach sites of the program for children with Down syndrome and other developmental delays. *Topics in Early Childhood Special Education, 5*(2), 78–87.

Phillips, D. C. (1983). After the wake: Postpositivistic educational thought. *Educational Researcher, 12*(4), 4–8.

Rogers, S. J., Herbison, J. M., Lewis, H. C., Pantone, J., & Reis, K. (1986). An approach to enhancing the symbolic, communicative, and interpersonal functioning of young children with autism or severe emotional handicaps. *Journal of the Division for Early Childhood, 10,* 135–149.

Rosenberg, S. A., Robinson, C. C., Finkler, D., & Rose, J. S. (1987). An empirical comparison of formulas evaluating early intervention program impact on development. *Exceptional Children, 54,* 213–219.

Sainato, D., Strain, P. S., & Lyon, S. L. (in press). Facilitating group instruction for handicapped preschool children. *Journal of the Division for Early Childhood.*

Sax, G. (1979). *Foundations of educational research.* Englewood Cliffs, NJ: Prentice-Hall.

Shonkoff, J. P., Hauser-Cram, P. (1987). Early intervention for disabled infants and their families: A quantitative analysis. *Pediatrics, 80,* 650–658.

Shuster, S. K., Guskin, S. L., Hawkins, B. A., & Okolo, C. M. (1986). Views of health and development: Six mothers and their infants. *Journal of the Division for Early Childhood, 11,* 18–27.

Simeonsson, R. J., & Weigerink, R. (1975). Accountability: A dilemma in infant intervention. *Exceptional Children, 45,* 474–481.

Simpson, R. G., & Eaves, R. C. (1985). Do we need more

qualitative research or more good research? A reaction to Stainback and Stainback. *Exceptional Children, 51,* 325–330.

Skrtic, T. M. (1986). The crisis in special education knowledge: A perspective on perspective. *Focus on Exceptional Children, 18*(7), 1–16.

Snyder-McLean, L. (1987). Reporting norm-referenced program evaluation data: Some considerations. *Journal of the Division for Early Childhood, 11,* 254–265.

Spieker, S. J. (1986). Problems of very insecure attachment found in samples of high-risk infants and toddlers. *Topics in Early Childhood Special Education, 6*(3), 37–53.

Stainback, S., & Stainback, W. (1984). Broadening the research perspective in special education. *Exceptional Children, 50,* 400–408.

Stainback, S., & Stainback, W. (1985). Quantitative and qualitative methodologies: Competitive or complementary? A response to Simpson and Eaves. *Exceptional Children, 51,* 330–334.

Tawney, J. W., & Gast, D. L. (1984). *Single-case research in special education.* Columbus, OH: Charles E. Merrill.

Tjossem, T. D. (1976). *Intervention strategies for high risk infants and young children.* Baltimore: University Park Press.

Ulman, J. D., & Rosenberg, M. S. (1986). Science and superstition in special education. *Exceptional Children, 52,* 459–460.

Walker, H. M., Hops, H., & Greenwood, C. R. (1984). The CORBEH research and development model: Programmatic issues and strategies. In S. C. Paine, G. T. Bellamy, & B. Wilcox (Eds.), *Human services that work: From innovation to standard practice* (pp. 57–77). Baltimore: Paul H. Brookes Publishing Co.

White, K. R., Mott, S., Pezzino, J., & Behl, D. (1987, May). *Longitudinal studies of the effects and costs of early intervention with handicapped children.* Paper presented at conference: Focusing on the Future: Linking Research, Policy, & Practice in Early Intervention, Washington, DC.

White, K. R., & Pezzino, J. (1986). Ethical, practical, and scientific considerations of randomized experiments in early childhood special education. *Topics in Early Childhood Special Education, 6*(3), 100–116.

Widerstrom, A. H., & Goodwin, L. D. (1987). Effects of an infant stimulation program on the child and the family. *Journal of the Division for Early Childhood, 11,* 143–153.

Winton, P. J., & Turnbull, A. D. (1981). Parent involvement as viewed by parents of preschool handicapped children. *Topics in Early Childhood Special Education, 1*(3), 11–19.

Wolery, M. (1983). Proportional change index: An alternative for comparing child change data. *Exceptional Children, 50,* 167–170.

Wolf, M. M. (1978). Social validity: The case for subjective measurement or how applied behavior analysis is finding its heart. *Journal of Applied Behavior Analysis, 11,* 203–214.

Zahorik, J. A. (1986). Acquiring teaching skills. *Journal of Teacher Education, 37*(2), 21–25.

Chapter 2

Assessment in Early Childhood Special Education

A Typology of Dependent Measures

John T. Neisworth and Stephen J. Bagnato

CLINICAL PRACTICE AND RESEARCH in early childhood special education (ECSE) can no longer be constrained by the assessment traditions of the past. Descriptions, predictions, placements, and prescriptions for special needs infants and preschoolers require specialized materials and practices. Further, behavioral and developmental research usually employs assessment measures as dependent variables to register the effects of independent or treatment variables. Too frequently practitioners have been without appropriate assessment tools or have been forced to use instruments not matched to the measurement purpose. Assessment devices and practices designed for older and nonhandicapped persons have been stretched and force-fitted to the needs of early childhood and special education. These practices and purposes are often at odds with the business of contemporary ECSE.

Over the past decade, necessity has been the mother of invention in ECSE. A confluence of social, legal, and professional forces has created both needs and instruments for assessing handicapped infants and preschool children. For example, the survival of low birth weight, small-for-gestational age babies has created the need and thus the instruments for earlier and more sensitive appraisal; the passage of Public Laws 94-142 and 99-457 requires and continues to generate multidimensional interdisciplinary evaluation procedures; the proliferation of infant/preschool intervention programs and the push for accountability has

necessitated the use of treatment-specific, curriculum-based assessment systems; and the legal, ethical, and practical realities of parent involvement have generated instruments that stress parent-child and family relations (Fewell, 1983; Neisworth & Bagnato, 1987; Paget, 1985).

The field of early childhood special education has now reached the point at which the diverse instruments available must be appraised and categorized according to the appropriate "fit" of assessment purposes and instruments. "Scores" or other indices produced by these instruments are used as the dependent measures in research and practice. It becomes crucial to employ the relevant dependent variable, and often several, in order to describe child status and to detect treatment effects. The wrong choices may result in failure to detect important changes or may provide misleading information. This chapter presents an eight-category scheme to assist the early intervention specialist in making appropriate selections of instruments. This framework offers a practical guide for matching assessment measures to clinical and research needs.

A MULTIDIMENSIONAL MODEL: MULTIPLE VARIABLES FOR ASSESSMENT AND RESEARCH

New and multiple dependent measures permit not only more comprehensive, reliable, and valid clinical assessments, but also the opportunity to pose more varied and refined research hypotheses. It is naive and often misleading to employ a singular criterion in clinical child assessment and research. The complexities of special needs children as well as the requirements of parents and professionals demand a *multidimensional approach* to assessment (Bagnato & Neisworth, 1981, 1985a, 1985b; Brooks-Gunn & Lewis, 1981; Fewell, 1983; Gresham, 1983; Simeonsson, 1986; Simeonsson, Huntington, & Parse, 1980).

Rationale

While a multitrait-multimethod approach has been recommended for years (Campbell & Fiske, 1959; Gresham, 1983), Public Law 99-457 *mandates* multivariate evaluation for all handicapped children. Many factors support the logic of this approach. Clinically, many young handicapped children have complex developmental needs and/or sensorimotor impairments that require alternative assessment practices that sample behavior over a wider range of tasks, situations, people, and time. This broad based appraisal not only more comprehensively and accurately defines child needs, but also establishes a richer basis for effective programming and treatment. Moreover, one form of assessment can serve as a "check" to challenge the accuracy of more traditional (but often misleading) forms of assessment. In short, the reliability and validity of child/environmental assessment is significantly enhanced by using a multidimensional approach.

Definition

Multidimensional assessment refers to a comprehensive and integrated evaluation approach that employs *multiple measures,* derives data from *multiple sources,* surveys *multiple domains,* and fulfills *multiple purposes.*

Multimeasures Multimeasures provide a broader based, more valid vehicle for assessing developmentally disabled preschoolers. Some recent research has demonstrated that diagnostic batteries that combine norm-based, curriculum-based, and clinical judgment scales have the greatest probability of accurately de-

scribing and prescribing the complex needs of multihandicapped preschoolers (Bagnato, 1984; Bagnato & Neisworth, 1981; 1985b). Others have argued for the prominent use of alternative or adaptive assessments, including play scales (Fewell, 1986), clinical judgment measures (Simeonsson et al., 1980), information-processing paradigms (Zelazo, 1982), curricular methods (Neisworth & Bagnato, 1986), and measures of attention (Brooks-Gunn & Lewis, 1981).

Multisource Multisource aspects emphasize that information must be gathered from several contexts (home, school, clinic) and sources (parents, teachers, therapists). Multisource measures are clearly synonymous with interdisciplinary team procedures for child and environmental assessment. Early intervention research supports the value of multisource assessment in investigations of such areas as parent-professional agreement (Blacher-Dixon & Simeonsson, 1981; Gradel, Thompson, & Sheehan, 1981; Sexton, Miller, & Murdock, 1984), team congruence in diagnosis and intervention (Bagnato, 1984), and the reliability and predictive validity of developmental assessments (Sciarillo, Brown, Robinson, Bennett, & Sells, 1986).

Multidomain Multidomain features refer to assessments that examine the child's capabilities and deficiencies within and across several developmental and behavioral areas or processes. Traditional assessment has emphasized cognitive capabilities. Infant and preschool programs, by necessity, have expanded assessment to include language, socioemotional, gross motor, fine motor, and self-care domains (Garwood & Fewell, 1983). Recently, researchers have urged clinicians to target such dimensions as mastery motivation (Jennings, Connors, Stegman, Sankaranarayan, & Mendelsohn, 1985); social competence (Neisworth, 1984); play (Fewell, 1986); temperament (Zeenah, Keener, Anders, & Levine, 1986); self-regulation (Kopp, 1982); attention (Brinker & Lewis, 1982); emotional expression (Emde, Katz, & Thorpe, 1978); and early coping behavior (Zeitlin, Williamson, & Szczepanski, 1984).

Multipurpose Multipurpose measurement refers to the several assessment functions: description, placement, prediction, and prescription. The Developmental Assessment Curriculum Linkage Model can serve as a blueprint to guide early intervention specialists in "linking" or synchronizing the instruments employed in diagnosis, intervention, and progress evaluation (Bagnato & Neisworth, 1981; Neisworth & Bagnato, 1987). Other researchers have built upon this framework to propose their own versions of a linkage approach (e.g., Bricker, 1986). The linkage model uses curriculum-based assessment as the focal point for planning treatment and monitoring progress. Additional measures in the multidimensional battery are chosen in terms of their congruence with curricular goals and content. This congruence between assessment and curriculum objectives leaves little doubt about the mutual content validity of testing and teaching. Through this method, both the descriptive and predictive validities of child assessments are enhanced.

In summary, the linkage model is most illustrative of multidimensional assessment in that it promotes the blending of philosophies (e.g., developmental/behavioral), purposes (e.g., prescriptive, evaluative), and practices (e.g., multidimensional assessment and treatment).

The body of this chapter deals with a heuristic framework or typology to guide in the selection and use of appropriate combinations of measures for multidimensional assessment applicable to both clinical practice and research. It is the authors' hope that this framework will prove useful for discriminating among types of measures useful for description, placement, prediction, and prescription in early childhood special education.

PROMINENT AND EMERGING DEPENDENT VARIABLES IN ASSESSMENT

Advances in early childhood assessment allow clinicians to describe, place, predict, and prescribe more accurately for young handicapped children. Yet, despite new developments, few resources are available to guide the early childhood specialist in selecting and using assessment measures as dependent variables. Much research, and certainly clinical practice, attempts to measure a change in or a relationship between a treatment (i.e., independent) variable and an outcome (i.e., dependent) variable. A treatment may or may not show an effect, depending on how the outcome is measured. Use of IQ change (i.e., norm-based assessment) to assess the influence of a 9-month preschool program would, at best, show slight effects. In this example, a curriculum-based dependent measure would be a wiser choice since it would be more sensitive to the content of the preschool program. Problems in research and practice do not exclusively reside with treatment circumstances, but are often associated with the use of inappropriate dependent measures that fail to register changes or relationships that may be present.

Available assessment instruments can be categorized into several classes based on the particular purpose for measurement. In Table 1, a *typology* of assessment devices that encompasses eight distinct categories of instruments is presented: curriculum-based, adaptive-to-handicap, process, norm-based, judgment-based, ecological, interactive, and systematic observation. Depending upon the clinical purpose or research question, certain types of instruments are more appropriate and may fit more closely the purpose or question than would others. Discussion of each type of measure includes definition and characteristics, examples of instruments within the measurement category, applicability of the measure in research and clinical practice, feasible research questions addressed by the measure, and research close-ups of instruments within the category.

CURRICULUM-BASED ASSESSMENT

Definition and Characteristics

Curriculum-based assessment (CBA), a form of criterion-referenced evaluation, is rapidly emerging as the preeminent diagnostic/ pre-

Table 1. Dependent variables in early intervention assessment

Type of dependent variable	Definition	Illustrative dependent measures	Appropriate purpose research/practice	Illustrative studies
Curriculum-based (CBA)	. . . child mastery of objectives within a continuum of objectives	Learning Accomplishment Profile (Sanford & Zelman, 1981) HICOMP Preschool Curriculum (Willoughby-Herb & Neisworth, 1983)	Identify individual treatment objectives. Track child progress/provide feedback for instructional changes. Offer common base for interdisciplinary diagnosis and treatment.	MacTurk & Neisworth, 1978 Bagnato, 1984
Adaptive-to-handicap (AH)	. . . modification of assessment content to include or permit alternative sensory or response modes	Oregon Project Curriculum (Brown, Simmons, & Methvin, 1979) Uniform Performance Assessment System (White, Edgar, Haring, Affleck, Hayden, & Bendersky, 1981) Early Intervention Developmental Profile (Rogers, D'Eugenio, Brown, Donovan, & Lynch, 1981) Carolina Curriculum (Johnson-Martin, Jens, & Attermeier, 1986)	Obtain valid assessment by circumventing handicap. Identify goals for instruction. Specify strategies for learning.	Kiernan & Dubose, 1974
Process (PA)	. . . detection of changes in child related to changes in stimulus events; qualitative changes in cognitive status	Information Processing Approach (Zelazo, 1982) Infant Learning (Dunst, 1981)	Probe possible capabilities when more direct, conventional assessment is not feasible.	Kearsley, 1981 Dunst, 1983
Norm-based (NBA)	. . . comparison of a child's skills and characteristics relative to an appropriate referent group	Battelle Developmental Inventory (Newborg, Stock, Wnek, Guidubaldi, & Svinicki, 1984) McCarthy Scales of Children's Abilities (McCarthy, 1972)	Diagnostic screening and description of child characteristics relative to peers.	Sciarillo, Brown, Robinson, Bennett, & Sells, 1986 Dubose, 1976

(continued)

scriptive approach in applied settings for young exceptional children (Fewell & Sandall, 1983). Firmly rooted in the traditions of programmed instruction and precision teaching, CBA involves a direct congruence among testing, teaching, and progress evaluation (Bagnato, Neisworth, & Capone, 1986; Neisworth & Bagnato, 1986). *Curriculum-based assess-*

Table 1. *(continued)*

Type of dependent variable	Definition	Illustrative dependent measures	Appropriate purpose research/practice	Illustrative studies
Judgment-based (JBA)	. . . impressions of developmental/ behavioral traits (e.g., reactivity, motivation, normalcy)	Carolina Record of Individual Behavior (Simeonsson et al., 1982) Perceptions of Developmental Status (Bagnato & Neisworth, 1987)	Detect perceptions and bias. Estimate nebulous/difficult to observe processes. Enhance scope of assessment battery.	Blacher-Dixon & Simeonsson, 1981 Bagnato, 1984
Ecological (EA)	. . . evaluation of the physical, social, and psychological features of a child's developmental context	Early Childhood Environment Rating Scale (Harms & Clifford, 1980) Home Observation for Measurement of the Environment (Caldwell & Bradley, 1978)	Describe nature of reciprocal interactives. Identify environmental variables that suggest needed changes in interactions.	Bailey, Clifford, & Harms, 1982 Dunst, Trivette, & Cross, 1986
Interactive (IA)	. . . examination of social capabilities of the infant and caregiver and the content and extent of synchrony between them	Brazelton Neonatal Behavioral Assessment Scale (Brazelton, 1984) Parent Behavior Progression (Bromwich, 1978)	Appraise parent-child reciprocity; discover match between child competencies and tasks presented.	Crockenberg & Acredolo, 1983 Mahoney, Finger, & Powell, 1985
Systematic observation (SO)	. . . structured procedures for collecting objective and quantifiable data on ongoing behavior	Pla-Check (Doke & Risley, 1972) Mapping (Ruggles, 1982)	Analyze functional relations among antecedents, child behavior, and consequences; provide close-ups of strengths and weaknesses, and detect small changes.	Madle, Neisworth, & Kurtz, 1980

ment traces a child's achievement along a continuum of objectives, especially within a developmentally sequenced curriculum.

CBA tracks individual child performance on specific program objectives; in essence, each child's current performance is compared to past performance in order to monitor progress and learning. The foundation of CBA is the sequence of developmental objectives that constitute a program's curriculum. Objectives may vary from general "landmark" goals in each developmental domain (e.g., walks independently) to finely graded sequences of prerequisite behaviors that constitute a given skill-

objective (e.g., turns head 30° to search for an auditory stimulus). CBA enables the teacher or diagnostic specialist to determine the specific breakdown of skills that a child has or has not acquired within the developmental task analysis. The scope, quality, and extent of individual learning can be described by profiling ranges of absent (−), fully acquired (+), and emerging (±) capabilities which then provide curriculum entry points for instruction and treatment. In regular progress evaluations teachers use these entry points as criteria to determine mastery of the skills that have been taught. The primary strength of curriculum-based assessment is its direct synchrony between testing and teaching. For this reason, CBA is referred to as the "test-teach-test" model; baseline assessments guide instruction and therapy to specific objectives that form the basis for evaluations of child mastery and program effectiveness.

Selected Examples of Dependent Measures

Thorough and current reviews of curriculum-based measures are available (Bagnato et al., 1986; Bailey, Jens, & Johnson, 1983; Neisworth & Bagnato, 1986). Two types of CBA instruments are *curriculum-imbedded* and *curriculum-referenced* measures. Curriculum-imbedded scales are those in which the assessment and curricular objectives are essentially identical; curriculum objectives *are* the assessment items. Curriculum-referenced scales sample objectives commonly emphasized in most developmental curricula, but not integral to any particular curriculum.

Curriculum-Imbedded Measures The *Learning Accomplishment Profile* (LAP) (Sanford & Zelman, 1981), with its related assessment components, the *Early Learning Accomplishment Profile* (ELAP) (Glover, Preminger, & Sanford, 1978), and the *Learning Accomplishment Profile: Diagnostic Edition* (LAP-D) (LeMay, Griffin, & Sanford, 1978) are perhaps the most widely used curriculum systems in preschool programs for young exceptional children. The LAP covers the birth-to-72-months age range with developmental objectives in six areas: fine motor, gross motor, language, cognition, self-help, and personal-social.

The HICOMP Preschool Curriculum (Willoughby-Herb & Neisworth, 1983) is a behaviorally based, developmentally sequenced curriculum system, appropriate for both normal and handicapped preschoolers, birth to 5 years old. The curriculum (800 objectives) and its assessment component, the *Track Record,* survey communication, self-care, motor, and problem solving skills. Unique features of the system include "linkage" of tasks from other developmental scales to objectives within the curriculum, and matching of behavioral strategies to teach clusters of related behavior.

Curriculum-Referenced Measures The *BRIGANCE Diagnostic Inventory of Early Development* (BDIED) (Brigance, 1978) is one of the best criterion-referenced measures of developmental functioning that is not, itself, a curriculum. The inventory samples brief task analyses of skills across the birth-to-84-month age range in 11 domains, including general knowledge and comprehension, fine motor skills, prespeech, and preambulatory motor skills.

The Developmental Activities Screening Inventory II (DASI) (Fewell & Langley, 1984) is most appropriately used as an interim screening of young children suffering sensorimotor impairments. The DASI analyzes skills through 55 uncategorized developmental tasks requiring such abilities as means-end relationships, cause-effect, association, fine motor coordination, and number concepts. The manual includes suggestions for modifying response modes for handicapped preschoolers and for designing strategies useful for teaching general goals compatible with many curricula.

Applicability of CBA Measures for Research and Clinical Practice

Appropriate Purposes Curriculum-based measures fulfill two primary research and clinical objectives: they *identify* a child's individual treatment objectives and *track* the child's progress within a curriculum. Curriculum-based instruments are sensitive to child change because goals are operationally defined and mastery criteria are clearly stated. Whereas norm-based assessment (to be discussed) provides comparative developmental age functioning, curriculum-based assessment makes explicit the child's strengths and weaknesses in terms of curricular objectives.

The second purpose of CBA is directly linked with the first (i.e., longitudinal analysis of child gain). Curriculum-based measures enable early childhood special educators to chart child change in a formative manner. Evaluation provides a *within-program* analysis of curricular objectives achieved. This evaluation can occur on a weekly, daily, or even per session basis and serves not only to assess learning as a function of treatment, but also to flag no-progress areas that may require changes in instructional methods. Summative evaluation allows a treatment team to form a broader perspective on child change and program effectiveness based on pretest/posttest analyses over a longer period of time (e.g., monthly, quarterly). The close relationship among assessment, goals, and methods provide a much more reliable and valid picture of intervention effectiveness.

Another valuable CBA dimension is its capacity to describe interdisciplinary team collaboration in practical terms. The use of a uniform curriculum-based instrument by members of a treatment team enables charting of the relative contributions of each discipline or therapy to specific aspects of child development progress. For example, specialists representing child development, speech/language, occupational therapy, physical therapy, psychology, pediatrics, nursing, or parents can complete those portions of the CBA measure that relate to their treatment content and objectives (e.g., physical therapy = gross motor). Formative CBA analysis can then determine status and progress in specific areas as a function of particular disciplinary treatment. Such analyses are invaluable guides to team decision-making about needed modifications in intervention approaches.

Some caveats must be considered in the use of curriculum-based assessment. CBA instruments and/or curricula on which they are based often have undetermined reliability and validity; moreover, many were developed to address the unique needs of particular programs and, consequently, may not encompass the content of another program. Finally, many CBA systems lack a clear theoretical and/or empirical base of support; thus, they may not show the necessary congruence across content, goals, and methods that must be present for progress and efficacy evaluations.

Feasible Research Questions Certain questions in clinical research and practice, such as those below, can be addressed through the use of criterion/curriculum dependent measures.

Is there a differential impact between a home-

and a center-based intervention program on the developmental progress of developmentally delayed infants?

Does the use of a uniform treatment-based diagnostic measure increase the consistency and correspondence of interdisciplinary team members' assessments of handicapped children?

Does any difference exist between the rates of developmental progress of children with Down syndrome and children with cerebral palsy enrolled in the same type of early intervention program?

Does a particular program show similar or dissimilar effectiveness within and across areas of development?

Research Close-Ups Research into curriculum-based developmental assessment has centered on two primary areas of study; concurrent validity studies and program efficacy research.

MacTurk and Neisworth (1978) designed a concurrent validity study to evaluate the relative sensitivity of a norm-based scale, such as the Gesell Developmental Schedules (GDS), and a curriculum-based scale, such as the HICOMP Preschool Curriculum, in evaluating the progress of both handicapped and nonhandicapped preschool children within a mainstreamed early intervention program. Two major questions guided the study: What is the correspondence between norm- and criterion-based scales? Of what utility are these two measures in program planning and progress monitoring? Results revealed high positive correlations between the GDS and HICOMP scales for the mainstreamed handicapped preschoolers. The authors emphasized the importance of using norm-based assessment (NBA) and CBA instruments interdependently within early intervention programs matched to summative and formative evaluation purposes, respectively.

A treatment efficacy study was conducted by Bagnato and Neisworth (1985a) on two etiologically distinct groups of brain injured infants and preschoolers (i.e., congenital and acquired injury). Formative and summative evaluations of child progress, team congruence, and therapeutic impact in each developmental domain were obtained using a multidimensional diagnostic battery composed of norm, curriculum, and clinical judgment scales. However, the primary index of progress and effectiveness was the curriculum-based Early Intervention Developmental Profile (EIDP) (Rogers, D'Eugenio, Brown, Donovan, & Lynch, 1981). The study revealed that an intensive treatment program, as demonstrated on a program-specific curriculum measure, could alter the functioning of severely handicapped infants in distinct ways. In addition, the study showed that functioning levels are not necessarily static, as was once believed. The CBA measure was invaluable as a weekly/monthly measure of progress and as a summative (3½ month) evaluation.

ADAPTIVE-TO-HANDICAP ASSESSMENT

Definition and Characteristics

Sensorimotor impairments usually obfuscate and depress estimates of a child's developmental capabilities. A young child with cerebral palsy is penalized, particularly, on cognitive items that require precise motor manipulation to solve problems. If the child fails to sort shapes, is it due to a lack of discrimination or concept formation or to the presence of the neuromotor limitation? Adaptive assessment strategies are used increasingly to circumvent the child's disability in order to obtain a more accurate appraisal of the child's functioning. *Adaptive-to-Handicap (AH) scales include or permit the use of alternative sensory or response modes to minimize false item failure.*

Three types of adaptive approaches are available. First, some scales simply permit modification of the items and procedures where necessary. The person administering the scale decides how and when to make such ad lib adaptations. Another type provides systematic guidelines for altering the stimulus characteristics of the task or the response mode of the child to provide a less biased assessment. Finally, some assessment devices have been designed and even standardized for a specific handicap; such instruments exclude tasks and

procedures that would limit the performance of a child with that handicap. Scales or curricula for young visually impaired children, for example, emphasize auditory and tactile modes of learning.

Selected Examples of Dependent Measures

One of the best designed and practical diagnostic/prescriptive curriculum systems with specific disability modifications is *Developmental Programming for Infants and Young Children* (DPIYC) (Schaefer & Moersch, 1981). The system includes the *Early Intervention Development Profile* (EIDP) (Rogers et al., 1981) to survey the birth-to-36-month age range and, for the 36–72 month age range, the *Preschool Developmental Profile* (PDP) (Brown et al., 1981). The DPIYC is best employed by an interdisciplinary team of three to seven specialists to assess youngsters in six developmental domains (512 behaviors): cognitive, perceptual/fine motor, gross motor, social-emotional, language, and self-care. The *Stimulation Activities* guide provides clear, practical intervention activities for parents and teachers. This guide details strategies for altering the stimulus dimensions and response modes for each task to circumvent visual, hearing, and motor impairments.

A diagnostic and curricular system designed especially for the young visually handicapped child is the *Oregon Project for Visually Impaired and Blind Preschool Children* (ORP) (Brown, Simmons, & Methvin, 1979). The ORP was designed and field-tested with children in the birth-to-72-month age range. The structure of the curriculum is the *Skill Inventory* which comprises 700 behavioral assessment tasks in such domains as cognitive, language, self-help, socialization, fine motor, and gross motor. Developmental tasks are included that emphasize alternate auditory and tactile channels for experiencing, orienting, and exploring.

Applicability of AH Measures for Research and Clinical Practice

Appropriate Purposes Scales and procedures that adapt to the handicap have two primary purposes. As already discussed, these scales are employed to obtain a more valid or "fair" estimate of the handicapped child's intact capabilities or level of functioning independent of the sensorimotor impairment. Procedures for excluding biased items and for rescoring performances in order to arrive at a more representative age range appraisal of developmental functioning are available.

Perhaps the most practical function of AH scales is diagnostic teaching. Various researchers and clinical specialists have written extensively on this practical function of adaptive procedures (Bagnato & Neisworth, 1981; Dubose, Langley, & Stagg, 1977; Fewell, 1984; Haeusserman, 1958). In essence, adaptive assessment blends testing and teaching within the same sequence of activities. The diagnostic specialist modifies tasks so that different stimulus characteristics and response modes can be incorporated as needed. For example, handles may be placed on formboards, and magnets may be used to allow easy movement of objects by cerebral palsied children. Once this has been accomplished, the clinician can systematically proceed to evaluate upper, then lower levels of developmental functioning in order to obtain a profile of the child's functional range. This appraisal accomplishes two objectives. First, the assessment identifies tangible goals for instructional planning that are within an easy to challenging range for the child. This helps to build motivation and provides the opportunity for nearly errorless learning. Second, adaptive procedures allow the clinician to specify the types of environmental arrangements, task modifications, and other alterations that are necessary to enable the young child to function and to learn optimally.

A major limitation of adapting formal diagnostic measures is the violation of standardized testing procedures. Whenever any variance from standardized procedures is introduced, the validity and interpretation of the results are compromised. A real dilemma exists, then, when deciding whether to adapt or not. On the one hand, failure to adapt will produce an underestimate of the child's capabilities; on the other hand, using adaptations departs from standardization procedures and prevents comparability with the available norms. Resolution of the dilemma may take two forms: use of a multidimensional diagnostic battery and/or the use of the few recently designed scales and curricula that are handicap-specific. A multidimensional diagnostic battery provides a broader evaluation and helps offset the underestimates produced by the handicap. The newly created handicap-specific measures already incorporate adaptations to accommodate various disabilities, and some even have limited norms for the disability group in question.

Feasible Research Questions AH assessment measures are useful as dependent measures in addressing issues such as:

Do blind and cerebral palsied toddlers differ in the age at which they acquire such cognitive concepts as object permanence, cause-effect, and means-end?

To what extent does a handicap such as deafness contribute to depressed scores on traditional measures of infant intelligence?

Within a catchment region, what percentage of handicapped preschoolers of various disabilities are misdiagnosed as retarded using a nonadaptive measure?

Will adaptive as opposed to traditional measures of the cognitive/ social/communicative abilities of handicapped preschoolers be in closer agreement with parental estimates of these abilities?

Research Close-Ups Research using AH measures is meager. but has focused primarily on demonstrations of changes in scores or diagnostic categories for handicapped children.

Kiernan and Dubose (1974) attempted to assess the intellectual performance of deaf-blind children on the Cattell Infant Intelligence Scale. Concurrently, items were selected from other infant scales and were adapted to accommodate the children's sensory deficits. Tasks were modified by increasing the size of some items, by altering textures, and by changing some items from two to three dimensions. In general, stimulus characteristics such as increased brightness and color were emphasized; also, other physical attributes were altered, such as changing the size of blocks and puzzle pieces to facilitate manipulation. This study

demonstrated that the children performed significantly better with the adapted scale compared to their own concurrent performances on
the traditional Cattell scale.

PROCESS ASSESSMENT

Definition and Characteristics

Frustrated by the limitations of traditional assessment practices for young handicapped children, early intervention specialists are
increasingly relying upon alternative approaches to evaluate the cognitive, adaptive,
affective, and social communication capabilities of such children (Bagnato & Neisworth, 1981; Brooks-Gunn & Lewis, 1981;
Dunst, 1981; Kearsley & Sigel, 1979; Simeonsson, Huntington, Short, & Ware, 1982;
Zelazo, 1979). Adaptive-to-Handicap measures, discussed above, represent one movement in this direction. Additionally, a more
recent option is *process* assessment, designed
to estimate the hidden capabilities of severely
impaired children. *Process assessment (PA)
examines changes in child reactions (e.g.,
smiling, vocalizing, heart rate, surprise, glee)
as a function of changes in stimulus events, to
produce, by inference, an indication of the
child's level of cognitive abilities, or a
qualitative advance in cognitive stage.*

Kearsley (1981) reports that the severely
handicapped child's reactions to sudden discrepant variations in the stimulus event (usually
visual) are "used to infer the infant's capacity
to attend to, process, and assimilate the information contained in the stimulus sequences"
(p. 47). It is important to note that the adaptive
quality of this assessment paradigm arises out
of the fact that the child does not need to use
speech or motor responses to demonstrate understanding of concepts or events.

Other, perhaps more familiar, forms of process assessment methods include Piagetian-
based evaluation. These methods often require
specific motor and speech behaviors to complete problem-solving tasks involving object
constancy, means-end, and cause-effect. Similar to the other process measures, these methods also examine the child's recognition of discrepancy (e.g., object once seen is now
hidden), memory, and recall in order to complete the tasks.

Selected Examples of Dependent Measures

Although Piagetian-based process assessment
scales have been used extensively in developmental research and clinical practice for many
years (Escalona & Gorman, 1966; Uzgiris &
Hunt, 1975), measures of dimensions such as
habituation, visual attention, and expectancy-
discrepancy are still being created and refined.

One of the most exciting and potentially valuable process assessment methodologies is the
information processing approach of Zelazo
(1982). With this approach, an attempt is made
to detect and gauge the cognitive, perceptual,
and affective/social capabilities elicited from
severely motor impaired children and premature infants. Zelazo's approach detects the
child's awareness of discrepancies among a series of visual events (e.g., car on inclined plane
topples a clown at the bottom unexpectedly
after repeated trials). These reactions are
judged to be "replacement" responses for the
child's impaired sensory and neuromotor
disabilities.

*Infant Learning: A Cognitive-Linguistic In-
tervention Strategy* (Dunst, 1981) is a practical
process instrument and intervention system
based on the Uzgiris-Hunt Infant Psychological Development Scale, a Piagetian-style assessment measure. Focused on children in the
birth-to-30-month range, this system blends
assessment and treatment goals and intervention methods by organizing process tasks into
several developmental domains, such as object
permanence, gestural and vocal imitation,
causality, and scheme actions. This approach
emphasizes the importance of the child's experience of "co-occurrences" or stimulus-re-
sponse connections between behavior and
outcome.

Applicability of PA Measures
for Research and Clinical Practice

Appropriate Purpose   The central purpose

of PA is to probe the assumed underlying perceptual-cognitive capacities of children when normal response modalities are absent or impaired. Very young infants and/or severely impaired preschoolers may not be able to respond to conventional assessment tasks. They are "untestable" through standard assessment techniques. The process approach attempts to discover capabilities, such as recognition of discrepancies, memory and recall, attention, and information-processing, through indirect and inferential means. Typically, these assessments rely upon such affective responses as surprise, glee, and upset as indirect indicators of the child's comprehension and memory.

When possible, assessment should be direct and noninferential. It is ideal to evaluate directly specific skills and knowledge taught within the preschool; however, when a child is too young and/or impaired, process assessment is, at least, a possible avenue for probing and identifying the existence of greater comprehension, discrimination, and recall than may be detected through more conventional assessment.

Feasible Research Questions   Process assessment measures most appropriately apply to three kinds of research and clinical questions: the screening/detection of subtle and obscured competencies, amenability to treatment, and the possible prediction of status. Possible research questions are as follows:

Is a newborn able to recognize discrepancies in a repeated series of complex visual events?

Will a given severely impaired child express recognition of an event in the same manner repeatedly? Can this expression be modified through operant means to a more sophisticated level?

Is a handicapped child's level of performance within a developmental curriculum predicted by earlier performance on a process assessment measure?

Research Close-Ups   In a series of clinical case studies, Kearsley (1981) reported attempts to assess the cognitive capacity of infants and toddlers suffering severe neu-

rodevelopmental disorders. Children who showed significant deficits in cognitive functioning as measured by the process approach failed to acquire normal language or to make appreciable gains on standard neurodevelopmental instruments. In contrast, a 22-month-old, cerebral palsied child was assessed with the process approach which, contrasted to conventional assessment, revealed cognitive capabilities that were intact and essentially normal. Based on the findings of the process assessment, speech stimulation and language teaching were implemented. At 3½ years of age, the child was regarded as intellectually normal.

Dunst and Rheingrover (1983) employed the Uzgiris-Hunt Scales of Psychological Development with four young children with different diagnoses: mental retardation, hydrocephalus, spastic diplegia, and Down syndrome. The longitudinal study covered a 33-month period. The infants ranged between 3 and 8 months of age at the outset. Cognitive growth curves were plotted for attainments in the object permanence domain. Dunst reported that despite diagnostic differences, the four infants showed "remarkably similar patterns of cognitive growth" (Dunst & Rheingrover, p. 53). He emphasized that the rates of acquisition of the four infants were considerably different; the largest variations were evidenced by the two infants with mental retardation. Dunst remarks that ordinal process scales may be useful in determining the average ages at which homogeneous groups of handicapped infants attain specific landmarks.

NORM-BASED ASSESSMENT

Definition and Characteristics

Without doubt, the most frequently used child performance measures for assessing cognitive and developmental attributes have been standardized/normative instruments. *Norm-based assessment compares a child's developmental skills and characteristics to those of a referent (normative) group that is comparable in child and demographic dimensions.* Diagnostic analysis with norm-based measures produces scores that gauge the child's status in cognitive and other developmental domains. The scores derived in the assessment are "standard" scores reflecting the child's relative position with respect to a normal distribution representative of the standardization population. Standard scores are reported as deviation scores such as developmental and intellectual quotients (DQ/ IQ), percentiles, and z and t scores.

Norm-based assessment has three major purposes: to *describe* the child's functioning in terms of developmental norms (e.g., walking, smiling, talking, problem solving); to *place* the child within a diagnostic category; and to *predict* the child's development. Knowing the performance of the average child of a given age on a given skill permits comparison of the child being assessed to such norms. Young children who deviate seriously from age expectations can thus be identified as exceptional in the skill areas sampled. When children exhibit a cluster of deviances (a syndrome), a diagnosis is possible (e.g., developmental retardation, cerebral palsy, autism). Predictions based on normative assessment are mixed and equivocal. Norm-based scales have been criticized for their lack of predictive validity for normal children despite the fact that they are adequate predictors for moderately and severely impaired children (Dubose, 1976; VanderVeer & Schweid, 1974). Presuming linearity of development and a typical environment, the child diagnosed as normal at 18 months will most likely be normal at 6 years of age. Similarly, the child diagnosed as abnormal at an early age will likely remain abnormal in the absence of any special efforts. It is important to emphasize, however, that the business of early intervention is to enhance developmental progress and thus invalidate predictions of poor development.

Selected Examples of Dependent Measures

The Battelle Developmental Inventory (BDI) (Newborg, Stock, Wnek, Guidubaldi, & Svinicki, 1984) is a recently developed, standardized scale that is the only current example of a norm-referenced diagnostic measure that also integrates adaptive and curriculum-referenced features into its structure. The BDI evaluates 341 critical developmental skills across children from birth to 8 years and within five functional domains and 22 subdomains.

A unique adaptive feature of the BDI is its inclusion of modifications for specific sensorimotor impairments and general guidelines for presenting test tasks to children with diverse developmental disabilities. In addition, the developmental and behavioral content of the BDI is congruent with the goals and tasks of frequently used developmental curricula. Normative and technical data on the BDI are equivocal at this time.

The Bayley Scales of Infant Development (BSID) (Bayley, 1969) are the most widely used and certainly technically adequate of the norm-referenced, developmental skill measures. The BSID surveys landmark skills across the 2–30-month age range through 244 tasks organized into mental and motor subscales. Both subscales cover such behaviors as sensory-perceptual skills, object permanence, classification, memory, expressive and receptive language, body control, eye-hand coordination, and socialization. The BSID was standardized on 1262 children; it reports comparative data in terms of standard developmental indexes, the Psychomotor Development Index (PDI), and the Mental Development Index (MDI).

The McCarthy Scales of Children's Abilities (MSCA) (McCarthy, 1972) are a developmentally based measure of cognitive functioning for children 2½ to 8½ years old. The MSCA surveys children's strengths and weaknesses across 18 subtests and six global scales. Normative and validity data are adequate for individual diagnosis and prediction.

Applicability of NBA Measures for Research and Clinical Practice

Appropriate Purpose Norm-based instruments provide a comparison against a standard. For example, an infant's weight can be compared to normative information on infant weight. This comparative information is descriptive and forms the data base for diagnosis. The diagnostic process includes three steps. First, a child is assessed with a scale that has norms for the particular attributes under examination. Second, the child's performance is represented by a standard score that places him or her within the distribution of scores generated by the reference group. This score or performance level describes the child's relative standing. Third, the clinician interprets the score in terms of some classification system that categorizes significant differences; these differences classify the performance of clinical subgroups. For example, a child given the Bayley Scales achieves an MDI of 50. This score permits the comparison of the child's score against the distribution of scores in the Bayley standardization sample. Then, a diagnosis of moderate mental retardation is made based on classification criteria superimposed on that distribution. Norm-based assessment is indicated when the purpose of assessment is to place a child within a diagnostic category. Unlike CBA, norm-based assessment does not portray the child in isolation from all other children; instead, it provides a frame of reference and a basis for interpretation (Lyon, 1982).

Diagnosis has both research and clinical applications. In research, it is often important to distinguish the relative performance, response to treatment, or unique characteristics of various diagnostic subgroups. For example, different subtypes of neurologically impaired children often show distinguishing behavioral characteristics. Clinically, diagnosis can offer teachers and therapists general information on a child's strengths and weaknesses and, in some instances, potential reasons for the child's problem. If the child is placed within a diagnostic category, the clinician or researcher should be alert for the presence of associated characteristics typically displayed by children with that diagnosis. Finally, perhaps the most productive use of norm-based assessment in research and clinical practice is for diagnostic screening. Technically adequate normative measures are vital in accurately identifying the child who is atypical. Strong reliability and validity in a test ensure that false positives and false negatives will be minimized (Mercer, Algozzine, & Trifiletti, 1979). Screening instruments such as the revised Denver Developmental Screening Test (DDST) (Frankenburg, Dodds, & Fandal, 1982) and other such systems are designed to differentiate abnormal from normal functioning and to indicate the need for evaluation.

All too often norm-based measures are used indiscriminately (Shonkoff, 1983). When the purpose of assessment is not diagnosis but program planning or monitoring of child progress during treatment, the use of such measures is unwarranted. Norm-based scales lack the precision to chart increments of change; in addition, the content of a program may not even be sampled by the norm-based measure. Also, norm-based developmental measures do not generally include handicapped children within standardization samples. Finally, the sensorimotor emphasis of many tasks biases the assessment of children with sensory and neuromotor impairments. Nevertheless, norm-based measures do permit early identification and differential diagnosis of developmental disabilities.

Feasible Research Questions Norm-based measures may address such questions of diagnosis and prediction as the following:

Which of several developmental screening instruments will yield the smallest number of false positives in a rural early identification effort?

Are infant intelligence tests reliable predictors of later cognitive functioning in multihandicapped children?

Is the Bayley Motor Scale administered at 3 months of age predictive of a subsequent diagnosis of cerebral palsy?

Do three subgroups of neurologically impaired children (cerebral palsy, spina bifida, and traumatic brain injury) differ with respect to normative assessments of temperamental lability?

What is the concurrent validity of a normative self-report measure to diagnose parent-child stress when compared with more time-consuming direct observation, interview, and anecdotal records of the interaction?

Research Close-Ups Controversy surrounds the predictive validity of infant intelligence scales. While such scales appear to be poor predictors for nonhandicapped youngsters, some researchers have suggested their predictive value for severely handicapped children. Dubose (1976) administered one of three mental measures to 28 multihandicapped children: the Cattell Infant Intelligence Scale, the BSID, or the Merrill-Palmer test. When the results were analyzed, children were divided into high/low IQ groups and younger/older age groups. Results demonstrated a nonsignificant correlation for the higher IQ group and a significant correlation for the lower IQ group. These findings indicate the stability of IQ for the lower group and the utility of infant intelligence tests for predicting subsequent intellectual functioning in severely impaired children. All children diagnosed as retarded on the first evaluation retained the retarded classification at second testing. Moreover, 81% of the children retained the same level of retardation as determined by their first initial diagnosis.

Recent research has examined the criterion validity of the Denver Developmental Screening Test for accurately identifying biologically at-risk infants (Sciarillo et al., 1986). Sixty-two neonatal intensive care unit graduates were assessed using the DDST in the home concurrently with a comprehensive evaluation including the BSID and pediatric and physical therapy assessments. The DDST results showed a false negative rate of 87.5% and a false positive rate of 13%. The authors discussed the results in terms of the unique needs of biologically at-risk infants with subtle problems compared to the more gross deficits of mentally retarded children—a population the DDST was designed to target. However, given the very young age of the children being studied, the authors failed to discuss the sparse sample of behaviors at the lower end of the scale on the DDST compared to the BSID, which could well have contributed to the screening inaccuracy problems.

JUDGMENT-BASED ASSESSMENT

Definition and Characteristics

One of the most unique and potentially valuable advancements in early developmental assessment is the use of structured clinical judgment devices. *Judgment-based assessment (JBA) collects, structures, and usually quantifies the impressions of professionals and caregivers about child environmental characteristics.*

A continuum of instruments exists within the category of JBA. Such measures range from those that require *in situ* observation and immediate judgment to those that ask for accumulated impressions over time and situations. For example, observers may be asked to document the degree of hyperactivity of a given preschool child. They might observe the child for 30 minutes in the preschool and then complete a checklist or a rating scale; although not truly objective, this procedure is a more structured form of gathering clinical impressions. Toward the more subjective end of the continuum, caregivers and professionals who know the preschool child might be asked to complete a scale regarding the child's activity level. Such opinions, while not based on immediate and guided observation, rely on a broader retrospective of accumulated impressions across time, people, and situations. Although retrospective and highly subjective, the longitudinal nature of these questions may provide important information.

JBA scales can be an important component in comprehensive assessment. First, many professionals assert that handicapped children, particularly children with severe and multiple handicaps, are shortchanged by formal assessment instruments that are insensitive to small increments in the child's capabilities (Simeonsson et al., 1980); JBA can be useful in this regard. Second, it is important to provide a means whereby clinical staff and parents can have personal input that either augments or challenges formal assessment; sole reliance on formal, more objective assessment neglects the invaluable opinions and impressions that can be offered by those persons who have known and worked with a child over time and contexts. This concern for *social validity* (Wolf, 1978) is addressed by JBA. People make value judgments about children that influence teaching, treatment, and child progress. It is, then, vital to detect and possibly adjust the perceptions of parents, teachers, therapists, and significant others in the child's environment. Third, judgment-based measures often tap ambiguous traits and behaviors that are not gauged by more objective instruments. Some examples of these traits and behaviors include reactivity, consolability, temperament, motivation, muscle tone/tension, reinforcement value of the child, normalcy of appearance and behavior, play style, attention, self-control, and self-esteem. Because of the definitional ambiguities of such traits, a few researchers have attempted to design systems that structure the collection of subjective impressions about the child. Instruments are now available that allow a Likert-type scaling of child traits under focus; each trait is operationally defined to enhance reliability of impressions.

Selected Examples of Dependent Measures

The *Perceptions of Developmental Status* (PODS) scale (Bagnato & Neisworth, 1987; Bagnato, Neisworth, & Eaves, 1978) was originally developed to detect discrepancies in parent-professional views of a handicapped preschooler's status. It proved to be a valuable procedure for standardizing interdisciplinary team decision-making based on clinical impressions. The revised PODS surveys 18 developmental/behavioral characteristics not frequently included on traditional assessment devices for children 2 to 6 years of age. These characteristics are organized within seven major clusters: communication, sensorimotor, physical, self-regulation, cognitive, self-social, and general development. Clinical ratings are obtained using a 5-point scale anchored to operational definitions for each point value. Current research within mainstreamed day care and preschool settings is ongoing to determine reliability and validity.

Focusing on capabilities in the birth-to-48-month age range, the *Carolina Record of Individual Behavior* (CRIB) (Simeonsson et al., 1982) measures the developmental skills and behavioral style of severely handicapped youngsters. A 9-point scale allows parents and professionals to rate their clinical perceptions in 15 operationally defined domains, including social orientation, frustration, activity, reactivity, object orientation, endurance, and reactivity. The CRIB also enables individuals to record their perceptions of the severity of various stereotypes or rhythmic habit patterns (RHP) such as body rocking, head banging, hand flapping, and rumination. Descriptive norms on these developmental and behavioral dimensions are based on over 600 young children exhibiting various disabilities.

Infant temperament assessment scales are another type of subjective or clinical judgment measure. These require the caregiver to provide accumulated observations and impressions about an infant on a rating scale that surveys various aspects of the infant's self-regulatory and affective capabilities. The most common temperament instruments employed are those developed by Carey and his colleagues: the *Infant Temperament Questionnaire* (ITQ) (Carey & McDevitt, 1977); the *Toddler Temperament Scale* (TTS) (Fullard, McDevitt, & Carey, 1978); and the *Behavioral Style Questionnaire* (BSQ) (McDevitt & Carey, 1975). These three scales sample capabilities in the age range from 4 to 84 months in various processes including activity and distraction level, persistence, threshold of response, approach/withdrawal, and rhythmicity. These judgment-based instruments are unique in that they have normative groups and allow the derivation of standard scores for diagnostic and comparative purposes.

Applicability of JBA Measures for Research and Clinical Practice

Appropriate Purposes Judgment-based measures seem best fitted for detecting perceptions rather than for determining objective facts of child status. When the question is how parents and staff view a child, these subjective measures are most appropriate. This phenomenological aspect is often neglected, but it may be an important dimension to highlight, since people's value judgments may be an important indication of how they will interact with the young handicapped child. It is often important to determine the correspondence of judgments among parents and professionals who work with the child. Significant discrepancies would suggest the need for a closer examination of differences. For example, counseling and education may be required to assist parents in becoming more informed or realistic about their child's capabilities, or perhaps team members' judgments differ due to the circumstances or limitations in the amount of time spent in contact with the child. For example, physical therapy may evoke unconsolable crying from the child; as a result, the physical therapist's perceptions of the child are likely to be very different from those of the parent or the developmental psychologist. Detecting these discrepancies in perception can help each team member to monitor and adjust personal views. These discrepancies may also underscore the need for programmatic or methodological changes.

A second major situation in which JBA instruments may be successfully applied is that in which the characteristics to be assessed are nebulous and thus refractory to objective assessment. As previously mentioned, attributes such as reactivity, object orientation, motivation, endurance, and self-control do not invite clear-cut observation and recording since they are processes or response classes rather than discrete behaviors. JBA procedures are particularly well suited for estimating such child traits.

Finally, some might argue that expediency is a rationale for the use of JBA. Certainly these measures are often more convenient, and are quicker and easier to employ than objective child performance instruments. Sheer expediency, however, does not constitute an acceptable rationale for child assessment when other more appropriate methods are available. Judgment-based scales are, then, most appropriate when they address phenomonological issues or augment more objective assessments.

Feasible Research Questions Measures of clinical impressions are employed appropriately as dependent variables in research and practice that examine issues such as those listed below.

What is the correspondence between parental and staff perceptions of child development and temperament?

Does increased therapy time with the child improve the correlation between subjective and objective measures?

Do a father's perceptions of his child's status differ from those of the mother?

Are parents' subjective ratings of global child traits more accurate than their parallel estimates of specific developmental skills?

Does the addition of a judgment-based device significantly improve the diagnostic/prescriptive accuracy of a multi-measure assessment battery for young severely handicapped children?

Can parents and professionals provide reasonably congruent estimates of children's developmental or mental ages?

Research Close-Ups Judgment-based scales seem to be a response to the mandate of the public laws to involve parents in the team assessment process and the need to assess severely handicapped children. Researchers have responded to these changes not only by developing new clinical instruments and methods but also by using them to answer specific research questions created by these cultural changes and needs as illustrated in the following two studies.

Blacher-Dixon and Simeonsson (1981) stressed that parents must be an integral part of the team child assessment process. Previous research had indicated that parents, compared to professionals, systematically overestimate children's capabilities. The authors asserted that this phenomena of "overestimation" may be largely due to limitations of the measures used and of questions asked when collecting parent judgments rather than to actual bias. In a study of mothers and teachers of 52 developmentally disabled infants and preschoolers, the researchers examined the degree of similarity between parent and teacher ratings on the Carolina Record of Individual Behavior (CRIB) and also the degree of consistency between parent/teacher estimates across time using both the CRIB and two measures of child temperament: the *Infant Temperament Questionnaire*

(Carey & McDevitt, 1977) and the *Toddler Temperament Scale* (Fullard et al., 1978). Results demonstrated significant correspondence between maternal and teacher judgments about child behavior as well as "extremely consistent" estimates of temperamental and some behavioral characteristics over time.

Bagnato (1984) addressed the issue of congruence among members of an interdisciplinary team, including mothers, in their assessments of developmental and behavioral progress within a treatment program for severely and multihandicapped infants and preschoolers ($n = 54$). Norm-based assessment, curriculum-based assessment, and judgment-based scales were administered. The Perceptions of Developmental Skills (PODS) (Bagnato et al., 1978), was the JBA scale completed by the teacher, occupational therapist, psychologist, and the mothers. Results clearly demonstrated that interdisciplinary team members maintained a high level of internal consistency in assessing both observed and perceived child skills and gains. (Only the child psychiatrist showed a significant underestimation of child capabilities in the social-emotional domain.) Three team professionals and the parents showed high levels of overall agreement on the PODS, with significant discrepancies only on the more nebulous dimensions such as attention, motivation, and attachment. The author concluded that mothers were better judges of changes in subtle behavioral characteristics than of discrete developmental skills.

ECOLOGICAL ASSESSMENT

Definition and Characteristics

Traditional assessment has focused almost exclusively on characteristics of the child. Such a perspective fails to account for the environmental factors that contribute to the child's status. Contemporary learning theory and instructional/therapeutic approaches have provided the impetus for broadening the concept of assessment to include environmental variables. These variables account for the antecedent, contemporaneous, and consequent events that influence a child's development. This trend has

been termed "ecological assessment." *Ecological assessment (EA) refers to the examination and recording of the physical, social, and psychological features of a child's developmental context.* Physical elements that are commonly evaluated when employing an ecological approach include room layout, materials available, lighting, temperature control, and the properties of toys. Common social features include extent of peer interaction, caregiver sensitivity and responsiveness, and provision of rewards and punishment. The psychological/ learning variables consist of setting events, discriminative stimuli, child's behavior, consequences, and the contingencies among these.

Ecological assessment is clearly built on an interactive model, a position that stresses that behavior is a function of personal variables interacting with environmental variables. Field theory (Barker, 1968; Lewin, 1951), operant learning theory (Bijou & Baer, 1978; Skinner, 1968), process-product studies of teacher effectiveness (Brophy, 1979; Flanders, 1970), and contemporary child development models emphasizing reciprocity in interactions (Bell, 1968; Sameroff, 1986) provide a strong rationale for ecological assessment.

Selected Examples of Dependent Measures

Generally, dependent measures are in the formative stages of development and vary in their technical adequacy and field-testing. These scales use combinations of different types of assessment formats to derive information (e.g., clinical ratings, anecdotal records, criterion checklists, and normative assessments).

Perhaps the most widely used measure of the content, quality, and responsiveness of young children's home environments is the *Home Observation for Measurement of the Environment* (HOME) (Caldwell & Bradley, 1978). The reliability and validity of the HOME Inventory for normal infants and preschoolers has been well established, but research on its application in populations of developmentally disabled children is only now emerging (Elardo & Bradley, 1981). The HOME Inventory is appropriate for children from birth to 72 months. The first section (0–36-month age range) appraises such clusters of home ecological attributes as emotional and verbal responsivity of the mother, avoidance of restriction and punishment, organization of the physical and temporal environment, provision of adequate play materials, and opportunities for variety in daily stimulation. Similar dimensions are tapped in section two for the 37–72-month-old child (i.e., provision of stimulation through equipment, toys, and experiences; stimulation of mature behavior; availability of a stimulating physical and language environment; avoidance of restriction and punishment, pride, affection, and thoughtfulness; masculine stimulation; and independence from parent control).

One exemplary approach for evaluating the ecological context for young exceptional children is the *Early Childhood Environment Rating Scale* (ECERS) (Harms & Clifford, 1980). The ECERS focuses on 37 items to rate the quality of the classroom setting for preschool children. Ratings are accomplished through a 7-point scale (1 = inadequate; 7 = excellent) for such items as furnishings for relaxation and comfort, dramatic play, free play, scheduled time for gross motor activities, room arrangement, and space to be alone. The scale has been used in some studies with handicapped preschools (Bailey, Clifford, & Harms, 1982). Results show that on 32% of the items, ratings for regular classrooms were significantly higher than those for special classrooms; this has implications for the impact on program decision-making and child progress. The ECERS will soon be available with additional items appropriate for day care centers that integrate handicapped youngsters. A similar instrument is designed for evaluating home day care settings and also has items for rating provisions for enrolled handicapped children.

Applicability of EA Measures in Research and Clinical Practice

Appropriate Purposes Ecological assessment can serve both to describe and to prescribe environmental factors for the young exceptional child. First, such measures describe the specific nature of the reciprocal interaction (i.e., the environmental variables that influence the child's development and the child's own effect upon persons and things within that environment). Second, ecological assessment identifies those child and milieu dimensions that permit manipulation of such variables to improve interactive outcomes. These measures are especially useful in examining the properties of daycare/preschool/hospital settings and family home circumstances. Among the features in child care settings and home circumstances that have been addressed are changes in the physical aspects of the environment (e.g., room arrangement, toys and learning materials, furnishings, number and characteristics of children, program content and sequence, and staff-child ratio), the social behaviors (e.g., communication between the child, peers, and adults), and stimulus-/response learning opportunities (e.g., the use of sound approximations instead of gestures to obtain a toy from the teacher) (Rogers-Warren, 1982; Smith, Neisworth, & Greer, 1978).

Family characteristics are another crucial aspect of the child's environment. EA samples such family attributes as qualities of the home environment (e.g., provision of toys, crowding), parent interactions with the handicapped child (e.g., presence of the father for active play and role modeling), changes in family coping skills (e.g., family's level of and response to economic hardship), social support systems (e.g., kinship and friendship networks), and health of family members.

Feasible Research Questions Illustrative clinical and research questions that might require an ecological dependent measure are:

Do alterations in the physical arrangement of the preschool classroom increase the handicapped child's frequency of self-management and independent acts?

Will handicapped children increase their level of involvement in lessons with a "zone" teacher supervision pattern (e.g., group circle time activities) versus "group" staffing patterns (e.g., teacher responsible for six children regardless of activity)?

Does *in situ* home counseling with the family

significantly increase their skills in managing resources (e.g., money, food), interacting with their handicapped child, arranging alternative social support systems, and coping with stress through preventive decision making?

Do direct instruction and videotape modeling significantly increase parents' skills in teaching and managing the behavior of their handicapped preschooler?

Research Close-Ups In a study of preschools for handicapped and nonhandicapped children, Bailey examined possible environmental differences that might contribute to children's progress (Bailey et al., 1982). ECERS (Harms & Clifford, 1980) was employed as the dependent measure to provide an overall account of the preschool setting. Twenty-five classrooms for handicapped and 56 classrooms for nonhandicapped children, ages 2–5 years, were involved. Analyses showed that the two kinds of settings differed significantly. Classrooms for handicapped preschoolers generally received lower ratings than those for nonhandicapped youngsters. Prominent differences were observed in room arrangement, especially for interest and relaxation centers, creative activities, and socialization. The authors noted the concerns their research uncovered regarding the qualities of preschools for handicapped youngsters.

Dunst, Trivette, and Cross (1986) studied the mediating influences of social support on personal, family, and child functioning and coping. The study employed the *Family Support Scale* (Dunst, Jenkins, & Trivette, 1984), the *Questionnaire on Resources and Stress* (Holroyd, 1974), and the *Parent-Child Interaction Rating Scale* (Dunst, 1984). The results of this complex study demonstrated that more supportive social networks were associated with greater individual well-being of family members, with more positive parental attitudes, and with greater impact of these attitudes on child-parent play interactions and overall child developmental progress. The authors noted the debilitating effects of a handicapped child on different family members' attitudes and functioning, but also the positive mediating impact of social support on the target child and the family's coping abilities.

INTERACTIVE ASSESSMENT

Definition and Characteristics

Interactive assessment may be viewed as a component of ecological assessment. However, since much research in the past decade has demonstrated the critical importance of reciprocal social interactions, a separate discussion of interactive assessment as a dependent measure is warranted. Formerly, it was presumed that parent behavior shaped infant behavior, and that the infant's limited capabilities produced little if no impact on parent behavior. The discovery of the clear reciprocal nature of parent-child interactions has led researchers to develop instruments to assess the content and effect of interactions as well as the capabilities of both partners in this dynamic process. This assessment allows interventionists to enhance the handicapped infant's ability to communicate and respond clearly and to increase the parent's ability to detect and respond to such cues. *Interactive assessment (IA) examines the social capabilities of the infant and caregiver and the content and extent of synchrony between them.* Does the handicapped infant send clear signals to the mother to express needs? Does the infant reinforce caregiving behaviors through contingent smiling, crying, frowning, and gestures? Likewise, does the caregiver read and provide cues and reinforcing consequences to the infant? What is the nature of the give-and-take or synchrony within the dyad? Field (1978) stressed the importance of the parents' facility in reading and responding to their infant's unique signals. The disabilities of handicapped children limit their ability to sustain interaction. Early intervention can enhance the skills of both partners to reinforce each other and to increase the enjoyable and nurturing quality of this social exchange.

Selected Examples of Dependent Measures

Early interventionists plan treatment goals and

activities aimed at shaping patterns of attachment and independence, teaching play-elicit-
ing behaviors to parents, managing child mis-
behavior, and altering patterns of stress and
coping. Newly developed scales that probe
these interactive relationships are now available for both research and clinical practice.

The premier measure of infant interactive
behavior is the *Brazelton Neonatal Behavioral Assessment Scale* (BNBAS) (Brazelton,
1984). Although primarily a research tool, the
BNBAS is employed extensively by developmentalists who study the organizational and
interactive capacities of prematures and new-
borns. Increasingly, the scale is being used to
assess severely impaired children who evince
low levels of arousal and impaired adaptive and
interactive capabilities (Bagnato, Mayes, &
Nichter, 1988; Simeonsson et al., 1980). The
BNBAS appraises 28 behavioral processes and
18 elicited, neurological integrity indicators
grouped into six clusters: habituation, orientation, motor, state variation, state regulation,
and physiological stability.

While most interactive scales assess the infant's contribution to the emerging attachment
relationship, some newly designed measures
probe maternal behaviors and characteristics
that promote or limit bonding. The *Parent Behavior Progression* (Bromwich, 1978) assesses status and change in parenting behavior
in the context of an infant intervention program
that focuses intensively on the mother-infant
dyad. Two forms of the scale cover targeted
behaviors for parents of children from birth to
36 months. The scale and related intervention
program emphasize such behaviors as reading
biological and temperamental cues, structuring
the environment for satisfying experiences, enhancing play, and anticipating next steps in
development.

Rosenberg, Robinson, and Beckman (1984)
developed the *Teaching Skills Inventory* (TSI)
for the specific purpose of evaluating concom-
mitant increases in child developmental capabilities and parent competencies as teachers/
therapists within an intervention program. The
TSI focuses upon a wide array of parent teaching competencies, including sensitivity to the

child, child versus child-initiated activities, developmental appropriateness of activities, appropriateness of verbal and nonverbal instruction, adjustment of task complexity, and
mutual mother/child enjoyment of the activity.

Finally, the *Parenting Stress Index* (Abidin,
1983) was designed as a screening and diagnostic assessment measure to detect the degree
of stress in the parent-child dyad. The PSI can
be completed by either parent, but generally
focuses on maternal stress, both personal and
perceived in their children. The PSI covers
child characteristics, maternal characteristics,
and situation/demographic life stress.

Applicability of IA for
Research and Clinical Practice

Appropriate Purposes   Research continues
to identify important dimensions of parent/
child interaction that promote developmental
progress (Rosenberg et al., 1984). Among the
purposes of interactive assessment are measurement of the following parent and/or child
characteristics: active versus passive behaviors
of the infant in the interaction; the responsivity
of the parent to the infant's moods; the extent to
which the infant initiates social exchange
rather than simply reacts; the nature of the caregiver's feedback to the infant (content, timing,
and reinforcement value); and finally, the
match between the infant's developmental
competencies and the complexity of the tasks
and communications presented.

Feasible Research Questions   Clinical research questions that emphasize the parent-
infant dyad and the reciprocity of interactive
exchanges are appropriately addressed by interactive dependent measures.

To what extent do structured teaching and therapy for depressed mothers alter both their
own and their infant's behavior during face-
to-face interactions?
In what ways do different styles of infant temperament and different types of sensorimotor handicaps influence the behavior
of mothers in interacting with their disabled
infants?
What is the relationship between different

styles of maternal interactive behavior and changes in the rate of development of their organically impaired, mentally retarded infants within an early intervention program (Mahoney, Finger, & Powell, 1985)?

To what extent do the perceptions of mothers about the vulnerability of their premature, high-risk infants (real or imagined) influence their motivation and behavior in social play?

Research Close-Ups Researchers continue to be interested in the transactional effects of infant characteristics and behavior, and maternal or caregiver attributes and behavior. It is widely believed that such evidence will be valuable in designing treatment strategies that can enhance relationships and thus promote child progress.

Crockenberg and Acredolo (1983) followed 56 mother-infant pairs through the first 3 months of life in order to study the extent to which infant temperamental characteristics were shaped by maternal behavior rather than or additional to constitutional attributes of the children themselves. The Neonatal Behavioral Assessment Scale (NBAS) was used to examine infant neurological and interactive behavior capabilities (conceptualized as constitutional in nature); the Infant Behavior Questionnaire (IBO) was used to assess maternal perceptions of infant temperament; direct 10-second recordings of dyadic behavior were used to assess synchrony between mother and child behavior. The primary results of this study supported the view that mothers modify the behavior of their infants in a specific "temperamental direction" and then rate those attributes accurately on infant temperament measures like the IBQ.

Since developmental gains in normal children (e.g., cognitive, social, and language) have been shown to be related to various aspects of maternal behavior, researchers have been interested in probing this relationship with handicapped infants as well. Mahoney et al. (1985) studied the relationship between the cognitive development of organically impaired mentally retarded preschoolers and maternal

behavioral style. The Bayley Scales of Infant Development were used to assess cognitive status. Videotapes of mother-child play behavior using selected toys were employed. Results from the study led the authors to draw two major conclusions: as the children aged, mothers became more sensitive and responsive, and a significant interrelationship existed between the children's cognitive abilities and maternal behavioral style. "Mother-dominated" interaction patterns were associated with greater deficits in child functioning; conversely, child-oriented maternal patterns were related to higher levels of child development status. Rather than posing a causal relationship between maternal style and child status, the authors discussed issues related to the effectiveness of direct teaching versus child-responsive strategies in early intervention programs.

SYSTEMATIC OBSERVATION

Definition and Characteristics

As evidenced by the preceding material, there are several forms of assessment, or dependent variables, that are available for describing, monitoring, and evaluating child functioning. *Direct observation* and *recording* of *behavior* have been considered fundamental procedures for an empirical science of behavior, the *sine qua non* of applied behavior analysis (Gelfand & Hartmann, 1975, p. 21).

Systematic Observation (SO) refers to structured procedures for collecting objective and quantifiable data on ongoing behavior. The observation of child behavior may occur under several circumstances or formats: 1) *in vivo* or naturalistic (e.g., as in observing children at play in their usual, ongoing settings); 2) simulated or staged, where a situation and materials are provided to permit or occasion the target behavior (e.g., placing toys and arranging typical conditions to structure observation); and 3) role-play or prompted settings, wherein the child is asked to show how he or she would behave given a particular circumstance (e.g., "Show me what you would do if Becky grabbed your blocks while you were playing with them").

Direct observation and recording should not include interpretations of behaviors, as is the case with verbal reports, ratings, and narrative descriptions such as anecdotal and running records. Systematic observation is thus congruent with behaviorism's focus on overt behavior, public events, quantification, low levels of inference, and environmentalism (Hartmann & Wood, 1982). Several dimensions of behavior are observable and can be systematically assessed and measured (White & Haring, 1980): frequency/rate, duration, latency, intensity, topography, and locus. Unlike anecdotal records, checklists, and rating scales, direct and systematic observation provides objective measures of actual instances of overt behavior. Techniques for data collection are of two types: continuous and sampling. Continuous data collection, of course, refers to the uninterrupted gathering of data over a specified period of time. Sampling methods involve data collection for representative portions of time. Samples may record the frequency of discrete instances of behavior or the presence or absence of behavior within a prespecified interval. Interval recording and time-point sampling are widely used methods to assess behavior when continuous records are not feasible (Craighead, Kazdin, & Mahoney, 1981).

Selected Examples of Dependent Measures

Researchers have developed methods for selective systematic observation of behavior. These include the Planned Activities Check (PLA-CHECK) (Doke & Risley, 1972), Scanning (Rogers-Warren, 1982), and Mapping (Ruggles, 1982).

The PLA-CHECK system is used to monitor the behavior of young children at preset intervals, for example, every 10 minutes. The procedure involves the establishment of both inappropriate and appropriate behaviors to be monitored during each daily activity period. Observations are made at the prespecified time of the number of children who are present and participating in the activity. Results from this measure indicate the percentage of appropriate activity-engagements evident for each activity throughout the entire day.

Scanning, or the "snap-shot technique," involves a similar activity and child observation strategy. By successively monitoring each child and teacher in a particular order for a set time (e.g., 5 seconds), an observer can record, for instance, interactive play behavior and the use of specific kinds of curricular materials. The teacher records behavior after a signal occurs. Scanning codes guide the evaluation of ongoing activities in several areas in sequence or at the same time.

Mapping also tracks children's experiences in a variety of classroom settings. Such a strategy enables teachers to observe whether a child was playing alone or was present in a particular area while also sharing toys with other children. The data sheet used is a diagram of the classroom area to be observed with a recording matrix for coded areas of observation times. More complicated coding systems are available (see Alberto & Troutman, 1986).

Applicability of SO for Research and Clinical Practice

Appropriate Purposes Direct, "on-line" observation of child behavior is most useful for describing and analyzing child behavior-environmental relationships (contingencies) and for providing a sensitive means of detecting the impact of treatment (Lovitt, 1975; Madle, Neisworth, & Kurtz, 1980). There are numerous appropriate uses for systematic observation:

1. Documenting if a perception concerning a child (clinical judgment) is factual (i.e., warranted by actual behavior)
2. Determining how a child behaves in a given setting under specified conditions
3. Clarifying the child's presenting problem
4. Selecting instructional materials and techniques
5. Providing a fine-grain analysis or close-up of curricular skill attainment
6. Evaluating progress (change) in specific aspects of development
7. Providing concurrent validity measures of other forms of assessment
8. Determining local or situational norms to

provide the parameters of "normality" and "abnormality"

9. Assessing low-functioning, nonverbal children who cannot or will not respond to traditional assessment situations.

Deciding exactly what behavioral measure to use depends on a number of factors. The aspect of behavior of concern (deficiencies or excesses in frequency, duration, intensity, and latency) is perhaps most basic (Kanfer & Grimm, 1977). The rate of behavior (e.g., too fast to count), incidence (e.g., only once a week), duration (e.g., lasts two hours), and discreteness (e.g., vague beginning or end) must be considered when selecting an observational/recording method. Other considerations include amount of time available for observation, the number of children to be observed, and the kind of behavior to be observed.

In summary, systematic observation of behavior is the dependent variable of choice when it becomes important to detect emerging or present behavior trends, when close-ups of specific strengths and weaknesses for given children are required, and when sensitive measures of even small change as a function of some treatment (independent) variable are needed.

Feasible Research Questions Consider the following illustrative research questions and note how they particularly invite systematic observation.

Will cooperative play that has been reinforced in classroom activities be generalized to the playground where no specific prompts for cooperation are provided?

How often will preschool children pick up litter with modeling? How often will this be performed with verbal prompting? How often will they pick up litter with reinforcement?

Can a high rate self-stimulatory behavior (with no apparent/accessible reinforcer) be reduced through deliberate reinforcement followed by sudden extinction procedures?

Given an operationalized definition of Attention Deficit Disorder (ADD) with hyperactivity, will children diagnosed as ADD by clinical methods exhibit observable differences in behavior?

Will the rate of prosocial interaction among nonhandicapped and handicapped preschoolers increase as a result of posting pictures of such children playing together in the classroom?

How does one determine which toys members of a preschool group will select when given free choices, so that the most motivating toys can be incorporated by the instructor into daily lessons?

Can the separation anxiety behaviors of a child be eliminated through the contingent presence of the mother during periods of nonanxious behavior?

Research Close-Ups Direct and systematic observation takes more effort than other assessment approaches, but is often the method of choice—especially when rater bias is an issue. A convincing study by Madle et al. (1980) strongly supports the use of direct and systematic observation over clinical judgment in assessment of preschooler hyperactivity. Twenty-four raters observed videotapes of two preschool children. Bogus diagnostic reports indicating hyperkinesis for one of the children (and not the other) were given to all of the raters. Twelve raters were randomly selected to use a clinical judgment instrument to assess hyperkinesis, while the other 12 used a time-sampling observation technique. For each group, half of the raters received special training on the instrument/approach they used. The clinical judgment scale employed was the Davids Scale of Hyperactivity (Davids, 1971) which includes six dimensions of behavior rated on a 6-point Likert scale. The time-sampling method involved a 15-second observation interval (signaled by audiotape); at the signal, observers noted if hyperkinetic behavior had occurred any time during that interval. Behaviors included within the hyperkinetic syndrome were operationalized to enable reliable observations. Results showed a clear biasing effect of diagnostic reports on clinical judgment ratings but no such effect with the time-sampling method. The investigators concluded that direct systematic observation (time-sampling) may be the most objective and valid means for assessing problematic behavior in the setting where it is suspected or alleged to occur. Perhaps, the authors speculate, direct observation is more trustworthy because it focuses the observer's attention away from global assessments of the child to actual exhibited behaviors.

SUMMARY

Assessment must fulfill a purpose. There are numerous applications for assessment that require specialized tools. Just as in other professions, it is important to select the right tool for the job. An assessment typology in ECSE can help to match the right tool or measure with a particular purpose or need. Major purposes for assessment in ECSE and their corresponding tools include the following: tracking child program progress (curriculum-based), modifying procedures to circumvent handicaps (adaptive-to-handicap), probing of inferred and undetected competencies (process), comparing child status with peers (norm-based), rating impressions of child status and progress (judg-

ment-based), appraising dimensions of the child's environment (ecological), analyzing social interchange between child and caregivers (interactive), and observing and recording behavior systematically (systematic observation).

Valid assessment of handicapped infants and preschoolers demands a multidimensional approach employing several measures. It involves surveying multiple functional domains and gathering data from diverse sources of information. Both clinical and research objectives can be accomplished by using a multidimensional approach that employs appropriate measures.

Creative advancements in ECSE assessment have generated an array of instruments and methods to address clinical and research needs. An organizational framework for sorting, selecting, and using these measures can advance research and treatment efforts for the young exceptional child; the typology described in this chapter is offered as a step toward that framework.

REFERENCES

Abidin, R. R. (1983). *Parenting Stress Index.* Charlottesville, VA: Pediatric Psychology Press.

Alberto, P. A., & Troutman, A. C. (1986). *Applied behavior analysis for teachers.* Columbus, OH: Charles E. Merrill.

Bagnato, S. J. (1984). Team congruence in developmental diagnosis and intervention: Comparing clinical judgments and child performance measures. *School Psychology Review, 13,* 7–16.

Bagnato, S. J., Mayes, S., & Nichter, C. (1988). An interdisciplinary neurodevelopmental assessment model for brain injured infants and preschool children. *Journal of Head Trauma Rehabilitation, 2*(4), 44–55.

Bagnato, S. J., & Neisworth, J. T. (1981). *Linking developmental assessment and curricula: Prescription for early intervention.* Rockville, MD: Aspen Systems.

Bagnato, S. J., & Neisworth, J. T. (1985a). Efficacy of interdisciplinary assessment and treatment for infants and preschoolers with congenital and acquired brain injury. *Analysis and Intervention in Developmental Disabilities, 5,* 107–128.

Bagnato, S. J., & Neisworth, J. T. (1985b). Assessing young handicapped children: Clinical judgment versus developmental performance scales. *International Journal of Partial Hospitalization, 3,* 13–21.

Bagnato, S. J., & Neisworth, J. T. (1987). *Perceptions of developmental status: A system for planning early intervention.* University Park: Penn State University.

Bagnato, S. J., Neisworth, J. T., & Capone, A. (1986). Curriculum-based assessment for the young exceptional child: Rationale and review. *Topics in Early Childhood Special Education, 6*(2), 97–110.

Bagnato, S. J., Neisworth, J. T., & Eaves, R. (1978). A profile of perceived capabilities for the preschool child. *Child Care Quarterly, 1*(4), 326–335.

Bailey, D. B., Clifford, R. M., & Harms, T. (1982). Comparison of preschool environments for handicapped and nonhandicapped children. *Topics in Early Childhood Special Education, 2*(1), 9–20.

Bailey, D. B., Jens, K. G. & Johnson, N. (1983). Curricula for handicapped infants. In S. G. Gardwood & R. Fewell (Eds.), *Educating handicapped infants* (pp. 387–415). Rockville, MD: Aspen Systems.

Barker, R. G. (1968). *Ecological psychology: Concepts and methods for studying the environment of human development.* Stanford, CA: Stanford University Press.

Bayley, N. (1969). *Bayley Scales of Infant Development.* New York: Psychological Corporation.

Bell, R. A. (1968). A reinterpretation of the direction of effects in studies of socialization. *Psychological Review, 15,* 81–95.

Bijou, S. W., & Baer, D. M. (1978). *Behavior analysis of child development.* Englewood Cliffs, NJ: Prentice-Hall.

Blacher-Dixon, J., & Simeonsson, R. (1981). Consistency and correspondence of mothers' and teachers' assessments of young handicapped children. *Journal of the Division for Early Childhood, 3,* 64–71.

Brazelton, T. B. (1984). *Brazelton Neonatal Behavioral Assessment Scale* (2nd ed.). Philadelphia: Spastic International Medical Publications, J. B. Lippincott.

Bricker, D. D. (1986). *Early education of at-risk and handicapped infants, toddlers, and preschoolers.* Glenview, IL: Scott, Foresman.

Brigance, A. H. (1978). *Brigance diagnostic inventory of early development.* Worcester, MA: Curriculum Associates.

Brinker, R. P., & Lewis, M. (1982). Discovering the competent handicapped infant: A process approach to assessment and intervention. *Topics in Early Childhood Special Education, 2*(2), 1–16.

Brooks-Gunn, J., & Lewis, M. (1981). Assessing young handicapped children: Issues and solutions. *Journal of the Division for Early Childhood, 3,* 84–95.

Bromwich, R. (1978). *Working with parents and infants.* (Appendices A and B, Parent Behavior Progression.) Austin, TX: PRO-ED.

Brophy, J. E. (1979). Teacher behavior and its effects. *Journal of Educational Psychology, 71,* 733–750.

Brown, D., Simmons, V., & Methvin, J. (1979). *The Oregon project for visually impaired and blind preschool children.* Medford, OR: Jackson County Education Service District.

Brown, S. L., D'Eugenio, D. D., Drews, J. E., Haskin, B. S., Lynch, E. W., Moersch, M. S., & Rogers, S. J. (1981). *Preschool developmental profile.* Ann Arbor: University of Michigan Press.

Caldwell, B. M., & Bradley, R. H. (1978). *Home observation for measurement of the environment.* Little Rock: University of Arkansas, Center for Child Development and Education.

Campbell, D. T., & Fiske, D. W. (1959). Convergent and discriminant validation by the multitrait-multimethod matrix. *Psychological Bulletin, 56,* 81–105.

Carey, W. B., & McDevitt, S. C. (1977). *Infant Temperament Questionnaire* (ITQ). Media, PA: Carey Associates.

Craighead, W. E., Kazdin, A. E., & Mahoney, M. J. (1981). *Behavior modification: Principles, issues and applications.* Boston: Houghton Mifflin.

Crockenberg, S., & Acredolo, C. (1983). Infant temperament ratings: A function of infants, of mothers, or both? *Infant Behavior and Development, 6,* 61–72.

Davids, A. (1971). An objective instrument for assessing hyperkinesis in children. *Journal of Learning Disabilities, 4,* 499–501.

Doke, L., & Risley, T. R. (1972). The organization of daycare environments: Required versus optional activities. *Journal of Applied Behavior Analysis, 5,* 405–420.

Dubose, R. F. (1976). Predictive value of infant intelligence scales with multihandicapped children. *American Journal of Mental Deficiency, 81,* 388–390.

Dubose, R. F., Langley, M., & Stagg, V. (1977). Assessing severely handicapped children. *Focus on Exceptional Children, 9*(7), 1–13.

Dunst, C. J. (1981). *Infant learning: A cognitive-linguistic intervention strategy.* Hingham, MA: Teaching Resources.

Dunst, C. J. (1983). Evaluating trends and advances in early intervention programs. *New Jersey Journal of School Psychology, 2,* 26–40.

Dunst, C. J. (1984). *Parent-Child Interaction Rating Scale.* Unpublished scale, Family, Infant, and Preschool Program, Western Carolina Center, Morgantown, NC.

Dunst, C. J., Jenkins, V., & Trivette, C. M. (1984). Family support scale: Reliability and validity. *Journal of Individual, Family and Community Wellness, 1*(4), 45–52.

Dunst, C. J., & Rheingrover, R. M. (1983). Structural characteristics of sensorimotor development among Downs Syndrome infants. *Journal of Mental Deficiency Research, 27,* 11–22.

Dunst, C. J., Trivette, C. M., & Cross, A. (1986). Mediating influences of social support: Personal, family, and child outcomes. *American Journal of Mental Deficiency, 91,* 403–417.

Elardo, R., & Bradley, R. (1981). The home observation for measurement of the environment (HOME) scale. *The Developmental Review, 1,* 113–145.

Emde, R. N., Katz, E. L., & Thorpe, J. K. (1978). Emotional expression in infancy: II. Early deviations in Down's syndrome. In M. Lewis & L. A. Rosenblum (Eds.), *The development of affect* (pp. 88–110). New York: Plenum.

Escalona, S., & Gorman, H. (1966). *Albert Einstein Scales of Sensory Motor Development.* New York: Albert Einstein College of Medicine.

Fewell, R. R. (1983). New directions in the assessment of young handicapped children. In C. R. Reynolds & J. H. Clark (Eds.), *Assessment and programming for young children with low incidence handicaps* (pp. 1–41). New York: Plenum.

Fewell, R. R. (1984). Assessment of preschool handicapped children. *Educational Psychologist, 19,* 172–179.

Fewell, R. R. (1986). *The Play Assessment Scale* (experimental edition). Seattle: University of Washington, Experimental Education Unit.

Fewell, R. R., & Langley, M. B. (1984). *Developmental Activities Screening Inventory II.* Austin, TX: PRO-ED.

Fewell, R. R., & Sandall, S. R. (1983). Assessment of high-risk infants. In E. M. Goetz & K. E. Allen (Eds.), *Early childhood education: Special environmental, policy, and legal considerations* (pp. 3–34). Rockville, MD: Aspen Systems.

Field, T. M. (1978). A first-year follow-up of high-risk infants: Formulating a cumulative risk index. *Child Development, 49,* 119–131.

Flanders, N. (1970). *Analyzing teacher behavior.* Menlo Park, CA: Addison-Wesley.

Frankenburg, W. K., Dodds, J., Fandal, A. (1982). *Denver Developmental Screening Test—Revised.* Denver, CO: Denver Developmental Materials.

Fullard, W., McDevitt, S. & Carey, W. (1978). *Toddler Temperament Scale.* Media, PA: Carey Associates.

Garwood, S. G., & Fewell, R. R. (Eds.). (1983). *Educating handicapped infants.* Rockville, MD: Aspen Systems.

Gelfand, D. M., & Hartmann, D. P. (1975). *Child behavior analysis and therapy.* New York: Pergaman Press.

Glover, M. E., Preminger, J. L., & Sanford, A. L. (1978). *The early learning accomplishment profile.* Winston-Salem, NC: Kaplan School System.

Gradel, K., Thompson, M., & Sheehan, R. (1981). Parental and professional agreement in early childhood assessment. *Topics in Early Childhood Special Education, 1,* 31–39.

Gresham, F. M. (1983). Multitrait-multimethod approach to multifactored assessment: Theoretical rationale and practical application. *School Psychology Review, 12*(1), 26–34.

Haeusserman, E. (1958). *Developmental potential of pre-school children: An evaluation in intellectual sensory and emotional functioning.* New York: Grune & Stratton.

Harms, T., & Clifford, R. M. (1980). *Early childhood environmental rating scale.* New York: Teachers College Press.

Hartmann, D. P. & Wood, D. D. (1982). Observational methods. In A. S. Bellack, M. Herson, & A. E. Kazdin (Eds.), *International handbook of behavior modification and therapy* (pp. 109–138). New York: Plenum Press.

Holroyd, J. (1974). The questionnaire on resources and stress: An instrument to measure family responses to a handicapped family member. *Journal of Community Psychology, 2,* 92–94.

Jennings, K. D., Connors, R. E., Stegman, C. E., Sankaranarayan, P., & Mendelsohn, S. (1985). Mastery motivation in young preschoolers: Effect of a physical handicap and implications for educational programming. *Journal of the Division for Early Childhood, 9*(2), 162–169.

Johnson-Martin, N. M., Jens, K. G., & Attermeier, S. A. (1986). *The Carolina curriculum for handicapped infants and infants at risk.* Baltimore: Paul H. Brookes Publishing Co.

Kanfer, F. H., & Grimm, L. G. (1977). Behavioral analysis: Selecting target behaviors in the interview. *Behavior Modification, 1*(1), 7–28.

Kearsley, R. B. (1981). Cognitive assessment of the handicapped infant: The need for an alternative approach. *American Journal of Orthopsychiatry, 51*(1), 43–54.

Kearsley, R. B., & Sigel, I. E. (1979). *Infants at risk: Assessment of cognitive functioning.* Hillsdale, NJ: Lawrence Erlbaum Associates.

Kiernan, D. W., & Dubose, R. F. (1974). Assessing the cognitive development of preschool deaf-blind children. *Education of the Visually Handicapped, 6*(4), 103–105.

Kopp, C. B. (1982). Antecedents of self-regulation: A developmental perspective. *Developmental Psychology, 18*(2), 99–114.

Kurtz, P. D., Neisworth, J. T., & Laub, K. W. (1977). Issues concerning the early identification of handicapped children. *Journal of School Psychology, 15*(2), 136–140.

LeMay, D. W., Griffin, P. M., & Sanford, A. R. (1978). *Learning Accomplishment Profile: Diagnostic edition* (rev. ed.). Winston-Salem, NC: Kaplan School Supply.

Lewin, K. (1951). *Field theory in social science.* New York: Harper & Row.

Lovitt, T. C. (1975). Applied behavior analysis and learning disabilities: II. Specific research recommendations and suggestions for practitioners. *Journal of Learning Disabilities, 8*(8), 504–518.

Lyon, R. (1982). Social and legal issues in testing. In H. Swanson & B. Watson (Eds.), *Educational and psychological assessment of exceptional children* (pp. 82–102). St. Louis: C. V. Mosby.

MacTurk, R. H., & Neisworth, J. T. (1978). Norm- and criterion-based measures with handicapped and nonhandicapped preschoolers. *Exceptional Children, 45*(1), 34–39.

Madle, R. A., Neisworth, J. T., & Kurtz, P. D. (1980). Biasing of hyperkinetic behavior ratings by diagnostic reports: Effects of observer training and assessment method. *Journal of Learning Disabilities, 13*(1), 35–38.

Mahoney, G., Finger, I., & Powell, A. (1985). Relationship of maternal behavioral style to the development of organically impaired mentally retarded infants. *American Journal of Mental Deficiency, 90*(3), 296–302.

McCarthy, D. (1972). *McCarthy Scales of Children's Ability: Manual.* Cleveland, OH: Psychological Corporation.

McDevitt, S., & Carey, W. (1975). *Behavioral Style Questionnaire.* Media, PA: Carey Associates.

Mercer, C. D., Algozzine, B., & Trifiletti, J. J. (1979). Early identification: Issues and considerations. *Exceptional Children, 21*(2), 52–54.

Neisworth, J. T. (Ed.). (1984). Social policy and young handicapped children. *Topics in Early Childhood Special Education, 4*(1), 1–111.

Neisworth, J. T., & Bagnato, S. J. (1986). Curriculum based developmental assessment: Congruence of testing and teaching. *School Psychology Review, 15*(2), 180–199.

Neisworth, J. T., & Bagnato, S. J. (1987). *The young exceptional child: Early development and education.* New York: Macmillan.

Newborg, J., Stock, J. R., Wnek, L., Guidubaldi, J., & Svinicki, J. (1984). *Battelle Developmental Inventory.* Allen, TX: Teaching Resource.

Paget, K. D. (1985). Assessment in early childhood education. *Diagnostique, 10,* 76–87.

Paget, K. D., & Bracken, B. A. (1983). *The psychoeducational assessment of preschool children.* New York: Grune & Stratton.

Rogers, S. J., D'Eugenio, D. B., Brown, S. L., Donovan, C. M., & Lynch, E. W. (1981). *Early intervention developmental profile.* Ann Arbor: University of Michigan Press.

Rogers-Warren, A. K. (1982). Behavioral ecology in classrooms for young, handicapped children. *Topics in Early Childhood Special Education, 2*(1), 21–31.

Rosenberg, S., Robinson, C., & Beckman, P. (1984). The Teaching Skills Inventory (TSI): A measure of parent performance. *Journal of the Division for Early Childhood,* Summer.

Ruggles, T. R. (1982). Some considerations in the use of teacher implemented observation procedures. In K. E. Allen & E. M. Goetz (Eds.), *Early childhood education: Special problems, special solutions* (pp. 77–104). Rockville, MD: Aspen Systems.

Sameroff, A. J. (1986). Environmental context of child development. *Journal of Pediatrics, 109*(1), 192–200.

Sanford, A. R., & Zelman, J. G. (1981). *Learning Accomplishment Profile* (rev. ed.). Winston-Salem, NC: Kaplan Press.

Schaefer, D. S., & Moersch, M. S. (1981). *Developmental programming for infants and young children.* Ann Arbor: University of Michigan Press.

Sciarillo, W. G., Brown, M. M., Robinson, N. M., Bennett, F. C., & Sells, C. J. (1986). Effectiveness of the Denver Developmental Screening Test with biologically vulnerable infants. *Journal of Developmental and Behavioral Pediatrics, 7*(2), 77–83.

Sexton, D., Miller, J. H., & Murdock, J. Y. (1984). Correlations of parental professional congruency scores in the assessment of young handicapped children. *Journal of the Division for Early Childhood, 8*(2), 99–106.

Shonkoff, J. P. (1983). The limitations of normative assessments of high-risk infants. *Topics in Early Childhood Special Education, 3*(1), 29–43.

Simeonsson, R. J. (1986). *Psychological and developmental assessment of special children.* Boston: Allyn & Bacon.

Simeonsson, R. J., Huntington, G. S., & Parse, S. A. (1980). Expanding development assessment of young handicapped children. In J. Gallagher (Ed.), *New directions for exceptional children* (pp. 51–74). Washington, DC: Jossey-Bass.

Simeonsson, R. J., Huntington, G. S., Short, R. J., & Ware, W. B. (1982). The Carolina record of individual behavior: Characteristics of handicapped infants and children. *Topics in Early Childhood Special Education, 2*(2), 43–55.

Skinner, B. F. (1968). *The technology of teaching.* New York: Appleton-Century-Crofts.

Smith, R., Neisworth, J. T., & Greer, J. (1978). *Evaluating educational environments.* Columbus, OH: Charles E. Merrill.

Uzgiris, I., & Hunt, McV. (1975). *Assessment in infancy: Ordinal scales of psychological development.* Urbana: University of Illinois Press.

VanderVeer, B., & Schweid, R. (1974). Infant assessment: Stability of mental functioning in young retarded children. *American Journal of Mental Deficiency, 79*(1), 1–4.

White, O. R., Edgar, E., Haring, N., Affleck, J., Hayden, A., & Bendersky, M. (1981). *Uniform performance assessment system.* Columbus, OH: Charles E. Merrill.

White, O. R., & Haring, N. G. (1980). *Exceptional teaching* (2nd ed.). Columbus, OH: Charles E. Merrill.

Willoughby-Herb, S. J., & Neisworth, J. T. (1983). *HICOMP preschool curriculum.* San Antonio, TX: Psychological Corporation.

Wolf, M. M. (1978). Social validity: The case for subjective measurement or how applied behavior analysis is finding its heart. *Journal of Applied Behavior Analysis, 11*(2), 203–214.

Zeenah, C. H., Keener, M. A., Anders, T. F., & Levine, R. (1986). Measuring difficult temperament in infancy. *Developmental and Behavioral Pediatrics, 7*(2), 114–119.

Zeitlin, S., Williamson, G., & Szczepanski, M. (1984). *Early Coping Inventory.* Edison, NJ: JFK Medical Center.

Zelazo, P. R. (1979). Reactivity to perceptual-cognitive events: Applications for infant assessment. In R. B. Kearsley & I. B. Sigel (Eds.), *Infants at risk: Assessment of cognitive functioning* (pp. 112–128). Hillsdale, NJ: Lawrence Erlbaum Associates.

Zelazo, P. R. (1982). An information processing approach to infant cognitive assessment. In M. Lewis & L. T. Taft (Eds.), *Developmental disabilities: Theory, assessment, and intervention* (pp. 229–255). New York: Spectrum.

Chapter 3

Research and Program Evaluation in Early Childhood Special Education

Glendon Casto

PRACTITIONERS AND POLICYMAKERS in the field of early childhood special education are constantly making decisions that have immediate and long-term effects on young children, their families, and ultimately their communities. In addition, state and federal governments create legislation and regulations that affect these same groups, as exemplified by the passage of PL 99-457 in the fall of 1986. By what process do these diverse groups obtain the information that leads them to prescribe a certain type of intervention or to urge the passage of a certain law? This important question can be addressed in part by identifying the sources of the information used to make early intervention decisions. These sources include expert opinion, tradition, personal experience, intuition, common sense, and finally, research and evaluation. Too often the field of early childhood special education has relied too extensively on sources of information such as expert opinion and personal experience rather than on research and evaluation. It is the purpose of this chapter to emphasize the importance of research and program evaluation as sources of information.

One approach to research is to relate it to the field of scientific inquiry. Scientific inquiry involves the search for knowledge using appropriate procedures in data collection, analysis, and interpretation. Although scientific inquiry is more an approach than a series of steps, the methods of scientific inquiry include: 1) identifying a research problem or question, 2) reviewing existing knowledge about the problem, 3) formulating research questions or hypotheses, 4) selecting an appropriate research design, 5) collecting and analyzing data, and 6) interpreting results and drawing conclusions.

In the field of early childhood special education, much of the evaluation research completed to date has been severely criticized (Bricker, Bailey, & Bruder, 1984; Dunst & Rheingrover, 1981; Odom & Fewell, 1983; Simeonsson, Cooper, & Schiener, 1982; White & Casto, 1984). Determining whether this criticism is entirely justified is somewhat problematic. In fact, many of the studies reviewed indicated that early childhood researchers were cognizant of the need for scientific methods of inquiry. What apparently has happened is that social policy mandated that large-scale early intervention programs be established quickly, and consequently the problems involved in applying scientific methods of inquiry to the field were never fully addressed. The criticism of much of the research conducted forces professionals in the field to once again consider the usefulness of methods of scientific inquiry in early childhood special education.

To infuse the methods of scientific inquiry

The work reported in this chapter was carried out in part with funds from the U.S. Department of Education (Contract #300-82-0367) awarded to the Early Intervention Research Institute at Utah State University.

into early intervention evaluation research, it is useful to consider the role that theory might play in research. Theories, or basic principles, are used to state relationships that are thought to exist between phenomena. For example, the notion that infant-mother attachment is crucial to later social-emotional development in a handicapped infant could be considered a theory. This theory, if validated through research, could be used by intervention personnel to devise interventions designed to strengthen the attachment between the infant and the infant's caregiver. Theories then provide a foundation for scientific research, especially if they include statements of relationships that can be scientifically tested.

TYPES OF RESEARCH

The purpose of basic and applied research and program evaluation in early childhood special education is to advance the knowledge base of the field. Although distinctions are often made between the three types of research, each method is important and has the potential to advance the field significantly. A brief explanation of the three research approaches follows in Table 1, which depicts the three approaches across the dimensions of purpose, subject, and utilization of findings.

Basic Research

To test theories like the attachment construct mentioned previously, and also to discover basic principles that operate in a given area, researchers typically conduct programs of basic research. Using the examples of attachment, a researcher could conduct a program of

research to test the importance of attachment as a guiding principle in early childhood special education, or could conduct research that would lead to a better understanding of attachment. Since basic research is concerned almost exclusively with discovering and understanding principles, the knowledge generated through basic research must be translated into applications that are usable by practitioners in the field. In the example mentioned above, the basic research findings about attachment would need to be transformed into intervention strategies. Thus, basic research in the field of early childhood special education would add to the general knowledge base in this field, but it might have limited practical application unless the necessary transformations were performed.

Applied Research

Applied research, in contrast to basic research, is usually concerned with the application of research knowledge and the testing of empirical relationships within a given field. Although applied research findings may not translate directly into intervention principles, the findings do produce a knowledge base that can have general implications for practice.

In early childhood special education, the basic research knowledge base related to growth and development in normal children has been utilized to a great extent to explain development in handicapped children. As more basic research is conducted with preschool handicapped samples, theorists may be forced to turn away from the knowledge base developed in research with normal children and to generate a more specialized view of develop-

Table 1.   Functions of research

Functions	Basic research	Applied research	Evaluation research
Purpose	Discover basic principles, test theories	Test causal hypotheses, determine functional relationships	Test usefulness of specific programs or practices
Subject of research	Social sciences	Early childhood special education	A given practice in early childhood special education
How findings are utilized	Develop a body of knowledge in social sciences	Develop a research-based body of knowledge in early childhood education	Develop "best practices" in early childhood special education

ment. This could have tremendous implications for basic and applied research in the field.

Evaluation Research

While both basic and applied research strategies have much to offer the field of early childhood special education, a third area of inquiry also has the potential to contribute to the field. This area, which is usually referred to as evaluation or action research, tends to focus on a particular practice at a given site and attempts to assess the value of a particular practice. Thus, evaluation research findings are designed to be immediately usable by practitioners at a given site. For example, one may test the efficacy of a specific practice that provides information leading to the adoption or rejection of the practice based upon objective data. Evaluation research findings are thus of great value to decision-makers and program planners in the field. In addition, evaluation research findings may also stimulate further basic and applied research in a field.

Evaluation researchers usually attempt to determine the worth of an early childhood program or product. In some cases, research is done to determine which of two programs or products are better. In early intervention research, for example, one type of intervention may be compared against another (e.g., home-based versus center-based), or one type of curriculum may be compared to another type of curriculum.

In attempting to design evaluation research, evaluation experts have developed a number of approaches (McMillan & Schumacker, 1984). These approaches have been designed to answer evaluation questions from a number of perspectives. Most evaluation approaches have an originator, a rationale for the approach, and explicit procedures for conducting evaluations using a particular approach. Two examples of evaluation approaches are presented here.

Objectives-Based Evaluation (Tyler, 1950)
Objectives-based evaluation attempts to determine the degree to which the objectives of a given educational practice are achieved. In this type of evaluation, learner outcomes are stated as behavioral objectives, and the evaluator attempts to determine whether the learners actually achieve the objectives set up for them in a given program. One may state the following objective: During a 9-month intervention program, students age 3–5 years mainstreamed into a cognitively oriented day care program will improve their standard scores by 20% on the 1985 revision of the Stanford-Binet. Given this objective, a pre- and posttest administration of the Stanford-Binet would provide some evidence as to whether the objective stated above was achieved by mainstreamed preschoolers.

A second type of evaluation design that is receiving increased attention is *economic evaluation* (Barnett, 1985a; Levin, 1981; Thompson, 1980). Two types of economic evaluation—cost-effectiveness and cost-benefit analysis—are most relevant for early childhood special education. *Cost-effectiveness* analysis simultaneously assesses efficacy and costs. Cost-effectiveness analysis can be used to determine which of several approaches produces the desired effects at the lowest cost, or which of several approaches produces the greatest effects with a given budget (Barnett & Escobar, in press). It can also be used to identify specific program characteristics that have the potential to significantly improve efficacy and to reveal how relevant changes in these characteristics would effect costs.

Using the objectives-based evaluation example given earlier, one might compare the cost-effectiveness of the mainstreaming program for a self-contained preschool program. Assuming the same objective, the evaluation would measure the gains on the Stanford-Binet and also the costs for both programs. The results of such an evaluation may or may not be easily interpretable. For example, one recent study (Innocenti, Morgan, Rule, & Stowitschek, 1985) found a mainstreamed program to be no less effective, but much less costly, than self-contained preschool special education programs. Clearly, the mainstreamed program was more cost-effective. Researchers are not always so fortunate, however. If the mainstreamed program had been slightly less effective as well as less costly, the results would have been less clear. Policymakers would be faced with deciding whether the self-contained program's somewhat greater effectiveness was worth the extra cost.

Cost-benefit analysis seeks to provide more clearly interpretable results by evaluating the monetary value to society of program outcomes as well as costs. This approach is particularly useful when the evaluator is faced with a dichotomous choice (to adopt a program or not) and when multiple outcomes are evaluated. For example, the mainstreaming and self-contained programs might be compared on gains in social skills as well as cognitive functioning. The chief difficulty in applying cost-benefit analysis to early childhood special education is that it is sometimes difficult to calculate the monetary value of program objectives such as improved Stanford-Binet scores. Successful cost-benefit analyses have tended to focus on more easily valued outcomes like decreased special education costs, which require longitudinal follow-up for assessment. For example, the Perry Preschool benefit-cost analysis (Barnett, 1985b) included outcomes such as later education cost reductions, delinquency, crime cost reductions, welfare cost reductions, and earnings increases as outcomes.

The important point regarding cost-effectiveness analysis and cost-benefit analysis is that they allow for the simultaneous consideration of the costs of a given practice and the outcomes produced by the practice. Although economic evaluation is in its infancy in early childhood special education, methods pioneered by the Perry Preschool Project (Barnett, 1985a, 1985b) and the Early Intervention Research Institute (Barnett & Escobar, in press) should result in broader application in the field.

DESIGN CONSIDERATIONS

An important point to be stressed is that research design represents an important aspect of scientific inquiry, and various designs are chosen because they appear to have utility in answering certain types of questions. For example, one of the best ways to investigate

cause and effect relationships would be a true experimental design so that the causes of behavior may be actively controlled in the experiment. Alternately, quasi-experimental designs are a reasonable alternative in educational settings where intact groups are being observed. While true experimental designs are more elegant, both types of design have their place in early childhood research. This is also true for single case designs. The type of design utilized should be based on the research question to be answered. The types of designs utilized in early childhood special education are fully discussed by Odom in Chapter 1 of this volume.

RANDOM ASSIGNMENT

One necessary condition for true experimental research is random assignment of subjects to experimental and control groups. This procedure, if carried out with a large enough sample, helps to ensure that there are no differences between the subjects in each group. Unfortunately, in the field of early childhood special education, the subject populations are diverse, and the potential sample sizes are usually so small, that stratification procedures are usually necessary to ensure comparability of groups before random assignment.

Stratification in selecting experimental and control groups begins by grouping or ranking the study subjects on what may be considered the critical or the most important variable or variables. Severity of handicapping condition or type of handicapping condition might be critical variables. For example, within a hearing impaired sample the variable might be degree of hearing loss. If degree of hearing loss is used as the critical variable, then all subjects would be rank-ordered on degree of hearing loss, and randomly sorted (odd/even) into two groups (e.g., first subject into group A, second subject into group B, third subject into group A). If these groups were not sufficiently comparable on certain important variables, such as age, socioeconomic status, maternal relationship, IQ, etc., then pairs could be switched from one group to the other (i.e., the places of members of a pair would be switched) until equality was achieved. This would hold the critical variable more or less constant. The two groups thus formed would be finally designated treatment or control at random, for example, by the flip of a coin.

The primary reason for using matching procedures prior to random assignment is, of course, to reduce variability within pairs and to help ensure comparability of groups. Although random assignment to groups, in and of itself, may accomplish these aims, stratification prior to assignment reduces the probability of producing groups that are not comparable.

The number of variables to use in stratifying groups is dependent on subject characteristics and sample size. As the sample size increases, it may be possible to match on more variables, but matching becomes less necessary with large samples. In general, it becomes increasingly difficult to obtain a high percentage of successful matches from a limited subject pool as the number of matching variables increases. However, matching on at least two variables with available subject pools is usually feasible. Using at least two matching variables has the promise of reducing the variability within subject pools significantly.

In sum, experimental designs that produce findings that are unambiguous have strategies in place to ensure that experimental and control groups are comparable on all variables except the variable under question. This may be done in a number of ways, but as mentioned earlier, random assignment plus matching on critical variables appears to be the best way to control for extraneous variables. Additionally, it is always a good practice to collect data on all variables thought to be critical, and then to compare the experimental and control groups on these variables to ensure that they are comparable.

DATA COLLECTION

Research emphasizes gathering information about the chosen variables in a given study. To collect the information, researchers have access to a wide variety of techniques. These techniques range from questionnaires and in-terviews to direct observations and standardized tests. Each method has advantages and disadvantages, and the value of research findings is not only a function of the design utilized, but also of the instruments utilized to assess the critical variables. In selecting instruments then, careful consideration should be given to the variables under study. The following brief guidelines are intended to make the selection more systematic (See Neisworth and Bagnato, Chapter 2, this volume, for a comprehensive description of assessment instruments).

Questionnaires

In order to know about current practice in a given area, questionnaires, surveys, and interviews can be very useful. Fine and Swift (1986), for example, assessed the prevalence of handicapping conditions among young children ages 0–4 using a telephone survey technique. They also collected information regarding parents' perceptions of the early intervention services that their children had received. The data generated by this survey will provide information that can be used in planning further research.

But questionnaires, surveys, and interviews need to be used carefully because they rely on self-reports: data which may or may not be accurate. When one uses these techniques, the findings should be cross-checked using other data sources. When one wants to know about current practices, the above techniques, if used properly, provide an easy and economical way to gather this information.

Observational Techniques

Observational techniques represent a more exacting system for collecting data on research variables. The primary advantage of observational techniques is that there are fewer problems of self-report bias or response set with which to deal. Behavior can be observed and recorded as it occurs naturally. Observational techniques work well when the variable under study is a behavior that can be defined operationally. Observational techniques are utilized extensively in single subject research and probably should be utilized more in group research. Good observational methods include precisely defining the behavior to be observed, determining the units of analysis, training observers, and performing frequent observer reliability checks to guard against observer drift (Kent & Foster, 1977).

Tests

Tests are probably the most frequently used technique for collecting information in early childhood special education research. They are widely used because of the large numbers of preschool instruments available, because tests are usually easy to administer and score, and because they possess an aura of objectivity, which researchers find irresistible. However, it would be wise to remember that preschool assessment devices have been criticized as being unreliable, and in many instances, invalid for the purposes for which they are being used (Zigler & Balla, 1982). The best advice for the researcher choosing tests is to begin with an operational definition of the dependent variables in the research and then to carefully select instruments using the following questions:

What is the rationale for selecting this instrument?
Will this instrument give the best information regarding the variables under study?
Is this instrument valid and reliable for the study sample?

Unobtrusive Measures

Two often overlooked sources of information that can be utilized in research are unobtrusive and archival data sources. Such sources have been called nonreactive because subjects and their families are not required to do anything out of the ordinary and are not aware of the data gathering. These information sources have been used infrequently in early childhood special education research but could provide valuable, inexpensive information. For example, a research project investigating the effects of a parent training program on parent behavior might use the number of books checked out of a parent resource library by experimental and control group parents as one measure of program effectiveness. Similarly, the number of visits made by parents to a toy lending library might serve as another unobtrusive data source.

Archival data sources abound in early childhood special education. Many infants and young children with developmental delays are graduates of neonatal intensive care units (NICUs). Most of these units have computerized data bases and routinely collect extensive information on NICU patients. Although one has to secure both parental and NICU permission to conduct a records review, the results can be worthwhile in terms of valuable information provided. NICU discharge summaries are particularly useful in this regard.

Borg and Gall (1983), while advocating the use of unobtrusive measures, pointed out that the reliability of many nonreactive measures is suspect because they may be similar to a one-item test. The validity of nonreactive measures must be demonstrated on a case-by-case basis. For example, one would want to determine, in the example given earlier, if the number of books checked out from a parent resource library represents evidence that a parent training program is successful. The researcher would also want to know that one could obtain the same kind of results consistently.

TREATMENT VERIFICATION

A researcher attempting to design experimental research may start out with an ideal design including random assignment of subjects and clear distinctions between experimental and control group in terms of the independent variable. Yet, the researcher may fail to find differences between the two groups at posttesting. That finding may mean that the treatment made no difference. Alternately, the researcher may find that the treatment made a difference, but unanticipated and uncontrolled-for variables influenced the results. Or, in a more common scenario in early childhood special education, the treatment was implemented differentially or not at all.

In a recent meta-analysis of the early intervention efficacy research, Casto and Mastropieri (1986) found that verification of treatment implementation was one of the most neglected aspects of efficacy studies. For example, research reports typically included inadequate descriptions of the treatment to be offered and provided almost no data on the degree of treatment implementation effected. To remedy this, the researcher can utilize a number of inexpensive procedures to verify treatment implementation. These procedures include:

Completing daily activity logs that depict, on a 15–30 minute interval, the intervention activities carried out

Conducting periodic classroom observations using a treatment implementation checklist

Having supervisory personnel verify the intervention activities of staff

Carta and Greenwood (1985) have proposed an ecological-behavioral assessment system for use in conducting classroom observations that could be used in documenting treatment implementation. This system is also useful for providing important information about classroom environments that are related to student gains in achievement. (See also Carta, Sainato, & Greenwood, Chapter 13, this volume.)

It is also important to monitor the experiences of the control group during the treatment period. Typically, parent questionnaires are utilized to document the experiences of the control group members during the treatment period. Parental self-report data can be verified by reviewing a sample of official records maintained by agencies in the research catchment area.

One key principle that should operate in both instrumentation and verification of treatment implementation areas is that multiple data sources must be used to cross-validate the results. These procedures, which have been labeled triangulation procedures (Denzin, 1978; Mercer, 1979), require that data from one source be verified or confirmed by data from other sources. In the case of instrumentation, the data obtained from a criterion-referenced motor development test might be cross-validated against observation of behavior. In the case of treatment implementation, records kept by intervention personnel provide one data source. Direct observations by impartial observers would be another source. A final source would be self-report data collected from the supervisors of intervention personnel. In sum, triangulation methods provide evidence of the validity of data collected from one source by comparing it to data collected from other sources. Figure 1 provides a graphic representation of the triangulation process.

IMPARTIAL DATA COLLECTION

For data collection to be impartial, it is necessary to use data collectors who are both uninformed and unaware of the purpose of a given research study, and who are unaware of the group membership of the subjects from whom they collect data. Casto and Mastropieri (1986) found that only about 20% of the findings in their review of efficacy research came from studies where "blind," that is, unbiased, examiners were utilized. Since procedures to ensure impartial data collection are easy to implement, and in most cases, add nothing to the cost of doing the research, the use of blind examiners should be encouraged in early childhood special education research.

ETHICS IN RESEARCH

A final critical issue in the field of early child-

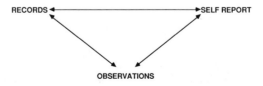

Figure 1. Triangulating the data collection process.

hood studies concerns ethical issues related to both research design and protection of human subjects.

There has been considerable controversy in the field as to whether randomized designs are possible and whether they are in fact ethical. Researchers at the Early Intervention Research Institute (White & Casto, 1984) demonstrated that randomization is possible by identifying over 80 randomized studies in the field of early intervention efficacy research. In fact, two of the most widely quoted studies with at-risk children (Ramey & Haskins, 1981; Weikart, Deloria, Lawser, & Wiegerink, 1970) were randomized experiments. Given that such studies are possible, a thornier dilemma is: are they ethical?

Certainly there are instances where randomization might be inappropriate. The most common argument in early childhood special education is that it is unethical to deny someone treatment. Consider, for example, a research study that is contemplating a treatment versus a no-treatment design beginning with two groups of three-month-old infants. The researcher randomly assigns neonatal intensive care infants who have suffered brain insults of varying severity to a treatment condition (e.g., a motor intervention) or to a control condition consisting of continuing medical care. If it is known that the motor program is an effective treatment, then it would be unethical to deny treatment. However, if it is not known at this point whether the motor intervention program is more effective than continued medical care for this particular group of infants, then the ethical issue is removed. If the evidence collected through this research suggests that the motor intervention program significantly benefits the intervention group, then it would be unethical to continue the study, and control group members would be offered the motor intervention program immediately.

The most important condition here is that information exists that unequivocally suggests that a given treatment is effective. Much has been learned from previous early childhood special education research. However, there are many information gaps that still exist, and most of these gaps can best be addressed by using randomized designs. It is an opportune time to conduct this kind of research now because there are still thousands of unserved children. If one enrolls 100 children, randomly assigns 50 to an intervention program of high intensity and 50 to a no-treatment control condition, both groups will benefit from being identified and assessed. If the treatment program is successful, then the control group can be immediately enrolled.

A final ethical issue is that of ensuring the protection of human subjects. The individuals included in this vulnerable population have benefited greatly in recent years from research that has focused on biological, chemical, surgical, and other medical advances. Infants who would have had little chance of survival 10 years ago are currently being saved in neonatal intensive care units. The federal government has also recently issued regulations to ensure that children born with congenital diseases are not discriminated against by withholding treatment (Department of Health and Human Services Regulations issued pursuant to Sec. 504 of the Rehabilitation Act of 1973). It is imperative that researchers observe a general code of ethics in conducting research in the field. Following is a brief list of guidelines:

Parents should receive a complete explanation of the research and should be given opportunities to ask questions.

All subjects should be informed of their rights to decline to participate in a study, or to withdraw at any time without prejudice.

Subjects should be protected from physical and mental discomfort, harm, and danger. If risks exist, subjects should be completely informed.

Information obtained about subjects must be held confidential.

Subjects should be provided an opportunity to receive the results of the study in which they are participating.

Fortunately, most research also comes under the surveillance of an institutional human subjects committee charged with protecting the rights of human subjects. These committees require signed informed consent documents for all subjects participating in the research and also provide further subject protection. Such protection is provided by the Privacy Act of 1974 which allows subjects to have access to all information pertaining to them.

FUTURE CONCERNS

The field of early childhood special education and program evaluation is rapidly evolving. How current issues are resolved will be an important determinant of future progress in the field. Issues include the problem of translating research findings into practice, the development of better techniques for integrating research findings into a body of knowledge, and finally, methods for developing and integrating theories into programs of research. These issues will be discussed briefly.

Translating Research to Practice

Getting research findings infused into educational practice in early childhood special education is an ongoing process. In this field, early practices were strongly influenced by social mandates and were not research-based. Still, there were ongoing research studies that generated information leading to changes in practices. The first research findings in the 1960s came from studies of programs for disadvantaged preschoolers. These findings were generalized to handicapped preschoolers—a questionable practice at best. Recently, however, more research is being focused on handicapped preschoolers who will meet PL 99-457 guidelines.

The development of a knowledge base depends on the combination of three interrelated areas: current educational practices, the findings from previous research, and advances in research methodologies and technology. It is instructive to use the construct of mother-infant attachment as an example of how the three areas interact. First, many current early intervention programs stress the importance of attachment. The intent is to promote mother-infant interaction through infant stimulation programs. Research findings have suggested that the development by the infant of a secure relationship with the mother is an important precursor to meeting developmental milestones (Smeriglio, 1981). Second, research has also elucidated some of the dimensions of attachment. Finally, the development of tests of attachment such as the Strange Situations Test (Ainsworth & Wittig, 1969) and new applications of videotaping technology have allowed for more systematic study of attachment. These three areas interact to produce new research problems that will, in turn, generate new studies. This interaction adds to the knowledge base and has the potential to change existing practices. Swan (1985) has suggested that the development of consortia combining colleges, universities, and service providers will encourage the implementation of research studies and will increase the relevance of research that is conducted.

Improvements in Methodology: Looking Toward the Future

The precise application of current research methodologies and the development of new methodologies will also be an area of important concern for the future. In the field of early childhood education research, the use of intensive or time series designs (Kratochwill & Piersel, 1983) will increase because these designs provide a format where a true experimental design can be used in a longitudinal study. It is expected that time series designs will receive increasing emphasis in both group and single case studies.

The use of multivariate analyses will continue to expand as researchers become more sophisticated and as improved statistical computer programs proliferate. The use of techniques such as multivariate analysis of variance and covariance, canonical correlations, discriminant function analyses, variant structure analysis, and path analysis will increase and new techniques will emerge to be tested. The use of exploratory data techniques (Hartwig & Dearing, 1979) will also enable researchers to get a better picture of the data to be analyzed.

The methods of naturalistic inquiry or ethnography will also receive increasing attention in the field (Guba & Lincoln, 1981; Wilson, 1977). Given the tentative nature of many current research findings, one may anticipate that ethnographic studies will be utilized to provide more qualitative data about certain aspects of the field, and to generate important research hypotheses for further study.

The integration of the findings of previous primary research studies in early childhood special education will continue to attract the interest of researchers. Narrative reviews of literature have helped to establish educational practices and to direct future research thrusts. Currently, the use of meta-analytic techniques (Glass, 1978) is gaining increasing favor because of its potential to test assertions made in narrative style reviews. Meta-analytic techniques utilize a rather complete and exhaustive collection of studies on a research topic, as well as the coding of each article across important dimensions, and the calculation of standardized mean difference effect sizes across studies. As an example, the assertion that "earlier is better" is a widely accepted axiom in early intervention. However, in a meta-analysis by Casto & Mastropieri (1986), it was found that there are few data to either refute or support this assertion when the data from primary research are aggregated across studies. Although the findings of this analysis are being questioned (Dunst & Synder, 1986; Strain & Smith, 1986), meta-analytic techniques have the potential to provide important information to the field. However, see Guralnick, Chapter 5, this volume, for a contrasting view.

The limitations of meta-analysis include the problems posed by incomplete data sets, possible inaccuracies in data analysis, the potential for unreliability in coding the information provided in the original research reports, and the possibility that certain across-study comparisons may not be valid. However, one should remember that any problems posed by meta-analysis are also present in any other effort to integrate research findings.

THEORETICAL, CONCEPTUAL FRAMEWORKS: SUMMARY

A final point to be made in this chapter is that there is a need to conduct research that is based on an explicit conceptual framework or theory. Because theories represent systematic attempts to explain phenomena, the importance of their use in developing a science of early childhood special education is evident. Basic research can then test theories and either verify or reject them. In doing so, the field moves toward the discovery of principles that govern the field.

In the discipline of early childhood special education, a systems model has been proposed by many researchers as a unifying framework from which to view early childhood special education. Briefly, systems theorists hold that an immense galaxy of variables govern human development. These variables can be best understood if one views the developing child as a complex system (Bertalanffy, 1968; Bowlby, 1969; Bunge, 1979; Casto, 1976; Denenberg, 1982; Frank, 1966; Ramey, McPhee, & Yeates, 1982). This orientation has important implications for early intervention because it differs from the cause-effect conceptual framework prevalent in the field. According to Frank (1966):

> To advance the study of infants we may formulate a model of the infant as a General Purpose system. Such a model would recognize the inherited potentialities of the young organism and the basic processes operating in this self-organizing, self-stabilizing, self-directing, largely self-repairing, open system which becomes progressively patterned, oriented, and coupled to the culturally established dimensions of his environment, natural and human. (p. 178)

Systems theory thus regards normal infants as competent organisms equipped with purposive behavior patterns, efficient effectors, and feedback mechanisms that facilitate goal-oriented behavior and adaptation to their environments. For handicapped children, insults to their systems make the development of goal-oriented behavior and adaptation to their environment problematic. Systems theory allows researchers to predict situations wherein handicapped infants require intervention and also to predict what form this intervention should take. Intervention should begin early, but it is recognized that the early intervention period represents only one link in an involved and intricate chain of development (Kagan, Kearsely, & Zalazo, 1980). In addition, systems theory holds that interventions should have child, family, and environmental emphases, and that outcome measures should be selected that reflect these broad emphases. Theories or conceptual frameworks thus permit the development of testable hypotheses and the advancement of the state of knowledge in the field of early childhood intervention.

REFERENCES

Ainsworth, M. D. S., & Wittig, B. A. (1969). Attachment and exploratory behavior of one-year-olds in a strange situation. In B. M. Foss (Ed.), *Determinants of infant behavior, IV* (pp. 111–136). London: Methuen.

Barnett, W. S. (1985a). Benefit-cost analysis of the Perry Preschool Program and its policy implication. *Educational Evaluation and Policy Analysis, 7*(4), 333–342.

Barnett, W. S. (1985b). *The Perry Preschool Program and its long-term effects: A benefit-cost analysis.* High/Scope Early Childhood Policy Papers, No. 2. Ypsilanti, MI: High/Scope.

Barnett, W. S., & Escobar, C. M. (in press). The economics of early educational intervention: A review. *Review of Educational Research.*

Bertalanffy, L. V. (1968). Chance or law. In A. Koestler & J. R. Smythie (Eds.), *Beyond reductionism* (pp. 78–94). Boston: Beacon.

Borg, W. R., & Gall, M. D. (1983). *Educational research* (2nd ed.). New York: Longman.

Bowlby, J. (1969). *Attachment and loss. Vol. 1: Attachment.* New York: Basic Books.

Bricker, D., Bailey, E., & Bruder, M. (1984). The efficacy of early intervention and the handicapped infant: A wise or wasted resource. *Advances in Developmental and Behavioral Pediatrics, 5,* Greenwich, CT: JAI Press.

Bunge, M. (1979). *Anthology II: A world of systems. Vol. 4: Treatise on basic philosophy.* Boston: D. Reidel.

Carta, J., & Greenwood, C. (1985). Expanding the evaluation of early intervention programs. *Topics in Early Childhood Special Education, 5,* 88–104.

Casto, G. (1976). *Final report: Affective behavior in preschool children.* Logan: Exceptional Child Center, Utah State University.

Casto, G., & Mastropieri, M. A. (1986). The efficacy of early intervention programs for handicapped children: A meta-analysis. *Exceptional Children, 52*(5), 417–424.

Denenberg, V. (1982). Early experience, interactive systems, and brain laterality in rodents. In L. A. Bond, H. Lynne, & J. Joffe (Eds.), *Facilitating infant and early childhood development* (pp. 78–79). Hanover, VT: University Press of New England.

Denzin, N. K. (1978). *The Research Act: A theoretical introduction to sociological methods* (2nd ed.). Chicago: Aldine Press.

Dunst, C. J., & Rheingrover, R. M. (1981). An analysis of the efficacy of infant intervention programs with organically handicapped children. *Evaluation and Program Planning, 4,* 287–323.

Dunst, C. J., & Snyder, S. W. (1986). A critique of the Utah State University early intervention meta-analysis research. *Exceptional Children, 53,* 269–276.

Fine, M., & Swift, C. (1986). Young handicapped children: Their prevalence and experiences with early intervention services. *Journal of the Division of Early Childhood, 10*(1), 73–83.

Frank, L. K. (1966). *On the importance of infancy.* New York: Random House.

Glass, G. V. (1978). Integrating findings: The meta-analysis of research. *Review of Research in Education, 5,* 351–379.

Guba, E. G., & Lincoln, Y. S. (1981). *Effective evaluation.* San Francisco: Jossey Bass.

Hartwig, F. E., & Dearing, B. E. (1979). *Exploratory data analysis.* Beverly Hills: Sage.

Innocenti, M., Morgan, J., Rule, S., Stowitschek, J. (1985, October). *Mainstreaming young handicapped children: A continuum of service and support.* Paper presented at a meeting of the American Association of University Affiliated Programs, Seattle, WA.

Kagan, J., Kearsely, R. B., & Zalazo, P. R. (1980). *Infancy: Its place in human development.* Cambridge, MA: Harvard University Press.

Kent, R. N., & Foster, S. L. (1977). Direct observational procedures: Methodological issues in naturalistic settings. In A. R. Ciminero, K. S. Calhoun, & H. E. Adams (Eds.), *Handbook of behavioral assessment* (pp. 279–328). New York: John Wiley & Sons.

Kratochwill, T. R., & Piersel, W. C. (1983). Time-series research: Contributions to empirical clinical practice. *Behavioral Assessment, 5,* 165–176.

Levin, H. M. (1981). *Cost-effectiveness: A primer.* Beverly Hills: Sage.

McMillan, J. H., & Schumacker, S. (1984). *Research in education.* Boston: Little, Brown.

Mercer. J. (1979). *System of multi-cultural pluralistic assessment technical manual.* New York: Psychological Corporation.

Odom, S. L., & Fewell, R. R. (1983). Program evaluation in early childhood special education: A meta-evaluation. *Educational Evaluation and Policy Analysis, 5*(4), 445–460.

Ramey, C. T., & Haskins, R. (1981). The causes and treatment of school failure: Insights from the Carolina Abecedarian Project. In M. Begab (Ed.), *Psychosocial influences and retarded performance: Strategies for improving social competence* (Vol. 2, pp. 89–112). Baltimore: University Park Press.

Ramey, C. T., McPhee, D., & Yeates, K. (1982). Preventing developmental retardation: A general system model. In L. Bond & J. Joeffe (Eds.), *Facilitating infant and early childhood development* (pp. 343–401). Hanover, NH: University Press of New England.

Simeonsson, R. J., Cooper, D. H., & Schiener, A. P. (1982). A review and analysis of the effectiveness of early intervention programs. *Pediatrics, 69,* 635.

Smeriglio, V. (1981). Effects of mother-newborn contact: Comparability and validity of measures. In V. J.

Smeriglio (Ed.), *Parent infant contact and newborn sensory stimulation* (pp. 97–101). Hillsdale, NJ: Lawrence Erlbaum Associates.

Strain, P. S., & Smith, B. J. (1986). A counter-interpretation of early intervention effects: A response to Casto & Mastropieri. *Exceptional Children, 53,* 260–265.

Swan, W. W. (1985). Implications of current research for the administration and leadership of preschool programs. *Topics in Early Childhood Special Education, 5*(1), 83–96.

Thompson, M. S. (1980). *Benefit-cost analysis for program evaluation.* Beverly Hills: Sage.

Tyler, R. (1950). *Basic principles of curriculum and instruction.* Chicago: University of Chicago Press.

Weikart, D., Deloria, D., Lawser, S., & Wiegerink, R. (1970). *Longitudinal results of the Ypsilanti Perry Preschool Project.* Ypsilanti, MI: High/Scope.

White, K. R., & Casto, G. (1984). An integrative review of early intervention efficacy studies with at-risk children: Implications for the handicapped. *Analysis and Intervention in Developmental Disabilities, 5,* 7–31.

Wilson, S. (1977). The use of ethnographic techniques in educational research. *Review of Educational Research, 47,* 245–265.

Zigler, E., & Balla, D. (1982). Selecting outcome variables in evaluations of early childhood special education programs. *Topics in Early Childhood Special Education, 1*(4), 11–22.

Chapter 4

Policy Factors Influencing Research in Early Childhood Special Education

Eugene Edgar

THE "JOB OF SCIENCE" IS TO ASK questions of nature (Cronbach, 1957), to solve the puzzles of nature (Kuhn, 1970), and all the while not to be "fooled" by nature (Pirsig, 1974). A big order! Yet professionals who claim the territory of "scientist" in the field of education accept the responsibility for asking relevant questions and attempting to solve some of the riddles posed by nature. Scientists pose and endeavor to resolve these questions by using a variety of methods that fall under the general rubric of scientific inquiry.

The purpose of this chapter is to scrutinize the forces that shape and direct research activities in the field of early childhood special education.

SOCIAL POLICY IN EARLY CHILDHOOD SPECIAL EDUCATION RESEARCH

Social policy has a direct impact on the research activities taking place in education. For the purpose of discussion, social policy is defined by the author as the sum of the prevailing societal attitudes toward a given topic, specifically: early childhood special education. Formal and informal manifestations of these attitudes include laws, rules, regulations, individual values, institutional values,

political influences, folklore, and social tradition. These influences shape and define that body of legislation known as policy. Federal, state, and local social services policies, for example, would be reflected in a plan for social agencies to distribute services.

The relationship between society and social policy is synergistic: each shapes and is shaped by the other. When the low school performance of poor children was recognized as a concern for society, for instance, research on the impact of early intervention upon the cognitive development of poor children proliferated. A specific example of this may be seen in the establishment of the Head Start program. As researchers began to report the benefits of early education for the cognitive development of poor children, the Head Start program was founded. The program was regarded as a general benefit to society, and as a solution for overcoming the problem of low academic performance by poor children as compared to the higher performance of children who were not poor. However, in the author's opinion, the decision to select education as the area of intervention rather than, say, deciding to provide financial stipends or free medical care for those families was a decision based on popular sentiment rather than on research. And, as Daniel Boorstin noted, the "religion" of education in

The author would like to thank his colleagues Sam Odom, Bud Fredericks, Kevin Cole, and Gray Garwood for commenting on an earlier version of this chapter. Their advice was always appreciated but not always followed. Jim Pruess added valuable editorial assistance.

America implies that education is the great leveler, the path to equality for all (Boorstin, 1974). So education as a solution to poverty was selected for reasons other than the research findings. Yet, research on how children learn did lead to the development of programs to respond to society's problems. Thus, through prevailing social attitudes, solutions for problems (e.g., education) are defined, and researchers then attempt to justify the policy decision. But the question remains; exactly what drives what: does research drive social attitudes, or does public sentiment drive research?

Special Education in the United States: The Important Questions

The impact of public sentiment on early childhood special education is closely tied to the role education has been given in society. The question of "what is the purpose of education?" was addressed in the writings of such American figures as John Dewey, Thomas Jefferson, G. Stanley Hall, William Clarke, and Samuel Gridley Howe (see Boorstin, 1974). Special education professionals may be spending too little time pondering larger questions such as those pondered by Jefferson and Dewey. A little thinking about the overall issue of education may help special education professionals to better understand what purpose education should serve in America. Daniel Boorstin frames the question in terms of equality and inequality:

> The debate over its [education] proper role in American democracy would focus once again on a question that had reoccurred throughout American History and that would bedevil the nation in the twentieth century. It was in some ways the central problem of modern democracy, for it was nothing less than the question of the meaning of human 'equality.' Was the good society one which allowed all citizens to develop their natural differences, including their natural inequalities? Or was it a society which tried to make men equal? Did 'equality' mean the maximum fulfillment of each, or did it mean the leveling of all?" (Boorstin, 1974, p. 491)

Relating this question of equality to the field of special education, one may ask: Is the purpose of special education to make children with disabilities the same as children who are without disabilities? Or is its purpose instead to effect the maximum fulfillment of each child *at his or her own ability level?* Should special educators endeavor to return their students to the mainstream of education or should a separate curriculum be created for them?

Chester Finn, Assistant Secretary of Education, raises a second issue. "Is formal education—the kind one gets in school—fundamentally an extension of the family? Or is it one of the premiere functions of the larger society?" (Finn, 1985, p. 17). Specifically, what is the role of parents in developing individualized education programs? Do parents or does society decide what and how children are to be taught? In the author's opinion, there are at present no clear-cut, agreed-upon objectives for the field of early childhood special education. For example, one of the most pressing policy questions is whether or not early intervention for handicapped students is effective. This question is difficult, if not impossible, to answer without an agreed-upon standard of effectiveness.

Furthermore, how can this basic question be answered without defining *who* the students with disabilities are? The problems with identification and classification of students as disabled have been discussed elsewhere (e.g., Edgar & Hayden, 1985), yet a few important points need to be reviewed. The definition of disability under federal regulations can be divided into: 1) disabilities that our technology can accurately measure (e.g., moderate to profound levels of retardation, orthopedic impairments such as cerebral palsy or spina bifida, and sensory impairments) and 2) disabilities that are inferred from low performance (e.g., speech-only problems, serious emotional disturbance, mild mental retardation, and learning disabilities). The clearly identifiable cases of disability represent less than 2% of the total population. The milder conditions become confused with the larger population of poor learners and low achievers. As a result, the primary goals of early childhood special education and early intervention programs for disadvantaged groups, such as in the Head Start program, become cloudy and overlapping. These two groups have been defined through artificial eligibility criteria that imply a difference in the *cause* of the learning problems. Thus, public sentiment determines which students are eligible for such programs; such attitudes are primarily responsible for much of the confusion about population characteristics. Repeatedly, careful researchers have pointed out the necessity of separating the data of those students with clear-cut central nervous system defects from the data of students with only low performance problems (Dunst & Rheingrover, 1981; Simeonsson, Cooper, & Scheiner, 1982). Yet, in the public mind, these groups continue to be confused.

So one returns to the question: What is the purpose of early childhood special education? What populations should be served, and what goals should be achieved?

Special Education Research: Asking the Right Questions

Garret Hardin, in a book of essays entitled *Stalking the Wild Taboo* (1978), discusses the importance of question-asking in science. By carefully asking the right questions, science can advance its knowledge base. However, correct answers to the wrong question result in incorrect conclusions. A good example of asking the right question may be found in the National Academy of Sciences report on equity in special education (Heller, Holtzman, & Messick, 1982). This blue ribbon committee debated the issue of why so many males and minorities were placed in special education by asking the question, "Are the placement procedures for special education discriminatory to minorities and males?" The committee's inquiry led to a review of nondiscriminatory testing, of referral procedures, and of the sticky issue of inequitable distribution of mild disabilities among ethnic groups. However, a satisfactory resolution to these issues has yet to be found. The issue was not clarified until the NAS committee reexamined the basic question and reworded it to read: "Why does regular education do such a poor job with males and

minorities?" This is one of the important issues that needs to be addressed: it is one of the "right" questions.

Societal Expectations and Data Analysis One sees what one wants to see. In his book, *The Mismeasure of Man* (1981), Stephen J. Gould provided an eloquent discussion on how scientists "see" in their data what society tells them should be there. Gould maintains this is not a case of overt data manipulation or misrepresentation, but rather a perceptual screen that filters out incompatible data from accepted theory. Kuhn (1970) described the same phenomena as a result of the prevailing paradigm: one can only "see" what one acknowledges as possible. The result is that one "looks for" indicators that confirm one's belief system, a system shaped as much by popular political beliefs as by scientific paradigms. (See Odom, Chapter 1, for an extended discussion of this issue.)

Permissible Solutions Public sentiment also dictates which solutions are and are not permissible. Education in the United States is widely regarded, according to Boorstin, as the "great leveler", the process by which, in theory, all individuals, regardless of ethnicity, gender, or social background, can come to enjoy the fruits of American society. The belief is that with hard work (another societal value), and equal opportunity to learn, each member of society can partake of the good life. So education is a very permissible solution to societal ills such as the effects of poverty on children's academic achievement. However, there are some solutions to societal problems that are not permissible and are thus not researchable. For example, financial stipends that ensure a guaranteed income to individuals are not considered a permissible solution in the United States, so one does not see studies comparing the outcome of giving a monetary stipend to poor families with preschool children as compared to offering these families enrollment in a Head Start program.

Currently Fashionable Research Topics

There are a number of "hot topics" or issues in science that are desirable research topics.

These issues tend to direct scientific research because they are "fundable" ideas and the scientific community finds studies on these topics suitable for publication. A number of these topics are identified below.

Education Can Make Unequal Events Equal If there is a population that has been denied equal academic experience (e.g., children from poor neighborhoods), a specially designed educational experience such as Head Start will allow them to perform as well as individuals who have been exposed to the "better experience" (e.g., middle class children). Similarly, if a child has a disability that inhibits normal development, special education at an early age can overcome or lessen the impact of the disability.

Education is an Extension of the Family Parents are the primary teachers of their own children; in home-based early intervention programs, parents should be regarded as the primary interveners. Methods to get parents more involved in the educational process are highly valued.

Early Intervention is Cost-Effective Studies demonstrating savings in public funds are in vogue. The reason for intervening is that money will be saved in the long run. This mode of thought suggests that an ounce of prevention is worth a pound of cure, which is a highly valued societal belief.

Integration is Desirable Demonstrating the positive effects of mingling various groups with nonhandicapped, nonpoor, mainstream, middle-class students is regarded as a desirable effort. Conversely, data indicating negative outcomes of segregation are considered to be "good" data.

Topics That are Taboo

There are topics that will not find favor among early childhood special educators. Regardless of the adequacy of the research design or the power of the outcomes, the following topics will not be accepted.

Taboos Society has defined some topics as too controversial to even question. These topics are treated as taboos, and as such, we do not even talk about them; we keep these issues bur-

ied in our subconscious. A taboo, according to Hardin (1978), "is a prohibition excluding something from use, approach, or mention . . ." (p. vii). When we refuse to discuss a subject, research a question, or even ask a question, we exclude these notions from our general thought patterns, and, in effect, we create a taboo on *thinking*. To violate a word or thinking taboo is bad taste.

Political Issues Other issues we have designated as being permissible only if the questions conform with prevailing political views on such matters as individual freedom and human dignity. For example, the debates between Piaget and Vygotsky are tinted with the innuendo of politics, as are the writings of Arnold Gesell, John Dewey, and Jean-Marc-Gaspard Itard. Political philosophy directs science, both overtly, as manifested in funding patterns and covertly, as manifested in the sanctions of colleagues by the academic community. The work and theory of Goddard (1913) was permissible up to World War II and the Holocaust, then the prevailing notions of inferior genetics were reviewed and ultimately rejected. As a current extension of this political belief, Arthur Jensen's (1969) work has been criticized, in part as a result of being politically impermissible. How can one espouse a democratic way of life if some subgroups are considered less capable, genetically, than others? Such a theory is unacceptable and questions related to it cannot be asked.

There is a Genetic/Hereditary/Internal Determinant of Learning Ability Not Amenable to Education This is the basic notion that all people do not have equal abilities and therefore equal opportunities. Exploration of this question can only lead to: 1) devaluing of a subgroup or 2) the need to treat this subgroup either better or worse than other groups. The political system and the scientific community in America cannot tolerate these theories and thus supports no research in this area.

Money as a Stipend is a Nonacceptable Intervention One can give advice, counseling, education, information, food, and materials, but one can never give money to individuals as the primary treatment. Often proposed facetiously, the idea involves dividing the number of clients by available funds and then giving clients direct stipends to do with as they please. This approach would entail few professional or administrative costs and would be, in effect, the ultimate voucher system.

Intellectual Capacity is Genetically Limited in Some Individuals   Perhaps there are some individuals, for whom education is *not* an effective intervention. For example, for those students who are not responsive to education, can one more effectively increase quality of life by altering the environment or by buying respite for their families rather than by expending the resources on therapists and teachers who may not be successful in teaching these students new skills? To make the recommendation that some people are not educable is in bad taste, results in criticism from other professionals (see Baer, 1981; Kaufman & Krouse, 1981), and causes us to be viewed as noncaring.

Does Federal Policy Need Research?

Federal policy clearly influences research. It directs research questions, provides funds for various types of research, limits the questions that are permissible for study, and limits the solutions that are proposed. Research affects federal policy in a much less direct manner. The belief that research dictates federal policy is not true (Garwood, 1983). First, scientists seldom make federal policy. Beliefs set federal policy, and then there is a search for data to support the beliefs. The prevailing attitude is not that statistics can be used to prove anything, but that there are probably data around (somewhere) that will support almost any federal policy. The problem is that scientists tend to use research to support what scientists already believe. One can always refuse to consider contradicting evidence if by no other means than by ignoring it.

However, a larger issue that should be addressed concerns the role of research in policy-making. Should federal policy be based on data? How should federal policy be determined about areas for which there are no clear data? There are instances when federal policy seems

the more logical road to take rather than to wait for data; early intervention for handicapped children is one such area. Federal policy has declared that these programs will exist. Research should be used to answer the more specific questions of how best to serve the population—not whether to serve it or not.

SCIENTIFIC INQUIRY IN EARLY CHILDHOOD SPECIAL EDUCATION

A common response to the basic question of why research is conducted is found, not surprisingly, in textbooks on educational research. The purpose of scientific inquiry is to better understand nature, to develop paradigms to explain nature, and to develop answers to everyday problems. The popular image of scientists is that of puzzle solvers: individuals who carefully collect information about nature in order to know what "is." In order to know what "is," scientists develop theories that explain how nature works. For example, consider this question: How do children learn to speak their native language? This is a fair question for scientists in education. First, a theory is needed: How does this very complex event occur so frequently with humans no matter where they live or what language they speak? So theories are developed of species-specific behavior (Lenneberg, 1967), developmental stages (Piaget, 1952), and environmental influences (Skinner, 1953). Kuhn (1970) defines this collection of theories—the beliefs the scientific community shares—as a paradigm. However, to really be scientific the paradigm must be able to predict events. It must answer questions such as: At what age does speech develop? What are the fixed rules of syntax across languages? What happens if certain usual events are altered, for example, if hearing is impaired? The power and credibility of a paradigm reside in its ability to correctly predict occurrences in nature.

Yet research is expected to provide answers for everyday problems. By developing theories to explain and predict nature, individuals attempt to "fix up" things when nature has made a mistake. Referring again to the language de-

velopment example, theories have been formulated that explain language development, that
predict behavioral occurrences, and provide
clues as to what to do when language does not
develop as predicted.

Thomas Kuhn, in his text *The Structure of
Scientific Revolutions* (1970), comments that
the popular notion that there is a gradual ac-
cumulation of facts leading always onward to
higher truths is an idea that is simply not supported by history. Instead, knowledge advances in jumps and spurts with each major
increase resulting in major shifts in the prevailing paradigms that are collectively regarded as
"science." Paradigms are, according to Kuhn
(1970), ". . . what the members of a scientific
community share, *and,* conversely, a scientific
community consists of men (scientists) who
share a paradigm" (p. 176).

As paradigms age, predictable events occur.
For example, there is a movement from less
accepted to more accepted explanations for
nature: a greater focus on more specific rather
than general problems, and the predominance
of the paradigm as the principal truth in textbooks of members of the profession. As the
paradigm becomes mature, the permissible explanations and investigative tactics become
more specific as does the roster of important
unsolved yet soluble questions. According to
Kuhn, a paradigm enters old age when the unsolved problems resist solution and hence are
removed from the permissible list of questions
to be asked and are replaced with solvable but
insignificant questions. A major sign of an
aged paradigm is when the questions being
asked by the scientists are so minute that the
answers are of no importance to anyone save
themselves. Kuhn describes this situation as
the precursor to a revolution: the old paradigm
will be replaced by a new, as yet unknown,
paradigm in the future.

The field of early childhood special education seems to be using a paradigm that can be
called the Environmental/Developmental Paradigm. Although there are competing theories,
all the theoretical underpinnings are based on
the notion that environmental events influence
learning and/or behavior. Other possible paradigms that could be used to address similar
issues are anthropological, medical/chemical,
or metaphysical. The environmental paradigm
dominates the research efforts in special education by dictating potential solutions to unsolved
problems and limiting the variable options for
problem solving. This paradigm also sets the
limits on acceptable research activities in the
field.

Developmental Psychology: Foundation of Early Childhood Special Education

One of the primary disciplines within the field
of ECSE is that of developmental psychology.
The classic debate of the relative influence of
nature versus nurture has been resolved within
the field of special education by the assumption
that there is an interaction between nature and
environment. Thus, educators need to focus on
the nurture aspect, that is, manipulating the
environment. In his definitive work, J. McV.
Hunt (1961) stated that our task is to focus on
the nurturing aspects of learning—to deal with
the observable world.

So research in early childhood special education deals with questions such as: which curriculum is best, how can researchers most efficiently get children to behave in predetermined
ways, what prosthetic devices can be used to
offset a damaged body or central nervous system, what sequence of activities produces the
best learning, how do researchers arrange environments? Investigators in early childhood
special education use the psychological paradigm to answer these questions. If a different
paradigm were being used, for instance an anthropological paradigm, different questions
would be asked and different approaches
would be tried. For example, questions that
might be asked include: What ideas do adults
have about what children should learn, how
they learn, and when they should learn (i.e.,
cultural influences on learning)? How do children feel about going to school? How is society
organized to care for families with handicapped children? These questions clearly lead
to different types of interventions than the
questions posed by psychologists (Becker,
1983).

In the psychological paradigm, the problems are both of theory building (i.e., predicting the occurrence or nonoccurrence of specific phenomena in specific contexts) and developing solutions for society's ills (e.g., evaluating young children who have language problems). Although there are debates between behavioral psychologists and pure developmental psychologists about which aspects of the environment should be manipulated or how learning should be defined, the general scientific community accepts environmental manipulation as the main currency of the science.

Like the field of developmental psychology, the field of education has benefitted from the work of such early leaders as Friedrich Froebel, Johann Guggenbühl, Jean-Marc-Gaspard Itard, Alfred Binet, and Maria Montessori (see Rosen, Clark, & Kivitz, 1976). But these advances have not been great. The notions advanced by the early paradigm builders have been refined but not substantially altered. Task analysis, discrimination learning, measuring performance, learning stages, and errorless learning are all old notions that have been refined rather than invented by Piaget (1952), Feuerstein (Feuerstein, Rand, Hoffman, & Miller, 1980), Engelman (Engelman & Carnine, 1982), Weikart (Weikart, Deloria, Lowsen, & Wiegerink, 1979) and other such leaders in the field.

The Environmental Paradigm and the Problem of Data Interpretation The research data continue to accumulate. In 1976, Gene Glass pointed out the overabundance of data facing educational researchers and the subsequent problems researchers face in making sense out of all this material. To assist researchers in understanding these data, he recommended a process called meta-analysis. Others try the time-honored approach of reviewing the literature, a careful reading of research reports followed by an analysis of the inherent soundness of the designs and the corresponding believability of the findings. Glass's laconic conclusion that studies lack even minimal experimental design prerequisites and thus produce questionable findings is, in the author's opinion, far too often true. The

field of special education has become overwhelmed with its own research findings and appears to be mired in its data overload.

Large questions continue to be asked (e.g., "Is early intervention effective?"), yet researchers know that these questions are not likely to be answered by a single study or even a series of studies (See Guralnick, Chapter 5, this volume.) Data are collected concerning more specific questions such as "What are the differential outcomes in reading between DISTAR and a cognitive mediated curriculum?" The findings are found to be mixed or definitive, and regardless of the outcome, new studies asking the same or very similar questions are generated (House, Glass, McLean, & Walker, 1978). One reason for this may be that the "scientific community" does not accept the answers that it generates. This could be due, in part, to the lack of clarity of the results. Far too many studies result in mixed results with only weak indications of main effect. A second explanation could be that a communication problem exists among scientists. Even though scientists all are working under the general rubric of the Environmental Paradigm, groups of researchers use different concepts to describe worldly events; these varying semantic structures and varying research methodologies prevent convergence of belief.

A third explanation could be that the environmental paradigm has aged to the point that no new socially important differences will or can be distinguished between experimental manipulations; or all we can *really* do in the context of arranging the environment we have done and researched already; or we have learned so much about discretely and effectively influencing learning that *all* of our studies are more or less equally effective. This paradigm has matured to the point where new advances are not likely, and additional breakthroughs in altering learning must await a new paradigm. The questions of researchers become redundant and more minute, and are significant only to those researchers who are debating the insignificant.

It is instructive to note the commentary provided by Kuhn (1970) on the common events that take place when the dominant paradigm has run its course. The predictive power of the theory has major problems that, despite countless efforts, remain unsolved. Those scientists working in theory building take on more and more specific and seemingly trivial questions, placing the more critical questions in the category of unsolvable at the present time. While findings continue to generate excitement among the inner circle of scientists, the general theory remains unchanged. Special education researchers should take note.

Among the group of applied research scientists that are attempting to devise solutions to problems, the glow of initial anticipation of what "will be, once we have the details worked out" has given way to the realization that the outcomes do not quite meet their expectations. Revisions follow modifications which followed alteration in procedures. The conclusion sections of the research reports are still optimistic, yet more and more we read words of caution and restraint. Positive results occur yet riddles remain. Growth or learning is not as powerful as we predicted. Significant numbers of children do not evidence educationally relevant gains although statistical significance may have been reached. Retention problems, washout effects, sleeper effects, lack of generalization, and regression to the mean become topics of debate. Society's ills, lack of funding, insensitive unions, along with further research and needed modification become cliches to explain why the results are not what was expected. The prospect that the paradigm might not provide the clues of what to do next does not seem to be considered. But how can this alternative be openly discussed *until* an alternative approach is proposed? The scientific method, which is so very helpful in preventing one from being fooled by nature and one's own intuition, also does not allow one to break out of the boundaries provided by the prevailing dominant paradigm. One's questions and methods of testing solutions are fixed by one's theory. When the theory has aged, the only way out is for a new, more powerful theory to replace the old.

It is the author's contention that the Environ-mental Paradigm has aged to the point that very few new answers will emerge. Problems such as finding ways to help severely retarded babies learn more rapidly, methods to help poor preschoolers develop cognitive skills, procedures to assist autistic preschoolers to relate to their environment, instructional alternatives for those students who do not learn from the current procedures will not be significantly answered within the framework of the Environmental Paradigm. The means of finding solutions simply are not present. Technology has peaked and new advances will only come from radically different ways of viewing the world.

Among the many indicators that the paradigm has aged is the proliferation of nontraditional treatments. A standard rule of thumb is that if traditional methods are effective there will be no opportunity for divergent activities. For example, in medicine the customary treatment for appendicitis is effective—there are few holistic or nutritional or spiritual clinics which specialize in treating the individual with acute appendicitis. On the other hand, with cancer one finds all types of divergent attempts to cure this disease ranging from laughter to laetrile. None of these treatments has a high cure rate. In fact, the lower the cure rate the more nontraditional the alternatives, which indicate a paradigm without answers.

Now, for example, in early childhood special education there are children with clusters of symptoms that are defined as autism. Our treatments include behavioral therapy, megavitamins, psychodynamic intervention, and sensorimotor integration. The cure rate is low regardless of intervention. The paradigm does not provide additional hints about which way to turn. Old ideas are tried again and again—sometimes with new names, often with new proponents, yet the results remain the same. This is not a disclosure on autism, for researchers could substitute cerebral palsy, Down syndrome, learning disabilities, or persons economically at risk and find the same results. Clearly, research has come a long way in the last 30 years. Researchers do a much better job now than they did then, but in the author's opinion, future advances under the Environmental Paradigm are unlikely.

A vivid scene from *The Right Stuff* by Tom Wolfe (1979) provides an example of this point. The pilots, led by Chuck Yeager, have been the gallant leaders of the attempt to reach space. Fixed wing flight was far ahead of rocket technology, and was far ahead in the race to space. But in the end fixed wing technology peaked before the ultimate goal, flight into space, was achieved, and rocket technology won the race.

Our situation is analogous. The Environmental Paradigm has peaked before the field of special education has reached its ultimate goal, that is, optimal learning for all. It is still the best thing researchers have; it was the only way to go in the past, and we did well. But now researchers must give way to another paradigm, one that is not yet clearly specified. So what should ECSE researchers do until the new paradigm comes along? We can model Chuck Yeager: we go out and do our best, day to day, remaining true to our values.

RESEARCH DEMANDS IN EARLY CHILDHOOD SPECIAL EDUCATION

A further influence on research activities revolves around professionals' behavior—the institutionalized ritual of what professionals are expected to do and how they ought to behave. An entire institution, the research university, is based on the search for knowledge through research. Entrance into this social system is highly regulated (e.g., sufficient academic degrees, courses of study, and mentor recommendations), and the standards of performance are clearly stated (e.g., publish, receive grant funds, obtain peer approval). These standards operate regardless of the final outcome of *new knowledge.*

So a major motivation for research activities is the need to be accepted or to maintain acceptance in the research community. Acceptance in this community means adhering to the rules prescribed in special education and psychology for identifying the types of research questions that may be asked and the types of intervention that may be attempted closely associated with professional membership. In maintaining job status, for example, publish or perish remains a factor even after tenure is awarded because professional colleagues often keep score of the number of publications others got last year. Clearly, the energy that drives much writing in special education is the need for peer approval, and the necessity of maintaining job status, rather than the desire to discover knowledge.

Few professionals would not like to make a positive contribution to the education of young handicapped children. A major impetus for individuals to enter the special education profession is to help others and to make a contribution to society. For researchers, the ultimate reward is to develop procedures, to produce research, to clarify issues, and/or to articulate ideas that result in better things happening to young children. I have no doubt that perhaps *the* major impetus for conducting research in early childhood special education is due to the drive of individual researchers to "do good."

Professional Communities: Competition and the Special Education Researcher

However, there are reasons other than helping society that drive researchers. As noted above, one is peer approval. As professional communities grow, an internal network of "insiders" develops. This network informally sets rules and establishes criteria for membership. Some of the interactions among members are self-serving (e.g., passing information on future grants, sharing confidential information, inviting each other to publish—often without peer review, recommending one another for positions, etc.). Other interactions, however, shape professional behavior. For example, current (unpublished) research is discussed, the latest ideas are openly debated and often new ideas are generated and shared. Sometimes there are negative outcomes. For example, there is the ongoing pressure to publish more papers, more chapters, more books—to get more than the others—to keep "score." This pressure to publish may result in publishing material that barely qualifies as noteworthy. But even more damaging is the control the "inner circle" maintains on its members to only ask permissible questions. This control, governed by the threat of ostracism for going against the flow, can be a serious barrier to innovative research. At times, eccentrics will break from the world but it is a lonely and often painful thing to do.

Publish or Perish

A distinction needs to be made between publishing and conducting research. At the very least, research is an attempt to answer a question by organizing data in some novel way. Publishing may include research articles or it may involve polemics—nondata-based speculations. However, the pressure to publish in research settings drives the writing behavior of researchers. There is a constant need to be in print, initially to get tenure and then to maintain professional standing. Some material is published only because of these needs and *not* because the information will be useful to anyone. The extent to which the professional literature becomes cluttered with trivia decreases the utility of the literature. However, I am the first to acknowledge that one person's trivia is another's truth.

The drive to publish in our profession may be a positive or a negative force. We all need to consider our own motives for producing words, for conducting research, and for publishing.

CONCLUSION

This chapter has attempted to present a logical exploration of the forces that drive research activities in early childhood special education. The author has attempted to present information in a way that might help all researchers consider their personal motives for doing research and writing. Each researcher, especially those who have reached the point in their careers when they have more personal freedom,

needs to devote a few minutes to reviewing the forces that shape professional behaviors. The author has great faith that a little "Eastern" introspection combined with "Western" deduction will continue to produce ideas that will benefit young handicapped children.

However, researchers must be constantly aware of the powerful influence of social policy on their thoughts. Political ideology must not unknowingly drive our research efforts, especially with regard to the questions we ask. Open, frank inquisitiveness is central to our well-being as educators and as human beings. Somehow researchers must attempt to keep asking relevant questions and to keep the open mind of a beginner, a mind capable of "seeing" things as they truly are (Suzuki, 1970).

The end of the educational paradigm is basically irrelevant to everyday research. If Kuhn is right at all, we simply have to wait for the next paradigm to arrive. This is not to imply that the environmental paradigm is wrong. A new paradigm will come along to replace our current theories but it will not negate what we have come to believe is true. Rather, "what we actually discover is that the way we have been looking at nature is no longer comprehensive enough to explain all that we can observe, and we are forced to develop a more inclusive view" (Zukav, 1979, p.19).

Finally, there is the issue of belonging to a professional community. I believe the advantages of a close-knit yet competitive professional community far outweigh the negative effects. How else could researchers function without the stimulation and pressure of professional colleagues? The exchange among colleagues adds much to the field. I am continually impressed with the energy and the capacity to give of oneself which predominates in the field of special education. Yet occasionally, researchers must pause and calmly reflect on the *reasons* behind their actions.

REFERENCES

Baer, D. M. (1981). A hung jury and a Scottish verdict: "Not proven." *Analysis and Intervention in Developmental Disabilities, 1,* 91–97.

Becker, H. (1983). Studying urban schools. *Anthropology & Education Quarterly, 14,* 99–108.

Boorstin, D. J. (1974). *The Americans: The democratic*

experience. New York: Vintage Books.

Boorstin, D. J. (1983). *The discoverers*. New York: Random House.

Cronbach, L. J. (1957). The two disciplines of scientific psychology. *American Psychologist, 12,* 671–684.

Dunst, C. J., & Rheingrover, R. M. (1981). An analysis of the efficacy of infant intervention programs with organically handicapped children. *Evaluation and Program Planning, 4,* 287–323.

Edgar, E., & Hayden, A. H. (1985). Who are the children special education should serve and how many children are there? *Journal of Special Education, 18,* 523–539.

Engelman, S., & Carnine, D. W. (1982). *Theory of instruction: Principles and applications*. New York: Irvington.

Feuerstein, R., Rand, Y., Hoffman, M. B., & Miller, R. (1980). *Instrumental enrichment: Redevelopment of cognitive functions of retarded performers*. Baltimore: University Park Press.

Finn, C. E. (1985). Our schizophrenic educational system. *The Peabody Reflection, 58,* 17, 36.

Garwood, S. G. (1983). National educational policy: Naive and cautious impressions from a temporary insider. *Newsletter* (Society for Research in Child Development, Inc.) Fall.

Glass, G. V. (1976). Primary, secondary, and meta-analysis of research. *Educational Researcher, 5,* 3–8.

Goddard, H. H. (1913). The improvability of feeble-minded children. Journal of Psycho-Asthenics, *17*(4), 121–131.

Gould, S. J. (1981). *The mismeasure of man*. New York: W. W. Norton.

Hardin, G. (1978). *Stalking the wild taboo* (2nd ed.). Los Altos, CA: William Kaufmann, Inc.

Heller, K. A., Holtzman, W., & Messick, S. (Eds.). (1982). *Placing children in special education: A strategy for equity*. Washington, DC: National Academy Press.

House, E. R., Glass, G. V., McLean, L. D., & Walker, D.

F. (1978). No simple answer: Critique of the Follow Through Evaluation. *Harvard Educational Review, 48,* 128–160.

Hunt, J. McV. (1961). *Intelligence and experience*. New York: Ronald.

Jensen, A. R. (1969). How much can we boost IQ and scholastic achievement? *Harvard Educational Review, 39,* 1–123.

Kaufman, J. M., & Krouse, T. (1981). The cult of educability: Searching for the substance of things hoped for, the evidence of things not seen. *Analysis and Intervention in Developmental Disabilities, 1,* 53–60.

Kuhn, T. S. (1970). *The structure of scientific revolutions* (2nd Edition). Chicago: University of Chicago Press.

Lenneberg, E. (1967). *Biological foundations of language*. New York: John Wiley.

Piaget, J. (1952). *The origins of intelligence in children*. New York: International Universities Press.

Pirsig, R. M. (1974). *Zen and the art of motorcycle maintenance*. New York: Bantam Books.

Rosen, M., Clark, G. R., & Kivitz, M. S. (Eds.). (1976). *The history of mental retardation*, Vol. 1. Baltimore: University Park Press.

Simeonsson, R. J., Cooper, D. H., & Scheiner, A. P. (1982). A review and analysis of the effectiveness of early intervention programs. *Pediatrics, 69,* 635–641.

Skinner, B. F. (1953). *Science and human behavior*. New York: The Free Press.

Suzuki, S. (1970). *Zen mind, beginners mind*. New York: Weatherhill.

Weikart, D. P., Deloria, D. J., Lowsen, S. N., & Wiegerink, R. (1979). *Longitudinal results of the Ypsilanti Perry Preschool Project*. Ypsilanti, MI: High Scope Educational Research Foundation.

Wolfe, T. (1979). *The right stuff*. New York: Farrar, Straus, Giroux.

Zukav, G. (1979). *The dancing Wu Li masters*. New York: Bantam Books.

Chapter 5

Efficacy
Research in Early Childhood
Intervention Programs

Michael J. Guralnick

ANY ATTEMPT TO ASSESS THE EFFEC-tiveness of early intervention programs for children with clearly documented handicaps is generally approached with considerable ambivalence. At one level, most professionals in the field recognize the public policy implications of such analyses and see their value in assisting early intervention programs to improve the quality of their services. Moreover, most understand the potential of efficacy analyses for contributing to our knowledge of child and family development, and even expect, in the distant future at least, that these outcome analyses will help form the basis for important educational and clinical decisions for individual children.

At the same time, however, the process of efficacy analysis has many troublesome characteristics for a field that is action-oriented. The fact is that circumstances surrounding efficacy research in early childhood special education have rendered it a most difficult and demanding task: one that must contend with many specific methodological problems as well as with the changing quality and nature of the early intervention approaches themselves. This latter point should be underscored: any evaluation of effectiveness must occur within the framework of a changing set of early intervention approaches. It is equally important to note that this continuous process typically proceeds through a well traveled developmental path, that is, moving from more global understandings to more differentiated ones.

An orientation such as this should not be construed as providing an excuse in advance for poorly designed or implemented studies. However, it does urge the early childhood professional to be cautious so that the press for human services does not lead to ill-conceived and overzealous statements regarding the ability of the field to demonstrate the efficacy of experientially based early intervention programs for children with documented handicaps. In fact, as the end of the first generation of systematic early intervention programs for handicapped children approaches, a transition from global to more differentiated questions can be detected. Professionals are beginning to ask not whether early intervention works, the global question, but rather for whom does it work, under what conditions, and toward what goals.

The fact has not gone unrecognized that the simplicity of the global question may have been replaced by a potentially unending stream of qualifications that may need to be placed on the more differentiated answers. Consider for a moment the vast diversity of *subject populations* that exist. The conventional grouping of children into the major handicapping conditions of hearing and visual impairments, cognitive (general) developmental delays, motor disabilities, autism and related problems, and communication and language disorders provides only an initial perspective of the characteristics of the children of concern. Clearly, the severity of each primary problem, the extent of

associated handicaps, related functional characteristics, and family attitudes and resources
are only some of the key factors that are certain
to govern the ultimate outcome of early intervention programs for individual children or
groups of children. Similarly, issues related to
the *program factors* under which intervention
may work include the optimal time to begin
early intervention and other parameters of a
program. The array of available program models (e.g., developmental or behavioral, home
or center-based, various forms and levels of
parent involvement, the intensity of a program)
must all be considered. Although many program models and variations are probably more
complex when described in written curricula
and program descriptions than in actual practice, the combination of possible program elements is nevertheless quite extensive.

Finally, whether or not early intervention
can be considered effective must be viewed in
the context of its *goals*. Will more limited
short-term effects be acceptable or are long-
term outcomes the only sensible criteria for
effectiveness? What of the relative importance
of child and family outcomes? What role do
factors such as improved social competence
and reduced levels of behavior problems have
in the array of outcome variables? As might be
expected, this subject population × program ×
goal matrix of variables for evaluating the effectiveness of early intervention soon expands
rapidly. Since these more differentiated questions are only beginning to be addressed, there
are still a vast number of scientifically acceptable answers that remain to be found. However, as will be seen, significant patterns and directions are emerging.

Interest in asking more differentiated questions has been paralleled by a rapidly expanding early intervention service system. Ironically, the availability of programs and
resources now serves to limit some of the issues
that can be addressed. Historically, for example, assessments of early intervention effects
have generally considered intervention occurring across the first 5 years of life. Ideally, a
test of intervention effectiveness would consist
of one randomly assigned group of subjects to a

systematic, well-defined, specialized, and
highly individualized program of services
based on prevailing best practice models.
These services would be available from the
point of diagnosis or clear documentation of a
handicap until 5 years of age. The other randomly assigned group would not receive these
systematic services during that time. Since early intervention programs were not available to
many children during this early period, the formation of a control group could occur without
delaying services. However, the widespread
availability of early intervention programs for
toddler and preschool-age children has drastically narrowed the ability to test the original
form of this early intervention paradigm. In
essence, "intervention versus no intervention" tests must now frequently rely on comparisons between the absence of intervention
for only the first year, or perhaps first 18
months of life, in contrast to services provided
during that same time period. Since children in
the control or contrast groups are likely to begin receiving services after this time in most
communities, the test actually evaluates the effects of *very early intervention*.

The point here is that it is important to bear in
mind the changing nature of early intervention
programs and their historical context in any
contemporary or future discussion of issues in
efficacy research for early intervention programs. As will be seen, vital and sophisticated
questions can still be addressed, but investigators must adapt their designs and pose research
questions that are compatible with changing
services and resources.

PURPOSES OF THIS CHAPTER

Efficacy research in the field of early childhood
intervention is concerned with analyses of the
effectiveness of individual intervention programs or clusters of such programs in comparison to some reasonable standard, as well as
with a determination of whether outcomes can
be linked directly or indirectly to specific features of intervention programs. Accordingly,
the domain of efficacy research is comprehensive, potentially involving many levels of anal-

ysis and maintaining a close association with what is often considered program evaluation (see chapter by Casto, Chapter 3, this volume). Given space constraints and the complexity of this issue, a comprehensive review of the current state of efficacy research in early intervention is not possible. However, many informative reviews can be found elsewhere (Bricker, Bailey, & Bruder, 1984; Casto & Mastropieri, 1986; Dunst, McWilliam, & Trivette, 1985; Dunst & Rheingrover, 1981; Ferry, 1981; Fewell, 1985; Gibson & Fields, 1984; Guralnick & Bennett, 1987b; Simeonsson, Cooper, & Scheiner, 1982). Nor will the important methodological and measurement problems that plague the field of early childhood intervention be discussed in any detail, as these are considered in other chapters in this volume (see Chapter 1 by Odom and Chapter 2, by Neisworth & Bagnato, this volume). Instead, the major issues in early intervention efficacy research that should be addressed to ensure progress toward greater clarity and specificity will be presented. Discussion will focus on the subject population × program × goal matrix.

The issues that will be discussed consist of: 1) specifying subject sample and program characteristics in efficacy research, 2) selection of educational/developmental models, 3) the nature of parent involvement, 4) intensity as an important factor in early intervention programs, and 5) the relevance of social competence and behavior problems. Where appropriate, individual studies or groups of studies will be discussed to illustrate specific issues.

Specifying Subject Sample and Program Characteristics

Evaluating the effectiveness of early intervention programs has been complicated by the unsystematic and generally fragmented manner in which the first generation of early intervention programs emerged. Program development, implementation, and evaluation were all occurring as part of a large dynamic process, with intervention activities ranging widely across poorly specified disability groups. Numerous factors prompted the establishment of intervention programs during this period, many of which were speculative and theoretical, relying on extrapolations from principles and research carried out in related domains (Guralnick & Bennett, 1987c; Horowitz, 1980). Given the absence of a clear framework for the development of these programs and given the real need to provide services to children and families, the high level of creativity and quality of these first generation programs was quite remarkable.

Within this framework, it is not surprising that existing efforts to review and evaluate the effectiveness of early intervention programs have taken more global approaches. The absence of sufficiently specific descriptions in the early studies and the lack of systematic evaluations of important program variables have yielded conclusions that tend to be based on outcomes aggregated across many different disability groups, intervention approaches, outcome measures, and numerous other subject, program, and goal characteristics. Compounding this situation, methodological problems characteristic of reviews in this area have been an additional challenge to the validity of many of their conclusions (see White, Bush, & Casto, 1985–1986). Nevertheless, various analyses of the literature have provided important perspectives on the field, presenting a sense of what was actually carried out and what could generally be expected to result (e.g., Dunst & Rheingrover, 1981; Simeonsson et al., 1982.)

Global Approaches   One recent attempt to cope with this complex array of studies while minimizing methodological problems common to reviews of this type has been to take a comprehensive statistical approach, referred to as meta-analysis (see Glass, 1976). In this method, all of the available published and unpublished research, including studies using only pre- and post- comparisons, as well as those using experimental and control groups, are analyzed in order to determine if any overall, "global" statistical patterns can be detected. In essence, the results from diverse studies are transformed to yield an "effect size" measured in standard deviation units. A common metric is thereby established to allow comparisons across studies and outcome measures. Certain assumptions are made, such as using pretest measures in the same way as control group measures, but the purpose here is not to debate the statistical and logical issues of the method.

The meta-analysis technique has recently been applied to the literature on early intervention for children with documented handicaps (Casto & Mastropieri, 1986). When 74 studies of heterogeneous groups of handicapped children meeting minimal criteria for inclusion were analyzed, an overall positive mean effect size was obtained. That is, the mean effect size for intervention groups exceeded the mean effect size for controls shortly after intervention ended. Most effect sizes were based on standardized intelligence test data or related cognitive assessments, as these have been the primary outcome measures for the vast majority of studies. In fact, for cognitive measures alone, the mean effect size was just less than one standard deviation (.85SD). When all measures (language, motor, etc.) were considered, the overall effect size was somewhat reduced (.68SD). However, when only those studies considered to have higher quality experimental designs were analyzed separately, the mean effect size was reduced even further to less than one-half of a standard deviation (.43SD).

As noted, this analysis was based on enormously heterogeneous groups of children, of programs, and of outcome measures. A global statement of immediate effects is only a first step toward an understanding of the detailed outcomes of early intervention. Unfortunately, despite avoiding the many methodological problems common to reviews, it is difficult at this time to go beyond global questions using the meta-analysis technique. For example, when questions of differential effects for disability groups arise, the subset of studies for analysis becomes unreliably small. Moreover, attempts to raise questions regarding the severity of a handicap, either across or within specific disability groups, is often confounded by the program type or age of start variables, thereby limiting conclusions that can be drawn.

Differentiated Approaches An alternative strategy is to organize efficacy analyses initially within disability samples themselves. Although such analyses must still contend with the methodological and design problems of existing studies, it may well be possible to develop different lines of evidence that take advantage of some special knowledge of the characteristics of a more limited subset of children. In one such approach, Guralnick and Bricker (1987) evaluated existing early intervention studies focusing exclusively on children with Down syndrome. Only published studies from peer-reviewed literature that met a variety of inclusion criteria were considered. Cognitive gains averaging one-half to three-quarters of a standard deviation (approximately 8–12 IQ points) were found in this analysis, and pretest measures did seem to serve as reasonable control group estimates. Since the predominant disability group in the meta-analysis discussed earlier was mental retardation (Casto & Mastropieri, 1986), it is not surprising that the overall short-term effects on cognitive development were highly similar in both approaches (Guralnick, 1985).

However, the overall conclusion from this more differentiated, non-statistical approach was strengthened by converging evidence from recent longitudinal studies (Berry, Gunn, & Andrews, 1984; Schnell, 1984). Specifically, these longitudinal studies revealed that the well documented decline in measured intelligence in Down syndrome children that occurs over the first few years of life (Carr, 1975; Connolly, 1978; Melyn & White, 1973; Morgan, 1979; Share, 1975) can be prevented by early and continuous participation in early intervention programs. That is, the projected decline served as the standard for evaluation, thereby avoiding the many problems associated with establishing control or contrast groups. Accordingly, by capitalizing on the special knowledge surrounding the development of children with Down syndrome, unique and, in my view, compelling evidence related to efficacy can be obtained. Similar, though far less compelling evidence for children with biologically-based delays other than Down syndrome can be noted as well (see Guralnick & Bricker, 1987). However, although additional analyses of other disability groups (e.g., children with motor disorders and delays, communication and language disorders, autism, visual and hearing impairments) have yielded much more variable findings (see Guralnick & Bennett, 1987b), there appears to be considerable merit in this more differentiated approach focusing on some dimension of subject characteristics.

Other definable groupings such as fragile X (Moser, 1985), fetal alcohol syndrome (Steinhausen, Nestler, & Spohr, 1982), or even Williams syndrome (Bennett, LaVeck, & Sells, 1978; Kataria, Goldstein, & Kushnick, 1984) may prove to be of similar value, although the circumstances for children with Down syndrome may be relatively unique. To be useful, however, careful attention must be given to subgroup characteristics. Unfortunately, existing research has too often been cavalier in this regard, even failing to document chromosomal abnormalities adequately in some instances (Rynders, Spiker, & Horrobin, 1978).

Despite the fact that confirmed etiological information is not available for a substantial number of children, it is nevertheless important to be much more comprehensive in characterizing study samples. Etiological and medical diagnostic information is only one aspect of this characterization. It is essential as well to be able to specify health issues, accompanying handicaps, the severity of delays or disabilities, behavior problems, family factors, and a whole host of related marker variables (see Kopp & Krakow, 1982). Only when these variables are adequately defined and described will it be possible to detect reliable and meaningful outcome patterns and to responsibly ask the important differentiated questions.

A similar argument can be made for the need to specify the range of program variables, including parameters related to duration, intensity, the developmental/educational model, service delivery approach, and numerous oth-

ers. Indicators of compliance to these program variables are of equal importance when evaluating the effectiveness of intervention programs. Unfortunately, protocols for these subject and program descriptions have not yet been developed but, as noted, it is clearly essential for protocols to be developed if efficacy research is to progress beyond global levels of analysis.

SELECTION OF EDUCATIONAL/ DEVELOPMENTAL MODELS

The philosophy and content of an educational or developmental model is central to any early intervention program. Although the structure and guidance provided by almost *any* reasonable model can be of value, it is also true that in certain instances the selection of a particularly well-suited educational/developmental model can have dramatic consequences. This is perhaps most apparent in the outcomes of early intervention programs for hearing impaired children. Until quite recently, research on the efficacy of early intervention for these children primarily assessed the effects of the "oral-only" model, emphasizing amplification of residual hearing, auditory training, speech reading, and oral skills. Overall, the progress of children following this educational model was slow by virtually any standard (Greenberg & Calderon, 1984; Meadow-Orlans, 1987). On the basis of the evidence from this model for hearing impaired children, the value of early intervention would be highly questionable.

However, the emergence of the "total communication" model in the last 10–15 years, which includes any one of a variety of artificial sign language systems and other supportive gestural techniques in conjunction with existing oral and auditory methods, has significantly altered expectations regarding the effectiveness of early intervention for hearing impaired children (Greenberg, Calderon, & Kusche, 1984; Moores, Weiss, & Goodwin, 1978). The Moores et al. report (1978) is particularly instructive as it describes a longitudinal study that spanned the transition period between the oral methods and those programs experimenting with manual supplements. The changing nature of many of the programs over the course of the 6 years of the study made it difficult to draw firm conclusions about comparative effects. However, the available evidence clearly pointed to the superiority of some combination of oral and manual approaches to oral-only approaches.

Greenberg and his colleagues (1984) evaluated the potential effectiveness of the total communication approach during the preschool years by comparing outcomes between two groups. An experimental group receiving a comprehensive and systematic early intervention program based on the total communication model was compared to a group receiving less systematic and less intensive services. Results revealed a clear superiority for the experimental group across a variety of domains related to communication abilities, parental communication style, and social competence.

This investigation was valuable not only for its contribution to the knowledge of the effects of total communication but also for its methodological approach (see also section in this chapter on intensity of the early intervention program). As suggested earlier, good efficacy research should be able to capitalize on certain circumstances and to establish experimental comparisons even in the absence of random assignment on a prospective basis. The "believability" of a phenomenon can be affected by data from many sources. In the previous section in this chapter it was pointed out how the prevention of a decline in measured cognitive functioning for children with Down syndrome was very compelling in view of the existing data for this group of children. In this instance, Greenberg and his colleagues took advantage of geographic restrictions to form their experimental and contrast groups. The experimental group lived near a major city and could thereby enroll in the comprehensive total communication program. The comparison group lived in more rural communities with only limited access to any systematic or intensive treatment. Accordingly, ethical concerns related to the denial of treatment to subjects in a control group were not issues. The key here, however, was the investigators' ability to match subjects on all critical variables in order to rule out rival hypotheses. The fact that the two groups appeared to differ only on the extent of manual communication training and the systematic nature of the intervention argues effectively that the differential outcomes could be attributed to these program factors. Systematic replications and evidence from converging lines of research would increase further the field's confidence in these findings.

Parent Involvement

For the majority of first generation early intervention programs, parents served primarily educational and instructional functions. In some programs, following training by professionals, they were the primary "service providers." In others, parents functioned to support and extend educational activities into the home. Parents have also benefited from the many programs providing various forms of parent counseling or sponsoring parent support groups.

In the last few years, the dominant didactic function of parents in early intervention programs has been called into question. There is no doubt that parents can be effective service providers or adjuncts to therapeutic treatment (Bruder & Bricker, 1985; Gross, Eudy, & Drabman, 1982). However, there is clearly a diversity of feeling among parents about their formal instructional role (Winton & Turnbull, 1981). Additionally, professionals have become sensitized to the wide variability of resources available to parents of handicapped children and to the impact of these factors on family functioning. In fact, these revised perceptions and contemporary family systems approaches (e.g., Bronfenbrenner, 1977) have the potential for radically restructuring the nature and role of parent involvement in many early intervention programs.

Perhaps the most significant change in the field of early childhood intervention in this area has been the increasingly systematic efforts to promote the coping strategies of parents of handicapped children, and to expand the resources available to these parents. Specifically, promoting social support networks to help mitigate some of the daily stresses experienced by parents is one important direction that early intervention programs are taking (Bailey & Simeonsson, 1984; Gallagher, Beckman, & Cross, 1983; Barber, Turnbull, Behr, & Kerns, Chapter 11, this volume).

Interestingly, this movement toward helping parents develop the needed resources and strategies to cope with the diverse problems they will inevitably encounter has been paralleled by alternative approaches to viewing parents as teachers, in the didactic sense, of their handicapped children. In fact, it has been suggested that specific teaching functions can, in many instances, prevent the development of appropriate parent-child relationships. For example, Affleck, McGrade, McQueeney, and Allen (1982) propose that the primary role of professionals is to foster natural, supportive, and reciprocal relationships between parents and children. To be sure, this ''relationship-focused'' approach includes the provision of important educational and developmental information as well as strategies to promote development where appropriate. However, it is the parent who is encouraged to take the initiative in utilizing that information in the natural context of parent-child relationships. In many respects, this model is consistent with a broad social systems approach in which parents and professionals establish a true partnership (Dunst, 1985).

Given that these changes are occurring, what are their implications for efficacy research? In one sense, helping to improve parents' abilities to cope with their daily problems may have a beneficial effect on the development of the handicapped child. It is reasonable to believe that more productive time will be available for parents to interact with all family members, including a handicapped child, as family functioning improves. But these changes also suggest that different dimensions of child development may be effected. Developing sensitive, warm, and reciprocal relationships through both relationship-focused models and through self-directed family participation may well have a positive impact on the social and emotional development of a handicapped child. As described in a later section of this chapter, effective measurement strategies must be available to assess these increasingly important noncognitive outcome variables.

Finally, these changes suggest that improved family functioning may well be a reasonable and appropriate outcome for early intervention programs, irrespective of their effects on child development. As this occurs, it adds yet another dimension to early intervention efficacy research, one that is complex and that will require early childhood specialists to carefully and sensitively examine value judgments as to what constitutes effective family functioning.

Intensity of the Early Intervention Program

It would seem that in order to produce substantial changes in the developmental course of children with significant handicaps, a correspondingly comprehensive and intensive series of early intervention experiences would be required. Yet, the typical early intervention program tends to take place over only a small proportion of a child's day. Infant and toddler programs usually range from 2–6 hours per week on average. Parent assistance extends this time, but the total contribution remains proportionally small. Even preschool programs tend to be relatively brief, perhaps 2½–3 hours per day in most instances. However, duration is only one aspect of intensity; actual instructional time or time engaged in productive early intervention activities is another. [Engagement time is used here as a process variable, but it also can be valuable as a product measure (see McWilliam, Trivette, & Dunst, 1985).] Although data on factors related to intensity (Carta, Sainato, & Greenwood, Chapter 13, this volume), are only beginning to be gathered, many directors of preschool programs in particular have commented on the lack of instructional and engagement time during the 2½–3 hour daily programs. The meta-analysis data for handicapped children suggested certain positive trends favoring more intensive programs (Casto & Mastropieri, 1986), and preventative intervention programs with disadvantaged children indicate that intensity is a critical factor (Bryant & Ramey, 1987). Clearly, one reasonable hypothesis is that intensity of a program, defined both in overall hours of intervention and in actual instructional or engagement time, may well be a variable that can alter significantly the outcomes of early intervention programs.

The intensity of any intervention is, of course, limited by the chronological age and accompanying physical capacities of the children involved. In addition, available resources, particularly personnel, may restrict the intensity of programs. Taken to the extreme, highly intensive interventions would extend into the home and neighborhood, requiring almost the total devotion of family members to assist with intervention activities.

The issue of intensity as a factor in altering developmental outcomes for handicapped children has been reported in a preliminary study by Lovaas (1982) focusing on children diagnosed as autistic. In this investigation, two groups of autistic children were formed and given treatments that varied substantially in terms of intensity. The intensive treatment group received a minimum of 40 hours of treatment per week on a one-to-one basis following well-established behavioral procedures (Lovaas, 1977, 1981). To carry out this level of intervention, 5–15 student therapists assisted with each child; parents were enlisted as cotherapists. In essence, the children in this group were in treatment 365 days a year for virtually all their waking hours for a period ranging from 1–4 years. Treatment intensity declined as children made progress.

In contrast, the children in the less intensive group received a similar treatment approach but for less than 10 hours of one-to-one intervention per week. It is important to note that both groups entered into treatment before they were 3½ years of age. Previous efforts with similar intervention strategies beginning with children at somewhat older ages had failed both to maintain gains following the termination of treatment and to generalize gains to new set-

tings. The younger children in this previous study seemed to do much better, consequently, the current project emphasized starting intervention at an earlier age.

Assignment of children to the two treatment groups was based on geographic proximity to the treatment center. Although random assignment would have been preferable, it was not possible for practical or ethical reasons. However, two factors argued for the position that any differences in outcomes could best be attributed to differences in intensity of treatment. First, the two groups were highly similar prior to intervention in relation to chronological and developmental age, language, play behaviors, aggression, and certain key motor milestones. Second, although not strictly comparable, existing longitudinal studies reported that the vast majority of children diagnosed as autistic at young ages did not recover spontaneously. In a manner similar to the longitudinal research for children with Down syndrome discussed earlier, these data can be used as a framework for evaluating any marked discrepancies from this pattern.

Children were considered to have "recovered" if they met the following criteria: 1) if they had moved from the first to the second grade without assistance from the project, 2) if they had achieved an IQ in the normal range, and 3) if they were rated by teachers as socially and emotionally adjusted. Remarkably, 10 of the 19 children in the intensive treatment group met these criteria, while no children in the less intensive treatment group did so. Furthermore, only 1 of the 19 children in the intensive treatment group were placed in classes for the autistic or mentally retarded, while 14 of the 17 children in the less intensive group were so placed. The remaining children were placed in small classes designed for children considered aphasic, that is, those with major language problems but not primarily socially or emotionally maladjusted. Accordingly, substantial improvement in approximately 90% of the children in the intensive treatment group occurred, whereas those children in the less intensive group progressed far more slowly; virtually all children remained significantly delayed and were placed in classes for autistic or retarded children.

A report of the outcome data for a somewhat similar group of children has also suggested that major developmental advances can occur as a consequence of intensive early intervention. Strain and his colleagues (Hoyson, Jamieson, & Strain, 1984; Strain, Jamieson, & Hoyson, 1986) developed a highly sophisticated service delivery model for classroom settings that permitted intensive individualized instruction and careful monitoring even within a group context. This model also emphasized, as did the Lovaas (1982) program, programmed generalization and the involvement of significant others in the child's educational/ developmental activities. Programmed classroom activities took place 3 hours per day, 5 days per week with strong parent involvement. Within this framework, six handicapped children, ages 30–53 months, were observed during a 1-week observation period. The children were selected after having provided evidence of repeated episodes of self-stimulation, limited or no functional speech, prolonged tantrums, and minimal or no positive interactions with peers. Children also scored in the mild to severe range of retardation based on a standardized intelligence test. Those children with mental retardation syndromes, evidence of central nervous system damage, or those receiving psychotropic medication were excluded. In contrast to the Lovaas (1982) group, these children were only considered as "autistic-like," and no firm diagnosis of autism was suggested.

Nevertheless, over the course of a 2-year period gains similar to that reported by Lovaas (1982) were obtained. Using the developmental rate on the Learning Accomplishment Profile (LeMay, Griffin, & Sanford, 1977) as the unit of assessment, children began the program at an average developmental rate of .71 across all developmental domains. By the end of the program, the rate of development increased markedly; in fact, on average the children's rate of development was doubled over the course of the intervention. Moreover, the use of multiple baseline techniques clearly indicated that gains in designated developmental domains were tied to specific activities of the program itself.

These studies of the effects of early intervention for highly intensive and structured programs have potentially important implications for efficacy research. But it is important that professionals in the field be mindful of the fact that a sound analysis of efficacy research, combined with good common sense, demand that we be a skeptical audience. The Lovaas (1982) study in particular is the first report of significant "recovery" for children diagnosed with a disorder considered to be organic in origin (see Ritvo & Freeman, 1984). The remarkable gains of these children contrast sharply with the modest gains obtained for children with biologically-based delays (see Guralnick & Bricker, 1987) but not classified as autistic. Whether the intensity or the nature of the program, perhaps in combination with certain characteristics of this population of children, can account for these findings is not known. Whatever the case may be, researchers must await formal publication of this work and, of course, replication by other investigators.

Taken together, these studies underscore once again the importance of examining current trends and findings in relation to efficacy. Significant advances in service delivery and important modifications in the content of educational programs deserve special consideration when evaluating the entire array of available research. As is generally the case, program development in the area of early intervention for handicapped children builds upon prior efforts and creates a historical account of its development. Evaluations of efficacy must be cognizant of this historical context, but they should also give proper consideration to contemporary models and findings. It is to be hoped that this process will continue as future efforts follow the usual scientific methods, especially independent replication. Of equal importance to the field of early intervention is the degree to which new approaches or models can be applied to different populations of children.

Social Competence and Behavior Problems

Recent research has suggested that handicapped children are at significant risk for developing social interaction difficulties and behavior problems (Baker & Cantwell, 1982; Eaton & Menolascino, 1982; Meadow & Trybus, 1979; Reiss, Levitan, & McNally,· 1982; Thompson, 1984). In addition, irrespective of the nature of the disability, young handicapped children tend to exhibit much lower levels of social competence, especially with peers, than would be expected on the basis of their developmental levels (see, for example, Guralnick, 1986). The extent to which these difficulties are due to the child's primary disability or whether they are secondary to inadequate relationships or restricted experiences is not known. Nevertheless, effective early intervention programs must consider these facts both in relation to therapeutic strategies and to outcomes.

The significance of these issues in evaluating the effectiveness of early intervention programs has certainly not gone unnoticed (Taft, 1983; Zigler & Trickett, 1978). In fact, in a recent longitudinal investigation of hearing impaired children, Watkins (in press) found that the only differences between a group who had received very early intervention (earlier than 2½ years) and a group that had received later intervention (after 2½ years) were on social and behavior measures after entry into public school. Initial differences in communicative and other developmental measures that favored the earlier intervention group during the intervention period apparently faded after the children entered public school. Although the processes of conducting and interpreting long-term follow-ups of children receiving early intervention are discussed in the concluding section of this chapter, the differences found for social and behavior domains are worthy of note.

The challenge, however, lies first in the ability of specialists to develop useful assessment instruments, and secondly in the development of corresponding therapeutic programs that can be effectively carried out within the context of typical early intervention programs. Successful efforts are occurring in certain areas (e.g., see Strain & Kohler, Chapter 8, this volume), but the absence of a comprehensive, integrated program designed to promote social competence and to reduce the occurrence and severity of behavior problems, firmly grounded in developmental principles, remains a task for the future. In conjunction with the need to develop evaluation instruments that can be adapted for early intervention programs, improving social competence and the prevention and amelioration of behavior problems for handicapped children may well be the most significant issues for efficacy research in the next decade (see Guralnick & Bennett, 1987a).

CONCLUSIONS

Research evaluating the effectiveness of early intervention programs has important implications for the current professional and political debate surrounding the impact of early intervention on children and families. This research, when joined with program evaluation, provides valuable information about a program's ability to achieve its goals and objectives. In addition, research on the malleability of development through systematic, experientially-based interventions has many implications for the field of child development.

Given the potential significance of efficacy research, it is essential that professionals recognize the historical context of intervention research and the changing nature of efforts to evaluate the effectiveness of early intervention. Intervention is a process that has evolved rapidly over the past 15 years as major changes have developed in assessment instruments, program content, service delivery strategies, program parameters, and preparation of personnel. As a consequence, these program development activities, combined with a nationwide effort to provide services to children and families, produced a situation that threatened the scientific credibility of a substantial number of efficacy studies. Some problems, to be sure, were due to investigator neglect, but many simply reflected limitations in resources as well as problems inherent in the processes required to provide reasonable early intervention services.

It is quite remarkable, in my view, that despite these very difficult circumstances, investigators have not only persevered but have been able to provide the field with important data concerning the effectiveness of early intervention. As has been seen, global analyses of these "first generation" studies have clearly suggested that research has been proceeding in a reasonable direction. Specifically, immediate though modest effects of early intervention have been demonstrated for a range of different programs and disability groups. In addition, these studies have been vital in identifying those variables, among a seemingly infinite supply, that seem most likely to significantly and positively influence the outcomes of early intervention programs.

Building upon this body of knowledge, researchers have entered a new era of efficacy research. The questions that are being asked are now much more focused, reflecting both an increased sophistication on the part of researchers as well as a recognition of the natural limitations imposed by changing service delivery patterns. Specific characteristics of children, defined in terms of disability status and a variety of other critical factors, continue to be seen as major sources of variability in outcome effectiveness. The improved ability to identify and define these characteristics will allow researchers to determine the responsiveness of specific subgroups of children to the best practice approaches. Even further, although the magnitude of the effects of early intervention is important, the ability to reduce the number of children unresponsive to those interventions is equally important. To accomplish this, information from intensive analyses of unresponsive children needs to be gathered and studied, and special experimental designs and intervention strategies need to be utilized in order to reduce this variability. Clearly, providing thorough subject definitions and descriptions is a necessary step in this process.

Now that potentially important program related variables, such as intensity or program content (in certain areas), have been identified, reasonable and ethical tests of the relative effectiveness of these factors can be carried out.

The small scale nature of studies comparing different approaches also increases the likelihood that random assignment on a prospective basis will occur. It is also more likely that resources will be available to ensure unbiased testing by evaluators unfamiliar with group assignment of children, that multiple outcome measures tied to specific program goals will be part of the evaluation plan, that process measures will be used to ensure that the model is being implemented effectively, and that the studies conform to all other aspects of sound scientific research. As has been seen, even if prospective random assignment is not possible, careful attention to rival hypotheses can establish the believability of many efficacy studies.

It is to be hoped that the new era of efficacy research will also be successful in helping professionals to understand and select appropriate goals for early intervention. The neglect of social competence and behavior problems as explicit goals of most early intervention programs must be reconsidered. The relative importance placed on either family or child outcomes, despite the interrelationships of these two groups, remains an issue that has not received adequate attention. Similarly, the expansion of efficacy research to include the long-term impact of early intervention must occur. However, there are numerous hidden assumptions and conceptual issues that must be examined when evaluating the impact of early intervention programs over substantial periods of time.

In fact, it can be argued that considerable caution should be exercised in accepting long-term effects as primary criteria for evaluating the impact of early intervention programs. The face validity of short-term effects must be recognized. Improvements in cognitive, language, motor, and social skills, or in family functioning, for example, are clearly of value by any standard. Any attempt to establish long-term impact as a final and perhaps primary measure of the value of an intervention program must recognize the options available and the variability in quality that exists in post-early childhood environments. Accordingly, unless the position is held that early childhood experiences are critical to subsequent development because they can overcome even nonsupportive and inadequate later experiences (see Rutter, 1980, for discussion), long-term effectiveness cannot be considered as a fair test of the ability or potential of early intervention programs to maintain any gains. Unfortunately, relatively little is known about those post-early childhood environments in relation to their ability to support, extend, or reduce any early gains. The initial task, then, should be to classify, define, and monitor these post-early childhood environments and to describe accompanying processes that may effect developmental and educational goals. There are certainly intricate linkages that need to be uncovered. For example, the puzzling nature of the so-called "sleeper effects" (i.e., those that appear long after systematic intervention has ended), reflect the lack of knowledge in the field about these effects and their processes. As the post-early childhood conditions that can alter and transform the effects of early intervention are analyzed, valuable questions regarding the long-term impact of early intervention can be addressed.

Finally, it is important to reemphasize that efficacy research in early intervention must be considered as an ongoing process, one that is dependent upon new knowledge, techniques, conceptualizations, intervention models, and approaches in the field. Reviews and analyses of effectiveness at various points in time can certainly help identify various stages in this process, can alert us to shifting emphases, and can perhaps even uncover biases that may exist in a process that is always dependent upon often unspecified value judgments. But in any analysis, however differentiated researchers' questions become, it will be the cumulative evidence brought together by experimental designs of varying quality, the consistencies in outcomes, the refinements produced by numerous small-scale comparative studies, and the persuasiveness of arguments to rule out competing explanations for one or another outcome that will be invoked when considering issues of efficacy. The process of efficacy research has many self-righting tendencies and, if carried out with integrity, this research will ultimately yield answers to the important questions regarding the effectiveness of early intervention.

REFERENCES

Affleck, G., McGrade, B. J., McQueeney, M., & Allen, D. (1982). Promise of relationship-focused early intervention in developmental disabilities. *Journal of Special Education, 16,* 413–430.

Bailey, D. B., Jr., & Simeonsson, R. J. (1984). Critical issues underlying research and intervention with families of young handicapped children. *Journal of the Division for Early Childhood, 9,* 38–48.

Baker, L., & Cantwell, D. P. (1982). Developmental, social and behavioral characteristics of speech and language disordered children. *Child Psychiatry and Human Development, 12,* 195–206.

Bennett, F. C., LaVeck, B., & Sells, C. J. (1978). The Williams elfin facies syndrome: The psychological profile as an aid in syndrome identification. *Pediatrics, 61,* 303–306.

Berry, P., Gunn, V. P., & Andrews, R. J. (1984). Development of Down's syndrome children from birth to five years. In J. M. Berg (Ed.), *Perspectives and progress in mental retardation: Social, psychological, and educational aspects* (Vol. 1, pp. 167–177). Baltimore: University Park Press.

Bricker, D., Bailey, E., & Bruder, M. B. (1984). The efficacy of early intervention and the handicapped infant: A wise or wasted resource. In M. Wolraich & D. K. Routh (Eds.), *Advances in developmental and behavioral pediatrics* (Vol. 5, pp. 373–423). Greenwich, CT: JAI Press.

Bronfenbrenner, U. (1977). Toward an experimental ecology of human development. *American Psychologist, 32,* 513–531.

Bruder, M. B., & Bricker, D. (1985). Parents as teachers of their children and other parents. *Journal of the Division for Early Childhood, 9,* 136–150.

Bryant, D. M., & Ramey, C. T. (1987). An analysis of the effectiveness of early intervention programs for environmentally at-risk children. In M. J. Guralnick & F. C. Bennett (Eds.), *The effectiveness of early intervention for at-risk and handicapped children* (pp. 33–78). New York: Academic Press.

Carr, J. (1975). *Young children with Down's syndrome.* London: Butterworth.

Casto, G., & Mastropieri, M. A. (1986). The efficacy of early intervention programs: A meta-analysis. *Exceptional Children, 52,* 417–424.

Connolly, J. A. (1978). Intelligence levels of Down's syndrome children. *American Journal of Mental Deficiency, 83,* 193–196.

Dunst, C. J. (1985). Rethinking early intervention. *Analysis and Intervention in Developmental Disabilities, 5,* 165–201.

Dunst, C. J., McWilliam, R. A., & Trivette, C. M. (Eds.). (1985). Special issue: Early intervention. *Analysis and Intervention in Developmental Disabilities, 5*(1–2), 1–209.

Dunst, C. J., & Rheingrover, R. M. (1981). An analysis of

the efficacy of infant intervention programs with organically handicapped children. *Evaluation and Program Planning, 4,* 287–323.

Eaton, L. F., & Menolascino, F. J. (1982). Psychiatric disorders in the mentally retarded: Types, problems, and challenges. *American Journal of Psychiatry, 139,* 1297–1303.

Ferry, P. C. (1981). On growing new neurons: Are early intervention programs effective? *Pediatrics, 67,* 38–41.

Fewell, R. R. (Ed.). (1985). Efficacy studies: Programs for young handicapped children. *Topics in Early Childhood Special Education, 5*(2).

Gallagher, J. J., Beckman, P., & Cross, A. H. (1983). Families of handicapped children: Sources of stress and its amelioration. *Exceptional Children, 50,* 10–19.

Gibson, D., & Fields, D. L. (1984). Early infant stimulation programs for children with Down syndrome: A review of effectiveness. In M. Wolraich & D. K. Routh (Eds.), *Advances in developmental and behavioral pediatrics* (Vol. 5, pp. 331–371). Greenwich, CT: JAI Press.

Glass, G. V. (1976). Primary, secondary, and meta-analysis of research. *Educational Researcher, 5,* 3–8.

Greenberg, M. T., & Calderon, R. (1984). Early intervention: Outcomes and issues. *Topics in Early Childhood Special Education, 3*(4), 1–9.

Greenberg, M. T., Calderon, R., & Kusche, C. (1984). Early intervention using simultaneous communication with deaf infants: The effect on communication development. *Child Development, 55,* 607–616.

Gross, A. M., Eudy, C., & Drabman, R. S. (1982). Training parents to be physical therapists with their physically handicapped child. *Journal of Behavioral Medicine, 5,* 321–327.

Guralnick, M. J. (1985, May). *Effectiveness of early intervention.* Paper presented at the Annual Meeting of the American Association of University Affiliated Programs, Seattle.

Guralnick, M. J. (1986). The peer relations of young handicapped and nonhandicapped children. In P. S. Strain, M. J. Guralnick, & H. M. Walker (Eds.), *Children's social behavior: Development, assessment, and modification* (pp. 93–140). New York: Academic Press.

Guralnick, M. J., & Bennett, F. C. (1987a). Early intervention for at-risk and handicapped children: Current and future perspectives. In M. J. Guralnick & F. C. Bennett (Eds.), *The effectiveness of early intervention for at-risk and handicapped children* (pp. 365–382). New York: Academic Press.

Guralnick, M. J., & Bennett, F. C. (Eds.). (1987b). *The effectiveness of early intervention for at-risk and handicapped children.* New York: Academic Press.

Guralnick, M. J., & Bennett, F. C. (1987c). A framework for early intervention. In M. J. Guralnick & F. C. Bennett (Eds.), *The effectiveness of early intervention for at-risk and handicapped children* (pp. 3–29). New York: Academic Press.

Guralnick, M. J., & Bricker, D. (1987). The effectiveness of early intervention for children with cognitive and general developmental delays. In M. J. Guralnick & F. C. Bennett (Eds.), *The effectiveness of early intervention for at-risk and handicapped children* (pp. 115–173). New York: Academic Press.

Horowitz, F. D. (1980). Intervention and its effects on early development: What model of development is appropriate? In R. R. Turner & H. W. Reese (Eds.), *Life-span developmental psychology: Intervention* (pp. 235–248). New York: Academic Press.

Hoyson, M., Jamieson, B., & Strain, P. S. (1984). Individualized group instruction of normally developing and autistic-like children: The LEAP curriculum model. *Journal of the Division for Early Childhood, 8,* 157–172.

Kataria, S., Goldstein, D. J., Kushnick, T. (1984). Developmental delays in Williams ("elfin facies") syndrome. *Applied Research in Mental Retardation, 5,* 419–423.

Kopp, C. B., & Krakow, J. B. (1982). The issue of sample characteristics: Biologically at risk or developmentally delayed infants. *Journal of Pediatric Psychology, 7,* 361–374.

LeMay, D., Griffin, P., & Sanford, A. (1977). *Learning accomplishment profile—Diagnostic edition.* Chapel Hill, NC: Chapel Hill Training-Outreach Project.

Lovaas, O. I. (1977). *The autistic child: Language development through behavior modification.* New York: Irvington.

Lovaas, O. I. (1981). *Teaching developmentally disabled children: The ME book.* Baltimore: University Park Press.

Lovaas, O. I. (1982, August). *An overview of the young autism project.* Paper presented at the meeting of the American Psychological Association, Washington, DC.

McWilliam, R. A., Trivette, C. M., & Dunst, C. J. (1985). Behavior engagement as a measure of the efficacy of early intervention. *Analysis and Intervention in Developmental Disabilities, 5,* 59–71.

Meadow, K. P., & Trybus, R. J. (1979). Behavioral and emotional problems of deaf children: An overview. In L. J. Bradford & W. G. Hardy (Eds.), *Hearing and hearing impairment* (pp. 395–403). New York: Grune & Stratton.

Meadow-Orlans, K. (1987). An analysis of the effectiveness of early intervention programs for hearing-impaired children. In M. J. Guralnick & F. C. Bennett (Eds.), *The effectiveness of early intervention for at-risk and handicapped children* (pp. 325–362). New York: Academic Press.

Melyn, M. A., & White, D. T. (1973). Mental and developmental milestones of noninstitutionalized Down's syndrome children. *Pediatrics, 52,* 542–545.

Moores, D. F., Weiss, K. L., & Goodwin, M. W. (1978). Early education programs for hearing-impaired children: Major findings. *American Annals of the Deaf, 123,* 925–936.

Morgan, S. B. (1979). Development and distribution of intellectual and adaptive skills in Down syndrome children: Implications for early intervention. *Mental Retardation, 17,* 247–249.

Moser, H. W. (1985). Biologic factors of development. In J. M. Freeman (Ed.), *Prenatal and perinatal factors associated with brain disorders* (pp. 121–161). Washington, DC: U.S. Department of Health and Human Services.

Reiss, S., Levitan, G. W., & McNally, R. J. (1982). Emotionally disturbed mentally retarded people: An underserved population. *American Psychologist, 37,* 361–367.

Ritvo, E. R., & Freeman, B. J. (1984). A medical model of autism: Etiology, pathology and treatment. *Pediatric Annals, 13,* 298–305.

Rutter, M. (1980). The long-term effects of early experience. *Developmental Medicine and Child Neurology, 22*, 800–815.

Rynders, J. E., Spiker, D., & Horrobin, J. M. (1978). Underestimating the educability of Down's syndrome children: Examination of methodological problems in recent literature. *American Journal of Mental Deficiency, 82*, 440–448.

Schnell, R. R. (1984). Psychomotor development. In S. M. Pueschel (Ed.), *The young child with Down syndrome* (pp. 207–226). New York: Human Sciences Press.

Share, J. B. (1975). Developmental progress in Down's syndrome. In R. Koch & F. De La Cruz (Eds.), *Down's syndrome (mongolism): Research, prevention and management.* New York: Brunner/Mazel.

Simeonsson, R. J., Cooper, D. H., & Scheiner, A. P. (1982). A review and analysis of the effectiveness of early intervention programs. *Pediatrics, 69*, 635–641.

Steinhausen, H., Nestler, V., & Spohr, H. (1982). Development and psychopathology of children with the fetal alcohol syndrome. *Journal of Developmental and Behavioral Pediatrics, 3*, 49–54.

Strain, P. S., Jamieson, B., & Hoyson, M. (1986). Learning experiences. An alternative program for preschoolers and parents: A comprehensive service system for the mainstreaming of autistic-like preschoolers. In C. J. Meisel (Ed.), *Mainstreamed handicapped children: Outcomes, controversies and new directions* (pp. 251–269). Hillsdale, NJ: Lawrence Erlbaum Associates.

Taft, L. A. (1983). Critique of early intervention for cerebral palsy. In T. B. Brazelton & B. M. Lester (Eds.), *New approaches to developmental screening of infants* (pp. 219–228). New York: Elsevier.

Thompson, R. J., Jr. (1984). Behavior problems in developmentally disabled children. In M. Wolraich & D. K. Routh (Eds.), *Advances in developmental and behavioral pediatrics* (Vol. 5, pp. 265–330). Greenwich, CT: JAI Press.

Watkins, S. (in press). A longitudinal study of early intervention with hearing impaired children. *American Annals of the Deaf.*

White, K. R., Bush, D. W., & Casto, G. (1985–1986). Let the past be prologue: Learning from previous reviews of early intervention efficacy research. *Journal of Special Education, 9*, 417–428.

Winton, P. J., & Turnbull, A. P. (1981). Parent involvement as viewed by parents of preschool handicapped children. *Topics in Early Childhood Special Education, 1*(3), 11–19.

Zigler, E., & Trickett, P. K. (1978). IQ, social competence, and evaluation of early childhood intervention programs. *American Psychologist, 33*, 789–798.

Chapter 6

Research in Early Language Intervention

Steven F. Warren and Ann P. Kaiser

THE ACQUISITION OF LANGUAGE IS one of the hallmarks of early childhood. Normal children have acquired virtually the entire language system by their fifth birthday. Five-year-olds may speak an average of 20,000 words daily and have an active vocabulary of 3,000 words (Wagner, 1985). This impressive accomplishment provides them with a multifaceted tool that is the key to other forms of symbolic learning (e.g., reading, math), as well as to an enormous range of complex social behavior.

Failure to acquire language normally is a developmental disaster. If unremediated, a language disorder will have pervasive effects on many aspects of a child's life, with educational and social consequences for years to come (Aram & Nation, 1975; Aram, Ekelman, & Nation, 1984; Hall & Tomblin, 1978; King, Jones & Lasky, 1982; Nippold & Fey, 1983; Weiner, 1974). Although precise prevalence data are unavailable, it is estimated that 10% of elementary school children have communication disorders of various types and severity (Owens, 1984).

In spite of the importance of language acquisition, the field of language intervention has a brief history. Most of the research that forms the basis of the field has been conducted in the past 25 years (Schiefelbusch & Lloyd, 1988). The purposes of this chapter are to characterize the basic findings of language intervention research with young children, to discuss the problems implicit in this research, and to identify the current directions of the field. The chapter will begin with a brief discussion of what language is and what the field of language intervention is all about.

WHAT IS LANGUAGE?

Communication is a signaling behavior that occurs in an interactional process (between two or more persons) and that provides a means to create shared understandings or meanings between persons. Language is a rule-governed system whereby meaningful intentions are represented through arbitrary, socially agreed-upon symbols that serve primarily the purpose of communication (Bryen & Joyce, 1985). Language is only one form of communication (other means include gestures, facial expressions, etc.), but it is an extraordinary flexible form upon which complex behaviors and symbol systems can be built.

The theories of how language is acquired and how it can best be taught when a child fails to acquire it normally have changed considerably in the past 2 decades. Fifteen years ago, there was still substantial debate among scientists concerning B. F. Skinner's proposition that language was strictly a learned behavior (Skinner, 1957) and Noam Chomsky's counter argument that language was a virtually innate

The development of this manuscript was partially supported by a grant from the National Institute of Child Health and Human Development (HD15051) and from the Special Education Program branch of the U.S. Department of Education (#G0084-00663). However, the views expressed are solely those of the authors.

behavior that essentially emerges as the child develops (Chomsky, 1957). Today, few researchers adhere tightly to either of these approaches. In recent years a broad-based approach, usually referred to as the "interactionist perspective" has emerged as arguably the most influential thesis in the field. The basic premise of this perspective is that at birth infants are prepared to learn to talk and the environment teaches them how to talk (McCormick & Schiefelbusch, 1984).

The emphases within the field of language intervention have also shifted substantially in the past 15 years. In the early 1970s there was much debate regarding the likely efficacy of a remedial (e.g., Guess, Sailor, & Baer, 1974) versus a developmental approach to language intervention (e.g., Miller & Yoder, 1974). The first comprehensive training programs were being published (e.g., Bricker & Bricker, 1974; Gray & Ryan, 1973; Guess et al., 1974; MacDonald & Blott, 1974; Miller & Yoder, 1974; Stremel & Waryas, 1974). Initial research was being conducted to determine whether operant methods could be used to teach linguistic rules (e.g., Baer & Guess, 1973; Wheeler & Sulzer, 1970) and to explore the relationship between receptive and expressive language (e.g., Guess, 1968; Guess & Baer, 1973). Early work on nonspeech communication approaches was in progress (e.g., Premack & Premack, 1974). In recent years there has been substantial research on language generalization (e.g., Hegde & McConn, 1981; Warren & Kaiser, 1986a), which has paralleled research on more naturalistic, less didactic ways to facilitate language development (e.g., Hart & Risley, 1980; Scherer & Olswang, 1984; Warren, McQuarter & Rogers-Warren, 1984). Theory, research, and intervention have reflected the increasing emphasis on the social basis of language in early mother-child interaction (Chapman, 1981a; Rogers-Warren &

Warren, 1984; Schiefelbusch & Bricker, 1981). Today, the field of language intervention is primarily concerned with facilitating the development of communicative competence (Rice, 1986; Schiefelbusch & Lloyd, 1988), not just language per se, and with ensuring the generalization of the child's communication skills across all environments the child inhabits (Duchan, 1986; Fey, 1986; Hughes, 1985; Warren & Rogers-Warren, 1985). In the current context, language intervention can be broadly defined as an *intentional attempt to stimulate or respond* to a child in a manner that will facilitate the development of new communication behaviors or will increase the appropriate use of existing communication skills (Fey, 1986; Schiefelbusch, 1983).

The Interactionist Perspective

Current interest in language intervention with young children is focused on what has been termed the "interactionist" perspective. This perspective incorporates certain operant and psycholinguistic notions with an overriding emphasis on the social bases of language acquisition and use. This approach is grounded in the increasing evidence that normal language acquisition is dependent on a variety of environmental processes and properties (Bates, 1976; Bates, Bretherton, & Snyder, in press; Bruner, 1975; Halliday, 1975; Hoff-Ginsberg, 1985; MacWhinney, in press; Nelson, in press).[1]

The interactionist perspective is not a fully developed theory of either language acquisition or intervention. It is a general approach to language development that concedes major roles for the nature and nuture concepts, and that accommodates a wide range of more specific ideas, theories, and approaches. From the interactionist perspective, competent use and understanding of language depends on a com-

---

[1]Despite movement toward an interactionist perspective, those studying normal language acquisition remain divided on many basic issues including the persistent controversy over the role of nature versus nurture (Bloom, 1983). By virtue of our primary concern in remediation, special educators are generally committed to some version of the interactionist perspective. An in-depth discussion of this perspective is beyond the scope of this chapter. Readers are referred to more detailed discussions in Bloom and Lahey (1978), Fey (1986), McCormick and Schiefelbusch (1984), McLean and Snyder-McLean (1978), or Rogers-Warren, Warren, and Baer (1983).

plex interaction between a child's skills with each of the three basic components of language: content (i.e., semantics), form (i.e., syntax), and use (i.e., pragmatics) (Bloom & Lahey, 1978; Fey, 1986). The child's major task in learning language is to infer the relationships between language content, form and use. In learning any part of the language system (e.g., form) the child must learn bits and pieces of all other parts concurrently (i.e., content and use) (Nelson, 1981). Language learning is viewed as beginning in early mother-infant interaction. During these interactions simple social routines are first established and the basic rules of human interaction are learned (e.g., turn-taking) (Bruner, 1978). The infant is an active participant in the social milieu from the first day of life (Thoman, 1981). As children develop sensorimotor skills, they actively explore the world, continually receiving feedback as to how things work and gradually gaining experience in regulating and controlling the environment for their own purposes. With experience, children come to understand symbols used in regularized and consistent ways and then to use specific gestures and symbols (Bricker & Carlson, 1981).

Researchers working from an interactionist perspective have developed a tentative description of how language is acquired in the context of normal mother-child dyadic interaction (e.g., Chapman, 1981b; Ervin-Tripp & Gordon, 1986). A number of interactional variables that appear to be important to the success of the learning process have been identified (e.g., turn-taking, build-ups, breakdowns, and expansions). The relative importance of specific variables to the language acquisition process is not well documented and will require additional research. However, during the past decade researchers have begun to examine the effects of intervening to modify interactional variables in combination with techniques previously shown to be useful in language intervention (e.g., differential reinforcement, modeling). The resulting "hybrid techniques," like the interactionist perspective itself, represent combinations of behavioral and developmental learning principles. From some per-

spectives, these intervention approaches may represent seemingly paradoxical combinations (e.g., using reinforcement to teach an abstract linguistic rule) that are not consistent with any coherent theoretical model (Johnston, 1983). Inconsistencies in terminology and in the relationship between the intent and actual result of many procedures abound (Rice, 1986). Such inconsistencies are to be expected in the early developmental stages of any major new theoretical reformation (Kuhn, 1970). At present there are indications that the field is beginning to coalesce toward a powerful set of intervention principles with an unusually high degree of external validity. The theoretical and empirical basis for this convergence will be discussed in a latter section of this chapter.

Parameters of this Chapter

In the remainder of this chapter the authors will: 1) describe the contributions and limitations of didactic intervention research, 2) review the theoretical and empirical bases for milieu intervention approaches, 3) discuss some problems inherent in conducting language intervention research, and 4) identify current directions for intervention research. The complexity of the language acquisition process makes it impossible to deal with all the research or even each of the research areas that are relevant to the remediation process in a single manuscript. For example, the authors will generally not deal with either basic research or specific aspects of the intervention process (e.g., the relationship between expressive and receptive language), or many important related topics, such as assessment and measurement. The authors have chosen to critique the intervention literature that has focused on teaching basic form-content relationships to young children in the early stages of productive language acquisition (i.e., mean length of utterance MLU 1.0 – 3.5). This literature has been selected for two reasons. First, it deals with the most fundamental issue of the field: how to remediate language deficits. Second, this literature has received far more clinical and research attention than any other area (Fey, 1986). Although primary emphasis is placed on early childhood, the authors will occasionally discuss relevant research conducted with chronologically older children still in the early stages of language acquisition.

THE CONTRIBUTIONS AND LIMITATIONS OF DIDACTIC RESEARCH

In the 1960s researchers began to systematically investigate procedures for remediating language disorders. They started with a simple question: Can elements of the linguistic system be taught to individuals with moderate to severe mental retardation? For the most part, these researchers were behaviorists working within a discrimination learning paradigm. Their initial subjects tended to be older children residing in institutional settings. Although operant theory emphasizes a functional approach to language (Skinner, 1957), through the 1970s most efforts to teach language behaviors using operant technology focused on the form and structure of language independent of normal function (Fey, 1986; McLean, 1983). These studies formed the basis of what is termed the "didactic approach" to language teaching.

Didactic training is characterized by use of the following: massed training trials, one-to-one highly structured, adult controlled training sessions, emphasis on precision and specificity of training procedures, and incorporation of a high ratio of differential reinforcement. Training typically occurs in a therapy room isolated from the child's classroom and is directed at teaching vocabulary, syntax, or morphology.

Early studies were promising. Well-controlled experiments demonstrated that children with mental retardation could be taught a variety of linguistic structures, skills, and words (Garcia, Guess, & Byrnes, 1973; Stephans, Pear, Wray, & Jackson, 1975; Welch & Pear, 1980; Zwitman & Sonderman, 1979). The experiments also demonstrated the children could be taught simple clausal constructions (Hester & Hendrickson, 1977; Jeffree, Whedall, & Mittler, 1973; Lutzker & Sherman, 1974), elements of verb phrase structure, such as auxiliaries (Gray & Fygetakis, 1968; Hegde, 1980; Hughes & Carpenter, 1983), articles, adjectives, pronouns, and other elements of noun phrase structures (Hegde & Geirut, 1979; McReynolds & Engmann, 1974; Smeets & Striefel, 1976), noun and verb inflections (Baer & Guess, 1973; Guess, 1968; Guess & Baer, 1973; Schumaker & Sherman, 1970), and complex sentences (Stevens-Long & Rasmussen, 1974; Tyack, 1981). Concurrent with these empirical demonstrations, a technology for language intervention was developed that relied largely on a didactic, adult-controlled, massed-trial approach incorporating teaching procedures such as shaping, fading, imitation, and differential reinforcement (cf. Gray & Ryan, 1973; Guess, Sailor, & Baer, 1978; Lovaas, 1977).

Operant research demonstrated that specific aspects of the content and form of language could be taught to children with specific language impairments as well as to children with moderate to severe mental retardation. The primary limit of this approach appears to be the extent to which it results in generalization of newly learned skills to appropriate communication situations (Costello, 1983; Harris, 1975; Leonard, 1981; Schiefelbusch & Lloyd, 1988; Spradlin & Siegel, 1982; Warren & Rogers-Warren, 1980). A few studies have extended the analysis of generalization to the child's natural environment. These investigations have reported either poor generalization (cf. Hughes & Carpenter, 1983; Jeffree et al., 1973; Mulac & Tomlinson, 1977; Warren, Baxter, Anderson, Marshall, & Baer, 1981; Zwitman & Sonderman, 1979) or mixed results (Hester & Henderickson, 1977; Warren & Kaiser, 1986a; Warren & Rogers-Warren, 1983a).

Generalization resulting from didactic training can be enhanced by the addition of specific procedures such as multiple examplar training (Hughes, 1985; Stokes & Baer, 1977). Nevertheless, there appear to be inherent problems with didactic training that make generalization and the attainment of communicative competence difficult to achieve. These problems result from several characteristics of the didactic approach that mitigate against generalization. These include: 1) an emphasis on structure and a corresponding lack of emphasis on normal function and use (Spradlin & Siegel, 1982), 2) difficulty in ensuring a high degree of child attention and interest (Bricker & Carlson, 1981; Dunlap & Koegel, 1980; Hart & Rogers-Warren, 1978), 3) difficulty in maintaining a communicative match with a child (Warren & Rogers-Warren, 1983a; Warren & Kaiser, 1986a), 4) difficulty in teaching the child to initiate language independent of specific adult cues (Bryen & Joyce, 1985; Charlop, Schreibman, & Thibodeau, 1985; Halle, 1987; Hubbell, 1977), 5) training that bears little resemblance to conditions in the natural environment (deVilliers & deVilliers, 1978; Fey, 1986; Seibert & Oller, 1981).

Despite the obvious problems with the didactic approach, there still may be many instances where it is the most appropriate approach to use (Carr & Kologinsky, 1983; Duchan, 1986). Didactic training may be necessary for initially establishing a skill in a child with moderate to severe mental retardation. It may be an efficient means to establish use of a skill with a zero baseline with children who typically require a large number of training trials to differentiate and produce the correct form of a response. Didactic training may be an especially useful approach for teaching an initial sound/label repertoire, for working on articulation and phonology, for rapidly training motor and vocal imitation, and for initially establishing linguistic rules such as pluralization and verb tense. However, the advantages offered by didactic instruction for teaching basic discriminations may become liabilities to promoting functional generalized language.

THE MILIEU APPROACH

Research on normal communication and language acquisition and the acknowledged limitations of the didactic training approach have encouraged researchers to investigate more "natural" methods for teaching language in recent years. The authors will use "milieu

teaching" (Hart & Rogers-Warren, 1978) as a generic term to represent the broad array of naturalistic approaches and techniques that have been proposed. Approaches included under this rubric are transactional teaching, (McLean & Snyder-McLean, 1978), conversational teaching (MacDonald, 1985), child-oriented teaching (Fey, 1986), pragmatic intervention (Duchan, 1986), the developmental interactive approach (Bricker & Carlson, 1981), unobtrusive training (Wulz, Meyers, Klein, Hall & Waldo, 1982), and the communicative competence approach (Rice, 1986). Milieu teaching approaches are characterized by the use of dispersed training trials, attempts to follow the child's attentional lead while teaching in the context of normal conversational interchanges, and an orientation toward teaching the form and content of language in the context of normal use. Milieu teaching encompasses a variety of more specific techniques, including incidental teaching (Hart & Risley, 1980), time delay (Halle, Marshall, & Spradlin, 1979), mand-model (Rogers-Warren & Warren, 1980), focused stimulation (Leonard, 1981), vertical structuring plus expansions (Schwartz, Chapman, Terrel, Prelock, & Rowan, 1985), and social language training (Haring, Rogers, Lee, Breen, Gaylord-Ross, 1986).

In the following section the theoretical and empirical support for a specific milieu teaching procedure, incidental teaching, and some variations of this procedure (i.e., mand-model and time delay) are reviewed. These procedures have much in common with procedures noted above. In this respect, they are representative of the remarkable recent convergence of the general field toward a more naturalistic child-oriented intervention approach. Behaviorists have arrived at this point through a generally inductive process based primarily on their attempts to obtain generalization. Developmentalists have followed the more deductive approach of applying recent theory and research with normal children to disordered children. But by whatever path, the implicit similarities between (for example) Hart and Risley's (1980) incidental teaching approach and MacDonald's (1985) conversation training approach are indicative of an unusual degree of convergent validity from two frequently disparate sources: behavior analysis research and developmental theory and research.

Incidental Teaching

Incidental teaching as language intervention involves a number of activities:

1. Arranging the environment to increase the likelihood that the child will initiate speech to the adult and will thus provide incidences for teaching
2. Selecting language targets appropriate to the child's skill level and interest, and to the environment
3. Responding to the child's initiations with requests for elaborate language resembling the targeted forms
4. Reinforcing the child's communicative attempts and use of specific forms with attention and access to the objects, actions, or events in which the child has expressed an interest (Hart, 1985).

Incidental teaching episodes are brief, positive, and oriented toward communication rather than toward language teaching per se. In many ways, incidental teaching resembles teaching that naturally occurs in mother-child dyadic interaction (Moerk, 1983; Schachter, 1979). Incidental teaching differs from naturally occurring teaching in two important ways: 1) communication or language targets are preselected for teaching (e.g., adjectives, nouns, and three-word sentence forms), and 2) a sequence of increasingly specific prompts are employed to ensure the child's use of the targets.

Why Incidental Teaching Should Be Effective With Young Children

Incidental teaching represents a systematic application of several variables and principles that should be effective from both behavioral and developmental perspectives. From a behavioral perspective, incidental teaching incorporates shaping, prompting, and differential reinforcement procedures that have been shown to be effective in the didactic literature. It also utilizes in the same teaching incidents the "loose teaching", the "programming common stimuli" and the "multiple exemplars" approaches that are effective in facilitating generalization (Stokes & Baer, 1977; Stremel-Campbell & Campbell, 1985). Because teaching occurs in the contexts and routines in which language is normally to be used, and because the cues are similar or identical to those the child will encounter in typical conversations, generalization is more likely (Hart, 1985). In addition, incidental teaching promotes the use of two specific learning strategies. First, imitation as a means of attending to and integrating new words with events is prompted and reinforced. Second, cross-modal transfer (i.e., spontaneous production of previously heard utterances) may be established through processes associated with generalized imitation. Repeated presentation of linguistically appropriate models, when the child's attention is focused on the immediate context, may teach the child to attend to words he or she hears spoken (Leonard, 1981). Practice in responding to formal models in naturalistic interactions may facilitate attention to and learning from models presented informally (Fey, 1986).

From a developmental perspective, several elements assumed to be critical for language learning are implicit in incidental teaching (Hart, 1985). The trainer follows the child's lead and teaches to his interests and intentions (Bruner, Roy, & Ratner, 1980; Muller, 1972; Schachter, 1979; Snow & Ferguson, 1977). The establishment of contiguity between the child's attention to an event and its linguistic representation by the trainer may be especially critical (Hoff-Ginsberg & Shatz, 1982; Murphy, 1978; Whitehurst, 1979). In addition, selection of appropriate targets slightly in advance of the child's productive competence and the explicit use of expanded models of the child's utterances ensures that there will be a communicative match between the teacher and the child (Newport, Gleitman & Gleitman, 1977). This represents application of the important Piagetian principle of "moderate novelty" (Piaget & Inhelder, 1969). Establishment of such a match with language disordered children may be especially conducive to language learning (Bricker & Carlson, 1981; Mahoney & Seely, 1976).

Equally important from both behavioral and developmental perspectives is the fact that incidental teaching focuses on successful communication, not on language per se. In incidental teaching, as in natural mother-child interaction, the consequences for talking are functional ones: control of the environment, continued interaction with the adult, and the realization of one's communicative intentions.

A basic component of incidental teaching is its emphasis on increasing children's frequency of talking (Hart & Rogers-Warren, 1978). There is some evidence that the use of language promotes the acquisition and use of more language (Hart & Risley, 1980; Nelson, 1973; Schachter, 1979). As a child begins to talk more, the need for more specific vocabulary and for more efficient means of encoding complex semantic notions also increases. For at least some children, then, initiating more frequent communicative attempts may prompt them to stretch the limits of their existing knowledge of language. It may also motivate their search for new forms that can more effectively and efficiently meet their needs (Fey, 1986).

Incidental teaching illustrates the importance of process: that language learning is facilitated not by specific principles, procedures, or techniques, but rather by the systematic but flexible arrangement of these elements within the ongoing stream of behavior-environment interaction (Prutting, 1983). The impact of any of the individual components of incidental teaching and of other broad milieu approaches does not predict the impact of the whole system. So while individual techniques (e.g., prompting, modeling, use of common stimuli, loose stimulus control) may have weak, even have weak, even transient effects, combinations of them may have powerful synergistic effects (Prutting, 1983).

Research on Incidental Language Teaching

The positive effects of incidental teaching procedures on targeted child responses have proven consistent across a range of linguistic responses for children of widely varying skills. Furthermore, results are consistent when procedures are applied by teachers, institutional staff, and parents. The effectiveness of incidental teaching was first demonstrated with disadvantaged preschoolers in a series of studies by Hart and Risley (1968, 1974, 1975, 1980). These researchers showed that while traditional group language training methods failed to produce generalized usage in other situations, incidental teaching resulted in significant increases in the use of target language in situations where the teaching procedures were not in effect. Hart and Risley (1980) reanalyzed data obtained in their 1975 study and compared data obtained during incidental teaching with longitudinal data on two comparison groups of preschool children (i.e., a group of middle-class children attending a university preschool and a group of children attending an inner city Headstart program). They found that incidental teaching resulted in substantial increases in the frequency of language use and in vocabulary growth. Disadvantaged children who had received the incidental teaching intervention showed acceleration in their rates of learning and using new language. After training, language use by the experimental group resembled that observed in advantaged university preschool children.

Incidental teaching has been adapted and modified in various ways for application with children who are low initiators and/or developmentally delayed or mentally retarded. Rogers-Warren and Warren (1980) and Warren et al. (1984) investigated an adapted version of incidental teaching termed the mand-model technique with socially isolated, language delayed preschool children. Halle, Baer, and Spradlin (1981) successfully applied another adaptation, the time delay procedure, to teach specific requesting strategies to six developmentally delayed preschool children. A number of other studies of incidental teaching variations have reported very positive results (Alpert & Rogers-Warren, 1984; Cavallaro & Bambara, 1982; Cavallaro & Poulson, 1985; Halle et al., 1979; McGee, Krantz, Mason, & McClannahan, 1983; McGee, Krantz, & McClannahan, 1985; Neef, Walters, & Egel, 1984; Oliver & Halle, 1982; Olswang & Coggins, 1984; Scherer & Olswang, 1984).

Four aspects of the results obtained from experimental applications of incidental teaching and its variations are significant. First, the effects on specific targeted language responses have been consistently strong and immediate across a range of subject populations (e.g., preschool disadvantaged, language delayed, mentally retarded, adolescent autistic, and severely mentally retarded) and experimenter populations (e.g., teachers, parents, and institutional staff experimenters) and a range of language responses (e.g., labels, adjectives, general requests, one- and two-word utterances, yes/no responses, compound sentences, specific requests). Second, there has been evidence of generalization across settings in each study in which this type of generalization was assessed (Alpert & Rogers-Warren, 1984; Cavallaro & Bambara, 1982; Halle et al., 1979; Halle et al., 1981; Hart & Risley, 1974; 1975; McGee et al., 1983; Warren et al., 1984). Third, except for the study by Cavallaro and Bambara (1982), every study in which frequency of subject initiation and responsiveness have been measured has reported increases in these two important dimensions of language use (Halle et al., 1981; Hart & Risley, 1980; Warren et al., 1984). Finally, studies that have measured the linguistic aspects of language use (complexity and vocabulary size were the aspects typically measured) have reported at least modest gains (Alpert & Rogers-Warren, 1984; Hart & Risley, 1975; 1980; Rogers-Warren & Warren, 1980; Warren et al., 1984).

Although the primary and generalized results of applications of incidental teaching are consistent in indicating the effectiveness of the teaching paradigm, research with young mentally retarded children and autistic children has been too narrowly focused (e.g., Cavallaro & Poulson, 1985; Halle et al., 1979; McGee et al., 1983) to determine if incidental teaching procedures can produce strong, consistent general effects on these children's language learning and use. To determine if this approach is viable with these children, evaluation of general effects on their language and communication is necessary.

Necessary Criteria for Evaluating Milieu Approaches

Two types of evidence are necessary to demonstrate that an intervention procedure is an effective language intervention strategy. First, there must be evidence that the primary effects of the intervention can be demonstrated consistently. Second, there must be empirical evidence that applications of the procedure result in significant changes in the general communication repertoire of the individual.

The issue of what constitutes remediation of a pervasive communication deficit is not widely discussed in current language intervention literature. Demonstrations of general effects would require evidence that formal and functional components of the communication system have been positively affected by the intervention. Communication depends on a formal system for expressing social intentions or functions. In order to acquire the formal and functional aspects of the communication system, children must have viable learning strategies that are applied in everyday learning situations. Remediation of general language deficits must include significant changes in the formal system for communication, evidence of increased expression of social intention and functional use of the expanded formal system, and implicit changes in the strategy employed in learning from natural contexts. Acquisition of specifically trained forms alone does not constitute evidence of significant remediation of a language deficit (Warren & Rogers-Warren, 1983a; Warren & Kaiser, 1986a). Generalization of trained forms and functions across settings, persons, and response classes is necessary but still not sufficient evidence of remediation by these criteria. Evidence of remediation should be reflected in increases in rate of acquisition and use of new forms and/or functions in functional communicative contexts. The new rate should exceed the level of increase attributable to the immediate effects of direct teaching to the extent that a change in the efficiency of learning can be assumed.

Based on this logic, a threefold criterion for evaluating the general effects of a comprehensive intervention consists of: 1) significant increases in the range of formal means of communication (e.g., syntax, vocabulary), 2) changes in the social use of language (i.e., increased functional communication), and 3) evidence suggesting that new forms and functions are being acquired and generalized more quickly than prior to the intervention. Few interventions with language-impaired or mentally retarded children have been evaluated in terms of these generalized types of changes or in terms of the general effects of the teaching procedures (Fey, 1986; Leonard, 1981; Warren & Rogers-Warren, 1980). Such stringent criteria have not been applied in the past, but given the importance of language and its role in social interaction, academic learning, and general cognitive functioning, use of these criteria in evaluating any technique suggested for widespread application is appropriate.

The General Effects of Incidental Teaching

The strongest evidence of general effects comes from incidental teaching studies with culturally disadvantaged and language delayed children. Positive effects on form and function have been reported. Increases in the use of targeted linguistic forms have been shown to be primary results of all incidental teaching studies. Generalized changes in the use of linguistic forms have been reported by Rogers-Warren and Warren (1980) (i.e., previously trained forms were shown to generalize to the classroom when incidental teaching was applied in that setting) and by Warren et al. (1984) (i.e., children's mean length of utterance increased following incidental teaching). Hart and Risley (1968, 1974, 1975) reported increases in novel examples of the classes of language forms trained via incidental teaching. Alpert and

Rogers-Warren (1984) reported significant changes in MLU, upperbound utterances (i.e., longest utterance in a speech sample), novel words produced, and total words produced by six language-delayed preschoolers following incidental teaching by their mothers, suggesting that the intervention may have had quite general effects on these subjects' use of linguistic forms. Increases in the use of specific language functions have been reported in all incidental teaching studies. These functions have included requesting (Halle et al., 1979; Halle et al., 1981; Hart & Risley, 1968), imitation and responses to questions (Rogers-Warren & Warren, 1980; Warren et al., 1984), and affirmation and negation (Neef et al., 1984). Hart and Risley (1982) have also described the use of incidental teaching to increase commenting and directive behavior by children.

There is no direct evidence of changes in language learning strategy as a result of incidental teaching. However, several studies have reported general acceleration in the acquisition of new words and forms that might be indicative of a learning strategy change by a child (Alpert & Rogers-Warren, 1984; Hart & Risley, 1980; Rogers-Warren & Warren, 1980). Additionally, accelerated generalized use of previously trained forms was evident in a study by Rogers-Warren and Warren (1980). Increasing generalization may indicate application by the child of a strategy learned through the incidental teaching intervention. Maintenance data reported by Alpert and Rogers-Warren (1984), Hart and Risley (1974), Rogers-Warren and Warren (1980), and Warren et al. (1984) might indicate that subjects had acquired strategies that they continued to apply after training was discontinued. Improved rates of initiations and responsiveness, sustained use of the trained classes of language behaviors, and in some cases, continued acquisition of new forms have been reported. However, these data may only indicate growth spurts by subjects and may not reflect a basic change of strategy.

In summary, incidental teaching appears to be a highly promising intervention approach that may affect children's communication repertoires in important general ways. It is clear from existing literature that incidental teaching: 1) teaches target skills effectively in the natural environment, 2) results typically in generalization of those skills across settings, time, and persons, and 3) results in gains in the formal and functional aspects of language. Because research with mentally retarded and autistic children is limited in both quantity and scope, the efficacy of this approach with these populations is less clear.

Limitations

Substantial research remains to be done on milieu teaching and its variations (Warren & Kaiser, 1986b). Milieu interventions that directly target pragmatic goals other than simple requests are needed. Examples of this would be topic continuation, turn-taking, and commenting. Research is also needed to determine the parameters of milieu effects with language-disordered children and how its effects are influenced by individual subject learning styles and differences. Research is also needed to determine ways to utilize this approach systematically within the present educational system and with parents.

There may ultimately be several limitations and restrictions on the use of milieu teaching, at least as a primary intervention approach. Some very specific linguistic devices, such as grammatical morphemes (e.g., verb copula, plurals, tense markers) may be difficult and inefficient to train incidentally. They might best be taught didactically first, with milieu teaching used to facilitate generalization. Conant, Budoff, Hecht, and Morse (1984) have expressed concern that teachers and clinicians might "drop back" to the use of didactic instruction because they simply can't "wait" for sufficient teaching incidents to occur naturally for specific structural forms and features. Several researchers have expressed concern that severely retarded children with limited response repertoires and passive learning and interaction styles may simply provide too few incidents (Baer, 1981; Bricker & Carlson, 1981; Carr & Kologinsky, 1983; Duchan, 1986).

FLEXIBLE COMBINATIONS OF DIDACTIC AND MILIEU APPROACHES: AN EVOLVING MODEL?

Didactic and milieu approaches each have strengths and weaknesses. Didactic instruction clearly has limitations that make it a poor choice for a comprehensive intervention approach. Milieu models may have limitations too, particularly with severely handicapped learners and in teaching very specific skills. In combination each model may complement the other. Milieu teaching strategies might be used exclusively with mildly delayed children needing general stimulation and as a teaching and generalization approach with all other children. Didactic instruction might be used to establish quickly and efficiently an initial baseline of either general skills with severely retarded children or specific skills (e.g., use of grammatical morphemes) with all types of children. Meanwhile, these children would receive milieu teaching of the same skills to teach functional use and to ensure generalization and integration into the child's natural usage repertoire.

Studies by Carr and Kologinsky (1983) and Rogers-Warren and Warren (1980) demonstrate the combined use of didactic and milieu teaching approaches. On the basis of their comparison between milieu and didactic approaches, Cole and Dale (1986) argued that a combined approach may prove superior to either approach used separately. Conant et al. (1984) demonstrated an interesting hybrid of milieu and didactic approaches. They used a games format that allowed many more teaching opportunities than is provided by milieu teaching; the format also allowed researchers to focus on very specific targets such as are provided by a didactic approach. Their hybrid approach retained many of the strengths of both didactic and milieu teaching within the same intervention session.

Current intervention research is clearly oriented toward the development of milieu techniques with an emphasis on communicative competence. The first truly comprehensive remediation model is yet to be developed. A comprehensive model would combine, when necessary, didactic and milieu approaches within an "acquisition-generalization-competence" sequential learning model that adapts to the point the child is at in development, the child's individual learning style, and the characteristics and uses of the specific skill being taught. Implementing this model would require an equally comprehensive and dynamic ongoing assessment approach.

RESEARCH PROBLEMS

Scientific research is a demanding and rigorous enterprise. Research on language development and remediation is one of the more complex and inherently hazardous branches of this enterprise. This is so because of the nature of the topic. Not only is language apparently the most complex form of human behavior, but it is also embedded in social and cognitive processes in ways that make it difficult if not impossible to untangle. In order to make language analyzable, researchers attempt to separate its individual aspects (e.g., syntax, semantics, and pragmatics) from each other. Yet it is evident that these distinctions do not reflect how humans produce and process language. Nor can language ultimately be understood separately from its context, that is, separately from social interaction. In short, research on language development and remediation presents a formidable challenge to the scientific method. In this section we will discuss some of the recurrent research problems in language remediation with young children. Some of these problems are manageable, others can only be acknowledged as recurring threats to the validity of our research.

The Slow Acquisition of Many Forms

With the exception of some lexical items, it is well documented that the period from emergence to the point of mastery is protracted for many linguistic forms for both normal children (Brown, 1973) and language impaired children (Cousins, 1979; Johnston & Schery, 1976; Morehead & Ingram, 1973). Extended acquisi-

tion periods make assessment difficult, compromise experimental designs that require temporally related increases in frequencies or appropriate use across situations, and complicate evaluation of generalization. To address these problems researchers must: 1) do comprehensive assessments and take long baselines under varying conditions, 2) know, if possible, how the form or skill they are studying typically emerges in a child's repertoire, and 3) take a multifaceted approach to generalization that may include samples and probes under a variety of naturalistic situations. Unfortunately, much of the intervention research to date can be criticized for utilizing relatively short baselines, superficial assessments, and narrow and highly restricted generalization measures.

Situational Constraints

Language is extraordinarily flexible. As a result, it is also highly influenced by context. In the authors' experience many teachers and even speech therapists consistently underestimate the productive abilities of some children because they seldom interact with them in truly give-and-take conversations. The mean length of utterance (MLU) of a child in a didactic situation is typically much shorter than their MLU in a free form conversational situation. Furthermore, a child will initiate a specific lexical item like "snake" only when that stimulus is present, desired, or an important element in some past or future event the child is describing. One might observe the child for hours, even days, and never observe the productive use of "snake," yet the child could have it in his or her repertoire. The same could apply to syntactic forms like passives. Situational constraints such as those noted often affect assessments as well as measures of generalization (cf. Warren & Rogers-Warren, 1983b). Like the slow emergence of forms, the primary control for them is to understand the "normal" constraints on the skill or behavior in question and to measure the skill or behavior in a multiplicity of ways including structured probes and elicited speech samples.

Inseparability of Related Processes

Language is a system. If one aspect of this system is manipulated all other aspects of the system are affected. When teaching a child something about syntax, semantics, pragmatics, and phonology are also taught. Production and comprehension may be similarly related. The inseparability of language components creates numerous analysis problems. First, what is being taught to the child and what the child is actually learning may not be identical. Second, when the child fails to generalize a form that was taught it may be impossible to discern the cause. Perhaps a form was taught for which the child has no natural function, or perhaps the child has a mnemonic problem that inhibits generalization. Finally, it may be difficult to control learning during baseline. If the child is truly "ready" to learn the training targets selected for him or her then he or she may begin to learn them independently of training (Olswang, Bain, Rosendahl, Oblak, & Smith, 1986). After all, the child is probably spending several hours a day in an environment that is sufficient to teach language to normal children. On the other hand, if a child has a stable zero baseline, training may be slow and arduous. Leonard (1981) has pointed out that training a child who shows no comprehension or use of a target form may represent something quite different from the same training with a child showing considerable comprehension of the form.

To control for effects caused by the interrelated nature of language components, a broad assessment of children's related skill base, both cognitive and social, and of their actual language competence and use is necessary. Unfortunately, much intervention research has been weak in terms of comprehensive assessment. The most obvious limitation has been the failure to assess comprehension skills in interventions designed to teach productive skills. Specific comprehension abilities may be related to children's success or failure in a given production learning task.

Heterogeneous Subjects

Samples with heterogeneous subjects are problems in research with handicapped children, but they are especially critical factors to consider when conducting language remediation research. Language acquisition, even in normal children, is a highly varied process. Nelson (1981) has identified substantial individual differences in how normal children go about the acquisition process. Klee and Fitzgerald (1985) have described how children at the same MLU can have different skills and conversational abilities. The problem of varying patterns of acquisition is accentuated with language disordered children. Menyuk (1975) has argued that these children may compensate for specific deficits in widely varying ways. Miller, Chapman and Bedorisan (1977) and others (Geschwind, 1979; Kirchner & Skarakis-Doyle, 1983; Naremore, 1979) have argued that research that has failed to establish its subjects' status on all relevant variables (e.g., cognition, comprehension, and production) may have inadvertently used groups or compared individuals so heterogeneous that the resulting data are useless for drawing conclusions about language and communication delays. The counterargument has been that if an intervention approach is powerful enough, it will overcome individual subject variability (Baer, Wolf & Risley, 1968). However, this argument is less compelling when the problem of differential and varied generalization patterns is considered. As with other problems noted above, the best management approach is comprehensive subject assessment and description. These descriptions would allow individual differences to be analyzed in relation to outcomes and for individual studies to be aggregated and compared. The problem of incomplete or poor subject descriptions has been a concern of the field in recent years (Wickstrom, Goldstein, & Johnson, 1985). It has caused some scholars attempting to do critical reviews of the field to disqualify large amounts of otherwise sound research from their comparative analyses (e.g., Arnold, Myette & Casto, 1986; Bryen & Joyce, 1985). The problem of limited subject description has probably been exacerbated by the traditional behaviorist assumption that individual differences may be unimportant (Baer et al., 1968).

Other problems in language intervention research are also reflective of its apparent complexity. These include: 1) lack of an experimental paradigm for establishing causal relationships in the context of a multi-causal dynamic and reciprocal system, 2) the practical management and analysis problems inherent in natural language studies, 3) use of inconsistent and poorly defined terminology that probably is indicative of the lack of a widely accepted strong, coherent theoretical model. These problems must be managed by researchers but presently they cannot be resolved completely. Such research issues are actually reflective of the complexity of the natural environments in which language must be studied as much as the language system itself. As research has moved out of the laboratory into the natural environment, ecological validity has been gained, but a degree of experimental control and precision has been lost.

RESEARCH DIRECTIONS

Although there are problems in doing high quality, ecologically valid research on language intervention, research must continue. Language is critical to everyday functioning and is basic to human expression. Regardless of an individual researcher's theoretical or experimental approach, the issues of understanding and producing specific generalization and general effects will drive future research. A diverse set of issues, including assessment, individual differences, timing of intervention, determination of stimulus control, the relationship of form to function and of comprehension to production, and the role of speech clinicians, must be evaluated according to how well they influence generalization and/or general effects. Obviously this implies a broad but systematic approach to generalization and efficacy that assumes that a multitude of variables may affect these outcomes in the real world. Within this context the authors suggest five research directions that seem likely to contribute substantial new knowledge about factors influencing generalization and general effects.

Individual Differences

Analysis of individual differences related to differential outcomes is a critically important area for future research. To date, there are almost no data on the differential affects of language intervention resulting from individual differences (Chapman, 1981a; Friedman & Friedman, 1980; Kirchner & Skarakis-Doyle, 1983; Rosenberg, 1982; Warren & Kaiser, 1986b). Different learning styles (e.g., expressive vs. referential styles or active vs. passive interactive styles) may interact with the same treatment approach in different ways (Nelson, 1981) and different cultural backgrounds may also have different affects (Rice, 1986). Generalization of training and general remediative effects may be influenced by these individual characteristics. These characteristics may not just represent idiosyncratic individual variance. They may represent systematic variance attributable to one or more specific attributes of an identifiable subgroup, for example, very young language delayed children. Analysis of individual differences requires dynamic assessment approaches to determine response and learning characteristics (e.g., Olswang et al., 1986). Static intelligence models (i.e., traditional IQ estimates) have not been enlightening because children with the same IQ can still respond to the same intervention in vastly different ways. Research on the relationship between individual differences and outcomes resulting from the same intervention approach may be one of the most productive research avenues of the future.

Stimulus Control

B.F. Skinner's (1957) position that behavior should be classified according to its controlling stimuli and not according to its topography is ultimately sensible. Unfortunately, as Skinner noted, this is not easy because language development is a complex process. Controlling stimuli are very difficult to discern except in the laboratory. Even the simplest language responses may be controlled by more than a single stimulus (Halle, 1987). Nevertheless, understanding stimulus control is critical to facilitating generalization and general effects. Behavior analysts are beginning to develop more complex models of stimulus control (e.g., Billingsley & Romer, 1983; Goldstein,

1985; Halle, 1987) that move beyond simplistic attempts to isolate single controlling variables. Indeed, Duchan (1986) has pointed out that "ironically, the behavioral approach, unlike more mentalistic approaches, comes to grip with the question of what is significant to the child. It does this by trying to determine the discriminative stimuli, or those parts of the context which control the child's response" (p. 198–199).

Analysis of Intervention Procedures

Research on naturalistic language teaching has been conducted for less than a decade. For all its potential, very little is known about many issues fundamental to the application of incidental teaching approaches (Warren & Kaiser, 1986b). Most other milieu procedures have either been the subject of just one or two studies or have only been proposed as potentially effective (e.g., teaching turn taking; using contingent imitation of the child to establish initial social responding). Hybrid procedures (e.g., the communication games approach investigated by Conant et al., 1984) that combine certain features of didactic and milieu approaches seem especially worthy of future research. Applications that teach a substantial repertoire of functional skills, especially with young mentally retarded and autistic children, are particularly lacking. For the foreseeable future, high quality intervention research leading to the development of new and improved techniques and packages is needed.

Very Early Intervention

Language disorders and delays typically have their genesis very early in development, due to an organic problem (such as Down syndrome), or to environmental insult or trauma, an abusive environment, or a combination of these factors. Whatever the etiology, intervention to correct communication and language deficits should begin as early as possible in order to avoid the cumulative effects of the deficit (Menyuk, 1975; Schiefelbusch & Bricker, 1981). Furthermore, as factors that contribute to disordered or delayed language are identified, it may be possible to intervene in preventative ways to limit some of the broader effects of the deficit. Language development takes place in the larger context of communication and social development that begins in mother-child dyadic interaction shortly after birth. For example, children learn to make crude requests long before they utter their first word (Bruner et al., 1980; Ervin-Tripp & Gordon, 1986). Appropriate prelinguistic intervention will likely focus on aspects of the social and communicative relationship between parent and child. To date, little research concerning direct attempts to facilitate prelinguistic development has been published. However, the bases for this type of research have been well specified (cf. Schiefelbusch & Bricker, 1981).

Timing of Intervention

The issue of readiness, or critical learning periods, as related to timing of intervention has not received much attention in applied research (Olswang et al., 1986). The combination of what treatment procedure is introduced and when may be critical variables for determining rate and success of change. Evidence supporting the nonlinearity of language learning, as defined by readiness and growth spurts, has continued to accumulate in the literature on normal children (e.g., Bates et al., in press; Bohannon & Leubecker, in press) and children with impairments (e.g., Gibson & Ingram, 1983; Olswang, Bain, Dunn, & Cooper 1983; Olswang et al., 1986; Olswang & Coggins, 1984). These data suggest that there may be optimum times for direct treatment and times when benefits of treatment may be negligible, at least with mildly handicapped children.

An experimental analysis of the effects of intervention timing was provided by Olswang et al. (1986). Static and dynamic assessment procedures (Feuerstein, 1979) were used to determine actual and potential levels of functioning of two preschool language impaired children at the single-word stage of development. The children were closely matched on the static assessment (the Sequenced Inventory of Communication Development), but one subject assessed much higher on a dynamic assessment of modifiability of novel lexical item production. The subjects' responses to treatment were successfully predicted by the dynamic assessment, but not the static assessment.

The Olswang et al., (1986) study involved only two subjects and a limited intervention target. This suggests that direct treatment may be most effective in changing behavior at different times during the language acquisition process. Systematic research is clearly needed to establish the potential usefulness of dynamic assessment in individualizing the timing of various intervention efforts.

Inappropriate Directions

There are some areas of research that are probably not worth pursuing. Siegel (1983) has argued that there is no need for research that simply asks "Does therapy work?" Obviously it "works," the important questions are how, with whom, and in what ways. Both Siegel (1983) and Baer (1981) have argued that comparative research in which two intervention approaches are directly compared (e.g., an incidental approach vs. a didactic approach) is inherently capricious and produces arbitrarily interpreted results. They suggest that by the time all relevant variables have been accounted for and controlled, it is nearly impossible to design a satisfactory comparison. Any group study that ignores, by statistical averaging techniques, individual variance resulting from an intervention approach may also be of limited value. Finally, component analyses of package approaches (such as incidental teaching) are probably not worth the inherent difficulty of such research. A better approach is to verify the independent effects of each component based on previous research, as has been done with most of the key components of incidental teaching.

Beyond the methodological constraints, there are also many important questions that fall outside the limits of scientific research on early language intervention. Siegel (1987) has divided these questions into three categories: those concerning social and personal values (e.g., is intervention worth the cost?); questions that call for logical rather than scientific analysis (e.g., the distinction between cogni-

tion and language); and questions for which the answers are already known or that would not be influenced by contrary findings (e.g., the general question: "Does treatment work?"). Research can influence questions of values and policy. But these are not fundamentally scientific issues; they are best treated from other perspectives "lest science be misused" (Medawar, 1984).

CONCLUSION

There has been a great deal of research on early language intervention over the past 25 years. In many respects, this research has been theoretically and procedurally fragmented, reflecting the general state of both evolution and ferment apparent in research on normal child language acquisition (Bloom, 1983). However, there is both theoretical and empirical evidence that the field is beginning to coalesce toward a more unifed intervention approach. This convergence of both inductive approaches, such as in applied behavior analysis, and deductive approaches such as in recent developmental theory and research on normal mother-child interaction suggests this evolving model may be characterized by an unusual degree of convergent validity.

Attempts by professionals to understand and to promote meaningful generalization will continue to drive both empirical work and theory. As for researchers' ongoing clinical and educational efforts, to the extent that a systems approach is applied, and to the extent that a variety of variables are combined to produce synergistic outcomes, researchers may anticipate increasing success at promoting generalized outcomes. Nevertheless, researchers remain a long way from actually understanding the process of generalization in either normal or handicapped children.

The overarching direction in intervention research is toward the application of more naturalistic techniques with an emphasis on communicative competence. Beyond this, researchers may be developing a more sophisticated overall intervention model that does not "reject" any effective technique but instead ties specific techniques to specific children with individual learning styles in the process of learning specific communication skills. The current research on individual differences and hybrid interventions seems indicative of this trend.

Science is by design a conservative approach to determining the "truth." Due to the pressing needs of young handicapped children, professionals have been forced to develop inter-

ventions that reflect "best guesses," because the ecologically valid research on which to base these interventions has not been available. As the needed empirical bases are developed, it is incumbent upon researchers to adjust and modify their educational and therapeutic practices. Building effective practice based on research is and will be a major challenge for the foreseeable future.

REFERENCES

Alpert, C. L., & Rogers-Warren, A. K. (1984). *Mothers as incidental language trainers of their language-disordered children.* Unpublished manuscript, University of Kansas, Lawrence.

Aram, D., Ekelman, B., & Nation, J. (1984). Preschoolers with language disorders: 10 years later. *Journal of Speech and Hearing Research, 27,* 232–244.

Aram, D., & Nation, J. (1975). Patterns of language behavior in children with developmental language disorders. *Journal of Speech and Hearing Research, 18,* 229–241.

Arnold, K. S., Myette, B. M., & Casto, G. (1986). Relationships of language intervention efficacy to certain subject characteristics in mentally retarded preschool children: A meta-analysis. *Education and Training of the Mentally Retarded, 21,* 108–116.

Baer, D. M. (1981). The nature of intervention research. In R. L. Schiefelbusch & D. D. Bricker (Eds.), *Early language: Acquisition and intervention* (pp. 559–574). Baltimore: University Park Press.

Baer, D. M., & Guess, D. (1973). Teaching productive noun suffixes to severely retarded children. *American Journal of Mental Deficiency, 77,* 498–505.

Baer, D. M., Wolf, M., & Risley, T. R. (1968). Some current dimensions in applied behavior analysis. *Journal of Applied Behavior Analysis, 1,* 91–97

Bates, E. (1976). *Language and context: The acquisition of pragmatics.* New York: Academic Press.

Bates, E., Bretherton, I., & Snyder, L. (in press). *From first words to grammar: Individual differences and dissociable mechanisms.* New York: Cambridge University Press.

Billingsley, F. F., & Romer, L. F. (1983). Response prompting and the transfer of stimulus control: Methods, research, and a conceptual framework. *Journal of The Association for Persons with Severe Handicaps, 8,* 3–12.

Bloom, L. (1983). Tensions in psycholinguistics. *Science, 20,* 843–849.

Bloom, L., & Lahey, M. (1978). *Language development and language disorders.* New York: John Wiley & Sons.

Bohannan, J. N., & Leubecker, A. W. (in press). Recent developments in speech to children: We've come a long way, baby talk. *Language Sciences.*

Bricker, D., & Carlson, L. (1981). Issues in early language intervention. In R. L. Schiefelbusch & D. D. Bricker (Eds.), *Early language: Acquisition and intervention* (pp. 477–516). Baltimore: University Park Press.

Bricker, W., & Bricker, D. (1974). An early language training strategy. In R. L. Schiefelbusch & L. L. Lloyd (Eds.), *Language perspectives: Acquisition, retardation, and intervention* (pp. 431–468). Baltimore: University Park Press.

Brown, R. (1973). *A first language: The early stages.* Cambridge, MA: Harvard University Press.

Bruner, J. S. (1975). The ontogenesis of speech acts. *Journal of Child Language, 2,* 1–19.

Bruner, J. S. (1978, September). Learning the mother tongue. *Human Nature,* 42–49.

Bruner, J., Roy, C., & Ratner, N. (1980). The beginnings of requests. In K. E. Nelson (Ed.), *Children's language* (Vol. 3). New York: Gardner Press.

Bryen, D. N., & Joyce, D. S. (1985). Sign language and the severely handicapped. *Journal of Special Education, 20,* 183–194.

Carr, E. G., & Kologinsky, E. (1983). Acquisition of sign language by autistic children II: Spontaneity and generalization effects. *Journal of Applied Behavior Analysis, 16,* 297–314.

Cavallaro, C. C., & Bambara, L. (1982). Two strategies for teaching language during free play. *Journal of the Association for the Severely Handicapped, 7,* 80–93.

Cavallaro, C. C., & Poulson, C. L. (1985). Teaching language to handicapped children in natural settings. *Education and Treatment of Children, 8,* 1–25.

Chapman, R. (1981b). Mother-child interaction in the second year of life: Its role in language development. In R. L. Schiefelbusch & D. D. Bricker (Eds.), *Early language: Acquisition and intervention* (pp. 201–250). Baltimore: University Park Press.

Chapman, R. (1981b). Mother-child interaction in the second year of life: Its role in language development. In R. L. Schiefelbusch & D. D. Bricker (Eds.), *Early language: Acquisition and intervention* (pp. 201–250). Baltimore: University Park Press.

Charlop, M. H., Schreibman, L., & Thibodeau, M. G. (1985). Increasing spontaneous verbal responding in autistic children using a time delay procedure. *Journal of Applied Behavior Analysis, 18,* 153–166.

Chomsky, N. (1957). *Syntactic structures.* The Hague, Netherlands: Mouton.

Cole, K., & Dale, P. (1986). Direct language instruction and interactive language instruction with language delayed preschool children: A comparison study. *Journal of Speech and Hearing Research, 28,* 205–217.

Conant, S., Budoff, M., Hecht, D., & Morse, R. (1984).

Language Intervention: A pragmatic approach. *Journal of Autism and Developmental Disorders, 14,* 301–317.

Costello, J. M. (1983). Generalization across settings: Language intervention with children. In J. Miller, D. E. Yoder, & R. L. Schiefelbusch (Eds.), *Contemporary issues in language intervention.* (pp. 275–297) Rockville, MD: American Speech-Language-Hearing Association.

Cousins, A. (1979). *Grammatical morpheme development in an aphasic child: Some problems with the normative model.* Paper presented at the 4th Annual Boston University Conference on Language Development.

deVilliers, J. G., & deVilliers, P. A. (1978). *Language Acquisition.* Cambridge, MA: Harvard University Press.

Duchan, J. F. (1986). Language intervention through sensemaking and fine tuning. In R. L. Schiefelbusch (Ed.), *Language competence: Assessment and intervention* (pp. 187–212). San Diego: College-Hill Press.

Dunlap, C., & Koegel, R. (1980). Motivating autistic children through stimulus variation. *Journal of Applied Behavior Analysis, 13,* 619–627.

Ervin-Tripp, S., & Gordon, D. (1986). The development of requests. In R. L. Schiefelbusch (Ed.), *Language competence: Assessment and intervention* (pp. 61–96). San Diego: College-Hill Press.

Feuerstein, R. (1979). *The dynamic assessment of retarded performances.* Baltimore: University Park Press.

Fey, M. (1986). *Language intervention with young children.* San Diego: College Hill Press.

Friedman, P., & Friedman, K. (1980). Accounting for individual differences when comparing the effectiveness of remedial language teaching methods. *Applied Psycholinguistics, 1,* 151–170.

Garcia, E., Guess, D., & Byrnes, J. (1973). Development of syntax in a retarded girl using procedures of imitation, reinforcement, and modeling. *Journal of Applied Behavior Analysis, 6,* 299–310.

Geschwind, N. (1979). Discussion of R. Naremore's "studying children's language behavior: Proposing a new focus." In C. Ludlow & M. E. Doren-Quine (Eds.), *The neurological basis of language disorders in children: Methods and directions for research.* (pp. 179–183) Bethesda, MD.: NIH Publication, #79-440.

Gibson, D., & Ingram, D. (1983). The onset of comprehension and production in a language delayed child. *Applied Psycholinguistics, 4,* 359–376.

Goldstein, H. (1985). Enhancing language generalization using matrix and stimulus equivalance training. In S. F. Warren & A. Rogers-Warren (Eds.), *Teaching functional language* (pp. 225–250). Austin, TX: PRO-ED.

Gray, B., & Fygetakis, L. (1968). The development of language as a function of programmed conditioning. *Behavior Research and Therapy, 6,* 455–460.

Gray, B., & Ryan, B. (1973). *A language program for a nonlanguage child.* Champaign, IL: Research Press.

Guess, D. (1968). A functional analysis of receptive language and productive speech: Acquisition of a plural morpheme. *Journal of Applied Behavior Analysis, 2,* 55–64.

Guess, D., & Baer, D. M. (1973). An analysis of individual differences in generalization between receptive and productive language in retarded children. *Journal of Applied Behavior Analysis, 6,* 311–331.

Guess, D., Sailor, W., & Baer, D. M. (1974). To teach language to retarded children. In R. L. Schiefelbusch & L. L. Lloyd (Eds.), *Language perspectives - Acquisition, retardation, and intervention* (pp. 529–564). Baltimore: University Park Press.

Guess, D., Sailor, W., & Baer, D. M. (1978). *Functional speech and language training for the severely handicapped.* Lawrence, KS: H & H Enterprises, Inc.

Hall, P. K., & Tomblin, J. B. (1978). A follow-up study of children with articulation and language disorders. *Journal of Speech and Hearing Research, 43,* 227–241.

Halle, J. (1987). Teaching language in the natural environment to individuals with severe handicaps: An analysis of spontaneity. *Journal of The Association for Persons with Severe Handicaps, 12,* 28–37.

Halle, J. W., Baer, D. M., & Spradlin, J. E. (1981). Teachers' generalized use of delay as a stimulus control procedure to increase language in handicapped children. *Journal of Applied Behavior Analysis, 14,* 387–400.

Halle, J. W., Marshall, A. M., & Spradlin, J. E. (1979). Time delay: A technique to increase language use and facilitate generalization in retarded children. *Journal of Applied Behavior Analysis, 12,* 431–440.

Halliday, M. A. (1975). *Learning how to mean: Explanations in the development of language.* New York: Elsevier/North Holland.

Haring, T. C., Rogers, B., Lee, M., Breen, C., & Gaylord-Ross, R. (1986). Teaching social language to moderately handicapped students. *Journal of Applied Behavior Analysis, 19,* 159–171.

Harris, S. L. (1975). Teaching language to nonverbal children—with emphasis on problems of generalization. *Psychological Bulletin, 82,* 565–580.

Hart, B. (1985). Naturalistic language training strategies. In S. F. Warren & A. Rogers-Warren (Eds.), *Teaching functional language* (pp. 63–88). Austin, TX: PRO-ED.

Hart, B., & Risley, T. R. (1968). Establishing the use of descriptive adjectives in the spontaneous speech of disadvantaged preschool children. *Journal of Applied Behavior Analysis, 1,* 109–120.

Hart, D., & Risley, T. R. (1974). Using preschool materials to modify the language of disadvantaged children. *Journal of Applied Behavior Analysis, 7,* 243–256.

Hart, B., & Risley, T. R. (1975). Incidental teaching of language in the preschool. *Journal of Applied Behavior Analysis, 8,* 411–420.

Hart, B., & Risley, T. R. (1980). In vivo language training: Unanticipated and general effects. *Journal of Applied Behavior Analysis, 12,* 407–432.

Hart, B., & Risley, T. R. (1982). *How to use incidental teaching for elaborating language.* Lawrence, KS: H & H Enterprises.

Hart, B., & Rogers-Warren, A. K. (1978). A milieu approach to teaching language. In R. L. Schiefelbusch (Ed.), *Language intervention strategies* (pp. 193–236). Baltimore: University Park Press.

Hegde, M. (1980). An experimental-clinical analysis of grammatical and behavioral distinctions between verbal auxiliary and copula. *Journal of Speech and Hearing Research, 23,* 864–877.

Hegde, M., & Geirut, J. (1979). The operant training and generalization of pronouns and a verb form in a language delayed child. *Journal of Communication Disorders, 12,* 23–34.

Hegde, M. N., & McConn, J. (1981). Language training: Some data on response classes and generalization to an occupational setting. *Journal of Speech and Hearing Disorders, 46,* 353–358.

Hester, P., & Hendrickson, J. (1977). Training functional expressive language: The acquisition and generalization of five-element syntactic responses. *Journal of Applied Behavior Analysis, 10,* 316.

Hoff-Ginsberg, E. (1985). Relations between discourse properties of mother's speech and their children's syntactic growth. *Journal of Child Language, 12,* 367–385.

Hoff-Ginsberg, E., & Shatz, M. N. (1982). Linguistic input and the child's acquisition of language: A critical review. *Psychological Bulletin. 92,* 3–26.

Hubbell, R. D. (1977). On facilitating spontaneous talking in young children. *Journal of Speech and Hearing Disorders, 42,* 216–231.

Hughes, D. (1985). *Language treatment and generalization.* San Diego: College-Hill Press.

Hughes, D., & Carpenter, R. (November, 1983). *Effects of two grammar treatment programs on target generalization to spontaneous language.* Paper presented to the American Speech-Language-Hearing Association Annual Convention, Cincinnati.

Jeffree, D., Whedall, K., & Mittler, P. (1973). Facilitating two-word utterances in two Down syndrome boys. *American Journal of Mental Deficiency, 78,* 117–122.

Johnston, J. R. (1983). What is language intervention? The role of theory. In J. Miller, D. E. Yoder, & R. L. Schiefelbusch (Eds.), *Contemporary issues in language intervention.* ASHA Reports, *12*(52–60). Rockville, MD: American Speech-Language-Hearing Association.

Johnston, J., & Schery, T. (1976). The use of grammatical morphemes by children with communication disorders. In D. Morehead & A. Morehead (Eds.), *Normal and deficient child language* (pp. 239–258). Baltimore, MD: University Park Press.

King, R., Jones, C., & Lasky, E. (1982). In retrospect: A fifteen-year follow-up report of speech-language-disordered children. *Language, Speech, and Hearing Services in Schools, 13,* 24–33.

Kirchner, D., & Skarakis-Doyle, E. (1983). Developmental language disorders: A theoretical perspective. In T. Gallagher & C. Prutting (Eds.), *Pragmatic assessment and intervention issues in language* (pp. 213–246). San Diego: College-Hill Press.

Klee, T., & Fitzgerald, M. D. (1985). The relation between grammatical development and mean length of utterance in morphemes. *Journal of Child Language, 12,* 251–270.

Kuhn, T. S. (1970). *The structure of scientific revolutions* (2nd ed.). Chicago: University of Chicago Press.

Leonard, L. B. (1981). Facilitating linguistic skills in children with specific language impairment: A review. *Applied Psycholinguistics, 2,* 89–118.

Lovaas, O. I. (1977). *The autistic child: Language development through behavior modification.* New York: Plenum Press.

Lutzker, J., & Sherman, J. (1974). Producing generative sentence usage by imitative and reinforcement procedures. *Journal of Applied Behavior Analysis, 7,* 447–460.

MacDonald, J. D. (1985). Language through conversation: A model for intervention with language delayed persons. In S. F. Warren and A. K. Rogers-Warren (Eds.), *Teaching functional language* (pp. 89–122). Austin, TX: PRO-ED.

MacDonald. J. D., & Blott, J. P. (1974). Environmental language intervention: The rationale for a diagnostic and training strategy through rules, context, and generalization. *Journal of Speech and Hearing Disorders, 39,* 244–256.

MacWhinney, B. (in press). Competition and language acquisition theory. In R. L. Schiefelbusch & M. Rice (Eds.), *The teachability of language.* New York: Cambridge University Press.

Mahoney, G. J., & Seely, P. B. (1976). The role of social agent in language acquisition: Implications for language intervention. In N. R. Ellis (Ed.), *International research in mental retardation* (Vol. 8, pp. 57–103). New York: Academic Press.

McCormick, L., & Schiefelbusch, R. L. (1984). *Early language intervention.* Columbus, OH: Charles E. Merrill.

McGee, G. G., Krantz, P. J., Mason, D., & McClannahan, L. E. (1983). A modified incidental-teaching procedure for autistic youth: Acquisition and generalization of receptive object labels. *Journal of Applied Behavior Analysis, 16,* 329–338.

McGee, G. G., Krantz, P. J., & McClannahan, L. E. (1985). The facilitative effects of incidental teaching on preposition use by autistic children. *Journal of Applied Behavior Analysis, 18,* 17–31.

McLean, J. (1983). Historical perspectives on the content of child language programs. In J. Miller, D. E. Yoder, & R. L. Schiefelbusch (Eds.), *Contemporary issues in language intervention* (pp. 115–126). The American Speech-Language-Hearing Association. Rockville, MD: ASHA Reports 12.

McLean, J. E., & Snyder-McLean, L. (1978). *A transactional approach to early language training.* Columbus, OH: Charles E. Merrill.

McReynolds, L., & Engmann, D. (1974). An experimental analysis of the relationship of subject and noun phrases. *ASHA Monographs, 18,* 30–47.

Medawar, P. B. (1984). *The limits of science.* New York: Harper & Row.

Menyuk, P. (1975). Children with language problems: What's the problem? In D. Data (Ed.), *Developmental psycholinguistics: Theory and applications* (pp. 129–144). Washington: Georgetown University Press.

Miller, J., Chapman, R., & Bedorisan, J. (1977). *Defining developmentally disabled subjects for research: The relationship between etiology, cognitive development, language, and communicative performance.* Paper presented at the 2nd Annual Boston University Conference on Language Development.

Miller, J. F., & Yoder, D. D. (1974). An ontogenetic language teaching strategy for retarded children. In R. L. Schiefelbusch & L. L. Lloyd (Eds.), *Language perspectives: Acquisition, retardation, and intervention* (pp. 505–528). Baltimore: University Park Press.

Moerk, E. L. (1983). *The mother of Eve as a first language teacher.* Norwood, NJ: Ablex Publishing.

Morehead, D., & Ingram, D. (1973). The development of base syntax in normal and linguistically deviant children. *Journal of Speech and Hearing Research, 6,* 330–352.

Mulac, A., & Tomlinson, C. (1977). Generalization of an operant remediation program for syntax with language-delayed children. *Journal of Communication Disorders, 10,* 231–244.

Muller, E. (1972). The maintenance of verbal exchanges between young children. *Child Development, 43,* 930–938.

Murphy, C. M. (1978). Pointing in the context of a shared activity. *Child Development, 49,* 371–380.

Neef, N. A., Walters, J., & Egel, A. L. (1984). Establishing generative yes/no responses in developmentally disabled children. *Journal of Applied Behavior Analysis, 17,* 453–460.

Naremore, R. (1979). Studying children's language behavior: Proposing a new focus. In C. Lublow & M. E. Doran-Quine (Eds.), *The neurological bases of language disorders in children: Methods and directions for research* (pp. 173–179). Bethesda, MD: NIH Publication #79-440.

Nelson, K. (1973). Structure and strategy in learning to talk. *Monographs of the Society for Research in Child Development, 38* (#1–2, Serial No. 149).

Nelson, K. (1981). Individual differences in language development: Implications for development and language. *Developmental Psychology, 17,* 170–187.

Nelson, K. E. (in press). Some observations from the perspective of the rare event cognitive comparison theory of language acquisition. In K. E. Nelson & A. Van Kleeck (Eds.), *Children's language* (Vol. 6). Hillsdale, NJ: Lawrence Erlbaum Associates.

Newport, E., Gleitman, L., & Gleitman, H. (1977). Mother I'd rather do it myself: Some effects and non-effects of motherese. In C. Snow & C. Ferguson (Eds.). *Talking to children: Language input and acquisition* (pp. 109–150). Cambridge, UK: Cambridge University Press.

Nippold, M., & Fey, S. (1983). Metaphonic understanding in preadolescents having a history of language acquisition difficulties. *Language, Speech, and Hearing Services in the Schools, 14,* 171–180.

Oliver, C. B., & Halle, J. W. (1982). Language training in the everyday environment: Teaching functional sign use to a retarded child. *Journal of The Association for the Severely Handicapped, 8,* 50–62.

Olswang, L., Bain, B. A., Dunn, C., & Cooper, J. (1983). The effects of stimulus variation on lexical learning *Journal of Speech and Hearing Disorders, 48,* 192–201.

Olswang, L. B., Bain, B. A., Rosendahl, P. D., Oblak, S. B., & Smith, A. E. (1986). Language learning: Moving performance from a context-dependent state. *Child Language Teaching and Therapy, 2,* 180–210.

Olswang, L., & Coggins, T. (1984). The effects of adult behaviors on increasing language delayed children's production of early relational meanings. *British Journal of Disorders of Communication, 19,* 15–34.

Owens, R. E. (1984). *Language development: An introduction.* Columbus, OH: Charles E. Merrill.

Piaget, J., & Inhelder, I. (1969). *The psychology of the child.* New York: Basic Books.

Premack, D., & Premack, A. (1974). Teaching visual language to apes and language-deficient persons. In R. L. Schiefelbusch & L. L. Lloyd (Eds.), *Language perspectives: Acquisition, retardation, intervention* (pp. 347–376). Baltimore: University Park Press.

Prutting, C. (1983). Scientific inquiry and communicative disorders: An emerging paradigm across six decades. In T. Gallagher & C. Prutting (Eds.), *Pragmatic assess-ment and intervention issues in language* (pp. 247–266). San Diego: College-Hill Press.

Rice, M. (1986). Mismatched premises of the communicative competence model and language intervention. In R. L. Schiefelbusch (Ed.), *Language competence: Assessment and intervention* (pp. 261–280). San Diego: College Hill Press.

Rogers-Warren, A. K., & Warren, S. F. (1984). The social bases of language and communication in severely handicapped preschoolers. *Topics in Early Childhood Special Education, 4,* 57–73.

Rogers-Warren, A. K., Warren, S. F., & Baer, D. M. (1983). Interactional bases of language learning. In K. Kernan, M. Begab, & R. Edgerton (Eds.), *Environments and behavior: The adaptation of mentally retarded persons* (pp. 239–266). Austin, TX: PRO-ED.

Rosenberg, S. (1982). The language of the mentally retarded: Development, processes, and intervention. In S. Rosenberg, (Ed.), *Handbook in applied psycholinguistics* (pp. 329–392). Hillsdale, NJ: Lawrence Erlbaum Associates.

Schachter, F. F. (1979). *Everyday mother talk to toddlers: Early intervention.* New York: Academic Press.

Scherer, N., & Olswang, L. (1984). Role of mother's expansions in stimulating children's language production. *Journal of Speech and Hearing Research, 27,* 387–396.

Schiefelbusch, R. L. (1983). Language intervention in children: What is it? In J. Miller, D. E. Yoder, & R. L. Schiefelbusch (Eds.), *Contemporary issues in language intervention* ASHA Reports 12 (pp. 15–26). American Speech-Language-Hearing Association. Rockville, MD.

Schiefelbusch, R. L., & Bricker, D. (1981). *Early language: Acquisition and intervention.* Baltimore: University Park Press.

Schiefelbusch, R. L. & Lloyd, L. L. (1988). *Language perspectives II:* Acquisition, retardation and intervention. Austin, TX: PRO-ED.

Schumaker, J., & Sherman, J. (1970). Training generative verb usage by imitation and reinforcement procedures. *Journal of Applied Behavior Analysis, 3,* 273–287.

Schwartz, R., Chapman, K., Terrell, B., Prelock, P., & Rowan, L. (1985). Facilitating word combinations in language-impaired children through discourse structure. *Journal of Speech and Hearing Disorders, 50,* 31–39.

Seibert, J. M., & Oller, D. N. (1981). Linguistic pragmatics and language intervention strategies. *Journal of Autism and Developmental Disorders, 11,* 75–88.

Siegel, G. M. (1983). Intervention context and setting: Where? In J. Miller, D. E. Yoder, & R. L. Schiefelbusch, (Eds.), *Contemporary issues in language intervention.* ASHA Reports 12 (pp. 253–260). Rockville, MD: American Speech-Language-Hearing Association.

Siegel, G. M. (1987). The limits of science in communication disorders. *Journal of Speech and Hearing Disorders, 52,* 306–312.

Skinner, B. F. (1957). *Verbal behavior.* New York: Appleton-Century-Crofts.

Smeets, P. M., & Streifel, S. (1976). Training the generative usage of article-noun responses in severely retarded males. *Journal of Mental Deficiency Research, 20,* 121–127.

Snow, C., & Ferguson, C. (Eds.). (1977). *Talking to chil-*

dren: Language input and acquisition. Cambridge: Cambridge University Press.

Spradlin, J., & Siegel, G. (1982). Language training in natural and clinical environments. *Journal of Speech and Hearing Disorders, 47,* 2–6.

Stephans, C. E., Pear, J. J., Wray, L. D., & Jackson, G. S. (1975). Some effects of reinforcement schedules in teaching picture names to retarded children. *Journal of Applied Behavior Analysis, 7,* 435–447.

Stevens-Long, J., & Rasmussen, M. (1974). The acquisition of simple and compound sentence structure in an autistic child. *Journal of Applied Behavior Analysis, 7,* 473–480.

Stokes, T. F., & Baer, D. M. (1977). An implicit technology of generalization. *Journal of Applied Behavior Analysis, 10,* 349–367.

Stremel-Campbell, K., & Campbell, C. R. (1985). Training techniques that may facilitate generalization. In S. F. Warren, & A. K. Rogers-Warren (Eds.), *Teaching functional language* (pp. 251–288). Austin, TX: PRO-ED.

Stremel, K., & Waryas, C. (1974). A behavioral-psycholinguistic approach to language training. In L. V. McReynolds (Ed.), *Developing systematic procedures for training children's language. ASHA Monographs, 18,* 96–130.

Thoman, E. (1981). Affective communication as the prelude and context for language learning. In R. L. Schiefelbusch & D. D. Bricker (Eds.), *Early language: Acquisition and intervention* (pp. 181–200). Baltimore: University Park Press.

Tyack, D. L. (1981). Teaching complex sentences. *Language, Speech and Hearing in the Schools, 12,* 49–56.

Wagner, K. R. (1985). How much do children say in a day? *Journal of Child Language, 12,* 475–488.

Warren, S. F., Baxter, D. K., Anderson, S. R., Marshall, A., & Baer, D. M. (1981). Generalization of question-asking by severely retarded individuals. *Journal of The Association for the Severely Handicapped, 6,* 15–22.

Warren, S. F., & Kaiser, A. P. (1986a). Generalization of treatment effects by young language-delayed children: A longitudinal analysis. *Journal of Speech and Hearing Disorders, 51,* 238–251.

Warren, S. F., & Kaiser, A. P. (1986b). Incidental language teaching: A critical review. *Journal of Speech and Hearing Disorders, 51,* 291–299.

Warren, S. F., McQuarter, R. J., & Rogers-Warren, A. K. (1984). The effects of mands and models on the speech

of unresponsive socially isolate children. *Journal of Speech and Hearing Disorders, 47,* 42–52.

Warren, S. F., & Rogers-Warren, A. K., (1980). Current perspectives in language remediation. *Education and Treatment of Children, 5,* 133–153.

Warren, S. F., & Rogers-Warren, A. K. (1983a). A longitudinal analysis of language generalization among adolescents with severely handicapping conditions. *Journal of The Association for the Severely Handicapped, 8,* 18–32.

Warren, S. F., & Rogers-Warren, A. K. (1983b). Setting variables affecting the display of trained noun referents by retarded children. In K. Kernan, M. Begab, & R. Edgerton (Eds.), *Environments and behavior: The adaptation of mentally retarded persons* (pp. 267–282). Austin, TX: PRO-ED.

Warren, S. F., & Rogers-Warren, A. K. (Eds.). (1985). *Teaching functional language.* Austin, TX: PRO-ED.

Weiner, P. (1974). A language delayed child at adolescence. *Journal of Speech and Hearing Disorders, 39,* 202–212.

Welch, S. J., & Pear, J. J. (1980). Generalization of naming responses to objects in the natural environment as a function of stimulus modality with retarded children. *Journal of Applied Behavior Analysis, 13,* 629–643.

Wheeler, A. J., & Sulzer, B. (1970). Operant training and generalization of a verbal response form in a speech-deficient child. *Journal of Applied Behavior Analysis, 3,* 139–147.

Whitehurst, G. J. (1979). Meaning and semantics. In G. J. Whitehurst & B. Zimmerman (Eds.), *The functions of language and cognition* (pp. 115–139). New York: Academic Press.

Wickstrom, S., Goldstein, H., & Johnson, L. (1985). On the subject of subjects: Suggestions for describing subjects in language intervention studies. *Journal of Speech and Hearing Disorders, 50,* 282–286.

Wulz, S. V., Meyers, S. P., Klein, M. D., Hall, M. K., & Waldo, L. J. (1982). Unobtrusive training: A home-centered model for communication training. *Journal of The Association for the Severely Handicapped, 7,* 36–48.

Zwitman, D., & Sonderman, J. (1979). A syntax program designed to present base linguistic structures to language-disordered children. *Journal of Communicative Disorders, 13,* 232–237.

Chapter 7

(Pre)Academic Instruction for Handicapped Preschool Children

Mark Wolery and Jeffri Brookfield-Norman

THE TITLE OF ANY CHAPTER SHOULD clearly communicate its primary topic or thesis. The title of this chapter, however, sends confusing messages about the nature of the skills being discussed. The two preceding and following chapters clearly identify the skills they address: language skills and social skills. Language skills are those needed to send and receive messages, social skills focus on interacting with others, and play involves pleasurable exchanges with materials and others. Academic skills, on the other hand, are those responses related to the traditional school curriculum (i.e., reading, computation, and written expression). This book focuses on preschool children with handicaps; thus, it would seem inappropriate to devote a chapter to reading, writing, and arithmetic. The "pre-" part of the title suggests that the chapter focuses on preparatory skills; thus, preacademic skills refer to the cognitive abilities that are necessary for later school learning. The "pre-" part of the title also refers to the identity crisis suffered by this domain; for example, terms such as "preoperational" and "readiness" are commonly used to describe the cognitive abilities/skills of children who are no longer infants, but who are not yet engaging in reading, writing, and arithmetic. This chapter addresses four questions:

What are academic skills?
What is meant by "readiness?"
What are preacademic skills?
How can preacademic skills be taught?

Infancy and sensorimotor skills will not be discussed; these issues have been addressed in other sources (e.g., Bailey & Wolery, 1984; Bricker, 1982; Dunst, 1981; Garwood & Fewell, 1983).

ACADEMIC SKILLS

The academic skills of reading, writing, and mathematics are three of many different skills (e.g., reasoning, social judgment, problem solving and others) that are acquired during the preschool years and primary grades. In this section, definitions of the academic skills are provided; characteristics shared by these skills, and the resulting implications for instruction, are listed. Readers interested in instruction of these skills with special populations should consult the following texts: (*The Fourth R: Research in the Classroom,* Haring, Lovitt, Eaton, & Hansen, 1978; *Evaluating Exceptional Children,* Howell, Kaplan, & O'Connell, 1979; *Tactics for Teaching,* Lovitt, 1984; *Teaching Students with Learning Disabilities,* Mercer & Mercer, 1985).

Preparation of this manuscript was supported in part by the Field Initiated Research Program, Office of Special Education and Rehabilitative Services, U.S. Department of Education, Grant number 8501281029. The opinions expressed do not necessarily reflect the position or policy of the U.S. Department of Education, and no official endorsement by the U.S. Department of Education should be inferred.

Reading

"Reading is the process of constructing meaning from written texts" (Anderson, Hiebert, Scott, & Wilkinson, 1985, p. 7). The act of reading may be further defined as a secondary receptive language system where the mode of transmission is graphic (including the use of Braille) and the receptors are visual or tactile; it is considered a secondary language system because a second level of symbolism (print) is used (Lerner, 1976). The communicative function of reading or the ability to "derive meaning" is not simply being able to decode printed words but includes integrating the information in print with information known to the reader from previous experiences. For discussions of reading and reading instruction see Durkin (1980), Osborn, Wilson, and Anderson (1985), and Pearson (1984).

Writing

Since reading can be conceptualized as a secondary receptive language system, writing can be viewed as a secondary expressive system (Lerner, 1976). Writing can be defined as an expressive form of language that conveys meaning through some graphic representation, such as manuscript, cursive, or calligraphic writing or through the manipulation of machines (e.g., typewriters, Braille writers, word processors) to produce graphic images. Content areas within writing include penmanship (handwriting), spelling, and composition (Hansen, 1978). Although the typical sequence of language development is thought to be listening, speaking, reading, and then writing, unclear relationships exist between these systems and, in fact, development may be parallel in some cases rather than serial (Lamme & Childers, 1983).

Mathematics

The science of mathematics involves analysis of quantity or amount. It may be defined as the science of numbers and the operations and relationships they involve. Mathematics is inherently logical and sequential; mastery of early skills is important for learning more advanced skills (Mercer & Mercer, 1985). It involves judgments about amount, time, monetary value, and across a number of stimulus dimensions such as weight, height, and length. It also involves computation of numbers using addition, subtraction, multiplication, and division.

Characteristics of Academic Skills and Implications for Instruction

Academic Skills are Means Rather than Ends   In general, academic skills are used for purposes other than their own performance. Reading is used to obtain information, writing to convey information, and mathematics to answer specific questions or solve particular problems. To be used in this manner, academic skills must be performed fluently (Anderson et al., 1985). Thus, instruction in academic and preacademic skills should focus on fluency building as well as acquisition.

Another implication of this characteristic is that many of the skills that are used as means may become obsolete. With the advances of technology, lengthy instruction in these skills may be adapted or sidestepped. For example, inexpensive hand-held calculators can currently perform the mathematical calculations that most people encounter daily. Perhaps the emphasis of instruction should be placed on use of the calculator and on when given operations are used rather than on how to perform them (Horton, 1985). Thus, rather than teaching students to add and subtract, they should be taught to discern when addition and subtraction are needed in real world situations. In the future, voice-activated word processors may alleviate the need for teaching the motor skills involved in writing; furthermore, the development of "reading machines" that will read narrative through synthesized speech for individuals with blindness may be applied to sighted persons with reading disabilities. Although most children will be required to learn academic skills, technological advances may be available as alternative response forms and as adaptions of skills that are used as means rather than ends.

Academic Skills Must be Highly Generalized Across Stimuli   Generalized performance is important in most skill domains, and it is particularly important with academics. Reading can be useful only when it can be applied accurately to many different print forms (e.g., italic, manuscript, Times New Roman, block print), and presentation formats (e.g., books, video and television screens, signs in the community). Likewise, math skills must be applied to a variety of stimuli. Almost anything can be counted, for example, and individuals need to make judgments about amounts such as weight, height, length, time, monetary value, and frequency in everyday life. Computation skills must be applied in instances that may be very different from traditional teaching formats, and in many cases, two or more operations are used in succession to solve the same problem. For example, a student may need to determine whether a 32-ounce bag of chips is cheaper than two 16-ounce bags. Such problems present themselves in very different formats from those encountered in a classroom, such as math problems on the chalk board or on a ditto sheet. Thus, instruction in academic and preacademic skills should be designed to facilitate generalization in "real life" situations. The type of generalization required is recombinative generalization (cf., Goldstein, 1983). Teachers carefully select teaching examples, use a variety of "best examples" and "general case" examples, and attend to the sequence in which examples are presented.

Academic Skills are not Form Specific; The Same Academic Skill can be Expressed through Different Indicator Behaviors The definition for "form" used in this chapter is borrowed from White (1980). Most academic skills involve discriminations and associations that can be demonstrated by a variety of different behaviors. For example, if children are presented with a simple addition problem (e.g., 2 + 2 = ?), they can answer a number of ways. They could write the correct answer, say the correct answer, point to the correct answer on a chart, say or nod "yes" or "no" to answers provided by the teacher, or push the "four" on a keyboard. Each of these are legitimate forms that communicate to other people that the correct discriminations and associations were made.

Some response forms are preferred over others due to efficiency or because a specific form will be expected more frequently in the natural environment, but the form used to show the presence of knowledge is not a critical element of that knowledge. This fact has at least four implications for instruction of preacademic and academic skills. First, when such skills are taught, one should be flexible concerning the forms used to determine whether a child can make the appropriate discriminations. Some children may have physical and/or speech disabilities that interfere with the performance of usual response forms; in such cases, alternative forms should be employed. Flexibility is also appropriate if a particular form is difficult for a given child to master. For example, if manuscript printing is difficult for a child and spacing problems persist, cursive writing should be considered as an alternative. Second, to facilitate generalization, multiple forms of responding to the same stimuli should be taught and reinforced. Third, children can learn the appropriate preacademic and academic skills even if they do not possess the usual response forms such as speech and physical dexterity. Thus, when typical response forms are absent, the teacher should find alternative forms for assessing the academic knowledge of the child. Fourth, since multiple response forms can be used to demonstrate that the same discrimination has been made, the teacher should be able to determine if functional equivalence across forms is evident. Functional equivalence refers to the situation wherein different response forms and different stimuli have equal functions. The numeral "3," the written word "three," and the oral statement "three" all are responses (and stimuli) that label the same quantity, yet they are all different response forms. These responses, or stimuli, are functionally equivalent because they mean the same thing. Teachers should not assume that students will respond correctly to these equivalent relationships, but should probe for generalization and provide instruction as necessary. This concept needs considerable attention from researchers.

Many Academic Skills are Discrete Re-

*sponses that are used in Many Different Re-
sponse Chains* Some of the skills that are
taught to children such as dressing, grooming,
and bed-making should be performed in fairly
consistent response chains. The actual sequences of those chains should be individually
determined for each child (cf., Bailey & Wolery, 1984), but once learned, the sequences
will be used in a fairly consistent pattern. With
academic skills, the response chains are more
fluid and variable. Students will be required to
read words or phrases in many different orders
and combinations; they will be required to apply their mathematics skills in some general
response chains that involve different stimuli.
For example, they may need to add the prices
of two different items to determine whether
they have sufficient money to purchase both.
While the steps involved would be consistent
(e.g., adding the one's column and then proceeding to add the ten's column, etc.) the stimuli they will be adding will vary greatly. Students must learn to form each letter of the
alphabet when learning to write, but they must
use those letters in many different combinations to write their name, address, social se-
curity number, and grocery list. Teachers
should teach these skills as discrete responses
and should also teach children to apply them in
different (multiple) response chains. A further
implication of this characteristic is that as soon
as a child learns discrete behaviors, the child
should learn how to combine them in a number
of different response chains. This will allow
children to practice discrete responses across a
variety of chains and will promote generalization of skills.

THE CONCEPT OF READINESS

The concept of readiness refers to a state of
being prepared to act or to learn specific behaviors. Two conceptualizations of readiness exist. One has its origins in maturational theory as
described by Gesell and his colleagues. In this
view of readiness, genetic factors and physiological maturation are seen as important determinants of readiness. The development of
skills is influenced by children's maturation

rather than by their interactions with the environment. It is closely tied to the notion that
children progress through inevitable, predetermined sequences and stages. Thus, readiness
implies a state or period when children are particularly sensitive and "primed for" developing new skills (Havinghurst, 1972). This view
of readiness has been quite popular, but it frequently serves as a casual explanation for children's behavior that may be injurious. Persons
proposing such causal relationships express
them through statements that begin with "he is
not ready to . . ." and end with "let's wait and
see what happens."

The second conceptualization of readiness
reflects a learning approach to the development
of skills. According to this interpretation, readiness is defined as the state wherein children
are capable of performing the prerequisite behaviors necessary for doing more complex or
advanced skills (Cohen & Gross, 1979,
pp. 44–45). This conceptualization suggests
that each complex skill can be broken down
into a set of component steps or behaviors that
are revealed by conducting a task analysis.
Once sequences are identified, children's current abilities can be assessed against them.
Children are considered "ready" to learn any
step or even more complex skills if they can
perform the necessary, less difficult responses
in the sequence.

Both conceptualizations may have proponents. If the former view is adopted in the extreme, then the course of intervention simply
involves providing children with safe, nurturing environments. If the latter is advocated,
then intervention involves the specification of
theoretically and logically consistent sequences through which children acquire the responses needed to perform the more complex
skills. Environmental manipulations will be
identified that will maximize the probability of
children acquiring those prerequisite skills.
These manipulations need not be rigid, artificial, mechanical procedures. For example,
Dunst's (1981) curriculum for the sensorimotor period is an example of highly natural, ecological intervention strategies that are
implemented to facilitate the development of

specific abilities, some of which are prerequisite responses for more complex skills. The second conceptualization of readiness is the more defendable and is more consistent with an intervention or treatment perspective; this definition is the one used in the remainder of this chapter.

PREACADEMIC SKILLS

Definition of Preacademic Skills

Given that the primary academic skills are reading, writing, and solving mathematical problems, and that readiness can best be defined as that state wherein one has the capability to perform prerequisite skills, the question then becomes "what are preacademic skills?" The authors would suggest that *preacademic skills are those skills that are logically and/or empirically needed to read, write, and engage in mathematics at the initial first-grade level.* The initial first-grade level means the point when intentional academic instruction begins (i.e., when a teacher begins instructing a student to read, compute math facts, or write meaningful words). Preacademic responses in this definition are tied directly to these academic skills. This definition excludes many activities that are commonly viewed as readiness activities. The following quotation from *Becoming a Nation of Readers* (Anderson et al., 1985) illustrates this point.

> In the past, under the belief that it would develop readiness for reading, kindergarten children were taught to hop and skip, cut with a scissors, name the colors, and tell the difference between circles and squares. These may be worthwhile activities for four- and five-year-olds, but skill in doing them has a negligible relationship with learning to read. . . . There are schools, nonetheless, that still use reading readiness checklists that assess kicking a ball, skipping, or hopping. Thus, reading instruction is delayed for some children because they have failed to master physical skills or other skills with a doubtful relationship to reading. (p. 29)

Thus, a general notion of "readiness" is not applicable to this definition of preacademic skills; rather, readiness refers to specific behaviors needed to perform more complex skills. This definition also excludes preschool cognitive skills other than those directly related to academic behaviors. For example, concept formation is a legitimate preschool cognitive domain, but in light of this definition, only concepts that relate directly to the academic skills are included. Thus, concept formation in general is not addressed. This restrictive definition is adopted to adhere to space limitations and to focus instruction on later, academic outcomes.

A further distinction is needed concerning this definition. "Directly leads" refers to prerequisite skills or component skills rather than to behaviors that may predict future academic failure or success. For example, Simmer (1983) reviewed warning signs that appear to identify students who are at risk for later academic failure. He listed five response categories as predictive warning signs: 1) in-class verbal fluency; 2) in-class attention span, distractibility, or memory span; 3) in-class interest and participation; 4) letter or number identification; and 5) printing errors. While each of these may be important instructional targets, letter or numeral identification may simply be a predictor behavior rather than a prerequisite skill. For example, learning to name the letters alone may not promote reading skills, but learning *both* the letter names and their associated sounds may facilitate reading development (Anderson et al., 1985). Thus, letter naming may be a measure of some other important prerequisite skill such as using two-dimensional stimuli or general language development. The implication of such findings is that predictor behaviors may not be prerequisite responses and may therefore constitute inappropriate instructional targets.

Description of Preacademic Skills

To identify common preacademic skills, the authors reviewed articles, the preacademic or cognitive sections of several texts, curricula, and criterion-referenced and curriculum-referenced assessment instruments that are frequently used in early intervention programs for

Table 1. Proposed preacademic behaviors for prereading instruction

Preacademic skill	Description	Relationship to academic skill	Usefulness to nonacademic children[a]
Well-developed language system (at least receptive language) (Smith, 1977)	Child demonstrates ability to understand what is being communicated to her/him.	Allows child to determine meaning in what will be read	Student can use language for communication with others
Predict future events (Smith, 1977)	Child answers questions about what will happen next	Allows child to anticipate what will occur in text being read and thus adds meaning	Allows child to engage in more complex communicative exchanges
Awareness of print, books, and purpose of reading (McCormick, 1983) (Wiseman, 1984)	Child demonstrates understanding that environmental print is symbolic and that books, etc. provide information	Allows child to approach print as though it is symbolic; thus, it is something from which information can be obtained	Allows child to be aware of environmental signs and symbols
Auditory discrimination of relevant phonetic sounds (Neisworth, Willoughby-Herb, Bagnato, Cartwright, & Laub, 1980; Palardy, 1984)	Child indicates that different but similar sounds are not the same	Foundation skill for learning that sounds are related to specific symbols	Minimal
Auditory blending of phonetic sounds (Cohen & Gross, 1979)	Child combines phonemes to produce words	Foundation for combining sounds to form words	Minimal
Auditory segmentation of series of phonetic sounds (Allan, 1982; Cohen & Gross, 1979)	Child separates phonemes or syllables within a word (presented auditorily)	Foundation for letter/sound training	Minimal
Visual discrimination of letters/words (Palardy, 1984)	Child indicates that different but similar letters/words are not the same	Allows child to learn skill needed for associating graphic symbols with referent	Allows child to learn important useful words needed in community
Matching letters/words (Brigance, 1978; Cohen & Gross, 1979)	Child indicates that same letters/words are the same	Allows child to learn skills needed for associating graphic symbols with referent	Allows child to learn important useful words needed in the community
Letter/word recognition and identification (Brigance, 1978; Cohen & Gross, 1979)	Child indicates letter/word when named by another, or names letter/word when asked	Allows child to learn that given graphic symbol has specific name, and in the case of words, specific meaning	Allows child to respond to words in the community
Sounds/letter match, recognition, and identification (Brigance, 1978; Neisworth et al., 1980)	Child indicates letter associated with given sound or indicates sound associated with given letter	Allows child to attempt new words and to learn their meaning	Minimal
Left-to-right sequence, top-to-bottom sequence, and front-to-back sequence (Neisworth et al., 1980)	Child interacts with sequenced materials using these sequences	Allows child to approach print as a source of information	May allow child to "read" picture books

[a]*Usefulness to nonacademic children* refers to the possible utility of the preacademic skill for children with whom later academic instruction in reading would be inappropriate; these statements indicate the potential usefulness of the skill despite the possiblity that the child may never use reading to obtain information.

handicapped children. Selected prerequisite behaviors from this review are shown in Tables 1, 2, and 3. This listing does not represent an empirical documentation of prerequisite behaviors; rather, responses have been listed that are, in the authors' judgment, logically related to later academic behaviors. Some students appropriately will not receive later instruction in academic skills; however, some of the preacademic behaviors may still have value for them. The right-hand column of the tables rep-

resents the potential relevance of skills for students who will not be taught to read, write, or compute math problems.

INSTRUCTION OF PREACADEMIC SKILLS

General Instructional Issues

As with any potential instructional target, several issues should be considered prior to imple-

Table 2. Proposed preacademic behaviors for prewriting instruction

Preacademic skill	Description	Relationship to academic skill	Usefulness to nonacademic children[a]
Grasps writing instrument and scribbles (LeMay, Griffin, & Sanford, 1977; Neisworth et al., 1980)	Child produces marks on paper with writing instrument	Allows child to learn that the writing instrument will produce marks	Minimal
Holds writing instrument with fingers and scribbles (Fredericks et al., 1976; Neisworth et al., 1980)	Child produces marks on paper with writing instrument	Allows child to learn that the writing instrument will produce marks	Minimal
Imitates specific strokes (e.g., circular, vertical, horizontal, diagonal) in isolation (Fredericks et al., 1976; Neisworth et al., 1980)	Child imitates another person making specific marks	Allows child to learn skill that will be used in forming letters or words	Minimal
Traces or copies from two-dimensional model specific strokes in isolation (Fredericks et al., 1976; Neisworth et al., 1980)	Child produces strokes that match a two-dimensional model	Allows child to learn skill that will be used in forming letters	Minimal
Imitates, traces, copies from models (live or two-dimensional) that combine strokes to form letters (Haring, White, Edgar, Affleck, Hayden, Munson, & Bendersky, 1981; LeMay et al., 1977)	Child produces combined strokes needed to print letters or numerals	Allows child to produce forms that can be labeled as letters or numerals	Minimal
Prints letters or numerals without model (Cohen & Gross, 1979; Fredericks et al., 1976)	Child produces letters or numerals without model	Allows child to produce letters without model; thus, will be useful for writing	Minimal
Prints combinations of letters using left to right sequence (Cohen & Gross, 1979)	Child produces letters to form words by moving from left to right	Allows child to print words	Minimal

[a]*Usefulness to nonacademic children* refers to the possible utility of the preacademic skill for children with whom later academic instruction in writing would be inappropriate; these statements indicate the potential usefulness of the skill despite the possibility that the child may never use writing to communicate.

Table 3. Proposed preacademic behaviors for premath instruction

Preacademic skill	Description	Relationship to academic skill	Potential usefulness to nonacademic children[a]
Rote counting (Baroody & Price, 1983; Fredericks et al., 1976)	Child verbally says numerals in sequence	Serves as a basis for counting objects	Minimal
Rational counting (Clements, 1984; Tawney, Knapp, O'Reilly, & Pratt, 1979).	Child counts objects, enumerating each object once and stopping at last object	Allows child to count objects and use counting to solve problems requiring counting	Allows child to count objects in real situations
Cardinal counting (Baroody & Snyder, 1983; Clements, 1984)	Child demonstrates that the last number counted in a set is the number of items in that set (i.e., responds correctly to "How many?"	Serves as foundation for working with numerals to solve computation problems	Allows child to determine how many objects, etc., are in a set
Matches/compares sets (Baroody & Snyder, 1983; Cohen & Gross, 1979; Tawney et al., 1979)	Child identifies sets of objects as same, more, or less	Allows child to make judgments about amount in computation problems	Allows child to make judgments of objects in sets
Recognizes and names numerals (Cohen & Gross, 1979; Fredericks et al., 1976; Neisworth et al., 1980)	Child responds correctly to "Show me (the numeral named)" and "what is this?" (numeral shown)	Provides foundation for using numerals in computation problems	Minimal
Matches numeral to set and correct number of objects to numeral (Cohen & Gross, 1979; Neisworth et al., 1980)	Child places correct numeral on set with correct number of objects; places correct number of objects on numeral	Foundation for using numerals to represent amount	Allows child to use numerals for solving everyday problems dealing with amount (e.g., recipes, directions)

[a]*Usefulness to nonacademic children* refers to the possible utility of the preacademic skill for children with whom later academic instruction in math would be inappropriate; these statements indicate the potential usefulness of the skill despite the possibility that the child may never use math for computation or problem solving.

menting instruction. Four such issues relative to teaching preacademic behaviors are discussed below.

Deciding Whether to Teach Preacademic Skills   Deciding to teach a behavior to a given child is, by practice and by legal mandate, an individualized decision, and should be based on a number of factors. Some of these factors include the child's current abilities, the current demands of the environment, the demands of probable future environments, other instructional priorities, and parents' perceptions about, and goals for, their child's current and future performance. In the case of preacademic skills, the probability that the student will eventually use the academic skills as the means

to obtain useful ends should be considered. Preacademic skills, as defined in this chapter, could be considered optional for some children. This statement would not be true of other skill domains such as social interaction, play, and communication. Children who will learn and use academic skills as generalized means to specific ends should probably be taught the preacademic skills as early as possible. Children with sensory handicaps will require adaptions in the nature of the preacademic behaviors and in the methods used for instruction. Other children may use some of the academic skills for narrow purposes but not use them as generalized means. For example, a student may learn to count and will find occasion to use that skill as an adult, but she or he may not learn computational skills sufficiently to apply them in everyday contexts. Still other children may never make use of the academic skills; therefore, instruction in the preacademic skills may be a waste of valuable intervention time and other more useful and meaningful behaviors should be targeted. One's ability to teach a given child specific preacademic behaviors clearly is insufficient justification for doing so. The decision about whether to teach preacademic skills must be made, at times, without the advantage of adequate predictors of future performance. In such cases, teams should consider parental desires, professional judgments, and the "principle of the least dangerous assumption" (Donnellan, 1984). This principle suggests that when faced with the absence of clear data, decisions should be made that will result in the least harm to the student if the decision is incorrect.

Selecting Appropriate Instructional Strategies With many of the preacademic skills, teams are faced with an interesting paradox: data suggest several procedures will be effective, but do not suggest which to use (Wolery, Ault, Doyle, & Gast, 1986). In the absence of clear data, several guidelines are suggested. First, procedures should be selected that are appropriate for the phase of learning that is evidenced by child performance. In general, procedures that provide ample antecedent information should be used during *acquisition* of skills. Increasing response rates and practice time by manipulating consequences appears to facilitate *fluency* building. Thinning and delaying reinforcement schedules, using natural reinforcers, and duplicating natural reinforcement schedules are likely to facilitate *maintenance* of acquired behavior. Carefully selecting examples for instruction, and varying examples, trainers, training formats, and instructional settings appear to facilitate *generalization* of learned responses. When the phase of learning is identified for a child, then the instructional strategies that best match that phase should be selected.

Second, procedures should be selected that are effective *and* efficient. Efficiency in pre-

academic skills instruction should include low rates or percentages of errors, few trials to criterion, small number of minutes in direct instruction time, and minimal teacher preparation time. Further, procedures that promote learning more than one skill at a time would be considered more efficient. Unfortunately, there has been minimal research comparing instructional strategies directly, and even fewer studies have presented data on the efficiency of procedures (Billingsley & Romer, 1983; Wolery et al., 1986; Wolery & Gast, 1984).

Third, procedures should be selected that allow student initiation and that minimize the artificial nature of the instructional sessions. While considerable research exists on the effectiveness of naturalistic teaching procedures for communication objectives (cf., Halle, Alpert, & Anderson, 1984), much less exists for preacademic skills as defined in this chapter. Nonetheless, to facilitate generalized use of the preacademic skills, naturalistic procedures should be selected and evaluated for effectiveness and efficiency. However, as noted elsewhere (e.g., Barton, Brulle, & Repp, 1983; Keith, 1979), natural or less intrusive procedures should be used only if they are effective.

Fourth, the principle of parsimony should be used when selecting instructional strategies (Etzel & LeBlanc, 1979). The principle of parsimony states that when two or more solutions exist for a problem, then the simplest procedure should be employed. If two instructional procedures are equally effective and efficient, equally intrusive, and appear to match the phase of learning displayed by the child, then the simpler of the two procedures should be used. A hierarchy of instructional strategies based on intrusiveness and simplicity for initial acquisition may be: 1) environmental manipulations, 2) trial and error procedures, 3) naturalistic teaching strategies, 4) response prompting procedures, and 5) stimulus modification strategies.

Making Decisions about Instruction Since the experiential history of each subject is different, no single instructional strategy is likely to be the most effective and efficient procedure for all children. Conversely, no instructional strategy will remain the most appropriate for a given child. The appropriateness will change as children progress through the learning phases. Teams should use a variety of information sources including their professional judgment, past experiences, and comments from parents and other team members as a basis for decision-making. In addition, teams should regularly collect and review data on children's performance. Application of data decision rules to children's data should increase the probability that the correct decisions will be made, and may decrease unnecessary delays between decision points (Eaton, 1978; Haring, White, & Liberty, 1980; Wesson, Skiba, Sevcik, King, & Deno, 1984; White & Haring, 1980).

Teaching Tool Skills and Content   Several preacademic skills such as matching, naming, and marking with a pencil are used as tool skills to assess and teach other preacademic skills and behaviors. For example, if the instructional objective is to have children name letters, the teacher initially would have them match different letters to ensure that they are discriminating between the different forms. If the children do not match the letters consistently, it may be because they cannot match, or because they can match but cannot make the correct visual discriminations of the forms being matched. To control for the first possibility, the teacher should attempt several matching trials with objects or pictures the children consistently name. If they can match these stimuli consistently, then the teacher can infer that problems exist in visual discrimination of the letter forms rather than in their matching skills. When performance difficulties arise during instructional programs, a child's ability with the tool skills should be assessed, since most young children will have acquired these skills recently.

Instructional Strategies

In this section, specific instructional strategies are described that can be used to teach the preacademic behaviors listed above. These instructional strategies represent a sampling of the available instructional repertoire. Each of these can be used as *intentional interventions* to teach specific preacademic skills. The importance of rich, less restrictive, experiential strategies should not be minimized (e.g., Hohmann, Banet, & Weikart, 1979). Most of the literature in math and premath skills suggests it is important for children to have self-initiated, multiple, and varied interactions with quantity-referenced materials (Forman & Kuschner, 1977; Kamii & DeVries, 1978). The literature in reading suggests that language skills are critical contributors to reading success (cf. Anderson et al., 1985) and reading aloud to children is seen as particularly important (McCormick, 1983). Opportunities for interacting with such materials and activities are an important part of the curriculum and should be provided. The procedures described below are supplements to the regular experiential curriculum. They should be used when specific preacademic targets are sufficiently important to warrant direct instruction. Thus, an interventionist perspective rather than a developmental/descriptive orientation has been adopted; procedures are described that can be used for establishing preacademic behaviors rather than for describing conditions that result in acquisition of those behaviors for typical learners (See Carnine, 1983, for a discussion of the ramifications of such orientations). The instructional strategies are presented in a general parsimonious hierarchy that goes from the least to most restrictive.

Environmental Arrangements   Different environmental structures can influence the amount of contact children have with preacademic activities. For example, Jacobson, Bushell, and Risley (1969) required children who switched activities frequently to stop at a centrally located table and complete a matching activity. Although this action reduced the number of activity switches, it also increased the number of times students engaged in preacademic activities. Similarly, Rowbury, Baer, and Baer (1976) applied the Premack principle to increase the number of preacademic tasks students completed. Children earned tokens for completing preacademic tasks and exchanged these tokens for access to 5 minutes of free play. Over time, the number of tasks completed increased. Kincaid and Weisberg (1978) used tokens with alphabet letters written on them; during token exchange times they taught children to recognize the letters on the tokens. Such informal instruction resulted in children acquiring letter recognition and facilitated later letter naming. Although extensive examples and data do not exist for recommending a variety of environmental manipulations, the minimal cost in terms of teacher time suggests they are viable supplements to both regular experiential instruction and direct instruction of preacademic behaviors.

Intermittent Scaffolds, Models, Direct Commands, and Practice The title of this instructional practice comes, in part, from Cazden's (1983) article describing assistance provided by parents when talking with their children. This descriptor could apply to situations where instruction in preacademic skills is relatively unsystematic and unplanned. Observations of many preschool classrooms suggest this type of instruction occurs frequently. Scaffolds, as used here, are teacher verbalizations intended to elicit more elaborate responses from children. Scaffolds are tied to children's previous responses, and are requests for more information (information already known by the teacher). For example, a child is counting several objects, and stops at four; the teacher might provide a scaffold such as "what's next?" or "Is that all?" Models refer to telling the student the answer, but in this practice fading the model is done unsystematically. Thus, the teacher does not appear to be planning the transfer of stimulus control from the model to the natural stimuli. Direct commands refer to specifically asking students to perform some preacademic task. The consequences of complying with the commands are varied and unplanned. In preschools and elementary special education programs, scaffolds, models, and direct commands frequently are accompanied by repeated practice with the same materials. There are no data, to our knowledge, on the effectiveness of this approach. While it is simplistic and unrestrictive, the use of this strategy

certainly should be accompanied by frequent data collection to verify that children are learning.

Trial and Error with Differential Feedback A considerable amount of preacademic and academic instruction appears to use a trial and error format with differential feedback for correct and incorrect responses. In general, reinforcement for correct responses should be descriptive and should be easily discriminated from consequences for errors. The combination of error correction plus reinforcement for correct responses appears to facilitate learning more than correct reponse reinforcement alone or error correction alone (Ollendick, Matson, Esveldt-Dawson, & Shapiro, 1980; Singh, Singh, & Winton, 1984; Trap, Milner-Davis, Joseph, & Cooper, 1978).

Naturalistic Teaching Strategies Two frequently used naturalistic teaching strategies are incidental teaching and the mand-model procedure. Incidental teaching involves a brief interaction that is initiated by the child during low-structure situations and is used by the adult to elicit and reinforce an elaboration of the child's initiation. Incidental teaching has been used to facilitate the generalization of language behaviors taught in more structured situations (Hart & Risley, 1968) and to teach new language forms to preschoolers from economically disadvantaged homes (Hart & Risley, 1974, 1975). More recently, it has been used effectively to establish language responses in preschoolers and young elementary students with identified handicaps (Cavallaro & Paulson, 1985; McGee, Krantz, & McClannahan, 1985; Neef, Walters, & Egel, 1984). In each of the above studies, incidental teaching was used to facilitate language development (See Warren & Kaiser, this volume, for further discussion of this topic). Its use with preacademic skills has not been documented, but appears to deserve investigation. The issue needing study is whether the child's initiation can be used to teach preacademic behaviors related or unrelated to the child's original initiation.

The mand-model procedure is a variation of incidental teaching. The critical elements of the mand-model procedure are:

1. The teacher rather than the child initiates the interaction in a low-structure setting.
2. The teacher provides a mand (request, demand, instruction) to perform some verbal response.
3. The teacher gives feedback if the child responds correctly.
4. The teacher models the correct response if the child does not respond or responds incorrectly (Warren, McQuarter, & Rogers-Warren, 1984).

The mand-model procedure also has been used to facilitate language responses. Rogers-Warren and Warren (1980) used the procedure with children who had severe language delays to obtain generalization of language forms trained in more structured situations. Warren et al. (1984) used it to increase the number of verbalizations in obligatory and nonobligatory situations by children described as "unresponsive language delayed preschoolers." Finally, McGee, Krantz, Mason, and McClannahan (1983) used a procedure that operationally was identical to the mand-model procedure to teach autistic children receptive object labels. Because the procedure involves teacher-initiated rather than child-initiated trials, it may be useful in the acquisition and/or generalization of pre-academic behaviors. In one initial study (Ault, Gast, Wolery, Godby, & Doyle, 1986), elementary-age students with mental retardation learned letter naming using the mand-model procedure. An important question for further investigation is whether the teacher's mand must be related to materials with which the child is engaged. Another important area needing study is the documentation of the effects, if any, on child-directed behavior when the mand-model procedure is used for pre-academic instruction. When these studies are completed, a better evaluation of the mand-model procedure for teaching preacademic behaviors can be made.

Model-Lead-Test, Antecedent Prompt and Test, or Demonstration-Prompt-Practice Procedure
These procedures are variations of trial and error instruction with feedback for re-

sponses. The model-lead-test and antecendent prompt and test procedures use a model or other prompt on initial trials (with or without subsequent imitation), and then provide trials where the child responds without a model/prompt (test trials). Corrective feedback may be provided for errors and reinforcement for correct responses (Becker & Carnine, 1981; Wolery et al., 1986). Thus, the teacher may present a series of stimuli (pictures or letters) to be named; she or he would show and name all of the stimuli, and then show the children the stimuli and ask them to provide the label. If children correctly labeled the picture, reinforcement would follow, and training would progress to the next stimulus. If errors occurred, the teacher would model the correct label and ask for imitation of that model. Although limited literature was found using the model-lead-test procedure with preschool handicapped children (cf. Fink & Sandall, 1978), it is commonly used with primary level children in academically oriented special education classrooms, and is a common element of direct instruction practices (Becker & Carnine, 1981). Thompson (1984) compared the model-lead-test procedure to a procedure wherein the Language Master (with daily tests) was used for teaching sight words to primary level children with diagnoses of learning disabilities. Both procedures were effective in establishing criterion level performance, but the model-lead-test procedure required less instruction time per word.

The demonstration-prompt-practice procedure is similar to the model-lead-test procedure in that a demonstration is provided, and then teachers engage in supervised practice where prompts are given as necessary to individual students. Independent practice without teacher supervision is also a critical element of this procedure. When errors occur during independent practice, demonstrations and supervised practice are reinstated (Stevens & Rosenshine, 1981).

Time Delay
Time delay is a procedure that has been widely used to teach language and other discrete responses to students with moderate to severe handicaps (Snell & Gast, 1981;

Wolery et al., 1986). Two types of time delay exist: progressive and constant. In both types initial trials are presented at a 0-second delay; the teacher presents the task direction and immediately provides a controlling prompt that elicits the response from the learner. On subsequent trials, the controlling prompt is systematically delayed after the presentation of the task request. With constant time delay, the prompt is delayed for a fixed amount of time (e.g., 4 seconds) on all subsequent trials. With progressive time delay, the prompt is delayed for progressively longer periods of time after the task direction. For example, the first session would be at 0-second delay, the next session at 1-second, the next at 2-seconds, and so on. The range of skills taught using the procedure include communication skills such as instruction following (Striefel, Bryan, & Aikens, 1974), manual sign production (Kleinert & Gast, 1982; Kohl, Wilcox, & Karlan, 1978), manual sign reading (Smeets & Striefel, 1976), and requesting (Charlop, Schreibman, & Thibodeau, 1985; Halle, Marshall, & Spradlin, 1979). It has also been used to teach domestic/ vocational skills such as bed-making (Snell, 1982) and task assembly (Walls, Haught, & Dowler, 1982).

Progressive time delay has been effective in teaching sight word reading to students with handicaps, but has not been used with preschool children. For example, Browder, Hines, McCarthy, and Fees (1984) taught eight adults with moderate retardation to read sight words in booklets describing daily living tasks. These students learned the trained sight words and generalized them to different booklets where the same words were used. McGee and McCoy (1981) compared trial and error training to both progressive time delay and to a fading procedure where picture referents were superimposed on the written word using slide projectors. Both time delay and the fading procedure were more effective than trial and error procedures, and subjects' learning history with either the delay or fading procedure appeared to influence their later performance. When students were introduced first to the fading procedure, then it appeared to be more effective

than progressive time delay; when delay was introduced first, then delay appeared to be more effective than fading. Bradley-Johnson, Sunderman, and Johnson (1983) compared stimulus fading to constant time delay and to a no treatment control group. They taught preschool children, who apparently did not have handicapping conditions, to discriminate between letters that are "easily confused." The fading procedure consisted of highlighting the relevant feature of each letter in red and then fading the intensity of the red cue over time. The constant time delay used a 4-second delay. However, it is unclear from the description of this study whether 0-second delay trials were provided. Although the fading resulted in a slightly higher mean number of letters learned, the difference was not statistically significant. The constant delay procedure, however, produced fewer errors on all letters from pre- to posttest performance and those differences were statistically significant. Touchette and Howard (1984) used progressive time delay to successfully teach three students (including a 6-year-old and a 7-year-old) with moderate retardation to point to alphabet letters when named by a teacher. Their study investigated the effects of different schedules of reinforcement for responding correctly before and after the prompt. A richer schedule of reinforcement for responding before the prompt produced the most rapid transfer of stimulus control to the task direction. However, transfer occurred even when responding after the prompt was on a richer schedule of reinforcement. This study suggests that the effectiveness of the time delay procedure cannot be attributed totally to the schedule of reinforcement. Constant time delay has been used to teach an 11-year-old student with learning disabilities to spell words correctly (Stevens & Schuster, 1987), and Johnson (1977) taught a 17-year-old student to identify pictures of animals, to answer addition problems, and to name geometric shapes. This acquisition occurred with minimal errors.

Three studies have compared progressive and constant time delay with sight word reading (Ault, Gast, & Wolery, in press; Precious, 1985; Thomas, 1986). Ault et al. (in press) used the two procedures to teach community-referenced words to primary-school-age children with moderate retardation; Precious (1985) and Thomas (1986) taught Dolch sight words to primary-school-age children with learning disabilities. In all three studies, both procedures were effective, and for most subjects both procedures were equally efficient in terms of sessions, trials, errors, and direct instruction time to criterion. With each study, one procedure appeared to be slightly more efficient with selected subjects. These differences, however, did not favor one procedure across all subjects, and no clear evidence existed for the differences, although variations in subjects' learning histories were suspected. No differences were noted for generalization of the trained words to sentences.

System of Least Prompts The system of least prompts, also called increasing assistance or least-to-most prompting (Billingsley & Romer, 1983), has been used extensively to teach older students with moderate and severe handicaps. The range of skills taught include toothbrushing (Horner & Keilitz, 1975), janitorial skills (Cuvo, Leaf, & Borakove, 1978), laundry skills (Cuvo, Jacobi, & Sipko, 1981), putting on a hearing aid (Tucker & Berry, 1980), mending skills (Cronin & Cuvo, 1979), and leisure skills (Neitupski & Svoboda, 1982).

The system of least prompts requires the development of a prompt hierarchy based on the intrusiveness of the prompt. Usually, three to four different levels of prompts are employed; the levels would include, for example, verbal prompts, modeling, and physical prompts. Each trial begins with a task direction; if there is no response, or an error occurs, the task direction is repeated and the least intrusive level of prompt is provided (e.g., verbal prompt); if no response or an error occurs, the next most intrusive level of prompt (e.g., model) is provided. This continues until the child responds correctly.

Limited data were found where the system of least prompts was used to teach preacademic skills to preschoolers with handicaps. Rynders, Behlen, and Horrobin (1979) attempted to teach 3-year-old children with Down syndrome to perform selected preacademic tasks. The results of this study were clearly mixed; that is, the system of least prompts was not always effective. Despite this questionable data, use of the system of least prompts to teach other skills has met with success. For example, Correa, Poulson, and Salzberg (1984) used three levels of prompts to teach three preschool children with blindness and severe to profound mental retardation to reach for and grasp toys. This procedure was effective in establishing reaching at midline and to the right or left. Mosk and Bucher (1984) taught preschoolers with moderate to severe retardation to place pegs in specific holes in a peg board. They compared a four prompt sequence to the same prompt sequence plus stimulus shaping (i.e., a sequence of boards that had progressively more holes in them). Combining stimulus shaping and the system of least prompts was more effective and more efficient than using the system of least prompts alone.

The system of least prompts also has been compared in effectiveness to that of progressive time delay for teaching discrete responses such as object identification to elementary-age students with severe retardation (Godby, Gast, & Wolery, 1987) and manual sign production to adolescent students with severe and moderate handicaps (Bennett, Gast, Wolery, & Schuster, 1986). Both procedures were effective, but progressive time delay was more efficient because it required fewer sessions, trials, errors, and minutes of direct instruction time to reach criterion. However, the system of least prompts has the potential of providing incidental information during the presentation of the prompt levels; this issue requires additional research.

Stimulus Modifications The instructional strategies previously described rely on response shaping (e.g., trial and error plus differential feedback), or on prompting correct performance, reinforcing the behavior in the presence of the appropriate stimulus, and then decreasing the prompt through some fading procedure. In the above strategies, the stimulus to which the child is expected to respond remains the same throughout instruction. With the stimulus modification procedures, the stimulus to which children respond is systematically changed (Etzel & LeBlanc, 1979; Goetz, 1982). There are three types of stimulus modifications: stimulus shaping, stimulus fading, and superimposition and shaping or fading. In stimulus shaping, the *relevant dimension* of the stimulus is changed over trials or sessions from a level where the child can initially make the correct discrimination to the level in the final objective. Thus, if the relevant or critical dimension is shape, then the shape of the stimulus is systematically changed. In stimulus fading, *irrelevant dimensions* of the stimulus are systematically changed; if the relevant dimension is shape, then an irrelevant dimension such as the color or size of the stimulus is manipulated. There are two types of stimulus fading: criterion-referenced fading and noncriterion-referenced fading. In criterion-referenced fading, the manipulation is made on the relevant dimension, but the relevant dimension does not change. For example, when discriminating letters from one another, shape is the relevant dimension; a color could be placed on the part of the letter that is needed for the discrimination (i.e., the distinctive feature). In noncriterion-referenced fading, the color would be placed on a redundant part of the stimulus rather than on the distinctive feature. In superimposition, the criterion or ultimate stimulus is shown and some manipulation of that stimulus is placed over it; stimulus shaping and fading are then employed in the modification of the superimposed stimulus.

Although stimulus fading and superimposition and fading are sometimes effective (e.g., McGee & McCoy, 1981), stimulus fading may not result in learning (Koegel & Rincover, 1976). Stimulus fading should be avoided because it requires children to shift the basis on which they make discriminations from an irrelevant dimension to the relevant dimension. Although considerable research has been conducted with stimulus modification procedures, we recommend that they be the strategy of last choice. Stimulus modification procedures can be costly in terms of materials and especially in

terms of teacher preparation time (LeBlanc, Etzel, & Domash, 1978). Further, when using the stimulus modification procedures, the teacher must make continuous decisions about whether the stimulus changes are occurring too quickly or too slowly (Bradley-Johnson et al., 1983).

Instructional Variables

In addition to the instructional strategies described above, several instructional variables appear to be important for teaching preacademic and academic responses. As with the instructional strategies, much of this information comes from special education programs with older students and from regular education, specifically the "teacher effectiveness" literature. These issues are summarized here under four headings: format, presentation (delivery), feedback, and performance levels.

Variables Related to Instructional Formats Although instruction should be individualized or targeted to the needs of each child, group presentation appears to be important (Stevens & Rosenshine, 1981). Small group instruction has practical benefits such as allowing children to receive instruction for larger portions of the instructional day. It also has potential for observational learning, more child-to-child interaction than one-on-one instruction, and perhaps facilitates generalization more than one-on-one instruction. The reader is referred to Reid and Favell (1984) for a comprehensive review of the types of group instruction and their efficacy with special populations.

Variables Related to Presentation or Delivery of Instruction Several variables related to presentation of examples influence children's learning. Regular review of previously learned material appears important for maintenance of skills. In addition, rapid presentation of trials appear to facilitate learning more than slower presentation rates (Brophy, 1983; Carnine, 1976; Koegel, Dunlap, & Dyer, 1980). Having increased opportunities to respond, both as a part of a group and individually, appears to promote learning (Brophy, 1983; Hall, Delquardi, Greenwood, & Thurston, 1982).

Presentation of a variety of "best examples," negative examples, and confirmatory examples appears to facilitate acquisition of concepts (Clark, 1971); further, varied examples that begin with a high degree of representiveness and proceed to a lesser degree should be presented (Rosenshine, 1983). Related to presentation of examples is whether distributed, massed, or spaced trial formats should be used. Generally, researchers recommend using distributed trial formats (Mulligan, Lacy, & Guess, 1982). Kaczmarek (1982) used motor activities as a basis for distributing opportunities for language instruction to other settings. Finally, monitoring children's performance is necessary for making accurate decisions about needed changes in instruction.

Variables Related to Feedback on Performance "Teachers with skill in providing immediate teacher feedback (e.g., reinforcement, prompts, or hints) following correct responses and errors produce greater learning than teachers who do not provide immediate feedback or who tell correct answers following errors" (Englert, 1984, p. 38). Rosenshine (1983) suggests classifying children's responses into four types: "correct—and quick and firm, correct—but hesitant, incorrect but careless, and incorrect but lacking knowledge of facts or a process" (p. 344). He indicates that all incorrect responses should be corrected. Careless incorrect responses should be simply corrected and incorrect responses that seem to indicate lack of understanding should be dealt with by providing hints or prompts or by reteaching. Firmly correct responses are not specifically responded to, but the fluency building activities should continue. The intent of this is to maintain the pace of the drill and practice and to keep children's attention focused on the activity (Anderson, Evertson, & Brophy, 1979). Correct but hesitant responses should be acknowledged with brief, positive feedback (e.g., "right") and followed by brief reiteration or expansion of the process used to arrive at the correct response. Clearly, teachers' feedback should be determined individually by the responses children produce.

Variables Related to Performance Levels Ideally, children will learn without errors

(Snell & Gast, 1981), but in reality some errors usually occur. For initial instruction, students should have success rates of at least 70%–80% (Brophy & Evertson, 1976) and between 95%–100% for independent work (Fisher, Berliner, Filby, Marliave, Cahen, & Dishaw, 1980). Rosenshine (1983) indicates that these success levels are reached by carefully providing instruction in small, sequenced steps, continuously monitoring children's progress, providing frequent reviews, and continuing child practice of skills to the point of overlearning so that responses become "automatic." This appears particularly important for younger children in initial academic skill instruction because of the hierarchical nature of the skills being learned.

RESEARCH NEEDS

Three general needs are easily identified from the current research on preacademic skill instruction for preschool children with handicaps. These needs are reflected in the following questions: 1) What are legitimate preacademic skills for preschoolers with handicaps? 2) In what sequences should those skills be taught? and 3) How can these skills be taught efficiently so that generalized outcomes result? By asking these questions, the authors are suggesting that much of what is currently known about preacademic skills and instruction of those skills with preschoolers who have handicaps comes from two sources: the special education studies of older children and academic instruction of typical children. The relevance of these data are open to question. In a review of the journals that are specifically devoted to early childhood special education, only a very small proportion of articles could be identified as being devoted primarily to instruction. An even smaller proportion of articles concern instruction of preacademic skills. Research in the field of early childhood education has examined many useful and relevant issues, but researchers have perhaps ignored one of their primary responsibilities as educational interventionists: determining how to effectively and efficiently teach important skills to specific learners.

REFERENCES

Allan, K. K. (1982). The development of young children's metalinguistic understanding of the word. *Journal of Educational Research, 76,* 89–92.

Anderson, L. M., Evertson, C. M., & Brophy, J. E. (1979). An experimental study of effective teaching in first-grade reading groups. *Elementary School Journal, 79,* 193–223.

Anderson, R. C., Hiebert, E. H., Scott, J. A. & Wilkinson, I. A. G. (1985). *Becoming a nation of readers: The report of the commission on reading.* Washington, DC: The National Institute of Education.

Ault, M. J., Gast, D. L., & Wolery, M. (in press). Comparison of delay procedures in teaching functional word reading to moderately handicapped children. *American Journal of Mental Retardation.*

Ault, M. J., Gast, D. L., Wolery, M., Godby, S., & Doyle, P. M. (1986). *A Comparison of progressive time delay and modified mand-model procedure in teaching letter and photograph identification.* Unpublished manuscript, University of Kentucky, Lexington.

Bailey, D. B., & Wolery, M. (1984). *Teaching infants and preschoolers with handicaps.* Columbus, OH: Merrill.

Baroody, A. J., & Price, J. (1983). The development of the number-word sequence in the counting of three-year-olds. *Journal for Research in Mathematics Education, 14,* 361–367.

Baroody, A. J., & Snyder, P. M. (1983). A cognitive analysis of basic arithmetic abilities of TMR children. *Education and Training of the Mentally Retarded, 18,* 253–259.

Barton, L. E., Brulle, A. R., & Repp, A. C. (1983). Aversive techniques and the doctrine of the least restrictive alternative. *Exceptional Education Quarterly, 4*(3), 1–8.

Becker, W. C., & Carnine, D. W. (1981). Direct instruction: A behavior theory model for comprehensive educational intervention with the disadvantaged. In S. W. Bijou and R. Ruiz (Eds.), *Behavior modification: Contributions to education* (pp. 145–210). Hillsdale, NJ: Lawrence Erlbaum Associates.

Bennett, D., Gast, D. L., Wolery, M., & Schuster, J. W. (1986). Time delay and system of least prompts: A comparison in teaching manual sign production. *Education and Training of the Mentally Retarded, 21,* 117–129.

Billingsley, F. F., & Romer, L. T. (1983). Response prompting and the transfer of stimulus control: Methods, research, and a conceptual framework. *The Journal of the Association for the Severely Handicapped. 8*(2), 3–12.

Bradley-Johnson, S., Sunderman, P., & Johnson C. M. (1983). Comparison of delayed prompting and fading for teaching preschoolers easily confused letters and numbers. *Journal of School Psychology, 21,* 327–335.

Bricker, D. D. (Ed.), (1982). *Intervention with at-risk and handicapped infants: From research to application.* Baltimore: University Park Press.

Brigance, A. H. (1978). *Inventory of early development.* Woburn, MA: Curriculum Associates.

Brophy, J. E. (1983). Classroom organization and management. *Elementary School Journal, 83,* 254–285.

Brophy, J. E., & Evertson, C. M. (1976). *Learning from teaching: A developmental perspective.* Boston: Allyn & Bacon.

Browder, D. M., Hines, C., McCarthy, L. J., & Fees, J.

(1984). A treatment package for increasing sight word recognition for use in daily living skills. *Education and Training of the Mentally Retarded, 19,* 191–200.

Carnine, D. W. (1976). Effects of two teacher-presentation rates on off-task behavior, answering correctly, and participation. *Journal of Applied Behavior Analysis, 9,* 199–206.

Carnine, D. W. (1983). Direct instruction: In search of instructional solutions for educational problems. In *Interdisciplinary voices in learning disabilities and remedial education* (pp. 1–66). Austin, TX: PRO-ED.

Cavallaro, C. C., & Paulson, C. L. (1985). Teaching language to handicapped children in natural settings. *Education and Treatment of Children, 8*(1), 1–24.

Cazden, C. B. (1983). Adult assistance to language development: Scaffolds, models, and direct instruction. In R. P. Parker, & F. A. Davis (Eds.), *Developing literacy: Young children's use of language.* (3–18). Newark, DE: International Reading Association.

Charlop, M. H., Schreibman, L., Thibodeau, M. G. (1985). Increasing spontaneous verbal responding in autistic children using a time delay procedure. *Journal of Applied Behavior Analysis, 18,* 155–166.

Clark, D. C. (1971). Teaching concepts in the classroom: A set of teaching prescriptions derived from experimental research. *Journal of Educational Psychology, 62,* 253–278.

Clements, D. H. (1984). Training effects on the development and generalization of Piagetian logical operations and knowledge of number. *Journal of Educational Psychology, 76,* 766–776.

Cohen, M. A., & Gross, P. J. (1979). *The developmental resource: Behavioral sequences for assessment and program planning* (Vol. 2). New York: Grune & Stratton.

Correa, V. I., Poulson, C. L., & Salzberg, C. L. (1984). Training and generalization of reach-graph behavior in blind, retarded young children. *Journal of Applied Behavior Analysis, 17,* 57–69.

Cronin, K. A., & Cuvo, A. J. (1979). Teaching mending skills to retarded adolescents. *Journal of Applied Behavior Analysis, 12,* 401–406.

Cuvo, A. J., Jacobi, E., & Sipko, R. (1981). Teaching laundry skills to mentally retarded students. *Education and Training of the Mentally Retarded, 16,* 54–64.

Cuvo, A. J., Leaf, R. B., & Borakove, L. S. (1978). Teaching janitorial skills to the mentally retarded: Acquisition, generalization, and maintenance. *Journal of Applied Behavior Analysis, 11,* 345–355.

Donnellan, A. M. (1984). The criterion of the least dangerous assumption. *Behavior Disorders, 9,* 141–150.

Dunst, C. J. (1981). *Infant learning: A cognitive-linguistic intervention strategy.* Hingham, MS: Teaching Resources.

Durkin, D. (1980). *Teaching young children to read* (3rd ed.). Boston: Allyn and Bacon.

Eaton, M. D. (1978). Data decision and evaluation. In N. G. Haring, T. C. Lovitt, M. D. Eaton, & C. L. Hansen (Eds.), *The fourth R: Research in the classroom* (pp. 167–190). Columbus, OH: Merrill.

Englert, C. S. (1984). Effective direct instruction practices in special education settings. *Remedial and Special Education, 5*(2), 38–47.

Etzel, B. C., & LeBlanc, J. M. (1979). The simplest treatment alternative: Appropriate instructional control and errorless learning procedures for the difficult-to-teach child. *Journal of Autism and Developmental Disorders, 9,* 361–382.

Fink, W. T., & Sandall, S. R. (1978). One-to-one vs. Group academic instruction with handicapped and non-handicapped preschool children. *Mental Retardation, 16,* 236–240.

Fisher, C. W., Berliner, D. C., Filby, N. N., Marliave, R., Cahen, L. S., & Dishaw, M. M. (1980). Teaching behaviors, academic learning time, and student achievement. In C. Denham & A. Lieberman (Eds.), *Time to learn.* Washington, DC: Department of Education.

Forman, G. E., & Kuschner, D. (1977). *The child's construction of knowledge: Piaget for teaching children.* Monterey, CA: Brooks/Cole.

Fredericks, H. D., Riggs, C., Furey, T., Grove, D., Moore, W., McDonnell, J., Jordan, E., Hanson, W., Baldwin, V., & Wadlow, M. (1976). *The teaching research curriculum for moderate and severely handicapped.* Springfield, IL: Charles C Thomas.

Garwood, S. G., & Fewell, R. F. (1983). *Educating handicapped infants: Issues in development and intervention.* Rockville, MD: Aspen.

Godby, S., Gast, D. L., & Wolery, M. (1987). Comparison of time delay and system of least prompts for teaching object identification. *Research in Developmental Disabilities, 8,* 283–306.

Goetz, E. M. (1982). Behavior principles and techniques, In K. E. Allen & E. M. Goetz (Eds.), *Early childhood education: Special problems, special solutions.* Rockville, MD: Aspen.

Goldstein, H. (1983). Training generatve repertoires within agent-action-object miniature linguistic systems with children. *Journal of Speech and Hearing Research, 26,* 76–89.

Hall, R. V., Delquadri, J., Greenwood, C. R., & Thurston, L. (1982). The importance of opportunity to respond in children's academic success. In E. B. Edgar, N. G. Haring, J. R. Jenkins, & C. G. Pious (Eds.), *Mentally handicapped children: Education and training* (pp. 107–140). Baltimore: University Park Press.

Halle, J. W., Alpert, C. L., & Anderson, S. R. (1984). Natural environment language assessment and intervention with severely impaired preschoolers. *Topics in Early Childhood Special Education, 4*(2), 36–73.

Halle, J. W., Marshall, G. M., & Spradlin, J. E. (1979). Time delay: A technique to increase language usage and facilitate generalization in retarded children. *Journal of Applied Behavior Analysis, 12,* 431–439.

Hansen, C. L. (1978). Writing skills. In N. G. Haring, T. C. Lovitt, M. D. Eaton, & C. L. Hansen (Eds.), *The fourth R: Research in the classroom* (pp. 93–126). Columbus, OH: Merrill.

Haring, N. G., Lovitt, T. C., Eaton, M. D., & Hansen, C. L. (Eds.). (1978). *The fourth R: Research in the classroom.* Columbus, OH: Merrill.

Haring, N. G., White, O. R., Edgar, E. B., Affleck, J. Q., Hayden, A. H., Munson, R. G., & Bendersky, M. (Eds.). (1981). *Uniform Performance Assessment System.* Columbus, OH: Charles E. Merrill.

Haring, N. G., White, O. R., & Liberty, K. A. (1980). Rules for data-based strategy decisions in instructional programs: Current research and instructional implications. In W. Sailor, B. Wilcox, & L. Brown (Eds.), *Methods of instruction for severely handicapped stu-*

dents (pp. 159–192). Baltimore: Paul H. Brookes Publishing Co.

Hart B., & Risley, T. (1968). Establishing use of descriptive adjectives in the spontaneous speech of disadvantaged preschool children. *Journal of Applied Behavior Analysis, 1,* 109–120.

Hart, B. & Risley, T. (1974). Using preschool materials to modify the language of disadvantaged children. *Journal of Applied Behavior Analysis, 7,* 243–256.

Hart, B., & Risley, T. R. (1975). Incidental teaching of language in the preschool. *Journal of Applied Behavior Analysis, 8,* 411–420.

Havinghurst, R. J. (1972). *Developmental tasks and education.* New York: Longman.

Hohmann, M., Banet, B., & Weikart, D. P. (1979). *Young children in action: A manual for preschool educators.* Ypsilanti, MI: High/Scope Educational Research Foundation.

Horner, D. R., & Keilitz, I. (1975). Training mentally retarded adolescents to brush their teeth. *Journal of Applied Behavior Analysis, 8,* 301–309.

Horton, S. (1985). Computational rates of educable mentally retarded adolescents with and without calculators in comparison to normals. *Education and Training of the Mentally Retarded, 20*(1), 14–24.

Howell, K. W., Kaplan, J. S., & O'Connell, C. Y. (1979). *Evaluating exceptional children: A task analysis approach.* Columbus, OH: Merrill.

Jacobson, J. M., Bushell, D., & Risley, T. R. (1969). Switching requirements in a Head Start classroom. *Journal of Applied Behavior Analysis, 2,* 43–47.

Johnson, C. (1977). Errorless learning in a multihandicapped adolescent. *Education and Treatment of Children, 1*(1), 25–33.

Kaczmarek, L. A. (1982). Motor activities: A context for language/communication intervention. *Journal of the Division for Early Childhood, 6,* 21–35.

Kamii, C., & DeVries, R. (1978). *Physical knowledge in preschool education: Implications of Piaget's theory.* Englewood Cliffs, NJ: Prentice-Hall.

Keith, K. D. (1979). Behavior analysis and the principle of normalization. *AAESPH Review, 4,* 148–151.

Kincaid, M. S., & Weisberg, P. (1978). Alphabet letters as tokens: Training preschool children in letter recognition and labelling during a token exchange period. *Journal of Applied Behavior Analysis, 11,* 199. Abstract.

Kleinert, H. L., & Gast, D. L. (1982). Teaching a multihandicapped adult manual signs using a constant time delay procedure. *Journal of The Association for the Severely Handicapped, 7*(4), 25–32.

Koegel, R. L., Dunlap, G., & Dyer, K. (1980). Intertrial interval duration and learning in autistic children. *Journal of Applied Behavior Analysis, 13,* 91–99.

Koegel, R. L., & Rincover, A. (1976). Some detrimental effects of using extra stimuli to guide learning in normal and autistic children. *Journal of Abnormal Child Psychology, 4,* 59–71.

Kohl, F. L., Wilcox, B. L., & Karlan, G. R. (1978). Effects of training conditions on generalization of manual signs with moderately handicapped students. *Education and Training of the Mentally Retarded, 13*(3), 377–385.

Lamme, L. L., & Childers, N. M. (1983). The composing processes of three young children. *Research in Teaching of English, 17*(1), 31–50.

LeBlanc, J. M., Etzel, B. C., & Domash, M. A. (1978). A functional curriculum for early intervention. In K. E. Allen, V. A. Holm, & R. L. Schiefelbusch (Eds.), *Early intervention - a team approach* (pp. 331–381). Austin, TX: PRO-ED.

LeMay, D. W., Griffin, P. M., & Sanford, A. R. (1977). *Learning Accomplishment Profile - Diagnostic Edition.* Chapel Hill, NC: Chapel Hill Training and Outreach Project.

Lerner, J. W. (1976). *Children with learning disabilities* (2nd ed.). Boston: Houghton Mifflin.

Lovitt, T. C. (1984). *Tactics for teaching.* Columbus, OH: Merrill.

McCormick, S. (1983). Reading aloud to preschoolers age 3–6: A review of the research. *Reading Horizons, 24*(1), 7–11.

McGee, G. G., Krantz, P. J., Mason, D., & McClannahan, L. E. (1983). A modified incidental-teaching procedure for autistic youth: Acquisition and generalization of receptive object labels. *Journal of Applied Behavior Analysis, 16,* 329–338.

McGee, G. G., Krantz, P. J., & McClannahan, L. E. (1985). The facilitative effects of incidental teaching on preposition use by autistic children. *Journal of Applied Behavior Analysis, 18,* 17–31.

McGee, G. G., & McCoy, J. F. (1981). Training procedures for acquisition and retention of reading in retarded youth. *Applied Research in Mental Retardation, 2,* 263–276.

Mercer, C. D., & Mercer, A. R. (1985). *Teaching students with learning disabilities* (2nd ed.). Columbus, OH: Charles E. Merrill.

Mosk, M. D., & Bucher, B. (1984). Prompting and stimulus shaping procedures for teaching visual-motor skills to retarded children. *Journal of Applied Behavior Analysis, 17,* 23–43.

Mulligan, M., Lacy, L., & Guess, D. (1982). Effects of massed, distributed, and spaced trial sequencing on severely handicapped students' performance. *Journal of the Association for the Severely Handicapped, 7*(2), 48–61.

Neef, N. A., Walters, J., & Egel, A. L. (1984). Establishing generative yes/no responses in developmentally disabled children. *Journal of Applied Behavior Analysis, 17,* 453–460.

Neisworth, J. T., Willoughby-Herb, S. J., Bagnato, S. J., Cartwright, C. A., & Laub, K. W. (1980). *Individualized education for preschool exceptional children.* Rockville, MD: Aspen Systems.

Nietupski, J., & Svoboda, R. (1982). Teaching a cooperative leisure skill to severely handicapped adults. *Education and Training of the Mentally Retarded, 17*(1), 38–43.

Ollendick, T. H., Matson, J. L., Esveldt-Dawson, K., & Shapiro, E. S. (1980). Increasing spelling achievement: An analysis of treatment procedures utilizing an alternating treatments design. *Journal of Applied Behavior Analysis, 13,* 645–654.

Osborn, J., Wilson, P. T., & Anderson, R. C. (1985). *Reading education: Foundations for a literate America.* Lexington, MA: Lexington Books.

Palardy, J. M. (1984). Some thoughts on systematic reading readiness instruction. *Reading Horizons, 24,* 167–171.

Pearson, P. D. (Ed.). (1984). *Handbook of reading research.* New York: Longman.

Precious, C. (1985). *Efficiency study of two procedures: Progressive and constant time delay in teaching oral sight word reading.* Unpublished master's thesis, University of Kentucky, Lexington.

Reid, D. H., & Favell, J. (1984). Group instruction with persons who have severe disabilities: A critical review. *The Journal of the Association for Persons with Severe Handicaps, 9,* 167–177.

Rogers-Warren, A., & Warren, S. (1980). Mands for verbalization: Facilitating the generalization of newly trained language in children. *Behavior Modification, 4,* 230–245.

Rosenshine, B. (1983). Teaching functions in instructional programs. *Elementary School Journal, 83,* 335–352.

Rowbury, T. G., Baer, A. M., & Baer D. M. (1976). Interactions between teacher guidance and contingent access to play in developing preacademic skills of deviant preschool children. *Journal of Applied Behavior Analysis, 9,* 85–104.

Rynders, J. E., Behlen, K. L., & Horrobin, J. M. (1979). Performance characteristics of preschool Down's syndrome children receiving augmented or repetitive verbal instruction. *American Journal of Mental Deficiency, 84,* 67–73.

Simmer, M. (1983). The warning signs of school failure: An updated profile of the at-risk kindergarten child. *Topics in Early Childhood Special Education, 3*(3), 17–28.

Singh, N. S., Singh, J., & Winton, A. S. W. (1984). Positive practice overcorrection of oral reading errors. *Behavior Modification, 8,* 23–37.

Smeets, P. M., & Striefel, S. (1976). Acquisition of sign reading by transfer of stimulus control in a retarded deaf girl. *Journal of Mental Deficiency Research, 20,* 197–205.

Smith, F. (1977). Making sense of reading—and of reading instruction. *Harvard Educational Review, 47,* 386–395.

Snell, M. E. (1982). Analysis of time delay procedures in teaching daily living skills to retarded adults. *Analysis and Intervention in Developmental Disabilities, 2,* 139–155.

Snell, M. E., & Gast, D. L. (1981). Applying the time delay procedure to the instruction of the severely handicapped. *The Journal of the Association for the Severely Handicapped, 6*(3), 3–14.

Stevens, K., & Schuster, J. (1987). Teaching spelling words using time delay. *Learning Disabilities Quarterly, 10,* 9–16.

Stevens, R., & Rosenshine, B. (1981). Advances in research on teaching. *Exceptional Education Quarterly, 2*(1), 1–9.

Striefel, S. Bryan, K., & Aikins, D. (1974). Transfer of stimulus control from motor to verbal stimuli. *Journal of Applied Behavior Analysis, 6,* 123–135.

Tawney, J. W., Knapp, D. S., O'Reilly, C. D., & Pratt, S. S. (1979). *Programmed environments curriculum.* Columbus, OH: Merrill.

Thomas, T. (1986). *A comparison of progressive and constant time delay in teaching oral sight word reading.* Unpublished master's thesis, University of Kentucky, Lexington.

Thompson, A. (1984). *Increasing sight word recognition: An analysis of treatment procedures utilizing a parallel treatments design.* Unpublished master's thesis, University of Kentucky, Lexington.

Touchette, P. E., & Howard, J. S. (1984). Errorless learning: Reinforcement contingencies and stimulus control transfer in delayed prompting. *Journal of Applied Behavior Analysis, 17,* 175–188.

Trap, J. J., Milner-Davis, P., Joseph, S., & Cooper, J. O. (1978). The effects of feedback and consequences on transitional cursive letter formation. *Journal of Applied Behavior Analysis, 11,* 381–393.

Tucker, D. J., & Berry, G. W. (1980). Teaching severely multihandicapped students to put on their own hearing aides. *Journal of Applied Behavior Analysis, 13,* 65–75.

Walls, R. T., Haught, P., Dowler, D. L. (1982). Moments of transfer of stimulus control in practical assembly tasks by mentally retarded adults. *American Journal of Mental Deficiency, 87,* 309–315.

Warren, S. F., McQuarter, R. J., & Rogers-Warren, A. K. (1984). The effects of teacher mands and models on the speech of unresponsive language-delayed children. *Journal of Speech and Hearing Research, 49,* 43–52.

Wesson, C., Skiba, R., Sevcik, B., King, R. P., & Deno, S. (1984). The effects of technically adequate instructional data on achievement. *Remedial and Special Education, 5*(5), 17–22.

White, O. R. (1980). Adaptive performance objectives: Form versus function. In W. Sailor, B. Wilcox, & L. Brown (Eds.), *Methods of instruction for severely handicapped students* (pp. 47–69). Baltimore: Paul H. Brookes Publishing Co.

White, O. R., & Haring, N. G. (1980). *Exceptional teaching* (2nd ed.). Columbus, OH: Charles E. Merrill.

Wiseman, D. L. (1984). Helping children take early steps toward reading and writing. *The Reading Teacher, 37,* 340–344.

Wolery, M., Ault, M. J., Doyle, P. M., & Gast, D. L. (1986). *Comparison of instructional strategies: A literature review.* (U.S. Department of Education, Grant Number G008530197). Lexington, KY: Department of Special Education.

Wolery, M., & Gast, D. L. (1984). Effective and efficient procedures for the transfer of stimulus control. *Topics in Early Childhood Special Education, 4*(3), 52–77.

Chapter 8

Social Skill Intervention with Young Children with Handicaps
Some New Conceptualizations and Directions
Phillip S. Strain and Frank W. Kohler

THE ABILITY TO GET ALONG WITH one's peers, to make friends, to learn from others, and to cooperate are hallmarks of socially skillful children. At the same time, the absence of these skills is a major defining characteristic of young handicapped children. Children with sensory impairments (Sisson, Van Hasselt, Hersen, & Strain, 1985), autism (Odom, Strain, Karger, & Smith, 1986), mental retardation (Guralnick, 1986), learning disabilities (Cooke & Apolloni, 1976), and behavioral disorders (Strain & Timm, 1974) have all been shown to exhibit significant social skill deficits.

The pervasiveness of social skill deficits, however, is overshadowed by its impact, both short- and long-term, on handicapped children. In the short-term, the social skill deficits of handicapped children are known to result in peer rejection and scapegoating, disproportionate placement in special classes, and poor self-esteem (Strain, 1981). In the long-term, there is good evidence to suggest that social deficits in childhood inhibit cognitive development (Hartup, 1979), predispose children to delinquency, sexual dysfunction, and adult conduct problems (Roff, Sells, & Golden, 1972), and generally promote immature and aggressive solutions to adult problems in living (Strain, 1985).

At one level, the social skill instruction of preschool handicapped children is relatively straightforward, rather like instruction in any other performance domain. For example, researchers assess students' social skills, select objectives, design appropriate training opportunities, and assess the effects of instruction. However, this surface analysis of similarities can easily hide the truth about ignorance and fledgling attempts to influence the social world of young handicapped children. As a preface to the discussion that follows, the authors will first consider some factors known to influence the development and maintenance of social skills.

The etiology of social skill deficits and their continuity across time represent a complex interplay of person, peer group, and environmental variables. A partial list of these variables might include the following:

Person Variables: developmental level, temperament, physical intactness, sensory intactness, toy use skills, and motor ability.
Peer Group Variables: tolerance for differences, social history with handicapped

Preparation of this chapter was supported by Contract No. 300-82-0368 (Early Childhood Research Institute) from the Department of Education to the University of Pittsburgh. However, the opinions expressed herein do not necessarily reflect the position or policy of the U.S. Department of Education and no official endorsement should be inferred.

children, access to appropriate role models, regularity of exposure to handicapped children, and prior training on how to interact with handicapped children.

Environmental Variables: availability and number of cooperative-use toys, teacher prompts to play together, fixed time and locale for peer interaction to occur, and dramatic-play opportunities.

At any point in time, one may suspect that *all* of the above listed variables exert influence on children's social skills. That being the case, a singular focus of intervention will, in all likelihood, fail to achieve optimal results.

Both the complexity and the controversy associated with children's social skills are readily apparent as one considers two fundamental issues: a) how one defines social skills, and b) how one conceptualizes skill problems.

DEFINING SOCIAL SKILLS

At the most basic level of conceptualization, one may consider the question, "What's 'social' about social skills?" The social dimension of skillfulness may be, as Asher and his colleagues suggest, that which is associated with popularity, friendship, and peer acceptance (Asher & Hymel, 1981; Oden & Asher, 1977). Alternatively, social skillfulness may be subsumed under a universal concept of adaptive behavior, as in the American Association on Mental Deficiency (AAMD) classification scheme. Here, the "socialness" of skills is defined by the individual's compliance with and adaptation to the demands and expectations of society. Finally, "social" may be defined simply as those skills that a person uses to perform competently in the presence of other people (Gresham, 1986). In truth, each of these attempts to distinguish the *social* character of certain skills may have merit. What is not known at this point is which approach is superior conceptually, and which definition of "social" eventually leads to the most robust interventions.

Before elaborating on the social character of certain skills, the reader should briefly consider what is meant by "skill." Here, too, uncertainty abounds. At one end of the conceptual continuum, skills have been thought of as representing underlying personality types or traits (McFall, 1982). That is, extrovert, passive, and gregarious, for example, are terms representing more or less skillful behavior. At the other conceptual extreme, skills are thought to be molecular units of behavior (e.g., eye contact, voice tone, body posture) that are used in the course of social interaction.

It is doubtful that any consensual agreement will ever be forthcoming on the definition of social skill. What is certain, however, is that the choice of definition will dictate the content of instruction, and its subsequent evaluation. For the sake of illustration, suppose that one defines social skillfulness within a peer-acceptance model. Being accepted and befriended is being socially skillful. Likewise, children who are rejected and isolated lack social skills. It also follows logically, though it is not necessarily the case, that the interpersonal actions of accepted children will be different from those of rejected children. Given these differences researchers may choose to teach that repertoire exhibited by accepted children to children who are rejected by their peers. Of course, the impact of such instruction would be evaluated, most cautiously, by examining whether the student is more accepted by his or her peers following training.

From a quite different definitional perspective, let the reader assume that social skillfulness comprises only those motor and verbal behaviors that are used in the course of interaction with peers (cf. Gresham, 1986). Operating within this framework, having certain motor and verbal behaviors in one's repertoire suggests skillfulness; not having these behaviors suggests the opposite. Peer acceptance per se is not relevant here, rather the focus of intervention and its evaluation is on increasing certain behaviors.

Of the various definitional approaches, what has been labeled in various quarters as a *social validity* (Gresham, 1986) or *performance-based* (Odom & McConnell, 1985) orientation seems best suited to the early intervention enterprise. According to Gresham (1986), the *social validity definition would focus on those behaviors in given social situations that lead to important social outcomes for children.* Such outcomes may include peer acceptance, significant others' judgments of liking for the child or the child's behaviors, and the child's receipt of desired behaviors from peers. Odom and McConnell (1985) expand this definition to include parents', teachers', and siblings' judgments. In addition, their performance-based approach places considerable emphasis on the situation-specific nature of skillfulness.

It should be mentioned at this point that the general concept of social validity has received great attention in recent years, particularly in the behavioral intervention literature. Under the general rubric of social validity three related concepts have emerged: 1) social significance of the target behaviors, 2) social acceptability of the intervention procedures, and 3) social importance of behavior change to the consumers (i.e., the individual child and those significant others who interact with the child) (Wolf, 1978).

According to Wolf (1978), the *social validation* of intervention goals addresses the question of whether these target behaviors are desired or valued by society. In practice, this validation has been determined by soliciting the subjective evaluations of persons who might be considered to be the *consumers* of the behavior change. For example, Sainato, Strain, and Lyon (1986) conducted an intervention study in which three developmentally delayed preschoolers were taught to sit appropriately and to answer questions correctly in a group with seven other children. Following intervention, 10 kindergarten teachers were asked to view videotapes of the group instruction and to determine if the three youngsters could function successfully in their teaching groups. All teachers reported that the target children's behaviors were satisfactory and appropriate for their respective classrooms. In this case, teacher consumers provided evidence that the behavior change was of value.

A second type of social validation relates to the *social acceptability* of behavioral pro-cedures. The relevant implementation agents (i.e., teachers or parents) may evaluate social skill teaching procedures on a wide range of possible dimensions, ranging from the amount of initial preliminary training to the daily response cost or effort needed to implement the intervention. Based on these considerations, these adults are likely to evaluate certain interventions as more preferred or *socially acceptable* than others.

The *social validation* of intervention outcomes addresses the question of whether or not the quantity and quality of behavior change makes a difference in the students' everyday life. In social skill research, social importance is often associated with changes in sociometric standing. That is, one concludes that certain skills have social importance if changes in their levels are correlated with less rejection and more friendship choices. Although used less frequently, there is an increasing trend to use *standards of competence* to judge the social importance of behavior change. Put simply, a range of competent or acceptable behavior is determined and this range becomes the target for intervention. If the child's behavior eventually falls within the range of competent performance, it can be argued that a socially important change has occurred.

CONCEPTUALIZING SKILL PROBLEMS

Assuming a working definition of social skills from a social validity perspective, we next turn our attention to how one might conceptualize skill problems. Seeing that a child does not engage in behaviors that lead to peer acceptance or that the child's social repertoire does not match that of nonreferred youngsters is an important but incomplete analysis. The relevant question for initial assessment is: "What contributes to the observation of poor social performance?"

According to Gresham's (1986) approach, we can identify three contributing factors: 1) a lack of essential behavior prerequisites, 2) a lack of environmental supports for skill display, and 3) avoidance behavior mediated by fear and/or anxiety.

Skill deficiencies in the social repertoire are quite common, even for the least handicapped child. To the observer of children with significant cognitive and physical disabilities it is readily apparent that many of these children do not possess the basic communicative responses (e.g., ability to say, "Hello") and motor responses (e.g., ability to pass and catch a ball) that are used in social exchanges between young children. For more developmentally capable children, their skill deficits may be subtle, but no less debilitating. Examples of typical yet subtle deficits include giving a compliment in a flat or monotone voice, and always insisting on going "first" at a game. If a child has never been observed to display a certain skill, it is probably safe to assume that the problem is one of a skill deficit.

Some children occasionally display effective social skills, but for many reasons, usually having to do with the social environment, they simply do not perform at acceptable levels or at the right time and place. For example, it is often the case that young handicapped children's skills (social or otherwise) do not generalize from a teaching context to more naturalistic situations. How much of this problem is a direct consequence of faulty instruction is an interesting matter for speculation. Nevertheless, it is clear that many children can and do display appropriate social skills in fairly limited situations where immediate and massive environmental support for these skills is available. Still, other children may attempt to use their newly acquired social skills in different situations but may be met with overt rejection by peers. Finally, one sees children who are exposed to environments that directly promote the antithesis of positive social behavior. For example, observational research has shown that young children may be *seven times* more likely to receive responses from teachers when the children are behaving inappropriately than when they are behaving appropriately (Strain, Lamber, Kerr, Stagg, & Lenkner, 1983).

Over extended periods of time, a lack of skill and an absence of support for social skill development can produce emotional responses in children that are as limiting as any primary disability (Gresham, 1986). Where poorly developed skills and punitive peer behavior interact, the stage is set for avoidance behavior and other fear- and anxiety-induced means of escaping social encounters. Since successfully avoiding contact is usually reinforced (i.e., it reduces anxiety and fear), a vicious cycle can emerge in which children become more and more isolated from their peers. The full-blown avoidance behavior associated with fear and anxiety is not often noted in preschool children. However, the lack of detection may be as much a reflection of measurement limitations as it is a function of any developmental process with a lower age/developmental limit.

The conceptualization of a social skill problem, whether it is a simple lack of skill, a lack of environmental support, the result of fear and anxiety, or some combination thereof, must be dynamic in order to be useful. Assuming that all children with certain conditions must have skill deficits, and skill deficits alone, is ludicrous. Similarly, assuming that a skill deficit is noted and that correction of the deficit alone will be sufficient is a limited view of the complexities of social behavior. The authors suspect that, in most situations, a complete and careful child assessment over time will reveal certain skill deficits, certain environmental inhibitors, and possibly a healthy dose of fear and anxiety.

In the authors' view, the *social validity* or *performance-based* orientations toward social skill instruction and performance are rather humble beginnings. The unknowns far outweigh the known and it is largely true that most social skill assessments and treatments, whether they are practiced by researchers or by teachers, represent narrowly focused efforts. Such narrowly focused assessments and treatments are problematic because they assume, falsely, that one or a few approaches are superior. Such comparative information is just not available. The authors' suggestion, which is elaborated in the balance of this chapter, is that researchers should consider a multimodal approach to assessment and treatment.

MULTIMODAL ASSESSMENT MODEL

As noted earlier, researchers in the field have not reached a consensus on a definition of social competence for young children. As a result of these varying definitions, there exist a variety of different techniques for assessing and teaching social skills, as well as for evaluating the outcomes of these efforts. This diversity presents a serious problem for early childhood personnel who must ensure that all children receive the best social skills education possible. Compounding this problem, educators must resolve a number of difficult program issues. At least nine different questions are crucial to the development and evaluation of the social skills teaching program:

1. Who needs social skills training?
2. What skills should be taught?
3. At what rates and contextual conditions should these skills be used?
4. Who should act as the teaching agent?
5. How and where should the skills be taught?
6. How long should teaching efforts persist?
7. Do the teaching efforts produce a behavior change?
8. Are these changes generalizable across settings, forms, and over time?
9. Are the new behaviors important for their users?

While most professionals would readily agree on the importance of asking the above questions, the methods used to provide their answers vary greatly. For example, the range of measures used to identify children in need of social skills training include:

1. Self-reports
2. Peer sociometric nominations or ratings
3. Teacher nominations or ratings
4. Observations of children's performance in behavioral rehearsal or script situations
5. Observations of children's performance in natural free play settings
6. Observations of the behaviors that peers direct towards target children in natural free play settings
7. Observations of peers in natural settings in order to establish normative behavioral standards

Despite the numerous features contained in this list, few researchers or intervention programs have included more than one or two measures to identify candidates for their educational efforts. Such a limited and rather narrow assessment focus may well explain the current ambiguity and lack of methodological congruence within the social skills field.

As a partial solution to the problem, the authors propose that researchers use a wider range of measures to develop and evaluate social skill teaching methods. Table 1 illustrates a multimodal assessment model. Presented vertically are a series of nine questions relevant to the development (Questions 1–6) and evaluation (Questions 7–9) of social skill interventions. Along the horizontal axis are 2 general assessment sources that could provide acceptable, yet potentially different answers to these questions (i.e., behavioral observations and social validation). Each assessment source has numerous distinct categories. For example, behavioral observations include assessing the target child's social interactions, the behaviors of peers who interact with this child, and the interactions of normative peers. The social validation source entails four separate categories of adult satisfaction. Adult consumers may screen or identify children in need of training, choose intervention objectives or goals, select the most acceptable teaching procedures, and express satisfaction with all intervention outcomes.

Notably absent from Table 1 are peer sociometric nominations and ratings. During the past decade, sociometric procedures have been used widely to assess children's peer relations and to evaluate the outcome of social skills training (Asher & Hymel, 1981; McConnell & Odom, 1986). Despite their popularity, however, these assessment procedures have at least four shortcomings when used with preschool-age children. First, children's nominations or ratings of their peers are influenced by numerous nonbehavioral variables (i.e., physical attractiveness, sex) that are beyond the

Table 1. Intervention questions and relevant measures

Questions	Behavioral observations			Social validation			
	Target child	Peers	Normative peers	Screen participants	Select goals	Select procedures	Evaluate outcomes
Who needs social skills training?	X	X	X	X			
What skills should be taught?	X	X	X		X		
At what rates and conditions should skills be used?	X	X	X		X		
Who should teach?	X	X				X	
How and where should skills be taught?	X	X				X	
How long should teaching continue?	X	X					X
Did the teaching efforts produce a behavior change?	X	X					X
Is the behavior change generalizable?	X	X					X
Is the behavior change important?	X	X	X				X

realm of social skills teaching efforts (Foster & Ritchey, 1979). Second, young children's reports generally result in poor test-retest reliability unless time consuming rating procedures with photographs are used (Asher, Singleton, Tinsley, & Hymel, 1979). Third, rating scales sometimes generate stereotypic responses from handicapped preschool-age children, such as giving everyone in the class the same rating (Odom & DuBose, 1981). Finally, some children are simply unable to identify their most unresponsive classmates or to accurately estimate their frequency of interaction with other children (Greenwood, Walker, Todd, & Hops, 1979; Kohler & Fowler, 1985b). For these reasons, the authors suggest that sociometric procedures should not be included as an assessment source for preschool-age children.

Although peers and adults *both* are involved in the multimodal assessment model, these two groups can provide different kinds of measures. For example, peers provide the relevant behavioral measures. In addition, they receive social interactions from the target children, direct social responses to target children, and demonstrate appropriate behavioral standards. Conversely, adults can screen intervention participants, select acceptable goals and procedures, and express satisfaction with training outcomes.

INTERVENTION QUESTIONS AND RELEVANT MEASURES

Table 1 lists nine questions that are pertinent to the development and evaluation of social skill interventions. To some degree, these questions are interdependent; answers to the intervention development questions (Numbers 1–6) will probably determine answers to the always important evaluation type questions (Number 7–9). For example, the choice to teach one particular social skill rather than another (Question 2) probably has implications for the later generalization and judged importance of the behavior change (Questions 8 and 9). Since these nine questions and their answers (especially 7–9) reflect the ultimate efficacy of social skills training for young children, the authors recommend that answers be obtained from a wide variety of different sources. A discussion of the various assessment categories follows.

Behavioral Observation Measures

Behavioral Observations of Target Children's Performance   The behavioral observations assessment category is appropriate for answering eight different questions, ranging from "Who needs social skills training?" to "Is the behavior change generalizable?" While some researchers have assessed target children's performance in rehearsal or role play type situations (e.g., Bornstein, Bellack, & Hersen, 1977), these skills do not always generalize to natural play situations (e.g., Berler, Gross, & Drabman, 1982). If an ultimate intervention goal is to teach social skills that persist in natural environmental conditions (i.e., free play, recess), then these settings should constitute the context for all skill assessment and training.

Behavioral observations of target children's performance are necessary to develop and evaluate social skill interventions. Any attempt to teach social skills should be based on reliable observations verifying that these particular behaviors were previously lacking. The observation of target children's performance also can indicate which skills require modification (Question 2), which teaching agents are most effective (Question 4), what training procedures and settings ensure optimal effects (Question 5), and so on. Finally, formal observations are necessary to determine the extent of a behavior change as well as its generalization to new settings and forms or maintenance over time (Questions 7 and 8). In summary, any decisions regarding the development or evaluation of social skills interventions should be based primarily upon observations of target children's performance.

Behavioral Observations of Peer Social Interactions   Many researchers have included peer behaviors in their assessment of target children's social skills. For example, Greenwood, Todd, Hops, and Walker (1982) and Strain, Shores, and Timm (1977) recorded the positive initiations and responses that target children directed towards their peers and vice versa. Fowler, Dougherty, Kirby, & Kohler (in press) and Kohler and Fowler (1985a) scored various prosocial behaviors (play suggestions, approval, etc.) and negative behaviors (hitting, rejection) that target children and their peers exchanged during play interactions. Similarly, Byrant and Budd (1984) scored peer acceptance or refusal of target children's share offers.

There are three reasons for including peer behaviors in the assessment of target children's social interaction. First, considerable experimental evidence indicates that young children can have a major influence on the behaviors of their peers (i.e., Strain & Shores, 1977; Strain et al., 1977; Wahler, 1967). Observations of peer behavior might suggest when these children's actions function to reinforce or to punish target children's treatment gains (e.g., Kohler & Greenwood, 1986). Second, the assessment of peer behaviors could promote the development of more effective interventions. For example, observations that a child is overtly rejected and ridiculed by peers might lead one to include both the target child *and* peers in the training process (Question 1), to teach the target child to initiate play activities and peers to accept these initiations (Question 2), and to continue training until the target child *and* peer exchanges are primarily positive in nature (Question 6). Conversely, evidence that a target child receives but rejects occasional positive initiations from peers prior to intervention might lead to different answers to Questions 1, 2, and 6. Third, peer observations may facilitate a more comprehensive evaluation of training procedures and outcomes (Questions 7–9). For example, observations that target children received high rates of play organizer bids (i.e., invitations to play) from peers after training suggests important training outcomes (Question 9). Conversely, observations that peers avoided, overtly rejected, and ridiculed the target child after intervention would suggest less optimistic conclusions about intervention importance.

Behavioral Observations of Normative Peers Numerous researchers have argued that naturalistic observations of "socially skillful" children are important to the development and evaluation of behavioral interventions (i.e., Foster & Ritchey, 1979; Kazdin, 1980; Nelson & Hayes, 1979; Van Houten, 1979; Walker & Hops, 1976). For example, Foster and Ritchey (1979) recommend that data should be collected on large samples of "normally skillful" children to provide information for future social skill interventions. Similarly, Van Houten (1979) suggests that observations of "competent" individuals could enable the more effective identification of treatment candidates (Question 1), target behaviors and their optimal rates and topographies (Questions 2 and 3), and evaluation of social importance (Question 9).

Normative observations, that is, observations of social interactions of "normal" children, have become more prevalent in the social skills field during the past several years. In order to identify the best target behaviors for social skill interventions, Tremblay, Strain, Hendrickson, and Shores (1981) observed the play interactions of 60 preschoolers in naturalistic free play settings. A 14-item observational code was developed to examine the impact that numerous types of social initiations had on peer responses. Results indicated that rough and tumble play and various types of play organizer bids generated the highest percentage of positive peer responses. Given these findings, Strain and his colleagues have included numerous types of play organizer initiations as a treatment objective for socially withdrawn children (Strain & Odom, 1986).

Although normative observations can undoubtedly provide useful information for the development and evaluation of social skill interventions, the ultimate premise of this assessment strategy is based on two assumptions: 1) the social behaviors of "normally skillful" children represent responses that have important and beneficial functions for their users, and 2) teaching "socially deficient" children to exhibit those same behaviors will ensure their more effective social interactions with peers. To date, neither of these assumptions has sufficient empirical support for preschool children with handicaps. Research that identifies the conditions under which normative data provides satisfactory answers to the questions in Table 1 will hasten a more effective technology for teaching social skills.

Overview of Behavioral Observation Measures Three types of behavioral observations are relevant to the development and evaluation of children's social skill interventions. Although all three observation types are apparent in the social skills literature, few studies have included more than one or two individual measures. When used collectively, however, these sources might provide different answers to the same research questions. For example, the question "What skills should be taught?" could be answered with at least three observational sources: 1) Assessment of target children's performance can pinpoint the specific responses that occur at problematic rates, 2) peer observations can determine which additional children and behaviors should be included in training, and 3) observations of normative peers can indicate which interaction behaviors are typical for a particular setting and age group, but are lacking from the target child and peer interactions. By collecting and considering data from all three observational sources, researchers are far more likely to design and implement the most effective intervention programs.

Social Validation Measures

Adults may contribute to the development and evaluation of social skill interventions in four different ways. They can: 1) screen or identify children to participate in social skills training, 2) choose the goals or objectives of intervention (e.g., target behaviors, optimal rates and conditions), 3) select the most acceptable procedures for teaching these skills, and 4) express satisfaction with all training outcomes. Each assessment category and its relevant research questions are illustrated in Table 1 and will be discussed below.

Screen Intervention Participants The purpose of screening is to identify children who exhibit problematic social behaviors and may be at-risk for poor social adjustment in later life (Garmezy, 1973). Teachers and parents have been the most frequent referral agents for social skill interventions (Hops & Greenwood, in press).

Two primary procedures have been used to screen children for training. A nomination technique allows teachers to simply select or "nominate" the most isolated or socially deficient children in their class (i.e., Shaffer, Egel, & Neef, 1984; Strain & Timm, 1974). In contrast, a ranking procedure allows teachers to rank and order numerous students along one or more particular dimensions of social skillfulness. For example, Greenwood et al. (1979) developed a three-step ranking method to identify preschool children in need of social skills intervention. First, 22 teachers listed all of the children in their class. Second, these students were divided into the least and most talkative groups. Finally, all children were rank ordered according to their frequency of interaction with peers. Formal behavioral observations indicated that 77% of the teachers were able to identify their least socially responsive child within the first five ranks. In contrast, peer sociometric nominations did not correspond with the social interaction observations.

In summary, the teacher ranking procedure is a cost effective method for identifying children for social skill interventions. By combining adult screening reports with the behavioral observations noted above, early childhood special educators may augment their scope of acceptable answers to the question "Who needs social skills training?"

Adults May Select the Goals or Objectives of Intervention As indicated in Table 1, this assessment strategy allows teachers, parents, and other adult consumers to select the most important social behaviors for training as well

as the most appropriate rates and stimulus conditions for their use (Questions 2 and 3). As noted by Wolf (1978), consumer preferences can be indicated through rating forms, questionnaires, or informal interviews.

Several social interaction studies have included systematic efforts to involve consumers in the goal selection process. For example, Dow (1985) paired 42 socially inadequate college students with peers of the opposite sex to engage in dyadic social conversations. After interacting with the client for 10 minutes, peers rated the degree of change they would recommend on 13 specific categories of their partner's interaction style. Similarly, in order to identify the crucial components of conversation, Minkin et al. (1976) observed 20 junior high to college-age females participating in dyadic social interactions. Videotapes of these conversations were then shown to adult judges, who were asked to rate each girl's social skillfulness on a seven-point scale. Results indicated that the behaviors of asking questions and providing positive feedback were positively correlated with the highest social skill ratings.

Unfortunately, the early childhood special education research literature contains few examples of this assessment methodology. While behavioral checklist and rating scales will identify socially deficient children, these instruments do not pinpoint children's specific training needs (Achenbach, 1978; Hops & Greenwood, in press; Spivack & Swift, 1973). The ultimate merit of a social skills intervention depends on identifying and teaching the most important skills at their optimal rates and stimulus conditions. Intervention programs that include adult-selected objectives may ensure more important and beneficial outcomes for target children and adult consumers.

Adults May Select the Most Acceptable Procedures for Teaching Social Skills As shown in Table 1, adults also may select the agents, settings, and procedures for teaching social skills (Questions 3 and 4). The early childhood special education research literature certainly contains a wide range of effective options from which adult consumers may choose. For example, Strayhorn and Strain (1986) noted that social skills can be taught by teachers, parents, peers, and a variety of nonprofessional adults. Similiarly, effective teaching procedures include behavioral rehearsal, modeling, instruction, positive reinforcement, antecedent prompting, positive correction, correspondence training, strategic placement, picture cue, and multimethod package (Barton, 1986). Finally, social skill training settings have ranged from structured behavioral script situations with adult instruction to unstructured freeplay activities with very little adult supervision (Hops & Greenwood, in press).

During recent years, a growing number of researchers have expressed interest in the social acceptability or validity of behavioral interventions (i.e., Kazdin, 1980; Witt, Elliot, & Martens, 1984). In fact, Wolf (1978) has argued that the social acceptability of an intervention may influence its overall effectiveness as well as its likelihood of being adopted and maintained over extended time periods. Since teachers and parents are ultimately responsible for young children's social education, their procedural satisfaction should be a top priority. Researchers who allow adult consumers to select their most acceptable teaching agents, procedures, and settings may well ensure the widespread adoption of social skill interventions.

Adults May Express Satisfaction with the Outcomes of Social Skills Training As shown in Table 1, adult satisfaction reports may answer four specific questions ranging from when social skills training should stop (Question 6) to the evaluation of various teaching outcomes (Questions 7–9). With respect to program evaluation, Wolf (1978) states that

> "behavior analysts may give their opinions, and these opinions may even be supported with objective behavioral data, but it is the participants and other consumers who want to make the final decision about whether a program helped solve their problems." (p. 210)

A growing number of social skill researchers are reporting the social validation of their teaching outcomes. For example, Walker, Hops, Greenwood, and Todd (1975) reported that six target children were perceived as more

skillful by their teacher after social skills training. Similarly, Shaffer et al. (1984) had three classroom teachers and one aide rate the interactions of four autistic children and their peers before and after social skill intervention. All four adults viewed these children as engaging in more interactions after treatment.

Consumer satisfaction is very important to the evaluation of social skill training programs. In particular, the assessment of outcome *importance* (Question 9) requires the judgement of adults such as parents and teachers who are responsible for their chidren's social skills education and welfare during the preschool years. Studies that continue to assess adult satisfaction with all intervention outcomes may lead to the development of teaching programs that provide the greatest benefits to young children.

Overview of Social Validation Measures
In summary, four types of social validation are useful for the development and evaluation of social skill interventions: 1) adults may screen or identify children to participate in social skills training, 2) adults may choose the objectives or goals of intervention (i.e., target behaviors, optimal rates and settings), 3) adults may select the most acceptable procedures for teaching these skills, and 4) adults may express satisfaction with the outcomes of social skills training. As indicated in Table 1, these four measures address different aspects of social skill interventions. The first three measures pertain exclusively to the intervention *development* (Questions 1–6 in Table 1) while the final measure evaluates training outcomes (Questions 7–9). Professionals who use all four validation measures will ensure maximum levels of adult satisfaction with all aspects of their social skill training programs.

Under ideal circumstances, all four adult validation measures should be combined with the three behavioral observation measures illustrated in Table 1. When used in this context, the observation and validation measures may provide *acceptable* and yet potentially *different* answers to the same research questions. The final section of this chapter discusses methods for integrating and analyzing these discrepancies.

PROCEDURAL
AND RESEARCH ISSUES

Up to this point in our discussion a certain level of agreement has been assumed between the various sources of information that may be tapped to answer particular questions about social skill assessment and intervention. However, there may be many occasions in which the various measurement methods produce an apparent disagreement or contradiction. For example, observations of the target child and peers may suggest that teaching resulted in a behavior change. At the same time, however, the target child's parents may express dissatisfaction about the direction or degree of the behavior change. Similarly, a parent may indicate that a behavior change has generalized, but target child behavior may suggest otherwise. As another example, researchers asking how and where to teach skills (Question 5) may obtain a different answer from each possible assessment source (see Table 1). Observations of target children may indicate maximum social improvements in freeplay settings with little teacher supervision. Conversely, peer observations might indicate that the children's prosocial behaviors that are directed towards target children require high levels of teacher prompts and reinforcement during freeplay. Finally, teachers may prefer to teach social skills during a group instruction activity that occurs 1 hour before the free play period. How should researchers respond to these inconsistencies and how can the probability of agreement in the first place be maximized? One thing that researchers can be sure of is that employing a broad array of information sources will inevitably lead to some disagreement in the data obtained.

Historically, the special education social skills research field has been dominated by a validation mentality that operates as follows. First, an assumption is made that a certain measurement method is preeminent. Second, the merit or validity of data from other measurement methods is dependent upon concordance with results derived from the preeminent method. Finally, the concordant measurement

methods acquire preeminent status, while the less fortunate methods are cast aside. In the authors' opinion, the foregoing process has not proven to be successful in promoting the view that there should be correspondence, covariation, or agreement between the multiple measures. At some time in the future researchers may find that the various data sources can and do, under some circumstances, covary in predictable directions. For now, however, much current validation work is based on speculation. As a strategy for eliminating this uncertainty, the authors propose the use of a multiple baseline analysis across dependent measures to understand, control, and predict the covariation of information from the various data sources.

Briefly, to demonstrate experimental control with a multiple baseline design, the investigator collects baseline data (i.e., no programmed intervention in effect) simultaneously across three or more behaviors, conditions, or individuals. After the data from each baseline are at an acceptable level and stable, an intervention is applied to the first "baseline" of the multiple baseline design. The behavior targeted in this baseline should change abruptly, while the other baselines remain unchanged. After some criterion level of performance is reached in the first baseline, intervention is applied to the second baseline, and so on.

The basic logic is that the baselines should change when and only when intervention is applied (see Odom, Chapter 1, this volume). Figure 1 illustrates the use of a multiple baseline design to answer the question, "Did our teaching efforts produce a behavior change?" (Question 7 in Table 1). It may be noted that Table 1 identifies three potential sources of information to answer this question; all of these are represented in Figure 1. In most cases, the multiple baseline design assumes a certain level of *independence* in the various legs of the baseline (Tawney & Gast, 1984). In accordance with this assumption, the hypothetical data in Figure 1 show that peers' behavior does not change fundamentally until a teacher-mediated intervention is directly applied to these individuals (solid vertical line in Figure 1).

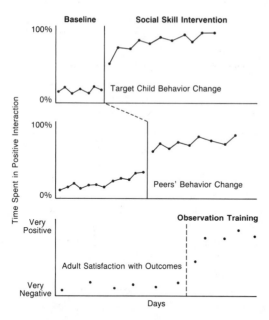

Figure 1. Sample multiple baseline design illustrating the effects of changing target child social behavior on peer behavior change and adult satisfaction.

fairs, some individuals have recommended that social skill researchers collect and analyze as many different sources as possible to develop and evaluate their interventions (i.e., McConnell & Odom, 1986). However, it is the authors' suspicion that these numerous data sources, especially the observational and social validation measures, will often disagree with one another. This disagreement is evident in Figure 1. Given this expectation, the authors recommend that researchers experimentally examine the relationships between the various data sources.

The multiple baseline design is an effective strategy to directly test the interdependence, or lack thereof, between the target children's behavior change, peer corollary responses to target children, and adult satisfaction. This design does not, however, speak adequately to the use of selected measures to "validate" others. The authors' suspicions about the wisdom of that tactic rest with the lack of answers to the following questions:

1. Do people sometimes say one thing and do another?
2. Do we know when and under what conditions peoples' verbal behavior and performance are likely to correspond?
3. Can we assume that changing the social behavior of target children will result in concomitant changes in the social behavior of peers (toward the target children)?
4. Do we know that peoples' qualitative judgements of good and bad outcomes are independent of their relationship and history with the individual who solicits their opinion?

This peer intervention might be something as simple as a teacher cueing peers that the target child may want to play with them.

Following this same logic, the figure also indicates that adult satisfaction with the target child's social skill does not change until this verbal behavior is subject to its own effective intervention. For example, the adult may be asked to observe the child while a second observer points out the new and improved behavior of the child. This example of independence is, admittedly, a radical departure from the usual "validation mentality" that assumes interdependence between measures and that certain confirmatory data, in this case peer behavior and adult satisfaction, will prove the worth of the target child's behavior change. Given researchers minimal understanding of the conditions that influence peer behavior and adult satisfaction reports, however, the authors feel that an independent position is the safer one.

As noted earlier, there exists a wide range of different methods for assessing and teaching social skills as well as for evaluating the outcomes of these efforts. Given this state of af-

Returning to Figure 1, the reader should review the hypothetical data arrays. It is clear that the onset of teaching produced an immediate change in the percent of time that the target child engaged in social behavior. When skill training began for this child, there was a small but relatively steady increase in the percent of time that peers engaged in positive social behavior with the target. Not until intervention was applied *directly* to peers, however, did their behavior change in a substantial fashion. During this same period of intervention with the target child and peers, adult satisfaction with the target child's behavior did not change from baseline. In an attempt to control this verbal behavior, the adult was exposed to a brief training regimen in which the target child's behavior was contrasted with that of normally developing children (vertical dashed line). By presumably making the adult consumer more aware of the "normalcy" of the target's behavior, subsequent evaluations of child outcomes were more positive.

The multiple baseline analysis in Figure 1 has several advantages over the more common method of selecting data from one or two presumed preeminent sources. First, this strategy provides a relatively unambiguous test of covariation between multiple measurement sources. It is the authors' opinion that in all cases a functional analysis is superior to a presumption of relation or effect.

Second, where some covariation between measures exists, the stage is set for new functional analyses that may identify an actual controlling relationship. As an example, assume the multiple baseline analysis shows that intervention on target children's behavior has a salutary effect on peers (nontarget children) as well. Since this relationship is not necessarily functional (i.e., the social skills intervention and target child's behavior change could both influence peer performance), one may next design a study to carefully regulate the social behavior of certain children and examine the concomitant effects on interacting peers. Similarly, one may also be able to design, a priori, an intervention scenario in which consumers can quickly discriminate or respond favorably to improvements in target child behavior. To follow the prior example, one may find that the multiple baseline strategy consistently reveals no or few positive evaluations of child performance until adults are taught to make the relevant discriminations. In this circumstance, it would be advisable to provide consumer evaluators with a keener sense of social behavior change *prior* to intervention.

Third, the multiple baseline design high-lights the fact that researchers often, if not always, have multiple audiences to please. One audience (e.g., target child) is not necessarily more important than others (e.g., peers, parents, teacher). What is important is to employ a strategy, such as the multiple baseline, that permits an assessment of those multiple audiences and that demands the employment of whatever intervention is necessary to influence children's behavior or consumers' opinions in a desired direction.

CONCLUSIONS

In this chapter the authors have attempted to highlight some of the complexities and uncertainties surrounding social skills programming for young handicapped children. It is the authors' belief that the social skills field will be more rapidly advanced by a fundamental change in current conceptualizations and directions for practice and research. The following conclusions are proposed:

1. The limited use of measurement methods to answer critical assessment and intervention questions, like those in Table 1, is responsible for the authors' limited treatment success. By limited treatment success, we refer to the relatively few demonstrations of social behavior maintenance and generalization, the relative absence of validated social skill interventions in everyday classroom practice, and the total absence of a consumer constituency that demands such interventions.

2. By expanding our professional repertoire of observational and social validation measures, we will surely create some confusion and mixed answers to the questions outlined in Table 1. However, our expansion will be worth the added burden if we become more aware and attentive to the multiple consumers of our interventions and the importance of their behavior change and positive evaluation.

3. The authors suggest that the logic and procedures inherent in the multiple baseline design are the best approach for utilizing

numerous data sources to answer the questions in Table 1. Rather than *assuming* covariation among measures, the multiple baseline design provides the necessary proof. It also requires that researchers employ appropriate interventions for each data source in case the target child behavior change does not result in wide-scale change across the other measures.

4. With repeated use of the suggested multiple baseline strategy, it is likely that some types of social skills, when taught, will covary predictably with the peer and adult measures. In such cases, we are obligated by our design to functionally analyze that covariation. That is, researchers must produce, withdraw, and reproduce the observed covariation in functional analysis fashion. It also seems likely that predictable inconsistencies between various measures will be found, particularly in the observational and social validation sources. In these cases, there are two important courses of action. First, the necessary intervention to bring data sources into aggreement needs to be identified. That is, those conditions under which these measures can covary in predictable directions need to be found. Second, the conditions must be provided to ensure that target children, peers, and adults can be the best predictors of their own treatment needs, procedural preferences, and posttreatment satisfaction (Wolf, 1978).

REFERENCES

Achenbach, T. M. (1978). Psychopathology of childhood: Research problem and issues. *Journal of Consulting and Clinical Psychology, 46*, 759–776.

Asher, S. R. & Hymel, S. (1981). Children's social competence in peer relations: Sociometric and behavioral assessment. In J. Wine & M. Smye (Eds.), *Social competence* (pp. 125–157). New York: Guilford Press.

Asher, S. A., Singleton, L. C., Tinsley, B. R. & Hymel, S. (1979). The reliability of a rating scale sociometric method with preschool children. *Developmental Psychology, 15*, 443–444.

Barton, E. J. (1986). Modification of children's prosocial behavior. In P. S. Strain, M. J. Guralnick, & H. M. Walker (Eds.), *Children's social behavior: Development, assessment, and modification* (pp. 331–372). New York: Academic Press.

Berler, E. J., Gross, A. M., & Drabman, D. S. (1982). Social skills training with children: Proceed with caution. *Journal of Applied Behavior Analysis, 15*, 41–54.

Bornstein, M. R., Bellack, A. S., & Hersen, M. (1977). Social skills training for unasserting children: A multiple baseline analysis. *Journal of Applied Behavior Analysis, 10*, 183–195.

Byrant, L. E., & Budd, K. S. (1984). Teaching behaviorally handicapped preschool children to share. *Journal of Applied Behavior Analysis, 17*, 45–65.

Cooke, T. P., & Apolloni, T. (1976). Developing positive emotional behaviors: A study in training and generalization effects. *Journal of Applied Behavior Analysis, 9*, 65–78.

Dow, M. D. (1985). Peer validation and idiographic analysis of social skill deficits. *Behavior Therapy, 16*, 76–86.

Foster, S. L., & Ritchey, W. L. (1979). Issues in the assessment of social competence in children. *Journal of Applied Behavior Analysis, 12*, 628–638.

Fowler, S. A., Dougherty, B. S., Kirby, K. C., & Kohler, F. W. (in press). Role reversals: Analysis of therapeutic effects achieved with disruptive boys during their appointments as peer monitors. *Journal of Applied Behavior Analysis.*

Garmezy, M. (1973). Children at risk: The search for the antecendents of sehizophrenia. Part I: Conceptual models and research methods. *Schizophrenia Bulletin, 8*, 14–90.

Greenwood, C. R., Todd, N. M., Hops, H. J., & Walker, H. M. (1982). Behavior change targets in the assessment and treatment of socially withdrawn preschool children. *Behavioral Assessment, 4*, 273–298.

Greenwood, C. R., Walker, H. M., Todd, N. M., & Hops, H. (1979). Selecting a cost-effective screening device for the assessment of preschool social withdrawal. *Journal of Applied Behavior Analysis, 12*, 639–652.

Gresham, F. M. (1986). Conceptual issues in the assessment of social competence in children. In P. S. Strain, M. J. Guralnick, & H. M. Walker (Eds.), *Children's social behavior* (pp. 143–179). New York: Academic Press.

Guralnick, M. J. (1986). The peer relations of young handicapped and nonhandicapped children. In P. Strain, M. J. Guralnick, & H. M. Walker (Eds.), *Children's social behaviors* (pp. 93–140). New York: Academic Press.

Hartup, W. W. (1979). Peer relations and the growth of social competence. In M. W. Kent & J. E. Rolf (Eds.), *Primary prevention of psycopathology* (Vol. 3, pp. 150–170). Hanner, NH: University Press of New England.

Hops, H., & Greenwood, C. R. (in press). Social skill deficits. In E. J. Mash & L. G. Terdal (Eds.), *Behavioral assessment of childhood disorders* (2nd edition), New York: Guilford.

Kazdin, A. E. (1980). Acceptability of time out from reinforcement procedures for disruptive child behavior. *Behavior Therapy, 11*, 329–344.

Kohler, F. W., & Fowler, S. A. (1985a). *An evaluation of the sociometric methodology: Some recommendations regarding its use in applied behavior analysis.* Paper presented at the Association for Behavior Analysis, Nashville, TN.

Kohler, F. W., & Fowler, S. A. (1985b). Training prosocial behaviors to young children: An analysis of reciprocity with untrained peers. *Journal of Applied Behavior Analysis, 18,* 187–200.

Kohler, F. W., & Greenwood, C. R. (1986). Toward a technology of generalization: The identification of natural communities of reinforcement. *The Behavior Analyst, 9,* 1926.

McConnell, S. R., & Odom, S. L. (1986). Sociometrics: Peer-referenced measures and the assessment of social competence. In P. S. Strain, M. J. Guralnick, & H. M. Walker (Eds.), *Children's social behaviors: Development, assessment, and modifications* (pp. 215–284). New York: Academic Press.

McFall, R. M. (1982). A review and reformulation of the concept of social skills. *Behavioral Assessment, 4,* 1–33.

Minkin, N., Braukmann, C. J., Minkin, B. L., Timbers, G. D., Timbers, B. J., Fixsen, D. L., Phillips, E. L., & Wolf, M. M. (1976). The social validation and training of conversation skills. *Journal of Applied Behavior Analysis, 9,* 127–140.

Nelson, R. O., & Hayes, S. C. (1979). Some current dimensions of behavioral assessment. *Behavioral Assessment, 1,* 1–16.

Oden, S., & Asher, S. R. (1977). Coaching children in social skills for friendship making. *Child Development, 48,* 496–506.

Odom, S. L., & DuBose, R. F. (April, 1981). *Peer rating assessments of integrated preschool classes: Stability and concurrent validity of the measure and efficacy of the peer model.* Paper presented at the National Conference for the Council for Exceptional Children, New York.

Odom, S. L., & McConnell, S. R. (1985). A performance-based conceptualization of social competence of handicapped preschool children: Implications for assessment. *Topics in Early Childhood Special Education, 4,* 1–9.

Odom, S. L., Strain, P. S., Karger, M. A., & Smith, J. D. (1986). Using single and multiple peers to promote social interaction of preschool children with severe handicaps. *Journal of the Division for Early Childhood, 10,* 53–64.

Roff, M., Sells, B., & Golden, M. M. (1972). *Social adjustment and personality development in children.* Minneapolis: University of Minnesota Press.

Sainato, D. M., Strain, P. S., & Lyon, S. R. (1986). Increasing academic responding of handicapped preschool children. Unpublished manuscript. University of Pittsburgh.

Shaffer, M. S., Egel, A. L., & Neef, N. A. (1984). Training mildly handicapped peers to facilitate changes in the social interaction skills of autistic children. *Journal of Applied Behavior Analysis, 17,* 461–476.

Sisson, L. A., Van Hasselt, V. B., Hersen, M., & Strain, P. S. (1985). Peer interventions: Increasing social behaviors in multihandicapped children. *Behavior Modification, 9,* 293–322.

Spivack, G., & Swift, M. (1973). The classroom behavior of children: A critical review of teacher-administered rating scales. *The Journal of Special Education, 4,* 55–89.

Strain, P. S. (1981). Modification of sociometric status and social interaction with mainstreamed developmentally disabled children. *Analysis and Intervention in Developmental Disabilities, 1,* 157–169.

Strain, P. S. (1985). Programmatic research on peer-mediated interventions. In B. H. Schneider, K. H. Rubin, & J. E. Ledingham (Eds.), *Children's peer relations: Issues in assessment and intervention* (pp. 193–206). New York: Springer-Verlag.

Strain, P. S., Lambert, D. L., Kerr, M. M., Stagg, V., & Lenker, D. (1983). Naturalistic assessment of children's compliance to teachers' requests and consequences for compliance. *Journal of Applied Behavior Analysis, 16,* 243–249.

Strain, P. S., & Odom, S. L. (1986). Peer social initiations: Effective intervention for social skills development of exceptional children. *Exceptional Children, 52,* 543–552.

Strain, P. S., & Shores, R. E. (1977). Social reciprocity: A clinical teaching perspective. *Exceptional Children, 43,* 526–530.

Strain, P. S., Shores, R. E., & Timm, M. A. (1977). Effects of social initiations on the behavior of a withdrawn child. *Journal of Applied Behavior Analysis, 10,* 289–298.

Strain, P. S., & Timm, M. A. (1974). An experimental analysis of social interaction between a behaviorally disordered preschool child and her classroom peers. *Journal of Applied Behavior Analysis, 7,* 583–590.

Strayhorn, J. M., & Strain, P. S. (1986). Social and language skills for preventive mental health: What, how, who, and why. In P. S. Strain, M. J. Guralnick, & H. Walker (Eds.), *Children's social behavior: Development, assessment, and modifications* (pp. 287–330). New York: Academic Press.

Tawney, J. W., & Gast, D. L. (1984). *Single subject research in special education.* Columbus, OH: Merrill.

Tremblay, A., Strain, P. S., Hendrickson, J. M., & Shores, R. E. (1981). Social interactions of normally developing preschool children: Using normative data for subject and target behavior selection. *Behavior Modification, 5,* 237–253.

Van Houten, R. (1979). Social validation: The evolution of standards of competency for target behaviors. *Journal of Applied Behavior Analysis, 12,* 581–592.

Wahler, R. G. (1967). Child-child interactions in free field settings: Some experimental analyses. *Journal of Experimental Child Psychology, 5,* 278–293.

Walker, H. M., & Hops, H. (1976). Use of normative peer data as a standard for evaluating classroom treatment effects. *Journal of Applied Behavior Analysis, 9,* 159–168.

Walker, H. M., Hops, H., Greenwood, C. R., & Todd, N. M. (1975). *Social interactions: Effects of symbolic modeling and individual and group reinforcement contingencies on the behavior of withdrawn children* (Report Number 15). Center at Oregon for Research in the Behavioral Education of the Handicapped, University of Oregon, Eugene.

Witt, J. C., Elliot, S. M., & Martens, B. K. (1984). Acceptability of behavioral interventions used in classrooms: The influence of teacher time, severity of behavior problem, and type of intervention. *Behavior Disorders, 10,* 95–104.

Wolf, M. M. (1978). Social validity: The case for subjective measurement or how applied behavior analysis is finding its heart. *Journal of Applied Behavior Analysis, 11,* 203–214.

Chapter 9

Play Skills Development
and Instruction for
Young Children with Handicaps

Rebecca R. Fewell and Ruth Kaminski

IN RECENT YEARS, THE DEVELOPMENT of research concerning play behavior in young children has attracted the attention of numerous researchers interested in child development. Many developmental theorists agree that play, a dominant developmental activity in young children, is an important medium for the intellectual, linguistic, emotional, and social development of the child. Play has a significant role in promoting cognitive growth in young children (Piaget, 1962) by providing a medium for the development of problem solving skills (Bruncr, 1972), the discovery of new combinations of behaviors with objects (Smith & Sutton, 1979), and the consolidation and strengthening of newly learned skills (Fein & Apfel, 1979). In addition, some theorists hypothesize that play facilitates creative and flexible thinking (Singer, 1973). The Russian psychologist, Vygotsky (1967), believed that play is also a primary source of linguistic development. According to Vygotsky (1967), play facilitates the development of language and symbolic representation by helping children to separate meanings from objects and actions. Still other theorists hypothesize that through play children learn social skills (Feitelson & Ross, 1973) and develop self-confidence and personality traits such as perseverance and motivation (Feitelson & Ross, 1973; Singer, 1973).

Recent studies of the development of play have indicated that play follows a regular developmental sequence in infancy and childhood (Lowe, 1975; Nicolich, 1977; Rosenblatt, 1977; Shimada, Kai, & Sano, 1981). Further, this sequence parallels, and thus may serve as a behavioral reflection of, social, linguistic, and cognitive development.

Accumulating data support the notion that play is, indeed, a developmentally important behavior. The data also suggest important implications for the use of play as an assessment tool with young children (Bromwich, 1985; McCune-Nicolich, 1980; Quinn & Rubin, 1984; Rogers, 1982a; Wolf, 1982). Assessment of children's play may yield more valid results than a standardized assessment procedure for a number of reasons. Because observation of play is an unobtrusive and nonthreatening procedure, children will more likely behave in a more typical manner than when asked to follow an unfamiliar adult's directions in a testing situation. In addition, responding to standardized test items may be impossible for some children with handicaps. Because play is such a natural and spontaneous action of children, it also holds promise as a medium of intervention. Thus, the study of the development of play clearly has both theoretical significance as well as practical implications for intervention with handicapped youngsters.

The purpose of this chapter is to summarize research that is relevant to the process of intervention and to the development of play behaviors in young children with handicaps. Before proceeding, however, it may be helpful to first define what is meant by the term "play."

WHAT IS PLAY?

Most people would agree that young children spend lengthy periods of time engaged in play. However, not all people would agree on a definition of play. This is due, in part, to the fact that play can take many forms. Consider, for example, the following: an infant bats at a mobile again and again; a group of children organize and engage in a game of kick-ball; a boy says "Sh, baby sleeping," as he sits rocking a doll; a girl builds a tower of blocks. Garvey (1977) asks the following questions about such varied occurrences: Are all of these events play? What characteristics do they have in common? Is there any feature unique to play?

Characteristics of Play

Some researchers and theorists have attempted to define play by describing its characteristics. Most agree to the following:

1. Play is intrinsically motivated—that is, it is done for its own sake, rather than as a means to an end.
2. It is spontaneous and voluntary—that is, it is undertaken by choice rather than compulsion.
3. Play is self-generated and involves active engagement on the part of the player.
4. Play involves enjoyment (Bruner, 1972; Garvey, 1977; Weisler & McCall, 1976).

In addition, it is generally held that play does not tend to occur when the organism is in a state of uncertainty or anxiety, and that play is not consistent from organism to organism and from situation to situation (Weisler & McCall, 1976). These generally agreed-upon characteristics of play help to restrict the definition of play and to differentiate play from other nonplay behaviors.

Types of Play

Play has also been described taxonomically by several theorists and researchers. For example, Chance (1979) divides play into four behavioral categories: 1) physical play, 2) manipulative play, 3) symbolic play, and 4) games.

Garvey (1977) likewise describes six types of play on the basis of behavioral categories: 1) play with motion and interaction, 2) play with objects, 3) play with language, 4) play with social materials, 5) play with rules, and 6) ritualized play.

Piaget (1962), on the other hand, divides play into three stages representing points where major changes in the child's growth become evident. For Piaget, it is the cognitive changes at each developmental period that are significant. *Sensorimotor* play involves the deliberate repetition of the application of some motor scheme to an object—the child shakes a rattle again and again. As children develop, they begin to apply action schemes to objects which are more and more remote from the initial object of focus. This leads to the emergence of *symbolic* play, in which children develop the ability to represent an absent object or experience through their own actions. Finally, in the period of concrete operations, *games with rules* replace individual symbolic make-believe as individual symbols and beliefs become modified by collective discipline and cooperation with others.

Another example of play taxonomy is that of Zelazo and Kearsley (1980) who examined a narrower segment of play behavior: play with objects prior to the development of representational play. These researchers have classified early play into four types on the basis of a child's behavior with objects at different developmental periods.

As is evident, these various taxonomies describe distinctly different types of play or play at different stages in development. Some of the taxonomies restrict the definition of play more narrowly than others. At any rate, such taxonomies help to define at least some aspects of play. This is helpful to the researcher in allowing for observations and measurement of these particular aspects of play.

Further Distinctions

A number of investigators make a distinction between play and exploration. Whereas play is intrinsically motivated, spontaneous, voluntary, and pleasurable, exploration consists of a "stereotyped perceptual-motor examination of an object, situation, or event the function of which is to reduce subjective uncertainty (i.e., acquire information)" (Weisler & McCall, 1976, p. 493).

According to Hutt (1979), play occurs only after children become familiar with the environmental properties of an object or situation. Prior to such familiarity, the behavior in which children engage is exploration. As long as the situation or the objects are novel, the behaviors will be less variable and more systematic than play behaviors (Hutt, 1979). As described by Rubin, Fein, and Vandenberg (1983), exploration is guided by the question "What is this object and what can it do?", while play is guided by the question "What can I do with this object?"

A further distinction is also made between play and games with rules. Game behavior is more restricted and formalized than play and is generally seen as a result of increased cognitive competence (Piaget, 1962). Likewise, play is also distinguished from peer interaction or social participation (Hartup, 1983; Parten, 1932).

For the purpose of limiting the scope of this chapter, these distinctions will be accepted; research concerning the development of exploration, games with rules, and social participation will not be discussed at length. For the authors' present purposes, discussion of play will be confined to the category of object play. The authors' working definition of play is as follows: play is a spontaneous activity that involves interaction with objects in a pleasurable manner.

DEVELOPMENT OF PLAY

Children's play skills, like their motor, language, cognitive and social skills, develop in an orderly sequence. In describing the development of play skills, researchers have tended to explore skills emerging within a given age period, for example from birth to 24 months (Fenson, Kagan, Kearsley, & Zelazo, 1976), from 9 to 15 months (Zelazo & Kearsley, 1980) or from 14 to 24 months (Watson & Fischer,

1977). Others focus more narrowly on the sequential development of a particular type of play such as the use of objects in symbolic play (Elder & Pederson, 1978; Lowe, 1975), constructive play (Rast, 1984; 1986) or agent use (Watson & Fischer, 1977). In keeping with the authors' definition of play, various aspects of child-object interactions that emerge in the first 3 years of life will be described.

Presymbolic Play

The changes in play behavior during the first year of life reflect development from visual to manipulative exploration of objects and from stereotypical to functional play.

Visual to Manipulative Exploration During the first few months of life, manipulative exploration is quite limited. From the moment of birth, however, infants are visually responsive to their environment. Throughout the first year, infants learn much about their environment visually. Although for the first 2 months visual interest is limited to stimuli that show high rates of change, infants soon begin to differentiate objects on the basis of perceptual attributes (e.g., color, size, shape) and to respond to visual events in terms of their meaning (e.g., photographs of human faces).

Beginning at 6 months of age, visually guided manual exploration expands markedly. Just as with visual exploration, infants will select and explore novel objects more frequently and to a greater extent than familiar ones (Rubenstein, 1976). As infants develop, their object manipulations also become more directly related to specific characteristics of the object such as shape, texture, and weight. By 12 months of age, infants display more interest in objects such as light switches, push buttons, and busy boxes that are responsive to the infant's manipulations (Fenson et al., 1976; McCall, 1974).

Stereotypical to Functional Play The other major shift in infant play behavior that takes place during the first year of life is an increase in behaviors that reflect the way objects are used in daily life. Prior to 7 months of age, infants engage predominantly in stereotypical play and tend to treat all similar sized objects alike. A child may bang a spoon and a rattle, for example (Fenson et al., 1976). Within the next 6 months there is a marked decrease in the amount of stereotypical play and an increase in play behavior with functional characteristics (Belsky & Most, 1981; Fenson et al., 1976; Largo & Howard, 1979; Zelazo & Kearsley, 1980). At this point, infants begin to act on objects in ways that are consistent with the function of the object. The infant might push a toy car rather than bang it or throw a ball rather than mouth it. Zelazo and Kearsley (1980) view the emergence of functional play around the first year as a major cognitive milestone. According to these investigators, the emergence of functional play underlies the cognitive ability to activate specific ideas.

Emergence of Symbolic Play

The development of symbolic play heralds a major transition in child development. According to many theorists, the ability to use symbolic representation in play signals the development of representational thought, which greatly increases the flexibility of a child's mental processes (Ungerer, Zelazo, Kearsley, & O'Leary, 1981).

The beginnings of symbolic play during the second year are initially marked by the continuing increase in play behaviors that mimic real-life activities. This occurs between 12 and 18 months of age with the first pretend gesture appearing at 12–13 months (Fein & Apfel, 1979; Fenson et al. 1976; Rosenblatt, 1977). For example, the 13-month-old child will often react appropriately to most toy feeding utensils, pretending to drink from a cup or eat with a spoon. Or the child will put her head down, close her eyes, and pretend to sleep. Such behaviors are the earliest forms of symbolic play in which young children simulate some of their own daily routines, showing awareness of pretense by using behavioral schemes playfully with realistic motions and sound effects (Nicolich, 1977; Rosenblatt, 1977).

During this period there is a corresponding decrease in behavior involving single objects as children develop the capacity to simultaneously consider and relate to two or more objects (Fein & Apfel, 1979; Fenson et al., 1976; Rosenblatt, 1977; Zelazo & Kearsley, 1980). A child may, for example, place a spoon in a cup or stack one block on top of another. The development of this ability is significant in that it allows the child to explore a wide array of interrelationships among objects and events including functional relations, spatial relations, causal relations, and categorical relations (Fenson, 1985).

Elaboration and Sophistication of Symbolic Play

The three processes that characterize the elaboration of symbolic play in children are decontextualization, decentration, and sequential combinations or integration.

Decontextualization The first process, decontextualization (Werner & Kaplan, 1963), refers to the child's ability to engage in behaviors without the usual objects and/or away from the usual contexts in which the behavior typically occurs. In the child's earliest pretend acts, when she pretends to drink from a baby bottle without actually doing so, decontextualization occurs. In these first pretend acts, the child merely expresses what she knows about how an object can be used (Fein, 1975). The materials used in these early forms of decontextualization are typically ordinary household objects. Use of such realistic objects in pretend acts increases until approximately 18 months of age. Between 18 and 24 months there is a gradual increase in the child's ability to use symbolic objects in play that are physically dissimilar from those used in real life (Elder & Pederson, 1978; Fein, 1975; Ungerer et al., 1981; Watson & Fischer, 1977). For example, Watson and Fischer (1977) found the first use of object substitution among children in their study to occur at approximately 18 months with the child using an object physically similar to the intended object. By 24 months of age, however, 75% of the children in the study demonstrated substitutions of a physically dissimilar object. These findings are consistent with those of Fein (1975), who found 70% of 24-month-old children in her study engaged in pretense (e.g., feeding a toy horse) when one dissimilar object (e.g., block) was substituted for another (e.g., cup). According to Ungerer et al. (1981), perceptual attributes appear to be of greater importance to the child than similar functions or action properties.

During the third year, children begin to use imaginary objects to symbolize absent objects. At first, a 3-year-old child might use a body part as an object substitute, such as a finger for a comb. Throughout the preschool years, imaginary representations of objects become more common. It is during the fourth or fifth year that the creation of imaginary playmates first occurs (Fenson, 1985).

Decentration Decentration (Piaget, 1962) refers to the child's ability to incorporate others into pretend activities. When symbolic play first emerges at about 12 months of age, the child acts as the agent and the action is involved with the child's own body. For example, the child picks up a cup and pretends to drink. Some researchers term this behavior "autosymbolic" (Nicolich, 1977). Following a developmental sequence, the child soon begins to incorporate others into her play, at first directing actions toward animate others (e.g., child pretends to give mother a drink) and then toward inanimate others (e.g., child pretends to give doll a drink) (Fein & Apfel, 1979). Eventually, the child's pretend actions involve inanimate objects as active agents rather than merely passive recipients of the child's actions (Corrigan, 1982). The child may place a telephone in a doll's hand and have the doll bring the telephone to its ear to listen. Watson and Fischer (1977) studied the developmental sequence of agent use in 36 infants between 14 and 24 months of age and confirmed the developmental sequence from self as agent to inanimate object as active other.

Sequential Combinations Initially, the child's symbolic play consists of a single pretend gesture such as drinking from a cup. However, as the child develops, the child's symbolic actions become linked to form sequences of behaviors. At first, these linkages involve single scheme combinations. That is, the same act is successively performed in relation to two

or more different agents or objects. The child may stir a spoon in a cup, then in a pot. Or the child may first feed herself, then, in turn, feed two different dolls or stuffed animals. Single scheme combinations are soon followed by the development of multischeme combinations. This type of sequence involves two or more different acts performed successively. For instance, the child may feed the doll with a bottle, pick the doll up and pat it on the back to "burp" it, then put the doll in bed (Belsky & Most, 1981; Fenson & Ramsay, 1981; McCune-Nicolich, 1981; Nicolich, 1977). After the third year, the child begins to plan out pretend situations in advance, organizing who and what will be required in the role enactment (Arnaud & Curry, 1973; Curry & Arnaud, 1974, 1984; Westby, 1980).

PLAY OF CHILDREN WITH HANDICAPS

Only recently has play become viewed as a viable instructional target in early interaction programs for handicapped children. These programs have typically focused on specific cognitive, language, self-care, gross motor, fine motor, and (to a lesser extent) social skills. Objectives in Individual Educational Planning conferences seldom reflect play behavior. Play has been viewed as "free time" and of little instructional value. However, the very critical role of play in the development of all children suggests a need for research into the development and facilitation of play in handicapped children. Such research would contribute to the understanding of the impact of various handicapping conditions on play and on other areas of development. This information would lead to the development of curricula and instructional strategies that could contribute to the development of skills in children with known impairments.

Unfortunately, studies of the specific characteristics of the play of particular handicap groups have no overall perspective. and have been sporadic (Mogford, 1977). In their review of the literature, Quinn and Rubin (1984) found most of the studies of handicapped children's play are "flawed either methodologically, statistically, and/or theoretically" (p. 77). The authors went on to express the possible impact such flaws might have in the future, leading ". . . to errors in judgment concerning the use of play as a diagnostic or training instrument" (p. 77).

Several factors contribute to the current state of research on the play behavior of handicapped children. The heterogeneity of the populations both within and across handicapping conditions is a major reason for the paucity of quality studies in the field. A second reason may be related to the earlier mentioned "value" of play for handicapped children as perceived by those who work with these children. Specifically, instructional priorities are determined by the objectives on a child's Individual Educational Plan. Objectives are drawn from deficits noted on the various assessments given to the child. These assessments are dominated in the early years by items from domains of the various developmental areas (i.e., gross motor, fine motor, language, cognition). Play is seldom included in the assessment experience, therefore it is overlooked as a critical objective for instruction or as a strategy for facilitating learning. The failure to focus on play in classroom settings may be a result of the minimal amount of research currently being generated on this topic. A third reason may have to do with timing. Only in the last 10 years have there been large enough populations of identified handicapped preschool-age children grouped in research settings. Without access to clusters of relatively homogeneous groups of young children, the environmental and economic difficulties of quality research make conducting such studies almost prohibitive.

Despite the problems that have plagued studies in the past, and despite the limited respect "play" has had as a viable developmental and instructional research domain, evidence substantiating the importance of play is emerging. As a result, many early childhood specialists are regarding play activity as a medium for the consolidation and acquisition of skills that relate to all areas of the child's early development.

Play of Mentally Retarded Children

Li (1981) surveyed the literature on play activities of mentally retarded children and concluded that their activities were characterized by a restricted repertoire of play skills that could be seen in the verbal language during play, in their pretend play, and in the play materials they selected. A number of studies support these conclusions.

Tilton and Ottinger (1964) compared the toy play behaviors of 18 normal, 12 retarded, and 13 autistic children using a 10-category play classification system. The researchers reported normal children engaged in more "combinatorial" play (e.g., puts cup on saucer, cup to doll's lips) than did retarded children. The retarded children engaged in more "undefined toy usage" (e.g., touching a toy without distinct manipulations) and more pounding activities than did the normal children. In a later study using Tilton and Ottinger's classification play scale, Weiner and Weiner (1974) again found combinational toy play to be the most discriminating category between normal and retarded children.

Odom (1981) observed preschool-age moderately and severely mentally retarded children during free play periods to determine the relationship between their developmental levels and their play levels. He found significant correlations between the mean play scores on three play scales and developmental levels, but no significant correlation between play scores and chronological ages. The author concluded that the play of mentally retarded children approximates their development in other areas. An earlier study (Hulme & Lunzer, 1966) of the play of retarded and nonretarded children matched for mental age (MA), sex, socioeconomic status (SES), and home life situation found no differences in the organizational levels of their play. This finding is in agreement with Odom's conclusion that play development will be similar to cognitive developmental age.

Hill and McCune-Nicolich (1981) examined play in 30 children with Down syndrome 20–53 months of age with mental ages of 12–26 months. They found four distinct levels of symbolic play and greater variability in the stage attainment patterns in the children with Down syndrome than in nonhandicapped children.

Udwin (1983) examined the impact of an intervention of imaginative play training on 17 children who had been removed from deleterious family backgrounds and were placed in an institutional care setting. They showed significant improvement in levels of imaginative play, positive emotionality, prosocial behaviors, and in measures of divergent thinking and storytelling skills, and decreases in levels of overt aggression.

Taken as a whole, these studies offer evidence that play skills, like other areas, are qualitatively and quantitatively less developed in retarded children than in nonretarded peers, although the relationship between cognitive development and play is similar for both groups.

Play of Physically Impaired Children

The movement limitations of children with physical handicaps reduce their opportunities for exploring their environments and for social play (Mogford, 1977). They appear to their parents and teachers as more passive, less persistent and less motivated than nonhandicapped peers (Greenberg & Field, 1982; Heffernan, Black, & Poche. 1982).

Insights into the play of physically handicapped children is offered in a recent study by Jennings, Connors, Stegman, Sankaranarayan, and Mendelsohn (1985). The researchers studied 69 preschool children, 25 with orthopedic handicaps. They assessed two aspects of mastery motivation (persistence and curiosity) using structured tasks and observed play in an unstructured setting. Results indicated the presence of the physical handicap affected the development of mastery motivation, particularly during play when the children had to structure their own activities. The play of the handicapped children was less complex. These children were also less involved in their play, as shown by larger amounts of time spent wandering about or blankly staring, and engaged in more solitary play and less social play with peers.

Play of Visually Impaired Children

Sandler and Wills (1965) identified three major differences in the play of blind and normal children: 1) blind children are delayed in exploring the environment and objects, 2) they are less likely to engage in elaborate play routines, and 3) they imitate actions and engage in role-playing later in their development. For some blind children these skills never emerge.

Case studies by Fraiberg and Adelson (1977) have also documented the delayed exploration of the environment by blind infants. These researchers described blind children's failure to use their hands to reach for and explore objects. At 5 months of age, when sighted infants are becoming skilled in intentional reaching, blind infants maintain their hands at shoulder height in a neonatal posture (Fewell, 1983).

Because they are receiving less visual input about how others play and develop play routines, it is not surprising that blind children are more likely to play in isolation or to develop play routines that provide physical manipulations and auditory stimulation. Tait (1972) found that blind children ages 4–9 years were more likely than their sighted peers to manipulate objects during free play.

Evidence for later development of imitation of actions and play routines has been found. Fraiberg and Adelson (1977) found that domestic doll play was delayed and qualitatively different from that of sighted peers in that the blind children failed to endow their dolls with personalities and pretend lives. Rogers and Puchalski (1984) reported a more optimistic picture. These researchers found evidence of some symbolic acts in blind children at a mean age of 25.9 months. Additionally, 3–4½-year-old blind children in their study began to represent themselves in play and to give their dolls personalities and imaginary lives.

It is well known that blind children begin to vocalize about past experiences and to create the presence of others through auditory fantasy. These episodes are often echolalic in nature and devoid of ideation in content. Sandler (1963) and Singer and Streiner (1966) report that children with sight score higher than children who are blind on imaginativeness of play, fantasies, and dreams.

Thus, it appears that the loss of sight means less input concerning play behaviors of other children, more solitary play by blind children, and fewer challenges and exchanges in play with others. The cognitive, social, language, and adaptive skills that are acquired and practiced in the play of children as they prepare for higher order skills cannot be expected to arise from these natural childhood experiences. The facilitation of play in blind children appears to be a challenge for teachers and parents.

Play of Hearing Impaired Children

The lack of hearing does not seriously impact a child's object play during the first 2 years of life. Deaf children observe others in their interactions with objects and they imitate these actions when they engage the same or similar objects. Deaf children explore the tactile, olfactory, visual, and spatial properties of the object world. It is at the age when the symbolic use of words begins to be included in play that differences are seen between the play of deaf children and of hearing children. Gregory (1976) reported the play of deaf children to be predominantly solitary, with delays in imaginative play becoming more obvious as the deaf child gets older.

In reviewing the literature on the object play of young hearing impaired children it is quite clear that researchers in this field have focused their investigations on the social interactions that occur between hearing impaired children and others (see Vandell & George, 1981; Vandell, Anderson, Ehrhardt, & Wilson, 1982). The impact of abbreviated forms of communication on all aspects of the child's development appears to be a much higher priority for study than is the young deaf child's interactions with objects during play.

One of the few observational studies of the play of young deaf children was reported by Kaplan and McHale (1980). The researchers observed a 50-month-old deaf boy and his normally hearing brother, age 38 months, during a series of free play sessions. Interactions be-

tween the siblings were initiated and maintained through proximal contact such as handing or gesturing something to the other child. The majority of contacts between the two focused on some play material. Communication was mainly through physical contact, signs, or gestures concerning objects, and was almost entirely void of symbolism. The researchers found many communicative attempts on the part of each sibling not perceived by the other. The researchers interpreted this departure from normal play interactions to be ". . . a direct result of the older child's low level of communicative competence" (p. 481).

McKirdy (1978) examined communication patterns and play in six dyads of young deaf or hearing children and found hearing children used higher levels of language abstractions, responded to social initiations, and engaged in more cooperative and less parallel play than deaf children.

Kretschmer (1972) studied the play habits of 71 hearing impaired and 71 normally hearing children playing in triads. Results indicated that hearing impaired children were more active, displayed more scanning behaviors using all sensory modalities, were more fearful, and engaged in little actual play. The triads of hearing impaired groups were less cohesive and produced fewer successful social contacts than the groups of normally hearing children.

Other Handicaps

The play behaviors of children with autism and other emotional disorders, (Terrell, Schwartz, Prelock, & Messick, 1984; Tilton, & Ottinger, 1964; Wing, Gould, Yeates, & Brierley, 1977) with speech and language deficits (Lovell, Hoyle, & Siddall, 1968), and with multiple handicaps (Gralewicz, 1973) have been studied by a few researchers. Although characteristics of the play behavior of children with various impairments differ, the play behavior of the handicapped child relates highly to each child's cognitive, language, and social skills. The complexity of the child's play increases over time as competency in other domains increases.

ASSESSMENT AND INTERVENTION THROUGH PLAY

Because play follows a regular developmental sequence from infancy through childhood, it is logical to use play behavior as a measure of competence and maturation and as a framework for determining instructional objectives. Assessment has occurred through observations of play behaviors, then classifying the behaviors according to levels described in the literature. A few researchers have developed play assessment scales and have used them with handicapped children, but these scales remain largely experimental; none of them are commercially available.

Classification and Assessment Procedures
Belsky and Most (1981) described twelve sequences of behavior that begin with infant explorations and conclude with pretend substitutions and double substitutions. Nicolich (1977) described levels of symbolic maturity through the analysis of pretend play. The five play levels (presymbolic schemes, autosymbolic schemes, single scheme symbolic games, combinational symbolic games, and internally directed symbolic games) are compared to Piagetian stages of development. For research purposes, the author has prepared *A Manual for Analyzing Free Play* (McCune-Nicolich, 1980), which describes a procedure for assessment of free play with specified toys, scoring criteria, and videotape analysis. Gowen and Schoen (1984) have prepared a method for evaluating play in an unstructured free play situation, categorizing and evaluating play using content, signifiers, and modes of representational analysis. Lunzer (1958) developed a scale of the organization of behavior for use in the study of play. This abstract measuring scale provides a 9-point developmental scale of the complexity of play and emphasizes adaptiveness, the use of materials, and integration of materials.

Jeffree and McConkey (1976) described an observation scheme for recording children's imaginative doll play. This scheme measures frequency and duration and investigates the diversity of imaginative play. A specified toy set is required; the procedure takes about 15 minutes. Another structured observation format is provided by Chappell and Johnson (1976). In this procedure, the child is presented with twelve objects and the observer records both unprompted and verbally cued responses.

Largo and Howard (1979) provided a list of play assessment procedures and play toys that can be used to help psychologists and educators learn about the developmental progress of play behavior in children. The Peer Play Scale (Howes, 1980) is a rating scale for five levels of interactive peer play: parallel, parallel with mutual regard, simple social play, reciprocal and complementary action, and reciprocal social play.

Both structured observation and parent or teacher reporting are allowed in the *Symbolic Play Scale Checklist* developed by Westby (1980). This checklist covers the period of 9 months to 5 years in both play and language. Lowe and Costello (1976) have provided an administrative manual along with a complete description of their *Symbolic Play Test*. Unfortunately, this test, published in England, is difficult to order.

Two other tests, used with handicapped children, are available only in experimental editions from the authors. Bromwich, Fust, Khokha, and Walden (1981) developed the *Play Assessment Checklist for Infants* to supplement widely-used infant development scales. The test requires a specific set of toys; the infant is videotaped interacting with them. Fewell (1984) has disseminated the *Play Assessment Scale* through workshops and for purposes of research. This scale is built around a sequence of play behaviors and produces a play age. Children are given opportunities to interact with various sets of toys and their interactions are scored using the scale. This scale also includes procedures for eliciting and scoring play at higher levels than the spontaneous play used in the measurement of play age.

Play Intervention

Curricula and intervention programs designed

to facilitate play behavior in young handicapped children have only recently begun to appear. Prior to this decade, curricula included a social skills section but the content of these sections has been quite variable. Self-care, adaptive, and some interactive skills appear in social subsections of these curricula, but have always been viewed as secondary to skills in other domains. Fewell and Vadasy's *Learning Through Play* (1983) was one of the first curricula to be devoted specifically to play. This publication has 192 developmentally sequenced (birth to 36 months) activities to stimulate play using several developmental domains. Activity adaptations are described for visually impaired, hearing impaired, and motor impaired children. A useful feature of this publication is that it provides permission to reproduce the activity pages; thus, activities can be conveniently shared with families.

Riddick's book, *Toys and Play for Handicapped Children* (1982), provides teaching strategies for children through the preschool years. The book contains information on children with special needs and suggests specific toys for various disabilities. McConkey and Jeffree (1981) have published a book, *Making Toys for Handicapped Children: A Guide for Parents and Teachers,* that is helpful in suggesting ways to prepare inexpensive toys. These same authors were involved in an earlier book *Let Me Play* (Jeffree, McConkey, & Hewson, 1977) that describes how to teach play at various levels.

The set of materials by MacDonald and Gillette (1984), *Ecological Communication System,* is language oriented and provides an extremely thorough guide of how play interaction and language can be taught. Much of the authors' work has grown out of long-term experiences with young handicapped children.

Although Musselwhite's (1986) recent book, *Adaptive Play for Special Needs Children,* is not a curriculum, it is extremely thorough in its description of strategies to enhance communication, interaction, and learning. She provides an excellent annotated bibliography, books, materials, and resources related to play and toy adaptations.

Several other publications, while not specific in terms of what to teach, are nevertheless valuable resources for teachers of young handicapped children who want to focus on play as a viable classroom instructional target. Pelz (1982) edited a monograph, *Developmental and Clinical Aspects of Young Children's Play,* that grew out of a symposium designed by Dr. Sally Rogers (1982b). These papers describe research on play and how it can be used to reflect a child's development.

A 1985 issue of *Topics in Early Childhood Special Education,* entitled ''Developmental Toys'' (Neisworth, 1985), contains numerous articles on play and toy adaptations for young handicapped children. Two recently published books by Yawkey and Pellegrini (1984a; 1984b), *Children's Play and Play Therapy* and *Children's Play: Developmental and Applied,* include chapters particularly relevant to play in handicapped children. Bretherton's edited book, *Symbolic Play: The Development of Social Understanding* (1984) offers a comprehensive review of the research on play in childhood. Readers will also find current thinking on toys and parents in play in two recent publications. Brown and Gottfried's edited book *Play Interactions: The Role of Toys and Parental Involvement in Children's Development* (1985) provides current thought and discussion of what research has reported and directions for the future. Interest in the play of young children with special needs resulted in *Play: a Skill for Life* (Pehoski, Exner, Holtman, Miller, & Warren, 1986), a topical monograph of the Developmental Disabilities Special Interest Section of the American Occupational Therapy Association.

From this brief review it is evident that the interest in play has mushroomed in recent years. While few specific assessments or systematic curricula have been published commercially, research and literature reviews are readily available. These sources can provide a sound basis for instructional programs for teaching play skills to young handicapped children.

FUTURE DIRECTIONS

Play as a means and measure of behavior in young handicapped children has a promising future. The research thus far has produced clear evidence of identifiable play milestones. The ecological validity of assessments conducted during play sessions is appealing because play represents a natural and relaxed condition. The interrelationship between play and behavior in other domains points to the generalization capabilities of new learnings within the context of play. Future research needs in the area of play in young handicapped children are apparent. A first need is for more information on the play of children with various disabilities. Such research might identify how play development in normal children differs from that of children with particular disabilities. Such research might also answer questions about variability in play development within populations.

If play is to be used as an intervention then we will need studies to compare the use of play to the more traditional curricula methodologies. At this point, play is not viewed as a major curriculum consideration. Such factors as settings, materials, and the number of participating peers or adults are all variables that will need to be considered in future investiga-tions. The variables of age, sex, intelligence, SES, and play styles might also be studied as researchers seek to identify how play can be used in the facilitation of child development.

SUMMARY

Play behaviors during the first few years of a child's life develop in a well documented sequence beginning with early visual and manual exploration and stereotypical play. The child's abilities to plan out a sequence of events and to engage in play with imaginary objects and people are the culmination of the variety of shifts and changes in the development of the child's play behavior.

Play provides an appropriate opportunity for observing development. It allows the child to engage in highly desirable activities at a pace of his or her own choosing. These environmental characteristics are particularly amenable to unobtrusive observations or assessments. Given the difficulties of following many traditionally administered infant and child assessments with handicapped children, the assessment of play offers a welcome alternative. Instructional strategies also can be implemented within the context of play.

REFERENCES

Arnaud, S. H. & Curry, N. E. (1973). Role enactment in children's play: A developmental overview [Film]. Valhalla, NY: Campus Film Distributors.

Belsky, J., & Most, R. K. (1981). From exploration to play: A cross-sectional study of infant free play behavior. *Developmental Psychology, 17*(5), 630–639.

Bretherton, I. (Ed.). (1984). *Symbolic play: The development of social understanding*. New York: Academic Press.

Bromwich, R. M. (1985). Play behavior of handicapped and nonhandicapped infants between 9 and 24 months. In S. Harel & N. J. Anastasiow (Eds.), *The at-risk infant: Psychological/social/medical aspects* (pp. 379–387). Baltimore: Paul H. Brookes Publishing Co.

Bromwich, R. M., Fust, S., Khokha, E., & Walden, M. H. (1981). *Play Assessment Checklist for Infants Manual*. Unpublished document. Northridge: California State University, Northridge.

Brown, C. C., & Gottfried, A. W. (Eds.). (1985). *Play interactions: The role of toys and parental involvement in childrens' development*. Skillman, NJ: Johnson & Johnson Baby Products Co.

Bruner, J. S. (1972). The nature and uses of immaturity. *American Psychologist, 27*, 687–708.

Chance, P. (1979). *Learning through play*. New York: Gardner Press.

Chappell, G. E., & Johnson, G. A. (1976). Evaluation of cognitive behavior in the young nonverbal child. *Language, Speech, and Hearing Services in Schools, 7*(1), 17–27.

Corrigan, R. (1982). The control of animate and inanimate components in pretend play and language. *Child Development, 53*, 1348–1353.

Curry, N. E., & Arnaud, S. H. (1974). Cognitive implications of children's spontaneous role play. *Theory into Practice, 8*, 273–277.

Curry, N. E., & Arnaud, S. H. (1984). Play in developmental preschool settings. In T. D. Yawkey & A. D. Pellegrini (Eds.), *Children's play: Developmental and applied* (pp. 273–290). Hillsdale, NJ: Lawrence Erlbaum Associates.

Elder, J. L., & Pederson, D. R. (1978). Preschool children's use of objects in symbolic play. *Child Development, 49*, 500–504.

Fein, G. G. (1975). A transformational analysis of pretending. *Developmental Psychology, 11*(3), 291–296.

Fein, G. G., & Apfel, N. (1979). Some preliminary observations on knowing and pretending. In N. Smith & M. Franklin (Eds.), *Symbolic functioning in childhood* (pp. 87–100). Hillsdale, NJ: Lawrence Erlbaum Associates.

Feitelson, W., & Ross, G. (1973). The neglected factor-play. *Human Development, 16,* 202–223.

Fenson, L. (1985). The developmental progression of exploration and play. In C. C. Brown & A. W. Gottfried, (Eds.)., *Play interactions: The role of toys in children's development* (pp. 31–38). Skillman, NJ: Johnson & Johnson Baby Products Co.

Fenson, L., Kagan, J., Kearsley, R., & Zelazo, P. (1976). The developmental progression of manipulative play in the first two years. *Child Development, 47,* 232–236.

Fenson, L., & Ramsay, D. (1981). Effects of modeling action sequences on the play of twelve-, fifteen- and nineteen-month-old children. *Child Development, 52*(3), 1028–1036.

Fewell, R. R. (1983). Working with sensorily impaired children. In S. G. Garwood (Ed.), *Educating young handicapped children* (2nd ed.) (pp. 235–280). Rockville, MD: Aspen Systems.

Fewell, R. R. (1984). *Play Assessment Scale* (4th ed.). Unpublished document. Seattle: University of Washington.

Fewell, R. R., & Vadasy, P. F. (1983). *Learning through play.* Allen, TX: Developmental Learning Materials.

Fraiberg, S., & Adelson, E. (1977). Self-representation in language and play. In S. Fraiberg (Ed.), *Insights from the blind: Comparative studies of blind and sighted infants* (pp. 248–270). New York: Basic Books.

Garvey, C. (1977). *Play.* Cambridge, MA: Harvard University Press.

Gowen, J. W., & Schoen, D. (1984). *Levels of child object play.* Unpublished coding scheme manuscript. Chapel Hill, NC: Carolina Institute for Research on Early Education of the Handicapped, Frank Porter Graham Child Development Center.

Gralewicz, A. (1973). Play deprivation in multihandicapped children. *American Journal of Occupational Therapy, 27*(2), 70–72.

Greenberg, R., & Field, T. (1982). Temperament ratings of handicapped infants during classroom, mother, and teacher interactions. *Journal of Pediatric Psychology, 7,* 387–405.

Gregory, H. (1976). *The deaf child and his family.* London: Allen & Unwin.

Hartup, W. (1983). Peer relations. In E. M. Hetherington (Ed.), *Handbook of child psychology: Socialization. personality and social development* (pp. 103–196). New York: Wiley.

Heffernan, L., Black, F. W., & Poche, P. (1982). Temperamental patterns in young neurologically impaired children. *Journal of Pediatric Psychology, 7,* 415–423.

Hill, P. M., & McCune-Nicolich, L. (1981). Pretend play and patterns of cognition in Down's syndrome children. *Child Development, 52,* 611–617.

Howes, C. (1980). Peer play scale as an index of complexity of peer interaction. *Developmental Psychology, 16*(4), 371–372.

Hulme, I., & Lunzer, E. A. (1966). Play, language and reasoning in subnormal children. *Journal of Child Psychology and Psychiatry, 7,* 107–123.

Hutt, C. (1979). Exploration and play. In B. Sutton-Smith (Ed.), *Play and learning* (pp. 175–194). New York: Gardner Press.

Jeffree, D. M., & McConkey, R. (1976). An observation scheme for recording children's imaginative doll play. *Journal of Child Psychology and Psychiatry, 17,* 189–197.

Jeffree, D. M., McConkey, R., & Hewson, S. (1977). *Let me play.* London: Souvenir Press Ltd.

Jennings, K. D., Connors, R. E., Stegman, C. E., Sankaranarayan, P., & Mendelsohn, S. (1985). Mastery motivation in young preschoolers. *Journal of the Division of Early Childhood, 9*(2), 162–169.

Kaplan, B. J., & McHale, F. J. (1980). Communication and play behaviors of a deaf preschooler and his younger brother. *The Volta Review, 82*(7), 476–482.

Kretschmer, R. R. (1972). *A study to assess the play activities and gesture output of hearing impaired preschool children. Final Report.* Cincinnati: Cincinnati Speech and Hearing Center. (ERIC Document Reproduction Services No. EC050522).

Largo, R. H., & Howard, J. A. (1979). Developmental progression in play behavior of children between nine and thirty months. I: Spontaneous play and imitation. *Developmental Medicine and Child Neurology, 21,* 299–310.

Li, A. K. F. (1981). Play and the mentally retarded child. *Mental Retardation, 19,* 121–126.

Lovell, K., Hoyle, H. W., & Siddall, M. Q. (1968). A study of some aspects of the play and language of young children with delayed speech. *Journal of Child Psychology and Psychiatry, 9,* 41–50.

Lowe, M. (1975). Trends in the development of representational play in infants from one to three years: An observational study. *Journal of Child Psychology and Psychiatry, 16,* 33–47.

Lowe, M., & Costello, A. J. (1976). *The symbolic play test.* Berkshire, England: NFER-Nelson Publishing Co., Ltd.

Lunzer, E. A. (1958). A scale of the organization of behavior for use in the study of play. *Educational Review, 11,* 205–217.

MacDonald, J. D., & Gillette, Y. (1984). *Ecological Communication System.* Toledo, OH: ECOLETTER.

McCall, R. (1974). Exploratory manipulation and play in the human infant. *Monographs of the Society for Research in Child Development, 39,* Chicago: University of Chicago Press.

McConkey, R., & Jeffree, D. (1981). *Making toys for handicapped children: A guide for parents and teachers.* Englewood Cliffs, NJ: Prentice-Hall.

McCune-Nicolich, L. (1980). *A manual for analyzing free play.* New Brunswick: Douglas College, Rutgers University.

McCune-Nicolich, L. (1981). Toward symbolic functioning: Structure of early pretend games and potential parallels with language. *Child Development, 52,* 785–797.

McKirdy, L. S. (1978). *Play and language in four-to-five-year-old deaf and hearing children.* New Brunswick: Rutgers University. (ERIC Document Reproduction Service No. EC113220).

Mogford, K. (1977). The play of handicapped children. In

B. Tizard & D. Harvey (Eds.), *Biology of play* (pp. 170–184). Philadelphia: J. B. Lippincott.

Musselwhite, C. R. (1986). *Adaptive play for special needs children.* San Diego: College-Hill Press, Inc.

Neisworth, J. T. (Ed.). (1985). Developmental toys. *Topics In Early Childhood Special Education, 5*(3).

Nicolich, L. (1977). Beyond sensorimotor intelligence: Assessment of symbolic maturity through analysis of pretend play. *Merrill-Palmer Quarterly, 23*(2), 89–101.

Odom, S. L. (1981). The relationship of play to developmental level in mentally retarded preschool children. *Education and Training of the Mentally Retarded, 16,* 136–141.

Parten. M. (1932). Social participation among preschool children. *Journal of Abnormal and Social Psychology, 27,* 243–269.

Pehoski, C., Exner, C., Holtman, P., Miller, K. S., & Warren, L. (1986). Play: a skill for life. *American Occupational Therapy Association Monograph.* Rockville, MD: The American Occupational Therapy Association, Inc.

Pelz, R. (1982). *Developmental and clinical aspects of young children's play* (WESTAR Series Paper #17). Monmouth, OR: Western States Technical Assistance Resource.

Piaget, J. (1962). *Play, dreams, and imitation in childhood.* New York: Norton.

Quinn, J. M., & Rubin, K. H. (1984). The play of handicapped children. In J. D. Yawkey & A. D. Pellegrini (Eds.), *Children's play: Developmental and applied* (pp. 63–80). Hillsdale, NJ: Lawrence Erlbaum Associates.

Rast, M. (1984). The use of play activities in therapy. *Developmental Disabilities Special Interest Section Newsletter, 7*(1), 4.

Rast, M. (1986). Play and therapy play or therapy? *American Occupational Therapy Association Monograph.* Rockville, MD: The American Occupational Therapy Association, Inc.

Riddick, B. (1982). *Toys and play for handicapped children,* (Available from Croom Helm, 51 Washington St., Dover, NH.).

Rogers, S. J. (1982a). Developmental characteristics of young children's play. In G. Ulrey & S. J. Rogers (Eds.), *Psychological assessment of handicapped infants and young children* (pp. 65–83). New York: Thieme-Stratton.

Rogers, S. J. (1982b, May). *Developmental and clinical aspects of young children's play.* Paper presented at symposium sponsored by the Playschool and funded by the U.S. Dept. of Education, Denver.

Rogers, S. J., & Puchalski, C. B. (1984). Social characteristics of visually impaired infants' play. *Topics in Early Childhood Special Education, 3,* 52–56.

Rosenblatt, D. (1977). Developmental trends in infant play. In B. Tizard & D. Garvey (Eds.), *Biology of play* (pp. 33–44). London: Wm. Heineman Medical Books Ltd.

Rubenstein, J. L. (1976). Concordance of visual and manipulative responsiveness to novel and familiar stimuli: A function of test procedure or of prior experience? *Child Development, 47,* 1197–1199.

Rubin, K. H., Fein, G. G., & Vandenberg, B. (1983). Play. In E. M. Hetherington (Ed.), *Handbook of child psychology: Socialization, personality, and social development* (pp. 693–774). New York: Wiley.

Sandler, A. M. (1963). Aspects of passivity and ego development in the blind infant. *Psychoanalytic Study of the Child, 18,* 343–361.

Sandler, A. M., & Wills, D. M. (1965). Preliminary rates on play and mastery in the blind child. *Journal of Child Psychotherapy, 1,* 7–19.

Shimada, S., Kai, Y., & Sano, R. (1981). *Development of symbolic play in late infancy.* The Research Institute for the Education of Exceptional Children, Research Bulletin, Tokyo Gakugi University.

Singer, J. L. (1973). *The child's world of make believe: Experimental studies of imaginative play.* New York: Academic Press.

Singer, J. L., & Streiner, B. I. (1966). Imaginative content in the dreams of fantasy play of blind and sighted children. *Perceptual and Motor Skills, 22,* 475–482.

Smith, P. K., & Sutton, S. (1979). Play and training in direct and innovative problem solving. *Child Development, 50,* 830–836.

Tait, P. (1972). Behavior of young blind children in a controlled play session. *Perceptual and Motor Skills, 34,* 963–969.

Terrell, B. Y., Schwartz, R. G., Prelock. P. A., & Messick, C. K. (1984). Symbolic play in normal and language-impaired children. *Journal of Speech and Hearing Research, 27,* 424–429.

Tilton, J. R., & Ottinger, D. R. (1964). Comparison of the toy play behavior of autistic, retarded and normal children. *Psychological Reports, 15,* 967–975.

Udwin, O. (1983). Imaginative play training as an intervention method with institutionalized preschool children. *British Journal of Educational Psychology, 53,* 32–39.

Ungerer, J. A., Zelazo, P. R., Kearsley, R. B., & O'Leary, K. (1981). Developmental changes in the representation of objects in symbolic play from eighteen to thirty-four months of age. *Child Development, 52,* 186–195.

Vandell, D. L., Anderson, I. D., Ehrhardt, G., & Wilson, K. S. (1982). Integrating hearing and deaf preschoolers: An attempt to enhance hearing children's interactions with deaf peers. *Child Development, 53,* 1354–1363.

Vandell, D. L., & George, L. B. (1981). Social interaction in hearing and deaf preschoolers. Successes and failures in initiations. *Child Development, 52,* 627–635.

Vygotsky, L. S. (1967). Play and its role in the mental development of the child. *Soviet Psychology, 5*(3), 6–18.

Watson, M. W., & Fischer, K. W. (1977). A developmental sequence of agent use in late infancy. *Child Development, 48,* 828–836.

Weiner, E. A., & Weiner, E. J. (1974). Differentiation of retarded and normal children through toy-play analysis. *Multivariate Behavioral Research, 9,* 245–252.

Weisler, A., & McCall, R. B. (1976, July). Exploration and play. *American Psychologist,* 492–508.

Werner, H., & Kaplan, B. (1963). *Symbol formation: An organismic developmental approach to language and the expression of thought.* New York: Wiley.

Westby, C. E. (1980). Assessment of cognitive and language abilities through play. *Language, Speech and Hearing Services in Schools, 11,* 154–168.

Wing, L., Gould, J., Yeates, S. R., & Brierley, L. M. (1977). Symbolic play in severely mentally retarded and in autistic children. *Journal of Child Psychology and Psychiatry, 18,* 167–178.

Wolf, D. (1982). Play as a mirror for development. In R. Pelz (Ed.), *Developmental and clinical aspects of young children's play* (pp. 15–26). Monmouth, OR: Western States Technical Assistance Resource.

Yawkey, T. D., & Pellegrini, A. D. (Eds.). (1984a). *Chil-dren's play: Developmental and applied.* Hillsdale, NJ: Lawrence Erlbaum.

Yawkey, T. D., & Pellegrini, A. D. (1984b). *Children's play and play therapy.* Lancaster, PA: Technomic Publishing Co.

Zelazo, P., & Kearsley, R. (1980). The emergence of functional play in infants: Evidence for a major cognitive transition. *Journal of Applied Developmental Psychology, 1*(2), 95–117.

Chapter 10

Interactions
of Parents with Their
Young Handicapped Children

Steven A. Rosenberg and Cordelia C. Robinson

RATIONALE FOR FOCUS ON
PARENT-INFANT INTERACTION

AN EMPHASIS ON PARENT INVOLVE-
ment has become an almost universal characteristic of early intervention programs for
handicapped infants and toddlers. Parent participation, and specifically parent-child interaction, have gained attention with the growing recognition that for infants and toddlers
most learning occurs in their homes. In the
past, relatively little information has been
available to guide efforts to shape parent-child
interaction in ways that enhance the parent and
child relationship and that promote child development. In recent years, however, a substantial
body of information has become available to
guide efforts to identify parent skill requirements, child learning needs, and to develop
interventions designed to enhance interaction
and promote child development. Use of this
information has been evident in the design of
intervention programs for handicapped infants
and toddlers and their parents.

The relationship between parental behavior
toward children and developmental outcomes
has been a subject of inquiry in the field of child
development for some time. Much of the early
work in this area examined parental attitudes
toward children and child-rearing practices that
might be expected to effect how children develop. These studies were usually correlational,
and the investigators only considered the im-

pact of parents' attitudes and behaviors. In
1968, Bell's article regarding the reinterpretation of the direction of effects had a tremendous
impact upon this field of inquiry. Bell reviewed
the parent-child relationship and interaction literature and concluded that there was no basis
for interpreting the literature in a unidirectional
manner; indeed, there was evidence to indicate
that child behavior substantially affects parent
behavior and in, turn, affects the type of care
that a child receives. Bell's paper, published
during a time when there was increasing interest in the study of infant behavior and growing awareness of the competencies of infants,
was to substantially change the nature of research in child development. Researchers began to look at younger and younger infants and
to emphasize direct observation of interaction
between parents and their infants and toddlers.
The research began to focus upon descriptions
of parent-child interaction as well as the implications of these interactions for children's
development.

A concurrent development in the child development field was the initiation, in the middle 1960s, of intervention efforts with children
considered to be disadvantaged or whose retardation was believed to be sociocultural in origin. Intervention efforts for children with biologically based disabilities also began to appear
shortly thereafter. In intervention efforts with
both of these populations of children, the em-

The authors wish to thank Paul Yoder for his valuable comments and suggestions.

phasis within the intervention programs was generally child-focused curricula. Hess and Shipman's (1965) work with families with poverty level incomes was an early exception to this emphasis. They examined the relationship of maternal teaching styles to children's language development.

The logic employed in the design of early intervention efforts for young children with disabilities has typically been that of drawing information from normal child developmental sequences and applying that knowledge to the design of curricula for children with disabilities. Most of these child development curricula, however, also include the assumption that parents should be given the information about the contents of these curricula, as they spend the majority of time with the child. Despite this fairly universal recognition that parents need to be knowledgeable about their children's development and the intervention programs in which their children are involved, it has taken some time within the early intervention movement for the study of parent-child interaction and the implications of the interaction to become a specific topic of inquiry in research.

In this chapter the topic of parent-child interaction with the child who has a developmental disability will be examined, and the implications of the findings for the design of intervention programs for young disabled children will be addressed. First, a selected review of literature on interaction between children and their parents will be provided, drawing from literature on mental retardation and sensory and physical impairments. In reviewing this literature, the authors will look for patterns in the findings that have influenced the design of intervention programs. Second, strategies for describing parent-child interaction will be examined, and measures in which investigators have specifically looked at interaction between parents and children when the child is disabled will be reviewed. Third, interventions that focus on the manner in which parents interact with their young children with handicaps will be examined.

RELATIONSHIP OF PARENT-CHILD INTERACTION TO CHILD DEVELOPMENT

In addressing the topic of the relationships between parent-child interaction styles and child development, studies in which the child in the dyad has a disability will be examined. Some of these dyads have been studied either descriptively for a specific population, such as children with Down syndrome, or in comparison to dyads in which the children are not handicapped. The authors have attempted to summarize findings regarding specific maternal and child variables. Where discrepancies among findings were found, the authors looked for methodological differences that might account for the differences. First, the contemporary origins of research on interaction between parents and their nonhandicapped infants will be summarized.

Impact of Parent-Child Interaction on Child Development

Maternal-child interaction has been studied in an effort to identify features of interaction that contribute to child growth and that also can be the targets of interventions designed to improve interaction and encourage child development. Underlying current research on parent-infant interaction is the idea that parent behavior affects child development (Ainsworth & Bell, 1973; Clarke-Stewart, 1973; Hunt, 1961; Lewis & Goldberg, 1969; Yarrow, Rubenstein, Pedersen, & Jankowski, 1972). Maternal styles, particularly the dimensions of warmth and affection, contingent responsiveness, sensitivity to the child's state and interests, and encouragement of achievement, have been found to be related to positive child outcomes in studies of nonhandicapped children. Alternately, maternal restrictiveness, punishment, and intrusiveness are negatively correlated with children's performance on tests of cognitive abilities. Very young children appear to develop most rapidly when parents respond to them frequently and give experiences that are appropriate to their developmental level (Hunt, 1961;

Stern, 1977). Research on language development has stressed the importance of the social environment in promoting the development of language. Research on nonhandicapped children suggests that a child's language is encouraged when a parent's speech is matched to the child's language abilities (Hess & Shipman, 1965; Nelson, 1973). Parents adapt to their children's understanding by simplifying their speech. In particular, parents adjust the length of their sentences to approach their child's own speaking style (Cross, 1977; Nelson, 1973; Phillips, 1973; Rondal, 1977). There is also some evidence that children's language development is associated with their parents' acceptance of their efforts to communicate (Moerk, 1975). These findings reflect a growing body of research that indicates that children develop more successfully when parents encourage rather than direct their children's efforts.

Methodological Issues

Matched Designs   Before discussing findings related to specific variables, a note about methodology seems in order. In this review the authors have tried to report studies that included comparisons of handicapped populations with groups of nonhandicapped children who were matched for ability. Often, ability is reported in terms of mental age. Mental age (MA) matches and chronological age (CA) matches provide different kinds of information. The CA match reveals whether a population of children with handicaps differs from a population of children of the same chronological age. It does not distinguish between effects associated with a disability versus the effects of child abilities on maternal behavior. A Mental Age match reveals the differences and similarities when the children are functioning at similar developmental levels. Clarity about the type of match used is required when making comparisons between the behavior of parents of handicapped and nonhandicapped children. In the past, several studies have made misleading generalizations about "faulty" parental behavior on the basis of data derived from CA-matched studies. A notable example comes

from the literature on the match between the mother's and child's mean length utterances. Buium, Rynders, & Turnure (1974) noted that mothers of children with Down syndrome used shorter utterances when talking to their children than did mothers of CA-matched nonhandicapped children. This finding led to the impression that mothers were providing a poor language model to their handicapped children. It was hypothesized that child language delays were at least partially the product of inadequate language models. However, when children were matched for linguistic abilities (e.g., Rondal, 1977), findings showed mothers of Down syndrome children displayed as strong a tendency to adjust their speech to the complexity of their children's speech as did mothers of nondelayed youngsters. Additional support for the importance of matching on child abilities may also be found. For example, Brooks-Gunn and Lewis (1984) argue for the use of a mental age match when studying the effects of handicapping conditions on maternal behavior. They based their argument upon the finding that increases in maternal responsivity were accounted for by mental age but not by chronological age.

Rate or Proportion Measures   In addition to examining the subject matching procedure in a given study, it is also important to examine the behavior recording system. In some studies, comparisons have been made in the frequency with which behaviors occurred independently for each dyad member. In other studies, instances of a behavior by one member has been considered as a proportion of the behaviors displayed by the other member of the dyad. For example, mother responsivity is sometimes measured in relationship to instances of child cues (Yoder, 1986). Proportion is particularly appropriate when comparisons are being made across populations of mothers on a variable such as responsivity. If such a proportion is not used, results are subject to the competing hypothesis that any differences in responsivity may be an artifact of differences in opportunities to be responsive.

Definition of Infant Cues   Another potential source of discrepant findings lies in the manner in which child initiations are measured. Yoder (1986) argued that behaviors mothers define as infant cues may be more subtle and may depend upon greater familiarity with the child than do researcher-defined infant cues.

Degree of Difference In any area of research when differences are found on a variable, consideration must be given to the size of those differences, and whether, given the context, those differences are large enough to be meaningful. For example, Wasserman and Allen (1985) found that mothers of children with physical handicaps tended to ignore their children at 24 months. They interpreted this ignoring as maternal withdrawal. However, the degree of ignoring they reported is very small, an average of 15 seconds in a 5-minute period. Similarly, Jones (1980) reported higher levels of directiveness by mothers of infants with Down syndrome than by mothers of nonhandicapped children. Here, too, the difference is small; mothers of infants with Down syndrome were less than 10 percent more directive than their counterparts in this study. It is important to put findings such as these in perspective. Some of the differences between groups of mothers are so small that their clinical significance is open to question.

Program Effects Another problem in interpreting research covered in this paper stems from the fact that many of the mother-child pairs involved in these studies were also enrolled in intervention programs. The effects of those interventions on the patterns of interactions reported in this research are largely unknown. Comparisons of interaction between mother-child dyads that have received intervention services and those that have not are needed to help clarify the source of differences in interactive style between parents of handicapped and nonhandicapped infants.

Dimensions of Parent and Child Behavior

Child Responsivity In general, parents of infants with handicaps must cope with infants who are less active and who provide less feedback than do their nonhandicapped counter-

parts (Ramey, Farran, Campbell, & Finkelstein, 1978; Walker, 1982). Overall level of activity of children with mental retardation and cerebral palsy is lower than their nonhandicapped peers (Hanzlik & Stevenson, 1986). Deafblind infants are also less responsive than are normal infants. Walker (1982) found deafblind infants were less active and had many fewer positive experiences with their parents than their nonhandicapped peers. Child responsiveness also is lower for infants and toddlers who are mentally retarded than for normal mental age matched peers (Cunningham, Reuler, Blackwell, & Deck, 1981; Eheart, 1982). Fraiberg (1975) found blind infants to be less responsive and less vocal than sighted infants. In proportion to their total behavior, normal infants smile more than handicapped infants (Brooks-Gunn & Lewis, 1982; Buckhalt, Rutherford and Goldberg, 1978).

Child Initiations Children with mental retardation initiate fewer interactions than MA-matched nonhandicapped peers (Cunningham et al., 1981). Children who are deaf attempt to initiate fewer interactions than hearing children. Wedell-Monnig and Lumley (1980) found that children who are deaf appeared to be more passive in the absence of input from their mothers. Hearing children were more likely to play independently, while deaf children sat and looked at their mothers. Jones (1977) studied several sets of parents and their babies with Down syndrome and found that these infants were less likely to yield a turn to their parents when interacting than were nonhandicapped infants. A later study found infants with Down Syndrome made eye contact with their parents less often than did normal babies (Jones, 1978).

Maternal Responsivity Studies of maternal responsivity have not yielded consistent findings. When children were matched on two MA levels, Cunningham, et al. (1981) found that mothers of nonhandicapped children are more responsive than mothers of children who are mentally retarded. The mean mental age of the group was 39 months. Eheart (1982) also found a difference in responsiveness between parents of handicapped and nonhandicapped children. Mothers of infants with average cognitive abilities but who were premature or had mild physical anomalies also appear to be less responsive than parents of nonhandicapped children (Wasserman, Allen, & Solomon, 1985). Other studies report no difference between handicapped and nonhandicapped groups of infants in degree of maternal responsiveness (Buckhalt et al., 1978). Hanzlik and Stevenson (1986) compared mother-positive responsiveness, that is, the proportion of child behaviors followed by positive maternal behavior, among three groups of mother-infant dyads. They found no differences among mothers of mentally retarded infants, or among infants who had both mental retardation and cerebral palsy and their MA and CA matched peers. Cunningham et al. (1981) found that mothers' levels of responsiveness were not different for infants with MA's of about 2 years. Data reported by Wasserman et al. (1985) are consistent with that finding.

Mothers of toddlers who were deaf were as responsive to their children's attempts to interact as were mothers of hearing children (Wedell-Monnig & Lumley, 1980). Parents of deaf-blind children have a greater tendency to repeat the actions of their infants than do parents of nonhandicapped infants. Moreover, parents of deaf-blind children try harder to solicit a response from their infants (Walker, 1982), perhaps because their infants respond less often and less positively. Still another trend has been reported; several studies have found mothers of more severely handicapped children to be more responsive than mothers of less handicapped children (Cunningham et al, 1981; Vietze, Abernathy, Ashe & Faulstich, 1978; Yoder, 1986).

As previously noted, some findings of differences among mothers are artifacts attributable to different methods of measurement of responsivity. Where responsivity has been measured as a count of mothers' responses to their infants, the relatively low rates of maternal responses may reflect nothing more than lower rates of child activity. For example, Eheart (1982) presents data indicating that mothers of children with mental retardation made fewer responses in interaction than did mothers of normal children. However, the proportion of maternal responses to child initiations or cues was similar for both groups, suggesting that the two groups display comparable levels of responsiveness.

The relationship of maternal responsivity to child abilities has been examined in several studies. Maternal responsiveness to handicapped infants has been shown to increase with the child's advancing mental age, not chronological age (Brooks-Gunn & Lewis, 1984). This finding may be a function of greater clarity in cues presented by children as they advance developmentally. Yoder (1986) addressed this methodological issue by examining those behaviors mothers identified as cues and the proportion of mother responses to parent identified cues. When he used this method with a sample of 15 mother-infant pairs in which the infants had varying conditions and severity of handicaps, the results indicated that mothers of severely handicapped infants were more responsive than were mothers of less handicapped infants to mother-defined infant communicative behaviors.

Maternal Directiveness Maternal directiveness and control of interactions have also been studied. Mothers of infants with handicaps give more commands to their children than mothers of MA-matched infants who are not handicapped; this relationship holds for infants who display mental retardation (Cunningham et al., 1981; Hanzlik & Stevenson, 1986; Jones, 1977, 1980) and infants who display both cerebral palsy and mental retardation (Hanzlik & Stevenson, 1986).

Evidence of differences in directiveness is seen in the language mothers use with their children. Mothers of prelinguistic 2 and 3-year-old children with Down syndrome matched to three groups of nonhandicapped children on mental age, chronological age, and level of language development, directed a substantially greater proportion of directives to their children than did the mothers of the three control groups of nonhandicapped children (Cardoso-Martins & Mervis, 1985).

The relationship of mother's directiveness to

child abilities has also been considered. Crawley and Spiker (1983) found no correlation between maternal directiveness and child Mental Developmental Index (MDI). Cunningham et al. (1981) found mothers of higher MA children used more command-questions, regardless of whether children were handicapped or not. However, they found mothers' use of controls and commands were not related to mental age for either group.

The impact of directiveness on child progress is currently being debated. Crawley and Spiker (1983) suggest that directiveness is not inherently undesirable. They have found indications that directiveness can have a positive effect on growth when applied by highly sensitive mothers. Such an effect may occur because mothers who are directive and sensitive help focus their children on interesting activities. Others, including Mahoney, Finger, and Powell (1985), see little evidence for the positive effects of directiveness. They have found that mothers who are both directive and insensitive may have a detrimental impact on their children's development. Apparently, insensitive and directive mothers can disrupt their children's pursuit of interesting topics by diverting children to activities that are poorly matched to child interest and abilities.

Maternal Affect   There have been some reports that mothers' use of praise does not differ between nonhandicapped infants and infants with mental retardation (Cunningham et al., 1981; Hanzlik & Stevenson, 1986), and infants who display both cerebral palsy and retardation (Hanzlik & Stevenson, 1986). Mothers of infants with handicaps smile less than mothers of normal infants (Brooks-Gunn & Lewis, 1982). The fact that infants with handicaps smile less than nonhandicapped infants is not thought to completely explain their mothers' low rate of smiling. Brooks-Gunn and Lewis (1982) note that increases in nonhandicapped infant smiling were accompanied by proportional increases in mothers smiling. However, increases in smiling by handicapped infants did not elicit proportional increases in smiling by their mothers. Tyler, Kogan, and Turner (1974) studied a group of 10 preschool-age

children who had cerebral palsy. When mothers and children engaged in therapy, both displayed greater amounts of negative behaviors than when they were playing together. Reductions in warm, positive maternal behaviors were also noted in both play and therapy sessions over a 3-year period.

Observations by Tyler et al. (1984) and by Brooks-Gunn and Lewis (1982) suggest that mothers of handicapped infants provide less positive responses to their preschoolers who are handicapped than do mothers of nonhandicapped children. It is not clear why this occurs. Perhaps these mothers are influenced by the child's condition and relative lack of developmental progress. Another possibility is that playful interactions are turned into work on educational and therapy goals.

Implications of Findings in Parent-Child Interaction Research

Information about how a handicap affects interaction between infants and parents is accumulating. Findings regarding handicapped children's behavior during interaction with their mothers tends to be fairly consistent across studies. When compared to nonhandicapped peers, young handicapped children are less active, less responsive to their mothers, initiate fewer interactions, and provide fewer communicative and affective cues. These differences make it more difficult for parents to establish rewarding interactions with their children.

The weight of the evidence suggests that most parents of handicapped infants share substantial similarities in their interaction styles with parents of nonhandicapped infants. It appears that mothers generally adapt to their children's interactional characteristics. However, these adaptations involve higher levels of directiveness and possibly lower levels of enjoyment than would typically occur in interactions with nonhandicapped children. Moreover, because handicapped children tend to initiate few interactions, the burden for maintaining an exchange falls to parents. Many intervention approaches attempt to redress this imbalance by helping parents secure their children's interest and active participation.

The extent to which particular parent-child pairs will have difficulty interacting will vary considerably and, consequently, so will their needs for assistance in improving interactions. Children with complex handicaps appear to present substantial challenges to their parents' efforts to interact (McCollum, 1984). As will be seen, interventions that enhance parents' interactional skills can affect child involvement in those interactions. For example, Rosenberg and Robinson (1985) found that increases in child interest in interaction with their mothers were associated with improvement in their mother's interactional skills.

ASSESSMENT SYSTEMS

At this point, efforts to evaluate procedures geared to enhancing parents' interactional skills have not been precise. Rather, the assumption frequently has been made that changes in parent skills will be reflected in measurable changes in child development. Such changes are certainly the ultimate criteria for judging the effectiveness of parent mediated interventions. However, assessments of child behavior neither provide specific information about the programs' impact on parenting nor prescribe strategies needed to refine intervention procedures. What is needed are measures of parents' interactional skills with respect to their handicapped infants.

A number of direct and indirect measures have been used to assess the quality of the interactions and the environments that parents provide their young children. Several measures have appeared recently in the literature. For interventionists, selecting an appropriate and sensitive measurement strategy can be difficult. To be useful, observational measures of parent-infant interaction should: 1) permit reliable assessment of dyads containing young children whose patterns of behavior may be ambiguous due to the effects of a handicap, 2) offer a system that is efficient and easily incorporated into an intervention program, and 3) aid in identifying strategies thought to foster effective interactions between parents and their young children who have a handicapping condition.

Approaches to Behavioral Observations

Systems for classifying behavioral observations vary in the size of the units of behavior recorded. *Molar* units are broad classes of behaviors such as responsivity or directiveness. Molar categories give the least information about specific behavioral exchanges and the highest level of summarization of what was seen. *Molecular* categories are more narrowly defined. These categories record specific behavioral events such as smiles, hugs, or vocalizations, and offer little condensation of information. The molar systems for recording behaviors use global rating scales to evaluate behavior after a period of observation. Checklists may contain either molar or molecular categories. Molecular systems use predetermined categories to record the occurrence of behaviors during a period of observation. Other systems use checklists to record the presence or absence of behaviors either during or after a period of observation.

Molar Rating Systems Molar ratings condense classes of behaviors that are presumed to reflect aspects of parent-child interaction (such as maternal sensitivity or child interest). Thus, a rating of a particular individual's sensitivity is an estimate of displays of sensitivity. The ratings eliminate many sources of variance such as peculiarities of the setting or idiosyncratic acts of individuals. They allow observers to make judgments based on a number of behavioral acts involving both parent and child. At their best, rating scales make complex events appear simple. This can give rise to the illusion that these devices are simple to construct (Helmstadter, 1964). Errors in the rating scales may stem from both the behaviors evaluated and the persons doing the ratings. For example, characteristics to be rated should be readily discernible and have consistent meanings for raters. In general, rating errors are minimized with well defined points on the rating scale and by training that insures reliability of raters.

Molecular Coding Systems As previously

noted, systems using molecular categories to record behaviors generally offer more detailed records than do ratings. As with rating scales, errors in coding molecular behaviors arise from problems in behavior definition and from observer performance. However, interobserver reliability is usually more easily obtained when coding molecular behaviors, because these behaviors are more easily defined and offer fewer opportunities for varying interpretation than do global ratings (Hollenbeck, 1978). In addition, molecular categories preserve much of the variance that is eliminated in global ratings; this is an important advantage when the analysis of a problem will benefit from the study of minute units of behavior, or where small shifts in rates of behaviors are of interest. Alternately, data derived from molecular categories may be difficult to summarize, because it can be hard to extract a common meaning from a set of narrowly defined behaviors. To cope with this problem, Gottman (1978) suggests a number of statistical procedures, including factor analysis, for reducing sets of behavioral categories into smaller, more readily interpreted clusters. Another drawback to the coding of molecular behaviors is the frequently laborious nature of this process. If a substantial number of molecular behaviors are to be coded, it is usually necessary to have a permanent record such as a videotape. The process of making a videotape may itself influence the nature of the interaction. Moreover, the logistics and costs of such a system may be prohibitive, particularly for home-based intervention programs. For example, the recording of molecular behaviors into categories can require substantial amounts of rating time, making the use of such a system impractical for clinical purposes.

Illustrations of Systems for Assessing Parent-Child Interaction

Molar Rating Scales Several rating scales of interaction between mothers and their infants with handicaps have appeared in the literature. The Maternal Behavior Rating Scale (Mahoney, Powell, & Finger, 1986) consists of 18 maternal behavior items and four child behavior items; these are rated on 5-point scales. The authors also have reported on a seven item version of the scale. The full scale assesses three components of parenting identified through factor analysis of the items. These three components are: child oriented/maternal pleasure, quantity of stimulation, and control. In the one study, interrater reliability obtained using a Pearson correlation ranged between .76 immediately after training and .81 on a random sample of 15 dyads. The authors did not report internal consistency for the scale. However, internal consistency should be adequate for each of the 3 component subscales if the subscales are limited to items with strong factor loadings. A revised manual would be helpful to potential users. For example, readers should be cautioned to reverse scoring on items with negative loadings.

The Teaching Skills Inventory (TSI)–Version 2 (Rosenberg & Robinson, 1985; Rosenberg, Robinson, & Beckman, 1984) consists of 15 items that are rated on 7-point scales. These items are designed to assess structure of the interaction, maternal responsivity, maternal instructional skills, and child interest. Interrater reliability for scale items was computed by a percentage of agreement procedure. With this procedure, the authors report an average interrater reliability of .86 for the 15 rating items. To evaluate internal consistency, the authors computed a coefficient alpha for the 13 rating items that assessed maternal responsivity and maternal instructional skills, which together form a single construct, maternal interactional skill. This analysis, based upon ratings of videotapes of 23 parent-infant dyads, yielded a coefficient alpha of .96. The remaining two items, structure and child interest, were not included in computation of coefficient alpha. The former was excluded because the 7-point scale was different for this item, the midpoint was considered to be the most positive rating, and the two extremes were viewed as equally negative in value. Child interest was excluded because the item is not a measure of mother's performance. When the content of the scale formed the basis for parent instruction, the TSI was sensitive to changes in parents' skill level. Also, the authors demonstrated that improvements in parent performance on the TSI related to increases in childrens' interest in activities with their parents (Rosenberg & Robinson, 1985).

Clark and Seifer (1985) reported on Interaction Rating Scales consisting of 10 items, each of which is based on a 5-point rating scale. The scale is recommended for use with children between birth and 18 months developmental age. Five of the items assess parental interaction style, three items assess the focus of parent and child attention during interaction, and two items assess the context of the interaction by rating parental effect and level of reciprocity in the interaction. The authors did not report internal consistency for this measure. Interrater agreement was assessed using tapes from 40 mothers of handicapped and at-risk infants. Three pairs of raters were used. Ratings on items were within one scale point for 91 percent of the ratings.

The Parent-Child Interaction Scale (Farran, Kasari, & Jay, 1984) and its predecessor, the Jay Scale (Jay & Farran, 1981), use 5-point rating scales to evaluate the quality of mother-child interaction. The original version of the scale contains seven items that assess involvement, maternal control, the extent of mothers' efforts to initiate activities, and maternal acceptance of child. In its present version, the scale contains 38 items and is composed of four subscales: amount, quality, appropriateness and impression of the interaction. The authors did not report internal consistency for these scales. Interrater reliability is reported in terms of generalizability coefficients ranging from .54 to .93 for the subscales; the total scale for a sample of 10 dyads with infants who were handicapped is reported to be .87 (Farran, Kasari, Yoder, Harber, Huntington, & Comfort-Smith, 1984). For a sample of 16 at-risk dyads, a G-coefficient of .77 was obtained for the total scale.

Molecular Coding Systems Many examples of molecular coding systems have been reported. Only a few examples are offered here. McCollum and Stayton (1985) summarize work on assessment and intervention with parents and infants using the Social Interaction Assessment/Intervention (SIAI) model. In this model, no formal measures are used during assessment; rather, this is a clinical process that makes use of observations of parent-infant dyads and expressions of parents' concerns. The goal of the assessment phase of the SIAI is to select a child behavior for which an increase is desired, and then to select parent behaviors that appear to affect the occurrence of the targeted child behavior. During intervention, the occurrence of the targeted behaviors are formally recorded by coding videotapes of parent-infant interactions made during baseline and treatment play sessions. Interobserver reliability was calculated by a percent of agreement method. The authors report average reliability of .97 for maternal behaviors and .93 for infant behaviors.

Kelly (1982) used an observational coding system to assess infant and caregiver behavior using videotapes of 10-minute teaching sessions. Behavior was categorized as initiating behavior, responding behavior, and controlling behavior. These behaviors were then rated as positive or negative, vocal or nonvocal. Both duration and frequency of the behaviors were recorded. The Pearson correlation was used to calculate interobserver agreement that ranged from .93 to 1.0 during the training of observers.

Kogan (1980) and Kogan and Gordon (1975) reported on the development of the Interpersonal Behavior Constructs System. This system permits the recording of the occurrence of 22 behaviors at 40-second intervals from videotaped parent-child play sessions. These behaviors are grouped under five headings: positive and negative affect, nonacceptance, control, and submissiveness. The authors offer limited information on interrater reliability, which they described as an "agreement with consensus." Where disagreements arose between two raters, a third rater reviewed the event in question, and the final rating was based on the agreement by two of the three observers. An average agreement with consensus of 85% was reported. It is difficult to know if this is an acceptable level of agreement without knowing how often disagreements requiring a third rater arose.

Checklists Checklists filled out after one or more periods of observations have also found a useful niche in the evaluation of parent-child interaction. The HOME Inventory for Infants and Toddlers, ages birth to 36 months, (Caldwell & Bradley, 1984) assesses aspects of the quality of care young children receive in their own homes. This measure makes use of both interview and observation methods to obtain information. After visiting a parent and child at home, interviewers record the presence or absence of the behaviors specified within the HOME scale. The HOME Inventory is composed of 45 items that are organized into 6 subscales: Responsivity, Acceptance, Organization, Play Materials, Parental Involvement, and Variety in Stimulation. The inventory focuses on several areas, including aspects of parent-child interaction. The HOME's six subscales are composed of items that assess aspects of the environment. However, these subscales are not independent home environment factors, and several scales are reported to share substantial common variance. Internal consistency as assessed by the K-R 20 was reported to be .89 (Caldwell & Bradley, 1984). Interobserver reliability, reported in many studies with the HOME (by percent agreement method), is generally reported above .90 for the total scale (e.g., Barnard, Bee, & Hammond, 1984). Several of the HOME's subscale have only modest interitem reliability. It may be advisable to use only the total HOME score, which has an acceptable level of internal consistency, when making decisions (e.g., screening) about individual children. Clinicians can use information from subscales to obtain valuable descriptions of households. It is worth noting that the relatively lower levels of internal consistency of several of the subscales does not preclude the use of subscale scores in studies involving groups of children, as group studies require substantially lower levels of internal consistency than do evaluations of individual cases.

The HOME has been recommended as a screening tool with which to identify children who are at-risk for developmental retardation.

Bradley and Caldwell (1977) used a discriminant function analysis to assess the utility of the HOME for identifying children in need of preventive educational experiences. Of the children who were classified by the discriminant function as being at-risk for retardation and who were therefore recommended for preventive services, only 43 percent were correctly identified. The remaining 57 percent of the children were found to be incorrectly identified. The discriminant function accurately identified 71% of the children who displayed retardation only by including a large number of children who did not need services. Moreover, readers attempting to use the HOME as a screening tool are hampered both by the absence of the discriminant function used in this study and by the tendency of these functions to lose accuracy when applied to groups of children subsequent to the original study.

Studies using the HOME demonstrate a relationship between child cognitive development and HOME scores (Wachs, 1976). One study found that handicapped and at-risk infants showing greater levels of pleasure in contact, greater soothability or less distress, were likely to reside in households receiving higher scores on the HOME (Affleck, Allen, McGrade, & McQueeney, 1982). Developed on at-risk and mildly handicapped populations, it appears, however, that the HOME may not be a suitable measure to assess the quality of care that severely physically handicapped children receive. For example, some of the items assess households based on the availability of toys that may be of little use to children with severe motor disorders.

Another checklist, the Parent Behavior Progression (PBP), Forms 1 and 2 (Bromwich, 1978), evaluates the quality of parenting provided to infants. Form 1 of the PBP spans the period from birth to 9 months, and Form 2 assesses parenting from 9–36 months. Form 1 is composed of 54 items organized into 6 levels. Form 2 contains 70 items that are grouped into 6 levels. For each form, the levels are: 1) enjoyment of the infant, 2) sensitivity/responsivity, 3) mutuality in interaction, 4) developmental appropriateness, 5) initiation of new activities based on those presented previously, and 6) independent generation of new developmentally appropriate activities. The PBP is meant to be completed by observers who are familiar with the family. No interobserver reliability data is available for the PBP, nor is there data indicating the relationship of individual items to the levels in which they are organized, nor to the sum of all items. The relationship of the PBP to the HOME has been examined with a group of handicapped and at-risk infants (Allen, Affleck, McQueeney, & McGrade, 1982). HOME total scores at age 9 months were found to be highly correlated with the total scores for the PBP at 4, 8, and 12 months. HOME total scores at 18 months were related to PBP totals at 12 and 18 months of age.

The Nursing Child Assessment Teaching Scales (NCATS) are described by Barnard, Booth, Mitchell, and Telzrow (1982) as consisting of 73 yes/no items that describe mother-child interaction during a period of teaching by the mother. The items are organized into six subscales. In addition, scores for infant behavior and mother behavior, as well as a total score, are provided. The infant behavior score summarizes the clarity of infant cues and responsiveness to caregivers. The mother behavior score summarizes maternal sensitivity, alleviation of infant distress, and activity to foster infant development. The authors report interrater reliability of 85%. Internal consistency was evaluated by coefficient alpha using a sample of 185 mother-infant pairs, observed at 3 and 10 months of age, and alphas are reported for both sets of observations. Internal consistency for the subscales ranged from .50 to .85. The alpha's for the infant and mother behavior scores were .86 and .87, respectively, at the 3-month observation point, and .82 and .91 at the 10-month observation point. The alpha's for the total score were .90 for observations at both 3 and 10 months. As with other observational tools, subscales that have modest reliabilities can be most appropriately applied to individual cases when used clinically as descriptors, rather than as quantitative measures.

The Nursing Child Assessment Feeding Scales (NCAFS) (Barnard et al., 1982) is sim-

ilar in construction to the NCAT Scales. NCAFS is composed of 76 yes/no items. Its subscales assess the same areas as the NCATS and yield subscale as well as infant, mother and total scores. Reliability assessment used the same population as NCATS. The average internal consistency for the 3 and 10 month observations were .84 for infants, .91 for mother behavior scores and .93 for total scores.

There have now been several articles calling for program evaluation strategies that address all the goals of an intervention program rather than just child developmental gains (Sheehan, 1982; Swan, 1981; Wang & Ellett, 1982; Zigler & Balla, 1982). As previously noted, the majority of infant intervention programs specify a role for parents in the intervention, but the impact upon the parent is not always measured directly. The reason for this is that until now, few measures were available. Several of the measures that are currently available have been presented here.

INTERVENTIONS WITH PARENTS

Rationale

Children's developmental capacities determine the content parents and professionals present as curricular activities to infants and toddlers, whereas children's and parent's interests, temperament, and personal style determine the manner in which content is presented. Intervention programs for young children with handicaps have directed considerable attention toward the identification of appropriate content. Procedures for assessing handicapped infants and toddlers for the purposes of program planning have been studied for some time and are now reasonably well established (see Neisworth & Bagnato, Chapter 2, this volume). A number of curricula are now available. These include: the Carolina Curriculum for Handicapped Infants and Infants At-Risk (Johnson-Martin, Attemeier, & Jens, 1986); Developmental Programming for Infants and Young Children (Rogers & D'Eugenio, 1981); the Hawaii Early Learning Profile (HELP) (Furuno, O'Reilly, Hosaka, Inatsuka, Allman, & Ziesloft, 1985); Infant Learning: A Cognitive-Linguistic Intervention Strategy (Dunst, 1981); the Macomb 0–3 Core Curriculum (Huntinger, Marshall, McCartan, & Smith-Dickson, 1983) the Marshalltown Project Parent/Child Home Stimulation (Donahue, Montgomery, Keiser, Roecker, Smith, & Walden, 1975); and the Portage Guide to Early Education (Bluma, Shearer, Frohman, & Hilliard, 1976). These curricula provide suggestions for developmentally appropriate activities for young children and often include adaptations for disabilities of individual children (Hutinger et al., 1983; Johnson-Martin, Attermeier, & Jens, 1986; Furuno et al., 1985). In contrast to the variety of curricula available, widespread interest has developed only recently in the strategies that parents are encouraged to use when interacting with their babies.

The importance of using interventions that include components that explicitly address interaction is demonstrated in a recent study by Rosenberg and Robinson (1985). These researchers found that participation in a program emphasizing developmental content does not necessarily improve parent interactional skills, and that those interactional skills increased only when training focused on enhancing the manner in which parents and children interacted. Intervention strategies that emphasize assessment and modification of parent-child interactions are based upon the assumption that important elements of children's social, cognitive, and communicative competence develop through the child's experience in dyadic interaction with the primary caregiver(s) (Bruner, 1975; Stern, 1977). Child development researchers have investigated the nature of these interactions in populations of normal, premature, and disabled children. While individual techniques have varied somewhat, the reports cited herein are consistent on several points. These points include: 1) an emphasis upon the style of interaction as the focus of the intervention, 2) less emphasis upon specific developmental content, and 3) an emphasis upon the need to examine the caregiver-child interaction for purposes of both individualizing and evaluating the effectiveness of the intervention strategies.

Recognition that children who are at-risk for or who display handicapping conditions do not interact with their parents as do nonhandicapped children has prompted interventions designed to change the pattern of parent-child interactions so that they more closely approximate that of nonhandicapped infant and parent dyads. As noted earlier, there is some evidence that infants with handicaps behave differently from normally developing infants and that their behavior in turn affects interaction between the parent and child. Using as a model the interactive style typical of dyads in which children seem to be developing well, a number of investigators have designed interventions for young infants and toddlers with disabilities.

The results presented in Table 1 allow for only a few conclusions regarding interventions that focus on interaction between parents and children who have handicapping conditions. It does seem that there is a growing emphasis upon interaction as a focus for intervention. Moreover, the impact of a variety of interventions on interaction has been evaluated in clinical and quasi-experimental studies. While far from conclusive, this work provides strong indications that parents' behaviors can be modified and the quality of parent-child interaction can be enhanced. Additional studies are needed to expand on this promising beginning. There is a need for experimental and quasi-experimental studies that evaluate the impact of these interventions on the manner in which parents and children interact. The range of outcomes and the time periods over which these measures are examined should also be expanded in order to provide information about the stability of changes in parent and child interaction and the effects of these changes on child development.

Parent Training Versus Relationship Focused Intervention

The intervention approaches addressed here have the common element of a focus upon parent-child interaction. Wright, Granger, and Sameroff (1984) distinguish between training parents to teach or engage in therapy with their children, and interventions that focus on effecting change in mother-child interaction. Parent

Table 1. Summary of interventions with parent-child interaction as the focus

Investigators	Population	Intervention	Control	Targeted behaviors and results	
				Parent	Child
Affleck, McGrade, Mc- Queeney, & Al- len (1982)	Medically high-risk pre- matures and children with known develop- mental disabilities, 0–2 years. Family characteristics not specified. 38 Treatment group 40 Control group	Home visitors supported by an interdisciplinary team. Focus of instruction: par- ent-child reciprocal in- teractions, generalized parental competence.	Contrast group; assign- ment to intervention contrast based upon town of residence. Both groups received services available in their community. In- tervention group re- ceived, in addition, the home visiting in- tervention.	Intervention group demonstrated great- er responsiveness in interactions and greater frequency of reciprocal activities between mothers & infants at 9-month follow-up.	No specific child out- comes reported.
Bromwich (1978)	Infants (0–3) with mild to severe delays, some with sensory or physical handicaps. Families also varied in so- cioeconomic status (SES), race, and educa- tional level.	Articulates a parent-infant interaction model as distinguished from par- ent education, parent therapy, or infant curric- ulum.	Case study approach.	Parent-child interac- tion—serial videotapes. Parent behavior progression. Individualized targets based upon staffing. No group analyses reported.	Diagnostic Assess- ments used to indi- vidualize programming. No group analyses re- ported.
Filler (1976)	2–4 year-old children who were mentally retarded. Mothers varied in educa- tional background, SES, and race. N = 21 (7 per group)	Instruction via investigator and mother viewing vid- eotapes of mother in a teaching session with her child.	Three groups: 1. Mothers instructed in giving positive feedback 2. Mothers instructed to manipulate task representation to maximize correct performance 3. Control—no specif- ic focus of instruction but same amount of time.	Changes in mothers according to strategy training they re- ceived, but formal analyses not re- ported.	Group 2: Manipulatory task presentation. Children showed positive changes in task performance.
Fraiberg (1971, 1975)	Parents and their blind in- fants.	Parents, primarily moth- ers, taught to read their children's behaviors. Lit- erature in blind chil- dren's developmental pathways used to guide instruction.	Case examples		

(continued)

Table 1. (continued)

Investigators	Population	Intervention	Control	Targeted behaviors and results	
				Parent	Child
Greenberg, Calderon, & Kusche (1984)	Preschool-aged children who were deaf. N = 24 (12 per group)	Total communication approach taught to families. Emphasis also placed upon interactive style in communication.	Comparison groups did not differ in age at diagnosis of hearing loss, age intervention started, or nonverbal intelligence score.	Experimental group maternal communication skills more positive, less directive & controlling, more in synchrony with child's behavior, more responsive.	Experimental group more advanced in communication skills and comprehension and in expression of time concepts.
Kogan (1980)	Children were infant and early preschool aged. Disabilities were mental retardation & cerebral palsy. N = 18	Investigator reviewed videotapes & gave feedback to mothers regarding their interactive behaviors. Also gave direct feedback on altering style in live interactions. Looked at play & therapy sessions.	No control group, pre/post individual cases.	Decreases in frequencies of negative behaviors in both members of dyad. In 14/18 cases the decreases maintained at 9-month follow-up with an additional 7 instances of decreases. Positive maternal behaviors remained stable. Given a total of 14 behaviors observed across 18 dyads, the meaning of 58 out of a possible 256 category changes is difficult to interpret.	
Mahoney, Powell, Finnegan, Fors, & Wood (1986)	Birth-to-3 year-old children, varying developmental disabilities. School-sponsored intervention program. N = 35	Parents taught to use two teaching paradigms: Turntaking & Interactional Match.	No control group. Classified parents as low, medium, or high directive, based upon videotape measures. Children did not differ in pretests across the three groups on the basis of maternal directiveness.	Pre- & postanalysis of videotapes of P-C interaction: 1. Turntaking (Kaye & Charney, 1981) 2. Matches 3. Maternal Behavior Rating Scale (MBRS) (Mahoney, Powell, & Finger, 1986). All groups made significant changes in interactive style. Low-directive parents implemented the procedures most faithfully.	Pre- & post Bayley Mental & Motor REEL. No pretest differences among the groups. Children of all 3 groups made significant changes in cognitive & language but not motor scores with the magnitude of change varying inversely with parent directiveness.

Table 1. (continued)

Investigators	Population	Intervention	Control	Targeted behaviors and results	
				Parent	Child
Mash & Terdal (1973)	Children 4–10 years of age who were mentally retarded. Mean IQ – 55, 90% free from motor impairment or identified syndrome. Families varied in SES. N = 45–50	Ten 1-hour training sessions, 2 of which devoted to strategies of interaction in free play. Videotape samples used to illustrate points.	Comparison group (N = 5) participated in multidisciplinary program for children but not in structured mothers' group.	Mothers receiving training decreased % of commands & increased % of questions & interaction. Comparison group increased commands, questions, & interaction.	Individual subject contingent analyses increases in positive behaviors by the child were related to differential responding by parents.
McCollum (1984, 1986) McCollum & Stayton (1985)	Infants with severe & multiple handicaps.	Social Interaction Assessment & Intervention model (SIAI). Target increase in behavior characteristic of pleasurable interaction.	Included subject designs if multiple parent behaviors are targeted, they are manipulated serially.	Individual case illustrations. All documented changes in parent- and infant-targeted behaviors.	
Rosenberg & Robinson (1985)	Infants 0–3 years with varied disabilities: retardation, physical, & sensory handicaps. Parents varied in SES, educational level. N = 16	Individualized parent-child, teacher instructional sessions. Instruction focused on sensorimotor tasks & teaching (interactive) style.	No control group. Pre-posttest design.	Pre- and post ratings of videotaped P-C interactions using the TSI (Rosenberg, Robinson, & Beckman, 1984). Parent's ratings increased significantly pre- to posttest & maintained at follow-up. Degree of gain did not differ according to severity of handicap of child or prior length of time in intervention.	Ratings of children's interest in the interaction were significantly higher at follow-up compared to preintervention ratings.

training is designed to integrate therapeutic activities into the child's daily routine. Its main drawback appears to be a tendency to produce more directive, less enjoyable interactions (Tyler et al., 1974). Several of the authors whose work was summarized in Table 1 contrasted their intervention approach with a parent training approach. Affleck, McGrade, Mc-Queeney, and Allen (1982) suggested a dichotomy between directive, curriculum focused and nondirective, relationship focused approaches. To lesser extents, Bromwich (1978), MacDonald and Gillette (1986), and Mahoney, Powell, Finnegan, Fors, and Wood (1986) have also made this distinction. However, despite their value, interventions focusing solely on interaction have not been shown to be sufficient to encourage a variety of aspects of child development. For this reason, it remains important to provide parents and infants with learning activities. Often this involves creating opportunities for children to explore new situations and materials. These activities can provide a context for enjoyable and productive interactions. The challange is to develop strategies for teaching parents to incorporate developmental activities into daily routines in ways that do not interfere with parents' efforts to be sensitive and responsive to their children.

SUMMARY

Responsivity and sensitivity, along with other parent characteristics, have become common elements in intervention strategies that emphasize parents' ability to read and respond to their children's communicative cues. Such an emphasis is appropriate, as there is evidence that infants' handicaps can alter their interactive capacities in ways that impair their ability to contribute to enjoyable exchanges with their parents. For example, they may respond slowly to their parents or use atypical modes for commu-

nicating their interest. As a result, interactions may be less enjoyable and may occur less frequently. Parents may be more directive toward their infants. They may also have difficulty recognizing and responding to their infants' communications and expressions of interest. It is readily evident that these responses by parents can easily result in decreases in child involvement in activities; this, in turn, may further complicate parental efforts to find mutually satisfying patterns of interaction. Fortunately, parents and their handicapped babies can be helped to establish mutually satisfying interactions that foster child growth. Following are several characteristics of enjoyable parent-infant interactions that promote child development.

1. Parents should be responsive to their children's interests and moods when interacting with them.
2. Wherever possible, children should be encouraged to initiate exchanges and select materials.
3. Active responding by children should be sought rather than the passive responding associated with extensive use of prompting or physical guidance.
4. There should be a match between children's developmental capacities and the developmental level of the tasks and communications presented to them.
5. Feedback regarding performance on curricular activities should be informative and positive.

Parents can be assessed on these dimensions. The information obtained during assessment can be used to give parents specific instructions and explanations for making the most of interactions with their children. In this connection, it is important to remember that interaction is a continually evolving process that serves as the foundation for all teaching efforts.

REFERENCES

Affleck, G., Allen, D., McGrade, B., & McQueeney, M. (1982). Home environments of developmentally disabled infants as a function of parent and infant characteristics. *American Journal of Mental Deficiency, 86,* 445–452.

Affleck, G., McGrade, B., McQueeney, M., & Allen, D. (1982). Promise of relationship-focused early intervention in developmental disabilities. *Journal of Special Education, 16,* 413–430.

Ainsworth, M. & Bell, S. (1973). Mother-infant interaction and the development of competence. In C. Connolly & J. Bruner (Eds.), *The growth of competence*. (pp. 97–118). New York: Academic Press.

Allen, D., Affleck, G., McQueeney, M., & McGrade, B. (1982). Validation of the parent behavior progression in an early intervention program. *Mental Retardation, 20,* 159–163.

Barnard, K., Bee, H., & Hammond, M. (1984). Home environment and cognitive development in a healthy, low-risk sample: The Seattle study. In A. Gottfried (Ed.), *Home environment and early cognitive development* (pp. 117–149). New York: Academic Press.

Barnard, K., Booth, C., Mitchell, S., & Telzrow, R. (1982). *Newborn nursing models*. Seattle: Department of Parent and Child Nursing, School of Nursing, University of Washington.

Bell, R. (1968). A reinterpretation of the direction of effects in studies of socialization. *Psychological Review, 75,* 81–95.

Bluma, S., Shearer, M., Frohman, A., & Hilliard, J. (1976). *Portage Guide to Early Education*. Portage, WI: Cooperative Educational Service Agency #12.

Bradley, R., & Caldwell, B. (1977). Home observation for measurement of the environment: A validation study of screening efficiency. *American Journal of Mental Deficiency, 81,* 417–420.

Bromwich, R. (1978). *Working with parents and infants: An interactional approach*. Baltimore: University Park Press.

Brooks-Gunn, J., & Lewis, M. (1982). Temperament and affective interaction in handicapped infants. *Journal for the Division of Early Childhood, 5,* 31–41.

Brooks-Gunn, J., & Lewis, M. (1984). Maternal responsivity in interactions with handicapped infants. *Child Development, 55,* 782–793.

Bruner, J. (1975). The ontogenesis of speech acts. *Journal of Child Language, 2,* 1–19.

Buckhalt, J. Rutherford, R., & Goldberg, K. (1978). Verbal and nonverbal interaction of mothers with their Down's syndrome and nonretarded infants. *American Journal of Mental Deficiency, 82,* 337–343.

Buium, N., Rynders, J., & Turnure, J. (1974). Early maternal linguistic environment of normal and Down's Syndrome language learning children. *American Journal of Mental Deficiency, 79,* 52–58.

Caldwell, B., & Bradley, R. (1984). *Home observation for measurement of the environment*. Little Rock: University of Arkansas.

Cardoso-Martins, C., & Mervis, C. (1985). Maternal speech to prelinguistic children with Down syndrome. *American Journal of Mental Deficiency, 89,* 451–458.

Clark, G., & Seifer, R. (1985). Assessment of parents' interactions with their developmentally delayed infants. *Infant Mental Health Journal, 6,* 214–225.

Clarke-Stewart, A. (1973). Interactions between mothers and their young children: Characteristics and consequences. *Monographs of the Society for Research in Child Development, 38,* (Serial No. 153).

Crawley, S., & Spiker, D. (1983). Mother-child interactions involving two-year-olds with Down syndrome: A look at individual differences. *Child Development, 54,* 1312–1323.

Cross, T. (1977). Mother's speech adjustments: The contribution of selected child listener variables. In C. Snow & G. Ferguson (Eds.), *Talking to Children* (pp. 151–188). Cambridge: Cambridge University Press.

Cunningham, C., Reuler, E., Blackwell, J., & Deck, J. (1981). Behavioral and linguistic developments in the interactions of normal and retarded children with their mothers. *Child Development, 52,* 62–70.

Donahue, M., Montgomery, J., Keiser, A., Roecker, V., Smith, L., & Walden, M. (1975). *Marshalltown Project Parent/Child Home Stimulation*. Marshalltown, Iowa.

Dunst, C. (1981). *Infant learning: A cognitive-linguistic intervention strategy*. Hingham, MA: Teaching Resources.

Eheart, B. (1982). Mother-child interactions with non-retarded and mentally retarded preschoolers. *American Journal of Mental Deficiency, 87,* 20–25.

Farran, D., Kasari, C., & Jay, S. (August, 1984). *Parent-child interaction scale: Training manual*. Chapel Hill, NC: Frank Porter Graham Child Development Center.

Farran, D., Kasari, C.,Yoder, P., Harber, L., Huntington, G. & Comfort-Smith, M. (1984). *Rating mother-child interactions in handicapped and at-risk infants*. Paper presented at the First International Symposium on Intervention and Stimulation in Infant Development, Jerusalem, Israel.

Filler, J. (1976). Modifying maternal teaching style: Effects of task arrangement on the match-to-sample performance of retarded preschool-age children. *American Journal of Mental Deficiency, 80,* 602–612.

Fraiberg, S. (1971). Intervention in infancy: A program for blind infants. *Journal of the American Academy of Child Psychiatry, 10,* 381–405.

Fraiberg, S. (1975). The development of human attachments in infants blind from birth. *Merrill-Palmer Quarterly, 21,* 315–334.

Furuno, S., O'Reilly, A., Hosaka, C., Inatsuka, T., Allman, T., & Ziesloft, B. (1985). *Hawaii early learning profile (HELP)* (rev. ed.). Palo Alto, CA: VORT Corporation.

Greenberg, M., Calderon, R., & Kusche, C. (1984). Early intervention using simultaneous communication with deaf infants: The effect on communication development. *Child Development, 55,* 607–616.

Gottman, J. (1978). Nonsequential data analysis techniques in observational research. In G. Sackett (Ed.), *Observing behavior volume 2: Data collection and analysis methods* (pp. 45–61). Baltimore: University Park Press.

Hanzlik, J., & Stevenson, M. (1986). Interaction of mothers with their infants who are mentally retarded, retarded with cerebral palsy, or nonretarded. *American Journal of Mental Deficiency, 90,* 513–520.

Helmstadter, G. (1964). *Principles of psychological measurement*. New York: Appleton-Century-Crofts.

Hess, R. & Shipman, V. (1965). Early experience and the socialization of cognitive modes in children. *Child Development, 36,* 869–886.

Hollenbeck, A. (1978). Problems of reliability in observational research. In G. Sackett (Ed.), *Observing behavior volume 2: Data collection and analysis methods* (pp. 79–98). Baltimore: University Park Press.

Hunt, J. (1961). *Intelligence and experience*. New York: Ronald Press.

Hutinger, P., Marshall, S., McCartan, X., & Smith-Dickson (1983). *Macomb 0–3 core curriculum*. (3rd ed.). Macomb, Il: Macomb Project, University of Western Illinois.

Jay, S. & Farran, D. (1981). The relative efficacy of predicting IQ from mother-child interaction using ratings versus behavioral counts. *Journal of Applied Developmental Psychology, 2,* 165–177.

Johnson-Martin, N., Attermeier, S., & Jens, K. (1986). *The Carolina curriculum for handicapped infants and infants at risk.* Baltimore: Paul H. Brookes Publishing Co.

Jones, O. (1977). Mother-child communication with prelinquistic Down's Syndrome and normal infants. In H. Schaffer (Ed.), *Studies in mother-infant interactions: Proceedings of the Loch Lomand Symposium* (pp. 379–402). London: Academic Press.

Jones, O. (1978). A comparative study of mother-child communication with Down's syndrome and normal infants. In H. Schaffer & J. Dunn (Eds.), *The first year of life: Psychological and medical implications of early experience* (pp. 175–195). New York: John Wiley & Sons.

Jones, O. (1980). Prelinguistic communication skills in Down's Syndrome and normal infants. In T. Field (Ed.), *High-risk infants and children: Adult and peer interactions* (pp. 205–225). New York: Academic Press.

Kaye, K., & Charney, R. (1981). Conversational asymmetry between mothers and children. *Journal of Child Language, 8,* 35–49.

Kelly, J. (1982). Effects of intervention on caregiver-infant interaction when the infant is handicapped. *Journal of the Division for Early Childhood, 5,* 53–63.

Kogan, K. (1980). Interaction systems between preschool handicapped or developmentally-delayed children and their parents. In T. Field (Ed.), *High risk infants and children: Adult and peer interactions* (pp. 227–247). New York: Academic Press.

Kogan, K. & Gordon, B. (1975). Interpersonal behavior constructs: A revised approach to defining dyadic interaction styles. *Psychological Reports, 36,* 835–846.

Lewis, M, & Goldberg, S. (1969). Perceptual-cognitive development in infancy: A generalized expectancy model as a function of mother-infant interaction. *Merrill-Palmer Quarterly, 15,* 81–100.

MacDonald, J., & Gillette, Y. (1986). Communicating with persons with severe handicaps: Roles of parents and professionals. *Journal of The Association for Persons with Severe Handicaps, 4,* 255–265.

Mahoney, G., Finger, I., & Powell, A. (1985). Relationship of maternal behavioral style to the development of organically impaired mentally retarded infants. *American Journal of Mental Deficiency, 90,* 296–302.

Mahoney, G., Powell, A. & Finger, I. (1986). The maternal behavior rating scale. *Topics in Early Childhood Special Education, 6(2),* 44–56.

Mahoney, G., & Powell, A., Finnegan, C., Fors, S., & Wood, S. (1986). The transactional intervention program, theory, procedures and evaluation. In D. Gentry & J. Olson (Series Eds.), *The family support network series: Individualizing family services* (Monograph 4) (pp. 8–21). Moscow, ID: Warren Center on Human Development, University of Idaho.

Mash, E., & Terdal, L. (1973). Modification of mother-child interactions: Playing with children. *Mental Retardation, 11,* 44–49.

McCollum, J. (1984). Social interaction between parents and babies: Validation of an intervention procedure. *Child Care, Health and Development, 10,* 301–315.

McCollum, J. (1986). Charting different types of social interaction objectives in parent-infant dyads. *Journal of the Division for Early Childhood, 11,* 28–45.

McCollum, J. & Stayton, V. (1985). Infant/parent interaction: Studies and intervention guidelines based on the SIAI model. *Journal of the Division for Early Childhood, 9,* 125–135.

Moerk, E. (1975). Piaget's research as applied to the explanation of language development. *Merrill-Palmer Quarterly, 21,* 151–170.

Nelson, L. (1973). Structure and strategy in learning to talk. *Monographs of the Society for Research in Child Development, 38,* (Serial No. 149).

Phillips, J. (1973). Syntax and vocabulary of mothers' speech to young children: Age and sex comparisons. *Child Development, 44,* 182–185.

Ramey, C., Farran, D., Campbell, F., & Finkelstein, N. (1978). Observations of mother-infant interactions: Implications for development. In F. Minifie & L. Lloyd (Eds.), *Communicative and cognitive abilities: Early behavioral assessment* (pp. 397–441). Baltimore: University Park Press.

Rogers, S. & D'Eugenio, D. (1981). *Developmental programming for infants and young children.* Ann Arbor: University of Michigan Press.

Rondal, J. (1977). Maternal speech in normal and Down's syndrome children. In P. Mittler (Ed.), *Research to practice in mental retardation: Education and training* (Vol. 3, pp. 239–243). Baltimore: University Park Press.

Rosenberg, S., & Robinson, C. (1985). Enhancement of mothers' interactional skills in an infant educational program. *Education and Training of the Mentally Retarded, 20,* 163–169.

Rosenberg, S., Robinson, C., & Beckman, P. (1984). Teaching skills inventory: A measure of parent performance. *Journal of the Division for Early Childhood, 8,* 107–113.

Sheehan, R. (1982). Infant assessment: A review and identification of emergent trends. In D. Bricker (Ed.), *Intervention with at-risk and handicapped infants: From research to application* (pp. 47–61). Baltimore: University Park Press.

Stern, D. (1977). *The first relationship: Infant and mother.* Cambridge, MA: Harvard University Press.

Swan, W. (1981). Efficacy studies in early childhood special education: An overview. *Journal of the Division for Early Childhood, 4,* 1–4.

Tyler, N., Kogan, K., & Turner, P. (1974). Interpersonal components of therapy with young cerebral palsied. *The American Journal of Occupational Therapy, 28,* 395–400.

Vietze, P., Abernathy, S., Ashe, M. & Faulstich, G. (1978). Contingency interactions between mothers and their developmentally delayed infants. In G. Sackett (Ed.), *Observing behavior, Vol. 1: Theory and application in mental retardation,* (pp. 115–132). Baltimore: University Park Press

Wachs, T. (1976). Utilization of a Piagetian approach in the investigation of early experience effects: A research strategy and some illustrative data. *Merrill-Palmer Quarterly, 22,* 11–30.

Walker, J. (1982). Social interactions of handicapped infants. In D. Bricker (Ed.), *Intervention with at-risk and handicapped infants: From research to application* (pp. 217–232). Baltimore: University Park Press.

Wang, M. & Ellett, C. (1982). Program validation. The state of the art. *Topics in Early Childhood Special Education, 1,* 35–49.

Wasserman, G., & Allen, R. (1985). Maternal withdrawal from handicapped toddlers. *Journal of Child Psychology and Psychiatry, 26,* 381–387.

Wasserman, G., Allen, R., & Solomon, R. (1985). At-risk toddlers and their mothers: The special case of physical handicap. *Child Development, 56,* 73–83.

Wedell-Monnig, J. & Lumley, J. (1980). Child deafness and mother-child interaction. *Child Development, 51,* 766–774.

Wright, J., Granger, R., & Sameroff, A. (1984). Parental acceptance and developmental handicap. In J. Blacher (Ed.), *Severely Handicapped Children and their Families* (pp. 51–90). Orlando, FL: Academic Press.

Yarrow, L., Rubenstein, J., Pedersen, F., & Jankowski, J. (1972). Dimensions of early stimulation and their differential effect in infant development. *Merrill-Palmer Quarterly, 18,* 205–218.

Yoder, P. (1986). Clarifying the relation between degree of infant handicaps and maternal responsivity to infant communicative cues: Measurement issues. *Infant Mental Health Journal, 7,* 281–293.

Zigler, E. & Balla, D. (1982). Selecting outcome variables in evaluations of early childhood special education programs. *Topics in Early Childhood Special Education, 1,* 11–22.

Chapter 11

A Family
Systems Perspective on Early
Childhood Special Education

Patricia A. Barber,
Ann P. Turnbull, Shirley K. Behr, and Georgia M. Kerns

ALL CHILDREN AFFECT AND ARE IN turn affected by their families. This chapter addresses, from a family systems perspective, the reciprocal nature of the relationship between young children with exceptionalities and their families. Each section addresses one of the four components of the family system: *family resources,* which are the means that families have to address the individual and collective needs of their members; *family interaction,* which refers to the relationships between individuals and subgroups of the family; *family functions,* which represent the different categories of needs families are responsible for addressing; and, *family life cycle,* which represents the sequence of changes that occur for families at different stages and time periods. These components, which are not mutually exclusive, provide the framework for the family systems concepts illustrated in Figure 1.

Two aspects of the chapter's organization warrant explanation. The Collins and Parades families introduced at the start are referred to throughout the chapter to illustrate or highlight concepts. Also presented in each section are "Fact or Fable?" statements that represent certain views often held by professionals regarding children with exceptionalities and their families. The status of each statement as a fact or a fable is examined within the context of the family systems framework, as well as the professional literature. After reading each state-

ment, the reader is encouraged to determine his or her own opinion before reading the authors' responses.

COLLINS FAMILY

Judy and Glenn Collins were married 12 years ago after their graduation from a university. Since then, Glenn has been moving up the corporate ladder of a large oil company, with his present position requiring extensive worldwide travel. Judy held several responsible positions conducting medical research until the birth of their child, Warren, took her off the "career-track." She now works part-time at temporary jobs in order to care for her son

Warren, age 4, was born with a rare genetic disorder. In addition to being legally blind, the doctors indicate he will probably remain non-ambulatory for life because of central nervous system damage. At first it was difficult to determine Warren's intellectual capacities because of his visual and motor problems. However, part-time attendance in a special education preschool coupled with Judy's commitment to home programs enabled him to progress further than anyone had anticipated. Because of his steady progress, his teachers are trying to prepare him for mainstreaming when he enters public school.

Judy has become a dedicated mother determined to do everything she can to help her son

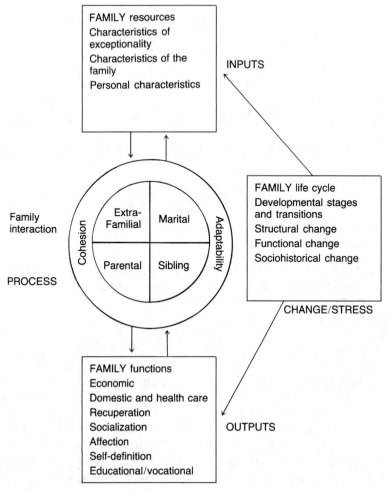

Figure 1.   Family Systems Conceptual Framework.

by home therapy, parent meetings, and by advocating for better services. However, she often wonders if she has sacrificed her career to care for her child. She had hoped to return to full-time work when Warren entered public school, but she knows that his success in a regular kindergarten will depend on her ability to tutor him at home.

Glenn tries to give Judy some respite from Warren's care and the household chores when he's at home. Yet, it is difficult for him to adjust to the hectic schedule Judy has established for herself and Warren, and it is difficult for him to learn and relearn how to care for his son. Glenn believes Judy's commitment to their son is a kind of martyrdom that has reduced their lives to a whirlwind of activities

related to Warren's needs, leaving no time for fun and relaxation. Most of all, Glenn misses the relationship that he and Judy once had. Falling asleep in front of "M*A*S*H" seems to be the extent of their personal and social life.

Not only do Judy and Glenn have little time to spend with each other or their friends, but they find little comfort in their interactions with their extended family. Theirs is an interfaith marriage—Judy was raised in a Jewish family and Glenn in a Methodist family—and both continue to practice their respective religions. The religious issue initially created some tension between the families which resulted in minimal communication between Judy and Glenn and their parents. But after Warren's birth, Judy and Glenn looked to their parents for support. Unfortunately, they found it even more difficult to communicate with their parents about Warren than they had about other family matters.

A difficult topic for Judy to broach with Glenn and other family members is that of future children. While Glenn would like to have another child, Judy believes a second child would rob Warren of the time and attention he needs, and would rob her of the chance to return to her career. How to balance the future—more children, career, Warren's needs, and her relationship with Glenn—is always stewing in her mind. Glenn, too, continually finds himself caught between his career, his need to pursue a normal family life, and his love for his son and his wife.

PARADES FAMILY

Bonita Parades left her homeland in South America 10 years ago to come to the United States after her husband deserted her and her two sons. Although it was difficult to leave her family, she knew that the move had given them a chance for a "better tomorrow." Both of her sons are doing well in school, and Bonita hopes to find the resources to send them to college. Victor, now 13, was identified as gifted in the second grade and has an insatiable curiosity about aerodynamics and anything mechanical. Dominick, age 11, also is doing well academically, although his primary interest is sports.

After several years of being a single parent, Bonita met Arthur, who had also come to the United States from South America. Because their church would not recognize a second marriage for Bonita, she and the boys moved in with Arthur, and they established themselves as a family.

Arthur is the owner of a small but successful construction company he has worked hard at for several years. At first he tried to teach the boys about the business, hoping that they would someday join him, but their lack of interest soon became apparent. He blames Bonita because of her preoccupation with the boys' education and her unrealistic expectations about sending them to college.

In the midst of these unresolved issues, Bonita gave birth to a daughter, Emily. Arthur quickly embraced his role as a father, and Emily seemed to draw the family closer together until it became apparent that she was ill. After she was hospitalized three times for respiratory problems, they diagnosed her condition as cystic fibrosis.

Bonita had worked prior to Emily's birth, but her daughter's chronic condition has required her constant attention over the last 11 months. With Bonita at home and with the extra medical bills, Arthur has been putting in extra hours at work to meet their financial needs. Since Arthur's company has an excellent medical insurance plan, however, and since the family has been able to reduce their expenses, Bonita believes he stays at work to avoid the family. The terminal nature of Emily's illness is an "unmentionable" topic in the family. Arthur refuses to discuss it, the boys have never been told about their sister's condition, and Bonita does not want to tell Emily the nature of her illness when she gets older.

The public health nurse who has been visiting Emily since her birth continually suggests to Bonita that Emily be enrolled in a hospital early intervention program, and that Bonita join the support group for mothers sponsored by the program. Bonita believes that Emily should be at home since her family and friends provide all of the help and support that's needed. This is especially true since Arthur and Bonita have decided to bring her mother from South America to live with them. Although Bonita is excited about her mother's arrival, she is also aware of the vast social and cultural differences to which her mother will have to adjust. In addition, as her mother gets older there is a possibility that she, too, will need to be cared for. For now, the entire family is hopeful that the arrival of her mother will solve all of their problems. Bonita hopes she will be able to return to work and save money for the boys' education. Arthur can then focus on the business of supporting his family, since Bonita will have someone else to help with Emily and the household tasks. The boys, who have received less attention since Emily's birth, are looking forward to spending more time with Bonita and to meeting their grandmother for the first time.

FAMILY RESOURCES

Resources, derived from the French word *resourdre* meaning to arise anew, commonly refers to a supply of something that is used to take care of a need. When professionals in early intervention use the word *resources,* they are usually referring to the funding, facilities, personnel, programs, techniques and special approaches that are used to improve or to change the status of young children with exceptionalities. In reference to families, *resources* means the characteristics and strengths that lie ready to be drawn upon to help them meet their needs and the needs of their child with an exceptionality. The needs and resources of families vary tremendously and can shape family interaction, including the way in which the family reacts to the child's exceptionality. Early intervention can be most effective when productive interactions take place between the resources of professionals and the resources of families.

This section describes family resources according to the characteristics of the exceptionality, the characteristics of the family, and the personal characteristics of individual family members.

The Characteristics of the Exceptionality

Fact or fable? The amount of stress experienced by a family is directly related to the severity of their child's exceptionality.

While it is true that the severity of a child's exceptionality can contribute to the stress experienced by the family, this fact is mediated by many other considerations. Assessments of the reactions of individual family members should include the following considerations related to the characteristics of the exceptionality: timing of the diagnosis; uninsured financial costs; the level of care-giving demands; the needs of the family members, including extended family; and the perception of stigma that may be at-

tached to the exceptionality (Fewell, 1986, Gallagher, Beckman, & Cross, 1983; Goffman, 1963; Lipsky, 1985). The family vignette that follows will help illustrate some of the ways in which the characteristics of the child's exceptionality can influence the family's reaction.

Judy and Glenn Collins anguish over the origin of their son Warren's multiple disabilities, and continue to search for a reason in their past behaviors and in their family histories. Each of them is certain that the genetic disorder was not transmitted from *their* side of the family, and they "secretly" place the blame for Warren's condition on one another. Their feelings are really not as secret as Judy and Glenn would like to think, and their behavior toward one another is often the cause of angry words and bitter arguments between them. Warren's grandparents also search for meanings and answers. On the one hand, Glenn's parents think that if Judy had taken better care of herself during her pregnancy, the outcome might have been different. On the other hand, Judy's parents question the competency of the professionals counseling them, and believe that Warren would receive more "expert" attention if Judy and Glenn moved to the city where her parents live. All of them are concerned about the potential diagnosis of mental retardation. They value intellectual achievement and attach a certain stigma to this diagnosis, which they fear might isolate them from their friends and neighbors and even affect Glenn's career. The care-giving needs associated with Warren's exceptionality place excessive demands on Judy and Glenn, resulting in a strain on their marriage, physical and mental health, social life, finances and careers.

The nature of this illustration might change if, from the beginning, Judy and Glenn had received adequate support and information from professionals to help them better understand the nature of Warren's exceptionalities. The awareness, knowledge and understanding by parents of their child's exceptionality is a most important factor in their adjustment (Weber & Parker, 1981). Stress in families is related to a number of factors. Once the sources of stress are identified, early intervention programs can emphasize the development of more positive attitudes in the family toward their child's exceptionality (Dyson & Fewell, 1986).

Sometimes professionals tend to emphasize family dysfunction. This emphasis may occur when they fail to recognize that families have many strengths and resources for effective coping. Families of children with exceptionalities, including those whose exceptionalities are severe, often believe their lives have been enriched by their children's presence (Cunningham, 1982; Evans, 1983; Fewell, 1986; Turnbull, 1985, Turnbull, Blue-Banning, Behr & Kerns, 1986).

The Characteristics of the Family

Fact or fable? Parents with higher levels of *education are able to cope more effectively with their child's exceptionality than are families with less education.*

It is the temperament of the family as a whole that shapes the family's responses to the exceptionality, and each characteristic serves as a potential resource to help the family cope (Turnbull & Turnbull, 1986). Educational level, usually associated with socioeconomic status, is only one of those family characteristics. Table 1 provides an overview of some of the features and issues associated with the four major family characteristics: family size and form, cultural background, socioeconomic status, and geographic location. This chapter examines some of the issues associated with only one of these family characteristics: cultural background. This focus should not suggest that one characteristic is more important than

Table 1. Family characteristics

Characteristic	Features	Associated issues
Family size and form	Large families	More people present to help with chores
		Intergenerational relationships
	Multiple siblings	May absorb parents' expectations for achievement
	Two-parent families	Supportive spouse
		More earning power
	Single-parent families	Less earning power
		Sole responsibility for child-rearing
		Social isolation
	Reestablished families	Emotional problems
		Ex-spouses
		Personal space
		Child discipline
Cultural background	Ethnicity	Stress of migration
		Spoken language
		Race
		Country of origin
		Religion
		Place of residence
		Upward mobility
		Political concerns
		Family roles
		Child-rearing
		Reactions to illness and exceptionality
Socioeconomic	Income and education level	Ability to pay for services
		Attitudes toward achievement and life expectations
		Sense of control over one's life
		Survival concerns
		Relationships with professionals
Geographic location	Region, state & community of residence	Family values
		Service scarcity
		Travel to services
		Frequent relocation
		Different service delivery approaches

Adapted from Anderson, Larson & Morgan (1981); McGoldrick (1982); Turnbull & Turnbull (1986).

the others. Each characteristic presents many different issues that professionals need to consider when working with families. Concentration on one characteristic provides an opportunity to explore it in more depth.

Cultural Background

The following is presented as background on the values generally associated with the South American culture that is the source of ethnic identification for the Parades family.

According to Bernal (1982), the family is considered the most important social unit, and a strong loyalty exists between nuclear and extended family members, friends, neighbors, and the community. The hierarchy in the family is generally traditional, with the man assuming the role of main provider. Individuals are more oriented toward other people than they are to concepts and ideas. They emphasize experiences that take place in the "here and now" rather than in the future. They feel "special" about themselves and their culture, and this feeling of specialness is often a driving force behind their important accomplishments. *Santeria,* one of their folk-healing traditions, combines the heritage of Spanish Catholic medical and religious practices with other belief systems and centers on a medium or healer who exorcises the spirits that cause illness.

The Parades' neighborhood is an ethnic community composed of other individuals from their country of origin. The women who are Bonita's neighbors take the place of the family she left behind. Bonita regularly seeks the counsel of one of the women who is a "medium," whom she trusts more than the doctors and nurses who claim there is no cure for Emily's illness. Bonita and Arthur's social life centers on the neighborhood, where Spanish is the spoken language. Arthur is respected by his friends and neighbors because he is a good provider. The neighbors, especially the women, look out for one another. Emily's illness is a matter for shared concern in the neighborhood, and prayers for her recovery are offered almost daily. It is to their friends and neighbors that Bonita and Arthur turn for interpretation of what the professionals tell them about Emily.

The combined "wisdom" of their community allows them to remain confident in themselves, maintain optimism and live only one day at a time.

If the professionals involved in Emily's care do not understand the cultural background of her family, they may fail to recognize the important resources for coping that are available to Bonita and Arthur from the support system provided through their ethnic identification. They may even consider them a "dysfunctional family." For example, professionals could become frustrated in their attempts to make Bonita understand the need for early intervention, for participating in the mother's group, and for planning for Emily's future. Arthur's pride could be misinterpreted as "arrogance" when he questions their advice and procedures. Observed signs of stress may be attributed to Emily's illness when they are in fact the result of conflict between the expectations of the professionals and the Parades' ethnic values, of unresolved issues related to the fact that they are a reestablished family, and of the need to preserve their family's ethnic identity in a "different" culture.

Personal Characteristics

Fact or fable? The personal resources that people bring to bear in coping can make a difference in their emotional well-being.

This statement is a fact. The personal characteristics of individual family members not only influence their reactions to the child's exceptionality, but make up the psychological resources that can help them withstand threatening events in their lives (Pearlin & Schooler, 1978). Two of these characteristics are physical/mental health and personality.

Physical and Mental Health There is an increasing emphasis in America on "wellness." The dimensions of wellness include physical fitness, which improves both physical and mental health, the ability to identify one's feelings and do something about them, and learning to deal with fear (Hettler, 1981). Wellness has important implications for professionals working with families in early intervention programs. Individuals who are in poor health find it difficult to cope with stressful situations (Turnbull & Turnbull, 1986). There are many competing demands on the physical and emotional resources of all families. The potential for even more demands and sources of stress exists among families who have a child with an exceptionality. The Collins family provides one example of the strain that excessive caregiving demands and unresolved conflict can place on a family's physical and emotional health. When the emphasis of early intervention is directed exclusively toward the achievement of developmental and educational objectives for the child, the family's wellness may be "at-risk." They may ignore their own health needs in an effort to help their child meet the program's expectations. Professionals need to recognize that the physical and mental health of families serve as an important resource. Asking family members "What are you doing to take care of *yourself* and to make yourself feel good?" is one way to indicate professional interest in their health. It also gives families the "permission" they may need to take the time and make the investment to replenish their own health resources. Concern for family wellness is often overlooked in early intervention programs, yet children benefit from the physical and emotional well-being of their families.

Individual Personality Characteristics
Personality characteristics reside within the "self" and can be effective barriers to the negative consequences of stressful circumstances and events. Three aspects of personality that have been identified with coping functions are self-esteem, self-denigration, and mastery (Pearlin & Schooler, 1978). Parents with marked feelings of inadequacy commonly see their feelings of rejection as the cause of their child's exceptionality (Mandelbaum & Wheeler, 1960). Mastery is described as the extent to which people believe the events in their lives are under their own control, rather than being ruled by fate. Self-esteem and mastery are two of the personality characteristics that serve as resources for developing effective coping strategies.

Professionals can nurture feelings of self-esteem and mastery in family members when they treat them as "equals," respect their right to have different and even conflicting opinions, and support their efforts to be in control of the decisions made for their child and for themselves as a family. It is also important to remember that individuals have different personal resources available to them. What is an effective coping strategy for one person may not be so for someone else—there is no one single coping strategy that works for everyone. Thus, family members should be encouraged to develop a wide range of coping strategies that work for them and are consistent with their individual personality characteristics.

Summary

Families have many resources to help meet their needs and the needs of their children with exceptionalities. Professionals can play an important role by encouraging families to identify and use resources effectively. First, every family must be considered individually in relation to the nature of their child's exceptionality, the characteristics of the family, and the characteristics of each family member. Each of these influences the family's reaction and serves as a potential resource. It also influences interactions within the family, which will be discussed next.

FAMILY INTERACTION

Early childhood specialists may be most familiar with the term "interaction" as it relates to parent/professional and parent/child relationships (Rosenberg & Robinson, Chapter 10, this volume). Since these types of interaction are most evident, professionals are often unaware of how the child is affected by the complex system of interactions within the family. They may thus neglect the importance of designing intervention strategies that take into account the multiple roles that family members play as they relate to each other.

Interaction is the tool that families use to accomplish the "work" or duties normally ascribed to the family system, such as sharing affection, planning for the future, resolving problems, accomplishing daily tasks, or teaching new skills. The interactional system within the nuclear family is a complex, interwoven set of reciprocal actions or influences between two or more family members. The various relationships within a family can be defined according to four subsystems: 1) *marital* (husband/wife interactions), 2) *parental* (parent/child interactions), 3) *sibling* (child/child interactions), and 4) *extrafamilial* (total family or individual relationships with extended family, friends, community, and professionals). The existence of some or all of these subsystems will depend on the actual makeup of any given family.

These subsystems are both coexisting and interrelated. That is, a father's relationship with his children will differ from his relationship, as a marital partner, with his wife. Yet, the nature of the relationship between the marital couple cannot be separated from other existing relationships within the family. External and internal forces that impinge on one set of interactions will affect the entire system.

Therefore, the interactional system functions for *all* family members—not just the child with disabilities. Efforts to assist families in providing a nurturing and supportive environment for the young child with disabilities should take into account the various interactional patterns that exist within the family and the multiple roles that family members play.

Family Subsystems

Fact or fable? Children with disabilities have a negative effect on normal family interactions.

Before determining the veracity of this statement it is necessary to examine the various types of interactions that constitute "family interaction." Children with disabilities do place additional demands on families which may stress established patterns of interaction between members. The manner in which families cope with the stress imposed by these demands and adapt their interactional patterns to accommodate the needs of all will determine the effect the child will ultimately have on family relationships.

The following discussion will examine the ways the child with disabilities can affect relationships within the four family subsystems.

Marital Subsystem   Several studies indicate that marital disharmony and divorce are more prevalent in families having members with disabilities than in those whose members do not have a disability (Gath, 1977; Tew, Payne, & Lawrence, 1974). Judy and Glenn Collins provide an example of how some couples find it problematic to maintain a healthy relationship while raising a child with special needs:

Although Glenn is sensitive to his son's needs, he is frustrated by the fact that Judy has made Warren the only source of interaction between them. Glenn misses his prior relationship with his wife, but he's unable to share these feelings with her. Considering his son's needs, Glenn feels guilty about even having needs of his own, and he is sure that Judy will accuse him of being selfish. On the other hand, Judy desperately needs for Glenn to participate in mutual discussions about their feelings, their future, and life in general.

The burden of care and other responsibilities imposed by the child can rob one or both parents of the time and energy to maintain a healthy relationship. Yet there is some indication that mothers, who generally assume most of the child-rearing responsibilities, are better able to deal with the stress of these responsibilities if they are secure about their marital relationships (Friedrich, 1979) and able to rely on their husbands for emotional support (Kazak & Marvin, 1984). The ability of married couples to share the emotional, psychological, and physical stress they experience appears to be a key to the family's ability to cope.

The assumption that marital relationships are at-risk because of the child with disabilities may be sound, but there is no evidence that all spouses will face marital disharmony. Kazak & Marvin (1984) found no significant differences in total satisfaction between couples who had children with spina bifida and matched couples with nondisabled children. Further analysis of the subscale data indicated slightly higher levels of satisfaction in the experimental group. Other studies have shown that the presence of the child with disabilities can actually strengthen marital relationships by drawing couples closer together over a mutual concern (Gath, 1977; Hare, Laurence, Paynes, & Rawnsley, 1966).

The authors conclude that the exceptionality can impose additional stress on marital interactions, but family reactions to this stress will vary. The child can be the direct cause of spousal problems, an additional burden to an already unstable and problematic relationship, or a positive influence on the marital subsystem.

Parental Subsystem The parental subsystem, generally the mother/child dyad, has received the most attention from professionals concerned with early education. Emphasis may be placed on how the mother affects the child's development rather than on the reciprocal nature of the relationship. Less attention has been paid to father/child interactions, thus ignoring the father's role in the child's development, the effects of the child's disabilities on the father, and the ultimate impact these relationships will have on others within the family.

Generalizations about the impact of the child with disabilities on mothers and fathers cannot be made, since there appear to be differences in how each will respond. For example, the sex of the child may be a relevant factor in how parents react to the birth of the child, with fathers showing a greater initial impact when the child is a boy, and mothers being more affected by the birth of a girl (Farber, Jenne, & Toigo, 1960).

Mothers and fathers appear to voice different concerns in relation to their child. Gumz & Gubrium (1972) found that mothers focus on matters related to the nuclear family, such as child care and other daily tasks, emotional strain, and family harmony, whereas fathers show more concern than mothers about societal acceptance and stigmatization of the family, the child's future, costs of care and similar matters. Although these concerns parallel traditional parental roles, some fathers, for example, who more actively participate in child raising activities, may show equal concern for home-related issues, whereas some mothers

may focus more on the child's eventual independence than on the day-to-day tasks.

Fathers of children with disabilities may feel inferior in their parental roles:

Glenn feels inadequate as a father since he has little time to interact with Warren, and when he does he must rely on Judy's instruction. At times he's jealous of how well Judy and Warren seem to get along, each one understanding the other. Yet for Glenn, simple interactions are a constant struggle.

It is not surprising that the primary caregiver will develop a system of communication with the child that meets their needs, but one that may not be well understood by others. For Glenn, and other fathers, it may be frustrating that they are unable to establish similar interactional patterns. Loss of self-esteem may occur when fathers are unable to fulfill traditional roles as models for their children (Cummings, 1976; Gath, 1977).

Arthur knew he could never be the father he wanted to be with Bonita's children. He was unable to enjoy the respect he needed from the two boys for his accomplishments and hard work over the past few years. He was sure that his own child, especially a boy, would follow in his footsteps and would accept and understand all of the things he believed in. For Arthur, the birth of a girl was a slight disappointment, but still something to be proud of. After his daughter was diagnosed, Arthur lost all hope of being a real "father."

Although some parents may find it difficult to adjust to the unexpected role of parent of a child with disabilities, the most important factor that may influence parents' attitudes is their interaction with their child, and it is through the interactional process that many parents learn to love and accept their child (Darling & Darling, 1982). Professionals can enhance relationships between parents and their children by acknowledging differences between fathers and mothers in relation to needs, expectations, roles, and interactions, and through the design of early intervention programs that will facilitate healthy parent and child relationships.

Sibling Subsystem Bonita is proud of how her sons have helped with Emily and the household chores, but it is becoming apparent that the novelty of playing "big brother" is beginning to wear off for both of them. In addition, Bonita is finding it difficult to respond to the boys' questions about Emily's health. In trying to protect the boys, Bonita and Arthur may actually be hampering the children's ability to adapt to the special problems of having a sister with disabilities.

As with parents, brothers and sisters must learn to make adjustments both initially and over the span of a life-time because of the special needs of their sibling. They must learn to contend with the fact that a disproportionate amount of their parent's time and energies and the total family resources must be deflected to meet the extra demands imposed by the child. Older children, especially daughters, may be given increased responsibilities in relation to household chores or the care of the child. In addition, siblings must learn to deal with the questions and positive and negative reactions of friends, neighbors, and strangers. These stressors, added to the normal problems of growing up, place siblings at-risk for psychological and emotional problems. Some negative reactions of siblings cited in the literature include: 1) attention-seeking behaviors (Kew, 1975), 2) siblings' fears of being disabled themselves, 3) feelings of guilt, shame, and neglect (Grossman, 1972), and 4) concerns about the future (McCullough, 1981). Some factors that appear to place siblings at greater risk for stress and other related problems include the age, sex, and birth order of the sibling, the type and severity of the disability, interactions between siblings and the child with disabilities in relation to parental norms, and the effect of the child on the family's future (Vadasy, Fewell, Meyer, & Schell, 1984).

Despite the potential negative effects, many siblings seem to make successful adjustments to their situations (McMichael, 1971; Schipper, 1959). In some cases, siblings cite the positive aspects of their experiences with disabled sisters and brothers, such as a greater understanding of other people, greater compassion and tolerance, and a greater appreciation of their own intelligence and good health (Grossman, 1972).

Does the child with disabilities have a negative impact on sibling interactions? For some siblings such an impact would be a fact, for others a fable. Much more needs to be known about why some siblings make better adjustments than others. What is known is that both parents and professionals are often unaware that siblings are experiencing problems in adjustment, since they rarely voice their concerns. Professionals can help by assisting parents in identifying and responding to the needs of siblings and by reinforcing early and ongoing communication with siblings about the child's disabilities.

Extrafamilial Subsystem   The extrafamilial susbsystem is defined by the interactions between the family or individual family members and members of the extended family, friends, the community, and professionals. Many families rely on members of this subsystem for emotional and psychological support, information, or assistance with child-care and other needed resources. Yet, many of these families have smaller and less supportive networks than families with nondisabled members (Kazak & Marvin, 1984). This may be due in part to the fact that families often pull away when they find that others are unable to understand their problems (Winton & Turnbull, 1981) and in part to the fact that friends and relatives may avoid interaction with the family because of their discomfort with the disabled person (Morton, 1985).

Many families prefer to look to their own kin for support. Grandparents, as well as other family members, often play an important role in assisting the family, but often interactions between family members and the extended family are strained. Parents may find that it is difficult for others to relate to the child or the special problems surrounding the child and it is therefore difficult for them to provide the needed support.

Judy and Glenn's relationships with their parents were already tenuous before Warren's birth, but their parents' inability to respond appropriately to their needs has created further tension. Since Judy and Glenn had never really established a strong system of communication with their parents, it is not surprising that both sets of grandparents are trying to provide the support they *assume* is needed.

Grandparents also may go through a process of grief and mourning for the expected grandchild, while simultaneously feeling sorrow because of the burden the child will place on their own children (Fewell, 1986). They may need assistance in working through their own feelings before they can play a supportive role. Open lines of communication and the continual sharing of information about the child and family will facilitate this process.

Families can play an active role in maintaining relationships with members of the extrafamilial system by encouraging others to interact with their child, by teaching them skills that will enhance these interactions, by sharing information about the child's condition, his or her school program and his or her interests, or by providing others with books and materials that will help them gain a better understanding of the needs of the child and family. Families may lose some members of their support systems but may gain others. The child's impact on the relationships of the family with these individuals may be negative in some cases but positive in others.

Summary

The manner in which the child with disabilities affects family members cannot be assumed, since families differ along a number of dimensions. Yet, if professionals can look at each family in relation to its own interactional system and the manner in which interactions are used as tools to fulfill the tasks of daily life, support and assistance can be provided that will more closely meet the needs of the total family, and therefore those of the child.

FAMILY FUNCTIONS

Families are very busy meeting daily needs. A glance through any family's daily schedule makes one wonder how everything is accomplished. Normal daily activities plus tasks added by early intervention and preschool programs often fill to overflowing the schedules of families of young children who have exceptionalities. Basic family tasks, or functions, can be categorized as follows: economic, domestic/health care, recreation, socialization, affection, self-identity, and educational/vocational (Turnbull & Turnbull, 1986). Table 2

Table 2. Tasks associated with family functions

Economic	Domestic/health care	Recreation
Generating income Paying bills and banking Handling investments Overseeing insurance benefit programs Earning allowance Dispensing allowance	Food purchasing and food preparation Clothes purchasing and preparation Health care and maintenance Safety and protection Transportation Home maintenance	Individual and family-oriented Setting aside demands Developing and enjoying hobbies

Socialization	Self-definition	Affection
Interpersonal relationships Developing social skills Engaging in social activities	Establishing self-identity and self-image Recognizing strengths and weaknesses Sense of belonging	Nurturing and love Companionship Intimacy Expressing emotions

Educational/vocational		
Continuing education for parents School work Homework Cultural appreciation Career choice Development of work ethic Support of career interests and problems		

From *Families, professionals, and exceptionality: A special partnership* (p. 68) by A. P. Turnbull and H. R. Turnbull, 1986. Columbus, OH: Charles E. Merrill.

provides an overview of some tasks associated with each family function. Some activities involve several functions, such as the bedtime ritual that many families of young children develop. Reading a bedtime story followed by a good-night kiss may involve socialization, self-identity, affection, educational/vocational, and recreational functions. Most tasks, when closely assessed, have elements of several functions such as this.

Although each family develops its own style of meeting its needs within these seven functional categories, little research has been conducted to assess how families of children with exceptionalities carry out their functions. The research available usually lacks a control group for the purpose of determining whether families of children with and without exceptionalities differ in how they function (Crnic, Friedrich, & Greenberg, 1983). This section of the chapter will look at factors that may affect the way families with young children who have exceptionalities address family needs and at the issues that families must face in determining priority needs and functions.

Addressing Family Needs

Fact or fable? Families with young children who have exceptionalities need professional help in meeting family needs.

Young children with exceptionalities may cause their families to change the way they address major functions. The characteristics of the exceptionality, family resources, and family interactions may each influence the manner in which the family adapts to meet its needs.

Before Emily's birth Bonita had always been responsible for the household chores such as cleaning and cooking, but with the extra care that Emily needs, Bonita is now unable to find the time to keep up the house alone.

Often, because of the extra caregiving requirements of the child, the routines that families had developed for meeting needs must be changed. Frequently, children with exceptionalities make greater demands on their families in having their basic needs met (Beckman-Bell, 1981; Schell, 1981) Depending on the characteristics of the exceptionality, there may

be greater degrees of dependency and physical incapacitation (Dyson & Fewell, 1986; Gallagher et al., 1983) which may continue for longer periods of time than for children without exceptionalities.

In many cases, the extra caregiving demands of the child may impinge on the family's ability to address other functions. For example, young children with autism may require extensive supervision such that it may become difficult for parents to meet some of the other needs of the family (Bristol & Schopler, 1984). Parents of children with chronic illnesses such as Emily's may have to take time from other daily tasks to transport their children to and from appointments with physicians or therapists (Doernberg, 1978), which often includes waiting for tests to be completed, or for time to talk with specialists. In addition, families also may be expected to provide some of the child's intervention at home.

Judy finds it difficult to find the extra minutes in each day to get everything done if something unexpected arises. She spends at least 2 hours each day providing an intensive program to support what Warren is doing in preschool and has her own schedule carefully blocked out around this time.

To incorporate the needs of the child, families may find it necessary to adapt not only their schedules, but their resources, as well. In some cases, parents may experience increased financial demands due to the special needs of the child (Gallagher et al., 1983). The cost of medical interventions, therapies, transportation, and adaptive equipment may cause one or both parents to seek a second job or some other means of meeting their financial needs, thus creating an impact on how the other functions may need to be met.

Families may make adaptations with the child's and family's needs in mind through several means. There is research to show that many families seek help in meeting the functions by relying on family members or other members of their informal support networks, such as friends and neighbors, to provide assistance (Berger & Fowlkes, 1980; Caplan, 1976).

Judy depends on Glenn, when he is home, to help with many of the household tasks. Glenn says that she has organized the menus and shopping lists so well that anyone could purchase the groceries and not forget a thing! He also assists with the laundry and cooking chores.

As in many families, grandparents may assume some of the care-giving or other tasks in order to provide parents with time to relax or to meet other needs (Schell, 1981).

Bonita's mother will help to provide the "extra hands" so that Bonita's sons Victor and Dominick can be relieved of many of their household chores, and spend more time on their schoolwork and sports activities. Bonita also sees the possibility of her own return to work once her mother is situated in their home.

In some cases, parents may exchange caregiving responsibilities with other parents in the neighborhood or those involved in the same early intervention program. These are just some of the ways families can adapt their own resources or utilize the assistance of extended family members, neighbors, and friends as they attempt to meet the multiple needs of the child and other family members.

Research has shown that families may prefer to use their informal support systems before they will take advantage of the formal support systems that are available (Brotherson, 1985; Schilling, Gilchrist, & Schinke, 1984). Yet, many families use formal support systems in addition to their informal networks to meet the family's needs. Physicians, nurses, social workers, teachers, therapists, and others all provide support, information, and aid for families of young children with exceptionalities.

Glenn has hired someone to help Judy with the household chores, allowing her to spend time on Warren's program. Judy was unable to keep up with the house alone while Glenn traveled, so this extra help has been a lifesaver in her eyes.

Some parents may need help with domestic functions, such as hiring someone to do household chores. They also may find it necessary to seek help through local, state or federal agencies (Berger & Fowlkes, 1980; Bricker & Ca-

suso, 1979; Gallagher et al., 1983; Winton, 1980). Visiting nurses may help with the child's health care needs, financial assistance for such expenses as modifying adaptive equipment can help relieve the strain on the family's economic resources, and respite and child care services allow family members extra time to attend to other needs.

Although families with young children with exceptionalities may seek the help of professionals to meet family needs, this is not the only way in which families may adapt. For many families, it is possible to change to meet the functional needs through the use of family members and informal support networks. Other families either lack informal support or are unable to gain access to this network. These families may need greater assistance from professionals in order to meet their total needs within the seven functional categories.

Family Function Priorities

Fact or fable? The education/vocation function should be the first priority for families of young children with exceptionalities.

Parents of young children with exceptionalities would usually agree that they wish their children could have the best education possible (Joworowski & Joworowski, 1978). Yet professionals should not assume that families view education as the first priority. Parents may have little choice as to what their first priority may be, or they may choose to deemphasize certain functions. Differing priorities between parents and professionals may at times cause conflicts in goal-setting for the child.

Parents may be restricted in determining priority family functions. The medical needs of the child may force choices because of the immediacy of the child's needs and the critical nature of the medical problem.

Emily has been rushed to the hospital several times, and each time Bonita and Arthur feared that she would die. Nothing else mattered to them until they knew the crisis was over. Only then could other issues be considered.

A medical crisis may force families to place the child's needs first at any given time. Emergency hospitalizations may require one or both parents to block out all other functions until the crisis has passed. Children with chronic illnesses may create situations such as this periodically or continually over a long time span. Aside from critical medical needs, other caregiving needs of the young child with an exceptionality may force parents to emphasize some functions over others. The economic, domestic, and health care functions are usually most affected.

Bonita sees Emily's medical needs as first priority for the family. She realizes that forgetting Emily's medicine or therapy will result in catastrophic effects on her health. Arthur agrees that Emily's medical needs may be the highest priority, but he is equally concerned about his ability to support the family if taxes, utilities and food costs keep rising.

For some families, the basic necessities are of the highest priority, and meeting those needs through informal and formal support is most critical. Professionals need to understand that families are often faced with responsibilities that must take precedence over the child's education and that the manner in which families rank by priority tasks and responsibilities may be dictated by the needs of one or more family members.

Families may consciously choose to deemphasize some of the family functions, almost to the point of omitting them. Some functions, such as economics, are necessary for the family to survive from day to day, but other functions that families deem less immediate and important can be "set aside" temporarily or even for long periods. For example, most families of infants and young children find it difficult to allocate time for activities to meet all of the family's needs, but this usually changes as schedules are developed and as children become more independent. Families who have children with chronic medical exceptionalities, severe behavior disorders, or other longterm disabilities may experience this same dilemma, but for longer periods of time. One function that is often deemphasized is recreation. It may seem that there is not enough time, money, or energy to devote to relaxation.

Glenn and Judy have not taken a vacation, or even hired a babysitter so that they could go to the movies, since Warren was born. Television has become their only recreation. Judy misses reading *The Wall Street Journal* but does not see how she can fit it into her schedule again without taking something away—and she can't imagine what that something would be. Glenn finds that the only recreation he now gets is taking care of the yard. Judy has suggested that they hire someone to do it, but Glenn feels that at least he is getting outside.

Another function that families may deemphasize is socialization. Families with young children with exceptionalities may choose to avoid activities in which they interact with families of children without exceptionalities. Issues related to the characteristics of their child's exceptionality, such as wheelchair accessibility, may create difficulties which some families would rather avoid. It may be easier to socialize with families who are similar and who form an informal support system (Darling & Darling, 1982), but such preferences may restrict the family's socialization network.

Regardless of how families decide to rank by priority their functions, they may experience difficulties when their priorities do not match those of professionals who are providing services to the family. Extensive interventions for the child may or may not be meeting the family's needs in the most appropriate way. Too much time devoted to interventions may force parents to slight other functions. Some parents may choose to rank socialization or the identity of the child as more important than educational intervention because they see the child's self-image and ability to interact with others as ultimately more valuable. When parents choose not to follow professional suggestions because of other priorities, they may be made to feel they do not have their child's best interests at heart (Foster, Berger, & McLean, 1981). Professionals may be unaware of other impinging needs that make it difficult and stressful, if not impossible, for families to place the child's educational needs first. With seven functional categories of needs to be met, families need to create a balance that continues to meet the needs of all members efficiently.

Summary

Families are busy meeting the needs of all members through the seven functional categories. These functions may be fulfilled in a variety of ways that are unique to each family. Young children with exceptionalities may create the need to change the way their families meet these functions, due to caregiving demands, increased financial demands, and other factors. Families may adapt by involving other family members and informal or formal support systems to help meet their needs. Factors such as financial needs or the health of the child may force families to place one function above all others. Or they may choose to deemphasize certain functions because of time, economics, or other restrictions. Finally, families may feel pressure if the functions they consider most important are seen as less important by helping professionals.

Professionals can support family functioning through aid in developing and strengthening informal support systems, through help in ranking by priority needs based on the family's viewpoint, and through providing access to formal services.

FAMILY LIFE CYCLE

The three perspectives that have been presented on family life—resources, interaction, and functions—provide a "snapshot" of family adaptation at any given time. This "snapshot," however, is misleading if its static nature is not complemented. The final perspective of a systems orientation, the family life cycle, involves the dynamic view that the "snapshots" of family life must be combined into a "motion picture," the scenes of which illuminate the everchanging nature of resources, interaction, and functions.

The key concepts in a family life cycle are *chronicity* and *change,* which interact over the entire life span of the family. These concepts can best be understood by an analysis of family life cycle stages and the transitions between them. An overview of developmental stages and transitions will be presented, their implica-

tions for family-professional interactions during the early childhood period will be described.

Family Life Cycle Stages

Fact or fable? Family life with a child with a disability should be a sprint for development during the early years.

Although many early childhood educators regard this assumption as a fact, the authors suggest that it is indeed a fable. This belief presumes that early childhood is the most important period of all, and that intense effort toward ameliorating the child's disability will undoubtedly yield dividends for the child and family. The chief problem with the assumption and the reason it is viewed by the authors as false, is that it does not adequately take into consideration the long-term implications of disability and the continuing impact of family coping over the entire life cycle. Consider the situation facing Judy and Glenn Collins:

In many ways Judy has approached Warren's first 5 years as if it were a sprint for development. Because of the time and attention she has invested in working with Warren at home and in actively participating in his early intervention program, Glenn feels their marriage is shortchanged. Both Glenn and Judy experience frustration over the fact that recreation, socialization, and affection have been sacrificed to developmental and educational needs. A major effect on the family life cycle is Judy's reluctance to have another child because of the time and attention she invests in Warren. Thus, the emphasis on the educational function with Warren has spin-off effects on the marital, parental, and sibling subsystems and on the overall nature of the family's satisfaction and quality of life in meeting a range of needs in different functional areas.

Six Developmental Stages Perhaps an awareness of life cycle issues and decision-making could have been shared with the Collins family by the professionals working with Warren to help them gain perspective on early childhood. Such a perspective would recognize that the family life cycle can be conceptualized as a series of developmental stages representing periods in which the needs of the family are generally similar and the services and programs offered are both similar and stable. Many conceptualizations of developmental stages have been described in the literature, ranging from as many as 24 stages to as few as 6 (Carter & McGoldrick, 1980). Typically the stages are defined in terms of the ages of children, particularly the oldest child. The conceptualization the authors propose consists of six stages: birth and early childhood, elementary

school years, adolescence, young adulthood, empty nest, and elderly years.

Each of these stages has special implications for every member of the family when any one member has a disability. Table 3 summarizes *possible* issues that parents and siblings may face at each of the six life cycle stages, particularly when the member has a severe disability. It is important to remember, however, that families vary and that one should not automatically expect these issues to be manifested.

Table 3.   Possible issues encountered at life cycle stages

Life cycle stage	Parents	Siblings
Early childhood, ages 0–5	Obtaining an accurate diagnosis Informing siblings and relatives Locating services Seeking to find meaning in the exceptionality Clarifying a personal ideology to guide decision-making Addressing issues of stigma Identifying positive contributions of exceptionality	Less parental time and energy for sibling needs Feelings of jealousy over less attention Fears associated with misunderstandings of exceptionality
School Age, ages 6–12	Establishing routines to carry out family functions Adjusting emotionally to educational implications Clarifying issues of mainstreaming versus special class placement Participating in individualized education program conferences Locating community resources Arranging for extracurricular activities	Division of responsibility for any physical care needs Oldest female sibling may be at-risk Limited family resources for recreation and leisure Informing friends and teachers Possible concern over surpassing younger sibling Issues of "mainstreaming" into same school Need for basic information on exceptionality
Adolescence, ages 13–21	Adjusting emotionally to possible chronicity of exceptionality Identifying issues of emerging sexuality Addressing possible peer isolation and rejection Planning for career/vocational development Arranging for leisure time activities Dealing with physical and emotional change of puberty Planning for postsecondary education	Overidentification with sibling Greater understanding of differences in people Influence of exceptionality on career choice Dealing with possible stigma and embarrassment Participation in sibling training programs Opportunity for sibling support groups
Adulthood, ages 21–	Planning for possible need for guardianship Addressing the need for appropriate adult residence Adjusting emotionally to any adult implications of dependency Addressing the need for socialization opportunities outside the family for individual with exceptionality Initiating career choice or vocational program	Possible issues of responsiblity for financial support Addressing concerns regarding genetic implications Introducing new in-laws to exceptionality Need for information on career/living options Clarify role of sibling advocacy Possible issues of guardianship

Alterations in Developmental Stages
Although families generally move through the life cycle stages from beginning to end, various alterations occur. The Parades family illustrates one type of alteration: Bonita was married previous to her relationship with Arthur; thus, Arthur did not experience the birth of Victor and Dominick, and entered their life midway through the early childhood stage.

Many families are reestablished (Visher & Visher, 1982); thus, parents enter the children's lives at various times. This can have major implications for the interactions that occur within families.

In the field of disability a new developmental stage is emerging which could be characterized as prebirth. As the identification of disability during fetal development becomes increasingly prevalent, would-be parents are provided with choices concerning the desirability of having a child with a disability.

Consider the scenario that Glenn and Judy Collins had sought amniocentesis during Judy's pregnancy and had been told that a disability existed. Would they have elected to be parents of Warren? Would they have elected abortion?

One study reported that 76% of the parents who sought amniocentesis for the purpose of determining if a disability existed elected to have an abortion when informed that disabling conditions existed (Laxova, 1980). Some of the ethical issues associated with this prebirth stage are discussed by Turnbull and Turnbull (1986).

Change and Chronicity in Developmental Stages As shown in Table 3, some of the issues in successive developmental stages are similar and some are different. Families need to be prepared to change as they face new issues associated with developmental growth. An example of this is change in parental advocacy as parents age and are unable to assume the intense responsibility they demonstrated at earlier life cycle stages. Assisting and supporting parents to make these changes is an important responsibility of professionals who work with them.

Families also need to be prepared for the fact that some issues do not change as much as

others, so that learning to live with chronicity is an important coping strategy. For example, Wikler, Wasow, and Hatfield (1981) compared parent and social worker responses to the expectation of parental adjustment across developmental stages. One of their findings was that social workers tended to over-estimate how upsetting the parents' early experiences were (e.g., the time when the child would normally learn to walk or the time the child would enter a special rather than a regular class) and to underestimate the stressful impact of later experiences (e.g., the child's 21st birthday). These data suggest that parental adjustment and adaptation to the child's disability may need to be made at the beginning of each developmental stage because of the new issues associated with that stage. The chronicity of adjustment is an important area for parents to be aware of so that when they have continuing periods of anxiety or depression about their child's disability they do not perceive it to be abnormal or unusual.

Life Cycle Transitions

Fact or fable? Many parents experience extreme stress when their child leaves preschool and enters kindergarten.

This statement is factual. Leaving preschool and entering kindergarten is a stressful transition in the lives of many families. (Transitions are the major periods of change that can occur between life cycle developmental stages [developmental transitions] or within the stages themselves [nondevelopmental transitions]). Changes invariably disrupt routines and patterns of carrying out family responsibilities and can be expected to result in greater stress in family life (Neugarten, 1976; Olson, McCubbin, Barnes, Larsen, Muxen, & Wilson, 1983).

Developmental Transitions Developmental transitions occur when families enter new life cycle stages largely characterized by the needs and activities of their children. At the birth of a child, family roles change drastically to provide care for the newest member. As the child grows through the early childhood stage and enters school, major changes occur in

moving from preschool to elementary programs and in adapting to the new issues and
demands of that period.

Judy and Glenn Collins will face new challenges as Warren leaves the preschool program
and enters either a mainstreamed or specialized
kindergarten. It is likely that this period of
change for the Collins family will be characterized by much greater stress than they are
presently experiencing, since the routine and
rhythm of their involvement in the preschool
program has become a family pattern. Even
prior to this transition period, Judy had already
felt stress when she contemplated the program
that would best accommodate Warren's needs.

Professionals can offer valuable assistance
to families as they help them anticipate the demands of the next developmental stage and
teach the skills to best ensure the child's and
family's success with that stage.

Nondevelopmental Transitions   As contrasted to developmental transitions that occur
between life cycle stages, nondevelopmental
transitions can occur at any time. These transitions can be changes in family resources or
functions. Either type of change has a rever-
berating effect on family interaction. Two examples of nondevelopmental transitions are
evident in the Parades family: A nondevelopmental transition occurred when Bonita and her
two children left their homeland in South
America and moved to the United States. This
geographic relocation caused major changes in
life-style due to separation from the extended
family, the need to learn a new culture and
language, and starting over in a different community and neighborhood. A second nondevelopmental transition will occur when
Bonita's mother moves from South America to
live with Bonita, Arthur, and her grand-
children. She will help Bonita around the house
and thus be a catalyst for changing the way
tasks are allocated.

Other examples of nondevelopmental transitions would include a major accident or illness,
the loss of a job, the employment of the mother
outside the home, an increase or decrease in
assistance with family responsibilities such as
babysitting or household cleaning, and an in-

crease or decrease in the social support available to the family in helping to solve problems.

Change and Chronicity in Transitions   A
major responsibility of families is to adapt to
transitions as constructively as possible so that
disruption and anxiety are minimized and the
development of new routines characterized by
adaptability and satisfaction are maximized. A
major barrier to effective adaptation is the
strong tendency of parents with children having disabilities to cope by "taking things one
day at a time." Many families whose children
have a disability tend to have a pervasive worry
about the future (Birenbaum, 1971; Bristol &
Schopler, 1983; Turnbull, Summers, & Brotherson, 1986). One of the ways that many families minimize this future worry is to try not to
think about the future.

Bonita provides a good example of not actively dealing with the future by her emphasis
on living in the "eternal now." By not thinking as much about Emily's illness, Bonita can
prevent feelings of grief and disappointment.

Transitions are often more difficult to make
if they are not anticipated and strategies are not
developed for dealing with them. An important
intervention for families during the early childhood years can be the sharing of problem-solving strategies they can use in approaching various developmental and nondevelopmental
transitional periods. Models have been developed for providing information to parents
through weekly group problem-solving sessions (Doyle, 1985; Intagliata & Doyle, 1984)
and through a self-help guide (Goldfarb,
Brotherson, Summers, & Turnbull, 1986). The
major issue for professionals to consider is how
they can provide support and assistance to families in learning to move into the future with
confidence, knowing that they can control their
own lives through effective problem-solving
strategies.

The issue of chronicity comes into play in
transitions in recognizing that there is a chronicity of issues associated with all types of developmental and nondevelopmental changes.
As families learn to make their child's transitions successfully from preschool to kindergarten, they can also recognize that these tran-

sitional skills can be generalized to transitions from elementary to junior high school or from secondary school to adult services. Thus, families do not need to learn new skills at every transition, but rather they need to generalize their transitional skills from one situation to another and to recognize that transitions are chronic.

In summary, an understanding of developmental stages and transitions suggests that family life with a child who has a disability is a marathon rather than a sprint. A crucial aspect of supporting families during the early years is to empower them with coping strategies that can help them to run the full course with their son or daughter and to avoid the trap of investing their energies heavily for a short period of time and then burning out. An important role for professionals is to encourage families to keep their eyes on the everchanging "motion picture" of family life as well as reflecting on the family "snapshot."

REFERENCES

Anderson, J., Larson, J., & Morgan, A. (1981). PPSF/ Parenting program for step-parent families: A new approach for strengthening families. In N. Stinett, J. Defrain, K. King, P. Knaub, & G. Rowe (Eds.), *Family strengths: Roots of well-being* (pp. 351–363). Lincoln: University of Nebraska Press.

Beckman-Bell, P. (1981). Child-related stress in families of handicapped children. *Topics in Early Childhood Special Education, 1*(3), 45–53.

Berger, M., & Fowlkes, M. A. (1980). Family intervention project: A family network model for serving young handicapped children. *Young Children, 35*(4), 22–32.

Bernal, G. (1982). Cuban families. In M. McGoldrick, J. K. Pearce, & J. Giordano (Eds.), *Ethnicity and family therapy* (pp. 187–207). New York: The Guilford Press.

Birenbaum, A. (1971). The mentally retarded child in the home and the family cycle. *Journal of Health and Social Behavior, 12,* 55–65.

Bricker, D., & Casuso, V. (1979). Family involvement: A critical component of early intervention. *Exceptional Children, 46*(2), 108–116.

Bristol, M. M., & Schopler, E. (1983). Stress and coping in families with autistic adolescents. In E. Schopler & G. B. Mesibov (Eds.), *Autism in adolescents and adults* (pp. 251–278). New York: Plenum

Bristol, M. M., & Schopler, E. (1984). A developmental perspective on stress and coping in families of autistic children. In J. Blacher (Ed.), *Severely handicapped young children and their families: Research in review* (pp. 91–141). New York: Academic Press.

Brotherson, M. J. (1985). *Future planning and its relationship to family functioning in families with sons and daughters who are disabled.* Unpublished doctoral dissertation, University of Kansas, Lawrence.

Caplan, G. (1976). The family as a support system. In G. Caplan & M. Killilea (Eds.), *Social support and mutual help* (pp. 19–36). New York: Grune & Stratton.

Carter, E. A., & McGoldrick, M. (Eds.). (1980). *The family life cycle: A framework for family therapy.* New York: Gardner Press.

Crnic, K. A., Friedrich, W. N., & Greenberg, M. T. (1983). Adaptation of families with mentally retarded children: A model of stress, coping, and family ecology. *American Journal of Mental Deficiency, 88*(2), 125–138.

Cummings, S. T. (1976). The impact of the child's deficiency on the father: A study of mentally retarded and chronically ill children. *American Journal of Orthopsychiatry, 46,* 246–255.

Cunningham, C. (1982). *Downs syndrome: An introduction for parents.* London: Souvenir Press (Education & Academic) Ltd.

Darling, R. B., & Darling, J. (1982). *Children who are different.* St. Louis, MO: C. V. Mosby.

Doernberg, N. L. (1978). Some negative effects on family integration of health and educational services for young handicapped children. *Rehabilitation Literature, 39*(4), 107–110.

Doyle, P. B. (1985). *The effects of problem-solving training programs for mothers of developmentally delayed children.* Unpublished doctoral dissertation, University of Washington, Seattle.

Dyson, L., & Fewell, R. R. (1986). Stress and adaptation in parents of young handicapped and nonhandicapped children: A comparative study. *Journal of the Division for Early Childhood, 10*(1), 25–35.

Evans, D. P. (1983). *The lives of mentally retarded people.* Boulder, CO: Westview Press.

Farber, B., Jenne, W., & Toigo, R. (1960). *Family crisis and the decision to institutionalize the retarded child* (NEA Research Monograph Series, Series A, No. 1). Washington, DC: Council for Exceptional Children.

Fewell, R. R. (1986). A handicapped child in the family. In R. R. Fewell & P. F. Vadasy (Eds.), *Families of handicapped children: Needs and supports across the life span* (pp. 3–34). Austin, TX: PRO-ED.

Foster, M., Berger, M., & McLean, M. (1981). Rethinking a good idea: A reassessment of parent involvement. *Topics in Early Childhood Special Education, 1*(3), 55–65.

Friedrich, W. N. (1979). Predictors of the coping behavior of mothers of handicapped children. *Journal of Consulting and Clinical Psychology, 47,* 1140–1141.

Gallagher, J., Beckman, P., & Cross, A. (1983). Families of handicapped children: Sources of stress and its amelioration. *Exceptional Children, 50*(4), 614–617.

Gath, A. (1977). The impact of an abnormal child upon parents. *British Journal of Psychiatry, 130,* 405–410.

Goffman, E. (1963). *Stigma: Notes on the management of spoiled identity.* New York: Jasson Aranson.

Goldfarb, L., Brotherson, M. J., Summers, J. A., & Turnbull, A. P. (1986). *Tapping the wellsprings: A problem-solving guide for families with disabled or chronically ill members.* Baltimore: Paul H. Brookes Publishing Co.

Grossman, F. K. (1972). *Brothers and sisters of retarded children: An exploratory study.* Syracuse: Syracuse University Press.

Gumz, E. J., & Gubrium, J. F. (1972). Comparative parental perceptions of a mentally retarded child. *American Journal of Mental Deficiency, 77*, 175–180.

Hare, E. H., Laurence, K. M., Paynes, H., & Rawnsley, K. (1966). Spina bifida cystica and family stress. *British Medical Journal, 2*, 757–760.

Hettler, W. (1981). Family wellness—your choice. In N. Stinett, J. DeFrain, K. King, P. Knaub, & G. Rowe (Eds.), *Family strengths: Roots of well-being* (pp. 165–176). Lincoln: University of Nebraska Press.

Intagliata, J., & Doyle, N. (1984). Enhancing social support for parents of developmentally disabled children. Training in interpersonal problem-solving skills. *Mental Retardation, 22*, 4–11.

Joworowski, S., & Joworowski, R. J. (1978). A baby goes to "school." In S. L. Brown & M. S. Moersch (Eds.), *Parents on the team* (pp. 25–29). Ann Arbor: The University of Michigan Press.

Kazak, A. E., & Marvin, R. S. (1984). Differences, difficulties, and adaptations: Stress and social networks in families with a handicapped child. *Family Relations, 33*, 67–77.

Kew, S. (1975). *Handicap and family crisis: A study of the siblings of handicapped children.* London: Pitman Publishing Company.

Laxova, R. (1980). Prenatal diagnosis of genetic diseases. *Comprehensive Therapy, 6*, 66–76.

Lipsky, D. K. (1985). A parental perspective on stress and coping. *American Journal of Orthopsychiatry, 55*(4), 614–617.

Mandelbaum, A., & Wheeler, M. A. (1960). The meaning of a defective child to parents. *Social Casework, 43*, 360–367.

McCullough, M. E. (1981). Parent and sibling definition of situation regarding transgenerational shift in care of a handicapped child. (Doctoral dissertation, University of Minnesota, 1981). *Dissertation Abstracts International, 42*, 1618.

McGoldrick, M. (1982). Ethnicity and family therapy: An overview. In M. McGoldrick, J. K. Pearce, & J. Girodano (Eds.), *Ethnicity and family therapy* (pp. 3–30). New York: Guilford Press.

McMichael, J. K. (1971). *Handicaps: A study of physically handicapped children and their families.* Pittsburgh: University of Pittsburgh Press.

Morton, K. (1985). Identifying the enemy—A parent's complaint. In H. R. Turnbull & A. P. Turnbull (Eds.), *Parents speak out: Then and now* (pp. 143–148). Columbus, OH: Charles E. Merrill.

Neugarten, B. (1976). Adaptations and the life cycle. *The Counseling Psychologist, 6*(1), 16–20.

Olson, D. H., McCubbin, H. I., Barnes, H., Larsen, A., Muxen, M., & Wilson, M. (1983). *Families: What makes them work.* Beverly Hills: Sage Publications.

Pearlin, L. I., & Schooler, C. (1978). The structure of coping. *Journal of Health and Social Behavior, 19*, 2–21.

Saenger, G. (1957). *The adjustment of severely retarded adults in the community.* Albany: New York Interdepartmental Health Resource Board.

Schell, G. C. (1981). The young handicapped child: A family perspective. *Topics in Early Childhood Special Education, 1*(3), 21–27.

Schilling, R. F., Gilchrist, L. D., & Schinke, S. (1984). Coping and social support in families of developmentally disabled children. *Family Relations, 33*, 47–54.

Schipper, M. T. (1959). The child with mongolism in the home. *Pediatrics, 24*, 132–144.

Tew, B. J., Payne, E. H., & Lawrence, K. M. (1974). Must a family with a handicapped child be a handicapped family? *Developmental Medicine and Child Neurology, 16*, 95–98.

Turnbull, A. P. (1985, May). *Positive contributions that members with disabilities make to their families.* Paper presented at 109th annual meeting of the American Association on Mental Deficiency, Philadelphia.

Turnbull, A. P., Blue-Banning, M., Behr, S. K., & Kerns, G. M. (1986). Family research and intervention: A value and ethical examination. In P. Dokecki & R. Zaner (Eds.), *Ethics of dealing with persons with severe handicaps: Toward a research agenda* (pp. 119–140). Baltimore: Paul H. Brookes Publishing Co.

Turnbull, A. P., Summers, J. A., & Brotherson, M. J. (1986). Family life cycle: Theoretical and empirical implications and future directions for families with mentally retarded members. In J. J. Gallagher & P. Vietze (Eds.), *Families of handicapped persons: Current research, treatment, and policy issues* (pp. 45–66). Baltimore: Paul H. Brookes Publishing Co.

Turnbull, A. P., & Turnbull, H. R. (1986). Stepping back from early intervention: An ethical perspective. *Journal of the Division of Early Childhood, 10*(2), 106–117.

Turnbull, A. P., & Turnbull, H. R., with Summers, J. A., Brotherson, M. J., & Benson, H. A. (1986). *Families, professionals and exceptionality: A special partnership.* Columbus, OH: Charles E. Merrill.

Vadasy, P. F., Fewell, R. R., Meyer, D. J., & Schell, G. (1984). Siblings of handicapped children: A developmental perspective on family interactions. *Family Relations, 33*, 155–167.

Visher, J. S., & Visher, E. B. (1982). Stepfamilies and step-parenting. In F. Walsh (Ed.), *Normal family processes* (pp. 331–353). New York: Guilford Press.

Weber, G., & Parker, T. (1981). A study of family and professional views of the factors affecting family adaptation to a disabled child. In N. Stinett, J. DeFrain, K. King, P. Knaub, & G. Rowe (Eds.), *Family strengths: Roots of well-being* (pp. 379–395). Lincoln: University of Nebraska Press.

Wikler, L., Wasow, M., & Hatfield, E. (1981). Chronic sorrow revisited: Attitude of parents and professionals about adjustment to mental retardation. *American Journal of Orthopsychiatry, 51*(1), 63–70.

Winton, P. (1980). *Descriptive study of parents' perspectives on preschool services: Mainstreamed and specialized.* Unpublished doctoral dissertation, The University of North Carolina, Chapel Hill.

Winton, P. J., & Turnbull, A. P. (1981). Parent involvement as viewed by parents of preschool handicapped children. *Topics in Early Childhood Special Education, 1*(3), 11–19.

Chapter 12

Home-Based Early Intervention

Donald B. Bailey, Jr. and Rune J. Simeonsson

TWO BROAD POLICY QUESTIONS ARE often asked in early childhood special education. The first regards the issue of documenting the overall effectiveness of early intervention. The second regards the nature and form of the services provided: What constitutes "best practice" in early intervention? Neither question has a simple answer. The effectiveness of early intervention is presently being debated in professional circles (Casto & Mastropieri, 1986 a,b,c; Dunst & Snyder, 1986; Meisels, 1985; Strain & Smith, 1986). Likewise, best practice in early intervention has yet to be well defined (Bailey & Wolery, 1984) and in fact continues to evolve as researchers and practitioners alike seek to find ways of providing quality services.

One fundamental question regarding best practice is whether early intervention services should be home-based or center-based (Halpern, 1986; Mueller & Leviton, 1986). As with most policy questions, the answer is not an either-or response, but rather "it depends." Gray and Wandersman (1980) suggested several years ago that the question "Are home-based programs effective?" must be rephrased to "What characteristics of home-based interventions are effective in facilitating which areas of competence for which members of the families in which social contexts?" (p. 995). The purpose of this chapter is to examine home-based intervention as a strategy for serving young handicapped children. Six questions are addressed:

1. What is home-based intervention?
2. What factors contribute to the provision of home-based services?
3. What are the costs and benefits of home-based versus center-based services?
4. What does research tell us about the effects of home-based intervention?
5. What is generally accepted as best practice in home-based services?
6. What are the needs for future research and policy analysis on this topic?

WHAT IS HOME-BASED INTERVENTION?

Broadly speaking, home-based intervention may be defined as an approach in which services are delivered in the home as opposed to a center. A more specific definition is difficult because of the extreme diversity across programs with respect to population served, philosophical orientation, and goals.

Prevalence of Home-Based Services

Halpern (1984) reports a rapid growth in home-based programs over the past decade as community service agencies and sometimes schools attempt to prevent child abuse and neglect, to help teenage parents, and to work with handicapped or at-risk infants and preschoolers. The opposite trend is reported in a recent study of home visiting by public health nurses (Coyner, 1985). Although home visiting has been the primary mode for supporting

Preparation of this manuscript was supported in part by Special Education Programs, Special Education and Rehabilitative Services, U. S. Department of Education, Contract Number 300-82-0366. The opinions expressed do not necessarily reflect the position or policy of the U.S. Department of Education, and no official endorsement by the U.S. Department of Education should be inferred.

maternal and child health since the late nineteenth century, most services are now clinic-based. However, data describing the extent to which home-based programs are provided or reporting the proportion of handicapped infants and preschoolers enrolled in home-based programs are not available.

In the 1984–1985 Directory of HCEEP (Handicapped Children's Early Education Program) Projects, only 10% of the model demonstration programs identified themselves as exclusively home-based. Many states, however, have chosen to provide home-based services for handicapped infants through Departments of Mental Health or Human Resources. For example, North Carolina's Department of Human Resources coordinates a statewide program of home-based services for handicapped and at-risk children from birth to approximately 2 years of age. Most children over 24 months are served in center-based programs, while very few infants have center-based specialized services as an option.

From an international perspective, recent reviews suggest that home-based programs constitute a major form of service delivery in many European countries (Odom, 1985; Pahud & Besson, 1985; Zucman, 1985), in the United Kingdom (Reader, 1984), and in Israel (Green & Cohen, 1979).

Nature of Home-Based Services

Since the Portage Project was first funded in 1969 to provide a home-based intervention program for handicapped children in rural Wisconsin, many different forms of home-based services have been developed and implemented. Just as few data exist describing the prevalence of home-based intervention programs, there are also few data that describe the nature and content of services. Although several approaches have been described in the professional literature, the authors do not know the relative implementation rates of each. Thus, to describe the "typical" home-based program is virtually impossible. However, the characteristics that differentiate programs can be described.

One differentiating characteristic is the actu-al frequency of home visits. Some programs make weekly or biweekly visits, whereas others may only visit at certain ages (e.g., at 6 months and again at 12 months). Another differentiating characteristic is staff. Some programs consist primarily of special educators; others are staffed by social workers or therapists, and still others use paraprofessionals. A third differentiating characteristic is philosophical orientation. Marfo and Kysela (1985) describe three prevailing models. The *parent training/infant curriculum model* is heavily child-focused. Typically this approach involves teaching parents to teach their children. The Portage Project (Shearer & Shearer, 1976) is an example of this model. The *parent therapy model* is more heavily parent-focused, and its primary goal is to provide counseling and guidance for parents to help them cope with having a handicapped child, and to resolve any feelings of stress associated with that child. Mueller and Leviton (1986) describe one such model of services provided by social work staff. The *parent-infant interaction model* emphasizes the enhancement of parent-child interactions through training of both parents and children. Examples have been described by Affleck, McGrade, McQueeney, and Allen (1982), Bromwich (1981), and Rosenberg and Robinson (Chapter 10, this volume).

What interventionists actually do during a home visit varies according to family needs and the philosophical orientation of the interventionist. In reality, even though a program may espouse one particular approach, the demands of interacting with parents in the context of the home frequently force the interventionist to play many roles, sometimes serving as teacher, other times as counselor or advocate. In a statewide survey of home-based interventionists in North Carolina, the authors asked interventionists to provide a record of the approximate percentage of time spent in each of several activities. On the average, about half of the typical visit was devoted to child-focused activities (developmental training activities, speech/language therapy, physical/occupational therapy) and about half of the visit was spent in parent-related activities (parent/caregiver training, education, or counseling). However, considerable variability was observed across families.

WHY HOME-BASED SERVICES?

The rationale for home-based services is two-fold. One set of reasons centers on the role of families in the intervention process. The other set focuses on practical issues of program implementation and service delivery.

Parent Involvement

Although several philosophical orientations have been adopted by home-based programs, all emphasize family involvement as a primary rationale for home-based as opposed to center-based services. Two arguments for family involvement have been suggested as central. One is that the child is a part of the larger family system, so that the only way to have a meaningful impact on the child's life is to strengthen that system (see Barber, Turnbull, Behr, & Kerns, Chapter 11, this volume). Gray and Wandersman (1980), for example, state that home-based programs are advantageous because:

(a) such programs begin at a formative period when patterns of interactions are being set and motivational tendencies influenced, but typically before severe difficulties or downward cycles emerge; (b) they focus on setting in motion transactional parent-child patterns that can continue beyond the intervention; and (c) they have the flexibility to work with each family individually, taking into account each family's social context, strengths, needs, and cultural background. (p. 993)

With respect to the second major argument for family involvement, which focuses more specifically on parents as teachers, Shearer and Shearer (1976) cite seven educational advantages:

(1) Learning occurs in the parent and child's natural environment. . . (2) There is direct and constant access to behavior as it occurs naturally. . . . (3) It is more likely that learned behavior will generalize and be maintained. . . . (4) There is more opportunity for full family participation in the teaching process. . . . (5) There

is access to the full range of behaviors. . . . (6) Training of parents, who already are natural reinforcing agents, will provide them with the skills necessary to deal with new behaviors when they occur. . . . and (7) Because the home teacher is working on a one-to-one basis with the parents and child, individualization of instructional goals for both is an operational reality. (pp. 336–337)

Practical Considerations

In addition to the central role of parent involvement, practical reasons also have contributed to the provision of home-based services. Karnes and Zehrbach (1977) describe several programs developed to accomodate specific characteristics of populations served. For example, rural areas where children are widely dispersed make it difficult to provide center-based programs that are accessible to all children. Some children have medical needs that preclude center attendance or that make attendance difficult. Many parents, particularly parents of infants, may prefer to keep their children at home. Home-based services provide a mechanism for early intervention that fits the values of such families. Furthermore, some families, such as low income families or families with teen-age mothers, may have special difficulties getting their children to a center. Thus home-based intervention is sometimes viewed as a means of bringing the program to the clientele.

Home-based programs are also viewed as attractive because they are potentially more economical. A large center-based facility with its associated equipment is not needed, and the problem of transporting children to a center is thus avoided (Bailey & Wolery, 1984). When Bailey and Bricker (1985) compared the costs of a home-based infant program (birth–15 months) with those of a center-based toddler and preschool program, they calculated a per-child cost for the home-based program of $1,059; the per-child cost of the center-based program, including rent, utilities, and other building maintenance costs, was $2,645. It is not clear whether the cost of office space and transportation expenses were included in the calculation of home-based expenses. Ross

(1984) reports an annual cost of $60,000 to run a home-based program for 40 premature infants, or approximately $1,500 per child. No other studies, however, have compared the costs of home-based and center-based services. Such studies are needed, since home-based programs often involve considerable travel expense and staff travel time.

WHAT ARE THE RELATIVE ADVANTAGES AND DISADVANTAGES OF HOME-BASED VERSUS CENTER-BASED SERVICES?

Any evaluation of home-based intervention as a service delivery option must consider a wide range of possible outcomes. What could be expected to vary as a function of home-based versus center-based services? Before reviewing the limited research evaluating home-based intervention, the advantages and disadvantages of each option are discussed under four categories of outcomes: 1) child development, 2) child behavior, 3) family functioning, and 4) child health.

Child Development

A primary rationale for early intervention is to produce changes in children's developmental status and to accelerate the acquisition of functional skills in at least five broad areas: cognition, communication, motor, self-help, and social/play skills. How might home- versus center-based programs affect developmental status and skill acquisition? Home-based programs require the parent to be the primary teacher of the child. This role can be advantageous for several reasons, as described above by Shearer and Shearer (1976). However, the fact that the parent must assume the teacher role in home-based intervention poses major disadvantages as well. First, many parents may not have the skills to teach their children effectively. Second, many prefer not to serve as teachers of their children (Winton & Turnbull, 1981), finding that such activities are time-consuming and sometimes stressful (Sloper, Cunningham, & Arnljotsdottir, 1983). Other

factors related to home-based intervention that may limit the overall effect on child development are: 1) limited access to therapists and other specialists, 2) limited opportunities for social and communicative interactions with peers, and 3) limited access to a wide range of toys and specialized equipment.

Center-based programs have several advantages over home-based programs. First, the child spends a substantial part of the day under the guidance of teachers who are trained in child development and who are proficient at strategies to facilitate learning and development. Second, the child probably has more access to related service personnel and may be engaged in more appropriate programming in specialized areas such as communication and motor development. Third, a center can have available a wide variety of developmentally appropriate toys and specialized learning and adaptive equipment. In addition, a child in a center-based program has more opportunities for engaging in social and communicative interactions with peers.

Center-based programs may, on the other hand, have several disadvantages. First, there is the possibility that center placement may have a negative impact on parent-child interaction by reducing time and opportunities for such interactions and may perhaps exert a negative influence on the attachment relationship (Belsky, 1986). Second, without careful planning, center-based learning may not generalize back to the home environment. Finally, many children may have to travel long distances or long periods of time to attend a center-based program, requiring time that could otherwise be spent in motor, play, or learning activities.

Child Behavior

A second important rationale for early intervention is to produce changes in children's behavior. Although "behavior" obviously could include anything the child does, the term is being used in this context to describe three basic domains (Simeonsson, Huntington, Short, & Ware, 1982). The first of these is *state variability,* which refers to the total time the child is in a "state" amenable to learning and social interactions; the term also refers to the rate or frequency of shifts from one state to another. One goal of early intervention is to increase the length of alert states and to decrease the number of shifts from alert to non-alert states. The second domain, *behavioral style,* encompasses a broad range of child characteristics, some of which are developmental (e.g., participation, motivation, endurance, consolability) and some of which are non-developmental (e.g., activity, reactivity, goal-directedness, frustration, attention span). In some of these areas the goal of early intervention is to increase the child's ability (for example, self-motivation), whereas in other areas the goal is to normalize functioning (for example, normalized levels of activity as opposed to significantly over- or under-active levels). The third domain, *rhythmic habit patterns,* refers to repetitive, nonfunctional, and inappropriate patterns of behavior such as body rocking, tongue thrusting, or head banging. Goals of early intervention in this area of child behavior may be to reduce or to eliminate inappropriate behavioral patterns.

How might home- versus center-based services differentially affect child behavior as the authors have defined it? Although no research has been conducted in this regard, several effects can be postulated. A number of advantages of center-based programs are possible. First, center-based programs may be more likely to emphasize the acquisition of behavioral skills such as attention span, participation, endurance, and goal-directedness due to the demands associated with group activities and the provision of structured learning experiences. Second, a center-based program may be more effective in preparing children to demonstrate appropriate behavioral skills in later school environments, since by its very nature a center-based program more closely approximates the school environment than does a home. Third, center-based programs may be less tolerant of aberrant behaviors since such behaviors may be disruptive to the program and have the po-

tential for inappropriate modeling. Also, center-based staff may be more knowledgeable and aware of procedures for controlling inappropriate behaviors. Fourth, a center-based program may be able to provide a broader range of stimulating, high-interest activities throughout the day, thus increasing the potential for longer alert states. Longer periods of stimulation and increased variability in activities are made possible by the larger number of staff who are involved with children in a center, as well as by the diversity of activities that may accrue from different disciplinary perspectives. Finally, assuming that alert states in children may be mediated by extrinsic environmental factors in addition to intrinsic neurological status, a center-based program may increase the amount of time a child spends in an alert state through at least three management procedures. First, working with medical staff, medication dosages may be systematically monitored and adjusted to enhance child responsiveness. Second, given the fact that medication may negatively influence state organization (Prechtl, Theorell, & Blair, 1973), a child's need for medication can be reduced by implementing behavior management techniques. Third, given the evidence of the relationship of posture to state (Muhiuden, Melville, Ferguson, & Mohan, 1984), a third management technique may be applied that involves appropriate positioning and placement of the child to optimize alert states.

Differential contributions to the improvement of child behavior may also be attributable to home-based programs. Parents who have the time and skills may be able to provide more intensive one-to-one interventions than are possible in a center. Furthermore, children at home may spend less time waiting to participate in activities, thus increasing alert, engaged time and reducing frustration. Evidence to the contrary, however, was found in a study by Phemister, Richardson, and Thomas (1978) in which handicapped children functioning at the infant level were characterized by a higher percentage of "empty" time if they were at home rather than in day care. Although handicapped children as a group also had a higher percentage of empty time than nonhandicapped children, these results suggest that both child and setting variables influence active involvement.

Family Functioning

Since its inception in the late 1960s, early intervention has been largely child-focused. When parents have been involved, it typically has been for the child's benefit. However, families of handicapped children may themselves need to be the focus of intervention. Although family impact should be addressed in evaluating intervention effectiveness, the research thus far has been limited (Bailey & Simeonsson, 1986). One area of family need that warrants attention is support for coping with the stress imposed by having a handicapped child. Although the birth of any child adds stress to a family, that stress appears to be intensified by the presence of a handicapped child (Gallagher, Beckman-Bell, & Cross, 1983). Stress may be associated with the shock of the birth of a handicapped child, additional caregiving demands, lack of community support and resources, rejection by neighbors and friends, marital tension, uncertainty about the future, and the pressure to seek out services and participate in their child's educational program.

Another area of family need is the family's perceived control over events. The birth of a handicapped child represents an uncontrolled event in the life of the family, and the loss of control may be accentuated by the parents' inability to work effectively with their handicapped youngster or to take advantage of needed community services and resources. Not knowing what to do or to whom to turn is frustrating for parents. These frustrations affect their feelings of competence and result in additional stress.

Finally, the fact that a child is handicapped may affect the nature and quality of parent-child or sibling-handicapped child relationships. Bailey and Wolery (1984), in a review of related literature, found numerous characteristics of young handicapped children that were likely to impair social interactions with parents or sib-

lings. These and other child characteristics of temperament and behavior have been shown to have a negative effect on parent-child interactions (Kelly, 1982; Stoneman, Brody, & Abbott, 1983), the ability of parents to deal adequately with developmental and behavioral difficulties (Firth, 1982), and the attachment relationship (Blacher & Meyers, 1983).

How might home- versus center-based services affect family outcomes? Home-based services can have a number of potentially advantageous effects. First, the use of parents as teachers should result in enduring changes in parenting behaviors, in parent knowledge about children, and in parental attitudes toward their children. Second, successful teaching may lead to an increased sense of competence as a parent and to a reduction of stress as certain child behaviors improve. Third, Mueller and Leviton (1986) argue that home-based programs are more likely to enhance an internal locus of control, since parents are more likely to be allowed to set the agenda and pace of treatment. Fourth, parent-child interactions may improve, particularly if those interactions are the target of interventions in which parents learn to "read" their children's social and communicative behaviors and to thereby respond effectively. Finally, mothers (and possibly fathers) of children treated at home may develop more positive and enduring relationships with their children due to significant differences in parent-child contacts (Belsky, 1986).

Home-based programs also have potential disadvantages that may be eliminated in center-based programs. For example, asking a parent to serve as the child's teacher may actually increase stress in families, since some parents prefer not to have primary responsibility for teaching (Barber et al., Chapter 11, this volume). Teaching may be a failure experience for some parents, particularly those with severely handicapped children; this failure would result in increasing stress for the parents, and would further reduce their sense of competence. Serving as teacher may also focus the parent's attention on formal aspects of the parent-child relationship, thus eliminating some of the spontaneity and joy. Finally, the full-time responsibility of taking care of a handicapped child can be extremely stressful. Center-based programs can relieve parents of both caregiving and teaching responsibilities. Center-based programs also provide greater opportunities for parents to meet and interact with other parents of handicapped children. On the other hand, center-based services may result in less intense emotional bonding for parents and thus may reduce parent-child interactions. Furthermore, many parents may feel guilty about placing a young infant in a day care center.

Child Health

An outcome of early intervention with handicapped infants and preschoolers that has yet to be documented pertains to health effects. Handicapped children as a group are more likely to experience medical crises or serious and recurring health problems than are nonhandicapped children. In some cases this is due to physiological structures. For example, children with Down syndrome or with a cleft palate are more likely to have frequent cases of otitis media (Paradise, 1980). Also, some children (e.g., Down syndrome children) are generally less resistant to infections and thus have frequent respiratory infections, runny noses, and conjunctivitis (Blackman, 1984). Other disabilities can lead to secondary health effects. For example, children with spina bifida are susceptible to frequent urinary tract infections (Wolraich, 1984).

How might home- versus center-based services affect the health status of handicapped infants? Recent research suggests that children in day care centers have higher rates of otitis media, diarrhea, and other infectious diseases than do children reared at home (Child Day Care Infectious Disease Study Group, 1984; Haskins & Kotch, 1986). Infants and toddlers in particular are at greater risk for increased infections. Not only are young children more susceptible to infections, but they also have behavioral characteristics that increase the likelihood of transmitting disease. Examples of such behaviors include:

Close, repeated person-to-person contact; lack of fecal continence prior to toilet training; frequent exploration of the environment with their mouths, offering opportunity for fecal-oral transmission as well as for spread of respiratory secretions; and requirements for frequent hands-on contact by staff. For these reasons, centers that care for infants and toddlers seem likely to be at greater risk for transmission of infectious agents. (Child Day Care Infectious Disease Study Group, 1984, p. 684)

Although these diseases are not usually debilitating in and of themselves, they can result in a variety of negative secondary effects. For example, otitis media often results in temporary hearing impairment, ranging from negligible to as much as 50 decibels (Paradise, 1981). Evidence suggests that chronic and continuous middle ear infections and subsequent hearing loss are related to temporary impairments in children's speech, language, and cognition (Paradise, 1980), and there is evidence that such impairments may also have long-term adverse developmental outcomes. Although Roberts, Sanyal, Burchinal, Collier, Ramey, and Henderson (1986) found no association between measures of early childhood otitis media occurrence and measures of intelligence and academic achievement with low income children, Roberts, Burchinal, Collier, Ramey, and Henderson (1987) found a relationship between sickness and attention span. Specifically, they found a significant relationship between number of days a child has otitis media before age 3 and teachers' ratings of children's attentional behavior in the classroom during the third year of elementary school. Thus, for children who are already at-risk for academic failure by virtue of their handicaps, frequent cases of temporary hearing loss may further prevent optimal school behavior. Furthermore, frequent occurrences of illness may result in a significant reduction in the number of days a child attends the center-based program. Center-based programs have the potential health disadvantage of promoting frequent infections in children during the first 2 years of the handicapped infant's life. The longitudinal health effects of early infections have yet to be documented. Recent data with nonhandicapped children suggest that day care children who have many infections during the infancy period subsequently have *fewer* infections during the preschool years (ages 2–5) than do home-reared children (Denny, Collier, & Henderson, 1986). However, the question of which pattern has fewer adverse long-term effects on development, particularly for handicapped infants, has yet to be examined.

Center-based services may also provide some health advantages for children. First, children from impoverished environments are more likely to receive diets that meet their nutritional needs. Second, teachers may be more observant of warning signs of infections (e.g., lethargy, restlessness) and children may thus receive earlier medical treatment. Furthermore, children whose parents smoke are exposed to significantly lower levels of passive smoke in center-based programs, since most day care centers do not allow staff to smoke in areas where children spend their time.

WHAT DOES RESEARCH REVEAL ABOUT THE EFFECTS OF HOME-BASED INTERVENTION?

Thus far the authors have painted a complex picture of home-based intervention. It has been shown that intervention can consist of many different approaches, can focus on different goals, can be implemented by different kinds of staff, and can occur at varying levels of intensity. Furthermore, it has been suggested that intervention can result in a multiplicity of outcomes: some positive and some negative. The question of whether home-based services are effective, then, is too broadly framed to answer. What might be appropriate for a single adolescent mother of a multiply handicapped child in the inner city, for example, may not be appropriate for a 38-year-old mother of a Down syndrome child, the sixth child in the family, living on a farm in the Midwest. Research simply has not examined the complexity of the issue from a multivariate perspective. Problems associated with home-based research, however, such as those already presented, are delineated by Gray and Wandersman (1980),

Bailey and Simeonsson (1986), and Halpern (1984). The following sections review: 1) research with low-income populations, 2) research documenting program effects with handicapped populations, 3) research on parent training, and 4) research documenting variables that enhance or modify program effectiveness.

Research with Low-Income Populations

Although a large number of studies have investigated the effects of either home-based or center-based services for low-income children, very few have compared the two approaches. Ramey, Sparling, Bryant, and Wasik (1982) reviewed 18 exemplary prevention-oriented early intervention programs designed for high-risk and normal infants. Only two studies compared home visits versus day care services, and at the time of publication the studies had followed children only to 24 months of age. At 2 years of age, both studies reported day care children were superior to home-visit children on Mental Scale scores of the Bayley Scales of Infant Development. In a later publication, Ramey, Bryant, and Suarez (1985) concluded that research to date supports the hypothesis that better outcomes are associated with more intense, that is, center-based, services.

Field, Widmayer, Greenberg, and Stoller (1985) compared home- and center-based intervention for teen-age mothers and their infants. At 4 months, infants in both home- and center-based groups weighed more and performed better on the Denver Developmental Screening Test than did a control group receiving no intervention. Mothers in both treatment groups were less likely to rate their infants as having a "difficult" temperament and received higher mother-infant interaction ratings than control mothers. Center-based mothers talked to their infants more and their infants exhibited less gaze aversion than home-based subjects. At 1 year, center-based infants received higher Bayley Motor Scale scores than did home-based babies. Also, mothers of center-based infants were more likely to return to work and less likely to repeat pregnancy during this first year.

In a recent study at the Frank Porter Graham Child Development Center, Ramey, Bryant, Sparling, and Wasik (1985) randomly assigned 64 high-risk (low-income) children at birth either to a center-based day care program with a family education component or to family education alone. Both groups were compared to similar high-risk children who were not receiving intervention. Results at 36 months of age indicated that gains in IQ scores were greater for the center-based intervention group than for the other two groups, which did not differ significantly from one another. The authors conclude that "intervention consisting of parent education alone was not intense enough to have a positive and measurable impact on intellectual scores during the first 36 months of age" (Ramey, Bryant, Sparling, & Wasik, 1985, p. 23).

Although earlier reviews concluded that day care rearing of children as opposed to home care has little effect on the attachment between parents and children, a recent review by Belsky (1986) suggests the possibility of negative consequences for center-based care:

> A relatively persuasive *circumstantial* case can be made that early infant care *may* be associated with increased avoidance of mother, *possibly* to the point of greater insecurity in the attachment relationship, and that such care *may* also be associated with diminished compliance and cooperation with adults, increased agressiveness, and possible even greater social maladjustment in the preschool and early school-age years. (p.6)

Additional research is needed, however, before the validity of these conclusions can be determined.

Research with Handicapped Populations

Research on home-based services for handicapped children is considerably less rigorous methodologically than similar research conducted with at-risk children. To date, no study has randomly assigned children to treatment conditions, has followed subjects longitudinally, or has examined the range of outcomes in child and family domains. Likewise, no study has systematically compared home- and center-based services. Thus the authors' confidence of conclusions in this area is low.

Studies in the United States, such as those reported by Greenberg, Calderon, and Kusche (1984); Hanson and Schwarz (1978); Maisto and German (1979); Shearer and Shearer (1976); and Solomon, Wilson, and Galey (1982), have typically compared progress in a home-based program with that observed in no-treatment groups or have simply documented progress with no comparison groups at all. All these studies conclude that home-based services have a positive impact on child development or family outcomes. Ross (1984) compared the effects of home-based services with those of no treatment settings for a population of premature infants from low-income families and found that after 12 months the treatment group infants had significantly higher Bayley Mental Scores and higher total HOME scores. Brassell and Dunst (1978) demonstrated that a home-based program of training conducted by parents could increase infant performance on object permanence tasks. Bailey and Bricker (1985) provided home-based services to infants from birth to 15 months and then center-based services to children from 15 to 36 months. Both home- and center-based services resulted in statistically significant MA changes, as measured by the Gesell Developmental Schedules, but not DQ changes.

In the United Kingdom, considerable research has focused on home-based intervention, but it is difficult to compare the results with research from the United States because the systems differ in several fundamental ways. Professionals providing home-based services in British studies have tended to possess less training than service professionals in the United States. Furthermore, home visits in Britain take place much less frequently, often occurring at 6 week intervals. Given these differences, however, findings are generally consistent with those already described, although the methodological problems associated with U.S. studies also are apparent in British studies. Bidder, Bryant, and Gray (1975) divided 16 Down syndrome children into two groups matched on CA, sex, and MA. The treatment group, which received home-based parent training, demonstrated significant differences in the Language and Performance subscales of the Griffiths Scales. Woods, Corney, and Price (1984) documented the progress of 28 Down syndrome children participating in a home-based program and observed that the decline in their developmental quotients over time was not as great as the decline reported in an earlier study in which children received a less structured intervention.

In regard to parent perceptions of home- versus center-based services, Moran (1985) interviewed 85 families of developmentally disabled infants in Massachusettes who had participated in a variety of types of intervention programs. She summarized her findings as follows:

> I found that no one program type was clearly superior in all ways: program types had startlingly different patterns of effects that have major implications for the development and evaluation of community early intervention programs and for policy decisions regarding early intervention. Whether early intervention services for developmentally disabled infants are offered in the client's home or in a center *does* make a difference for families. Mothers participating in home-based programs had more positive attitudes toward their special needs children and sought child care advice from a relatively large number of sources. Trends in the data also suggested that mothers in home-based programs, compared to those involved in other types of early intervention, may develop stronger, possibly more dependent, relationships with service providers and are also more apt to follow through with their children on program suggestions. Center-based intervention was associated with larger social networks for mothers. Mothers of children in primarily center-based intervention reported decreased homemaking stress, but evaluated their marriages as more stressful than those in primarily home-based intervention. (p. 11)

Research on Parent Training

As opposed to the small number of general studies of home-based intervention, a plethora of studies exists in which the effects of parent training are documented. It is beyond the scope of this chapter to review this research in any detail. Several recent reviews, however, have described the results of many studies in which parents have been trained to address the behav-

ioral/emotional problems evidenced by children (Breiner & Beck, 1984; O'Dell, 1985; Sanders & James, 1983), to serve as teachers of their handicapped children (Snell & Beckman-Brindley, 1984), to serve as speech-language therapists for their children (Howlin, 1984), and to be physical therapists with their physically handicapped child (Gross, Eudy, & Drabman, 1982). In brief, these reviews all have concluded the following:

1. Parents can be taught to implement correct and consistent behavior change programs, educational interventions, and specific therapeutic techniques.
2. Parent training programs often result in subsequent changes in children in accordance with desired child outcomes.
3. Generalization and maintenance of training effects has not been adequately documented.
4. Effective training techniques most frequently incorporate modeling, practice, and specific feedback, as well as a system for monitoring performance.
5. Parent and child variables often serve to mediate or to limit the effectiveness of parent training programs.

PARENT AND CHILD VARIABLES ENHANCING OR MEDIATING PROGRAM EFFECTIVENESS

The effectiveness of home-based intervention can be modified or enhanced by both child and family variables. In regard to child variables, one might expect that more severely handicapped children would profit least from intervention. Two studies have confirmed this expectation in home-based intervention (Barna, Bidder, Gray, Clements, & Gardner, 1980; Brassell, 1977). Maisto and German (1979), however, found more dramatic changes in the behavior of children participating in a home-based program who initially scored in the severely handicapped range than in the behavior of the children initially scoring in the mildly delayed range. This finding may be due to regression to the mean.

Family demographic variables related to

poorer outcome in home-based intervention include low socioeconomic status (Brassell, 1977; Dumas & Wahler, 1983; McMahon, Forehand, Griest, & Wells, 1981) and low maternal and paternal education (Brassell, 1977; Sharav, Collins, & Shlomo, 1985). Piper and Ramsay (1980) found that scores on the Home Observation for Measurement of the Environment (HOME) Inventory correlated significantly with the mental development of Down syndrome infants. Children showing the least decline in total developmental quotient lived in homes rated as having better organization of the physical and temporal environment. In a similar study, Best and Roberts (1976) found that specific cognitive skills of hearing impaired toddlers were correlated with HOME scores. Griest and Forehand (1982) reviewed the literature on the role of family variables in child behavior therapy and suggested that: 1) a positive relationship exists between child behavior problems and parental maladjustment, marital difficulties, and dysfunctional extrafamilial interactions and 2) the outcome of parent training is affected adversely when parents suffer from poor personal, marital, and extrafamilial adjustment. For example, McMahon et al. (1981) found that depressed mothers were more likely to drop out of parent training groups. Similarly, Dumas and Wahler (1983) found "insularity" of mothers to be negatively related to treatment outcome in parent training. Insularity is defined as "a specific pattern of social contacts within the community that is characterized by a high level of negatively perceived coercive interchanges with kinfolk and/or helping agency representatives" (Dumas & Wahler, 1983, p. 302). Allen, Affleck, McQueeney, and McGrade (1982) found that ratings of the mothers of handicapped infants using the Parent Behavior Progression (Bromwich, 1981) were more likely to decline or show nonlinear trends in father-absent families. Finally, Maisto and German (1981) found that maternal locus of control accounted for a substantial portion of variance in the developmental gains of handicapped infants following a home-based intervention program.

WHAT IS BEST PRACTICE IN HOME-BASED EARLY INTERVENTION?

In addition to asking "Does home-based intervention work?" one may also ask "How should home-based services be provided?" Some data exist on specific strategies or components of home-based programs.

Studies of Home-Based Practices

One question warranting attention concerns the frequency of contacts necessary for effective home-based intervention. To the authors' knowledge, only one study has addressed this issue. Sandow, Clark, Cox, and Stewart (1981) assigned two matched groups of 16 subjects to home visits at either 2 week or 8 week intervals. The less frequently visited group made greater progress after 2 years than the group receiving more visits, but this difference disappeared after 3 years. Both treatment group children made more gains than a third no-treatment comparison group.

In regard to the content of parent training, Moxley-Haegert and Serbin (1983) compared parents of delayed infants (all of whom were participating in a home-based intervention program). The parents were randomly assigned to one of three groups: developmental education for parents, child management education for parents, and no parent training. Children whose parents participated in the developmental education group gained a greater number of skills; their parents participated more in the assigned home treatment programs than did parents in either of the comparison groups. This greater rate of participation was maintained 1 year after treatment.

Bidder, Hewitt, and Gray (1983) compared three methods of implementing the Portage Project model in a home-based program. Under one condition, activity charts as prescribed in the model were required. Under a second condition, specific targets were set, but parents were not required to complete daily activity charts. Under the third condition, parents were simply given general suggestions for working with their children. A slight advantage for activity charts was observed in weekly skill acquisition, but there were no overall differences on prepost checklist performance. Visits tended to be longer when activity charts were used, and parents generally preferred the activity charts over other procedures.

Holsworth and Currie (1982) evaluated three modes of home-based parent training (i.e., a videotaped program discussing and demonstrating home teaching strategies, illustrated activity guides, and both videotapes and activity guides) and compared acquired parent training skills with those of a no-treatment (waiting list) control group. The combination of print and audiovisual material resulted in greater acquisition of training skills than did either method alone.

New Directions in Home-Based Intervention

Existing studies of best practice have primarily examined effective strategies for enhancing parent teaching and child outcomes. Recent publications, however, have called for a re-examination of the mission of the early interventionist, particularly those working in home-based programs (Bailey & Simeonsson, 1984). Although each has offered a different approach or direction, all have several common themes. First is a recognition of the role of the family in making decisions regarding intervention. Cadman, Goldsmith, and Bashim (1984) found that parents and professionals often disagreed on values and goals for children with developmental disabilities. Whereas clinicians rated family interaction as the most important area for intervention, parents typically placed the greatest value on a child's "prognosis for normal role fulfillment in later years" (p. 62). Rosenberg, Reppucci, and Linney (1983), in a case study of a parent-training project for high-risk families, cite discrepancies between professional and client perception of needs as a major problem affecting implementation of home-based programs. Cadman, Shurvell, Davies, and Bradfield (1984) found that family compliance with consultant recommendations was enhanced if several factors were present: 1) a complete explanation of the rationale for therapy, 2) feasibility of the rec-

ommendation given the individual family situation, 3) clarity of roles in implementation, 4) overall agreement with recommendation, 5) client perception of own qualifications to fulfill the recommendation, 6) adequate time to discuss the recommendation with the therapist, and 7) consideration of the parent's opinion in the assessment.

A second general theme of the recent literature is the need to extend the target of intervention from the child alone to the family (Barber et al., Chapter 11, this volume). More enduring and perhaps more important changes should occur if the child is viewed as a part of a larger system.

A third general theme is the need to individualize services for families in the same way that professionals now individualize services for children. Not every family needs or wants a support group; likewise not every family wants training in child management skills. The effective interventionist assesses the needs of each family and designs an individualized program of services to meet those needs. Recent models for intervention embodying these principles include: 1) relationship-focused early intervention (Affleck et al., 1982), 2) proactive empowerment (Dunst, 1985), and 3) Family-Focused Intervention (Bailey et al., 1986).

Relationship-Focused Early Intervention   According to Affleck et al. (1982), relationship-focused intervention differs from traditional parent training programs in both goals and intervention procedures. The goals of relationship-focused programs are "(a) encouragement of warm parent-infant reciprocal interactions; and (b) promotion of generalized parental competence and problem-solving skills" (Affleck et al., 1982, p. 416). The approach draws on the work of Bromwich (1981), Fraiberg (1970), and Goldberg (1977) to promote these goals through home visits whose content is largely determined by parents. The role of the home-based interventionist or consultant is to support constructive ideas suggested by parents, to identify and reinforce positive parent-child interactions, to help parents develop their own goals and problem solving skills, and to encourage use of family and community support networks. In a study of the effects of this approach, Affleck et al. (1982) found that treatment group mothers were more responsive to their children, participated in more reciprocal activities, and demonstrated greater overall involvement with their children.

Parent Empowerment Dunst (1985) argues for a family systems approach to early intervention that is a proactive model focusing on child and family strengths, not weaknesses. The primary goal of this model, referred to as Proactive Empowerment through Partnerships (PEP), is to "empower" parents to "make informed decisions and take control over their lives" (p. 170). Dunst suggests that traditional approaches to early intervention are paternalistic, usurp control over decision-making for families, and create dependency and learned helplessness. Parent empowerment, on the other hand, is accomplished "through provision and mediation of support that strengthens families as well as other normal socializing agents (relatives, friends, neighbors, the church, etc.) but which neither replaces or supplants them" (pp.181–182). Dunst goes on to suggest that "the process of strengthening families consists of imparting information, knowledge, skills, and competencies through provision or mediation of support that proactively influences child, parent, and family functioning" (p.182). In view of data showing that early intervention is but one of many aspects of social support, Dunst argues that the task of the early interventionist should be to help parents secure other, more enduring support systems.

Family-Focused Intervention Our own work with early interventionists in home-based programs has led to the development of a functional model for planning, implementing, and evaluating individualized services for families of handicapped infants (Bailey et al., 1986). Called Family-Focused Intervention, the model draws on the "goodness-of-fit" concept (Thomas & Chess, 1977) to shift the goal of intervention from a focus on children or families alone to an emphasis on the consonance or "fit" between characteristics of children and families and the coping demands they experi-

ence. The interventionist's task thus becomes one of individualizing services to families in order to optimize fit. The model has four goals:

1. To help family members cope with special needs related to caring for and raising a child with a handicap
2. To help family members grow in their understanding of the development of their child both as an individual and as a member of the family
3. To promote warm, enjoyable, and stimulating parent-child interactions
4. To preserve and reinforce the dignity of families by respecting and responding to their desire for services and by incorporating them as partners in the assessment, planning, and evaluation process.

These goals are accomplished through a sequence of activities similar to those used in planning, implementing, and evaluating family services. The steps include functional assessment of family needs, planning and conducting a focused interview, specifying objectives for families, planning and implementing services for families, and evaluating program effectiveness.

NEEDS FOR FUTURE RESEARCH

What can be said about the status of knowledge regarding home-based intervention? First, the topic is extraordinarily complex. Home-based intervention can take many forms and can occur at varying levels of intensity. It can be provided by many different kinds of professionals for many different kinds of children and families. It can be provided alone or in combination with center-based services. It may be for one month or for 3 years. Second, because of its complexity, it is difficult to make generalizations about the effects of home-based intervention, about the best ways of providing it, or about who might best profit from it. Third, it is clear that home-based intervention can result in a multiplicity of outcomes, only some of which have been studied or documented. Finally, studies have rarely shown sufficient levels of methodological rigor to warrant confidence in the conclusions.

From a public policy perspective, the provision of home-based services clearly meets the needs and personal value systems of some but not all families with young handicapped children. In an ideal world both center- and home-based services would be available to meet the needs of individual families and children. We appear, however, to be entering an age of scarce resources for human service programs. Policymakers must come to grips with these issues and must often make tough decisions about how resources should be allocated. These decisions affect the nature and intensity of services available to children and families. What information must researchers continue to provide policymakers and practitioners regarding home-based intervention?

Child-Related Issues

Historically, the primary target of intervention has been the handicapped child. Although it is now recognized that families constitute a major focus of intervention, child effects remain of fundamental importance. A number of studies with handicapped children provide evidence that home-based services can influence child outcome more than no intervention at all. It must be reiterated, however, that no study has assigned children randomly to treatment and no-treatment conditions with longitudinal follow-up. Of more fundamental concern, however, is the fact that research with low-income families is yielding seemingly consistent findings that center-based services result in significantly better child development outcomes than may be found in home-based programs. These findings should not be used as an argument to stop home-based programs for handicapped children. Rather, they point to the critical need for carefully controlled studies to determine their relevance to policy decisions regarding handicapped children. One argument, of course, is that low-income children in impoverished environments constitute a different population from handicapped children. But a large percentage of handicapped children do live in low-income families. This combination is potentially devastating to child outcomes and may argue for center-based services for those children.

Research has not examined the "age-at-entry" question, nor has it addressed the comparative appropriateness of home-based and center-based services for infants versus preschool-age children. One scenario is that although center-based programs in infancy produce more substantial child change than home-based programs, those differences do not endure, particularly if home-based children enter a high quality center-based program at 2 or 3 years of age. Thus, there is a need for longitudinal follow-up research on child effects.

Family-Related Issues

Family outcomes other than parent teaching skills have yet to be documented adequately. This documentation is essential, given Moran's (1985) findings that mothers in home-based programs had more positive attitudes toward their children. It is likely that home-based programs, particularly during the infancy period, are preferred by many parents and may result in more positive parent outcomes. Many professionals would argue that in the long run, positive parent outcomes at an early age are more important than changes in children's developmental status. Longitudinal studies are needed to examine this issue.

Of additional interest is the question of best practice in family-focused home-based intervention. Are specific procedures or approaches better than others (e.g., parents as teachers versus parent-child interaction model), or is the most appropriate strategy to focus on individualized needs assessment and values clarification?

Finally, to what extent are the skills required of the home-based interventionist different from those required of the center-based teacher? The home-based professional is required to interact with parents as well as children. With the parent as primary client, the interventionist often is confronted with complex case management demands (Halpern, 1986), counseling responsibilities, and adult education tasks.

SUMMARY

The issues discussed in this chapter reveal that the setting in which early intervention should be delivered for maximal benefit is not reducible to a single dimension. At least two additional dimensions of significance are the *qualitative* role of the caregiver and the *availability* of the caregiver. In homes where the quality and intensity of caregiving is high and the parent is satisfied with the caregiving role, home-based services may be the most appropriate approach. In homes where the quality and intensity of caregiving is low and the parent is not satisfied with the caregiving role, center-based services are essential. Future research must continue to examine the multiple dimensions and outcomes of each system.

REFERENCES

Affleck, G., McGrade, B. J., McQueeney, M., & Allen, D. (1982). Promise of relationship-focused early intervention in developmental disabilities. *Journal of Special Education, 16,* 413–430.

Allen, D., Affleck, G., McQueeney, M., & McGrade, B. (1982). Validation of the Parent Behavior Progression in an early intervention program. *Mental Retardation, 20,* 159–163.

Bailey, D. B., & Simeonsson, R. J. (1984). Critical issues underlying research and intervention with families of young handicapped children. *Journal of the Division for Early Childhood, 9,* 27–37.

Bailey, D. B., & Simeonsson, R. J. (1986). Design issues in family impact evaluations. In L. Bickman & D. L. Weatherford (Eds.), *Evaluating early intervention programs for severely handicapped children and their families* (pp. 209–230). Austin: PRO-Ed.

Bailey, D. B., Simeonsson, R. J., Winton, P. J., Huntington, G. S., Comfort, M., Isbell, P., O'Donnell, K. J., & Helm, J. M. (1986). Family-focused intervention: A functional model for planning, implementing, and evaluating individualized family services in early intervention. *Journal of the Division for Early Childhood, 10,* 156–171.

Bailey, D. B., & Wolery, M. (1984). *Teaching infants and preschoolers with handicaps.* Columbus, OH: Charles E. Merrill.

Bailey, E. J., & Bricker, D. (1985). Evaluation of a three-year early intervention demonstration project. *Topics in Early Childhood Special Education, 5*(2), 52–65.

Barna, S., Bidder, R. T., Gray, O. P., Clements, J., & Gardner, S. (1980). The progress of developmentally delayed preschool children in a home-training scheme. *Child: Care, Health, and Development, 6,* 157–164.

Belsky, J. (1986). Infant day care: A cause for concern. *Zero to Three, 6*(5), 1–7.

Best, B., & Roberts, G. (1976). Early cognitive development in hearing impaired children. *American Annals of the Deaf, 121,* 560–564.

Bidder, R. T., Bryant, G., & Gray, O. P. (1975). Benefits to Down's syndrome children through training their mothers. *Archives of Disease in Childhood, 50,* 383–386.

Bidder, R. T., Hewitt, K. E., & Gray, O. P. (1983). Evaluation of teaching methods in a home-based training scheme for developmentally delayed preschool children. *Child: Care, Health, and Development, 9,* 1–12.

Blacher, J., & Meyers, C. T. (1983). A review of attachment formation and disorder of handicapped children. *American Journal of Mental Deficiency, 87,* 359–371.

Blackman, J. A. (1984). Down Syndrome. In J. A. Blackman (Ed.), *Medical aspects of developmental disabilities in children birth to three* (pp. 91–96). Rockville, MD: Aspen.

Brassell, W. R. (1977). Intervention with handicapped infants: Correlates of progress. *Mental Retardation, 15*(4), 18–22.

Brassell, W. R., & Dunst, C. J. (1978). Fostering the object construct: Large scale intervention with handicapped infants. *American Journal of Mental Deficiency, 82,* 507–510.

Breiner, J., & Beck, S. (1984). Parents as change agents in the management of their developmentally delayed children's noncompliant behaviors: A critical review. *Applied Research in Mental Retardation, 5,* 259–278.

Bromwich, R. M. (1981). *Working with parents and infants: An interactional approach.* Baltimore: University Park Press.

Cadman, D., Goldsmith, C., & Bashim, P. (1984). Values, preferences, and decisions in the care of children with developmental disabilities. *Developmental and Behavioral Pediatrics, 5,* 60–64.

Cadman, D., Shurvell, B., Davies, P., & Bradfield, S. (1984). Compliance in the community with consultants' recommendations for developmentally handicapped children. *Developmental Medicine and Child Neurology, 26,* 40–46.

Casto, G., & Mastropieri, M. A. (1986a). Much ado about nothing: A reply to Dunst and Snyder. *Exceptional Children, 53,* 277–279.

Casto, G., & Mastropieri, M. A. (1986b). Strain and Smith do protest too much: A response. *Exceptional Children, 53,* 266–268.

Casto, G., & Mastropieri, M. A. (1986c). The efficacy of early intervention programs: A meta-analysis. *Exceptional Children, 52,* 417–424.

Child Day Care Infectious Disease Study Group. (1984). Public health considerations of infectious diseases in child day care centers. *Journal of Pediatrics, 105,* 683–701.

Coyner, A. (1985). Home visiting by public health nurses: A vanishing resource for families and children. *Zero to Three, 6*(1), 1–7.

Denny, F., Collier, A., & Henderson, F. (1986). Acute respiratory infections in daycare. *Reviews in Infectious Diseases, 8,* 527–532.

Dumas, J. E. & Wahler, R. G. (1983). Predictors of treatment outcome in parent training: Mother insularity and socioeconomic disadvantage. *Behavioral Assessment, 5,* 301–313.

Dunst, C. J. (1985). Rethinking early intervention. *Analysis and Intervention in Developmental Disabilities, 5,* 165–201.

Dunst, C. J., & Snyder, S. W. (1986). A critique of the Utah State University early intervention meta-analysis research. *Exceptional Children, 53,* 269–276.

Field, T., Widmayer, S., Greenberg, R., & Stoller, S. (1985). Home- and center-based intervention for teen-age mothers and their offspring. In S. Harel & N. J. Anastasiow (Eds.), *The at-risk infant: Psycho/socio /medical aspects* (pp. 29–39). Baltimore: Paul H. Brookes Publishing Co.

Firth, H. (1982). The effectiveness of parent workshops in a mental handicap service. *Child Care, Health, and Development, 8*, 77–91.

Fraiberg, S. (1970). Intervention in infancy: A program for blind infants. *Journal of the American Academy of Child Psychiatry, 16*, 381–405.

Gallagher, J. J., Beckman-Bell, P., & Cross, A. H. (1983). Families of handicapped children: Sources of stress and its amelioration. *Exceptional Children, 50*, 10–19.

Goldberg, S. (1977). Social competence in infancy: A model of parent-infant interaction. *Merrill-Palmer Quarterly, 23*, 163–177.

Gray, S. W., & Wandersman, L. P. (1980). The methodology of home-based intervention studies: Problems and promising strategies. *Child Development, 51*, 993–1009.

Green, H. A., & Cohen, J. (1979). *Research in action.* Jerusalem: School of Education, Hebrew University of Jerusalem.

Greenberg, M., Calderon, R., & Kusche, C. (1984). Early intervention using simultaneous communication with deaf infants: The effects on communication development. *Child Development, 55*, 607–616.

Griest, D. L., & Forehand, R. (1982). How can I get any parent training done with all these other problems going on? The role of family variables in child behavior therapy. *Child and Family Behavior Therapy, 4*(1), 73–80.

Gross, A. M., Eudy, C., & Drabman, R. S. (1982). Training parents to be physical therapists with their physically handicapped child. *Journal of Behavioral Medicine, 5*, 321–327.

Halpern, R. (1984). Lack of effects for home-based early intervention? Some possible explanations. *American Journal of Orthopsychiatry, 54*, 33–42.

Halpern, R. (1986). Home-based early intervention: Dimensions of current practice. *Child Welfare, 65*, 387–398.

Hanson, M., & Schwartz, R. (1978). Results of a longitudinal intervention program for Down syndrome infants and their families. *Education and Training of the Mentally Retarded, 13*, 403–407.

Haskins, R., & Kotch, J. (1986). Day care and illness: Evidence, costs, and public policy. *Pediatrics, 77*, 950–982.

Holsworth, T. E., & Currie, R. J. (1982). An evaluation of the efficacy of televised home instruction: Teaching parents to be trainers of their preschool handicapped children. *Journal of the Division for Early Childhood, 6*, 36–41.

Howlin, P. (1984). Parents as therapists: A critical review. In D. J. Miller (Ed.), *Remediating children's language: Behavioral and naturalistic approaches* (pp. 197–229). San Diego: College-Hill Press.

Karnes, M. B., & Zehrbach, R. R. (1977). Alternative models for delivering services to young handicapped children. In J. B. Jordan, A. H. Hayden, M. B. Karnes, & M. M. Wood (Eds.), *Early childhood education for exceptional children* (pp. 20–65). Reston, VA: Council for Exceptional Children.

Kelly, J. F. (1982). Effects of intervention on caregiver-

infant interaction when the infant is handicapped. *Journal of the Division for Early Childhood, 5*, 53–63.

Maisto, A. A., & German, M. L. (1979). Variables related to progress in a parent infant training program for high-risk infants. *Journal of Pediatric Psychology, 4*, 409–419.

Maisto, A. A., & German, M. L. (1981). Maternal locus of control and developmental gain demonstrated by high risk infants: A longitudinal analysis. *Journal of Psychology, 109*, 213–221.

Marfo, K., & Kysela, G. M. (1985). Early intervention with mentally handicapped children: A critical appraisal of applied research. *Journal of Pediatric Psychology, 10*, 305–324.

McMahon, R. J., Forehand, R., Griest, D. L., & Wells, K. C. (1981). Who drops out of treatment during parent behavior training? *Behavioral Counseling Quarterly, 1*, 79–85.

Meisels, S. J. (1985). The efficacy of early intervention: Why are we still asking this question? *Topics in Early Childhood Special Education, 5*(2), 1–11.

Moran, M. (1985). Families in early intervention: Effects of program variables. *Zero to Three, 5*(5), 11–14.

Moxley-Haegert, L., & Serbin, L. A. (1983). Developmental education for parents of delayed infants: Effects on parental motivation and children's development. *Child Development, 54*, 1324–1331.

Mueller, M., & Leviton, A. (1986). In-home versus clinic-based services for the developmentally disabled child: Who is the primary client—parent or child? *Social Work in Health Care, 11*(3), 75–88.

Muhiuden, H. A., Melville, T. G., Ferguson, S. D., & Mohan, P. (1984). The postures exhibited by 3-day-old full-term neonates. *Early Human Development, 20*, 57–66.

O'Dell, S. L. (1985). Progress in parent training. *Progress in Behavior Modification, 19*, 57–108.

Odom, S. L. (1985). Early intervention for handicapped children in Germany and the United States: A comparative view. *Journal of the Division for Early Childhood, 9*, 215–218.

Pahud, D., & Besson, F. (1985). Special education in Switzerland: Historical reflections and current applications. *Journal of the Division for Early Childhood, 9*, 222–229.

Paradise, J. L. (1980). Otitis media in infants and children. *Pediatrics, 65*, 917–943.

Paradise, J. L. (1981). Otitis media during early life: How hazardous to development? A critical review of the evidence. *Pediatrics, 68*, 869–873.

Phemister, M. R., Richardson, A. M., & Thomas, G. V. (1978). Observations of young normal and handicapped children. *Child: Care, Health, and Development, 4*, 247–259.

Piper, M. C., & Ramsay, M. K. (1980). Effects of early home environment on the mental development of Down syndrome infants. *American Journal of Mental Deficiency, 85*, 39–44.

Prechtl, H. F. R., Theorell, K., & Blair, A. W. (1973). Behavioral state cycles in abnormal infants. *Developmental Medicine and Child Neurology, 15*, 606–615.

Ramey, C. T., Bryant, D. M., Sparling, J. J., & Wasik, B. H. (1985). Project CARE: A comparison of two early intervention strategies to prevent retarded development. *Topics in Early Childhood Special Education, 5*(2), 12–25.

Ramey, C. T., Bryant, D. M. & Suarez, T. M. (1985). Preschool compensatory education and the modifiability of intelligence: A critical review. In D. K. Detterman (Ed.), *Current topics in human development* (pp. 247–296). Norwood, NJ: Ablex.

Ramey, C. T., Sparling, J. J., Bryant, D. M., & Wasik, B. H. (1982). Primary prevention of developmental retardation during infancy. *Journal of Prevention and Human Services, 1*(4), 61–83.

Reader, L. (1984). Preschool intervention programmes. *Child: Care, Health, and Development, 10,* 237–251.

Roberts, J. E., Burchinal, M. R., Collier, A. M., Ramey, C. T., & Henderson, F. W. (1987). *Otitis media in early childhood and cognitive performance, academic achievement, and classroom behavior in school children.* Manuscript submitted for publication.

Roberts, J. E., Sanyal, M. A., Burchinal, M. R., Collier, A. M., Ramey, C. T., & Henderson, F. W. (1986). Otitis media in early childhood and its relationship to later verbal and academic performance. *Pediatrics, 78,* 423–430.

Rosenberg, M. S., Reppucci, N. D., & Linney, J. A. (1983). Issues in the implementation of human service programs: Examples from a parent training project for high-risk families. *Analysis and Intervention in Developmental Disabilities, 3,* 215–225.

Ross, G. S. (1984). Home intervention for prenatal infants of low-income families. *American Journal of Orthopsychiatry, 54,* 263–270.

Sanders, M. R. & James, J. E. (1983). The modification of parent behavior: A review of generalization and maintenance. *Behavior Modification, 7,* 3–27.

Sandow, S. A., Clark, A. D. B., Cox, M. V., & Stewart, F. L. (1981). Home intervention with parents of severely subnormal preschool children: A final report. *Child: Care, Health, and Development, 7,* 135–144.

Sharav, T., Collins, R., & Shlomo, L. (1985). Effects of maternal education in prognosis of development in children with Down syndrome. *Pediatrics, 76,* 387–391.

Shearer, D. E., & Shearer, M. S. (1976). The Portage Project: A model for early childhood intervention. In T. D. Tjossem (Ed.), *Intervention strategies for high risk infants and young children* (pp. 335–350). Baltimore: University Park Press.

Simeonsson, R. J., Huntington, G. S., Short, R. F., & Ware, W. B. (1982). The Carolina Record of Individual Behavior: Characteristics of handicapped infants and children. *Topics in Early Childhood Special Education, 2*(2), 43–55.

Sloper, P., Cunningham, C. C., & Arnljotsdottir, M. (1983). Parental reactions to early intervention with their Down syndrome infants. *Child: Care, Health, and Development, 9,* 357–376.

Snell, M. E., & Beckman-Brindley, S. (1984). Family involvement in intervention with children having severe handicaps. *Journal of The Association for Persons with Severe Handicaps, 9,* 213–230.

Solomon, G. S., Wilson, D. O., & Galey, G. S. (1982). Project DEBT: Attempting to improve the quality of interaction among handicapped children and their parents. *Journal of The Association for the Severely Handicapped, 7*(2), 28–35.

Stoneman, Z., Brody, G. H., & Abbott, D. (1983). In-home observations of young Down Syndrome children with their mothers and fathers. *American Journal of Mental Deficiency, 87,* 591–600.

Strain, P. S., & Smith, B. J. (1986). A counter-interpretation of early intervention effects: A response to Casto and Mastropieri. *Exceptional Children, 53,* 260–265.

Thomas, A., & Chess, S. (1977). *Temperament and development.* New York: Brunner/Mazel.

Winton, P. J., and Turnbull, A. P. (1981). Parent involvement as viewed by parents of preschool handicapped children. *Topics in Early Childhood Special Education, 1*(3), 11–20.

Wolraich, M. L. (1984). Myelomeningocele. In J. A. Blackman (Ed.), *Medical aspects of developmental disabilities in children birth to three* (pp. 159–166). Rockville, MD: Aspen.

Woods, P. A., Corney, M. J., & Pryce, G. J. (1984). Developmental progress of preschool Down's syndrome children receiving a home-advisory service: An interim report. *Child: Care, Health, and Development, 10,* 287–299.

Zucman, E. (1985). Early childhood programs for the handicapped in France. *Journal of the Division for Early Childhood, 9,* 237–245.

Chapter 13

Advances in the Ecological Assessment of Classroom Instruction for Young Children with Handicaps

Judith J. Carta, Diane M. Sainato, and Charles R. Greenwood

ADVANCES IN ECOLOGICAL ASSESSMENT

HOW SHOULD ONE DETERMINE QUALITY educational environments for preschool children with handicaps? Defining good programs is not necessarily an easy task. Opinions vary on what the outcomes of early education should be, what the role of preschool teachers is, and what students should do in preschool. In spite of this lack of consensus, there is no shortage of popular advice regarding how a "good" program should look. For example, this list of considerations for evaluating a preschool was taken from a book on child care and development written for parents:

> Does the classroom feel good? Do the children seem happy and involved? Are the children doing interesting work? Are the teachers warm, attentive, and relaxed with the children? Are the teachers working with the children or talking to other adults, doing paperwork, etc.? Is there a reasonable amount of sturdy, age-appropriate equipment readily accessible to all the children and arranged so as to be inviting? (Samuels & Samuels, 1979, p. 216)

A similar list of criteria for evaluating preschool programs written for teachers included the following:

1. A good program values the child's healthy, happy, responding, secure approach to living.
2. A good program provides for the emotional growth of the child.

3. A good program provides appropriate opportunities for children to grow in self-direction and independence.
4. A good program is challenging to children's intellectual powers.
5. A good program provides media for self-expression.
6. A good program encourages children's verbal expression (Hildebrand, 1971, p. 297).

While these may be helpful indicators for persons needing only a rough yardstick of program quality, they are obviously inadequate for professionals striving to design and improve programs for young children with special needs. Persons examining early intervention programs need more precise ways of describing program variables. Methods are needed for determining whether specific program dimensions are present and for quantifying the impact of those dimensions. Additionally, ways of ensuring that programs are "delivering" as promised are needed. For children with handicaps, the early years are too critical for the professional to be "loose" about program description and monitoring.

In spite of this urgency for quality programs, the science of describing programs and of determining their ecologies is weak. In this chapter, some of the literature related to the ecological variables that have been used to describe and contrast preschool environments will be

217

explored. While this literature provides some indication of dimensions that may be useful for quantifying behaviors in the preschool classroom, it falls short in pointing to the most crucial program variables or those that are most likely to affect developmental outcomes. No studies have linked specific program variables to any of the outcome measures that are typically employed as indicators of effective early intervention programs (e.g., gains on norm-referenced or criterion-referenced tests [Bricker & Dow, 1980; Kopp, 1979]; program graduates' success in subsequent school environments [Karnes, Schwedel, Lewis, Ratts, & Esry, 1981; Schweinhart & Weikart, 1980]; or improvement in children's social competence or behavioral adjustment [Strain, 1981; Zigler & Balla, 1982]). Therefore, a critical link is missing in determining which ecological variables will have an important later effect on children's development. This specification awaits a more sophisticated methodology, the beginnings of which are spelled out in the two studies described in the latter section of this chapter.

In summary, the reader of this chapter will first review some of the representative findings of researchers who have examined the ecological variables that characterize preschool. As part of this discussion, the methodological and technological limitations of these studies will be described. Second, examples of some new ways for assessing ecological variables in preschool classrooms that will provide direction for designing more effective programs will be discussed.

Definition of Ecological Variables

Ecology is a term shared by many disciplines, yet few can agree on its precise definition. Rogers-Warren and Wedel (1980) have pointed out that the term "human ecology" is presently used by psychologists in at least two ways. One approach focuses on the way the stationary or topographical features of the physical milieu influence the subject. Proponents of this conceptualization (Barker, 1968; Gump, 1971; Wright, 1967) view the relationship between environment and the subject

as static, that is, the ecology affects the subject's behavior. A more recent perspective on human ecology views the environment-subject relationship as a dynamic interplay in which changes in one affect changes in the other (Patterson & Moore, 1979); furthermore, changes in behavior affect changes in other behaviors, either within an organism or between two organisms (Patterson, 1976). Trickett, Kelly, and Todd (1972) have described this "principle of interdependence" by stating that "whenever any component of a natural ecosystem is changed, there are alterations between all other components of the ecosystem" (p. 377). Preschool classrooms are excellent examples of this type of "interdependent" system.

REVIEW OF RESEARCH CONCERNING PRESCHOOL ECOLOGICAL VARIABLES

In this review, the effects of both static and dynamic ecological variables on preschool classrooms will be examined. First, studies that have investigated the stationary and topographical features of the environment and their effects on child behavior will be highlighted. These studies embracing the *static* notion of ecology investigate the impact of various materials, spatial arrangements and classroom composition. Second, studies of *dynamic* ecological variables (i.e., teacher behavior variables) and their effects on students' behavior will be described.

Static Features of the Environment

A number of features of the classroom environment are fairly stable and relatively unaffected by student behavior. These static aspects of preschool classroom environments include the types of materials present and their arrangement, the spatial configuration, the student-teacher ratio, the number of peers present, and their level of functioning. Some of these variables are discussed below.

The Effect of Materials The static variable that has received the most attention in the literature is the effect of materials on student behavior. Naturalistic studies document that children's behavior in preschools varies as a result of the type, the number, and the arrangement of materials in classrooms. First, some materials have more "holding power" over children, that is, children will attend and interact with certain toys for longer periods of time than with other toys. Among these play objects are: blocks and sand (Hulson, 1930); art materials (Rosenthal, 1973); and role play materials (Kounin & Sherman, 1979). Kounin and Sherman (1979) proposed that attractiveness of certain materials may be a by-product of the behaviors they provoke. Materials with high "holding power" (art, role play, books, and sand) seem to evoke either a wide range of behaviors or they result in a product or a clear sense of progress.

Several studies have documented that preschoolers' social behavior varies as a function of the type of play materials that are available. Typically, these have been naturalistic studies of free play situations in which the number of students playing together or the specific social interactions of students are investigated. For example, Shure (1963) found differences in play behaviors depending on the type of play area that was made available to children. Subjects engaged in social interaction most frequently and at most complex levels when they played in the doll play area. They engaged in the lowest degree of social interaction when they played in the art area. These findings have been replicated in a number of naturalistic studies of play materials and their relationship to social behaviors. A selection of these studies and their findings are summarized in Table 1.

In a study that digressed from the typical naturalistic/descriptive framework in exploring the effect of materials on social behaviors, Quilitch and Risley (1973) experimentally manipulated the types of materials made available to a group of children. Materials had previously been defined as "social" toys (i.e., most often played with by two to four children simultaneously) or "isolate" toys (i.e., most often engaged in by children playing alone). Children engaged in social play 78% of the time when they were involved with social toys (e.g., games that involved competition such as checkers, playing cards, Pick-Up Stix, and board games). The same children engaged in social play only 16% of the time when isolate toys (e.g., puzzles, crayons, play dough) were made available. Because these differences were obtained after a deliberate manipulation of the environment, a functional relationship between materials and behavior was demonstrated. This, of course, provided a much stronger case for the effect of materials than the correlational relationships obtained from the previously discussed naturalistic studies.

Arrangement and the *number* of toys simultaneously available are other aspects of materials that influence specific behaviors of preschoolers. Arranging toys on shelves rather

Table 1. Play behaviors and materials found to set the occasion for their occurrence

Play behavior	Materials	Study
Solitary play	Blocks, games	Shure, 1963
	Jigsaw puzzle, crayons	Quilitch & Risley, 1973
	Modeling clay, crayons, sand and water toys	Rubin, 1977
	Puzzles, vehicles, clothing	Rosenthal, 1973
	Library materials, fine motor toys, art materials	Stoneman, Cantrell, & Hoover-Dempsey, 1983
Parallel play	Sand and water toys, crayons, Play Doh	Rubin, 1977
Cooperative play	Clay	Updegraff and Herbst, 1933
	Doll corner	Green, 1933
	Blocks	Markey, 1938
	Doll corner	Shure, 1963
	Reading and number materials	Rubin, 1977
	Blocks, vehicles, water play, housekeeping, music	Stoneman, Cantrell, and Hoover-Dempsey, 1983

than in toy boxes increases the amount of time children will engage in manipulating toys (Montes & Risley, 1975). Allowing children open access to materials instead of limited access to the materials does not seem to affect the amount of time children interact with them.

The *number* of materials made available affects a variety of children's behaviors during play. Naturalistic studies indicate that when the number of toys available to a group of children falls below a certain critical point, children in the group tend to engage in more social contacts, teasing, crying, and quarreling (Johnson, 1935), and more aggression and rough and tumble play (Smith & Connolly, 1972). When Krantz and Risley (1977) experimentally manipulated the number of materials available to a group of eight children, they found the lowest levels of disruptions when all eight children had the materials. When half the group needed to wait for materials, disruptions were most frequent within the group. especially among the children who had no materials.

These results are derived mostly from studies of non-handicapped children. While few studies have replicated these findings for young children with handicaps, the literature that does exist indicates that there are few differences between handicapped and nonhandicapped children and the ways in which toys affect their behaviors (Rogers-Warren, Ruggles, Peterson, & Cooper, 1981; Stoneman, Cantrell, & Hoover-Dempsey, 1983). Teachers of handicapped preschoolers should be aware that the toys and instructional materials made available may affect children's engagement with play objects and the ways children interact.

The Effect of Spatial Variables Like the materials variable, the ecology of spatial arrangements in the preschool classroom has received considerable attention in the literature. Several aspects of classroom "space" have been shown to affect students' behavior in numerous ways. For example, the actual *physical location* of children in relationship to other children in the classroom may affect the way they behave. Krantz and Risley (1977) demonstrated that the on-task behavior of kindergar-

teners was significantly higher when they were spaced equidistantly on chairs or assigned spaces on the floor than when they were allowed to crowd together on a small rug. Similarly, Eck (1975) pointed out that children exhibited fewer disruptions during nap time when children's cots were spaced and staggered than when the children were allowed to face each other.

The arrangement or *organization of the classroom* is another spatial variable related to preschool environments. The traditional folklore about how classroom spatial organization affects student behavior is that children tend to play more cooperatively in enclosed spaces and tend to be less restrained and run around more in large open spaces (Huston-Stein, Friedrich-Cofer, & Susman, 1977). This bit of teacher wisdom is, in fact, born out in studies related to this issue. Well-defined areas led to smaller groupings of children and quieter interactions (Fitt, 1974; Sheehan & Day, 1975), more task involvement and child-equipment interactions (Fitt, 1974; Pollowy, 1974) and an increase in cooperative behaviors. Larger play areas, on the other hand, led to the gathering of larger groups of children, noisier interactions, and a decrease in cooperative behaviors.

The *number of children in a classroom* (i.e., the spatial density) is a variable to which researchers have directed considerable attention. The results of these studies have been mixed (Phyfe-Perkins, 1980; Rogers-Warren & Wedel, 1980). A number of researchers have noted an increase in the level of different types of social interaction including aggressive behaviors as space per child decreases (Hutt & Vaizey, 1966; Smith, 1974; Smith & Connolly, 1972). On the other hand, some researchers have found that as classroom areas become more densely populated, children will make fewer contacts (McGrew, 1972) and exhibit fewer aggressive responses (Loo, 1972). Apparently, the effects of spatial density depend on how the density was achieved. For example, when a classroom has become more densely populated by increasing the number of children in a fixed amount of space, children are more likely to keep their distances from one another (McGrew, 1972), and exhibit more aggressive behaviors (Hutt & Vaizey, 1966). However, they may also exhibit more imaginative play (Peck & Goldman, 1978). Alternatively, when a classroom or play area has become more crowded because its space has been reduced by adding partitions, children engage in less physical contact, less aggression (Loo, 1972) and fewer instances of social interaction (Preiser, 1972). One confounding variable in these studies may be the way in which teacher behaviors interact with spatial density. Fagot (1977) discovered that teachers in crowded classrooms exhibited more control over their students. Similarly, Perry (1977) found that Head Start teachers who had crowded classrooms exhibited more than three times the amount of controlling behaviors. In summary, it appears as though spatial density has some effects on preschoolers' behavior in educational settings, but the effects are very likely mediated by the amount of direction employed by the teacher.

The Effect of Teacher-Pupil Ratio

One factor related to classrooms that receives considerable attention from state regulators and school administrators is the *number of adults* present and the general *staffing pattern* in the classroom. Here the conventional wisdom seems to be that it is advantageous to have more rather than fewer adults available, because a lower staff-child ratio will allow more individual attention to students. However, the limited number of studies conducted on this topic do not necessarily support this advantage. Shapiro (1975) examined the relationship between *teacher-child ratio* and the number of child-teacher contacts. She discovered that more individualization occurred in situations with fewer students when classes ranged in size from 16–22 students. When classes contained fewer than 16 students, however, fewer teacher-child contacts occurred as the number of students was reduced.

Examining the effect of *teacher-child ratio* on student behavior, Stodolsky (1974) found that in preschools with more adults per student, children engaged in shorter periods of activity and more time in transition between activities.

Similarly, O'Connor (1975) reported that in classrooms with lower teacher-child ratios (1:3.5), students engaged in more frequent bids for adult attention than in settings with higher teacher-child ratios (1:7). At least one study has suggested that the number of staff present in the classroom may not be as important as the way that staff are deployed. LeLaurin and Risley (1972) found that assigning staff to "zones" or areas in a day care center provided teachers with more opportunities to interact with children in comparison to a "man-to-man" assignment when staff were responsible for specific groups of children. In addition, the "zone" method increased the average amount of participation in activities per child and reduced the average amount of waiting time between activities.

The Effect of the Ratio of Handicapped to Nonhandicapped Children

One final topographical variable related to preschools that has been the object of much scrutiny is the ratio of handicapped to nonhandicapped students in the classroom. This research is part of the larger issue of the effectiveness of mainstreaming young children with special needs. The literature on this issue reveals no clear advantage for integrating handicapped students with nonhandicapped students (Tawney, 1981). The reasons for the "mixed bag" of results on the effectiveness of mainstreaming at the preschool level are many, although among the primary difficulties in this literature are the following: 1) the range of research designs, 2) flaws in some research designs (e.g., comparing students behavior in nonequivalent groups, and 3) differences in definitions of similar dependent variables (e.g., social interaction). For a more complete discussion of this literature, see Chapter 14 by Odom and McEvoy in this volume.

This section has reviewed studies that concerned the static features of the preschool environment. While only a few of these variables were discussed, there are clearly many other variables, such as daily schedule, furniture and its arrangement, use of routines, and so on. The literature that was discussed mentioned several behaviors that may be affected by the multitude of static variables. These vary from play, on-task, and academic behaviors to language and positive and negative social behaviors. The point to this review is that topographical features of the classroom ecology affect the ways in which preschoolers behave on a daily basis.

This conclusion is only tentative, however, because of the nature of these studies. Almost without exception, these studies were descriptive; they described the behaviors emitted by preschoolers when a specific ecological variable was present in a classroom. Studies that demonstrate behavioral changes as a function of specific manipulations of environmental features (Krantz & Risley, 1977; Montes & Risley, 1975; Quilitch & Risley, 1973) are rare in the preschool literature. If early intervention programs are to be designed based on scientific evidence about the variables that influence behavior, more experimental studies of ecological variables in preschool classrooms will be essential.

Dynamic Features of the Environment

Some variables not only affect student behavior but are also affected by changes in student behaviors. Prime examples of these dynamic, interdependent features of the classroom environment include teacher behaviors and peer behaviors (See Strain & Kohler, Chapter 8, this volume). In order to provide an illustrative review of the literature on dynamic ecological features in preschool settings, this section will focus solely on teacher behavior.

The Effect of Teacher Behavior   Teachers have long been recognized as a potent force in determining the nature of the preschool experience for children (Anderson, 1943). The role of the teacher in early childhood settings is extremely complex. The teacher not only has an impact on children through direct interactions, but also influences children indirectly through the arrangement of the learning environment (Phyfe-Perkins, 1981). In controlling the learning environment, the teacher selects and arranges the materials, determines the schedule, groups children for instruction, and also serves as the pivotal focus for all instructional interaction in the preschool. The general

class of teacher behavior sets the occasion for the majority of observed child behavior. The most researched variable within this set has been the impact of teachers' verbal behavior on the behavior of young preschool children.

The study of teachers' verbal behavior has most often focused on the effects of behaviors such as praise or criticism on children's performance in a classroom or play setting. Three types of studies have examined these interactions. The first group of studies explored the effects of experimenter behavior on child performance in a contrived work or play situation. Examples of *experimental studies* of this type can be found in the work of Allen (1966); Farnham-Diggory and Ramsey (1971); McCoy and Zigler (1965); Taffell, O'Leary, and Armel (1974); and Wyer (1986). Second, studies of the effect of various teacher verbal behaviors on children's social and task-performance can be found in the *applied behavior analysis* literature. These studies are exemplified by the early work of Allen, Hart, Buell, Harris, and Wolf (1964); Hart, Reynolds, Baer, Brawley, and Harris (1968); Madsen, Becker, and Thomas (1968) and more recently in the work of Odom and Strain (1986). These studies offer detailed analysis of the functional relationship between observed teacher behavior (e.g., prompts or praise) and subsequent child performance (e.g., social interaction or on-task behavior) following the experimental manipulation of the quantity and/or type of teacher behavior.

A third type of study involved *naturalistic observations* of teacher-child interactions. These studies attempt to relate, in a more ecological sense, the specific types of teacher verbal behavior to variations in child behavior. These studies will be discussed in more detail.

The impact of teachers' verbal behavior on children's *task persistence* has been a recurrent theme throughout the literature on early childhood settings. In a complex observational study, Stallings (1975) examined four early childhood models to identify the effects of certain teaching practices on child behavior. Stallings noted that children's task persistence was positively correlated with individual instructions by adults. Stallings further noted that verbally responsive, nondidactic teachers who interacted with small (one or two) groups of children promoted task persistence, independence, verbalization, cooperation and self-esteem in young children.

Fagot (1973) observed preschool children and their teachers during free play periods in three separate investigations. In each study, children with the *less* directive, less critical teachers showed a higher rate of task behavior. In the same study, teachers of children with a high rate of task engagement responded more to children's questions and offered unrequested information less.

The results of the Fagot (1973) study were supported by Hamilton and Gordon (1978), who utilized a combined methodology of naturalistic observation of preschool teacher's interactions with their students and laboratory observation of children's persistence on a predetermined individual task. Results of this investigation suggested that children who received *more criticism* and directing statements from teachers in the classroom had lower scores on experimental tasks. In addition, it was noted that children who received *more suggestions* had higher experimental task scores. Similar results occurred from observations of teachers' verbal behaviors and child performance in the classroom. Hamilton and Gordon concluded that teachers should distinguish between the use of suggestions and directions and be aware that these behaviors may be related to children's development of task behaviors.

Interestingly, the findings from the observational studies seem to suggest that *less* directive teachers encourage more task engagement in their students. This finding is in direct contrast to research on instructional processes, which suggests that academic engaged time (linked to subsequent student achievement) is enhanced through *direct* instruction by teachers (Rosenshine, 1977).

SUMMARY

This review makes it clear that the research literature suggests that many specific variables affect preschoolers' behavior in classrooms. Some of these are static variables and set the occasion for students to respond. Other more dynamic variables, like teacher behaviors, may affect the ways in which students behave but may themselves be affected by student behavior.

While this past research is interesting, it does not inform the researcher conceptually or empirically about the best ways to plan preschool environments for children with handicaps. These earlier ecological studies fall short in two respects. First, they examine only one variable at a time. Program providers know that the behavioral differences that are observed among preschool children are most likely the result of an interaction between the teacher and the child and the specific aspects of the instructional situation. Those interactions must be described and quantified if children's classroom behavior is to be understood.

A second and more important drawback in the earlier ecological studies is that while they describe a host of variables they fail to inform researchers about which of these are important or are most related to significant outcome variables. If effective classrooms for preschoolers are to be arranged, it will be necessary to step beyond the facts that certain ecological variables affect behaviors in certain ways. Specifically, researchers will need to know which of these ecobehavioral interactions are most important and will thus effect preschoolers' development in significant ways. The studies presented below describe two important methodologies that may lead to a more effective analysis of the critical aspects of early intervention programs.

TWO ECOLOGICAL APPROACHES FOR QUANTIFYING PRESCHOOL ENVIRONMENTS

In this section, two approaches to the study of preschool instruction are examined. The first is an ecological approach for contrasting preschool environments in light of the skills required for independent functioning in future mainstream environments. The second is an ecological approach for linking ecological variables, student behavior variables, and program outcomes. Both approaches seek to improve our knowledge of preschool programs by providing quantified descriptions across a wide range of variables related to the environment, the teacher, and the student. More importantly, they both link these rich descriptions to other significant socially valid measures.

An Approach for Contrasting Preschool Environments

The ecological perspective has been used to quantify important classroom variables within regular and special education classrooms at the Early Childhood Research Institute at the University of Pittsburgh. For this particular investigation, an ecological approach was used to provide a descriptive analysis of the requirements for independent performance in handicapped and nonhandicapped early childhood settings. The focus on independent functioning was based on three basic premises: 1) students' behavior and classroom performance are determined by their degree of fit in their educational environments, 2) students' success in functioning in mainstream classrooms will depend on their ability to fit into those environments, 3) teachers need descriptions of those mainstream environments and knowledge of the student behaviors necessary for fitting into those environments in order to prepare students for functioning in regular classroom settings.

Necessity for Child Environment Fit The necessity for child environment fit between-classroom differences and the differential impacts of classrooms has been part of the educational lore for some time. Each classroom may be viewed as a singular ecosystem in which the physical arrangement of the room, the available materials, individual children (and their competencies), and teachers (and their competencies) continuously interact to form a unique environment (Rogers-Warren & Wedel, 1980). A child's success or failure in a particular classroom may be a function of his or her ability to fit into a particular environment (Fowler, 1982). Attention to setting variables (e.g., quantity or

quality of teacher instruction, praise and feedback, size of instructional groups) and the child-environment "fit" in the educational literature represents a shift from an approach that is strictly skill-based to a more interactional view of a child's performance in educational settings (Morrison & Oxford, 1978).

Necessity for Kindergarten Survival Skills Although integration of preschool handicapped students with their normally developing peers has been accepted as public policy, it is typical for school systems to mainstream only those students who do not demand inordinate amounts of teacher attention or drastic alteration in the school's accepted curriculum. In addition, the specialized nature of preschool programs for handicapped students, (i.e., level of supervision, degree of independence, complexity of task [Vincent et al., 1980]) may inadvertently undermine the handicapped students' chance for success in the regular classroom. Handicapped preschoolers receive a great deal more instruction and supervision in specialized settings than do normal peers of handicapped children in mainstreamed classrooms (Kaufman, Agard, & Semmel, 1985). The discrepancy between regular and special learning environments may actually increase the incidence of behavior problems and decrease generalization of skills as the child moves across them (Vincent et al., 1980).

Necessity for Information about the Next Environment Several authors have addressed the problem of preparing handicapped preschool children for transition to the "next environment" (Fowler, 1982; Le Blanc, Etzel, & Domash, 1978; Vincent et al., 1980). Transitional programming has at its roots the assumption that teachers will prepare children to meet the demands of future mainstream environments by instructing them in the necessary skills in their present (special) classroom.

The first step is to identify the critical skills needed by children to succeed in mainstream environments. The identification of these critical skills may be accomplished by focusing on the children who perform competently in these future environments, on the "receiving" teacher's priorities for children functioning in these classrooms and on the ecological features (e.g., materials, classroom structure, teacher-child ratio, instructional interactions) that differentiate specific classrooms.

Teacher Priorities in Mainstream Kindergartens Using an adaptation of the Vincent et al. (1980) "Survival Skills Checklist," Sainato and Lyon (1983) interviewed fourteen regular preschool and kindergarten teachers. Children who were rated as being "most independent" were those who could work independently, and who completed tasks within the allotted time and worked in the absence of teacher direction. The appropriate behavior of children during group instruction (e.g., appropriate sitting, responding to questions, participation, following directions) was noted to be very important by 100% of the teachers. These skills were also exhibited by 100% of all highly rated children in the mainstreamed classrooms. In addition to the skills of being able to work independently and also behaving appropriately during group instruction, teachers noted that 90% of all children rated as most independent followed class routine, complied with two or three step directions, and remained engaged in either work or play behavior with peers in the absence of teacher direction. In contrast, 100% of the children rated as "least independent" by teachers were only occasionally noted to engage in the highly rated skills of following directions and behaving appropriately during group instruction, independent work times, or in peer interaction.

Observational Assessment In order to quantify the various ecological structures operating in the preschool classrooms, an observational instrument was developed to capture the activity structures in special and mainstream classrooms. In addition to observing the type of activity taking place, teachers' and children's behavior and interactions within those activities were also observed. Specific observational measures were categorized in six major areas:

1. *Topographic features* including type of activity, presence of teacher(s), the physical arrangement, instructional grouping
2. *Materials* including type, location and access
3. *Teaching Codes* including categories of instruction
4. *Response Codes* including engagement and quantity and/or quality of response
5. *Classroom Interactions* for peers and teachers
6. *Transition Codes* These measures were collected by five trained observers using a partial interval recording procedure across three days in each classroom.

One Classroom: Two Educational Experiences In order to illustrate the various dynamic features operating within a single classroom environment, a single case example of two children's educational experiences within the same special education classroom will be discussed. For this purpose, three dimensions of the classroom ecology: *type of activity, classroom structure or grouping,* and *type of instruction* will be examined.

For the moment, Child A is described as the child rated as "most independent" by the special education teacher. Child B will be known as the "least independent" child in the classroom. Discussion will focus first on the quantity and *type of activities* in which these children engaged during the preschool day.

As can be seen in Figure 1, the "least independent" child and the "most independent" child had extremely different schedules. While Child A (most independent) spent 71% of her time in free play, Child B (least independent) was engaged in free play only 14% of the time. The second most frequent activity for Child A was eating. Interestingly, Child B spent no time in either preacademic or language instruction. This finding seems quite distressing since a major instructional emphasis in this particular classroom was language development. Another interesting comparison is the observation that Child A had little or no observed time in fine motor activities while Child B spent 33% of her time engaged in this type of activity. Although the reader might suspect that these

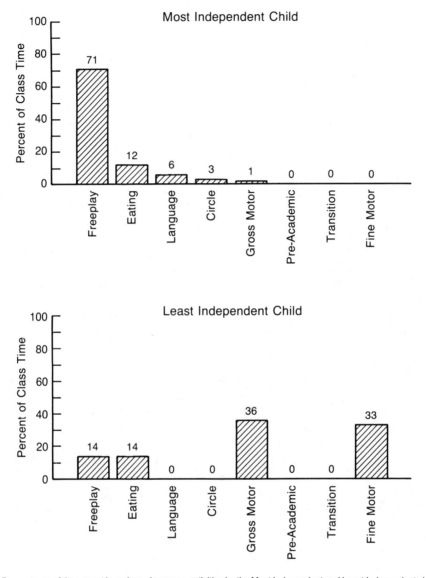

Figure 1.   Percentages of time spent in various classroom activities by the Most Independent and Least Independent children in the same preschool special education classroom.

very discrepant schedules of these two children might reflect individual education plans and specific child needs, a look at the teacher's planned schedule and the amount of time allocated for these instructional activities showed that the time allotted for each activity was equally distributed across the school day for each child.

A second category of observations concerned with *grouping* also yielded interesting results. Within the same special education classroom, children spent varying amounts of time in instructional groups (see Figure 2). Children A and B spent a great deal of their time not engaged with either teachers or peers (46% and 42% respectively). In addition, Child A spent only 12% of the time engaged in either a small or a large group even though these are common instructional arrangements in mainstream environments. It is also interest-

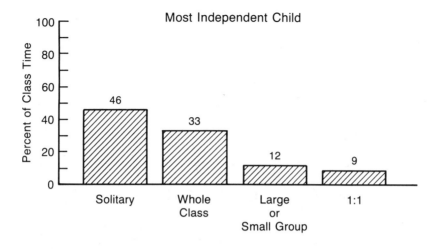

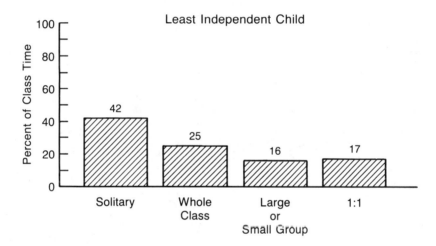

Figure 2.   Percentages of time spent in various grouping arrangements by the Most Independent and Least Independent children in the same preschool special education classroom.

ing to note that the amounts of time Child A and B spent in any type of instructional group was less than 20% of all available instructional time. (Whole class time was most frequently spent eating or in free play.)

The third classroom dimension that was studied was *instruction*. In examining the findings, the authors note very discrepant amounts of time spent in instruction for both Child A and Child B. Instruction is divided into three basic forms: *child-guided,* in which children choose the activity and are free to disengage at will; *teacher-guided,* in which the teacher presents the framework for the activity, monitors

the activity, but provides little or no instruction, prompting, or feedback; and *teacher-directed,* in which the teacher presents specific content, controls the materials and gives feedback and praise (see Figure 3).

In this particular classroom, it is quite surprising to note that the least independent child (Child B) spent the *most* time (42%) in *child-guided* activities and the *least* amount of time (17%) in *teacher-guided* activities. Given the definition of independence, one might think that this child would demand the *most* teacher attention. In addition, Child A, our most independent child, received the most teacher atten-

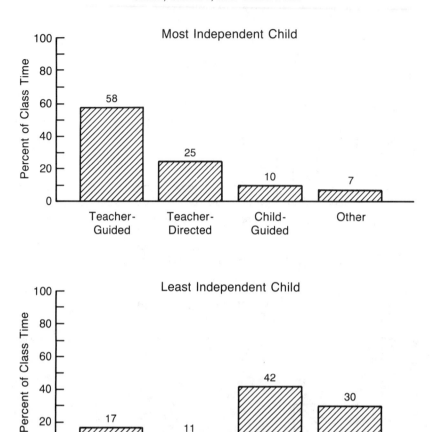

Figure 3.   Percentages of time spent in various instructional arrangements by the Most Independent and Least Independent children in the same preschool special education classroom.

tion, spending a total of 35% of the allocated instructional time in teacher-guided activities. Once again, this finding is quite puzzling given this child's rating as "most" independent.

Implications for Integration into the Least Restrictive Environment   From the data displayed in Figures 1, 2, and 3, it appears that the two handicapped children being educated in the same classroom received varying amounts of teacher attention, instruction, and time in instructional groups. While this finding is quite interesting, it is also important to examine the differences in two areas between this special education classroom and the mainstream environment.

Let us assume that we are ready to main-

stream our most independent child. If we examine the critical differences found in grouping and instruction between the regular and special education preschools seen in our study, we find that even our most independent child has not been given the opportunity to practice certain skills. Figure 4 depicts the differences in the instruction between a regular and special preschool for a "most independent" child.

As can be seen in this bar graph, children in the regular preschool are required to be more independent and to engage in more child-guided instructional time than is allotted in the special preschool. This child in special preschool spent 65% of the available time in either teacher-guided or teacher-directed activities.

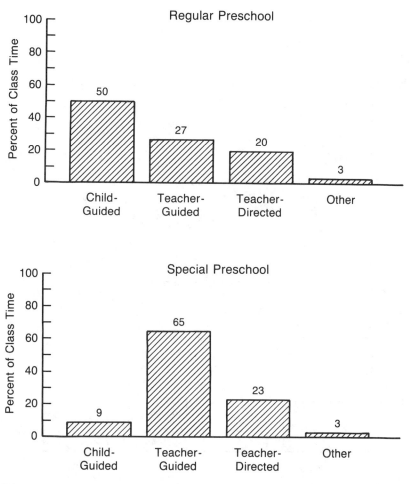

Figure 4. Percentages of time spent in various instructional arrangements by the Most Independent child in a regular preschool classroom and in a special education classroom.

The opportunity to work or play independently existed for only 9% of the time. These children may have great difficulty rising to the demands of the regular classroom even if they are among the most competent children in the special preschool.

Another example of the differing instructional ecology of mainstream and special preschool settings can be seen in Figure 5. With regard to instructional grouping, one can see that in this instance, 86% of the instructional time in the regular preschool was spent in large or small group configurations. The least independent child in the regular preschool spent approximately three times the amount of time in a large or small group than his special educa-

tion counterpart. This discrepancy in the regular and special preschool instructional environments diminishes the probability for successful transitions into the mainstream without special adaptations.

The preceding discussion illustrates only a fraction of the data that Sainato and her colleagues have collected in their observations of regular and special education settings. It is our contention that the methodology employed here is an advance over previous research on preschool environments. This research shows that: 1) individual children's experiences in a single classroom vary considerably and may not be related to their specific needs, 2) the ecologies of special and regular preschools dif-

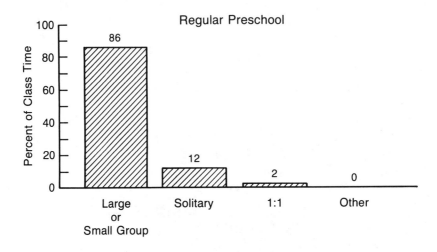

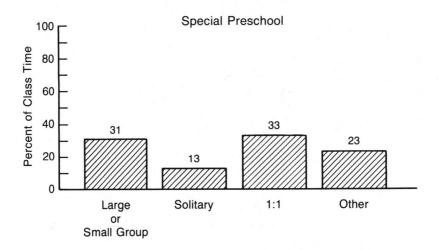

Figure 5.   Percentages of time spent in various grouping arrangements by the Least Independent child in a regular preschool classroom and in a special preschool classroom.

fer across many variables, and 3) the ecologies of special preschools may not be arranged to foster the independent functioning that will be required in mainstream settings. In short, we have presented a new approach for linking descriptions of classroom environments and behavior to important instructional outcomes. It is this type of information that will enable us to create settings that will allow young handicapped children to participate in the mainstream of regular education.

An Approach for Linking Ecological Variables, Student Behavior Variables, and Program Outcomes

The literature review and the study described above demonstrate that numerous static and dynamic variables affect children's behavior in preschool classrooms. What is not clear is how these different dimensions interact temporally within the classroom, how this interplay of variables sets the occasion for children to behave, and how these ecobehavioral interactions affect children's development and achievement over time (Carta & Greenwood, 1985). The Ecobehavioral System for Complex Assessment of Preschool Environments (ESCAPE) has been developed at the Juniper Gardens Children's Project at the University of Kansas in order to address these issues (Carta, Greenwood, & Atwater, 1985). This coding system is based on two relatively recent methodological advances in the educational literature: process-product research on teacher effectiveness (Brophy, 1979; Rosenshine, 1977) and ecobehavioral assessment (Greenwood, Delquadri, Stanley, Terry, & Hall, 1985).

Process-product research on teacher and classroom effectiveness is a means of quantifying classroom environments, teachers' behaviors, and students' behaviors, and relating those measures to academic gains (Brophy, 1979). Typically, process measures are similar to the ecological variables described throughout this chapter. They are often systematic observations of the dynamic interactions of teachers and students (Flanders, 1970; Medley & Mitzel, 1963) and other more static aspects of the classroom (e.g., size of instructional grouping [Soar, 1973; Stallings & Kaskowitz, 1974]). These measures are used to explain students' academic products (outcome gains) resulting from instruction. Many process-product studies have been conducted to determine the specific classroom variables that are related to student achievement. Instructional processes that are positively and significantly related to school achievement include: observed time spent directly on instruction as opposed to non-academic activities (Stallings & Kaskowitz, 1974); frequency of direct factual single answer questions by teachers instead of complex divergent questions (Brophy & Evertson, 1974; Stallings & Kaskowitz, 1974); student attention or on-task behavior as opposed to disruptive off-task behavior (Brophy & Evertson, 1974; Stallings & Kaskowitz, 1974). By linking process variables like these to important student outcomes, the process-product approach has begun to provide information about

which classroom instructional variables are critical to a program's success (Greenwood, 1985).

The other methodological advance incorporated into the ESCAPE system is ecobehavioral assessment. Ecobehavioral assessment is the simultaneous measurement of both static or situational factors (setting events) and dynamic or related subject behaviors. It differs from traditional forms of behavioral assessment in that situational factors are reflected in the observational record on par with behavioral occurrences.

This type of measurement allows researchers to examine classrooms and behaviors in an important diversity of ways. First, it can be used to generate the percentages of time that each coded event occurs in a given period of time. We refer to this type of analysis as a *molar description*. These descriptions, like those used in the study described above, are helpful in making comparisons between settings or specific children within settings. Second, this type of ecobehaviorally-based observation instrument allows researchers to examine the conditional probabilities of jointly occurring coded events. These types of *molecular descriptions* measured by the ESCAPE are helpful in revealing which classroom ecological variables are likely to occur together in time (e.g., when the classroom activity is preacademic, the most probably grouping configuration is small group). What may be even more interesting, however, is that these molecular descriptions allow researchers to examine the most probable student behavior, given a specific ecological variable or set of variables (e.g., when the classroom activity is gross motor, the most likely student response is attending to task).

Using an ecobehavioral observation instrument in elementary grade classrooms, Greenwood and his colleagues found that specific ecological variables increased the probability of student's academic responding to twice its base probability rate (Greenwood et al., 1985). The ESCAPE system has been used to provide molar and molecular descriptions of classroom environments. It is currently being employed in a process-product framework to link certain student behaviors and ecobehavioral interactions to outcome measures. Some examples of these analyses will be described below.

The results presented are derived from a pilot study completed with ESCAPE in which nine handicapped and three nonhandicapped students were observed for the entire school day between 5 and 10 times. The children were located in one of four preschools that differed with respect to both program philosophy and the types of children they served. Of the four sites, three were university-affiliated and one was community-based and privately funded. The ratio of handicapped and nonhandicapped students varied across settings: one site served only students with handicaps, a second site was also totally segregated with the exception of lunch and free play activity, a third site incorporated all nonhandicapped students and mainstreamed one physically handicapped student, and a final site contained all handicapped students and one nonhandicapped peer model. Two of the programs were half-day programs and two were full-day programs.

In each setting, observations were conducted for the entire length of the school day with only nap and bathroom times being eliminated as opportunities for data collection. ESCAPE categories and codes are summarized in Table 2.

Molar Descriptions of Classrooms   The analyses presented below illustrate the most global level of analysis. They reflect all four classrooms, all 12 children across those classrooms, and a total of 87 days of data. This analysis was conducted to examine a typical preschool day, and the data, like the data from Sainato and Lyon (1983) described above, are represented as percentages of the classroom day. Figure 6 shows that transition was the

Table 2.   Preschool observation system for measuring ecobehavioral interactions

	Description	Code examples
Ecological categories		
Designated activity	Subject of instruction	Free play, pre-academics, language, fine motor
Activity initiator	Classification of person choosing activity	Teacher, child, no one
Materials	Objects with which the student engages	Manipulatives, art materials, large motor equipment
Location	Physical placement of the observed student	On floor, at tables, on equipment, in chairs
Grouping	Size of group in same activity as observed student	Small group, large group, one-to-one
Composition	Mix of handicapped and nonhandicapped students in instructional group	All handicapped, mixed, all nonhandicapped
Teacher behavior categories		
Teacher definition	Primary adult interacting with observed student	Teacher, aide, student teacher, ancillary staff
Teacher behavior	Teacher behavior relative to observed student	Verbal instruction, physical assisting, approval, disapproval
Teacher focus	Direction of teacher's behavior	Target child only, target child and entire group, other than target child
Student behavior categories		
Appropriate behaviors	Specific on-task responses	Fine motor, gross motor, academic work
Inappropriate behaviors	Behaviors which compete with appropriate behaviors	Acting-out, off-task, self-stimulation
Talk	Verbalizations	Talk to teacher, talk to peer

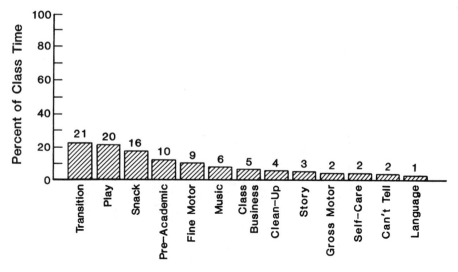

Figure 6. Percentage of time designated activities were observed to occur across four preschools.

most frequently occurring classroom activity. More than 20% of the typical day was spent either between activities or in no activity. Play was the second most frequent activity, occurring for 20% of the day. Preacademic activities took place for only 10% of the typical day.

This general picture of noninvolvement and noninstruction is also reflected in the data on the materials to which children were observed to be attending or engaged. Figure 7 shows that children were most frequently observed to be engaged with no materials at all (30% of the average day). The most common type of materials coded was food or food preparation materials (18% of the typical day). Instructional materials were coded in fewer than 11% of the total number of intervals.

Data on student behavior continue this pattern of non-engagement. Figure 8 illustrates that the most frequently occurring behavior was attending, for example, looking at a teacher who was instructing or discussing, or at an

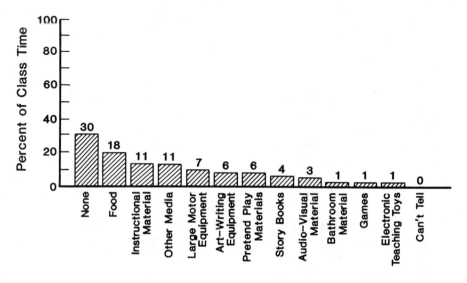

Figure 7. Percentage of time various materials were used by students across four preschools.

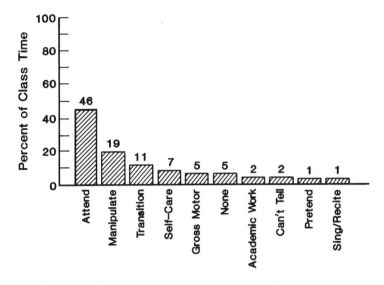

Figure 8.   Percentage of time appropriate student behaviors were observed to occur across four preschools.

interacting peer, or at some play or instructional material. Attending took place for 46% of the entire day. Children were engaged in some type of active behavior (i.e., manipulating objects, performing self-care or gross motor activities, engaging in academic work, or singing/reciting) for only 36% of a typical day. Children spent only 2% of the average day in academic work behavior.

Collectively, the results presented so far suggest a general pattern of nonpreacademic instructional emphasis and of student nonengagement. Children spent most of the average day in transition, with no materials, and passively attending. This first level of analysis provided descriptions of the "typical" day but masked some striking differences across the four preschools. For example, while approximately 10% of the total time was spent in preacademics across preschools, this varied from a mean percentage of 1.8% of a typical day at a special preschool to 19.6% at a mainstream preschool.

What is missing even in this analysis is an analysis of the relationships of student behavior to these ecological variables. Classrooms may be shown to provide considerable amounts of time for preacademics, but if students do not make use of this time and are off task or are uninvolved, this dimension of the classroom ecology may be insignificant. The interactions between ecological variables and student behavior can only be obtained from observation systems that are designed to capture temporal and sequential relationships. The following section will illustrate the advantages of such an ecobehavioral analysis.

Molecular Descriptions of Preschools
The advantage of molecular analyses of classroom interaction is that they permit the determination of the temporal correlations between ecological and behavioral variables, and are thus a first step in the examination of functional relationships. Table 3 presents one such analysis based upon a consolidation of 10 days of observation for one child with developmental delays.

This analysis was prompted by a teacher concerned that this child was spending too much time during the day sitting and waiting. This molecular description of student behaviors across class activities was completed to determine the situations in which this child was actively engaged versus those when he was merely attending or doing nothing. To simplify the analysis, an engagement composite score was formed consisting of several single student behavior codes (i.e., manipulation, self-care, gross motor, pretend, academic work, singing/reciting).

Table 3. Appropriate student engagement as a function of ESCAPE Tasks

Activities	Manipulate	Self-care	Gross motor	Pretend	Academic work	Sing/Recite	Engagement composite	Attend
			Appropriate student engaged responses[a]					
Transition	.082	.028	.016	.002	.004	.004	.136	.502
Play	.338	.013	.177	.051	—	—	.579	.241
Snack	.090	.385	.003	—	—	—	.478	.393
Fine motor	.543	—	—	—	—	—	.543	.371
Preacademic	.111	—	.005	—	.087	—	.203	.681
Gross motor	.064	—	.085	—	—	—	.145	.681
Class business	.148	—	—	—	—	.016	.164	.738
Music	.093	—	.041	.041	—	.208	.383	.486
Clean-up	.174	.044	.029	—	—	—	.247	.420
Story	.118	—	—	—	—	—	.118	.882
Self-Care	.140	.512	—	—	—	—	.652	.191
Language	.182	.091	—	—	.091	—	.364	.556
All activities/ All day	.139	.102	.037	.011	.012	.022	.323	.470

[a]All scores represent the conditional probability of a response—p (Ri | Ai) defined as the joint occurrence of a response (Ri) and a specific activity (Ai) divided by the total frequency of the activity (Ai), or (Ri | Ai)/Ai. For the purpose of this investigation, conditional response probabilities were computed for seven specific student responses (i.e., manipulating, self-care, gross motor, pretending, academic work, singing/reciting, and attending) and for the engaged response composite containing the first six of these responses. Scores are based on 1768 intervals (minutes) of data.
    ——— = 0 probability

The analysis confirmed the teacher's concern about the lack of engagement. The base level for engagement for this student (i.e., the probability that an engaged response would occur at any point throughout the day) was .323. This student was much more likely to be attending ($p=.470$). The conditional probabilities within the table indicate that an engaged response was much more likely to occur during certain activities. For example, an engaged response was much more likely during self-care, play, and fine motor activities: .652, .579, and .543, respectively. Engagement was much less likely during story, transition, and gross motor activities at .118, .136, and .145, respectively.

These data were used by the classroom teacher as the basis for restructuring the classroom to promote more active student engagement. The data also provide some evidence that the ecological variables that are in place within a classroom have a profound effect on student behaviors. Currently, the classroom teacher is implementing a revised schedule of classroom activities that is designed to promote high levels of engagement. Ecobehavioral analysis of this intervention will reveal: 1) whether more time was spent in those "engagement-pulling" activities and 2) whether higher levels of engagement did indeed occur with this revised schedule.

Future Directions: Process-Product Analysis

What has been discussed up to this point are two observation systems for describing classroom ecologies and teacher behaviors, and for explaining student behaviors. Both of these systems can be used to compare and contrast various types of preschools, individual children's experiences and performance within the same preschool, or even one child's experiences across several days. The second of these observational instruments can also be used to examine the interactions between ecological variables and student behaviors.

What is still missing is an indication of which ecological variables or ecobehavioral interactions are most important in affecting important outcome measures. The process-product methodology will allow one to examine the relationship between specific aspects of the preschool environment, teacher behaviors, and student behaviors and scores that reflect change in significant aspects of children's development (e.g., developmental test scores, achievement tests, or measures of social competence). The data from this new methodology will yield a new level of ecological explanation of student performance in preschools. Previous studies of preschool ecologies allowed for simple descriptions of specific aspects of the environment and their correlated effects on behavior. These new systems will expand the ability to examine and explain classroom environmental effects in a number of ways. They will allow researchers to look at students' current and future placements and their response requirements. This information will enable researchers to select target behaviors and target ecological goals. Finally, these systems will be the means used to monitor both classroom and behavioral interventions as changes in targeted ecological and student behavior variables and corresponding outcomes are being tracked. In short, these new methodologies promise to advance the knowledge of effective and optimal practices in classrooms that serve young children with handicaps.

SUMMARY

Ecological variables are directly related to the ways children behave in preschool classrooms. In this chapter, we have presented two ways of analyzing classroom environments and student behaviors and have demonstrated that considerable variation exists in these ecological dimensions across preschool classrooms and across individual students. We expect that these variations will have important implications with regard to students' achievement. By including ecological variables in our efforts to evaluate preschool programs, we will add considerably to our power to explain why early intervention programs are successful, why they fail, and what specific aspects of these programs contribute to their success.

Ecological variables will add to our descriptive power in a number of ways. First, they can form the basis for defining the program variables across different types of preschool settings in a quantifiable manner. For example, programs embodying different service delivery models, such as special preschools or mainstream programs, or half-day versus full-day

preschools can be contrasted across a wide range of variables such as the activities and materials provided, and the behaviors engaged in by teachers and students. In a similar fashion, programs that reflect different philosophies (e.g., behavioral, cognitively-oriented, or Montessori) can be quantified and contrasted.

Second, quantifications of programs based on ecological descriptions can be used to examine the fidelity of program replications. If an original program can be quantifiably described across a variety of dimensions (e.g., the activities that are presented, the materials used), then those quantified dimensions can become a template against which replications can be compared.

Third, ecological descriptions can provide a means of documenting effects of specific changes in programs for groups and for individual students. Some examples of programming shifts that could be monitored are changes incurred by the institution of a new curriculum, changes brought by a shift in the classroom population (e.g., the integration of nonhandicapped peers into a program), or changes brought about when a teacher decides to alter the classroom environment or some dimension of teaching behavior (e.g., the rate of "approval" statements). Traditionally, when specific aspects of programs are altered, data are gathered on the altered variable and the student behavior targeted for change. The behavioral approach allows for a description of several aspects of the program and of teacher and student behaviors both before and after the intervention is implemented. In this way, the effect of the program change can be reflected across those dimensions that are targeted for change as well as those that may be indirectly affected.

Fourth, descriptions of student behaviors can be used in process-product analyses to determine the specific classroom behaviors that are most related to developmental gain. This type of information will help program developers to choose the behaviors (e.g., academic work, free play, language) that will be the focus of the early intervention program.

Fifth, molecular descriptions of eco-behavioral interactions can then be used to make precision diagnoses of instruction, that is, the determination of specific combinations of ecological and teacher variables that are most related to the classroom skills that are critical to the enhancement of developmental outcomes. These instructional variables can then be the variables targeted for improvement.

In summary, we contend that classroom ecological variables do effect the way children be-have in preschool settings, and these daily in-teractions, whether they are instructional or non-instructional, have a profound affect on children's developmental outcomes. As we de-velop improved ways of describing preschool environments, and the ways in which they af-fect students' behavior on a short- and long-term basis, we will begin to make program decisions based upon "what works." In this way, researchers will take the first step toward a real "science of early intervention."

REFERENCES

Allen, K. E. (1966). The effects of verbal reinforcement on children's performance as a function of type of task. *Journal of Experimental Psychology, 3,* 57–73.

Allen, K. E., Hart, B., Buell, J. S., Harris, F. R., & Wolf, M. M. (1964). Effects of social reinforcement on isolate behavior of a nursery school child. *Child Development, 35,* 511–518.

Anderson, H. H. (1943). Domination and socially inte-grative behavior. In R. G. Barker, J. Kounin, & H. F. Wright (Eds.), *Child behavior and development,* (pp. 459–483). NY: McGraw Hill.

Barker, R. G. (1968). *Ecological psychology.* Stanford, CA: Stanford University Press.

Bricker, D., & Dow, M. (1980). Early education with the young severely handicapped child. *Journal of The Asso-ciation for the Severely Handicapped, 5,* 130–142.

Brophy, J. (1979). Teacher behavior and its effects. *Jour-nal of Educational Psychology, 71,* 733–750.

Brophy. J., & Evertson, C. (1974). *Process-product cor-relations in the Texas Teacher Effectiveness Study: Fi-nal Report* (Research Report 74-4). Austin: University of Texas, R & D Center for Teacher Education (ERIC Document Reproduction Service No. ED 091 094).

Carta, J. J., & Greenwood, C. R. (1985). A methodology for the evaluation of early intervention programs. *Topics in Early Childhood Special Education, 5,* 88–104.

Carta, J. J., Greenwood, C. R., & Atwater, J. B. (1985). *ESCAPE: Ecobehavioral system for complex assess-ment of preschool environments.* Kansas City: Juniper Gardens Children's Project, Bureau of Child Research, University of Kansas.

Eck, R. (1975). *Removing the time-wasting aspects of nap time for young children.* Unpublished master's thesis, University of Kansas, Lawrence.

Fagot, B. I. (1973). Influence of teacher behavior in the preschool. *Developmental Psychology, 9,* 198–206.

Fagot, B. I. (1977). Variations in density: Effect on task and social behaviors of preschool children. *Develop-mental Psychology, 12*(2), 166–167.

Farnham-Diggory, S., & Ramsey, B. (1971). Play per-sistence: Some effects of interruption, social reinforce-ment and defective toys. *Developmental Psychology, 4,* 297–298.

Fitt, S. (1974). The individual and his environment. *School Review, 8,* 617–620.

Flanders, N. (1970). *Analyzing teaching behavior.* Read-ing, MA: Addison-Wesley.

Fowler, S. A. (1982). Transition from preschool to kinder-garten for children with special needs. In K. E. Allen & E. M. Goetz (Eds.), *Early childhood education: Special problems, special solutions* (pp. 309–330). Rockville, MD: Aspen Press.

Greenwood, C. R. (1985, May). *An ecobehavioral in-teraction approach in behavior analysis: Refinement of the issues and the data.* Presented at the Annual Conven-tion of the Association for Behavior Analysis, Colum-bus, OH.

Greenwood, C. R., Delquadri, J., Stanley, S., Terry, B., & Hall, R. V. (1985). Assessment of ecobehavioral in-teraction in school settings. *Behavior Assessment, 7,* 331–347.

Gump. P. V. (1971). Milieu, environment, and behavior. *Design and Environment, 2*(4), 49.

Hamilton, V. J., & Gordon, D. A. (1978). Teacher-child interactions in preschool and task persistence. *American Educational Research Journal, 15,* 459–466.

Hart, B., Reynolds, N. J., Baer, D. M., Brawley, E. R., & Harris, F. R. (1968). Effects of contingent and non-contingent social reinforcement on the cooperative play of a preschool child. *Journal of Applied Behavior Analy-sis, 1,* 73–76.

Hildebrand, V. (1971). *Introduction to early childhood education* (2nd ed.). New York: Macmillan.

Hulson, E. L. (1930). An analysis of the free play of ten four-year-old children through consecutive observa-tions. *Journal of Juvenile Research, 14,* 188–208.

Huston-Stein, A., Friedrich-Cofer, L., & Susman, E. J. (1977). The relation of classroom structure to social be-havior, imaginative play, and self-regulation of eco-nomically disadvantaged children. *Child Development, 48,* 908–916.

Hutt, C., & Vaizey, M. (1966). Differential effects of group density on social behavior. *Nature, 209*(5030), 1371–1372.

Johnson, M. W. (1935). The influence of verbal directions on behavior. *Child Development, 6,* 196–204.

Karnes, M. B., Schwedel, A. M., Lewis, G. F., Ratts, D. A., & Esry, D. R. (1981). Impact of early programming for the handicapped. *Journal of the Division of Early Childhood, 4,* 62–79.

Kaufman, M. J., Agard, J. A., & Semmel, M. I. (1985). *Mainstreaming: Learners and their environments.* Cambridge, MA: Brookline Books.

Kopp, C. B. (1979). Mildly to moderately handicapped

infants. What should influence your approach to measurement? In T. Black (Ed.), *Perspectives on measurement: A collection of readings for educators of young handicapped children* (pp. 32–38). TADS Series Paper No. 1. Chapel Hill, NC: Technical Assistance Development System, Frank Porter Graham Child Development Center.

Kounin, J. S., & Sherman, L. W. (1979). School environments as behavior settings. *Theory into Practice, 12,* 65–91.

Krantz, P., & Risley, T. R. (1977). Behavior ecology in the classroom. In K. D. O'Leary & S. G. O'Leary (Eds.), *Classroom management: The successful use of behavior modification* (pp. 349–366). New York: Pergamon Press.

LeBlanc, J. M., Etzel, B. C., & Domash, M. A. (1978). A functional curriculum for early intervention. In K. E. Allen, V. A. Holm, & R. L. Schiefelbusch (Eds.), *Early intervention—A team approach* (pp. 332–382). Baltimore: University Park Press.

LeLaurin, K. D., & Risley, T. R. (1972). The organization of day care environments: "Zone" versus "man-to-man" staff assignments. *Journal of Applied Behavior Analysis, 5,* 225–232.

Loo, C. M. (1972). The effects of spatial density on the social behavior of children. *Journal of Applied Social Psychology, 2*(4), 372–381.

Madsen, C. H., Jr., Becker, W. C., & Thomas, D. R. (1968). Rules, praise and ignoring: Elements of elementary classroom control. *Journal of Applied Behavior Analysis, 1,* 139–150.

McCoy, N., & Zigler, E. (1965). Social reinforcer effectiveness as a function of the relationship between child and adult. *Journal of Personality and Social Psychology, 1,* 604–612.

McGrew, P. L. (1972). Social and spatial density effects on spacing behavior in preschool children. *Journal of Child Psychology and Psychiatry, 2,* 197–205.

Medley, D. M., & Mitzel, H. E. (1963). Measuring classroom behavior by systematic observation. In N. L. Gage (Ed.), *Handbook of research on teaching.* Chicago: Rand McNally.

Montes, F., & Risley, T. R. (1975). Evaluating traditional day care practices: An empirical approach. *Child Care Quarterly, 4,* 208–215.

Morrison, S. B., & Oxford, R. L. (1978). *Classroom ecology and kindergarten students' task-related behaviors: An exploratory study.* Paper presented at the Annual Meeting of the American Educational Research Association, Toronto, Canada.

O'Connor, M. (1975). The nursery school environment. *Developmental Psychology, 11*(5), 556–561.

Odom, S. L., & Strain, P. S. (1986). A comparison of peer-initiation and teacher-antecedent interventions for promoting reciprocal social interaction of autistic preschoolers. *Journal of Applied Behavior Analysis, 19,* 59–71.

Patterson, G. R. (1976). The aggressive child: Victim and architect of a coercive system. In L. A. Hamerlynck, L. C. Handy, & E. J. Mash (Eds.), *Behavior Modification and Families: Theory and Research* (Vol. 1, pp. 267–316). NY: Brunner/Mazel.

Patterson, G. R., & Moore, D. (1979). Interactive patterns as units of behavior. In S. J. Suomi, M. E. Lamb, & G. R. Stephenson (Eds.), *Social interaction analysis:*

Methodological issues (pp. 77–96). Madison: University of Wisconsin Press.

Peck, J., & Goldman, R. (1978). *The behaviors of kindergarten children under selected conditions in the social and physical environment.* Paper presented at the meeting of the American Education Research Association, Toronto, Canada. ERIC Document Reproduction Service ED 152 436.

Perry, G. (1977). *Cross-cultural study on the effect of space and teacher controlling behavior.* ERIC Document Reproduction Service No. ED 131 351.

Phyfe-Perkins, E. (1980). Children's behavior in preschool settings: A review of research concerning the influence of the physical environment. In L. G. Katz (Ed.), *Current topics in early childhood education, Vol. III* (pp. 91–125). Norwood, NJ: Ablex Publishing.

Phyfe-Perkins, E. (1981). *Effects of teacher behavior on preschool children: A review of research.* Urbana, IL: ERIC Clearinghouse on Elementary and Early Childhood Education. ERIC Document Reproduction Service No. ED 211 176.

Pollowy, A. M. (1974). The child in the physical environment: A design problem. In G. Coates (Ed.), *Alternative learning environments* (pp. 370–382). Stroudsburg, PA: Dowden, Hutchinson, and Ross.

Preiser, W. F. E. (1972). Work in progress: The behavior of nursery school children under different spatial densities. *Man's Environment Systems, 2,* 247–250.

Quilitch, H. R., & Risley, T. R. (1973). The effects of play materials on social play. *Journal of Applied Behavior Analysis, 6,* 575–578.

Rogers-Warren, A. K., Ruggles, T. R., Peterson, N., & Cooper, A. Y. (1981). Playing and learning together: Social interaction among normal and handicapped preschoolers. *Journal of the Division of Early Childhood, 3,* 56–63.

Rogers-Warren, A., & Wedel, J. W. (1980). The ecology of preschool classrooms for the handicapped. *New Directions for Exceptional Children, 1,* 1–24.

Rosenshine, B. (1977). Review of teaching variables and student achievement. In G. D. Borich (Ed.), *The appraisal of teaching: Concepts and process* (pp. 114–120). Reading, MA: Addison-Wesley.

Rosenthal, B. A. (1973). An ecological study of free play in the nursery school (Doctoral dissertation, Wayne State University). *Dissertation Abstracts International, 37*(7-A), 4004.

Rubin, K. H. (1977). The social and cognitive value of preschool toys and activities. *Canadian Journal of Behavioral Science, 9,* 382–385.

Sainato, D. M., & Lyon, S. R. (1983, December). A descriptive analysis of the requirements for independent performance in handicapped and nonhandicapped preschool classrooms. In P. S. Strain (Chair), *Assisting behaviorally handicapped preschoolers in mainstream settings: A report of research from the Early Childhood Research Institute.* Paper presented at the HCEEP/DEC Conference, Washington, D. C.

Samuels, M., & Samuels, N. (1979). *The well baby book.* NY: Summit Books.

Schweinhart, L. J., & Weikart, D. P. (1980). Young children grow up: The effects of the Perry Preschool Program on youths through age 15. *Monographs of the High Scope Research Foundation, 7.*

Shapiro, S. (1975). Preschool ecology: A study of three

environmental variables. *Reading Improvement, 12,* 236–241.

Sheehan, R., & Day, D. (1975). Is open space just empty space? *Day Care and Early Education, 3,* 10–13.

Shure, M. B. (1963). The psychological ecology of the nursery school. *Child Development, 34,* 979–992.

Smith, P. K. (1974). Aspects of the playgroup environment. In D. Canter, & T. Lee (Eds.), *Psychology and the built environment.* England: Architectural Press.

Smith, P. K., & Connolly, K. J. (1972). Patterns of play and social interaction in preschool children. In N. B. Jones (Ed.), *Ethological studies of child behavior* (pp. 65–96). London: Cambridge University Press.

Soar, R. S. (1973). *Follow-through classroom process measurement and pupil growth (1970–71): Final report.* Gainesville: College of Education, University of Florida.

Stallings, J. (1975). Implementation and child effects of teaching practices in follow-through classrooms. *Monographs of the Society for Research in Child Development, 40,* 7–8.

Stallings, J., & Kaskowitz, D. (1974). *Follow Through classroom observation evaluation, 1972–73.* Menlo Park, CA: SRI International.

Stodolsky, S. S. (1974). How children find something to do in preschool. *Genetic Psychology Monographs, 90*(2), 245–303.

Stoneman, Z., Cantrell, M. L., & Hoover-Dempsey, K. (1983). The association between play materials and social behavior in a mainstreamed preschool: A naturalistic investigation. *Journal of Applied Developmental Psychology, 4,* 163–174.

Strain, P. (1981). Conceptual and methodological issues in efficacy research with behaviorally disordered children. *Journal of the Division for Early Childhood, 4,* 110–124.

Taffel, S. J., O'Leary, K. D., & Armel, S. (1974). Reasoning and praise: Their effects on academic behavior. *Journal of Educational Psychology, 66,* 291–295.

Tawney, J. W. (1981). A cautious view of mainstreaming in early education. *Topics in Early Childhood Special Education, 1,* 25–36.

Trickett, E. S., Kelly, J. G., & Todd, D. M. (1972). The social environment of the school: Guidelines for individual change organizational redevelopment. In S. Golann & C. Eisdorfer (Eds.), *Handbook of community mental health* (pp. 331–406). NY: Appleton-Century-Crofts.

Updegraff, R., & Herbst, E. K. (1933). An experimental study of the social behavior stimulated in young children by certain play materials. *Journal of Genetic Psychology, 42*(2), 372–391.

Van Alstyne, D. (1932). *Play behavior and choice of play materials.* Chicago: University of Chicago Press.

Vincent, L. J., Salisbury, C., Walter, G., Brown, P., Gruenwald, L. J., & Powers, M. (1980). Program evaluation and curriculum development in early childhood/special education: Criteria of the next environment. In W. Sailor, B. Wilcox, & L. Brown (Eds.), *Methods of instruction for severely handicapped students* (pp. 303–328). Baltimore: Paul H. Brookes Publishing Co.

Wright, H. F. (1967). *Recording and analyzing child behavior.* NY: Harper & Row.

Wyer, R. S. (1968). Effects of reinforcement and task difficulty on perseverance. *Journal of Personality and Social Psychology, 8,* 269–276.

Zigler, E., & Balla, D. (1982). Selecting outcome variables in evaluations of early childhood special education programs. *Topics in Early Childhood Special Education, 1*(4), 11–22.

Chapter 14

Integration of Young Children with Handicaps and Normally Developing Children

Samuel L. Odom and Mary A. McEvoy

IN THE BEGINNING, THERE WERE NO services for young children with handicaps. By the turn of this century, some isolated programs began to appear, such as the *Casa dei Bambini* operated by Maria Montessori in Italy, but until the late 1960s young children with noticeable handicaps generally stayed home with their mothers or were sent to institutions. As early intervention programs emerged in this country, center-based educational programs routinely occurred in nonintegrated settings. But with the passage of PL 94-142, in the 1970s, professionals in the field advanced closer toward considering the integration of all children with handicaps into programs for normally developing children.

Given this historical context, the mainstreaming movement can be seen as an evolutionary trend in early childhood special education. This mainstreaming trend continues today, with advocacy groups proposing that education in the least restrictive environment, as defined by proximity to normally developing peers, should be the cornerstone for any educational program for young children with handicaps (e.g., Division for Early Childhood, 1987; The Association for Persons with Severe Handicaps, 1987). Yet many of these policy statements occur without an examination of the research base that could support them. In this chapter the authors will critically examine the research on the mainstreaming and integration

of young children with handicaps and children who are normally developing. The authors will review the various reationales proposed for mainstreaming, the parameters that these rationales set for research, the natural social interaction and friendship patterns that develop in mainstreamed and integrated special education settings, the developmental and educational affects of mainstreaming on young children with handicaps and normally developing children, procedures for socially integrating children in mainstreamed and integrated settings, and the attitudes that parents and teachers have about mainstreaming. Last, the results of this research and its implications for social policy and practice will be summarized.

DEFINITIONS

Researchers who conduct investigations on mainstreaming experience difficulties similar to those who investigate the efficacy of early intervention (Guralnick, Chapter 5, this volume): the procedural variables associated with mainstreaming are so great that there is probably not one singularly agreed upon "mainstreaming" intervention (Guralnick, 1981a). Yet agreement does exist about the general concept. *Mainstreaming* refers to the placement of children with handicaps into educational programs for and with normally developing children (Karnes & Lee, 1979; Safford &

Preparation of this chapter was supported in part by a grant (number G008302979) from the Department of Education.

Rosen, 1981; Tawney, 1981; Turnbull & Blacher-Dixon, 1981). *Integration* is a more generic term that will be defined as the process for actively mixing the two groups of children. According to Kaufman, Gottlieb, Agard, and Kukic (1975), mainstreaming must include not only the physical integration of children with handicaps into the regular education class, but also social and academic integration (i.e., active involvement in social and academic activities with peers).

A variation on the mainstreaming intervention is a process by which nonhandicapped children are placed in classes for handicapped children. This process has been termed *reverse mainstreaming* (Guralnick, 1981b; Turnbull & Blacher-Dixon, 1981; Wynne, Brown, Dakof, & Ulfelder, 1975) and *integrated special education* (Odom & Speltz, 1983). The differences between mainstreaming and integrated special education programs have more than just semantic importance. These programs typically differ on such procedural variables as ratio of handicapped to nonhandicapped children, teachers' background and training, child to teacher ratio, curricular orientation, and total number of children in the class (Odom & Speltz, 1983). When trying to determine the affects of mainstreaming, the specification of such variables is critically important. Thus, in this chapter, the authors will refer to the programs in which more than 50% of the children are normally developing as *mainstreamed*, and programs in which more than 50% of the children have handicaps as *integrated special education* (ISE) programs. The more generic term, *integrated programs,* will be used to refer to any program(s) that enroll both children who are normally developing and children who are handicapped (i.e., mainstreamed and ISE programs).

RATIONALES FOR THE INTEGRATION OF CHILDREN WITH HANDICAPS AND CHILDREN WHO ARE NORMALLY DEVELOPING

Researchers, program developers, and policy-makers have proposed numerous rationales for

integrating young children with handicaps and normally developing children. These rationales serve as a base from which research questions may be generated and the literature examined.

Legalistic Rationales

A basic rationale for preschool mainstreaming and integration has been established by federal and state legislation (Bricker, 1978; Turnbull, 1982). The intent of PL 94-142 was to ensure that an appropriate education was provided for children with handicaps in a setting with or in close proximity to children who were not handicapped. PL 99-457 carries a similar provision for placement in the least restrictive environment. As stated above, the social policy dictated by this federal law, and other state laws, was established in advance of an empirical base to support mainstreaming. Yet research can be conducted *post hoc* to establish the best ways for ensuring that the intent of the law is met.

One problem encountered when trying to educate young children with handicaps in mainstreamed settings is the absence of a mainstreamed counterpart associated with the public schools (public school services usually start at 5 or 6 years of age for children without handicaps). Thus, to provide a mainstreamed placement at the preschool level, public schools must collaborate with private agencies that provide preschool or day care services for normally developing children. Although several survey studies have indicated that private day care programs are willing to accept young children with handicaps (Gorelick, 1973; Sullivan, Shuster, & Sherif, 1987), the experiences of the present authors indicate that the public school/private mainstream program option is not one often made available to parents.

For years, Project Head Start has been the only public mainstreamed program. In 1972, the Amendment to the Economic Opportunity Act mandated that at least 10% of the children enrolled in Head Start be classified as handicapped. However, one limitation to Head Start as a public mainstreamed program is that only children with handicaps from low-income families qualify for their services.

Given the legal imperative to provide education in the least restrictive setting, usually interpreted as an integrated setting, several research questions arise: Is there evidence that children are placed in mainstreamed or ISE classes? Given the definition of mainstreaming cited above, does social integration occur when children are physically integrated or do segregated groups form within the integrated settings? Last, given an additional intent of the law that parents become closely involved in their children's programs, what are the parents' perspectives on their child's inclusion in programs for normally developing children?

Moralistic/Philosophical Rationale

The least restrictive environment provision in PL 99-457 is an institutionalized reflection of the normalization philosophy (Wolfensberger, 1972). Following this rationale, mainstreaming would be considered the best practice because it best exemplifies the principles of normalization (Vincent, Brown, & Getz-Sheftel, 1981). Similarly, placement in a nonintegrated classroom could be viewed as a violation of a child's civil right because he or she is segregated from normally developing children (Safford & Rosen, 1981), and thus presumably from a more effective program. Although this rationale is based on a philosophical imperative, research questions may address issues related to this position. For example, do normally developing children actively reject their peers who have handicaps? Again, are young children with handicaps socially integrated in mainstreamed or ISE settings? Do children with or without handicaps enrolled in mainstreamed settings perform as well on developmental measures as comparable groups of children in nonintegrated settings?

Educational Benefits

Researchers have also proposed that there may be developmental or educational benefits to placement in mainstreamed or ISE settings. Normally developing children in mainstreamed class may model age-appropriate behaviors that less advanced children with handicaps might acquire through observational learning (Bricker & Sandall, 1979; Karnes & Lee, 1979; Turnbull, 1982). Similarly, by creating a more advanced cognitive and linguistic environment, children with handicaps might be "pushed", in a developmental sense, to acquire more advanced skills (Bricker, 1978; Guralnick, 1981c). This rationale is less value oriented than the normalization argument, and does not have the a priori legalistic imperative of the legislative rationale. Research can determine whether there are developmental benefits to children in mainstreamed and ISE programs and can identify the most effective approaches for achieving positive benefits. Questions that might address this rationale include: Do young children in mainstreamed programs perform at a higher rate on developmental measures than comparable groups of children in nonintegrated settings? Do children with moderate or severe handicaps benefit as much from mainstreaming as children with mild handicaps? What procedures are available for promoting social integration?

REVIEW OF RESEARCH

The rationales for integration and related research questions may be used as a guide for examining the research on mainstreaming and integration of young children with handicaps. Across rationales, the research questions seem to fall into several categories; these will serve as the basis for our review. These include: frequency and availability of mainstreamed and ISE settings, patterns of social interaction between children with handicaps and normally developing children in mainstreamed and ISE settings, the impact of integration on children's attitudes, procedures for promoting integration in preschool classes, the developmental outcomes of integration, and the attitudes of parents toward mainstreaming their handicapped child.

AVAILABILITY OF MAINSTREAMED AND ISE PROGRAMS

Little data exist on the nationwide availability of mainstreamed and ISE programs, although there is some information on the potential access to mainstreamed settings. In a survey of preschools for normally developing children in the Los Angeles area, Gorelick (1973) found that 83% of the responding preschools were willing to accept handicapped children. In a more recent survey of parents with normally developing children enrolled in preschools, all of the parents interviewed expressed a willingness to have children with handicaps enroll in their children's program (Gallagher, 1987). Similarly, in interviewing day care providers about their willingness to enroll handicapped children, Sullivan et al. (1987) found that of the sites preselected as high quality preschools in the community, 100% were willing to accept children with handicaps. Last, in a large study of the implementation of this Head Start mandate to integrate children with handicaps, Ensher, Blatt, and Winschel (1976) observed 28 centers and found that 13% of the population was classified as handicapped, although only 2% were identified as having substantial handicaps.

Less information is available on ISE programs. From data collected over a 3-year period in the Handicapped Children's Early Education Program network, ISE programs represented 33%, 24%, and 29% of the center-based model demonstration programs funded, while mainstreaming programs represented 58%, 63%, and 60% of the total (Assael, 1985; Decker, 1986). From these data, it appears that models for ISE programs do exist, although mainstreamed model programs occur more frequently. Interestingly, only 9%, 12%, and 11% of the model programs for whom integration was appropriate reported having no normally developing children in their programs. Thus, the models for integration are available, but the data on how frequently school systems make them available to children or how frequently parents choose them has yet to be reported.

PATTERNS OF SOCIAL INTERACTION

The interactions that occur between children with handicaps and normally developing chil-

dren in integrated settings has relevance for both the philosophical and educational rationales. If the normalization principle is to be achieved, children with handicaps should become socially integrated (i.e., interact with normally developing peers in the class) in the integrated setting and should develop positive social relationships with normally developing children.

Social interaction patterns may also be relevant to the educational rationale. According to Bricker (1978), the integration of young children with handicaps with their normally developing peers may provide an important avenue of stimulation and subsequent learning. Proponents of mainstreaming argue that the naturally occurring patterns of interaction that arise out of mainstreamed settings are beneficial to the development of social interaction and communication skills for children with handicaps (Cooke, Apolloni, & Cooke, 1977; Guralnick, 1981c).

Social Interaction Patterns

The investigations of the patterns of social interaction between children with handicaps and normally developing children represents the most active research literature on integration. The majority of these studies have used direct observational methodology (see Table 1 for list of studies reviewed). The general conclusion to be drawn from these studies appears to be that normally developing children tend to interact more frequently with peers who are also normally developing or mildly handicapped than with peers who are moderately or severely handicapped, regardless of the ratio of handicapped to nonhandicapped children. For example, Cavallaro and Porter (1980) observed seven children who were at-risk for handicapping conditions and 13 normally developing children in an integrated free play setting. They concluded that the normally developing children initiated gazes toward and interacted more with other normally developing peers. Interestingly, handicapped children tended to interact more with other handicapped children. Similarly, Porter, Ramsey, Tremblay, Iaccobo, and Crawley (1978) observed six groups

Table 1. Summary of social interaction studies

Author(s)	Subjects (#,HC)	Information recorded/ Behaviors observed	Results
Apolloni, Cooke, & Cooke (1977)	3 HC[a] (delayed) 1 NHC[b]	Peer imitation training Four behaviors: —spoon feeding —cup drinking —peek-a-boo —knee patting	Placing NHC with HC will not necessarily result in cross group peer imitation or initiation Peer imitation by HC is feasible
Beckman (1983)	4 groups of children —NH 4-yr-olds —NH 3-yr-olds —HC (moderate) —HC (severe)	Observed in integrated preschool during free play	Interactions occurred: —NH 4-yr-olds—mostly with NH4, then to mod. HC —NH 3-yr-olds—mostly NH 3, then —NH 4 —Frequency of interactions —NH 4 > NH 3 > Mod HC > Sev HC NHC exhibit preference for same age peers to exclusion of HC Severely HC interact least
Blackmon & Dembo (1984)	32 NHC 13 HC (mild/moderate devel. delayed)	Measured empathy, helping, and altruism	The milder HC, the more adjusted Number of behaviors observed: altruistic, helping, empathy HC were recipients of altruism only (never received help from NHC)
Cavallaro & Porter (1980)	7 HC (at-risk) 13 NHC	Observed during free play Behaviors: —parallel play —mutual obj. manipulation —gaze	NHC initiated more gazes towards other NHC NHC interacted with other NHC more often HC interacted mostly with HC
Dunlop, Stoneman, & Cantrell (1980)	6 HC (mild); 2 BD[c]; 1 Downs; 3 dev) 6 NHC	Observed during selected free choice Behaviors: —solicited act —direct interaction/dominant —direct interaction/cooperative —adult-child interactions	Mainstreaming is beneficial to development of social competence

(continued)

Table 1. (continued)

Author(s)	Subjects (#,HC)	Information recorded/ Behaviors observed	Results
Faught, Balleweg, Crow, & van den Pol (1983)	5 NHC 7 HC (mild, mod, sev with lang del)	Observed integrated program Patterns looked at: —isolate —facing —parallel —touching —cooperative —speaking —proximity	Trend towards less complex interactions between HC and NHC Clear preference of NHC for NHC More advanced behavior won't occur without active progress
Fenrick, Pearson, & Pepelnjak (1984)	6 HC (mild)	Observed integrated and segregated settings Parten scale Verbal or physical interactions Appropriate and inappropriate play Attention to task Language	HC had more "no play" in integrated setting HC had more solitary in segregated setting No difference in parallel play HC low coop. beh. No difference in frequency of interaction, in attending or on language measures
Field, Roseman, DeStefano, & Koewler (1981)	16 HC (mild) 18 NHC	Observed integrated and segregated settings	NHC relate more frequently with own classmates HC related more to peers and less to teachers when integrated (opposite when segregated) HC should be placed according to developmental level inst. C.A.
Guralnick (1980)	12 NHC 9 HC (mild) 5 HC (mod) 11 HC (severe)	Looked at homogeneous (mile and NHC, mod and sev) versus heterogeneous (all 4) grouping	Severe HC played less inappropriately when play group included mild and NHC NHC and mild HC interacted more often than moderate and severely HC Mod HC and sev HC played with all 4 groups—failed to differentiate
Guralnick & Paul-Brown (1984)	8 NHC 12 HC (mild, mod, sev)	Peer tutors Observed in integrated setting Behavior—request episodes Communication exchanges	NHC obtained compliance > 50% with mild and moderate; 28% with HC NHC justify or mitigate their requests almost exclusively to NHC NHC capable of adjusting communication interactions to listener's functioning.
Ispa (1981)	8 HC (4 language, 4 lang, Downs, CP) 21 NHC (2 classrooms)	Parten scale Emotional tone with 23 categories	NHC interacted with HC less NHC involved HC in extended interaction more than HC did HC received more help and affection from peers than NHC

Study	Subjects	Method	Findings
Ispa & Matz (1978)	5 NHC 7 HC (mild, mod, severe)	Behaviors: —isolate —parallel —cooperative play —proximity —facing —touching —speaking	NHC appeared socially well integrated Conclude little evidence that NHC and HC not well socially integrated Specific teacher strategies did not appear necessary
Kohl, Beckman, & Swenson-Pierce (1984)	6 NHC 6 HC (mild-mod)	Four activities: —free play —gross motor —fine motor —snack	Level of social interaction is equivalent for HC and NHC in all activities but free play In free play, NHC interact 2 times as much as HC
Novak, Olley, & Kearney (1980)	5 preschools: 1– 7 HC (BD) 2– 7 NHC 3–18 NHC 4–10 HC (HI)[a] 5–16 HC (BD)	Free play Naturalistic observation 19 Behavior categories	HC played more with objects and less with other children
Peterson & Haralick (1977)	8 HC 5 NHC	Observed during free play	Rejection of and discrimination against HC not found NHC more preference for NHC NHC chose HC 51.9% time (29% solely with HC, 22% in group) NHC chose NHC 70.6% of the time (48% solely with NHC, and 22% NHC and HC)
Peterson, Peterson, & Scriven (1977)	14 HC (dev delay) 15 NHC	Peer model	Similar amount peer imitation between NHC and HC, but both more likely to imitate NHC peer
Porter, Ramsey, Tremblay, Iaccobo, & Crawley (1978)	15 NHC 12 HC (mod MR)	Free play separated from class Observed interpersonal proximity and social interactions	NHC maintained proximity to NHC more and interacted more with NHC HC were indiscriminate as to whom they played with
Raver, Cooke, & Appolloni (1978)	2 NHC 2 HC (delayed)	Peer imitation training Observed during structured and free play	Interactions were higher and could be increased in structured play only
Rogers-Warren, Ruggles, Peterson, & Cooper (1981)	4 HC (Downs) 4 NHC	Free play in class and on playground observed Recorded and observed: —play areas —types of play —nature and frequency of interactions	HC and NHC prefer to play with NHC HC selected HC playmates NHC selected NHC playmates HC engaged in more solitary play

(continued)

Table 1. (continued)

Author(s)	Subjects (#,HC)	Information recorded/ Behaviors observed	Results
Sebba (1983)	6 HC 4 NHC	Observed during free play Behaviors: —imitation —responses —interactions —motor-gestural —vocal-verbal	Overall, patterns of interaction or preference of choice for playmates showed no significant difference between HC and NHC Children developmentally similar interacted most often Familiarity increased interacting
Strain (1984a)	140 children/10 preschools 68 NHC 72 HC (sev)	Observed: early a.m., free choice, fine motor, late p.m. Behaviors: —8 positive categories —2 negative categories	NHC selected NHC of same age and sex or an older HC Normally developing children's interactions not affected by HC presence
van den Pol, Crow, Rider, & Offner (1985)	12 HC (mod-sev) 5 NHC	Observed during free play Observed spontaneous social integration Recorded behaviors: —isolate —facing —parallel —touching —cooperative —touching —proximal —vocalizing	NHC preferred NHC in more sophisticated play No differences in proximity

[a]HC = handicapped children
[b]NHC = nonhandicapped children
[c]BD = behavior disorder
[d]HI = hearing impaired

of equal numbers of normally developing children and children with moderate handicaps. Again, results indicated that the nonhandicapped children showed a clear preference for other nonhandicapped children. However, the handicapped children interacted with both their handicapped and nonhandicapped peers. Finally, Faught, Balleweg, Crow, and van den Pol (1983) observed seven children with mild, moderate and severe handicapping conditions in an ISE classroom. They reported a trend toward less complex interactions among children with handicaps and a clear preference of the normally developing peers for other normally developing children. Similar results have been reported by Apolloni, Cooke, and Cooke (1977); Field, Roseman, DeStefano, and Koewler (1981); Raver, Cooke, and Apolloni (1978); Rogers-Warren, Ruggles, Peterson, and Cooper (1981); and van den Pol, Crow, Rider, and Offner (1985).

The above studies, while important, must be viewed cautiously. For example, the term social interaction is defined differently across the studies. In addition, a number of developmental levels (mild, moderate and severe) were evaluated. Taken as a group, the studies reviewed above seem to indicate that advanced social interaction skills will not occur without active programming. However, there is evidence to suggest that social integration does occur for children with mild handicaps in integrated programs, especially when integration is examined over time. In one of the few experimental studies evaluating the effects of integration on the development of social interaction skills, Guralnick (1980a) investigated heterogeneous (i.e., integrated) and homogeneous (i.e., nonintegrated) groupings of children. In every instance, children who were normally developing or had mild handicaps interacted more with one another than they did with the children with severe handicaps. Guralnick concluded that social integration did occur for the children with mild handicaps.

In one of the earliest observational studies, Peterson and Haralick (1977) observed an ISE classroom consisting of six normally developing children and eight children with mild to moderate handicaps. Rejection and discrimination against the handicapped child was not found. While the normally developing children showed a preference for their normally developing peers, interaction with mildly handicapped students was reported. Other researchers have reported similar results, thus supporting the notion that social integration for mildly handicapped students may occur naturally in integrated settings (Blackmon & Dembo, 1984; Dunlop, Stoneman, & Cantrell, 1980; Guralnick & Paul-Brown, 1977, 1980; Ispa, 1981; Ispa & Matz, 1978; Sebba, 1983).

In contrast to these findings, Guralnick's (1984; 1986) later research has suggested that though the frequency of social interactions between normally developing children and children with mild handicaps approaches those of normal dyads, the nature of the interactions may not be coequal. His examination of communication patterns in integrated activities suggests that the social behaviors of normally developing peers toward their peers with mild handicaps may be directive and often tutorial in purpose (Guralnick & Paul-Brown, 1984). Although these findings may be influenced in part by the nature of the particular context in which the researcher observed the children (i.e. in an instructional task), Guralnick's research points out the need for examining the content of the social interaction among peers in integrated settings as well as the frequency of interaction.

While the results of research on natural patterns of social interaction in mainstreamed and ISE settings is not entirely consistent, there seems to be considerable evidence that social integration may occur for children with mild handicaps, but that it will not occur spontaneously for children with moderate and severe handicaps. However, this finding is not without significant limitations. This research has been conducted in a variety of settings, with differing ratios of handicapped and nonhandicapped students, differing levels of teacher training, varying levels of observational periods, and a wide variety of social interaction codes. Given this methodological heterogeneity, it is not surprising that some inconsistency exists.

Friendship Patterns

The social relationships that develop between children with handicaps and normally developing children in integrated settings is an important aspect of mainstreaming and ISE, but they have been examined less actively than have patterns of social interaction. The study of social relationships differs from research on the patterns of social interactions in that a child must in some way exhibit a preference for or rejection of a peer, as revealed usually through sociometric assessment. In a sociometric study of a small mainstreamed classroom, Gerber (1977) used a peer nomination scale to examine the social relationships between class members. Low acceptance and high rejection of the children with handicaps occurred, although rejection was tied most closely to the visibility of the handicap. Using a peer rating scale, Strain (1984a) examined the friendship patterns of children in 10 mainstreamed preschool classrooms. He found that friendship patterns between the normally developing children and children with handicaps was related to the types of prosocial behaviors that occurred during social interactions, a finding that Field (1984) corroborated in her examination of handicapped friendship pairs. In a subsequent examination of his data, Strain (1985) found that general acceptance by normally developing peers was also determined in part by such nonsocial factors as physical appearance and attractiveness.

In an ISE class, Odom and DuBose (1981) used a peer rating scale to examine the acceptance of the normally developing children enrolled in the class. Three of the four normally developing children enrolled as peer models were in the upper 25% of the ranked scores, making them among the most popular children in the class. The authors suggested that this high rating for three of the normally developing peers contributed to their efficacy as peer models. These studies generally indicate that although positive social relationships do not automatically develop between children with handicaps and normally developing children in integrated settings, such relationships can oc-

cur and may be dependent on the types of social interactions that occur between the children and the visibility of the handicapping condition. These studies should be interpreted with caution. The reliability of sociometric assessments of young children, especially peer nomination scales, is suspect (McConnell & Odom, 1986). Of the studies cited above, only Odom and DuBose (1981) provided any evidence of reliability.

INTERVENTIONS TO PROMOTE INTEGRATION

Although some researchers and program developers accomplish integration by simply placing children with handicaps and normally developing children together in the same classroom, direct interventions have been developed to promote the social integration of the two groups and to optimize the potential outcomes of mainstreamig. These interventions include preparing normally developing children before the integration begins, arranging environmental aspects of the classroom to promote social interaction between the two groups, and utilizing teacher- or peer-mediated strategies for promoting social integration.

Preparing Normally Developing Children

Normally developing children may benefit from training that precedes actual integration. While there is evidence that the attitudes of normally developing elementary-age children about handicapping conditions can be modified via information given prior to mainstreaming (e.g., Cohen, 1977; McHale & Simeonsson, 1980; Westerwelt & McKinney, 1980). There have been few investigations of the effects of prior training on the attitudes and action of preschool nonhandicapped children. In fact, we are aware of only two studies to date that have empirically evaluated the use of preenrollment activities. Raab, Nordquist, Cunningham, and Bliem (1986) trained six normally developing preschool children using a variety of simulation activities prior to the admission of a girl with autism to their preschool program. Specifically, the children participated twice daily, for two weeks, in training that consisted of information about similarities and differences, simulation of handicapping condition (e.g. the children transported materials while riding in a wheelchair, tried to eat blindfolded, etc.), and specific information about the autistic child, including videotapes of the child and an opportunity to talk with her mother. Teacher incident reports of children's actions toward and comments about the child with autism after mainstreaming as well as sociometric ratings indicated that these children, in comparison to a control group in the classroom, interacted more with the autistic child and named her more often as a friend.

In contrast, Vandell, Anderson, Ehrhardt, and Wilson (1982) provided a series of informational activities to normally developing children about preschoolers with hearing impairments who were to be integrated into their class. The activities included information about the meaning of deafness, opportunities to practice communication techniques, and opportunities for including the hearing impaired children in activities during free play. These researchers found that normally developing children involved in the training activities engaged in significantly less social interaction with peers who were hearing impaired, as compared to a control group of children not receiving the training sessions. They cautioned against the use of preenrollment training for normally developing children who were involved in mainstreamed programs with children who are hearing impaired.

The dramatically different outcomes for these two studies could be attributed to a number of factors. The nature of the handicapping conditions were substantially different, different training activities were used, there could have been different teacher reactions, and there may have been idiosyncracies in the peer groups. However, these studies strongly suggest the need for more research to determine how much and what kinds of information are necessary to promote positive attitudes. In addition, the effects of such training should be closely monitored.

Environmental Arrangements

One aspect of programming for mainstreamed settings that has not been explored fully is how to design the classroom to facilitate learning and service delivery (Rogers-Warren & Wedell, 1982). Although there have been a number of experimental evaluations on the effects of various environmental arrangements on the behaviors of normally developing preschool children (see Carta, Sainato, & Greenwood, Chapter 13, this volume) the fact remains that "the relationship between programmatic factors and child-child social interactions can only be speculative because of the absence of systematic research" (Guralnick, 1981a, p. 79).

Despite the limited amount of research in this area, a few researchers have evaluated organizational variables and their affects on the interactions of children with handicaps and normally developing preschoolers. In a systematic evaluation of four mainstreamed classes, Burstein (1986) observed three organizational arrangements: grouping, center time, and outdoor play. Observers coded the involvement of nine preschoolers with handicaps and nine normally developing children in tasks and teacher and peer interaction. The settings differentially affected the integration of the handicapped children. During rug time (i.e., adult-directed, large group activities), few opportunities for social interaction occurred for either the handicapped or nonhandicapped children. However, time-on-task for handicapped children was low. In center and outdoor play periods, the handicapped children spent time with other children when prompted by adults only. In all instances, handicapped children interacted more with adults. The author concluded that informal settings (e.g., center time) do not foster social integration, and teacher supervision was necessary to maintain the task engagement and social interaction of children with handicaps.

According to Peterson and Haralick (1977), the types of toys available during freeplay periods will influence the patterns of social interactions in integrated classrooms. Beckman and

Kohl (1984) evaluated the effect of social and isolate toys on the interactions of preschoolers in integrated and nonintegrated settings. Despite limited observations, the results indicated that in both settings, interactions increased when toys that had been rated as "social" were available. However, in these same situations, toy play decreased. The authors concluded that toy manipulation may be a simple and non-obtrusive way to facilitate interaction. However, it is possible that some children may not have the know-how to play with toys. To examine this possibility, Kohl, Beckman, and Swenson-Pierce (1984) evaluated the effects of functional toy use on the interactions of handicapped preschoolers. Using a multiple baseline design across subjects, four children with handicaps were taught to use toys for which normally developing children had shown a preference. As a result, for two of the subjects, social interaction with peers increased as toy play increased. No change was observed for one subject, and one subject withdrew from the project.

Stoneman, Cantrell, and Hoover-Dempsey (1983) observed six children at-risk for special education placement and six normally developing children in an integrated setting to determine the rate of social interaction during play with various types of materials. The authors found that play materials which require cooperative interaction (e.g., blocks and vehicles, water play, housekeeping and music) were instrumental in facilitating peer interactions. Finally, DeKlyen and Odom (1987) assessed the extent to which play activities were structured and their effects on peer interactions. Eight normally developing children and 28 children with mild to moderate handicapping conditions were observed during free play activities. The activities were given a rating from 1–4 according to the amount of teacher structure present. The authors reported that peer interaction rates increased with the activity structure ratings. However, teacher interaction was not significantly related to the rating of activity structure.

Taken together, these studies indicate that simple environmental manipulations may increase the frequency of social interactions in integrated settings. However, as Strain and Kohler (Chapter 8, this volume) point out, patterns of social interactions are additionally influenced by the interventions that occur with the children with handicaps and the nature of the peer group. Future research should be directed toward the cumulative effects engendered by the interaction of these three variables.

Direct Interventions to Promote Social Integration

From the myriad social interaction studies cited above, one consistently replicated finding has been that when children with moderate and severe handicaps are placed in programs with normally developing children, the two groups will separate themselves and social integration will probably not occur. Most researchers agree that some form of programming must occur if social integration is to be achieved (Snyder, Apolloni, & Cooke, 1977), although the types of interventions have varied.

Teacher Prompt and Reinforcement A frequently used procedure for promoting social integration is for the teacher to give instructions for the children with handicaps to interact with their peers and then to provide teacher praise when interaction occurs. Guralnick (1976) described a study in which he provided reinforcement to a child with a handicap for interacting with a normally developing child, and documented increases in play. Similar increases in social interaction between children with and without handicaps occurred in a study in which Devoney, Guralnick, and Rubin (1974) had teachers "structure" the play activities of the children. In an integrated play session Strain, Shores, and Kerr (1976) prompted and reinforced social interactions between normally developing children and children with behavior disorders. They found an increase in the social interactions of the children in the intervention and collateral increase in social interaction for children in the play setting with whom the intervention had not been implemented. In a more recent single case study, van den Pol et al. (1985) instructed aides to "get the children to play together,'' through, for example, prompting and reinforcement, and then the teachers were provided feedback on the children's level of social interaction. Increases in social interactions in the integrated groups occurred during this prompting and feedback phase of the study. Teacher prompting and/or reinforcement represents a powerful intervention for promoting social integration. However, from these and other studies, there is limited evidence that the teacher's support can be faded in an efficient manner (Timm, Strain, & Eller, 1979).

Peer-Mediated Approaches A similar approach to promoting social integration is to teach the normally developing children to engage their peers with handicaps in social interactions. These peer mediated interventions make take three forms: 1) proximity interventions in which children of different developmental levels are simply mixed in a social group, 2) prompt and reinforce interventions in which the normally developing children prompt or reinforce the social interactions of their peers with handicaps, and 3) peer-initiation interventions in which the normally developing child directs social interactions toward peers with handicaps (Odom & Strain, 1984). In an example of a peer-initiation intervention occurring in an ISE class, Odom, Hoyson, Jamieson, and Strain (1985) taught normally developing children to initiate interactions with three peers who were autistic and had behavior disorders. They noted increases in the latter children's behavior in the three classroom settings in which the intervention was implemented.

Group Affection Activities Another approach to promoting social integration is the use of activities that teach and encourage affectionate interactions between children. Building upon an observational study of affection behavior in day care providers and children (Twardosz, Schwartz, Fox, & Cunningham, 1979), and a study using affectionate behaviors to intervene with a socially isolate child (Twardosz, Nordquist, Simon, & Botkin, 1983), McEvoy, Nordquist, Twardosz, Heckaman, Wehby, and Denny (1987) adapted typical

group activities occurring in day care centers so that they would elicit affectionate behaviors between the normally developing children and their peers who were autistic. Across three studies, McEvoy et al. (1987) documented increases in social interactions outside of the affection activities for the peers who were autistic, which demonstrated that social integration was in fact resulting. Using a similar affection training approach for children in two preschool classrooms who were socially isolated and had accompanying handicaps, Brown, Ragland, & Fox (in press) reported similar generalized increases in social interaction.

Curricular Interventions Although isolated intervention procedures have been developed to promote social integration, few have been translated into treatment packages that teachers can use to promote social integration. The *Integrated Preschool Curriculum* (Odom et al., in press) is one package that is designed to promote social integration. In this curriculum, a large number of play activities are provided to serve as a basis for social integration, and specific directions are given for teachers to prompt social interaction, to vicariously reinforce interaction, and to prompt imitation of appropriate social and play behavior. Techniques are provided for assessing social integration and for intervening directly when social skill deficits occur. In an examination of the implementation of this curriculum, Odom, Jenkins, Speltz, and DeKlyen (1982) found that significantly greater levels of social integration occurred in ISE classes in which the Integrated Preschool Curriculum was implemented, as compared to comparable classes exposed to a contrast condition.

The Social Competence Intervention for Preschool Youngsters (Day, Powell, & Stowitschek, 1980) The Social Competence package was designed to teach normally developing children to promote the social interactions of their peers who are handicapped. In this package, a number of activities are provided for teaching the normally developing peers targeted social initiations that have a high likelihood of producing a social response from their peers with handicaps. In a single subject design field test of this intervention package with three integrated dyads, Day, Powell, Stowitschek, and Dy-Lin (1982) found reliable increases in social initiations from normally developing children and in social interactions of the children with handicaps when the intervention was implemented. From these studies, it appears that treatment packages for promoting social integration have been developed and validated; however, data on the frequency of their use in the field are not available.

Interventions to Promote Imitation

A cornerstone of the educational benefits rationale for integration is the premise that young children with handicaps will acquire, through imitation and observational learning, the more advanced skills modeled by normally developing peers. Because children with substantial handicaps often do not have good imitation skills, interventions in integrated settings have been developed to teach imitation. Using a vicarious reinforcement approach, Guralnick (1976) reinforced a normally developing peer in an integrated situation for using a correct language form, which resulted in increases in correct usage by the peer in the group who was handicapped.

To directly train imitation skills, Apolloni and Cooke (1978) have developed a peer imitation training procedure for integrated settings. In this intervention, a normally developing classmate demonstrates a behavior that the peer who is handicapped is to imitate. If the child does not imitate the behavior, the teacher prompts and reinforces the imitation behavior. The purpose of this intervention is to teach the children with handicaps to imitate the behaviors of their normally developing peers. Across a series of single case studies, these researchers and their colleagues have demonstrated the immediate and generalized effects of peer imitation training in integrated settings (Apolloni et al, 1977; Peck, Apolloni, Cooke, & Raver, 1978).

To promote imitation skills of a preschooler with autism enrolled in a mainstreamed class, Nordquist (1978) designed a prompting and re-

inforcement intervention in which the teacher or the parent who assisted in the classroom would wait until the child chose an object with which to play, required the child to stop playing and imitate the motor behavior of the researcher, and then allowed the child to return to the object in which he was engaged. After the child learned the imitation skills from the adults, the teacher trained two normally developing peers to conduct the procedure with the child. Spontaneous imitation increased when this procedure was implemented, especially when the peers served as the trainers. However, Nordquist also documented increases in stereotypic behavior and decreases in sustained peer interaction as a collateral change associated with this intervention.

OUTCOMES OF INTEGRATED PROGRAMS FOR CHILDREN WITH HANDICAPS AND NORMALLY DEVELOPING CHILDREN

The effects of integrated educational experiences on all children in the program has relevance for all three of the rationales cited above. For the normalization rationale, the children with handicaps, at a minimum, would be expected to perform as well as they would in a nonintegrated environment. For the legalistic rationale, the appropriateness of an integrated educational program, as recommended by PL 99-457, would be questioned if the children did not perform as well in a nonintegrated environment. For the educational benefits rationale, researchers would expect the children with handicaps to perform better in the integrated setting. Moreover, if deleterious effects occurred for the normally developing children in integrated programs, the ethics of running such programs would be questioned.

Developmental Outcomes for Children with Handicaps

Over the past decade and a half, researchers have closely monitored the effects of integrated programs upon young children with handicaps. Such outcome studies are listed in Table 2. As can be seen, researchers have used a range of

Table 2. Developmental outcomes for children with handicaps in integrated programs

Authors	Program type	Age of children	Design	Outcome measures	Results
Bricker & Bricker (1971)	MS[a]	Toddler	Single group	Bayley scales	Children made consistent gains, although there was no basis for comparison (no control group or prediction design)
Bricker, Bruder, & Bailey (1982)	ISE[b]	Toddler, Preschool	Single group Ed. sign. gains	Bayley scales McCarthy student progress record Uniform performance assessment system	Educationally significant gains on the Student Progress Record (SPR) and Uniform Performance Assessment System (UPAS) for all preschoolers. Educationally significant gains for one of the preschool classes on the McCarthy. Educationally significant gains on SPR & UPAS for toddler class, but Bayley > 50 on pretest prevented comparison
Cooke, Ruskus, Apolloni, & Peck (1981) Study 1	MS	Preschool	Noncomparable control group	Peabody picture vocabulary test (PPUT) Vineland test of social maturity (VSM) Alpern Bolls developmental profile (AB)	Children in mainstreamed & nonintegrated class did equally well on most measures. Mainstreamed children did significantly better on VSM
Study 2	MS	Preschool	Noncomparable control group	PPVT VSM AB	Children in both groups made gains on all measures across the year. Children in the mainstreamed classes were significantly higher on VSM and the AB Physical scale. Children in the nonintegrated class were significantly better on the AB social scale.
Study 3	MS	Preschool	Noncomparable control group	PPVT VSM AB	All children made significant gains across the year. Children in the mainstreamed class scored significantly higher on AB communication scale.
Hoyson, Jamieson, & Strain	ISE	Preschool	Single group regression	Learning accomplishment profile	Mean rate of development was significantly higher at end of the year, relative to entry level rate, for all children.
Ispa & Matz (1978)	MS	Preschool	Noncomparable control group	McCarthy Scale	Children made gain in test scores similar to the normally developing children in their class.
Jenkins, Speltz, & Odom (1985)	ISE	Preschool	Random group design	Woodcock Johnson Brigance and Language UPAS	Few differences between children in integrated and nonintegrated classes

(continued)

Table 2. *(continued)*

Authors	Program type	Age of children	Design	Outcome measures	Results
Jenkins, Odom, & Speltz (1986)	ISE	Preschool	Random group design	Preschool language scale (PLS) UPAS PreAcademic scale Peabody motor scale Calif. Scale of Social Competence (CPSCS)	Children in social integration classes scored significantly higher on PLS. Children in integrated social integration class scored higher than all others on CPSCS.
Galloway and Chandler (1978)	MS	Preschool	Single group re-gression	AB Developmental Profile	Children with mild mental retardation showed one month gain for each month in program. Gains were substantially less for children with moderate and severe mental retardation.

[a]MS = Mainstream

[b]ISE = Integrated special education

developmental measures to examine the outcomes associated with enrollment in mainstreamed and ISE classes. Generally, the children with handicaps enrolled in these programs make significant developmental gains that would not be attributed to maturation alone. Unfortunately, most of the researchers were unable to establish a comparison group against which to gauge the effects of program outcomes. Within subject, regression designs (see Odom, Chapter 1, this volume) while controlling for the maturation threat to interval validity, lack the experimental control required to make firm statements about the effects of integrated placement. Without such controls, the researchers cannot state effects of the program were due to the exposure to normally developing children, the classroom curriculum, or an interaction of the two.

The studies by Cooke, Ruskus, Apolloni, and Peck (1981) did include a comparison group of children with handicaps in nonintegrated settings, and found that the children in the integrated and nonintegrated settings, in general, performed comparably well on a range of outcome measures. However, these researchers were unable to randomly assign children to the experimental conditions, thus they could not rule out effects due to extraneous variables. Only two studies have randomly assigned children to integrated and nonintegrated programs. The first study by Jenkins, Speltz, and Odom (1985) randomly assigned children with developmental delays and children with communication handicaps to ISE and nonintegrated classes, but provided essentially no programming for social integration. The findings of these authors, across a number of developmental measures, confirmed the findings of most previous studies: integration alone, at least in ISE classes, has negligible effects, although the children do seem to benefit from the educational program. In a second study, Jenkins, Odom, and Speltz (1986), again randomly assigned children with handicaps to ISE and nonintegrated classes, but provided programming for social integration in half the classes, using the Integrated Preschool Curriculum (Odom, DeKlyen, & Jenkins, 1984), and

a contrast curriculum (Hohmann, Banet, & Weikert, 1979) for the other children. As compared with children in the contrast group, children in the classes receiving the social integration curriculum scored significantly higher on the measure of language development, and children in the ISE-social integration classroom scored significantly higher on the teacher rating measure of social competence. These findings suggest that children with handicaps enrolled in integrated classes seem to perform as well as children in nonintegrated classes, although there may be some developmental benefits to integration if programming for social integration is provided. As several researchers have suggested, the curriculum employed and the quality of instruction may have a more powerful effect upon developmental outcome and skill acquisition than the presence or absence of normally developing peers (Bricker, Bruder, & Bailey, 1982; Peck & Cooke, 1983).

Behavioral Outcomes for Children with Handicaps

Placement in integrated classes may also have immediate behavioral effects for children with handicaps. In a study cited above, Guralnick (1980b) examined the effect of grouping normally developing children and handicapped children with different levels of severity. He found that when children with severe handicaps were grouped with normally developing peers, they engaged less frequently in appropriate play behaviors. Similarly, Rogers-Warren et al. (1981) noted initial differences in the levels of social interaction for children with handicaps enrolled in nonintegrated classes as compared to normally developing children. However, when placed in ISE classes that programmed for social integration, the social interaction levels of the children with handicaps approximated those of the normally developing children, although the changes seen in this study could be attributed to the program effects or to exposure to the normally developing peers, or both.

In an investigation of children with handicaps in nonintegrated and mainstreamed settings, Field, Roseman, DeStefano, and Koewler (1982) found that children engaged in more peer-directed behavior and less teacher-directed behavior in mainstreamed free play settings. However, in a similar study with fewer subjects, Fenrick, Pearson, and Pepelnjak (1984) noted few differences in the social behavior of children with handicaps across mainstreamed and nonintegrated settings. Conversely, in a mainstreaming study with four mildly handicapped children, Smith and Greenberg (1981) found more positive increases in social behavior with peers and adults for a comparison group of children who remained in the nonintegrated special education setting.

Although these studies contain methodological problems (e.g., the use of small numbers of children in a group experimental design), one major confounding variable was that, with the exception of Rogers-Warren et al. (1981), children with handicaps were placed together to study grouping effects, but were never fully enrolled in the integrated classes. Possibly, when full and continuous enrollment occurs, different effects on social behavior may be found.

Intervention Effects

Because of the availability of normally developing peers in integrated settings, it is possible that certain types of behavioral interventions for children with handicaps may be more or less effective. Using single case designs to examine the effects of peer-initiation interventions, Strain (1983, 1984b) found that young children with autism and other behavior disorders more often generalized their newly acquired social interaction skills to mainstreamed settings than to nonintegrated settings, especially if the normally developing children in the mainstreamed setting had been taught to promote the generalization. However, these results were not replicated by Hecimovic, Fox, Shores, and Strain (1985).

In one of the earliest studies of integration, Allen, Benning, and Drummond (1972) found that simply integrating a child with a behavior disorder into an ISE class did not reduce the

behavior problems, but that when a behavior modification intervention was implemented, the presence of normally developing peers as appropriate models contributed to the positive outcome. With the exception of Hecimovic et al. (1985), these studies suggest that integration may contribute to the positive effects of behavioral interventions for certain types of social behavior, although this conclusion is based on observations of a small number of subjects.

Future Class Placements

The objective of most early intervention programs is movement of the children with handicaps into the mainstream of public education. Integrated programs have been seen as an effective way to achieve this transition because children with handicaps are given experience with a normally developing peer group (Turnbull, 1982). Several researchers have tracked the placement of graduates from integrated programs. In a large mainstreamed program for children with hearing impairments, Northcott (1978) found that 44% of their program graduates moved into full-time mainstream classes and 6% moved into partial mainstreamed placements. The ENCOR program, a mainstreamed program for preschool children with substantial handicaps, also has produced data on program graduates (Galloway & Chandler, 1978). Of the graduates for whom there was follow-up data, 44% moved into regular preschool or kindergarten programs. Although none of these studies had comparison groups against which to compare their results, the findings are encouraging because both programs enrolled children who are not typically mainstreamed in regular elementary settings. However, because of experimental design restrictions, the successful placement into a mainstreamed setting could be attributed to the instructional quality of the programs, and their transition practices, as well as to the process of integration itself.

Developmental Outcomes with Normally Developing Children

The presence of children with handicaps in

mainstreamed programs and the enrollment of normally developing children in ISE programs are actions that often raise concerns for parents of normally developing children. The concern is that exposure to the children with handicaps may have a negative effect on their children's development or acquisition of skills.

Researchers and program developers have been sensitive to such concerns and have monitored the effects of mainstreamed and ISE programs on normally developing children. Studies that have examined the effects are listed in Table 3. These studies reflect the trends seen in the outcome studies for children with handicaps. Children in the integrated programs make significant developmental gains during the year that are on par with or that exceed the gains that would be expected from maturation, and there are few negative or positive differences that could be attributed to integration. The only exceptions are the studies by Cooke et al. (1981) in which the effects of mainstreaming on normally developing preschool children were examined in three year-long studies, using a noncomparable control group design. Although their findings are for the most part varied across studies, one consistent finding was that the normally developing children in mainstreamed settings seemed to score less well on measures of social abilities.

This finding was not supported in a somewhat similar study by Odom et al. (1984). These researchers compared the performances of normally developing children enrolled in four ISE classes with a matched group of children in preschool classes for normally developing children. Although both groups made significant gains during the school year on measures of intelligence, language development, preacademic skills, or social competence, no between-group differences were found.

Across the studies in Table 3, the cumulative evidence suggests strongly that normally developing children are not adversely affected by enrollment in integrated classes, and in fact benefit developmentally from the curriculum and instructional strategies. However, further systematic research is needed on the effects of integration on the social development of normally developing children.

Other Outcomes for Normally Developing Children

As well as possibly influencing the acquisition of developmental skills, participation in integrated classes may affect other aspects of normally developing children's behavior. Strain, Hoyson, & Jamieson (1985) tracked the social behavior of the normally developing children in their ISE class and compared it to a select group of "star" students from regular kindergarten classes in the public school. They reported that the ISE students' inappropriate social behaviors were at a low rate but actually decreased during the year in the program, and that their students' behavior at the end of the year was comparable to the star comparison group's behavior. Also, they reported that while all of their normally developing program graduates moved on to kindergarten, four out of ten of their program graduates moved on to enter gifted student programs in the public schools.

In two studies that assessed the effects of participation in a mainstreamed program across a one-year period, Nordquist, Twardosz, & McEvoy (1986) observed directly the social behavior of normally developing children enrolled in different mainstreamed classes into which several children with autism had been integrated. Their data revealed that the social interactions of the normally developing peers were not inhibited by the presence of the children with autism, even when social integration interventions were implemented in the classroom. In fact, their social interactions with the peers with autism and with peers in general increased during the year. These researchers also found that the normally developing children did not imitate the unusual stereotypic behavior of the children with autism, and that generally the teachers distributed their attention evenly across the children.

To measure the effect of integration on the attitudes of normally developing children toward persons with handicaps, Esposito and Peach (1983) administered the Primary Student

Table 3. Developmental outcomes for normally developing children in integrated programs

Authors	Program type	Age of children	Design	Outcome measures	Results
Bricker & Bricker (1971)	McCarthy Scales (MS)	Tod	Single group	Bayley Scales Stanford-Binet	Children made consistent gains across the year, although there was no method of comparison (control group or prediction design)
Bricker, Bruder, & Bailey (1982)	ISE	Tod, Pre	Analysis of educational significance	Bayley Scales McCarthy Scales Student Progress Record (SPR) Uniform Performance Assessment System (UPAS)	Educationally significant gains on all measures
Bricker & Sheehan (1981)	ISE	Tod, Pre	Analysis of educational significance	McCarthy Scales SPR UPAS	Educationally significant gains on all measures
Hoyson, Jamieson, & Strain (1984)	ISE	Pre	Single group Regression	Learning Accomplishment Profile	Children made 2 months gain for each month in the program.
Ispa & Matz (1978)	MS	Pre	Single group Norm & Regression	McCarthy Scales	Children made 2 months gain in mental age for every month in the program
Cooke, Ruskus, Apolloni, & Peck (1981) Study 1	MS	Pre	Noncomparable control group	Peabody Picture Vocabulary test (PPVT) Vinel and Test of Social Maturity (USM) Alpern Bolls Developmental Profile (AB)	Children in the nonintegrated classes made more significant gains on developmental measures
Study 2	MS	Pre	Noncomparable control group	PPVT USM AB	Children in mainstreamed classes scores significantly higher on VSM and AB physical. Children in nonintegrated classes score higher on AB subscale social.
Study 3	MS	Pre	Noncomparable control group	PPVT VSM AB	Children in mainstreamed classes made significantly higher scores on seven measures. Children in nonintegrated classes were higher only on VSM.
Odom, DeKlyen, & Jenkins (1984)	ISE	Pre	Noncomparable control group	Stanford Binet Preschool Language Scale (PLS) UPAS-Preacademic Subscale Calif. Preschool Social Competency Scale (CPSCS)	No significant differences were found across measures.

Survey of Handicapped Persons to nine normally developing children who had been enrolled in a mainstreamed kindergarten. They found that the children exhibited generally more positive attitudes toward handicapped persons during the course of the year, although again the absence of a comparison group limited the interpretability of the study. Taken together, these studies suggest that the presence of children with handicaps in mainstreamed and ISE classes does not negatively affect the behavior of the normally developing children.

PARENT ATTITUDES
TOWARD INTEGRATION

Parents of children in integrated programs may be substantially influenced by integration. Parents of children with handicaps may be reminded daily of their child's difference when they observe the normally developing children in the program. In addition, they may feel that they share the stigma that may be associated with their children's handicap or may feel that they do not have interests in common with the parents of the normally developing children in the program (Turnbull & Blacher-Dixon, 1980).

In one of the first integrated programs, Bricker and Bricker (1971, 1976) monitored the satisfaction of parents of both the children with handicaps and of the normally developing children. One hundred percent of the parents stated that they would put their child in the program again. Of the parents of handicapped children, all indicated that they would prefer to place their child in an integrated or "mixed" program, as compared to a nonintegrated program, in the future. Six out of seven of the parents of the normally developing children indicated a similar preference, and all parents felt that their children experienced no negative effects from interacting with "less capable" children.

To measure parents' concerns about the preschool programs for their children, Winton and Turnbull (1981) interviewed parents of children with handicaps enrolled in both mainstreamed and nonintegrated programs. Their primary concerns were with the logistics of the program, the nature of professional involvement, the parental relationship with professionals, parental involvement in the program, and the impact of the peer group upon their child. In a similar study, Turnbull and Winton (1983) found that mothers of children with handicaps in mainstreamed settings felt that their children needed exposure to a normally developing peer group, whereas mothers of children in the nonintegrated programs felt that their children were too young for exposure to a "regular" peer group. Overall, mothers of integrated children reported more benefits of the program for their child, fewer drawbacks, and a higher percentage of their child's needs being met in comparison to mothers of nonintegrated children.

To determine how active and informed parents are in mainstreamed programs, Blacher and Turnbull (1983) conducted telephone interviews of parents of children with handicaps and of normally developing children. The parents of children with handicaps interacted with the parents of normally developing children as often as they did with other parents of children with handicaps. Parents reported that these interactions occurred most often around matters not related to the school. In a second survey of 101 parents, again of children with and without handicaps, Turnbull, Winton, Blacher, and Salkind (1982) reported that all parents were concerned about the quality of the program. Parents of normally developing children saw the value of having their children in a mainstreamed program, and parents of handicapped children felt that the mainstreamed program made their children work harder. However, a survey study of parents of children in mainstreamed kindergartens revealed that parents of children with handicaps, as compared to the parents of normally developing children, were less satisfied with the mainstreamed program and felt more often that the program did not meet all the needs of their children. Both groups emphasized the importance of being able to communicate with their teachers (Winton, Turnbull, & Blacher, 1985).

As a group, these studies indicate that the

parents of both groups of children have common concerns about their children's instructional program, that the parents of children with handicaps appear to be well integrated, and that the parents see integration as valuable for their children. However, parents of children with handicaps, especially in mainstreamed settings, admit concerns about the programs' ability to meet the needs of their children.

TEACHER ATTITUDES TOWARD INTEGRATION

According to Safford and Rosen (1981), one general advantage of mainstreaming is the effect that mainstreaming purportedly has on the attitudes of teachers about mainstreaming. While limited in number, a few studies in the literature address the issue of teacher attitude toward mainstreaming. McEvoy, Nordquist, and Cunningham (1984) evaluated regular and special education teachers' judgments about children with handicaps portrayed on videotapes in three integrated conditions: fully integrated, partially integrated, and minimally integrated. For regular education teachers, judgment ratings depended both on the characteristics of the target child and the integration ratio. Special education teachers' judgments also were influenced by characteristics of the child but not the integration ratio.

In a survey of teachers in mainstreamed programs, Blacher and Turnbull (1982) found that there appears to be strong support for mainstreaming from teachers and parents. Similarly, Clark (1974) reported that teacher preconceptions and attitudes about mainstreaming were alleviated when children with handicaps were mainstreamed into a class for normally developing preschoolers. Only slight adaptations were necessary to accommodate the handicapped children, and the competencies of the regular teachers proved to be adequate to accommodate the handicapped children. Finally, Tait and Wolfgang (1984) examined teacher attitudes toward the mainstreaming of a child who was blind. Teachers reported that they lacked appropriate equipment, that the blind child interacted infrequently with his peers,

and the adults were unable to keep the child occupied. From these studies, it appears that teacher attitudes toward including children with handicaps in mainstreamed settings were generally positive. In most situations, teachers have the skills for integrating children. However, to integrate children with certain handicaps, additional training and support for the teacher is needed.

CONCLUSIONS AND FUTURE DIRECTIONS FOR RESEARCH

Conclusions drawn from the research literature can be related directly to the rationales for integration that dictate the research questions.

Legal Rationale

With regard to the legal rationale for integration: public law recommends that children be integrated into the least restrictive environment; the authors found very little data on the frequency with which mainstreaming occurred, although there appears to be an abundant supply of model demonstration programs for accomplishing the process. There was good evidence that children with handicaps can receive an appropriate education in mainstreamed and ISE preschool programs, although the gains children make appear to be attributable to the quality of instruction that they receive rather than to integration. Although parents of children with handicaps enrolled in mainstreamed preschools generally expressed satisfaction with the mainstreaming experience that their child received, parents of kindergarten-age children with handicaps stated some concerns about the mainstreaming experience.

Future research directed to the legal rationale should examine the frequency with which the mainstreaming placement option is offered to parents of young children with handicaps, how often such options are chosen, and the factors associated with efficiently providing individualized instructional programs for children in those settings. Furthermore, given the broad range of instructional practices associated with early childhood special education in general (Carta, Sainato, & Greenwood,

Chapter 13, this volume), investigations of ecobehavioral variables associated with positive outcomes in mainstreamed settings could well be productive areas of research.

Philosophical Rationale

The normalization rationale would dictate that not only should children with handicaps be placed in programs alongside normally developing children, but that some form of social integration also occur and that positive social relationships develop among these children. The literature suggests that mainstreaming and ISE can accomplish this goal, in part. Although there is some recent evidence to the contrary, a number of studies suggested that for children with mild handicaps, social integration will occur either immediately or during the school year. For children with moderate and severe handicaps, such social integration does not appear to occur spontaneously, and programming must be instituted to accomplish it. Other studies suggested that normally developing children in mainstreamed preschools and kindergartens develop positive attitudes toward at least some of their peers with handicaps, and may, for some, assign high sociometric status. Social status appears to be related to both social behavior and nonsocial determinants.

Future research related to the normalization rationale for mainstreaming should take several directions. More information needs to be obtained about the qualitative nature of the interactions between normally developing children and children with mild handicaps. For children with more substantial handicaps, further investigations of intervention packages to promote social integration would appear to be very important. Finally, more precise measurement of young children's social relationships (i.e., sociometric analyses) and attitude formation in mainstreamed settings could contribute to the existing support of a normalization rationale for integration.

Educational Benefits

The least support was found for the educational benefits rationale for integration. Despite the theoretical suggestions that exposure to developmentally advanced peers could contribute substantially to skill acquisition for children with handicaps, no studies demonstrated that physical integration alone contributed to positive developmental outcomes. One study did suggest that when programming for social integration occurred in ISE classes, there were benefits for language and social development, and a number of studies revealed immediate positive effect on social and play behavior in integrated groupings. Also, across several studies of normally developing children, the consistent finding was that placement in classes with children who have handicaps did not have a deleterious effect on the normally developing children's development. However, the general conclusion to be drawn from the literature is that developmental outcomes for children enrolled in integrated educational programs are attributable to the specific curriculum employed and the quality of instruction rather than to integration.

Research associated with the educational benefits rationale would be most important for future integration efforts. Specifically, development of instructional programs that could take advantage of the advanced developmental skills exhibited by the normally developing children in integrated settings (e.g., incidental teaching, peer imitation training) could contribute substantially to the practice of integration in early childhood special education. Also, further studies that systematically control the variables of integration and curriculum for mainstreamed settings, as Jenkins et al. (1986) did for ISE settings, could reveal that educational benefits actually do exist but have gone undetected.

REFERENCES

Allen, K. E., Benning, P. M., & Drummond, W. T. (1972). Integration of normal and handicapped children in a behavior modification preschool: A case study. In

G. Semb (Ed.), *Behavior analysis and education* (pp. 127–141). Lawrence: University of Kansas.

Apolloni, T., & Cooke, T. P. (1978). Integrated programming at the infant, toddlers, and preschool levels. In M. Guralnick (Ed.), *Early intervention and the integration of handicapped and nonhandicapped children* (147–165). Baltimore; University Park Press.

Apolloni, T., Cooke, S. A., & Cooke, T. P. (1977). Establishing a normal peer as a behavioral model for developmentally delayed toddlers. *Perceptual and Motor Skills, 44*, 231–241.

Assael, D. (Ed.). (1984). *Handicapped children's early education program directory* (1983–1984). Chapel Hill, NC: TADS.

Assael, D. (Ed.). 1985. *Handicapped children's early education program directory, 1984-85*. Chapel Hill, NC: TADS.

Beckman, P. J. (1983). The relationship between behavioral characteristics of children and social interaction in an integrated setting. *Journal of the Division for Early Childhood, 7*, 69–77.

Beckman, P. J., & Kohl, A. K. (1984). The effects of social and isolate toys on the interactions and play of integrated and nonintegrated groups of preschoolers. *Education and Training of the Mentally Retarded, 19*, 169–174.

Blacher, J., & Turnbull, A. P. (1982), Teacher and parent perspectives on selected social aspects of preschool mainstreaming. *The Exceptional Child, 29*, 191–199.

Blacher, J., & Turnbull, A. P. (1983). Are parents mainstreamed? A survey of parent interactions in the mainstreamed preschool. *Education and Training of the Mentally Retarded, 18*, 10–16.

Blackmon, A. A., & Dembo, M. H. (1984). Prosocial behaviors in a mainstreamed preschool. *Child Study Journal, 14*, 205–215.

Bricker, D. D. (1978). A rationale for the integration of handicapped and nonhandicapped preschool children, in M. Guralnick (Ed.), *Early intervention and the integration of handicapped and nonhandicapped children* (pp. 3–26). Baltimore: University Park Press.

Bricker, D. D., & Bricker, W. A. (1971). Toddler Research and Intervention Project Report - Year 1. *IMRID Behavioral Science Monograph No. 20*, Nashville, TN: Institute on Mental Retardation and Intellectual Development.

Bricker, D. D., Bruder, M. B., & Bailey, E. (1982). Developmental integration of preschool children. *Analysis and intervention in Developmental Disabilities, 2*, 207–222.

Bricker, D. D., & Sandall, S. (1979). Mainstreaming in preschool programs: How and why to do it. *Education Unlimited, 1*, 29.

Bricker, D. D., & Sheehan, R. (1981). Effectiveness of an early intervention program as indexed by measures of child change. *Journal of the Division for Early Childhood, 4*, 11–28.

Bricker, W. A., & Bricker, D. D. (1976). The infant, toddler, and preschool research and intervention project. In T. D. Tiossem (Ed.), *Intervention strategies for high risk infants and young children* (pp. 545–572). Baltimore: University Park Press.

Brown, W. H., Ragland, E. V., & Fox, J. J. (in press). Effects of group socialization procedures on the social interactions of preschool children. *Research in Developmental Disabilities*.

Burstein, N. D. (1986). The effects of classroom organization on mainstreamed preschool children. *Exceptional Children, 52*, 425–434.

Cavallaro, S. A., & Porter, R. H. (1980). Peer preferences of at-risk and normally developing children in a preschool mainstream classroom. *American Journal of Mental Deficiency, 84*, 357–366.

Clark, E. A. (1974). Teacher attitudes toward integration of children with handicaps. *Education and Treatment of Children, 11*, 333–335.

Cohen, S. (1977). Fostering positive attitudes toward the handicapped: A new curriculum. *Children Today*, November-December, 7–12.

Cooke, T. P., Apolloni, T., and Cooke, S. A. (1977). Normal preschool children as behavioral models for retarded peers. *Exceptional Children, 43*, 531–532.

Cooke, T. P., Ruskus, J. A., Apolloni, T., & Peck, C. A. (1981). Handicapped preschool children in the mainstream: Background, outcomes, and clinical suggestions. *Topics in Early Childhood Special Education, 1*, 73–83.

Day, R. M., Powell, T. H., & Stowitschek, J. J. (1980). *Scippy: Social competence intervention package for preschool youngsters*. Nashville, TN: Vanderbilt University.

Day, R. M., Powell, T. H., Stowitschek, J. J., & Dy-Lin, E. G. (1982). An evaluation of the effects of a special interaction training package on handicapped preschool children. *Education and Training of the Mentally Retarded, 17*, 125–130.

Decker, M. (Ed.). (1986). *Handicapped children's early education program directory, 1985-86*. Chapel Hill, NC: TADS.

DeKlyen, M., & Odom, S. L. (1987). *Structure and preschool peer interaction. Beyond the mainstream.* Manuscript submitted for publication.

Devoney, C., Guralnick, M. J., and Rubin, H. (1974). Integrating handicapped and nonhandicapped preschool children: Effects on social play. *Childhood Education, 50*, 360–364.

Division for Early Childhood. (1987). *Least restrictive environment and social integration for young children with handicaps.* DEC White Paper. Reston, VA: Council for Exceptional Children.

Dunlop, K. H., Stoneman, Z., & Cantrell, M. L. (1980). Social interaction of exceptional and other children in a mainstreamed preschool classroom. *Exceptional Children, 47*, 132–141.

Ensher, G. L., Blatt, B., & Winschel, J. F. (1976). Head Start for the Handicapped Congressional Mandate Audit. *Exceptional Children, 43*, 202–210.

Esposito, B. G., & Peach, W. J. (1983). Changing attitudes of preschool children toward handicapped persons. *Exceptional Children, 49*, 361–363.

Faught, K. K., Balleweg, B. J., Crow, R. E., & van den Pol, R. A. (1983). An analysis of social behaviors among handicapped and nonhandicapped preschool children. *Education and Training of the Mentally Retarded, 18*, 210–214.

Fenrick, N. J., Pearson, M. E., & Pepelnjak, J. M. (1984). The play, attending, and language of young handicapped children in integrated and segregated settings. *Journal of the Division for Early Childhood, 8*, 57–67.

Field, T. (1984). Play behavior of handicapped children who have friends. In T. Field, J. Roopnarine, & M. Segal (Eds.), *Friendships in normal and handicapped children* (pp. 153–162). Norwood, NJ: Ablex Publishing Corp.

Field, T., Roseman, S., DeStefano, L., & Koewler, J. H.

(1981). Play behaviors of handicapped preschool children in the presence of and absence of nonhandicapped peers. *Journal of Applied Developmental Psychology, 2,* 49–58.

Field, T., Roseman, S., DeStefano, L. J., & Koewler, J. (1982). The play of handicapped preschool children with handicapped and nonhandicapped peers in integrated and nonintegrated situations. *Topics in Early Childhood Special Education, 2,* 28–38.

Gallagher, T. A. (1987). *Assessing the needs of families of preschool children.* Unpublished master's thesis. Vanderbilt University, Nashville, TN.

Galloway, C., & Chandler, P. (1978). The marriage of special and generic early education services. In M. Guralnick (Ed.), *Early intervention and the integration of handicapped and nonhandicapped children* (pp. 261–287). Baltimore: University Park Press.

Gerber, P. J. (1977). Awareness of handicapping conditions and sociometric status in an integrated preschool setting. *Mental Retardation, 15,* 24–25.

Gorelick, M. C. (1973). *Are preschools willing to integrate children with handicaps? Careers in integrated early childhood programs.* Northridge: California State University (ERIC Document Reproduction Service No. ED 097 794).

Guralnick, M. J. (1976). The value of integrating handicapped and nonhandicapped preschool children. *American Journal of Orthopsychiatry, 46,* 236–245.

Guralnick, M. J. (1980a). The social behavior of preschool children at different developmental levels: Effects of group composition. *Journal of Experimental Child Psychology, 31,* 115–130.

Guralnick, M. J. (1980b). Social interaction among preschool handicapped children. *Exceptional Children, 46,* 248–253.

Guralnick, M. J. (1981a). Programmatic factors affecting child-child social interaction in mainstreamed preschool programs. *Exceptional Education Quarterly, 1,* 71–91.

Guralnick, M. J. (1981b). Mainstreaming young handicapped children. In B. Spodek (Ed.), *Handbook of research on early childhood education* (pp. 456–500). New York: The Free Press.

Guralnick, M. J. (1981c). Peer influences on development of communicative competence. In P. Strain (Ed.), *The utilization of peers as behavior change agents* (pp. 31–68). New York: Plenum Press.

Guralnick, M. J. (1984). The peer interactions of young developmentally delayed children in specialized and integrated settings. In T. Field (Ed.), *Friendships between normally developing and handicapped children* (pp. 139–152). Chicago: Society for Research in Child Development.

Guralnick, M. J. (1986). The peer relations of young handicapped and nonhandicapped children. In P. Strain, M. Guralnick, & H. Walker (Eds.), *Children's social behavior: Development, assessment, and modification* (pp. 93–140). New York: Academic Press.

Guralnick, M. J., & Paul-Brown, D. (1977). The nature of verbal interactions among handicapped and nonhandicapped preschool children. *Child Development, 48,* 254–260.

Guralnick, M. J., & Paul-Brown, D. (1980). Functional and discourse analysis of nonhandicapped preschool children's speech to handicapped children. *American Journal of Mental Deficiency, 84,* 444–454.

Guralnick, M. J., & Paul-Brown, D. (1984). Communicative adjustments during behavior-request episodes among children at different developmental levels. *Child Development, 55,* 911–919.

Hecimovic, A., Fox, J. J., Shores, R. E., & Strain, P. S. (1985). An analysis of developmentally integrated and segregated free play setting and the generalization of newly-acquired social behaviors of socially withdrawn preschoolers. *Behavioral Assessment, 7,* 367–388.

Hohmann, M., Banet, B., Weikart, D. P. (1979). *Young children in action: A manual for preschool children.* Ypsilanti, MI: High/Scope press.

Hoyson, M., Jamieson, B., & Strain, P. S. (1984). Individualized group instruction for normally developing and autistic-like children: The LEAP curriculum. *Journal of the Division for Early Childhood, 8,* 157–172.

Ispa, J. (1981). Social interactions among teachers, handicapped children, and nonhandicapped children in a mainstreamed preschool. *Journal of Applied Developmental Psychology, 1,* 231–250.

Ispa, J., & Matz, R. D. (1978). Integrating handicapped and preschool children within a cognitively oriented program. In M. Guralnick (ed.), *Early intervention and the integration of handicapped and nonhandicapped children* (pp. 167–190). Baltimore: University Park Press.

Jenkins, J. R., Odom, S. L., & Speltz, M. L. (1986). *Effects of integration and structured play on handicapped preschoolers.* Manuscript submitted for publication.

Jenkins, J. R., Speltz, M. L., & Odom, S. L. (1985). Integrating normal and handicapped preschoolers: Effects on child development and social interaction. *Exceptional Children, 52,* 7–18.

Karnes, M. D., & Lee, R. C. (1979). Mainstreaming in the preschool. In L. Katz (Ed.), *Current topics in early childhood education* (Vol. 2, pp. 13–42). Norwood, NJ: ABLEX Publishing Co.

Kaufman, J. J., Gottlieb, J., Agard, J. A., & Kukic, M. B. (1975). Mainstreaming: Toward an explication of the construct. *Focus on Exceptional Children, 7,* 1–12.

Kohl, F. L., Beckman, P. J., Swenson-Pierce, A. (1984). The effects of directed play on functional toy use and interactions of handicapped preschoolers. *Journal of the Division for Early Childhood, 8,* 114–118.

McConnell, S. R., & Odom, S. L. (1986). Sociometrics: Peer-referenced measures and the assessment of social competence. In P. Strain, M. Guralnick, & H. Walker (Eds.), *Children's social behavior: Development, assessment, and modification* (pp. 215–284). New York: Academic Press.

McEvoy, M. A., Nordquist, V. M., & Cunningham, J. L. (1984). Regular and special education teachers' judgements about mentally retarded children in an integrated setting. *American Journal of Mental Deficiency, 89,* 167–173.

McEvoy, M. A., Nordquist, V. M., Twardosz, S., Heckaman, K., Wehby, J. H., Denny R. K. (1987). *Promoting autistic children's peer interaction in mainstreamed settings using affection activities.* Manuscript submitted for publication.

McHale, S., & Simeonsson, R. J. (1980). Effects of interaction on nonhandicapped children's attitudes toward autistic children. *American Journal of Mental Deficiency, 85,* 19–24.

Nordquist, V. M. (1978). A behavioral approach to the analysis of peer interaction. In M. Guralnick (Ed.), *Early intervention and the integration of handicapped and nonhandicapped children*. Baltimore: University Park Press.

Nordquist, V. M., Twardosz, S., & McEvoy, M. A. (1986). *Some longitudinal effects of behavioral interventions on nonhandicapped children in two mainstreamed preschools*. Manuscript submitted for publication.

Northcott, W. H. (1978). Integrating the preprimary hearing-impaired child: An examination of the process, product, and rationale. In M. Guralnick (Ed.) *Early intervention and the integration of handicapped and nonhandicapped children* (pp. 207–238). Baltimore: University Park Press.

Novak, M. A., Olley, J. G., & Kearney, D. S. (1980). Social skills of children with special needs in integrated and separate preschools. In T. Field, S. Goldberg, D. Stern, & A. Sostek (Eds.), *High risk infants and children: Adult and peer interaction* (pp. 327–346). New York: Academic Press.

Odom, S. L., Bender, M., Stein, M., Doran, L., Houden, P., McInnes, M., Gilbert, M., DeKlyen, M., Speltz, M., & Jenkins, J. (in press). *Integrated preschool curriculum*. Seattle: University of Washington Press.

Odom, S. L., DeKlyen, M., & Jenkins, J. R. (1984). Integrating handicapped and nonhandicapped preschoolers: Developmental impact on the nonhandicapped children. *Exceptional Children, 51*, 41–49.

Odom, S. L., & DuBose, R. F. (1981, April). *Peer rating assessments of integrated preschool classes: Stability and concurrent validity of the measures and efficacy of the peer model*. Paper presented at National Convention for the Council for Exceptional Children, New York.

Odom, S. L., Hoyson, M., Jamieson, B., & Strain, P. S. (1985). Increasing handicapped preschooler's peer social interactions: Cross-setting and component analysis. *Journal of Applied Behavior Analysis, 18*, 3–16.

Odom, S. L., Jenkins, J. R., Speltz, M. L., & DeKlyen, M. (1982). Promoting social integration of young children at risk for learning disabilities. *Learning Disabilities Quarterly, 5*, 379–387.

Odom, S. L., & Speltz, M. L. (1983). Program variations in preschools for handicapped and nonhandicapped children: Mainstreamed vs. integrated special education. *Analysis and Intervention in Developmental Disabilities, 3*, 89–104.

Odom, S. L., & Strain, P. S. (1984). Peer-mediated approaches to increasing children's social interaction: A review. *American Journal of Orthopsychiatry, 54*, 544–557.

Peck, C. A., Apolloni, T., Cooke, T. P., & Raver, S. (1978). Teaching retarded preschool children to imitate nonhandicapped peers: Training and generalized effects. *Journal of Special Education, 12*, 195–207.

Peck, C. A., & Cooke, T. P. (1983). Benefits of mainstreaming at the early childhood level: How much can we expect? *Analysis and Intervention in Development Disabilities, 3*, 1–22.

Peterson, N. L., & Haralick, J. G. (1977). Integration of handicapped and nonhandicapped preschoolers: An analysis of play behavior and social interaction. *Education and Training of the Mentally Retarded, 12*, 235–245.

Peterson, C., Peterson, J., & Scriven, G. (1977). Peer imitation by nonhandicapped and handicapped preschoolers. *Exceptional Children, 43*, 223–224.

Porter, R. H., Ramsey, B., Tremblay, A., Iaccobo, M., & Crawley, S. (1978). Social interactions in heterogeneous groups of retarded and normally developing children: An observational study. In G. P. Sackett (Ed.), *Observing Behavior, Vol. 1: Theory and Applications in Mental Retardation* (pp. 311–328) Baltimore: University Park Press.

Raab, M. M., Nordquist, V. M., Cunningham, J. L., & Bliem, C.D. (1986). Promoting peer regard of an autistic child in a mainstreamed preschool using pre-enrollment activities. *Child Study Journal, 16*(4), 265–284.

Raver, S. A., Cooke, T. P. & Apolloni, T. (1978). Developing nonretarded toddlers as verbal models for retarded classmates. *Child Study Journal, 8*, 1–8.

Rogers-Warren, A. K., Ruggles, T. R., Peterson, N. L., & Cooper. A. Y. (1981). Playing and learning together: Patterns of social interaction in handicapped and nonhandicapped children. *Journal of the Division for Early Childhood, 3*, 56–63.

Rogers-Warren, A. K. & Wedell, J. W. (1982). The ecology of preschool classrooms for the handicapped. *New Directions for Exceptional Children, 1*, 1–24.

Safford, P. L., & Rosen, L. A. (1981). Mainstreaming: Application of a philosophical perspective in an integrated kindergarten program. *Topics in Early Childhood Special Education, 1*, 1–10.

Sebba, J. (1983). Social interactions among preschool handicapped and non-handicapped children. *Journal of Mental Deficiency Research, 27*, 115–124.

Smith, C., & Greenberg, M. (1981). Step by step integration of handicapped preschool children in a daycare center for nonhandicapped children. *Journal of the Division for Early Childhood, 2*, 96–101.

Snyder, L., Apolloni, T., & Cooke. T. P. (1977). Integrated settings at the early childhood level: The role of the nonretarded peers. *Exceptional Children, 43*, 262–266.

Stoneman, Z., Cantrell, M. L., & Hoover-Dempsey, K. (1983). The association between play materials and social behavior in a mainstreamed preschool: A naturalistic investigation. *Journal of Applied Developmental Psychology, 4*, 163–174.

Strain, P. S. (1983). Generalization of autistic children's social behavior change: Effects of developmentally integrated and segregated settings. *Analysis and Intervention in Developmental Disabilities, 3*, 23–34.

Strain, P. S. (1984a). Social behavior patterns of nonhandicapped and nonhandicapped-developmentally disabled friend pairs in mainstreamed preschools. *Analysis and Intervention in Developmental Disabilities, 4*, 15–28.

Strain, P. S. (1984b). Social interactions of handicapped preschoolers in developmentally integrated and segregated settings: A study of generalization effects. In T. Field (Ed.), *Friendship between normally developing and handicapped children* (pp. 187–208). Chicago: Society for Research in Child Development.

Strain, P. S. (1985). Social and nonsocial determinants of acceptability in handicapped preschool children. *Topics in Early Special Education, 4*, 47–58

Strain, P. S., Hoyson, M., & Jamieson, B. (1985). Normally developing preschoolers as intervention agents for autistic-like children: Effects on class deportment and social interaction. *Journal of the Division for Early Childhood, 9*, 105–115.

Strain, P. S., Shores, R. E., & Kerr, M. M. (1976). An experimental analysis of "spillover" effects on the social interaction of behaviorally handicapped preschool children. *Journal of Applied Behavior Analysis, 9,* 31–40.

Sullivan, C., Shuster, S., & Sherif, G. (1987). *Identifying placements for young children with handicaps: A survey of day care providers.* Unpublished manuscript, Indiana University—Developmental Training Center.

Tait, P. E., & Wolfgang, C. (1984). Mainstreaming a blind child: Problems perceived in a preschool day care program. *Early Child Development and Care, 13,* 155–167.

Tawney, J. W. (1981). A cautious view of mainstreaming in early education. *Topics in Early Childhood Special Education, 1,* 25–36.

The Association for Persons with Severe Handicaps (1987). *Reauthorization of the Education of the Handicapped Amendments of 1986: Committee Paper.* Seattle, WA: TASH.

Timm, M. A., Strain, P. S., & Eller, P. H. (1979). Effects of systematic, response dependent fading and thinning procedures on the maintenance of child-child interaction. *Journal of Applied Behavior Analysis, 12,* 308.

Turnbull, A. P. (1982). Preschool mainstreaming: A policy and implementation analysis. *Educational Evaluation and Policy Analysis, 4,* 281–291.

Turnbull, A. P., & Blacher-Dixon, J. (1980). Preschool mainstreaming: Impact on parents. *New Directions for Exceptional Children, 1,* 25–46.

Turnbull, A. P., & Blacher-Dixon, J. (1981). Preschool mainstreaming: An empirical and conceptual review. In P. Strain and M. Kerr (Eds.), *Mainstreaming children in schools* (pp. 71–100), New York: Academic Press.

Turnbull, A. P., & Winton, P. (1983). A comparison of specialized and mainstreamed preschools from perspectives of parents of handicapped children. *Journal of Pediatric Psychology, 8,* 57–71.

Turnbull, A. P., Winton, P. J., Blacher, J., & Salkind, N. (1982). Mainstreaming in the kindergarten classroom: Perspectives of parents of handicapped and nonhandicapped children. *Journal of the Division for Early Childhood, 6,* 14–20.

Twardosz, S., Nordquist, V. M., Simon, R., & Botkin, D. (1983). The effects of group affection activities on the interaction of socially isolate children. *Analysis and Intervention in Developmental Disabilities, 3,* 311–338.

Twardosz, S., Schwartz, S., Fox, J., & Cunningham, J. L. (1979). Development and evaluation of a system to measure affectionate behavior. *Behavioral Assessment, 1,* 177–190.

Vandell, D. L., Anderson, L. D., Ehrhardt, G., & Wilson, K. S. (1982). Integrating hearing and deaf preschoolers: An attempt to enhance hearing children's interactions with deaf peers. *Child Development, 53,* 1354–1363.

van den Pol, R. A., Crow, R. E., Rider, D. P., & Offner, R. B. (1985). Social interaction in an integrated preschool: Implications and applications. *Topics in Early Childhood Special Education, 4,* 59–76.

Vincent, L. J., Brown, L., & Getz-Sheftel, M. (1981). Integrating handicapped and typical children during the preschool years: The definition of best educational practice. *Topics in Early Childhood Special Education, 1,* 17–24.

Westerwelt, V., & McKinney, J. D. (1980). Effects of a film on nonhandicapped children's attitudes toward handicapped children. *Exceptional Children, 46,* 294–296.

Winton, P. J., & Turnbull, A. P. (1981). Parent involvement as viewed by parents of preschool handicapped children. *Topics in Early Childhood Special Education, 1,* 11–19.

Winton, P. J., Turnbull, A. P., & Blacher, J. (1985). Expectations for and satisfaction with public school kindergarten: Perspectives of parents of handicapped and nonhandicapped children. *Journal of the Division for Early Childhood, 9,* 116–124.

Wolfensberger, W. (1972). *The principles of naturalization in human services,* Toronto: National Institute on Mental Retardation.

Wynne, S., Brown, J. K., Dakof, G., & Ulfelder, L. S. (1975). *Mainstreaming and early childhood education for handicapped children: Review and implications of research.* Washington, DC: Wynne Associates. (ERIC Soc. Reproduction No. ED 108–426).

Chapter 15

Research in Teacher Education

Issues and
Future Directions for Early Childhood Special Education

Jeanette McCollum and Kathleen McCartan

RESEARCH RELATED TO TEACHER EDucation in early childhood education is meager. While much relevant information is contained in detailed descriptions of preservice and inservice programs, current practice in ECSE personnel preparation has not been subjected to research validation either by describing what exists or by relating what exists to outcomes for teachers and children. If the question is "How much of what we do in teacher education in ECSE is supported by research?" the answer is "Not much."

Since teacher education in ECSE is a relatively new area, a large research base should not be expected. But a similar state of affairs exists in other areas of teacher education. In special education, a 1980 review covering 5 years of seven special education journals (Schofer & Lilly, 1980) yielded only 14 research articles on teacher education; these were so diverse that few conclusions could be drawn. Spodek and Saracho (1982) encountered a similar problem in reviewing research in regular early childhood education.

By far the most comprehensive body of research related to teacher education comes from regular education. Monetary support over a number of years has resulted not only in a larger number of studies but in a more coherent and synthesized body of knowledge than in other areas of teacher education. Even here, however, "not only is the body of research small, it is methodologically and theoretically anemic" (Evertson, Hawley, & Zlotnik, 1984, p. 2). Regardless of its limitations, this re-

search has greatly influenced research and practice in other areas of teacher education. An older and larger body of information, it includes within its boundaries most of the theoretical positions and approaches to research selected by researchers in newer areas of teacher education. It therefore provides a larger framework for interpretation of research outcomes than would be possible from the limited research in any one of these areas alone. Furthermore, many issues addressed within this larger framework may have implications for teacher education in ECSE but may not have been examined within this more narrowly defined context.

For these reasons, this chapter will begin with an overview of the approaches to teacher education research that appear in the regular education literature. The remainder of the chapter will consider aspects of teacher education that have been the target of past research, including in each case a discussion of what is known from research in ECSE and an overview of current issues in teacher education research. Finally, the applicability of these issues to teacher education and teacher education research in ECSE will be considered.

A FRAMEWORK FOR TEACHER EDUCATION RESEARCH IN ECSE

Teacher education research can be categorized according to the aspect of teacher education being studied: context/input variables (characteristics of students and of teacher educators;

organizational structures within which programs reside); content variables (what is or should be taught or learned); and process variables (how content is or should be presented). A review of the literature further suggests that each of these aspects can be related to a continuum representing the stage in the teacher education process at which it occurs: preservice (prior to entry into teaching), induction (first 1–2 years of teaching), and inservice. The matrix in Figure 1 correlates these two dimensions.

Although the quality and quantity of existing research are not equal for all cells of the matrix, the matrix is useful in establishing parameters. Similar approaches have been suggested by others as a way to identify research questions in teacher education (Cruickshank, 1984; Egbert, 1984; Katz & Raths, 1985). The matrix can also serve as a framework for synthesizing research; areas in which research is needed become obvious. The matrix serves both as an impetus to researchers and as a way to tie new research into existing knowledge.

In this chapter, one dimension of the matrix, the aspect of teacher education, serves to organize the issues discussed. Few questions, however, can be asked about any cell of the matrix without encountering questions of influence or of relationships with other cells. Relationships can be studied, for instance, across levels of teacher education; for example: How do effective personnel preparation processes differ for teachers in different stages of their careers? Relationships can also be studied for

any one stage across different aspects of the teacher education program; for example: How do entry characteristics of students affect what content is taught? Many research questions also address interactions between cells along both dimensions (are the relationships between content and process similar for preservice and inservice teachers?).

Although research in teacher education in ECSE is too sparse and diverse to yield comprehensive syntheses or guidance to programs, there are reasons for optimism. First, funding patterns stimulating the development of service delivery and teacher education programs in ECSE have resulted in a body of knowledge and minimal standards for program planning. Hence, many teacher education programs include what is currently regarded as best practice. A second and related reason is that teacher education in ECSE is a relatively new field and may not yet be firmly entrenched in the power and resource structures of universities and colleges; there may yet be time, given an adequate research base, to avoid some of the ills affecting other areas of teacher education. Hence, the present appears to be a prime time for conducting research in teacher education in ECSE. The purpose of this chapter is to provide impetus and direction for doing so.

THE CURRICULUM CONTENT OF TEACHER EDUCATION

Research on content attempts to describe what is taught and what is learned in teacher educa-

| | | Focus of research | | |
		Program input/context	Program content	Program process
	Preservice training			
Career stage	Induction			
	Inservice training			

Figure 1. An organizational framework for research in teacher education.

tion, to compare teacher education programs that vary in content, to determine the outcomes of variations in content for teachers and for the recipients of their services, and to identify what content should be included. Few studies directly related to the content of teacher education in ECSE are available in the published literature.

ECSE Teacher Education: What Do We Know?

Studies of content in ECSE teacher education have relied on surveys; most often, the purpose is to gather information on broad questions of current practice or to obtain opinions on what content should be included.

A recent survey by Bricker and Slentz (in press) examined the structure of ECSE teacher education programs to identify current practices and beliefs affecting the preparation of personnel who work with handicapped infants and their families. Two similarities related to content were found. First, personnel were purportedly being trained for a variety of positions, including teacher, infant specialist, team collaborator, and facilitator/consultant. Most programs reported preparing students for multiple roles. Second, several areas of common content appeared in the curricula of these programs, including knowledge of normal and atypical child development, assessment and individual program development, intervention strategies, data collection and monitoring skills, and parent training and family involvement.

The Bricker and Slentz study further indicated that particular roles are of special importance in birth–3 programs. However, despite general agreement that roles of personnel in programs for children from birth–3 years and children 3–5 years old differ in important ways, and despite the belief that these differences should be reflected in training, few distinctions were found in required curricula for these two types of personnel.

Competency validation studies are a second type of survey used extensively in ECSE. Lists of statements concerning knowledge, skills,

and attitudes needed by ECSE teachers are compiled by the teacher education program using other lists and relevant literature, and are then rated by experts for their relevance to teacher education. Results are generally not available in the literature. However, careful examination of three such studies (Hutinger, 1984; Ryan, 1982; Walker & Hallau, 1981) indicated that the content covered tends to be similar, including statements related to instructional areas (e.g., assessment, planning, teaching), parent involvement, and team functioning, as well as more general foundation areas such as knowledge of child development and the ability to communicate professionally with other adults. Despite variations in the types of experts chosen to respond and in the geographic areas from which they were drawn, the most important statements tended to fall into the areas of normal development, handicapping conditions, and individualized instruction. These results fit well with the curriculum areas included in the programs surveyed by Bricker and Slentz (in press).

Competency validation studies have a number of serious limitations. Aside from some broad commonalities, results usually are idiosyncratic and unique to the particular program conducting the study, since statements chosen for inclusion reflect that program's philosophy. Moreover, because the statements included have been drawn from best practice and current thinking, consensus finds most of them to be important; each program, regardless of its orientation, is shown to have "validity." A related problem is that content *not* contained in the statements is not subjected to review. Another limitation is that no observational/descriptive research has been done to compare survey results with reality. For instance: does "demonstrating" or "knowing" what is contained in these listings make any difference at all in the quality of teaching once the student is on the job, or even in whether the student ever uses that knowlege or skill? Finally, these studies generally do not yield information on priorities for preservice preparation. Instead, the outcomes tend to be almost overwhelming arrays of needed content.

Selected Content Issues

Research in the areas of teacher education most closely related to ECSE, special education, and early childhood education, has been scattered across a wide range of questions. Hence, research from other areas, primarily from regular education, provides the most abundant and pertinent information. It should be noted, however, that many other areas of research, which could not be included here, also are relevant. Primary among these is research on the development and learning of young children. Moreover, while research in ECSE teacher education must eventually examine a range of teacher roles, the issues presented below are limited to the role of instructional agent, since that is the one addressed most directly in the preponderance of available research.

Issue 1: What is Learned in Teacher Education? The effective teacher has been described as one who is flexible and reflective in formulating and implementing plans to fit particular situations (O'Neal, 1983a). The reality, in contrast, is that practicing teachers tend toward inflexibility, conservatism, and preoccupation with immediate problems (Lanier, 1986; Nemser, 1983). A primary concern occupying researchers in teacher education is therefore the contrast between what teacher educators want their students to learn and what apparently *is* learned. Katz and Raths (1982) have stated that preservice teacher education seems to have had little if any effect on the quality of teaching. Lanier (1986) has concluded that if anything at all is learned in teacher education, it may be negative and detrimental to teaching.

Both course work and student teaching have been implicated in students' learning this "unplanned" curriculum. In both cases, undesirable content seems to be a by-product of program structure and process as much as of planned content. It should be noted, however, that few causal connections have been established between specific program content (intended *or* unintended) and later outcomes.

Content of Course Work What teachers do is to make decisions, using many sources of data, both as they are planning and as they

move from moment to moment during the teaching process (O'Neal, 1983a). O'Neal and others (Lanier, 1982; Zeichner & Tabachnick, 1981) contend that it is this very process that is ignored in teacher education. Courses emphasize the learning of "how-to's," usually from one model espoused by the program or by a professor. Two problems result: no model alone fits reality, and future teachers are not taught to reflect on what they are doing. Thus, when the model works, it is grasped as the way to approach not only the particular but the general; when the model doesn't work, there are few available alternatives.

The application of results from research on teaching to teacher education (to be discussed under Issue 2) is often equated with technical as opposed to reflective teaching, since particular teaching behaviors are learned and used in a prescriptive manner. In contrast, researchers who espouse the application of these results to teacher education feel that many of the problems of today's teachers stem from their *not* having skill in research-derived teaching techniques (Rosenshine, 1983). From this point of view, inflexibility and conservatism are more related to teachers' not having been taught to incorporate new research results from research on teaching than from an inability to reflect on what they do.

Content of Student Teaching Student teaching has the express purpose of enabling students to experiment, explore alternatives, and engage in reflection. The unintended content appears instead to teach dependence, inflexibility, and poor habits (Zeichner, 1982). Hence, the curriculum of student teaching, like that of course work, may be counterproductive to the goals of teacher education (Lanier, 1986).

Research on what students actually do in student teaching reinforces this pessimism. Griffin's review (1983) indicates that student teachers have little practice in making decisions about the activities in which their pupils will engage and have little chance to explore the reasons for doing things in particular ways. Most decisions are made by the teacher prior to the student teacher's entry into the classroom;

the student's role is to fit into that structure. Not only does the student not participate in curriculum planning, but usually he or she is not privy to the teacher's thinking when the decisions were made (O'Neal, 1983b). Teaching decisions made by the student teacher tend thus to be narrow in scope and consequence.

All too often, supervision and feedback do little to overcome these handicaps. Conferences with cooperating teachers are few, and students take a passive role (O'Neal, 1983b). Cooperating teachers do most of the talking, and feedback centers on classroom routines and control rather than on the student's teaching behavior. University supervisors also focus on procedural issues rather than on teaching behavior (Zeichner, 1982). The smoothness with which activities are implemented may come to be seen as the goal rather than as the means to educational gains (Nemser, 1983; Zeichner, 1980).

The conflict between technical and reflective approaches to teacher education reappears in many guises (e.g., whether or not the approach should be competency-based teacher education or not). It is also apparent that these two approaches reflect contrasting philosophies. There are problems with each view (Howsam, Corrigan, & Denemark, 1985; Koehler, 1985), and an integration of extremes is needed. Inflexible thinking can result from a focus on *any* one model: programs that teach technical skills may in fact teach reflection and problem-solving. Techniques from any model of teaching can serve as legitimate alternatives for problem-solving and decision-making (Zumwalt, 1982). Teacher education course work must present an array of alternative models of teaching and should engage students in reflecting on the "whys" of these models in relation to different situations. The problem is how to integrate these foci in ways that meet teachers' survival needs *and* prepare them for continued growth. Programs that seem to provide teachers with a variety of alternative techniques and that help them develop abilities and attitudes conducive to reflection and professional self-development need to be described.

Research is needed to determine whether course work and student teaching in ECSE suffer from limitations similar to those reported in regular education. Research is also needed to identify to what program characteristics these limitations are related, and how programs without these limitations function. Is the balance of influence between cooperating teacher and program similar under conditions where the program is more tightly structured, where course work and student teaching are interwoven, and/or where university supervisors also teach core courses? ECSE programs with these characteristics tend also to be organized around a list of core performance statements: Is rigidity in thinking one of the outcomes? Are most ECSE programs limiting the knowledge and skills of students to a narrow range of "right" alternatives? What can be done during preservice programs, and during the induction and career periods, to counteract these outcomes? Collaborative research across teacher education programs in ECSE is needed to reveal the interplay between and among programmatic variables.

Issue 2: Teacher Effectiveness Research as a Source of Teacher Education Content Strong arguments have been made both for and against equating application of the outcomes of teacher effectiveness research with a prescriptive, technical approach to teaching. But there is a point quite aside from that issue that needs to be addressed. Even if teacher educators do accept that teacher effectiveness research is appropriate content for teacher education, the current results of this body of research do not necessarily describe teacher effectiveness in ECSE.

This is an issue of considerable importance. The results of teacher effectiveness research are being applied to developing generic procedures for evaluating and even certifying teachers. Presumably, unless research shows otherwise, this blanket will cover ECSE teachers, as well. The results of teacher effectiveness research are congruent with common sense (McIntyre, 1980). Because they also emphasize teaching techniques similar to those considered best practice in special education, they have had extensive impact in ECSE. However, the very logic and simplicity of these techniques may belie their potential dangers: Quite simply, the applicability of outcomes to ECSE has not been tested (but see Carta, Sainato, & Greenwood, Chapter 13, this volume, for current research in this area).

Teacher effectiveness research is concerned with uncovering and describing teacher behaviors that influence student learning. The major teacher effectivenss research projects have been large-scale studies that include groups of regular education teachers from one or more grades, usually at the elementary level. The typical approach has been to observe these teachers throughout an academic year on a multitude of teaching variables. At the end of the year, teachers are grouped into "good" and "poor" categories based on the achievement scores of the children in their classes. Analyses are then aimed at identifying differences between the two groups of teachers, using observational data obtained throughout the year. The major results of this research are therefore correlational: teachers who display more of a particular behavior have students who score higher on achievement tests, and vice versa.

Most of this research can be placed in one of two categories: 1) interactive teaching or 2) classroom organization and management. The first tends to be a slightly older body of research; in general, interest in the second category grew from observations made during that earlier period (Emmer, 1984). This research has been reviewed extensively (cf. Berliner, 1984; Brophy, 1983); very brief summaries are included here.

Interactive Teaching   The instructional ingredients that characterize the effective teacher in this research are 1) teacher directed learning and 2) a high level of interaction between teacher and students (Gee, Shulman, & McReynolds, 1983). As summarized by Gee et al., interactive teaching (or active teaching) consists of a clear focus on academic goals, active presentation of information (explaining, summarizing, reviewing, outlining), promo-

tion of high engagement rates, a check of understanding before moving on, and immediate academically oriented feedback. Rosenshine's list includes small steps, daily review and reteaching if necessary, a rapid pace, a high frequency of questions/answers, immediate correction of errors, and a high rate of student success (1983).

High correlations have been found between interactive teaching and the time students spend in active engagement with learning activities. Furthermore, both active teaching and academic learning time (ALT) are related to the development of academic skills (Bruning, 1984).

Classroom Organization and Management   As one might expect, and since the effect of good management is to maximize the time available for learning, there is a close relationship between classroom management and student engagement with the learning task. Outcomes of this research indicate that the effective teacher is one who organizes and manages the classroom in ways that prevent disruptive behavior and nonproductive use of time. Effective management contains elements of both planning and implementation (Emmer, 1984). The effective teacher communicates expectations and initiates planned routines and procedures. Rules are discussed, procedures are presented gradually and in context, rehearsal and demonstration are used as needed, and feedback is immediate and specific. Activities at the beginning of the year involve the whole group, with more individual activities introduced gradually. Activities focus on academic content but are not difficult, thus ensuring a high level of success. The effective manager constantly monitors student activity, maintains eye contact, and handles inappropriate behavior promptly. Responses to student behaviors are timely and accurate. Furthermore, they do not interrupt the flow of the ongoing activity; rather, the teacher deals with the behavior while maintaining a high level of student involvement with the task.

Teacher effectiveness research leaves little doubt that what teachers do has an impact on how much students learn. It is also clear that teachers can learn the behaviors identified by this type of research and can thereby influence student achievement. For ECSE, the major issue is to determine which of the behaviors identified in this research also apply to teaching young children with handicaps, and under what conditions. The small number of studies examining variations in teacher behavior as compared to variations across subgroups of students and types of learning have yielded few generalizations that hold up under all conditions (Edwards, 1981). Results reviewed by Bruning (1984), for instance, indicate that lower SES students learn more than higher SES students (as measured by achievement) when teachers are more structured, more supportive, when they wait for a response, and when they praise more, even if responses are not completely accurate. In contrast, students at higher SES levels learn more when given occasional negative feedback and when the teacher structures the activity to reduce competitiveness. Similarly, Gee et al. (1983) reported that there is no set criterion for adequate academic learning time; rather, the time required varies according to the students' learning ability. Soar and Soar (1976) found that greater structure in learning activities led to gains in low cognitive objectives but not necessarily to gains in higher objectives such as creativity. Moreover, the relationships between structure and achievement were positive only up to a certain point and then became negative, affecting both student achievement and self-concept. Finally, relationships between teaching variables and achievement and self-concept were not consistent across grade levels. Much research is needed on what determines effectiveness for a wider array of children and for outcome measures of different types (e.g., cognitive, communication, affective) and different levels (e.g., mastery of basic skills, proficiency, creative application).

It is clear that teaching behaviors identified by teacher effectiveness research cannot be assumed to be directly applicable to ECSE; rather, differences in the population and in program goals demand direct research with this population. Therefore, the inclusion of these

techniques in teacher education programs as the *only* way to approach teaching is not warranted. As sources of hypotheses for studies and/or as data for decision-making about individual children, however, these results are valid (Fenstermacher, 1984). From this point of view, they are not only appropriate conduct for teacher education but essential content.

The literature indicates that ECSE teacher education programs must at the very least engage in self-examination in relation to their content. Moreover, research is needed that examines the characteristics of effective teaching in ECSE. Do philosophical differences between programs influence how teachers teach? What variations are there in teaching roles, and how do they relate to differences in service delivery systems or to the ages and severity levels of the children? Given the extreme individuality in the population, this research may have to rely on many collaborative small-scale studies directed toward testing hypotheses concerning age, level of development, handicap, and program goal. Finally, many areas outside teacher education are relevant to ECSE, both in relation to the teachers' instructional roles and in relation to roles such as family involvement and interdisciplinary teaming. In most cases, these areas remain to be synthesized and examined for their applicability to ECSE.

THE PROCESS OF TEACHER EDUCATION

Research on processes that teacher education employs to transmit content to students has dealt with both specific and general aspects of training programs. Typically, this research describes what exists or explores the effects of particular processes on the acquisition of knowledge, skills, and/or attitudes by students, or on the satisfaction or attitudes of instructors, supervisors, cooperating teachers, or others providing training.

Process in ECSE: What We Know

Empirical information on processes of teacher education in ECSE is even more limited than that on content. What is known is almost exclusively descriptive in nature: what courses are offered, the extent and location of field experiences, and the philosophical orientations of programs.

From the Bricker & Slentz study (in press) it is apparent that a large percentage of ECSE training programs rely on field experiences as a critical part of the training process. In addition, 92% of the respondents indicated that their training programs were competency-based. However, despite similarities in content across programs, there were extreme differences among programs in the amount of time devoted to ECSE as an area of specialization. These differences varied from one course to a full year program and from no specialized practicum to two full semesters.

What is missing in ECSE research are efforts to determine the effects of these program characteristics on students, to document more specifically what actually occurs within courses and field experiences, and to make comparisons between different processes and their outcomes. Does the number, extent, or type of program make any difference? What effects do different approaches to course teaching have? Do some teaching techniques result in faster acquisition than others? It is clear from the previous section that responses to process questions relate not only to how *well* content is learned but also to *what* content actually is learned.

Selected Process Issues

With so little empirical information available on the process of teacher education in ECSE, the best guidance on how to proceed must again come from other fields. The myriad process issues needing to be explored include two that have been selected by the authors as examples of how research in other areas can shed light on processes in ECSE teacher education. The issues selected are inextricably related to those identified earlier in the chapter.

Issue 1: The Influence of Teacher Education Activities   Field experiences for teacher education students have received considerable attention from researchers. In light of the sup-

port for such experiences from teacher educators in ECSE (Bricker & Slentz, in press), this particular component of the training process will be examined more closely.

Although the efficacy of field experience is supported in the literature, Haberman (1982) has noted that there are no widespread practices in student teaching that have resulted from research, nor have any widespread practices been dropped as a result of research. Both research and thoughtful analysis, however, have documented many problems in the field experience process. Applegate (1985), in a review of recurring issues related to field experience, differentiated individual dilemmas (problems experienced by students, cooperating teachers, and university supervisors because of differences in roles and performance expectations) and institutional dilemmas (the relationship between field experience and the expenditure of program resources) as areas of concern. To counteract the individual dilemma, Painter and Weiner (1979) instituted an inservice training program for cooperating teachers, resulting in reports of improved relations between student teachers and cooperating teachers, and increased respect for cooperating teachers by university supervisors. Institutional dilemmas may be more difficult to counteract, since they are often grounded in long-term organizational structures of colleges of education (Lanier, 1986).

Potentially negative outcomes of student teaching were introduced earlier in this chapter. Not only is there little evidence that student teaching is integrated into the general program (Griffin, Hughes, Defino & Barnes, 1981), but views of teaching may actually conflict. One issue discussed repeatedly in the literature is the tendency of student teachers to finish their field experiences with their teaching behaviors and philosophies closely resembling those of their cooperating teachers, even if such views are at odds with what the students have been taught in their course work (Mahan & Lacefield, 1978; Zevin, 1974). Zeichner's (1980) perception is that the influence of the cooperating teacher on attitudes and behavior is particularly strong because without the experience or background for asking why or for considering alternatives, students tend to accept what they see as the only reality. If what the teacher does works in that environment, the student teacher is likely to adopt it; if it works for the student teacher (in that same environment), then it is likely to be carried over into other environments. Hence, without opportunities for reflection, the unintended curriculum of student teaching may be the learning of inflexible patterns of behavior.

The teacher education program is not without some influence. Several researchers have found evidence that matching student teachers and cooperating teachers for conceptual levels and philosophical orientations provides a better situation than when significant mismatches occur (Bocher & Ade, 1982; Copeland, 1977; Mahan & Lacefield, 1978; Thies-Sprinthall, 1980). Griffin et al. (1981) have noted that student teachers make greater gains if there is congruence between course work and the classroom. Further, students will try methods learned in course work if: 1) the cooperating teacher has been trained in supervision and/or 2) the cooperating teacher uses the same methods. If neither of these conditions exists, the methods are not likely to be tried (Copeland, 1977).

Relating these findings to the question of what students learn from cooperating teachers, Fenstermacher (1984) emphasizes that cooperating teachers can influence students' use of reflection by using similar processes themselves, thereby modeling ways to think about alternatives. Teacher education programs should either seek cooperating teachers with these traits or should train them to use these processes. A study by Barnes and Edwards (1984) indicated that the primary characteristics distinguishing good from poor cooperating teachers were a proactive stance, clear, specific communication, verbal/behavioral consistency, positive problem-solving, and analytical reflection.

In Haberman's view (1982), the underlying problem is that student teaching is thought of as teaching experience (application of what has been learned) rather than as learning experi-

ence; hence, few opportunities for learning are provided. The outcome for the student teacher is an experience in which interpersonal comfort, rather than the tension created by reflecting on and learning from one's experience, appears to be the primary goal.

McIntyre (1984) believes that student teachers are also influenced by university supervisors, but in ways that have not yet been well defined or measured. University supervisors do influence students' satisfaction with the experience (Griffin et al., 1981).

Griffin et al. (1981) summarized the literature as indicating the existence of communication problems between supervisors and students, the need for training of supervisors, particularly in the area of self-awareness, and the need for further research on the effects of supervisors' training and background on student teachers.

Bonar (1985) compiled six recommendations on the structure of field experiences:

1. Assuring that field experiences serve as natural extensions of the curriculum
2. Targeting specific skills and concepts for reinforcement
3. Articulating content from course to course and from field experience to field experience
4. Organizing field experiences around highly structured activities based on target concepts and skills
5. Training cooperating teachers, students, and supervisors in their respective roles and responsibilities (cooperating teachers, for instance, should learn techniques for facilitating the student's development of target skills and concepts)
6. Having university supervisors conduct debriefing sessions with students to assist them in reflecting on their experiences

Research does support the preference of students for a directive style of supervision (Copeland & Atkinson, 1978). However, students also become more accepting of an indirect approach as they gain experience (Copeland, 1982).

Student teaching is not the only type of

teacher education activity studied in process research. A variety of activities have been examined in both noncomparative (pre/post) and comparative studies (Koehler, 1985). The teacher education literature is replete with information on activities that enhance content acquisition. In general, it appears that when information and feedback are clear and precise, students are able to acquire teaching skills regardless of the teaching model being learned. However, congruence between skills taught in simulated settings (such as microteaching) and those practiced in the classroom leads to greater gains (Griffin et al., 1981).

This review of processes used in teacher education raises many questions for teacher educators and researchers in ECSE. What characteristics of student teaching influence teaching behavior? A high percentage of ECSE programs responding to the Bricker and Slentz study (in press) indicated that their programs were competency-based: What impact do competencies have on training? What activities have been generated to assist in competency attainment? Do competencies form the basis of expectations for student behavior in field experiences? If so, how does the competency basis influence the student's drift toward conformity with the cooperating teacher? How are particular types of activities matched to particular types of content? These are a few of the questions that need to be asked in relation to the specific activities of teacher education in ECSE.

Issue 2: Adults as Learners Research in staff development and adult learning appears to have broad implications for teacher education programs across the spectrum of preservice, induction, and inservice training. Most of this work has been concerned with inservice audiences. The implications of this research need to be carefully investigated before it is applied to preservice training and induction.

Hutson (1981) conducted an extensive analysis of staff development/inservice research and then formulated guidelines in three areas, procedural, substantive, and conceptual, which should guide the development and delivery of inservice training. Key points included:

Procedural Issues   Decision-making should proceed as a collaboration between clients, providers, and others.

Incentives for participation should emphasize intrinsic professional rewards.

Support for change must be given by administrators.

Implementation strategies should include continual growth activities and local development of materials.

Program should be designed in response to assessed needs, interests, and strengths and should be complex and ambitious, clear and specific.

Program should be conducted on site.

Substantive Issues   Content should be directed at changing teacher, not student, behavior. Inservice process should model good teaching (encourage active learning, use self-instruction methods, allow freedom of choice, involve demonstrations, supervised trials, and feedback, and adapt to the life conditions of the involved adults).

Conceptual Issues   Inservice training should be based on an adult development model, rather than a skill deficit model. Program should be an integral part of the total school program.

Edwards' review of several recent large-scale efforts on teacher change supports many of Hutson's conclusions (1981). A 5-year study of teacher change by the Institute of Development of Education Activities, Inc. (I/D/E/A), used peer groups as a basis for intervention. Teachers and administrators were helped to think, plan, decide, and act together in solving their own problems. The school in which supportive peer groups were formed had staff who were more willing to attempt change. Edwards' perception was that peer groups facilitated the development of change-oriented group norms and expectations.

A study by the Rand Corporation, a survey and case analysis of federally funded projects, also reviewed by Edwards, indicated the need to adapt staff development to the locale and to characteristics of the district and the staff. Mutual adaptation between innovation and the characteristics of the setting were essential to change. This provides additional support to Hutson's recommendation that inservice training should be based on assessed needs and should utilize locally developed materials.

The issue of adult development is addressed in numerous discussions of staff development and inservice programs. A variety of developmental models have been proposed, some pertaining to adults in general and some to teachers. The Concerns-Based Adoption Model (Hall & Louk, 1978, as cited in Edwards, 1981) approaches inservice as a series of stages that recognize that change is a personal experience. This model posits seven stages through which individuals move in relation to innovation. From an early stage of limited awareness and concern, teachers increase their awareness of the need for and the consequences of innovation.

Katz (1984) described four stages of teacher development: survival (primary concern is control and management), consolidation (concern moves from group to individuals), renewal (seeking of new information to refresh career), and maturity (concern with more philosophical issues of education). Katz encourages teacher educators to familiarize trainees with the stages, to assist them in developing survival strategies, and to encourage their personal development for later stages. She suggests that initial preservice training should be very practical, with later courses focusing on theoretical issues to correspond with the developmental model.

Christensen, Burke, Fessler, and Hagstrom (1983) have described a sequence similar to the one provided by Katz; they also make specific suggestions for training (primarily inservice) to correspond to the developmental stages of teachers. Teachers in the survival stage (induction period) need assistance with the technical aspects of teaching, with clarifying expectations for acceptable teaching behaviors and with understanding the personal changes they might be undergoing. Teachers in the middle years (Katz's consolidation and renewal phases) should be provided with individualized professional opportunities to support their quest for alternatives, new ideas, and perhaps

career advancement. For the teacher in the mature stage, formalized, traditional inservice training has little appeal. Other opportunities, such as mentoring, supervision, or individualized professional development, are appropriate.

While there appear to be many applications of this literature to preservice preparation, it is not yet clear which principles and recommendations can be applied directly. Information on the survival needs of beginning teachers can be used to develop content for preservice programs. But application of these principles also needs to reflect the cautions discussed previously. In equipping teachers to survive their first years of teaching, care should be taken not to foster rigid, conforming thought processes. Further investigation is needed to determine what can be done during preservice teacher education both to warn teachers against allowing survival needs to solidify into rigid behavior patterns and to provide them with self-examination techniques that will lead to growth once the survival period is over.

It appears that the most effective efforts for change have several characteristics in common. For example, they account for levels of development and are aimed at teachers' perceptions of their own needs. Successful efforts also help teachers develop evaluative and analytical skills. Finally, successful efforts socialize teachers with a value system in which change is desirable, necessary, and ongoing (Edwards, 1981).

Collaboration and support appear to be the passwords to professional development (Hutson, 1981). Collaborative inquiry models have recently been used by a number of projects as a way of providing inservice training to practicing teachers. In these models, teachers are engaged as researchers systematically examining their own concerns (Gee et. al, 1983; Lanier & Glassberg, 1981). A similar approach is appealing for preservice preparation. Howsam et al. (1985) have recommended that students work with research faculty, while McIntyre (1980) suggests that systematically forming and testing hypotheses about their own teaching should be a part of students' field experiences. A model for this approach may be found in literature related to resource/consulting teacher preparation (Nevin, Paolucci-Whitcomb, Duncan, & Thibodeau, 1982).

Many questions remain. At what levels are preservice teachers functioning? What processes will help them toward more mature ways of thinking? Are there processes that will teach them to function collaboratively with other teachers? How can activities be matched to teachers' current levels of development and at the same time help them grow? Much research is needed to examine applications of these theories and processes to different stages of teacher education in ECSE.

INPUT AND CONTEXT VARIABLES IN TEACHER EDUCATION

Issues in personnel preparation are not restricted to the "how" and "what" of the training process. Research on the people involved in training and on the institutional contexts in which training occurs indicates that both of these greatly influence teacher education. Context variables, those organizational and environmental factors that influence the way training programs are organized and implemented, are as diverse as the level of training offered (associate through doctoral), the type of training (preservice, induction, inservice), the size and type of the institution, the departmental and college affiliation of the program, and certification standards in the state. Input variables represent characteristics of the students and faculty involved in training. Each of these places limits on content and process and hence on the outcomes of teacher education.

ECSE: What We Know

Information on the input and context variables of teacher education programs in ECSE, while often consistently collected, is not readily available for review. Data are typically collected as part of the evaluation of federally funded personnel preparation projects and are reported in continuation proposals and in final

reports. The data that do receive wider dissemination are usually contained in descriptions of training programs reported in journals (cf. Geik, Gilkerson, & Sponseller, 1982; Mallory, 1983). Other more general surveys (Hirshoren & Umansky, 1977; Stile, Abernathy, Pettibone, & Wachtel, 1984) have reported on broader context variables such as training and/or certification requirements across states.

The most comprehensive information on context variables in ECSE programs is provided by Bricker and Slentz (in press). Seventy-two percent of the respondents reported that the ECSE program was housed in a special education department. An additional 16% were in child study departments. The remainder reported a variety of affiliations (e.g., early childhood, elementary education, psychology). Smaller departments were found to be less specialized in the programs offered, and there was much variability in the extent and variety of course work and field experience required. Programs decreased in the number of students involved from the bachelors to masters to doctoral level of training.

Although several input variables were explored, the primary variable was the number of faculty associated with the program and the roles and responsibilities of the respondents. Two thirds of those responding indicated multiple responsibilities, including instruction, supervision, advising, coordination, and program direction. Another third indicated a single role, typically instruction. The number of faculty associated with ECSE programs showed a wide range, from 1–14, with a mean of 2.5 per program; 77% of the respondents reported six or fewer associated faculty members. When asked about the availability of resources outside special education, respondents most often cited psychology, family and child development, and elementary education for bachelor's and master's programs. Not until the doctoral level were resources such as medicine, communication disorders, social work, and counseling/educational psychology frequently reported. This is an interesting finding in light of the respondents' strong agreement on the need for coordination of input from many disciplines.

Bailey, Lillie, and Paul (1981) compared students in on-campus and in field-based programs. The field-based group was found to have more teaching experience and to be older than on-campus students, but they represented the same male/female ratio. Off-campus students scored lower on the Graduate Record Examination (GRE) and had a lower undergraduate grade point average. Mallory (1983) described the students enrolling in one master's degree program as characterized by diversity in undergraduate and professional backgrounds (Head Start graduates, elementary and home economics teachers, nurses, occupational therapists, and speech/language pathologists), in years of experience (2–15), and in career goals. This diversity speaks for the challenge of developing content and process variations that match the needs of all students.

Selected Input/Context Issues

Information on input and context variables in ECSE programs is limited to a small number of surveys and program descriptions. Little or no effort has been made to look at these variables in relation to specific research questions, either within or across individual training programs.

This type of effort is more readily evident in research from general special education and even more from regular education. A review of research from these areas indicates that the questions raised may also be important in relation to ECSE teacher preparation, particularly since these variables may determine both the content of programs and the processes that most influence students.

Judith Lanier (1986), in her survey of research in teacher education over the past decade, reviews numerous demographic studies of students but expresses concern over the lack of thoughtful analysis of student characteristics. With increasing public concern over the quality of teachers in public education, a careful investigation into the factors contributing to successful performance is needed.

Researchers have found that there are proportionally more education majors scoring in the lower ranges on measures such as the Scholastic Aptitude Test (SAT) and National Teacher's Exam (NTE) than there are nonteacher education majors. Vance and Schlechty (1982) found that "32% of the college graduates scoring lowest on the SAT verbal and math measures were recruited to education." Weaver (1979) showed that the mean test scores for education majors were in roughly the 40th percentile. Longitudinal work by Schlechty and Vance (1981) indicated that the most capable students were the ones most likely to leave teaching early. However, the implications of such findings are unclear. Shim (1965) found that students taught by teachers who had lower undergraduate grade point averages scored higher than did the students of teachers with higher undergraduate grade point averages.

Sprinthall and Thies-Sprinthall (1983) and Christensen et al. (1983) have approached student characteristics contributing to quality teaching performance from a conceptual developmental perspective. Sprinthall and Thies-Sprinthall (1983) cite a number of studies which show that:

> Teacher behaviors consistently associated with high conceptual level scores are described as flexible, responsive, adaptable, empathic. Such teachers employ different levels of structure according to pupil needs, use a wide variety of teaching "models" in their classrooms, are "indirect," and "read and flex" with pupils. In short, high conceptual level teachers perform in the classroom in a manner that fits closely with clusters of behaviors associated with effective teaching. (p. 19)

The "high conceptual level" referred to by Sprinthall and Thies-Sprinthall reflects developmental levels mentioned by a number of theorists. These include stages of cognitive development (Piaget, 1963), moral development (Kohlberg, 1969), ego/self development (Loevinger, 1966), conceptual development (Hunt, 1974), and epistemological/ethical development (Perry, 1970). Sprinthall and Thies-Sprinthall assert that no single model pulls together all aspects of adult development; rather, application of each theory can shed light on various aspects of adult functioning.

One examplar of research in adult development and its application to teacher education was conducted by Walter and Stivers (1977), who found a measure of stage identity formation (Ericksonian model) to be the single most powerful predictor of success in student teaching. They administered instruments measuring identity diffusion and resolution and found that undergraduate student teachers scoring high in resolution and low in identity diffusion received higher grades in student teaching, accepted more ideas from their students, and asked their students a greater number of higher order questions.

Since functional level appears to be predictive of teacher performance, an important research question is whether increasing the cognitive/conceptual functioning of preservice teachers is possible. This question was addressed by Hurt and Sprinthall (1977) and by Glassberg and Sprinthall (1980). Hurt and Sprinthall, in an effort to increase emphathy and responsiveness to others, taught counseling skills to preservice teachers. Students received information on skills (e.g., active listening, responsiveness to nonverbal behavior, peer counseling) and practiced the skills in role-playing situations. They were then taught to use the skills with children in classrooms. The group receiving this training was found to be significantly different from a control group that received no training. The trained group exhibited increased self-evaluation, concern for communication, and greater cognitive complexity.

Glassberg and Sprinthall (1980), working with a small sample of undergraduate student teachers, instructed the students to analyze and process their own and their peers' teaching. At the end of the training the student teachers showed significant increases in self-direction and independence and in their use of 'principled thought' (a Kohlberg construct).

The effectiveness of teacher education is also influenced by the characteristics of the faculty and by the structure of the program itself. Students may enter teacher education programs already accustomed to conservative thought

patterns, but teacher educators may exhibit similar characteristics (Lanier, 1986) and hence may reinforce them in their students. Lanier (1986) also has pointed out that the structure of teacher education programs, in which students generally proceed through their required work as individuals rather than as a group of future professionals, may prevent students from developing a professional identity or collegial behavior patterns. Lanier found little relationship among courses within teacher education programs, and characterized the curriculum as a disarray of survey courses. Structural aspects of programs may contribute to the lack of relationship between course work and student teaching (Griffin, 1983; Nemser, 1983), since there is often little communication between individuals teaching core courses and those persons charged with arranging and supervising student teaching.

The findings raise questions for those involved in ECSE personnel preparation. How do ECSE students compare with teacher education students and all other college students on such measures as the NTE, GRE, SAT, and grade point average? How do ECSE students perform on measures of cognitive/conceptual development? How does performance on such measures relate to performance in student teaching, and later, to job performance? What experiences will facilitate the continuing development of students? Do ECSE programs exhibit the same problems in terms of faculty characteristics and program structure as those found in regular education, and what distinguishes the programs that do have these problems from those that do not? Many ECSE programs are small ones in which students do move through the program in cohort groups: Does this have any impact on their development as professionals? These questions have significance for defining entry and exit criteria of students and for examining the role of faculty characteristics and program structure in shaping preservice teachers. Moreover, these input and context variables have obvious relationships with both content and process; these, too, need to be studied.

CONCLUSION

There are many more questions than answers in research on teacher education in early childhood special education. In this chapter, issues have been selected primarily from teacher education research in regular education. This is the area in which most research has been done. The range of issues examined has been broader than in other areas of teacher education, and many of the issues appear to have implications for teacher education in early childhood special education.

A major theme reiterated throughout the chapter is the question of direct applicability of research in other areas to teacher education in ECSE. In terms of research on teaching, ECSE is oriented toward a very special population that differs critically from those that have been the focus of this type of research in the past. Although the research in teacher education seems directly applicable, researchers do not know how ECSE teacher education differs from more general teacher education. Building a research base in ECSE teacher education is therefore essential, despite the many difficulties.

Given these caveats, there do appear to be a number of implications for teacher education in ECSE. First, it is clear that what students learn from teacher education programs is as much a function of the processes used as of the content presented. Furthermore, there are complex interactions between content, process, characteristics of students and faculty, and the parameters of programs in relation to the contexts in which they function. At the very least, teacher educators should be aware of and should examine these interactions, and then use this understanding to systematically match process to content and to change aspects of their programs that interfere with these efforts.

Second, many of the issues selected for review indicate that reflection and problem solving are essential content for teacher education. It is critical that programs present students with varied approaches and models; this will help them not only to be aware of conflicting views

but to draw on different knowledge bases for hypotheses to test in relation to individual children and/or to more general concerns. Learning to use a wide range of knowledge, to generate hypotheses, to evaluate the impact of interventions based on these hypotheses, and to reflect on the outcomes may not only be desirable, but necessary as the only way students can be adequately prepared for the heterogeneous populations and roles encountered by early childhood special education teachers. It is clear, however, that teacher education programs cannot expect to provide ECSE teachers with all of the alternatives they may need. Another critical component of teacher education content appears therefore to be techniques for effective searching, synthesis, and use of available literature. Activities within course work and systematic planning for self-analysis within field experiences can help ensure that students gain these abilities and areas of knowledge.

Finally research indicates that teacher educators should devise mechanisms whereby students can be socialized to collegial and mutually supportive professional relationships; these will encourage growth and will protect them against the rigidity that they may encounter on the job. Moving through programs as cohorts (Lanier, 1986) rather than as individuals, and engaging in joint planning and reflection are two approaches to this goal.

From a comparison of the cells of the matrix shown in Figure 1 and in the available research, it is apparent that current research in ECSE teacher ecuation is extremely limited. A number of research questions have been noted for each issue examined. There are many more questions yet to be addressed. There are also issues that may be unique to ExSE, including how to prepare teachers for the wide variety of roles in EXCSE programs. Two viable approaches to answering these questions are possible. First, the applicability of existing research from other areas to ECSE must be tested. Second, important questions not yet addressed must be identified and pursued.

There are a number of obstacles to conducting meaningful and cohesive research in teacher education in ECSE. Koehler (1985) noted that much research in teacher education has been of a "bootstrap" nature, that is, it is added to a full teaching load by teacher educators who receive little support. Furthermore, good teacher education research is difficult to do: variables are difficult to control, criteria for program success are unclear, and programs vary in many ways (Bricker & Slentz, in press), inhibiting comparison of outcomes in relation to any particular program characteristic.

A collaborative effort between teacher educators at different institutions appears to be the most feasible approach to overcoming these limitations. Research must be coordinated around common questions so that results can be aggregated. A first step is to identify priority research issues and areas of literature related to each. For some issues, much research may already be available but may not be synthesized in relation to specifi questions. For other areas, collaborative projects can be planned and implemented jointly by ECSE teacher programs. Planned variations in both content and process are possible, as are variations in existing program structures and inputs; these can be compared by using standard outcome measures across programs. A variety of designs and measures is not only possible but desirable; both large- and small-scale studies, when coordinated around the same issues, can contribute to and can enrich the research base in early childhood special education teacher education.

REFERENCES

Applegate, J. (1985). Early field experiences: Reoccurring dilemmas. *Journal of Teacher Education, 37*(2), 60–63.

Bailey, D., Lillie, D., & Paul, J. (1981). Field-based degree training in special education. In O. Stedman & J. Paul (Eds.), *New directions for exceptional children: Professional preparation for teachers of exceptional children* (p. 8.) San Francisco: Jossey-Bass.

Barnes, S., & Edwards, S. (1984). *Effective student teaching experience: A qualitative-quantitative study.* Austin, TX: Research and Development Center in Teacher Education.

Berliner, D. C. (1984). The half-full glass: A review of research on teaching. In P. L. Hosford (Ed.), *Using what we know about teaching* (pp. 51–77). Alexandria, VA: Association for Supervision and Curriculum Development.

Bocher, R., & Ade, W. (1982). The relationship of field placement characteristics and students' potential field performance abilities to clinical experience performance ratings. *Journal of Teacher Education, 33*(2), 24–33.

Bonar, B. (1985). Needed: Structured activities in early field experience programs. *Action in Teacher Education, 7(3),* 43–47.

Bricker, D., & Slentz, K. (in press). *Personnel preparation: Handicapped infants.* Elmsford, NY: Pergamon Press.

Brophy, J. (1983). Classroom organization and management. *Elementary School Journal, 83,* 265–285.

Bruning, R. H. (1984). Key elements of effective teaching in the direct teaching model. In R. L. Egbert & M. M. Kluender (Eds.), *Using research to improve teacher education: The Nebraska symposium* (pp. 75–88). Washington, DC: ERIC Clearinghouse on Teacher Education.

Christensen, J., Burke, P., Fessler, R., & Hagstrom, D. (1983). *Stages of teachers' careers: Implications for professional development.* Washington, DC: ERIC Clearinghouse on Teacher Education. (ERIC #SP 021 495).

Copeland. W. D. (1977). Some factors related to student teacher classroom performance following microteaching training. *American Educational Research Journal, 14,* 147–157.

Copeland, W. D. (1982). Student teachers' preference for supervisory approach. *Journal of Teacher Education, 32(2),* 32–36.

Copeland, W. D., & Atkinson, D. R. (1978). Student teachers' perceptions of directive and nondirective supervisory behavior. *Journal of Educational Research, 71,* 123–127.

Cruickshank, D. R. (1984, November-December). Toward a model to guide inquiry in preservice teacher education. *Journal of Teacher Education,* 43–48.

Edwards, S. (1981) *Changing teacher practice: A synthesis of relevant research.* Austin, TX: Research and Development Center in Teacher Education.

Egbert, R. L. (1984). The role of research in teacher education. In R. L. Egbert & M. M. Kluender (Eds.), *Using research to improve teacher education: The Nebraska symposium* (pp. 9–21). Washington, DC: ERIC Clearinghouse on Teacher Education.

Emmer, E. T. (1984). *Classroom management: Research and implications.* Austin, TX: Research and Development Center in Teacher Education.

Evertson, C., Hawley, W., & Zlotnik, M. (1984). *The characteristics of effective teacher preparation programs: A review of research.* Unpublished manuscript, Peabody College, Vanderbilt University, August 1984.

Fenstermacher, G. D. (1984). On getting from here (research) to there (practice). In R. L. Egbert & M. M. Kluender (Eds.), *Using research to improve teacher education: The Nebraska symposium* (pp. 22–27). Washington, DC: ERIC Clearinghouse on Teacher Education.

Gee, E. W., Shulman, J., & McReynolds, B. (July, 1983).

Synthesis of research on instructional effectiveness in elementary schools. San Francisco: Far West Laboratory for Educational Research and Development.

Glassberg, S., & Sprinthall, N. (1980). Student teaching: A developmental approach. *Journal of Teacher Education, 31,* 31–38.

Griffin, G. A. (1983). *Using research in preservice teacher education.* Paper prepared to the Improving Preservice Teacher Education Project, Detroit, Michigan.

Griffin, G. A., Hughes, R., Defino, M. E., & Barnes, S. (1981). *Student teaching: A review.* Austin, TX: Research and Development Center for Teacher Education.

Haberman, M. (1982). Research needed on direct experience. In D. C. Corrigan, D. J. Palmer, & P. A. Alexander (Eds.), *The future of teacher education: Needed research and practice* (pp. 69–84). Denton: College of Education, Texas A & M University.

Hirshoren, A., & Umansky, W. (1977). Certification of teachers of preschool handicapped children. *Exceptional Children, 44*(3), 191–196.

Howsam, R. B., Corrigan. D. C., & Denemark, G. W. (1985). *Educating a profession: Reprint with postscript 1985.* Washington, DC? American Association of Colleges for Teacher Education.

Hunt, D. (1974). *Matching models in education.* Toronto: Ontario Institute for Studies in Education.

Hurt, B., & Sprinthall, N. (1977). Psychological and moral development for teachers. *Journal of Moral Education, 6.* 112–120.

Hutinger, P. L. (1984, April). *Infant and preschool handicapped personnel competencies: Results of a survey.* Paper presented to the annual meeting of the Council for Exceptional Children, Washington, DC.

Hutson, H. M. (1981). Inservice best practices: The learning of general education. *Journal of Research and Development in Education, 14*(2), 1–10.

Katz, L. (1984). The education of preprimary teachers. In L. G. Katz, P. J. Wagemaker & K. Steiner (Eds.), *Current topics in early childhood education* (Vol. 5). Norwood, NJ: Ablex Publishing Corporation (ERIC Document Reproduction Service No. ED 220 197).

Katz, L. G., & Raths, J. D. (1982). The best of intentions for the education of teachers. *Action in Teacher Education* (Special Issues: The role of research in education), *4(1),* 8–16.

Katz, L. G., & Raths, J. D. (1985, November-December). A framework for research on teacher education programs. *Journal of Teacher Education,* 9–15.

Koehler, V. (1985, January-February). Research on preservice teacher education. *Journal of Teacher Education,* 23–30.

Kohlberg, L. (1969). Stage and sequence: The cognitive developmental approach to socialization. In D. Goslin (Ed.), *Handbook of socialization theory and research* (pp. 347–480). Chicago: Rand McNally.

Lanier, J. E. (1982). Teacher Education: Needed research and practice for the preparation of teaching professionals. In D. C. Corrigan, D. J. Palmer, & P. A. Alexander (Eds.), *The future of teacher education: Needed research and practice* (pp. 13–35). Denton: College of Education, Texas A & M University.

Lanier, J. E. (1986). Research on teacher education. In M. C. Wittrock (Ed.), *Handbook of research on teaching* (3rd ed., pp. 527–569) New York: Macmillan.

Lanier, J. E., & Glassberg, S. (1981). Relating research in classroom teaching to inservice education. *Journal of Research and Development in Education, 14*(2), 22–33.

Loevinger, J. (1966). The meaning and measurement of ego development, *American Psychologist, 21,* 195–206.

Mahan, J. M., & Lacefield, W. D. (1978). Educational attitude change during year-long student teaching. *Journal of Experimental Education, 46,* 4–15.

Mallory, B. C. (1983). The preparation of early childhood special educators: A model program. *Journal of the Division for Early Childhood, 7,* 32–40.

McIntyre, D. (1980). The contribution of research to quality in teacher education. In E. Hoyle & J. Megarry (Eds.), *World Yearbook of Education* (pp. 293–307). New York: Nichols Publishing Company.

McIntyre, D. J. (1984). A response to the critics of field experience supervision. *Journal of Teacher Education, 35*(3), 42–45.

Nemser, S. F. (1983). Learning to teach. In L. S. Shulman & G. Sykes (Eds.), *Handbook of teaching and policy* (pp. 150–170). New York: Longman Publishing.

Nevin, A., Paolucci-Whitcomb, P., Duncan, D., & Thibodeau, L. A. (1982). The consulting teacher as a clinical researcher. *Teacher Education and Specail Education, 5(4),* 19–29.

O'Connell, J. (1983). Education of handicapped preschoolers: A national survey of services and personnel requirements. *Exceptional Children, 49*(6), 538–539.

O'Neal, S. F. (1983a). *Developing effective instructional planning and decision making skills: Are we teaching teachers or technicians?* Austin, TX: Research and Development Center in Teacher Education.

O'Neal, S. F. (1983b). *Supervision of student teachers: Feedback and evaluation.* Austin, TX: Research and Development Center in Teacher Education.

Painter, L. H., & Weiner, W. K. (1979). Developing competent cooperating teachers. *Improving college education and university teaching, 27*(1), 13–15.

Perry, W. (1970). *Forms of intellectual and ethical development during the college years.* New York: Holt, Rinehart & Winston.

Piaget, J. (1963). *Psychology of intelligence.* Patterson, NJ: Littlefield Adams.

Rosenshine, B. (1983). *Teaching functions in instructional programs. Elementary School Journal, 83,* 335–351.

Ryan, S. B. (1982). *Competencies necessary for work with preschool handicapped children: Teachers' perceptions.* Submitted to Temple University Graduate Board in partial fulfillment of the requirements for the degree of Doctor of Education, March, 1982.

Schlechty, P., & Vance, V. (1981). Do academically able teachers leave education? The North Carolina case. *Phi Delta Kappan, 63,* 106112.

Schofer, R. C., & Lilly, M. S. (1980). Personnel preparation in special education. In L. Mann & D. A. Sabatino (Eds.), *The fourth review of special education* (pp. 367–390). New York: Grune & Stratton.

Shim, C. P. (1965). A study of four teacher characteristics on the achievement of elementary school pupils. Journal of Educational Research, 59, 33–34.

Soar, R. S., & Soar, R. M. (1976). Attempts to identify measures of teacher effectiveness from four studies. *Journal of Teacher Education, 27,* 261–267.

Spodek, B., & Saracho, O. N. (1982). The preparation and certification of early childhood personnel. In B. Spodek

(Ed.), *Handbook of research in early childhood education* (pp. 399–425). New York: The Free Press.

Sprinthall, N., & Thies-Sprinthall, L. (1983). The teacher
as an adult learner: A cognitive developmental view. In
G. A. Griffin (Ed.), *Staff development* (Eighty-second
Yearbook of the National Society for the Study of Edu-
cation) (pp. 13–35). Chicago: University of Chicago
Press.

Stile, S. W., Abernathy, S. M., Pettibone, T. J., &
Wachtel, W. J. (1984). Training and certification for
early childhood special education personnel: A six-year
follow-up study. *Journal of the Division for Early Childhood, 8(1)*, 69–73.

Thies-Sprinthall, L. (1980). Supervision: An educative or
miseducative process? *Journal of Teacher Education,
31*, 17–20.

Vance, V., & Schlechty, P. (1982). The distribution of
academic ability in the teaching force: Policy implications. *Phi Delta Kappan, 6(1)*, 2–27.

Walker, J. A., & Hallau, M. G. (1981, April). *Teacher
competencies in Early Childhood Education of the
Handicapped: A survey of expert opinion.* Paper presented at the annual meeting of the Council for Exceptional Children, New York.

Walter, S., & Stivers, E. (1977). The relation of student

*teachers classroom behavior and Erickson an ego iden-
tity. Journal of Teacher Education, 38*, 47–50.

Weaver, W. (1979). In search of quality: The need for
talent in teaching. *Phi Delta Kappan, 6(1)*, 29–46.

Zeichner, K. M. (1980). Myths and relaities: Field-based
experiences in pre-service teacher education. *Journal of
Teacher Education, 31(6)*, 45–55.

Zeichner, K. M. (1982). Reflective teaching and field-
based experiences in teacher education. *Interchange,
12(4)*, 1–22.

Zeichner, K. M., & Tabachnick, B. R. (1981). Are the
effects of university teacher education 'washed out' by
school experience? *Journal of Teacher Education,
32(3)*, 6–11.

Zevin, J. (1974). *In thy cooperating teacher's image: Convergence of social studies student teachers' behavior
patterns with cooperating teachers' behavior patterns.*
(ERIC Document Reproduction Service No. ED 087
781).

Zumwalt, K. K. (1982). Research on teaching: Policy implications for teacher education. In A. Lieberman &
M. W. McLaughlin (Eds.), *Policy making in education*
(pp. 215–248). 31st Yearbook of the National Society
for the Study of Education, Pt. 1. Chicago: University of
Chicago Press.

Chapter 16

Considerations and Future Directions for Conducting Research with Young Handicapped and At-Risk Children

Merle B. Karnes and Lawrence J. Johnson

THE PURPOSE OF THIS BOOK IS TO PRE-sent the most current information from research in important areas of early intervention with young handicapped children and to provide directions for future research. Until relatively recently, there has been little research with young handicapped children and little awareness of the importance of early identification and programming for them. This is not surprising, since financial resources for conducting research on programming for the young handicapped population were scarce. As DeWeerd (1981) aptly pointed out, service programs for young handicapped children were so scarce in the United States that one could visit all of them in less than 2 weeks.

In the middle 1960s, when the federal government began to invest in intervention programs for children from low-income families, very little effort was directed toward research. These early programs for the handicapped were preoccupied with providing services. Whether the services were effective in bringing about change received little attention. Frequently, the only evaluation data collected were reports of parent or teacher satisfaction with child progress. In some cases an intelligence test was given, usually the Stanford-Binet, on a pretest/posttest basis. Today, researchers would

never consider using an intelligence test as the sole or even the primary indicator of impact (see Neisworth & Bagnato, Chapter 2, this volume). Researchers now recognize the importance of assessing an intervention program and its effects not only on the handicapped child but also on family, peers, and teachers. Research designs and methods of collecting and analyzing data must be very rigorous if they are to produce reliable and valid results.

As reflected by the chapters in this book, researchers have become more sophisticated in conducting research with handicapped populations, and professional knowledge has grown to match this sophistication. Much of what is known about early intervention is due to support from federal and, to a lesser extent, from state and private agencies. Although the federal government has laudably supported research in early intervention (e.g., the funding of eight research institutes since 1977 to enhance services to handicapped children and their families), there is a great need to continue encouraging policymakers to support early intervention research. Without continued research funds, the empirical base for early childhood special education will not continue to grow in sophistication.

Years ago researchers asked, ''Does early

programming for the handicapped make any difference?'' In the late 1940s, Kirk (1958) started a preschool program to answer this question, and found the answer was "Yes, of course." Efforts to find the one best approach to educating children with problems have not been fruitful, however. As suggested by Lazar (1983), there probably is no one best method but rather a continuum of methods that can be successful, depending on the needs of the community and the resources available to the program. A more appropriate question may be "What approach is best for what children?" To continue to grow, researchers must now ask what intervention options are available, what situations are most conducive to implementing the option, and what resources are needed to implement it adequately (Guralnick, Chapter 5, this volume).

Throughout this book, the authors have made recommendations regarding directions research should take within specific content areas. As indicated, the growth in knowledge parallels the increased understanding of the research process. Indeed, our sophistication as researchers must also continue to grow if we are to continue to build on this knowledge base and to grow as a field. Although many current research issues require examination, the authors have identified several themes that emerged across chapters and that, one may predict, signal the form that much research will take in the future. These themes included: social validity, triangulation, replication, selection of dependent measures, descriptions of and implementation of independent measures, and expanding the impact of research on practitioners and policymakers. In the remainder of this chapter each of these issues will be discussed in greater detail.

SOCIAL VALIDITY

It is not enough to develop interventions that can efficiently change behavior in some desired direction. The social validity of the intervention must also be considered. As introduced by Wolf (1978), the assessment of social validity entails the determination that an interven-

tion produces meaningful changes in the individuals who are its focus. There are two considerations when determining the social validity of an intervention: 1) the magnitude of change in the behavior of individuals who are the target of the intervention, and 2) the degree to which their behavior deviates from that of their normally functioning counterparts. For example, if an intervention were developed that reduced the self-biting of an autistic child from 50 to 10 incidents per hour, the intervention would not be socially valid. Although the magnitude of the change would be significant, 10 incidents of self-biting per hour would still be injurious to the child and sufficiently deviant from normal behavior to be considered maladaptive.

In the example, the criterion of social validity is obvious: complete elimination of the behavior is the only acceptable option. In practice, however, criteria are less clear-cut. Kazdin (1977) has suggested several procedures that can help determine the social validity of a procedure.

Social Comparisons

Using the social validity procedure, one must first identify a set of peer counterparts for individuals who are the targets of the intervention. Behavior samples are then taken of this group to establish a normative level of performance on the target behavior. This information is used to determine reasonable goals for the intervention program. In this way normal behavior can be determined empirically rather than proceeding on an assumption.

In theory, this procedure prevents researchers from establishing unrealistically high or low standards for the intervention. As Kazdin (1982) points out, however, there are issues that must be given careful consideration by researchers before they adopt a social comparison procedure. First, depending on the level of the peer group and the individual who is the intervention target, it may be impossible for the individual's behavior ever to be equivalent to that of the peer group. Second, it may be difficult to identify an appropriate peer group. And third, the behavior of the peer group may not be the behavior that should be emulated. The fact that a particular behavior occurs in many children, for example, does not make it appropriate.

Subjective Evaluation

The subjective evaluation procedure consists of soliciting the opinions of experts or of individuals experienced with the child and the setting in which the program is going to be implemented in order to determine reasonable levels of behavioral change to consider indicative of social validity. These experts set goals for the intervention based on their previous experience and knowledge. Strain (1984) has suggested that "consumers" of the skills acquired by those targeted for intervention should be used to determine how great a change represents a socially valid change. In other words, teachers or parents would be asked to determine the effectiveness of the intervention.

Using experts or consumers, however, makes this procedure susceptible to the misperceptions that these individuals may hold. The level of behavior established for the intervention may not be realistic. Moreover, placing too great an emphasis on the desires of consumers rather than on the needs of the child can lead researchers to intervene in behaviors that are disturbing or annoying to consumers but that are not necessarily the child's greatest problem. For example, parents and teachers often rate highly the need for techniques to reduce acting-out behaviors, which may be a mere symptom of a child's actual problem. Rather than working solely on the acting-out behavior, it may be more helpful to provide parents and teachers with skills that will aid them in meeting the needs of the child, thus reducing the child's need for attention and corresponding attention-seeking behavior.

Combined Validation Procedures

Social comparison and subjective evaluation provide complementary methods of examining the social validity of the intervention (Kazdin, 1982). Used together, they can make a defensible and convincing case. Combining these methods, the development of unrealistic or un-

important goals can be prevented by using both the opinions of consumers and normative samples of behavior from peers of the individual who is the target of the intervention.

Practical Interventions

Defining social validity in terms of the outcomes of the intervention is far too limiting. Of equal concern is the practicality of the intervention. If, in the previously cited self-biting example, self-biting incidents were successfully reduced to zero but only as a result of intervention requiring such intensive resources that it was impossible to implement in applied settings, the intervention would still lack social validity because it would be impossible for practitioners to implement. This is not to say the intervention does not have merit; rather, some modification is needed so that the intervention is more effectively implemented by the practitioner. If at the outset the importance of developing a practical intervention is recognized, researchers will give careful consideration to factors affecting their ability to implement it in an applied setting. With practice, a disposition may be developed for interventions that are reasonable and practical by selecting options that can be easily adapted to applied settings.

TRIANGULATION

A continual problem in early childhood special education research is the difficulty of identifying appropriate measures to determine the impact of intervention on the children, their families, and others who may be targets (Neisworth & Bagnato, Chapter 2, this volume). As a rule, measures of behavior are used to make inferences about the impact of intervention. Most of these behaviors, however, are only indicators of a theoretical construct like intelligence or task persistence that researchers are interested in affecting. Because only indirect measures are available to make such judgments, it is difficult to determine the actual impact of an intervention.

A solution to this problem may be found in nautical history. For centuries, navigators had a similar problem when they attempted to pinpoint their positions at sea. Their solution was to apply basic trigonometric principles. By taking multiple measures on known positions (i.e., the stars), they were able to triangulate and determine their own positions.

The same principle can be applied to early intervention research. As navigators use multiple measures to determine their position indirectly but precisely, so researchers can use multiple measures to enhance scientific understanding of the impact of specific interventions. Borrowing from the geometric principle on which it is based, this use of multiple measures is called triangulation (Denzin, 1978).

By using several sources of data, researchers may be better able to determine accurately the impact of an intervention. Furthermore, confidence in an intervention is increased if positive impact from more than one data source can be documented. For example, researchers would have greater faith in an intervention that parent reports, teacher reports, and child change data indicated was effective than in an intervention not supported by parents and teachers even though the child change data indicated effectiveness.

Beyond using multiple sources of data, researchers can also triangulate on the impact of the intervention by using multiple methods of research. Experimental, quasi-experimental, single-subject, and qualitative methods, to name a few, have inherent characteristics that make each method better suited than the others to answer certain types of questions. For example, single-subject methods provide specific and objective measures of impact on individuals over time. These methods provide researchers with a "navigational log" of the daily impact of the intervention. As Kazdin (1982) points out, some researchers question the generalizability of such data because of the small sample size. Also, single-subject methods are less efficient when multiple interventions are being examined, or when quantifiable dependent measures that can be collected frequently over time are lacking.

Large sample (quasi- or experimental) methods provide researchers with indications of the average impact of the intervention across a large group of individuals and help them determine if differences between nonintervention and intervention groups are systematic or a result of change (Borg & Gall, 1983). These designs are also useful when the impact of multiple interventions are being compared. However, many researchers question the usefulness of information obtained from these designs, since no individual within the intervention group is likely to demonstrate the average effect (Kazdin, 1982; Patton, 1983). Moreover, some individuals within the intervention group may not have benefitted from the intervention and may actually have lower scores after the intervention. As a result, information may be obtained regarding the average impact of the intervention *across* groups but less information is available about how the intervention influences individuals *within* groups.

Qualitative methods provide researchers with rich portrayals of the influence of interventions on variables that are not easily quantified. Furthermore, they allow researchers to find influence in areas unanticipated at the onset of the intervention (Patton, 1983). Researchers who do not support the use of qualitative methods point to the potential for bias and the intensive labor requirements for data collection (Borg & Gall, 1983).

Each of these methods is powerful and can be a useful tool when examining the controlling variables related to early intervention. Used alone, each method limits the questions that can be asked and the data that can be collected. On the other hand, combining these methods into a systematic line of research can greatly broaden the kinds of questions that can be posed and can enhance scientific understanding of specific testing phenomena and of early intervention in general.

REPLICATION

A second data verification process that is related to triangulation is the systematic replication of research. Critical to the generalization of the findings of a particular investigation to other situations is its replication with different subjects, behaviors, settings, or methods. Although one would be hard pressed to find researchers who do not feel that replication is important, rarely does one see studies of early intervention systematically replicated. The stated or implied policies of refereed journals may be the most significant cause of this flaw in the research process. In replicating research, a nonsignificant finding can be as important as a significant finding, but rarely do editors accept manuscripts that do not produce significant findings.

If replication is to be encouraged, the field of early childhood special education must be more tolerant of nonsignificant findings. Researchers may expedite this process by clearly reporting that their investigations are replications, or by more explicitly delineating the ways in which their research differs from original investigations. Reviewers of research should not be quick to label what is being read as "old news," but should consider instead whether the replication refines scientific knowledge of the phenomena under study. In addition, ECSE educators could also encourage their graduate students to conduct replication studies. Graduate students are new to the research process, and a replication study can guide them, help them avoid design errors, and provide a good learning experience.

EXAMINATION OF DEPENDENT MEASURES

As previously discussed, one of the most perplexing problems in early intervention research is the identification of appropriate instruments and procedures to determine impact (Neisworth & Bagnato, Chapter 2, this volume). Following is a discussion of three dependent measures: tests, program cost, and effect size.

Tests

For many years, tests of all kinds have been developed to determine the impact of early intervention, and researchers have often relied too heavily on them as sources of data. While data from standardized and criterion-referenced tests are valuable, any single test taps only a small sampling of an individual's abilities. A broader spectrum of information and other, less formal sources of information should be sought. Moreover, too heavy a reliance on tests restricts the questions that can be asked about early intervention. Problem-solving, creative and productive thinking, self-esteem, task persistence, and self-concept are all important goals, yet the nature of these variables raises doubts about whether they will ever be validly measured with standardized tests.

Particularly abused are intelligence tests. Their use to document and track the impact of early intervention programs has come under serious attack (Meisels, 1985; Zigler & Trickett, 1978). The data from the Perry Preschool Project are an example (Berrueta-Clement, Schweinhart, Barnett, Epstein, & Weikart, 1984). One of the outcome measures in this project was IQ. Although there were initial gains in IQ scores by the intervention group over the comparison group, by the time students were in the second grade the IQ scores of the comparison and intervention children were equivalent. Meisels (1985) asks whether this finding reflects the efficacy of early intervention or the validity of using IQ as an indicator of impact. This uncertainty is partially settled by the other data collected in the Perry Project. Fortunately, IQ scores were not the only indicator of impact, and examination of the other indicators revealed that the program had a positive impact on children that was maintained through late adolescence (Schweinhart, Berrueta-Clement, Barnett, Epstein, & Weikart, 1985).

IQ increases are no longer considered sufficient evidence of program impact. The authors have concluded that in many instances, well-organized and monitored observations will produce more relevant data than will instruments that have not been rigorously validated, or whose reliability is questionable. No longer do researchers use instruments to assess facets of a program that are not compatible with its goals.

Another problem with the outcome measures in studies is their tendency to concentrate on child data to the exclusion of measures of the impact on families. It has become generally accepted that early intervention has influences that extend beyond the child and that it is important to consider the impact on the family when determining the effectiveness of the intervention (Zigler & Balla, 1982). Early intervention research to date, however, has generally ignored the family. Simeonsson, Cooper, and Scheiner (1982), in their review of 27 studies describing early intervention for biologically impaired infants and young children, reported that measures of family and sibling adjustments were almost nonexistent. This is a critical omission, since: 1) changes in the adjustments and functioning of parents and siblings constitute an appropriate and essential measure of effectiveness, and 2) these factors may influence the developmental status of the handicapped child.

Program Cost

Recently, a great deal of attention has been directed to the savings that can accrue from early intervention. Generally, the argument is that savings result from young children's needing less intensive and therefore less expensive services after early intervention. Cost-effectiveness data seem to be one of the most powerful sources of information regarding the impact of early intervention; however, as Strain (1984) points out, there are a number of dangers with such an economic argument.

First, the technical expertise to control all the variables to be considered in the cost-effectiveness equation is lacking. When establishing a program's cost effectiveness, the impact of the program is generally determined, and costs associated with this impact are identified. However, as indicated, measures to determine impact are imprecise. As a result, only indirect indicators of impact are obtained. Furthermore, if the variables to be considered when determining program impact are broadened, and if observations, interviews with parents and teachers, and other more qualitative measures are used, how will these variables be included in the cost effectiveness equation? Most likely what will happen is that such variables

will not be considered and cost effectiveness will be determined based on only part of the data. Strain (1984) has suggested that because researchers do not have a complete understanding of the interventions to be delivered, such sophisticated economic analysis must be applied cautiously.

Second, placing too much emphasis on the cost of programs detracts from the original intent of education and leads researchers to treat children as commodities. For instance, suppose two alternative treatments were being considered: Treatment A, at a cost of $10 per child, resulting in an average 15-point IQ increase over a year's time, and Treatment B, at a cost of $200 per child, resulting in an average 30-point IQ increase over a year's time. On economic grounds, Treatment A would be chosen because it produced a 1.5-point IQ increase for every dollar spent, whereas Treatment B produced only a .15-point increase for every dollar spent. From an ethical standpoint, however, Treatment B might have the advantage of providing children with a fuller opportunity to realize their potential.

Finally, focusing arguments on the money to be saved from early intervention may work against researchers in the long run. Educating children because it saves money, instead of educating children because they have a right to certain opportunities, is a dangerous policy. Those who allocate resources solely on an economic basis may someday decide to decrease their support to handicapped children and instead may place greater emphasis on regular or gifted education, since these children have far greater potential for giving society a return on its investment. To justify this shift, they may turn the argument against researchers and demonstrate through a cost/benefit analysis that money lost by not intervening early with handicapped children is offset by the money gained from the greater social contributions of gifted children due to the greater expenditure toward their development.

The authors do not advocate the abandonment of cost effectiveness studies, but we do advise caution in their application. The economic benefits of early intervention must be demonstrated, but ethical responsibility and the positive impact of early intervention on the child, family, and community should also be stressed.

Effect Size

The technique of meta-analysis, as developed by Glass (1977), synthesizes the findings of a broad range of studies in terms of a common metric called the "effect size." The effect size is the difference between the intervention or experimental group and the comparison or control group divided by the standard deviation of the comparison or control group. From its first appearance, meta-analysis has generated a great deal of discussion and debate. Many researchers have been highly supportive (Casto & Mastropieri, 1985a, 1985b; Cooper, 1982; Kavale, 1984; Rosenthal & Rubin, 1982), while others have been highly critical (Dunst & Snyder, 1985; Eysenck, 1978; Guskin, 1984; Slavin, 1984; Strain & Smith, 1985; Wortman, 1983).

Proponents of meta-analysis explain that it was developed because of flaws in traditional qualitative methods of synthesis research. Traditional qualitative reviews were criticized as overly subjective (Light & Pillemer, 1982) and vulnerable to reviewers' biases (Glass, McGaw, & Smith, 1981; Jackson, 1980; Light & Smith, 1971). The box score method of synthesizing research by counting significant positive, negative, or no difference findings in a large body of research was seen as equally limited. As Slavin (1984) pointed out, frequently cited limitations include the fact that this procedure does not indicate anything about the magnitude of a particular effect (Cooke & Leviton, 1980; Glass et al., 1981; Jackson, 1980) and that studies with large samples have a greater chance than those with small ones to be statistically significant (Light & Smith, 1971).

One criticism of meta-analysis is that it is similar to "comparing apples and oranges." Some researchers have asserted that combining results from different studies produces a conglomerate that makes little conceptual sense and is susceptible to misinterpretation (Gallo,

1978; Presby, 1978; Strain & Smith, 1985; Wortman, 1983). However, Glass et al. (1981) argued that combining results across diverse studies is no worse than combining data across subjects within a study. Glass proposed that if one suspects interactions between study characteristics and effect sizes, these interactions should and can be examined as part of the meta-analysis.

A second criticism of meta-analysis is that it tends to emphasize main effects, whereas the interactions between conditions are often more important (Cooke & Leviton, 1980; McGlynn, 1982). Supporters of meta-analysis respond that main effects do not need to be emphasized, and that interactions can and should be emphasized in the meta-analysis, if appropriate (Cooper & Arkin, 1981; Glass et al., 1981).

Perhaps the most serious criticism of meta-analysis is that it may involve the aggregation of poorly designed studies with well-designed ones (Dunst & Snyder, 1985; Eysenck, 1978; Mansfield & Busse, 1977; Strain & Smith, 1985). Glass et al. (1981) argued that the inclusion of strong and weak studies give researchers better understanding of the general impact of the intervention. Several authors have suggested (Cooper & Arkin, 1981; Glass et al., 1981) that studies may be coded on quality, and interactions between study quality and effect sizes may be examined. If such an interaction exists, main effects would have to be interpreted and qualified in view of the interaction.

Although there is much disagreement as to the merit of meta-analysis, the interest in meta-analysis, in the author's opinion, is not likely to abate in the near future. In fact, there is a recent movement to apply the logic of meta-analysis to single-subject research. Again, there is much debate both "pro" (Center, Skiba, & Casey, 1985–1986; Scruggs, Mastropieri, & Casto, 1987) and "con" (Salzberg, Strain, & Baer, 1987; White, 1987). Even more surprisingly, there has been a call for the development of meta-analytic techniques for qualitative and naturalistic studies (Guskin, 1984).

Without a doubt, more and more published studies in the field of early childhood special education will use meta-analysis to synthesize the extant literature. As Slavin (1984) points out, meta-analysis has great merit as a method to synthesize research. In practice, however, it may receive disproportionate weight because of its mischievous appearance of objectivity. Researchers need to use caution in using and interpreting meta-analytic procedures. It is the authors' belief that findings should be treated in much the same way as in other methods of synthesis, and should not be given undue credence for seeming to be objective. Such actions are not supported by practice or principle, and will obscure the truth rather than reveal it. However, as aptly stated by Slavin (1984), there is nothing inherent in meta-analysis that makes misleading conclusions inevitable; rather, it is the way it is used and interpreted that causes confusion.

At this time, it may also be prudent to examine the "best-evidence synthesis" proposed by Slavin (1986). This method is an alternative to both meta-analytic and traditional reviews. It combines the quantification of effect sizes and the systematic study selection of meta-analysis with the examination of methodological and qualitative issues typical of the good traditional reviews. This process is designed to help researchers focus on the "best evidence" available for examination. Using well specified and defined a priori criteria for inclusion, the studies highest in internal and external validity are selected for detailed qualitative review. Effect size is also included as an adjunct to the full qualitative discussion of the literature being reviewed. Although this is a new procedure, and time is needed to determine its efficacy, it appears to hold great promise because it combines the strengths of meta-analytic and traditional review procedures.

GREATER EMPHASIS ON INDEPENDENT MEASURES

The terminology applied to various facets of educational programs for the handicapped is highly developed. Surprisingly, most early intervention studies have provided neither good descriptions of the interventions nor documentation of how they were implemented. Attention is given instead to the appropriateness of dependent variables, but the key independent variable—the intervention—is inadequately addressed. Furthermore, there is a lack of comparability among intervention strategies (Meisels, 1985). Positive findings from one set of instructional strategies, service delivery models, or curricula cannot be generalized to other situations. For instance, home-based programming in recent years has been very popular, yet often the developer or researcher does not define what he or she means by home delivery and leaves many questions unanswered. Is the service weekly, semi-monthly, or monthly? Does the parent receive training, or does the paraprofessional have primary responsibility delivering the service? What instruments are used to make formative decisions? These are only some of the key variables that differentiate home-based programs. Greater care must be given to describing independent measures. Without knowing the details of a program, researchers run the risk of unknowingly comparing "apples to oranges."

Beyond knowing the goals, researchers must also become more rigorous in determining how the intervention is implemented. Sometimes there is a radical difference between a description of a program or a component for young handicapped children and what actually is being implemented in the center. Yet research results may be interpreted based on what the researcher thinks was going on rather than on what was actually happening. Both the degree to which the treatment is implemented and the quality of implementation are crucial in interpreting the results. Without knowledge of how the intervention is implemented, researchers have no indication whether a lack of significant findings means that the intervention lacks merit or that it is not being implemented properly (See Odom, Chapter 1, this volume).

Until the same consideration is given to independent measures that is given to dependent measures, intervention research will not advance much farther.

GREATER EMPHASIS ON EXPANDING THE IMPACT OF RESEARCH

The ultimate purpose of ECSE research is to provide users with the knowledge to meet the special needs of handicapped children and their families more efficiently and effectively than before. Publishing results in refereed research-oriented journals is one way of disseminating knowledge, but the result of this is that the literature is being read only by other researchers. Procedures must be developed that enable practitioners to understand findings and to incorporate them readily into practice. Practitioners need help in preservice courses and inservice training to bridge the gap between research and practice.

The rules governing promotion and tenure are partially at fault for the limited dissemination of findings by researchers. In the charge toward tenure and recognition, researchers attempt to publish in the most "prestigious" journals. Often these are the journals least likely to be read by practitioners. Teachers rarely have the time and training to understand the research presented there. But publications geared to practitioners are viewed as second-rate and less desirable.

Such restrictions are largely self-imposed. One might think that researchers are attempting to hide their work from practitioners, who would in fact profit most from the researchers' findings. Universities and colleges must be enlightened as to the importance of publishing our work in journals that will be read by the people we hope will use our innovations. In contrast to some of the more recondite disciplines, educators are attempting to influence people beyond our colleagues. Perhaps educators need a different set of standards for promotion and tenure that would encourage a balance between refereed, "prestigious" journals and practitioner-oriented outlets.

It appears at times that researchers feel little or no responsibility for bridging the gap between research and practice. Researchers are quick to indict the practitioner for not keeping up with research, but they do little to make research findings more interpretable or meaningful to the practitioner. Many research reports do not have a section on implications, so that readers have to ferret the implications out for themselves. Perhaps a journal for practitioners is needed that focuses on how research findings can improve practice. No wonder research reports gather dust on shelves if only other researchers find the reports meaningful.

The use of multidisciplinary teams in diagnosing and arriving at educational plans for young handicapped children is already a standard practice in early childhood special education. Perhaps a team approach is also needed in identifying research problems, conducting research, and deciphering what the research findings mean to practice. For example, in addition to a person or persons with research skills, a highly trained teacher or ancillary worker, and in some cases, a parent of a handicapped child may each have important roles. These individuals can be instrumental in defining the research questions, in implementing the research, in monitoring the treatment (if treatment is part of the research plan), in presenting the findings to the appropriate audience, and in interpreting how the findings can be appropriately used.

Research is too often viewed by practitioners as a mystical operation beyond their comprehension. As a result, they may avoid familiarizing themselves with research studies, or may be skeptical of the findings that come to their attention. Courses at the undergraduate and graduate levels on reading research may help. Courses at the graduate level often concentrate on conducting research, but not on reading research, which involves a different set of skills.

Another group requiring access to research findings is policymakers. As with practitioners, the information must be presented in a manner that is easily understood and is readily utilized for decision-making in persuading others to endorse, carry out, or reinforce existing policies, or in developing new policies based on new information. Policymakers will not be willing to spend much time pouring over detailed research reports in which elaborate statistics prevent them from getting the answers they need in order to make policy decisions.

Innovative ways of disseminating information need to be developed. Many of the exemplary programs for young handicapped children funded by OSEP under Outreach have developed effective blueprints for dissemination that are useful to researchers who are disseminating their own results. In addition, other disciplines may have to be called upon to market intervention research findings. If it is true that there is a gap of some 10 to 20 years between research findings and practice, it seems evident that help is needed from outside the field of ECSE to get the attention of the practitioner or policymaker, to show these persons our "products" (the research findings), and to motivate the appropriate audience to use the findings.

Information dissemination is time-consuming, however, and requires funds. In the authors' experience, one area that is often not fully funded in research projects is the information dissemination process. In the summer of 1986, for instance, the federal government held a 2 day conference for all directors of federally funded research projects. One day of this conference was spent in discussion of the importance of disseminating findings. That same summer we were awarded a research grant, and the area receiving the greatest budget cut was dissemination. It is pointless to spend money developing innovations if they are going to sit on a shelf. Researchers and supporters of research must be willing to pay the price of disseminating innovations. Funding sources must be informed of the importance and costs of adequately disseminating findings. Researchers should not accept cuts in the dissemination budget passively, but should instead fight for those funds or should suggest trade-offs with other areas of the budget.

CONCLUSIONS

The knowledge base in early childhood special education has expanded at an amazing pace. It is the authors' contention that this growth is

due in large part to our increased sophistication as researchers. If the field is to continue to grow, our research skills must also grow. Most importantly, a major purpose of educational research, that of improving practice, must be kept in mind. There are a number of steps that can and should be taken to achieve this goal.

1. *Better trained researchers* Some of the flaws that undermine confidence in research can be avoided if researchers receive more rigorous training. Research is becoming much more sophisticated, and new methods and techniques are constantly being developed. Researchers have a responsibility to keep up with these innovations. Journals should give space to discussing new methods to help researchers refine their skills. Finally, the author suggests caution in the use and interpretation of new and controversial techniques and procedures. Over time the flaws in such procedures usually present themselves. Perhaps costly errors can be avoided by moving cautiously with new procedures, and carefully evaluating their effects.

2. *Better trained consumers* The practitioner must be better trained to understand and use research findings. As a general rule, teachers know very little about research methodology and thus avoid reading research reports. A course on reading research should be a part of their preservice programs. Greater knowledge and understanding of the research process usually promotes greater respect for scientific research and should lead to greater use of research findings.

3. *Greater effort to encourage the use of research findings* As previously mentioned, a journal for practitioners is needed whose purpose is to present research findings and methods of incorporating findings into practice in a way that will motivate practitioners to use the results.

Inservice training is still another way to keep the practitioner abreast of new knowledge. At such meetings, researchers and practitioners may discuss findings, what the findings mean to practice, how the findings can be applied, and areas for study that are of interest to the practitioner. This kind of dialogue should reduce the time gap between the generation of new knowledge and the use made of it.

4. *More innovative ways of marketing research results* The federal government has allocated millions of dollars for research, but it has provided very little for dissemination. Money should perhaps be allocated for the development of innovative means of disseminating the information that is already available about early intervention. More innovative ways of marketing research findings will also narrow the gap between research and practice.

REFERENCES

Berrueta-Clement, J. R., Schweinhart, L. J., Barnett, W. S., Epstein, A. E., & Weikart, D. P. (1984). Changed lives: The effects of the Perry Preschool programs on youths through age 19. *Monographs of the High/Scope Educational Research Foundation* (No. 8). Ypsilanti, MI: High/Scope Press.

Borg, W., & Gall, M. (1983). *Educational research: An introduction* (4th ed.). New York: Longman.

Casto, G., & Mastropieri, M. A. (1985a). Strain and Smith do protest too much: A response. *Exceptional Children, 53,* 266–268.

Casto, G., & Mastropieri, M. A. (1985b). Much ado about nothing: A reply to Dunst and Snyder. *Exceptional Children, 53,* 277–279.

Center, B. A., Skiba, R. J., Casey, A. (1985–1986). A methodology for the quantitative synthesis of intra-subject design research. *Journal of Special Education, 19,* 387–400.

Cooke, T., & Leviton, L. (1980). Reviewing the literature: A comparison of traditional methods with meta analysis. *Journal of Personality, 48,* 449–472.

Cooper, H. (1982). Scientific guidelines for conducting integrative research reviews. *Review of Educational Research, 52,* 291–302.

Cooper, H., & Arkin, R. (1981). On quantitative reviewing. *Journal of Personality, 49,* 225–230.

Denzin, N. K. (1978). *The research act.* New York: McGraw Hill.

DeWeerd, J. (1981). Early education services for children with handicaps—Where have we been, where are we now, and where are we going? *Journal of the Division for Early Childhood, 2,* 15–25.

Dunst, C. J., & Snyder, S. W. (1985). A critique of the Utah State University early intervention meta-analysis research. *Exceptional Children, 53,* 269–276.

Glass, G. V. (1977). Integrating findings: The meta-analysis of research. *Review of Research in Education, 5,* 351–379.

Glass, G., McGaw, B., & Smith, M. L. (1981). *Meta-analysis in social research.* Beverly Hills, CA: Sage Publications.

Guskin, S. L. (1984). Problems and promises of meta-analysis in special education. *The Journal of Special Education, 18,* 73–81.

Jackson, G. B. (1980). Methods for integrative reviews. *Review of Educational Research, 50,* 438–460.

Kavale, K. A. (1984). Potential advantages of the meta-analysis technique for research in special education. *The Journal of Special Education, 18,* 61–73.

Kazdin, A. E. (1977). Assessing the clinical or applied significance of behavior change through social validation. *Behavior Modification, 1,* 427–452.

Kazdin, A. (1982). *Single-case research design: Methods for clinical and applied settings.* New York: Oxford University Press.

Kirk, S. A. (1958). *Early education of the mentally retarded: An experimental study.* Urbana: University of Illinois Press.

Lazar, I. (1983). Discussion and implications of the findings. In the Consortium for Longitudinal Studies, *As the twig is bent: Lasting effects of preschool programs* (pp. 461–465). Hillsdale, NJ: Lawrence Erlbaum.

Light, R., & Pillemer, D. (1982). Numbers and narrative: Combining their strengths in research reviews. *Harvard Educational Review, 52,* 1–26.

Light, R., & Smith, P. (1971). Accumulating evidence: Procedures for resolving contradictions among different research studies. *Harvard Education Review, 41,* 429–471.

Mansfield, R., & Busse, T., (1977). Meta-analysis of research: A rejoinder to Glass. *Educational Researcher, 44*(9), 3.

McGlynn, R. (1982). A comment on the meta-analysis of goal structures. *Psychological Bulletin, 92,* 184–185.

Meisels, S. J. (1985). The efficacy of early intervention: Why are we still asking the question? *Topics in Early Childhood Special Education, 5*(2), 1–11.

Patton, M. Q. (1983). *Qualitative evaluation methods.* Beverly Hills, CA: Sage Publications.

Presby, S. (1978). Overly broad categories obscure important differences between therapies. *American Psychologist, 33,* 514–515.

Rosenthal, R., & Rubin, D. (1982). Comparing effect sizes on independent studies. *Psychological Bulletin, 92,* 500–504.

Salzberg, C. L., Strain, P. S., & Baer, D. M. (1987). Meta-analysis for single-subject research: When does it clarify, when does it obscure? *Remedial and Special Education, 8,* 43–48.

Schweinhart, L., Berrueta-Clement, J., Barnett, W., Epstein, A., & Weikart, D. (1985). Effects of the Perry Preschool program on youths through age 19: A summary. *Topics in Early Childhood Special Education, 5*(2), 26–35.

Scruggs, T. E., Mastropieri, M. A., & Casto, G. (1987). The quantitative synthesis of single-subject research: Methodology and validation. *Remedial and Special Education, 8,* 24–33.

Simeonsson, R., Cooper, D., & Scheiner, A. (1982). A review and analysis of the effectivensss of early intervention programs. *Pediatrics, 69*(5), 635–641.

Slavin, R. E. (1984). Meta-analysis in education: How has it been used? *Educational Researcher, 13,* 6–15.

Slavin, R. E. (1986). Best-evidence synthesis: An alternative to meta-analytic and traditional reviews. *Educational Researcher, 15,* 5–11.

Strain, P. (1984). Efficacy research with young handicapped children: A critique of the status quo. *Journal of the Division for Early Childhood, 9*(1), 4–10.

Strain, P. S., & Smith, B. J. (1985). A counter-interpretation of early intervention effects: A response to Casto and Mastropieri. *Exceptional Children, 53,* 260–265.

White, O. R. (1987). Some comments concerning "the quantitative synthesis of single-subject research." *Remedial and Special Education, 8,* 34–39.

Wolf, M. M. (1978). Social validity: The case for subjective measurement, or, how applied behavior analysis is finding its heart. *Journal of Applied Behavior Analysis, 11,* 203–214.

Wortman, P. (1983). Meta-analysis: A validity perspective. *Annual Review of Psychology, 34,* 223–260.

Zigler, R., & Balla, D. (1982). Selecting outcome variables in evaluations of early childhood special education programs. *Topics in Early Childhood Special Education, 1*(4), 11–22.

Zigler, E., & Trickett, P. K. (1978). IQ, social competence, and evaluation of early childhood intervention programs. *American Psychologist, 33,* 789–798.

Index